The Traditional Tunes
of the
Child Ballads

THE
TRADITIONAL TUNES
OF THE
CHILD BALLADS

*With Their Texts, according to the Extant Records
of Great Britain and America*

BY

BERTRAND HARRIS BRONSON

*Volume I
Ballads 1 to 53*

PRINCETON, NEW JERSEY
PRINCETON UNIVERSITY PRESS
1959

❖

BERTRAND H. BRONSON is a professor in the Department of English at the University of California in Berkeley. This project represents many years of work. He has received several Guggenheim fellowships for research on ballads, and has worked through the major collections of ballads and popular songs in the English-speaking world. Mr. Bronson has made significant contributions to analytical method in the comparative study of folk-melodies, has written a number of articles on the subject, and has addressed various meetings of ballad specialists both in this country and abroad.

❖

Printed in the United States of America

by Princeton University Press, Princeton, New Jersey

Second Printing, 1968

Third Printing, 1971

CONTENTS

[v]

INTRODUCTION

1. THE PRIMARY IMPORTANCE OF THE TUNES

Question: When is a ballad not a ballad?

Answer: When it has no tune.

It is too late in the day to be offering fresh definitions of The Ballad and there is little likelihood that any reader will come to the present work in order to find one. We know already that the term has meant very different things in different ages and that the history of the word Ballad, though fascinating, complicates without clarifying its significance for us. That the Greeks and the Romans used such a word ($\beta\alpha\lambda\lambda\iota\zeta\omega$, *ballo*) to signify dancing proves nothing about our Ballads or their origin: the ancients may not have had anything of the kind in mind, any more than we, when we think of a Ball. At various times, each of the elements now considered essential to the form—narrative verse, traditional transmission, tune—has been ignored in current uses of the word. In the end, precise definition must set limits arbitrarily: we cannot dispense with the qualifying epithet, whether it be *traditional, communal, folk, popular, vulgar*, or another. No more than the term *Song* can *Ballad* by itself sharply determine a *genre*. But since none of the epithets that has gained wide currency includes the musical component, the little riddle so negatively put and so dogmatically answered above may call attention to a fundamental but often neglected truth. For ballads without tunes are as unfulfilled, as paradoxical, as songs without words. Harvy Hafter puts the emphasis where it belongs when, in Skelton's *The Bowge of Court*, he cries:

> Wolde to God it wolde please you some daye
> A balade boke before me for to laye,
> And lerne me to SYNGE *Re, mi, fa, sol!*
> And, whan I fayle, bobbe me on the noll.

And it is regrettable, although explicable historically, that the noll of so many a scholar has gone unbobbed for putting asunder, and then forgetting to reunite, the partners of an alliance so essential to the survival and vital continuance of both. For only by fruitful marriage can they be self-perpetuating in living tradition.

The present collection should at least make it difficult to overlook the fact that scholars who disregard the continuous interplay of tune and text in the ballads are guilty of a very one-sided approach to their subject. However it be with the partial study of the formal elements of ballad-texts—with metre, stanzaic patterns, refrain, or rhetoric—the influence of the ballad-music on ballad-form and general ordonnance has never been sufficiently scrutinized. The processes of natural selection have been at work here for many generations, and have clearly resulted, through unremitting pressures, in most of the typical characteristics of the ballad-style. It is the music which has dictated and controlled the stanzaic habit of ballads, suggesting a normal and consistent length to correspond with each repetition of the tune, and restraining impulses to overstep the regular limits or to abridge them. Abnormalities, when they occur, are felt as abnormal, and the pattern is reestablished as soon as possible. The textual line of the ballad, in singing, is seized by the ear as a *musical phrase*: it is this which has discouraged suspensions of meaning and kept the sentence-structure uncomplex. Each typical line of a ballad yields its total content as it is sung: if the sense is partial, the part is usually contained within the single phrase, and completed rather than resolved or reversed by what follows. The conjunctions between the phrase-lines are habitually progressive; *and, or, for, nor, till*; and *if* is likely to come before, not after, the apodosis. The units of thought are thus made commensurate with the four-stress musical phrase so generally typical of Western folk-melody. The mid-cadence and final cadence of a folk-tune are a kind of musical rhyme—conspicuously so in a tune like "Barbara Allen"; and typically chime on the dominant and tonic, the two points of greatest repose in a scale. When reinforced, as they usually are, by the cadential pause or held note, they almost automatically prompt a corresponding verbal rhyme.

The music, again, has governed the strategy of the dialogue in ballads. Typically, the whole length of the tune is allotted to a single speaker; so that question and answer, statement and reply, are in obvious parallel. Without becoming confusing, however, the speeches may be limited to half this length, the mid-cadence providing a natural break between two speakers, who are most often identified in a parenthetical clause. It is seldom that a speaker is given less than half the tune; and where a speech is shorter, the two musical phrases are filled out with narrative or descriptive matter, or with a refrain line, so that the new speaker can start at the second half of the tune or at the beginning. It would be very hard to find an instance of a *single* musical phrase divided between speakers: musical drama has a slower pace than spoken, and needs more time for its effects. The lack of flexibility—or, to put it positively, the formal gravity of the ballads, which lends characteristic dignity and an effect of ceremonial behavior to even the most trivial, violent, or abandoned expression of emotion—is mainly music's bequest: the result of pouring everything in turn into a small, arbitrary mold of sound, with regular divisions, each of which holds so much and no more, and which must be successively refilled at the same temporal pace. Structure and meaning must be immediately seized by the ear. The speed of narrative or dialogue can be further slowed by refrain-lines interpolated at fixed points. The conception of a refrain is itself musical, and its recurrence must conform to the shape of the tune. Whether the refrain is internal or external, it is of course a concession wrested from narration by music—most obviously so if aphoristic or merely syllabic interruption of the narrative flow, but not less truly so when lines of text are repeated.

The musical conditioning of dialogue, set forth in *melodic* units as above described, has psychological as well as formal consequences. It leads to simple confrontations of agreement and disagreement, to the obvious balance of repetitional statement in formulaic reply and, at a deeper level, discourages the subtleties of indirect statement because these cannot be conveyed without interpretive assistance. The relatively impassive outlines of a folk-tune suggest no latent shades of verbal meaning. Psychological implication, innuendo, irony cannot be heard in the straight rendition of a genuine folk-singer, and this is, of course, a source of strength as well as a limitation. Officious nods and becks, theatrical hints of a sub-surface understanding shared between singer and hearer, are an offense to that powerful impersonality which makes good folk-singing so uniquely impressive: they belong rather with the dramatic reading of words-without-notes which makes of the ballads an alien art. That almost marmoreal inviolability of the ballad as traditionally sung subdues insinuations and forbids intimacy. Suggestive inflections of stated meaning, even broadly ironic, find no foothold on this smooth surface. Thus, for example, in a version of "Eppie Morrie" (Child No. 223), the ironic threat of marauding Willie, demanding an instant marriage to his stolen and unwilling partner, is clear enough when read:

> He's taken out a pistol,
> And set it to the minister's breast:
> "Marry me, marry me, minister,
> Or else I'll be your priest."

But when sung, the accent refuses to fall on the emphatic *your* in the last line, and the point is lost in the hearing:

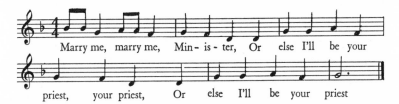

Marry me, marry me, Min - is - ter, Or else I'll be your priest, your priest, Or else I'll be your priest

A more flexible medium is necessary for such effects; consequently, over the centuries, music and words have collaborated in evolving a style that makes few demands beyond the powers of either to supply. This has meant that the persons of balladry should also maintain a directness and simplicity of character incapable of sophistication. One may justly suspect the non-singing Sir Walter of inventing Thomas the Rhymer's biting rejection of the Elfland Queen's gift of "the tongue that can never lee":

> "My tongue is mine ain," true Thomas said;
>   "A gudely gift ye wad gie to me!
> I neither dought to buy nor sell,
>   At fair or tryst where I may be.
>
> "I dought neither speak to prince or peer,
>   Nor ask of grace from fair ladye."
> "Now hold thy peace!" the lady said,
>   For, as I say, so must it be."

Thomas' insistence here on the crippling effects of truth-telling may be obvious enough to the reader, but it is too subtle for the musical phrase. The irony of the interchange is lost in the singing, and the hearer is baffled by the long explanation.[1] In many more ways than the foregoing the ballad-music exerts, and has always exerted, its powerful and unremitting influence upon the words, the phrase, the rhetoric, the verse, the narrative method and length, the range of character delineation and habit of expression of the *dramatis personae* of ballads. It is surely time to give it due weight with the texts in any comprehensive study of Balladry.

It is necessary to be thus insistent because of the inveterate and, until recently, almost universal indifference of the learned to the musical half of their subject. Such a one might say, reading the above, that mere assertion proves little, and why may not the influence have gone the other way, a traditional poetic art gradually shaping a musical vehicle to its needs? The question perhaps deserves a fuller discussion than can be allowed here, if proportions are to be kept. The answer can be no more than suggested. It is that the influences mentioned are *musical* influences. They could hardly move in the opposite direction: this is a one-way street. There is nothing peculiar about ballad-music to distinguish it from other folk-music. The same melodic conventions are observed in many other kinds of song. By nature, in fact, narrative is the least likely of all kinds to be drawn into the orbit of lyrical statement. Narrative travels toward a goal, along a path where fresh objects are successively encountered, incommensurate in urgency and importance. A constantly varying pace and emotional pitch is therefore all the while affecting, without obliterating, the underlying drive to get to the end. To impose upon such disparate matter an arbitrary and relatively rigid, brief but inevitably delaying, levelling, and equalizing, unit of melodic statement, repeated from start to finish regardless of changes of idea, is a procedure radically inimical to the needs of narrative and could not arise from them alone. The music has its own logic and the rationale of the traditional ballad can be understood only in the light of that logic.

The origins of rhyme, indeed, are almost as obscure as the origins of the ballad. There is no need to argue that they arose out of melodic suggestion. Rhyme in the ballads may be richer or poorer, as chance may have determined. But it is significant that, in the common ballad-quatrain, rhyme has seldom been sought except at the end of lines two and four. These correspond to the two emphatic and melodically balanced cadences of the ordinary folk-tune. The first and third cadences of the tune have no obvious mutual reference, and if there is a balance between them, it is inconspicuous and unnoticed. It is a fact that simple Western folk-tunes are built this way, and appear to have been so for centuries, whether with or without words. We cannot argue, in reverse, that the characteristic, lowest-common-denominator rhyme of the ballad-quatrain has influenced the structure of the tunes. And it is hardly necessary to insist that the ballad-refrain, whatever pattern it takes, is an effect derived from singing; not independently conceived and prompting to musical accompaniment:

> Seven lang years he served the King,
> *With a hey lillelu and a how lo lan;*
> And it's a' for the sake of his dochter Jean,
> *And the birk and the brume blooms bonnie.*

[1] The doubter may be convinced by asking anyone who has not recently read the words to listen to Ewan MacColl's very clear singing of the ballad on Riverside LP 12/622, Side 3, no. 1.

Lady Nancy died of pure pure grief,
Lord Lovel he died of sorrow, *-orrow, -orrow,*
Lord Lovel he died of sorrow.

There were three rauens sat on a tree,
Downe a downe, hay downe, hay downe
There were three rauens sat on a tree,
With a downe.
There were three rauens sat on a tree,
They were as black as they might be.
With a downe derrie, derrie, derrie, downe, downe.

§2. THE CHILD CANON

Since the contents of the present work are limited by, and lie well within, the compass of Child's great collection, the current editor will be expected to declare his position with respect to the canon of authenticity in British popular balladry. It is very noticeable that of late students are becoming increasingly restive under Child's authority, more and more unwilling to grant a mere second-class citizenship to the ballads in their own collections which missed of his royal accolade.

Child's views of what to include, and what not, were slow in crystallizing—if, indeed, they could be said ever to have arrived at final assurance. His correspondence with Grundtvig,[2] extending over the decade 1872-1882, shows that for years he worried about two problems above all others: the "compass" and the "arrangement" of his collection. The negative results of his efforts to collect anything new from oral sources gradually convinced him that everything of this kind in existence was preserved somewhere in writing or print, and probably in better state there than in late oral tradition; so that the chief questions were, How much of the record to admit? and What order to put it in? In 1872 he declares himself no clearer in his answers than he had been in 1860, when his first collection was revised and republished; and in 1877 he confesses that by that date he believes he would "have made a beginning" on the new definitive edition, "if I had been able to satisfy myself with a good order." In 1874 he wrote that the distinction between "genuine national or people's ballads" and "all varieties of base kind" is "easier to feel than to formulate"; and when finally the first part of the great collection appeared (late in 1882), he referred to it as "nine-years-put-off." He now set little store by his earlier collection, declaring that it was a publishers' venture in which saleability and speed of completion were essential considerations. "I felt obliged to include everything that the English had been accustomed to call *Ballad*, at least in specimens."[3] "I never pretended that the arrangement was founded on a deeper principle than convenience. Some sort of classifica-

---

[2] Cf. Sigurd B. Hustvedt, *Ballad Books and Ballad Men*, 1930, pp. 241-300.   [3] *Op.cit.*, p. 262.

tion everybody expects."[4] Deprived, however, of such an excuse for the later series, he kept begging his friend Grundtvig for his ideas on arrangement, and postponing his own final decision. In the end, Grundtvig reluctantly complied with his wishes ("I thought that you ought to make it yourself," he wrote) and sent him a list of 269 ballads with their preferred variants, arranged in four classes, and grouped according to the stanza-form. The two-lined couplet with four accents and a refrain after each line Grundtvig considered the oldest of the stanzaic patterns. Child conceded that this was "an approach to a rational arrangement" which had not occurred to him; and in the first part of the work as published, he followed it, only modifying so far as to group variants of a single ballad-complex together, whatever the formal scheme. "I was only too glad to have *any* way proposed," he wrote in 1882, "and thought your suggestion a very convenient one, and have adopted it." As to the order of the first group, he continues, "I do not deviate far from that which you sketched, and when I deviate (excepting *Sir Lionel*) I do not think my reasons very material."[5]

Without the evidence above, it would be plausible to infer that Child had planned his first part (Nos. 1-28), as well as his second (Nos. 29-53), as inviting samples of what prospective subscribers might expect. They show no clear indication of any scheme of arrangement: the stanzaic principle of Part I is obscured by the non-conforming variants of several ballads, by much metrical difference among those in couplets, by the variety of intervening refrains, as well as by the absence of any signal of future divisions. On the other hand, there is an obvious tentative linking of similar themes, short of any attempt to gather together all of a kind. Child begins with three varieties of riddling ballads, then passes to the theme of bride-stealing by "unco" wooers, magic and treachery playing a part. The range of foreign analogues can be fully displayed in headnotes to some of these, and several of the most striking illustrations of the supernatural are here presented for examination. From the tenth to the sixteenth ballad, interesting domestic tragedies, including incestuous connections, are exhibited. Nos. 17 to 19 have affiliations with medieval romance. Nos. 20 and 21 are matricidal, and related also in the penance predicted. Nos. 22 and 23 are scriptural apocrypha. Nos. 24 to 26 show further love-relations, grim or gay. Nos. 27 and 28 are scraps that terminate the first part—so as not to throw all the left-overs to the end of the work. Most of these varieties reappear two years later in the second part: romance-themes, the supernatural in love, more riddles, bride-stealing, familial relations with incestuous implications, romantic love ("Young Beichan") in a ballad analogous to "Hind Horn," ending in happy recognition and reunion. Had the religious group Nos. 54-57 been included, Part II would pretty well have recapitulated the whole range of Part I. Robin Hood, historical or pseudo-historical themes, and demonstrably late ballads of romantic love are the chief classes omitted so far, and there were obvious reasons for postponing these large categories. Thus, the first two parts were repetitive cross-sections that could hardly have been bettered had they been solely designed to display variety, to win readers, and to establish the scope and importance of the work as a whole.

Even before the first part was printed Child wrote: "If I ever come to a second edition, I may modify the arrangement."[6] Once in a while, as he goes, he indicates dissatisfaction with the

---

[4] *Ibid.*, p. 254.   [5] *Op.cit.*, p. 292-3.   [6] *Op.cit.*, p. 293.

present order. Thus, in a footnote to No. 234, he says the ballad should have come in with Nos. 221-25.[7] In view of the surprising ways in which ballads get modified and transformed, it might have been more systematic to put the derivative and secondary ballads regularly under their elder or parent forms, whether in appendices or sub-classes. Thus Nos. 17 and 252 have connections; 53, 62, 73, and 253; 78, 248, and 255; 99 and 251; 115 and 249; 167 and 250. In cases such as these, Child separated because of the undoubted modernity of the later numbers. But to do so is to become involved in contradictions. The earliest recorded text of No. 10 is obviously perverted, burlesqued, and "modern," yet Child gives it the post of honor. No. 250 is still widely sung traditionally and with intermixtures of its earlier condition. It is, in fact, a better representative of "Sir Andrew Barton" (No. 167) than is 10A of the "Two Sisters" tradition; yet it is separated by almost a hundred places in the series from its parent stock. There is no strictly logical way to separate the new from the old, since the old is always being renewed and what looks newest may have immemorial roots. Ignorance of the full history of a ballad is no sound principle of distinction. If we will, we may make qualitative judgments on aesthetic or anthropological grounds, or on the basis of date of record, but the argument lies then in a very different area. Agelessness in ballads is not a figure of speech. Like Keats's nightingale, they were not born for death; but the species, not the individual, is meant.

When, shortly before he died, Child sat down to draft the Introduction he did not live to complete, he commenced with the following sentence: "In the moderate compass of less than five vol[ume]s there has now been gathered everything in the Engl[ish] language that by the most liberal interpretation could be called a popular ballad, and all the known versions of such."[8] Clearly, he thought that, in a rigorous accounting, he had exceeded rather than fallen short of the mark. His own occasional comments can be cited to justify the exclusion of a large number of pieces in the collection from the traditional *genre*; and it would not be difficult to make a case for relegating to appendices some sixty of the pieces that now carry independent numbers. This is not the place to enter a formal demonstration but a few instances may be cited in support of the assertion. One may refer to Child's headnotes to Nos. 147, 149, 150, 151, 152, 153, 154, all patently ballads individually composed and existing only in untraditional broadsides, sometimes even flouting the lore of their subject. Some two dozen—or two-thirds—of the Robin Hood cycle are in comparable case.

From a *canon* of authentic popularity would also be excluded those pieces covered by Child's remark on "Young Ronald" (No. 304): "In this and not a very few other cases, I have suppressed disgust, and admitted an actually worthless and a manifestly—at least in part—spurious ballad, because of a remote possibility that it might contain relics, or be a debased representative, of something genuine and better." Sometimes, as with Buchan's variant of "Young Waters," he has reduced the spurious piece to an appendix. But jury-texts do not belong in a canon: if nothing has independently survived of a genuine anterior *ballad* (as distinct from a tale) either fragmentary or by testimony, it is idle to substitute the possibility for the fact. The existence, even, of foreign analogues will not greatly help, for the canon of traditional verse is not identical for all countries. No one assumes that there must have been a British analogue

[7] *E.S.P.B.*, IV, 309 n.   [8] Child MSS., Harvard Library, Vol. XVI, p. 132.

for every foreign ballad. Tact and knowledge might justify a suspicion that truly popular matter lies behind a spurious piece, but not an assurance that such matter was earlier incarnated in a genuine ballad.

Another category that Child sets apart from the truly popular, in his sense of the term, is the "minstrel ballad," e.g., Nos. 29, 30, 31, 111, 175, 176. All these are professional work. Many others of a similar kind, some of which were included in his first collection, are dismissed without remark from the second. But, if so, should not the pieces of those later minstrels, the inferior broadside writers from the sixteenth to the nineteenth century, also in strictness be excluded? Their work is not so truly popular as that of the earlier men: it has printer's ink in its veins.

It is not to be imagined that Child, who knew more about ballads than any man living, was blind to these and other inconsistencies and contradictions in his collection. They were the result of conflicting purposes and claims. There was the wish, lingering from his earlier work, to see that all historical varieties of respectable popularity—in the absence of clean boundary lines—should be represented. There was the wish to exclude everything that was not genuinely popular. There was the wish to keep only the best and most lyrical of the mass of possibilities. There was the wish, strongly reinforced by Grundtvig's counsel, to include (in Grundtvig's words) "every bit of genuine ballad lore, and consequently all that *may be* genuine, and I might say, also all that *has been so.*"[9] This last meant the inclusion of much dubious matter, and notably much of Peter Buchan's pinchbeck balladry, to which Grundtvig, approaching it as a foreigner interested in Scandinavian analogues, was much less hostile than Child. It meant the admission of late Robin Hood ballads "*essentially* vulgar," which Child confessed he had "scarcely patience or stomach to read." It meant an arbitrary distinction between short romances and ballads. "Is *Arthur and the King of Cornwall* a ballad?" he asked. "*The Horn of King Arthur* I incline to exclude, and yet I fear that my reasons are vague." What should he do about *King Arthur's Death*? or *The Suffolk Miracle*? "*The Outlaw Murray* and *Auld Maitland* . . . try me sorely. I wish I could rid myself of them."[10]

It is quite clear that if Child had felt able to obey his own inclinations, he would have drawn a much stricter line, and have done so mainly on grounds of intrinsic interest. There was literally no end to vulgar balladry. Like concentric rings widening from a primary impulse, it was by nature inimical to limiting command. How much of it was he then forced to admit? Obviously, as he saw the task, he was not compiling a fixed and final canon of authenticity but culling from the undiscriminated mass of possibilities a rationally comprehensive selection, inevitably arbitrary yet judicious, circumscribed wherever possible by negative considerations yet responsive to special pleading of various sorts in many individual cases. At the end, he had admittedly taken in too much to please himself, but there had always been some particular reason to tip the scale and overcome his repugnance. Purity in popular balladry is always relative: it no more exists in the natural world than absolute zero. The canon of the exclusively popular is therefore not to be found in Child's collection and neither, by the same token, could

---

[9] *Op.cit.*, p. 260.   [10] *Ibid.*, p. 254.

it ever have existed in his mind as other than an abstract concept. Actually, it was a fiction invented by the awe of his disciples and falsely equated with his collection as he left it.[11]

Such a misconception of Child's achievement was the result of special circumstances that no longer exert their full potency. It was born in a fostering climate of Teutonic romanticism somewhat belatedly reinforced in this country by ideas of literary evolution carried over by analogy from the Darwinian theory of organic evolution. The Ballad was, it was felt, a *genre* that had arisen, flourished, and declined in response to historic conditions that would not be repeated. Child, gifted with most miraculous organ, had been able to discover all the extant examples and traces of this now all-but-extinct phenomenon and had bequeathed the collection to posterity as a definitive record, adorned and illustrated by the light of his supreme knowledge. The reception of it as inviolable and entire was easy and natural to those who had worked day after day in the personal inspiration of his omniscient presence. "These three-hundred-odd ballads," wrote F. B. Gummere with a show of reason born of perfect conviction, "are either the surviving specimens of a genre, a literary species, which is called popular because in its main qualities it is derived from the 'people,' or else they are the somewhat arbitrary collection of poems which had in some way become favorite and even traditional, apart from print, with mainly unlettered folk. In the first case they can be treated as a closed literary account, and, like the medieval romance, the ancient epic, as an outcome of conditions which no longer exist and cannot be revived. In the second case, while conditions of oral transmission may be changed, there is nothing to prevent the daily production of ballads which may become in time as popular as any in our collections.[12]

Dismayed by the latter alternative, Gummere came to the unlucky conclusion that the only convincing way in which the Child ballads could ultimately be differentiated from other pieces speciously similar was by assuming a difference in their beginnings. "It is clear," he roundly declares, "that only a definition by origins really defines."[13] It seems equally clear today that such a contention with regard to ballads is utterly chimerical unless one starts with the critical issue already settled: that is, with the body of authentic materials already set apart from the spurious—with, in fact, the Child collection as Gummere conceived and received it. Had Gummere had to perform Child's task of sifting the true and genuine from the welter of popular and pseudo-popular matter, written and oral, no definition by origins would have helped him to establish a canon. Obviously, such a definition rests on a theory that can never be put to the test in any particular case. To make the hypothetical beginnings a fundamental point of definition is to beg the whole question, Whether there is a radical distinction between Child's three-hundred-odd ballads and all the other verse now or formerly in traditional circulation.

Subsequent opinion has inclined more and more to adopt Gummere's rejected alternative, that, "while conditions of oral transmission may be changed"—be it *via* cinema, television, radio, or phonograph!—"there is nothing to prevent the daily production of ballads which may become in time as popular as any in our collections." And this, we may feel, is a view to which

---

[11] Cf. "Mrs. Brown and the Ballad," *Western Folklore*, IV (1945), pp. 129-40.

[12] F. B. Gummere, *The Popular Ballad*, 1907, pp. 15-16.

[13] *Ibid*., p. 14.

Child, in face of his lonely and protracted struggles and uncertainties, his inability to find a close working definition, with his unrivalled knowledge of the incalculable paths of oral tradition, and his modest sense of what he had accomplished, might have become reconciled. But his sympathy, tolerance, and patience would surely have been exhausted long before that later orbit had been described: "the declension is so gradual from the freshest and raciest to the . . . absolutely mean and stupid. . . . It is a pity one can't consistently insist on the lyrical, or singable, character as a criterion."[14]

§3. BASIS, SCOPE, AND AIM

Why, then, it will be asked, if Child provides no dependable canon of authenticity; if, in fact, a considerable cantle of his pieces would have to be lopped from the truly popular by his own testimony; and if, relying for criterion of admission on indisputable evidence of prolonged circulation by oral transmission through the medium of song, in multiform versions, it is possible to compile a different and an even larger collection of "popular" ballads: why, then, persist in confining such a work as the present within Child's arbitrary limits?

The challenge must be met; and it can be met with confidence. In the first place, the Child collection has been the indispensable anchorage of all serious study of its subject for more than half a century. As the standard and authoritative work on British balladry and its Continental relationships, it is so far in the lead that its rivals are not even in sight. Child's work on his chosen texts, and his staggeringly learned comparative notes, subject only to minor correction in the light of subsequent evidence, stand as solid today as ever. So far as he carried it, his work is complete and sufficient, and will never have to be redone. Moreover, precisely because no final canon of the authentic can ever be constructed, it is an inestimable advantage to all students in this field to have in hand a work universally accepted as surrogate and point of departure. It is by his own merits that Child stands where he does, and not by virtue of a thesis that may in time be modified or superseded. The monumental stature of his achievement has given it a prescriptive right to be consulted before all else; its judgments, as reflected in inclusion and exclusion, carry inevitably the weight of its total *Anschauung* and are thus significant not merely as disconnected items but in relation to the whole work. It is not a simple question of right or wrong in individual cases: that Child omitted *this* may have a bearing on his having included *that*; and altogether the anfractuosities visible in the work are those of a single mind unquestionably master of the field.

But if the importance of Child's work has been truly represented, a more compelling answer to the challenge above stems from that fact. Ballads, as we have recognized, are songs, and the

[14] Hustvedt, *op.cit.*, p. 254. Child's views have been assessed by many students. The fullest collation and summary is still the very valuable article by W. M. Hart, "Professor Child and the Ballad," *PMLA*, xxi (1906), 755-807. More recently, Thelma G. James has compared Child's early and late collections for indications of changing or crystallizing standards. Cf. "The English and Scottish Popular Ballads of Francis J. Child," *JAF*, xlvi (1933), 51-68.

music that carries the words and keeps them alive in tradition is an integral and ultimately inescapable half of the subject. Text and tune are interdependent and interactive. Formally and stylistically, as we must finally acknowledge, ballad-texts cannot be adequately explained without reference to their proper music; and not infrequently acquaintance with the melodic tradition of a ballad will be found to throw valuable light on its history.[15] In a sense, therefore, Child left his work unfinished. The attempt to round it out by presenting the musical record alongside the texts with a fullness comparable to his—in so far as that may at this date be possible, in a different kind and distribution of evidence—is easily understood to be not merely natural but even necessary.

Unfortunately, the task is not a simple one of recovering the proper tunes of Child's printed texts and adding them to his work with appropriate editorial comment. Relatively few of the tunes sung to those texts were transmitted to posterity, at least in identifiable form. The great bulk of our records of the music for the Child ballads has been gathered in the half-century since Child's death from oral sources he was unable to reach. This later harvest is, of course, traditional and may be centuries old but it comprises a mass of newly collected versions of the texts along with the tunes. To print the tunes by themselves would therefore not be to supply the missing half of Child's work. It would be to commit the same old error in reverse, isolating the tunes from their mated texts and ignoring the latter, perpetuating that divorce which only among scholars has been traditional. And since there can be no historical justification for matching chosen tunes arbitrarily to chosen words, it is clearly essential to give each tune with its individual text, wherever both have survived, so that each may be studied in the light of the other, as the product of influences mutually exerted. It follows that although the present work is by intention complementary to Child's, it is also in large part necessarily supplementary on the textual side, taking in all such fresh copies of words as have been recorded with their proper tunes. Not much, in fact, of Child's copy can find place here, for reasons which we can only lament. Texts without their own tunes do not meet our primary objective. But the scarcity of the earlier musical record results in at least one small present comfort, namely, that the size of the present work is not owing to its having swallowed Child whole!

On the other hand, for the sake of rendering a full musical account to atone for previous neglect, tunes properly avouched as genuine will be allowed entrance even when their words are lost. There is the more excuse for such latitude in that, like the ballad-texts which have connections with other kinds of traditional matter—tales, riddles, lyrics—and which do not always cling to the same melody, the tunes also have other associations and a life of their own. They may often unite with other ballad-texts or with non-narrative lyrics secular or sacred, and may be sometimes followed independently through a series of unmistakable reappearances back into the Middle Ages and the traditional music of the Church. Whether Gregorian Chant has common roots with other folk-song or not, sacred and secular meet and cross over at many points in the winding course of the centuries; and, while we must not allow ourselves to be distracted in the mazes of musicology, the modal character of the ballad-tunes is a continual

[15] Cf. "The Interdependence of Ballad Tunes and Texts," *Western Folklore*, III (1944), pp. 185-207.

reminder that we are dealing with a tradition far more ancient than any of its surviving records. As with the ballad-texts, so with the tunes: there is no dependable evidence, either internal or external, for their ultimate age. We need not therefore be unduly cast down by the failure of earlier generations to preserve a mass of melodic testimony in dated records, much as we may regret the fact.

The effort to recover the singing tradition of the Child ballads throws interesting light on the degree and nature of their popularity. Ample record of their circulation as songs is the best possible confirmation of their belonging truly to the "people." It is of the highest interest, therefore, to discover which ballads have been favorite in this sense in recent times. Recognizing that favoritism waxes and wanes, and that whole classes, like the Robin Hood ballads which must at one time have borne away the bell, are no longer in fashion, one must yet regard it as significant that many of the songs put foremost by Child as among the oldest and most authentic are still among the most beloved and widespread. The musical record is, by far, most abundant for Child's first hundred ballads, generally speaking; least abundant in the second hundred, comprising the Robin Hood cycle and most of the historical subjects; and again more abundant for the later romantic Scottish and various unclassed ballads of the third hundred, where often the influence of print has clearly been strongly at work as a preservative.

There is some sort of evidence, good or bad, for the musical tradition of slightly more than two-thirds of the Child collection. All told, there must be on record in one or another medium—print, manuscript, disc, or tape—perhaps 5,000 independently derived versions of the Child ballad-tunes. These are very unevenly distributed both in time, space, and proportion. Of some of the ballads but one musical setting has survived; of others there are a hundred or even two hundred. Geographically, the amplest gatherings are those of England, of Scotland, and of the Appalachians and New England. In time, sad to say, much the greater proportion belongs to the present century. The only flattering unction to be found for this historical loss is that the great mass of evidence lies where the record is most dependable. Dependability is of course a very relative matter: no transcriptions into musical notation can be absolutely dependable, even from a hand so impeccable as Béla Bartók's. But live recordings reach a very high degree of accuracy in these "electronic" days. Moreover, they preserve the total song, from one end to the other, as music; and can be transcribed far more correctly than singing to the ear alone. Even without mechanical aids, however, twentieth-century records, because of a change of attitude among collectors and editors toward this kind of music, which has made them more knowing, more respectful, more critically aware, are far more faithful than what was set down in the nineteenth century, which preferred parlor versions with major-minor piano accompaniment; or in the eighteenth century, when the tunes were adapted to new ballad-opera texts; or in the seventeenth century, when they were seldom written down except as airs for country dances; or in the sixteenth century, when they served primarily, so far as the record is concerned, as themes for virtuoso variations by the masters of the Elizabethan keyboard instruments.

Broadly speaking, it is to the collectors of the present century alone that we are indebted for anything like a representative body of genuinely traditional ballad- and song-tunes, faithfully recorded from the lips of actual folk-singers. Earlier, there is but a meagre scattering of tunes casually preserved from anonymous sources and for the most part carelessly set down by amateur transcribers. Such records, to be sure, are precious; but we treasure them more because they are the only traces we possess of what was then sung than because of any reliance we can place in them. The list of remembered names is not long: Thomas Ravenscroft, to whom we owe our earliest records of Child ballad-tunes with their texts, one of the best musicians of the lot but little concerned with editorial fidelity; the Playfords, only interested in them as phrasal units for dancing; D'Urfey, who treated them as he pleased; Ramsay and Thomson, who saved them for social uses; Burns, who had an ear for a good tune, ballad words or no, and was fortunately not musician enough to sophisticate those he learned; Charles Kirkpatrick Sharpe, Kinloch, and Motherwell, who, though technically handicapped, loved them *in puris naturalibus* and took care to leave them so; Christie, who vitiated an almost unrivalled collection by bad editorial principles; his Northumbrian contemporary, John Stokoe, a safer authority; John Broadwood, Baring-Gould, and Frank Kidson, later and more knowledgeable English counterparts of the Scottish trio previously named: these are our principal benefactors during three whole centuries. Rimbault and Chappell were library men to whose antiquarian zeal we owe much in another kind.[16]

To the enthusiasm and energy and sound judgment of the founders and early members of the Folk-Song Society (London), established as the present century opened, we owe a fresh start, a clear direction and purpose in the investigation of British folk-song, and a huge accession of priceless melodic beauty seldom equalled in any time or country. It is ironic, and a little sad, that this society, devoted primarily to the salvage of traditional *music* but springing into life so soon after Child's death, should have been the means of bringing to light an ample harvest of the very kind that Child had vainly sought through so many years. It had the benefit, before the outbreak of the First World War, of the active participation of a considerable number of very gifted men and women, outstanding among whom were Vaughan Williams, Percy Grainger, Cecil Sharp, Lucy Broadwood, Anne G. Gilchrist, Frank Kidson, Gustav Holst, George Butterworth, E. J. Moeran, and Clive Carey. In the inspiration of its example, and at first spurred by the galvanizing spirit of Cecil Sharp, a series of regional societies was established in the United States by a sort of chain reaction. Several of these have made substantial additions to our knowledge of folk-song in this country, by published volumes and by recordings contributed to the national archive of American Folk-Song in the Library of Congress. Meanwhile, two most energetic and successful collectors had been independently at work in their native regions: Gavin Greig in the Northeast of Scotland, and Phillips Barry in New England. These men, and Cecil Sharp, must by their individual efforts have amassed in the aggregate easily half of all that was gathered in the first quarter of the present century. Indeed, it is unlikely that Cecil Sharp's contribution, assisted in life and faithfully carried forward after his death by his tireless co-worker, Maud Karpeles, will ever be approached. The

[16] Cf. the analytical roster in the editor's article, "On the Union of Words and Music in the 'Child' Ballads," *Western Folklore*, XI (1952), pp. 233-49.

magnitude and extraordinary versatility of his talents and accomplishments put him as far above competition in British Folk-Song and Dance as Child is in his own separate demesne. There has never been a collector with such quickness and tact in seizing and accurately reporting essential melodic characteristics from individual singing. His copy strikes a mean between the typical and idiosyncratic that is almost ideal. (There is a limit of refinement beyond which the subtle notation of nuances obscures all but the single rendition of an individual performance, and renders an account too cumbersome for comparative use in the study of melody, valuable though it be in the analysis of style.) Sharp enriched his national heritage by recovering some 5,000 records directly from the lips of country singers in England and America. Of these, something approaching a fifth are versions of the Child ballads. In Scotland, Greig, probably his nearest rival in collecting, gathered some 3,000 similar records, of which perhaps a tenth are versions of the Child ballads. It is difficult to estimate the size of Barry's collection, which was less systematically kept and less homogeneous. A good deal still remains on wax cylinders yet untranscribed. Barry and Percy Grainger were pioneers in field-recording but Barry was unable to take full advantage of the method, partly because of primitive equipment and the consequent difficulties of transcription. Much also of his collection came from chance correspondents and casual print. But his interests ranged more widely, and were more given to theory, than those of most British collectors.

The present collection pursues a graduated course among the various records now available. The editor has tried to make his accounting exhaustive to the end of the nineteenth century, scouring Child's own kingdom for musical remains. After that point, the treatment of the mass of materials is increasingly selective. For the first quarter of the current century, the aim has been to take account of whatever has been found in print. Available manuscripts and phonographic records also have been used whenever they seemed trustworthy as traditional evidence and could be deciphered by such lights as the editor could bring to bear. In the second quarter of the century, sound-recordings have tended to take over more and more of the burden of responsible preservation and transmission of evidence; and, while the editor has striven to keep abreast of the printed records and such manuscripts as he has been privileged to use, it has seemed unnecessary, even if it were possible, to make a complete report of everything that is more perfectly preserved in live vocal image and in that form can be made accessible to multitudes not musically trained. The right procedure for a future editor, once the past has been fully surveyed, will probably be to prepare a series of vocal recordings from authentic sources, and accompany them with critical and analytical notes, illustrated where desirable by selected passages transcribed for comparative study. It seems idle to reduce the living, truthful record with dogged persistence to a dim reflection, except where discussion may be facilitated.

There is, of course, no possibility in any case of absolute completeness. While the work is passing through the press, its hypothetical finality has been disproved by new books and recordings, and of the latter every month brings a fresh and larger supply. It may, on the other hand, be asked what justification there is for printing so many variants of the same melodic idea. The answer to this question is of central importance. It is in the variants alone that we can study the processes of melodic tradition and transmission; and through them alone can we hope to arrive at sound generalizations as to the laws or forces that find expression in these forms. Any theorist on the subject may easily promulgate his notions, and select and order the evidence so as to demonstrate their correctness. His readers, to prove him either right or wrong, will have to work through the bulk of the evidence which he for the most part omits but upon the totality of which his conclusions have presumably been based. But until that corpus of evidence has been made readily accessible, with a fullness not conditioned by thesis or theory, few will be able, even among specialists, to traverse the ground for themselves. It is therefore of primary importance to gather and present in a single view a body of materials sufficient and convenient, to which interested students may confidently refer as a basis for whatever conclusions their special insights may reveal. This is the merit of the great sweep of Child's collection, and it is this merit to which the present collection aspires in so comprehensively representing the ballad-music. The morphology of the subject can be established only by dint of the most detailed and laborious comparative analysis of traditional variation as revealed in the mass of recorded examples.[17] A nearly identical but independent variant can be a significant link in a chain of evidence. Tradition is essentially a centripetal force, a principle not of experiment but of stability; and in the study of it, variety is usually less revealing than homogeneity. No verbal language, obviously, could exist if the meanings of words changed abruptly rather than by imperceptible degrees. Just so, continuity is the fundamental consideration in the oral transmission of a melodic language.

§4. EDITORIAL PROCEDURE

Child, who followed Grundtvig's great Danish work in the plan of his volumes, has in turn provided the structural framework of the present collection—the sequence of headnotes, lists of versions, and gathered examples; has set the inclusive limits of the contents, and the numerical series and order of the ballad-complexes to be admitted. Where there is a gap in the sequence, it occurs because the editor has found no music and no musical traces of the number omitted.

The variant copies of the numbers included are usually more abundant than in Child for the reason suggested earlier, that melodic tradition has to be studied in its resemblances as well as differences. It is a point of significance to determine the *frequency* of a mode, or metre, or phrasal pattern, or cadence, in a melodic tradition. The habits of our folk-tunes cannot be safely described until we have enough evidence to identify them as *habits* and to determine their relative inveteracy.

The general intention of the headnotes is to perform for the melodic tradition of each ballad a service analogous to that of Child's headnotes for the text. The aim is to amass the pertinent information on the ballad's musical history in the English-speaking world, and to describe

[17] Cf. "The Morphology of the Ballad-Tunes," *JAF*, 67 (1954), pp. 1-13.

briefly the main outlines of its recorded tradition apart from the verbal text. The latter has not been entirely ignored: beyond its constant function as primary means of identifying ballads, it has not infrequently supplied useful pointers and checks upon melodic connections. Everywhere, however, Child's own headnotes are assumed to be indispensable for the fuller study of the ballad. There is no attempt here either to supersede or to summarize them. But as touching the verbal texts the editor has permitted himself much latitude, discussing them or not as might suit the occasion, or as he had later evidence to add to Child's, or, rarely, to enter an objection to Child's disposal of the case.

In these headnotes will be found no range of foreign reference such as gives weight and distinction to those of Child. Whether from insufficient knowledge or lack of perception, or because of the actual absence of evidence, foreign melodic resemblances have not often been found. Textual analogues, of course, with British ballads are abundant throughout Europe. Their relationships, being multiform permutations of a common underlying narrative theme or idea, are usually easy to establish, and Child's citations identify them by the score. But the case of the tunes is more vexatious. The foreign tunes found with analogous ballads are clearly irrelevant unless a common melodic idea can be demonstrated. Where such melodic affiliates exist, they need to be quoted note for note in order to convince. A general community of melodic idea is in fact exhibited in connection with three ballad-tunes in Walter Wiora's *Europäischer Volksgesang*,[18] a work which sweeps a very wide compass. The correspondence is always the large one of "gemeinsame Formen," and involves no sharing of textual affiliations. Melodic patterns or ideas may certainly pass from land to land, and have been held in common between peoples, as Wiora abundantly proves and as we shall observe in the case of a few more tunes that lead us far back in time. But it can seldom be shown that a distinct foreign tune has entered the British ballad-tradition, and perhaps never with an analogous text. Foreign tunes may from time to time come into favor just because they are foreign and therefore flavorsome. But they do not seem readily to be taken into the folk-tradition of their adopters, and if any are so, they are probably untypical of their own native tradition. Wider familiarity with the folk-song of other peoples than it is this editor's happiness to enjoy might disclose scattered instances, apart from quasi-universal Western forms, of borrowing or migration. But what chiefly strikes one in reading through the great representative collections of various cultures is their *otherness*, their nationalism. On the whole, the alien traditions would ill agree or assimilate with the simple rhythmic patterns and diatonic modal configurations of the British folk-style.

The capital difficulty of an editor of materials like these is to find an objective method of classifying and ordering them on musical grounds. Dates of record will not serve: these are misleading and unworkable. When far apart, they may promote an untruthful, sophisticated copy before a genuine traditional one. When close together, they may separate near relations. Again, however, to make the verbal text the principle of arrangement is in effect to leave the question of melodic resemblances untouched, or under impossible handicaps of cross-reference.

[18] Köln, n.d. but ?1955. Cf. pp. 32 ("The Douglas Tragedy"), 38 ("Lord Thomas and Fair Ellinor"), 52 ("The Gypsy Laddie").

The music itself, therefore, must be the basis of whatever scheme is to be followed, wherever order is a significant consideration.

Classifying is one problem and ordering is another. The crucial difficulty of the first involves the essential identity of a melody. How far apart, in rhythm and metre, in range, in modality, in phrasal scheme, in the succession of notes employed, may two tunes diverge and still be regarded as statements of the same melodic idea? Whatever the limits, they are narrower in folk-music than in art-music. In the latter, variation of a given entity is the deliberate and controlled intention of the composer. In the former, discernible resemblance is our only assurance of kinship. Within a tradition, variation is almost subliminal. The traditional tune, like the hand of the dial, "steals from his figure and no pace perceived." But the starting-point can never be ascertained: we must start where we happen to be. It is impossible to eliminate the subjective elements from our particular judgments, which are, moreover, never quite constant even in themselves because affected by their immediate melodic environment in the hearer's mind. The more rigidly we try to impose an arbitrary, objective scheme of classification, the more the essential identity, as we come to feel, tends to elude our predetermined tests. And since, in a normally homogeneous musical folk-tradition there will be many common features, it will not always be easy to decide whether a shared trait is peculiar to a group or belongs to a more inclusive society.

Yet, as we know, the gravitational force of tradition is on the side of stability; and when tunes attached to variant texts of the same ballad-complex show melodic resemblances in even a single phrase, it is more natural to infer a connection than to attribute the fact to mere accident. In obedience to this simple doctrine, we shall be reluctant to divide the tunes of a given ballad into distinct classes, so long as we can find plausible reasons for relating them. Hence, the grouping of tunes in this work is admittedly unscientific, open to debate; and even such consistency as it aspires to has at times been modified by convenience. It will be time to be strict when a scientific and reliable blood-test for tune families shall have enabled us to set up accurate and exclusive categories.

The crucial difficulty of *ordering* lies in finding a rationale of precedence for a series of tunes much alike. On what inherent grounds should one tune be placed before another? Our literal alphabet is non-rational but objective, and upheld by universal acceptance. A comparable invention for melody, collapsible or expansive at need, and certain for every user, would be of inestimable advantage in sorting and finding tunes. But the identity of folk-tunes does not inhere simply in a given succession of notes, like the correct thematic statements of authors' compositions. Consequently, to be valuable, the system would have to contain some of the properties of an analytical thesaurus as well. The perfect scheme would provide both a point of departure, a sequence objectively fixed, and a way of ensuring that tunes intrinsically alike, or related, would be found close together in the series. It is hardly surprising that no method combining such diversities has yet been devised.

Any large group of tunes comprised of variant statements of a melodic idea will probably reveal upon close analysis that the essential identity of the tune lies in the two related factors of mode and contour. As within the cycle of keys certain relationships inhere, so in the modal system we can find an analogous chain. Referring to the modes by their medieval names, because these are accepted and easier to remember than numbers, we discover that the Ionian heptatonic scale—our modern diatonic major with semitones between the third and fourth, seventh and eighth, degrees—in the octave segment from its lower dominant to upper dominant gives a scale coinciding with the Mixolydian, the half-tones now occurring between the third and fourth degrees, and between the sixth and seventh. Similarly, the scale that commences on the fourth below the Mixolydian tonic is the Dorian, with half-steps between two and three, and six and seven. And again, the scale a fourth below the Dorian is the Æolian—our modern melodic minor—with half-steps between two and three, and five and six. A fourth below the Æolian comes the Phrygian, with half-steps between one and two, and five and six. Thus, with each shift, the position of one of the half-steps in the octave sequence is altered, the other remains unchanged. If we omit the half-step where the alteration occurs, we have a hexatonic scale equally sharing all the notes held in common by the heptatonics on either side. The series of hexatonics therefore lies between the adjacent members of the heptatonic series. Similarly, when we omit both half-steps, we are left with a series of pentatonic scales, each one of which coincides in its full extent with two hexatonic, and three heptatonic, scales.

By virtue of the position of the semitones with relation to the tonic, or by their absence, each scale has a character of its own; and consequently, the tunes made out of those notes, and only those, which a particular modal scale offers for use, reflect the quality of that mode; but with diminishing force—or, conversely, with increasing neutrality—in the hexatonic system with its double, and in the pentatonic with its triple, reference. The gapped scales thus provide the channels through which with fewest obstacles a tune may pass from mode to mode.

Contour, obviously, is partly dependent on the notes at its disposal. The mode of a tune is therefore a primary fact in its delineation. It will ordinarily be found that a large group of variant tunes will show a numerical preference for one mode or another, but will perhaps spread to adjacent modes on either side, through gapped scales, toward statements more strongly minor or more positively major, as the case may be. In ordering our series of variants, therefore, we may give first place to the statements in the favorite modal position, holding back the strays unless for other reasons they claim immediate admission in the sequence of related tunes.

Coming now to consider contours with closer attention, we recognize at once that not all the notes have equal weight in fixing the character of a tune. Notes with metrical emphasis are more important, and of these the ones at the beginnings and ends of phrases are again outstanding. But neither are these latter of equal emphasis. We know that the tonic is the very root of every tune, and that all the other notes used in the tune get their basic meaning from their relation to it, directly or indirectly. Most tunes, therefore, end on the tonic, as the point of utmost insistence and stability. Again, it can be proved by statistical count that, next to the final, the point of a tune least likely to vary—we speak of typical folk-tunes in our British-American melodic tradition—is the mid-cadence, the last note of the second phrase of an ordinary four- or five-phrase tune. Thereafter, in any large mass of homogeneous tunes, it is possible to assign a relative weight of emphasis, by a similar analysis of stability, to all the other positions of stress.

Some of these may be nearly equal, like the first and last accented notes of the first phrase. Least stable is likely to be the third phrase of the tune—which is another way of saying that the popular memory is weaker in the third phrase than anywhere else. Most readers have probably experienced this fact in themselves. The fourth phrase is strongly conditioned by its approach to the concluding tonic, and so less individualized. It follows from these natural phenomena that tunes are likely to get themselves defined as identities by the time they have reached the mid-cadence. We can take advantage of such considerations as the foregoing in setting up a moderately consistent practice in the ordering of our variant copies of related tunes. This method has been put to use in the present work, though not with absolute and scientific rigor. Folk-tunes, one soon finds, are like living beings, recalcitrant to rigid rule, and seldom quite normal or typical. In studying them, moreover, we all too frequently find ourselves woefully short of specimens and unable to connect the tally of scattered bits of evidence in a solid account.

So far, we have been discussing matters as if the records, where they exist, gave a faithful account of the tune that was sung. This, of course, is never the case in a written transcription. The only way to experience the truth is in a live rendition or sound-recording, and the latter has until recently been impossible. All other records are in the final analysis a *pis-aller*. At the very best, we are working with suggested images, hardly closer to their originals than a skillful pen drawing of an oil painting on canvas. But once the fact has been frankly acknowledged, we can pick up the pieces and get on with our work. Unless we are content to reduce the study to one of contemporary folk-singing rather than a historical study of folk-song, the nature of our total mass of evidence leaves us no choice in the matter. And there are compensations.

No two renditions of the same song by the same singer on the same day and in the same hour can be identical, by laboratory standards of cents and bels. Moreover, no two stanzas of a *single* rendition can be musically identical. The singer, however, "knows the tune," and thinks he is singing it all the time. Actually, he is singing variations on a musical idea. These variations are scientifically interesting, but too synchronous and diminutive to be of much historical interest as between themselves. If we possessed a complete account of them, we should have to synopsize it to something approximating what the singer "had in mind," before we could employ it in a large-scale comparative study of the song. The task of reducing it, from the scientific data, to its typical form for that singer would be both arduous and puzzling, and probably, in the event, quite subjective. Most of our existing records, of course, simply by-pass such problems by starting at the end: with a subjective notion of the singer's melodic idea, and an attempt to suggest it on paper. When the transcriber has the ear, the skill, and the wide knowledge of a Cecil Sharp, the single approximation is more useful for comparative and historical inquiry than a more exact picture of a single rendition, stanza by stanza, with plus and minus signs suggesting sharpened flats and flattened sharps at particular notes on that particular occasion, and with all the other details of a meticulous record. The aims of the two kinds of transcription are divergent. As suggested above, one is directed toward the abstract, the song; the other toward the individual act of singing. And since musical notation, when all is said, is so desperately clumsy the latter aim can now best be furthered by the continuous study of sound-recordings.

It seems unnecessary to make a census of the comparative reliability of our records in this place. We have used everything we could find, good or bad; and it is part of an editor's business to estimate dependability, and where necessary to put the reader on his guard. Once we realize that all records must be partial and suggestive only of a continually fluctuating melodic design, we can proceed with a fair amount of confidence. Not to be forgotten is the fact that the folk-singer never is faced with the reader's problem of fitting the words of each successive stanza into the straitjacket of the time-values printed at the head of his text in such a work as this. As he sings, words and notes are continually making little mutual and natural concessions, comfortably adapting to each other's needs to gain their common object, within the narrow limits established. It is this relative freedom that gives vitality to each fresh statement, and saves the repetitions from intolerable monotony. But when the words of a single stanza are printed directly below the notes, the reader's difficulty is only increased: the music is thereby fixed in an inflexible, authoritative paradigm to which all that follows must conform. This is to compound our handicaps; and in order to remind ourselves constantly of the reality, we have chosen to print the tunes unattached to particular syllables, only indicating the phrasal cadence by a mark coinciding with the end of a verse. The phrase-marks are of different lengths, according to the weight of the cadence. To the same end, syllabic ties are generally removed from the notes, except for constant refrains.

For ease of comparison, the tunes are usually transposed, but the pitch of the original copy is indicated in a catch-signature with the initial note. Similar notice is given where the time-signature has been altered. Flats or sharps have been removed without notice from signatures when they are denied by the mode of the tune, unless the pitch has also been changed. An inverted fermata sign indicates a shorter pause than the usual hold, but has no fixed metrical value in relation to the note-length.

The modal terminology is that generally familiar to students of British folk-song, the names deriving from ecclesiastical use in the Middle Ages. It has been found unnecessary to employ the hypo- series, but the system has been extended to take in the hexatonic scales lying between each two heptatonics and sharing the scale-pattern of each. This is shown by the initial of each mode with a slash, thus: I/M, the hexatonic between the Ionian and Mixolydian heptatonics. The pentatonic scales have been numbered according to their relations with the diatonic series, with the symbol π and a superior figure. Thus, π^1 is the pentatonic lacking fourth and seventh, and therefore agreeing in all its notes with the two hexatonics Ly/I and I/M, and with the three heptatonics Ly, I, and M. Similarly with the rest.[19]

To the identifying symbol of the mode at the top of each printed tune is added a letter indicating the range: a for *authentic*, from tonic to octave and above; p for *plagal*, roughly from lower to upper dominant; m for *mixed*, the other two ranges combined. The range has a significant relation to the shape of the tune, and cannot safely be ignored in comparative analysis.

[19] Cf. "Folk-Song and the Modes," *Musical Quarterly*, xxxii (1946), pp. 37-49.

The knowing reader will object to the editor's use of the terms *duple* and *triple* to cover all multiples of two and of three in metrical reference. This is deliberate. There are no other terms equally self-explanatory. The unsatisfactoriness of "compound duple" to express a metre that in the ballad-world is much more strongly felt as triple than as duple is too obvious to be discussed. To our folk-singers, 6/8 time is hardly distinguishable from a faster 3/4. It has seemed desirable to avoid all unnecessary complexity; and for similar reasons 12/8 has usually been taken as simple 6/8, the refinement in this context, and considering the state of most of our records, appearing quite needless. The extraordinary rhythmical precision and awareness of some Continental folk-musics is not native to our tradition. British folk-song, unaccompanied, is by preference free and unhurried; its rhythmical complexities, when they occur, are more likely to be accidental than deliberate. Even so simple a metre as 5/4 has rather the feeling of chance than of controlled intention, and usually alternates somewhat irregularly between 3/4 and 2/4. Subtler patterns like 7/4 are almost never established. Freedom combines with simplicity to produce the characteristic rhythmical effects of this tradition.

Some of the musical texts have been corrected by the editor but seldom without due notice, and only where correction appeared necessary and obvious. The versions of Dean William Christie are a special case. Christie was given to swelling out his tunes by adding a second strain of his own and inserting turns and graces. These are usually clearly editorial and have frequently been omitted in this work, though the second strains are sometimes given in smaller notes. Christie's verbal texts, moreover, are all too frequently merely "epitomized" from Buchan's copies, and have no independent standing in tradition. Hence, more than the first stanza of them is not usually printed. It should also be mentioned that Sharp's practice was not so scrupulous with words as with music. He did not always transcribe the full words of a common song if it showed no unusual features as sung; and, of course, in his anxiety to restore to the English their heritage of folk-music, he did not hesitate to print more polished and acceptable texts than the rough and ungrammatical ones he had often taken down. But he used what he could, and never wrote fresh words on a different theme, as did Baring-Gould and A. P. Graves, for example, to supplant the originals.

In the punctuation of the verbal text, the sources of the present collection exhibit the utmost editorial diversity. Where the original was in print and easily accessible, the present editor has felt that punctuation was subject to his jurisdiction if he wished to assert his right. The heavy use of quotation-marks and the grammatical relation of refrains to context seem somehow to belie the facts of oral rendition and tend to assume undue importance. On the other hand, the frequent scantiness of punctuation in manuscript sources perhaps goes too far in the other direction and might well have been regularized had the collector reduced his copy to print. But the editor has found it repugnant to alter copy being printed now for the first time, feeling that in its untouched state it presented no real difficulties to the reader and perhaps even brought him closer to collector and singer. For the most part, therefore, manuscript has been left scrupulously uncontaminated by editorial rehandling. And, while the copy from print has been treated with somewhat less respect, the reader even yet may possibly feel that it still bears too many evidences of the variety of tastes that took part in its concoction.

The lists of ballad-variants have been gathered into groups, and sometimes into sub-groups, where such a division seemed justifiable. But for convenience of reference, each variant copy is designated by a number or a letter in a continuous series. Where the numerical sequence is interrupted by a letter, the alphabetical symbol signifies that the variant belonging there is not reprinted in the present work, either because its resemblance to its neighbor is too close, or because it is not sufficiently trusted as tradition, or because its notation is musically too illiterate to be corrected with assurance. It is perhaps worth repeating here explicitly that throughout the book the order of variants is not chronological either in fact or conjecture, is not geographic or regional, is not often affected by the verbal text, but is determined by the music alone.

The favorite configurations of British-American ballad-music will no doubt become evident in the course of this work. Clearly, there is no jealous regard for proprietary rights among the ballad-tunes, but everywhere a free and generous give and take. It is obvious that some types thrive in favorable localities and tend to crowd out the less hardy organisms. In this way, in a community of continuous ballad-singing, favorite tunes will tend to assume a great part of the work. Probably, as the creative elements of the community grow less interested in balladry, or more sophisticated, the older melodic tradition tends to become more and more homogeneous and stereotyped. Thus, instead of drifting farther and farther away from a primary base, the course of oral tradition, if uninterrupted by alien influences, would appear, as tributary streams are swallowed by rivers, to be tending toward fewer and fewer basic patterns. But, fortunately, that ultimate reduction is still far away. And if it comes, the records gathered in collections like the present one, will still enable us to repossess and solace ourselves with some portion of the wealth of the past.

BERTRAND H. BRONSON

ACKNOWLEDGMENTS

A WORK OF THIS KIND is necessarily the beneficiary of the time-consuming effort and skill of many individuals. Fortunately, the people who collect or concern themselves with folk-songs are likely to be motivated by affectionate enthusiasm for these nomads and not by hopes of monetary reward, and are as a rule glad to share their discoveries. To my requests to be allowed to print or reprint, I have met almost everywhere with the kindest responses, alike from collectors, librarians, and publishers. Indeed, their liberality has been so universal that I have come to attribute any exception rather to some mistaking of the purpose of this work than to reluctance to further its successful completion. Consequently, though my list of obligations is long, it is a list of genuine favors, almost unclouded by material conditions. Hence, the acknowledgments that follow are rendered with a more than ordinary warmth of gratitude, in the full consciousness that my work owes its very existence to the host of its benefactors; for it must be obvious that an insistence on individual fees would have been a death-sentence to the whole enterprise. To the names ensuing, therefore, I offer sincerest thanks; and in superlative degree to those that stand foremost in the list.

The vertebrate column of this work is that portion of Cecil J. Sharp's vast collection which belongs among the Child ballads. Without the free use of Sharp's variants there would have been little use in pursuing my task. The absence of so large, so trustworthy, so essential a portion of the extant record would have been absolutely crippling. My debt, therefore, to those responsible for the Sharp MSS and their publication is impossible to overstate. From all concerned I have met with a liberality commensurate with the magnitude of the favor conferred. Before the Second World War, I was hospitably welcomed at Clare College, Cambridge, and allowed the unhampered use of Sharp's original MSS deposited there, subject to no restrictions of time save those imposed by my own occasions. Thereafter, Miss Maud Karpeles, Sharp's indefatigable collaborator, editor, and executrix, put at my service her unrivalled knowledge, her encouragement, her constant and invaluable support, counsel, and practical assistance, with a generosity hard to match but familiar to many who share her friendship. To Miss Karpeles I owe permission to include the variants hitherto unpublished from Sharp's MSS; and a further favor as well, the advantage of reprinting in their original state some of the songs which she collected in Newfoundland. Latterly, with that munificence proper to "Her of the Book, the tripled Crown"—"down from whose towers a ray" has glanced upon this "passer-by"—the Oxford University Press has allowed the use of many songs recently reprinted in the authoritative work of Sharp, edited by Maud Karpeles, *English Folk-Songs from the Southern Appalachians*, 1932 and 1952. And to all these favors must be added the kindred generosity of Messrs. Novello & Co. in permitting the use of a number of Sharp's songs controlled by them in various publications: *English Folk-Songs*, Selected Edition, 1921; *School Songs (Folk-Songs of England)*, Sets II, VI, VII, IX, X, *Ballads, Folk-Song Carols*, and *Folk-Songs of English Origin collected in the Appalachian Mountains*, 1919-1921.

An obligation only less vast than the foregoing and in itself inestimably valuable is the permission granted me by Dr. W. Douglas Simpson, Librarian of Aberdeen University, to make free use of the great collection amassed in the Northeast of Scotland by Gavin Greig and the Reverend J. B. Duncan and housed in the Library of King's College, the hospitality of which in the Autumn of 1938 I recall with lively gratitude. Most of the songs in question were published in *Last Leaves of Traditional Ballads*, 1925, edited by Alexander Keith, but I have transcribed directly from the MSS themselves or from microfilm, or from the transcripts at King's College made by William Walker from the combined collections of Greig and Duncan of Child-variant tunes.

To the publishing-houses now to be named I am greatly indebted for courteous permission to reprint one or more—and in some cases a good many—of the ballad-versions first appearing in their various publications. Since every song is identified where it appears in this work, and also in the lists of variant copies, individual items are not specified here again, but only the titles of books whence they are drawn:

Messrs. Ascherberg, Hopwood & Crew, Ltd.: Frank Kidson and Alfred Moffat, *A Garland of English Folk Songs*, 1926. Messrs. Augener, Ltd.: Alfred Moffat, *Fifty Traditional Scottish Nursery Rhymes*, 1933. J. J. Augustin, Inc.: Mellinger E. Henry, *Folk-Songs from the Southern Highlands*, 1938, and Mary O. Eddy, *Ballads and Songs from Ohio*, 1939. Messrs. Albert and Charles Boni, Inc.: Songs Sung by the Fuller Sisters, "The Two Sisters," 1927. Messrs. Boosey & Hawkes, Inc.: Lucy Broadwood, *English Traditional Songs and Carols* (copyright 1908 by Boosey & Co., renewed 1936); Josephine McGill, *Folk-Songs of the Kentucky Mountains* (copyright 1917 by Boosey & Co., renewed 1944); and Charles V. Stanford, *The Complete Collection of Irish Music*, 1902-5. The Boston Music Co.: Mary Wheeler and Clara Bridge, *Kentucky Mountain Folk-Songs*, 1937. Columbia University Press: Dorothy Scarborough, *A Song Catcher in the Southern Mountains*, 1937. Messrs. J. B. Cramer & Co., Ltd.: Lucy Broadwood and J. A. Fuller-Maitland, *English County Songs*, 1893; and M. H. Mason, *Nursery Rhymes and Country Songs*, 1908. Messrs. J. Curwen & Sons, Ltd.: Clive Carey, *Ten English Folk Songs*, 1915; Alice Gillington, *Eight Hampshire Folk Songs*, 1907; and Sir R. R. Terry, *The Shanty Book*, 1921. Messrs. J. M. Dent & Sons, Ltd.: Helen Creighton, *Songs and Ballads from Nova Scotia*, 1933. Duke University Press: *The Frank C. Brown Collection of North Carolina Folklore*, 1952-. The Educational Company of Ireland, Ltd.: P. W. Joyce, *Old Irish Folk Music and Songs*, 1909. Friendship Press: James W. Raine, *The Land of Saddle Bags*, 1924. Alexander Gardner, Ltd.: Robert Ford, *Vagabond Songs and Ballads of Scotland*, 1899-1901. H. W. Gray Co.: Loraine Wyman and Howard Brockway, *Lonesome Tunes*, 1916. Greenberg, Publ.: Ethel P. Richardson, *American Mountain Songs*, 1927. Messrs. Harcourt, Brace & Co.: Carl Sandburg, *The American Songbag*, 1927. Harvard University Press: John H. Cox, *Folk-Songs of the South*, 1925; Arthur K. Davis, Jr.: *Traditional Ballads of Virginia*, 1929; Elisabeth B. Greenleaf and Grace Y. Mansfield, *Ballads and Sea-Songs of Newfoundland*, 1933; W. Roy Mackenzie, *Ballads and Sea-Songs from Nova Scotia*, 1928; Dorothy Scarborough,

On the Trail of Negro Folk-Songs, 1925; and Reed Smith, *South Carolina Ballads*, 1928. W. Wilbur Hatfield: Jean Thomas, *Devil's Ditties*, 1931. Hogarth Press, Ltd.: Norah and William Montgomerie, *Scottish Nursery Rhymes*, 1946. Messrs. Houghton, Mifflin & Co.: Francis James Child, *The English and Scottish Popular Ballads*, 1882-1898. Indiana University Press: Paul G. Brewster, *Ballads and Songs of Indiana*, 1940. Messrs. Methuen & Co., Ltd.: Sabine Baring-Gould and H. F. Sheppard, *A Garland of Country Song*, 1895. Messrs. Novello & Co., Ltd.: William A. Barrett, *English Folk Songs*, n.d.; and *Novello's School Songs*, Nos. 1133, 1134, 1331, 1413, 1414. Messrs. Routledge & Kegan Paul, Ltd.: Charlotte S. Burne, *Shropshire Folk-Lore*, 1883. Ryerson Press: Helen Creighton and Doreen Senior, *Traditional Songs from Nova Scotia*, 1950. E. C. Schirmer Music Co.: Lyle R. Ring, *New England Folk-Songs*, 1937. G. Schirmer, Inc.: Maurice Matteson and Mellinger E. Henry, *Beech Mountain Folk-Songs and Ballads*, 1936; John J. Niles, *Ballads, Love-Songs, and Tragic Legends from the Southern Appalachian Mountains*, 1938; and John J. Niles, *More Songs of the Hill Folk*, 1936. Messrs. Sidgwick & Jackson, Ltd.: Ella M. Leather, *The Folk-Lore of Herefordshire*, 1912. Messrs. Charles Taphouse & Son, Ltd.: Frank Kidson, *Traditional Tunes*, 1891. University of Alabama Press: Byron Arnold, *Folksongs of Alabama*, 1950. University of Florida Press: Alton C. Morris, *Folksongs of Florida*, 1950. University of Michigan Press: Elizabeth E. Gardner and Geraldine J. Chickering, *Ballads and Songs of Southern Michigan*, 1939. University of Missouri Studies: H. M. Belden, *Ballads and Songs*, 1940. University of Pennsylvania Press: George Korson, *Pennsylvania Songs and Legends*, 1949. Joseph Williams, Ltd.: Alice E. Gillington, *Songs of the Open Road*, 1911. Yale University Press: Phillips Barry, *et al.*, *British Ballads from Maine*, 1929; and Helen H. Flanders, *et al.*, *The New Green Mountain Songster*, 1939.

Many collectors and editors have generously granted personal consent to my inclusion of songs preserved by their efforts; and I have, in the course of this work, incurred many obligations of a more personal kind which it is a pleasure to specify:

Dr. Marius Barbeau for a song in *Come a Singing*, 1947. Mrs. Phillips Barry for several songs in the *Bulletin of the Folk Song Society of the Northeast*; and in her husband's *The Maine Woods Songster*, 1939. Professor Paull F. Baum for permission to use texts in *The Frank C. Brown Collection of North Carolina Folklore*, 1952-. Professor Samuel P. Bayard for songs contributed by him to the *Bulletin of the Folk Song Society of the Northeast*; and to *Pennsylvania Songs and Legends*, 1949. Mr. Clive Carey and Father George B. Chambers for a song in the *Journal of the English Folk Dance and Song Society*. Professor Louis W. Chappell for songs from *Folk-Songs of Roanoke and the Albemarle*, 1939, and for other favors. Mr. Richard Chase for a song in *Old Songs and Singing Games*, 1938. Mr. Francis M. Collinson for contributions to the *Journal of the English Folk Dance and Song Society* and a song in *Folk Songs from Country Magazine*, 1952, and other kindness. Mrs. Sidney Robertson Cowell for songs collected by her in California for the University of California and the Library of Congress, and for the benefit of her wide knowledge and friendly interest. Miss Helen Creighton for songs from *Traditional Songs from Nova Scotia*, 1950. Mrs. Allston Dana for much personal trouble in my behalf. Professor Arthur K. Davis, Jr., for valued communications. Miss Mary O. Eddy for songs in her *Ballads and Songs from Ohio*, 1939. Mr. Samuel Eskin for leave to use songs recorded by Sierra Records (Berkeley). Mrs. Helen Hartness Flanders, for substantial donations from *A Garland of Green Mountain Song*, 1934; *The New Green Mountain Songster*, 1939; *Ballads Migrant in New England*, 1953. Miss Marguerite Olney for particular courtesies relating to the Flanders Archive. Mr. A. Martin Freeman for a song in the *Journal of the Folk Song Society*. Mr. Rolf Gardiner, for a contribution by G. B. Gardiner to the *Journal of the Folk Song Society*. Mr. Theodore Garrison for songs included in his unpublished thesis, *Forty-five Folk Songs Collected from Searcy County*, 1939. Mr. Percy Grainger for songs printed in the *Journal of the Folk Song Society*; and for MSS material in the New York Public Library. Professor Herbert Halpert for material recorded for the Library of Congress. Professor Lester A. Hubbard for songs published in the *Journal of American Folklore*. Professor Arthur P. Hudson for selections from *Folk-Tunes from Mississippi*, 1937. Mr. Peter Kennedy for a song from the *Journal of the English Folk Dance and Song Society*. Mrs. Eloise H. Linscott for five songs from *Folk Songs of Old New England*, 1939. Mrs. Ruby T. Lomax for a song in John Lomax and Alan Lomax, *American Ballads and Folk Songs*, 1934. Professor David S. McIntosh for songs in his unpublished thesis, *Some Representative Southern Illinois Folksongs*, 1935. Miss Mabel Major for songs in *The Publications of the Texas Folklore Society*. Mr. Francis C. Merrick for material gathered by W. P. Merrick in the *Journal of the Folk Song Society* and the *Journal of the English Folk Dance and Song Society*. For the use of a song from Miss Mabel Peacock in the *Journal of the Folk Song Society*, by permission accorded by her nephew. Dr. John S. McLaren Ord and Mrs. Lockhart for songs from John Ord, *Bothy Songs and Ballads*, 1930. Dr. Donal O'Sullivan for a song in the *Journal of the Irish Folk Song Society*. Mr. William A. Owens for songs from *Texas Folk Songs*, 1950. Mrs. C. S. Parsonson for a contribution by C. S. Parsonson to the *Journal of the Folk Song Society*. Mr. Vance Randolph for songs collected by him in the Ozarks. Miss Jean Ritchie for a phonographically recorded song from family tradition. Mr. Charles Seeger, for interest, advice, and encouragement. Mr. Patrick N. Shuldham-Shaw for songs printed in the *Journal of the English Folk Dance and Song Society*. Mr. Elmer G. Sulzer for a song from *Kentucky Folk Ballads*, 1936. Mr. Asher E. Treat for several songs published in the *Journal of American Folklore*. Professor Randall Thompson, for wise counsel early and late, for ears patient and discerning, and for all the good offices of life-long friendship. Miss Evelyn K. Wells for songs from *Notes from The Pine Mountain Settlement School*, 1935; and *The Ballad Tree*, 1950; and for friendly help and counsel. Mr. Winston Wilkinson for songs in *The Winston Wilkinson Folklore Collections*, at the University of Virginia, and the generous offer of his private collections. Dr. Ralph Vaughan Williams for permission to use his own and the H. E. D. Hammond songs in the *Journal of the Folk Song Society*, and for other personal kindnesses. Dr. Harry M. Willsher for his transcriptions of a number of early Scottish songs from MSS.

To the following Societies and their editors I owe particular acknowledgment:

To the English Folk Dance and Song Society, for songs in its authority, from Lucy and Ada Broadwood, Dr. Clague, Walter Ford, Anne G. Gilchrist, and Esther B. White. Miss Sara E.

Jackson, Librarian of the Society and Editor of its Journal, has put me deeply in her debt by tracing out the present copyright holders of a large number of songs originally published in the *Journal of the Folk Song Society* and in the *Journal of the English Folk Dance and Song Society*, and in many cases by securing for me permission to reprint. Without this assistance, voluntarily undertaken and diligently prosecuted by Miss Jackson, I must have foundered in my efforts to win consent for the inclusion of many contemporary English records.

To the American Folklore Society, and its Editor, Mr. Thomas B. Sebeok, for materials published in the *Journal of American Folklore*. To the Folk-Song Society of the Northeast, through Mrs. Phillips Barry, for the use of songs from its Bulletin. To the Society of Antiquaries of Newcastle upon Tyne, and its Secretary, Mr. Herbert L. Honeyman, for the use of songs published in J. C. Bruce and J. Stokoe, *Northumbrian Minstrelsy*, 1882. To the Southeastern Folklore Society, and the Editor of its publication, the *Southern Folklore Quarterly*, Mr. Alton C. Morris, for similar favors. Likewise, to the Tennessee Folklore Society, and the Editor of its Bulletin, Mr. William J. Griffin, for contributions by Dorothy Horn and Dr. G. W. Boswell. To the Texas Folklore Society, and the Editor of its publication, Mr. Mody C. Boatright. To the Vermont Historical Society, and its Director, Dr. Arthur W. Peach, for permission to quote songs from Helen H. Flanders, *Vermont Folk-Songs and Ballads*, 1931, and *A Garland of Green Mountain Song*, 1934. To the Royal School of Church Music, Croyden, Surrey, for permission to reprint material by Dr. Sydney Nicholson which appeared in the *Journal of the Folk Song Society*.

Many libraries have furthered my investigations with their cooperative and efficient assistance and friendly harborage according to need. To some I am indebted for permission to use MS material in their keeping. I owe special thanks to Harvard and Houghton, unrivalled in all that pertains to ballads, for extracts from the Barry MSS, the Child MSS, the Harris MSS, the Macmath MSS, the White MSS, the Ritson-Tytler-Brown MS. My obligations to Clare College, Cambridge, and King's College, Aberdeen, have already been expressed above. I would also thank the Trustees of the National Library of Scotland for permission to quote from the Blaikie MS, C. K. Sharpe's MSS, the Margaret Sinkler MS, and Lady John Scott's Collections; and Dr. L. W. Sharp, Librarian of the Edinburgh University Library, for the use of MS Dc 1.69 and other courtesies. I owe thanks to the Libraries Department of the Glasgow Corporation for permission to draw upon the Kidson MSS in the Mitchell Library; and to the Plymouth Public Libraries for the use of Sabine Baring-Gould's MSS. To Dr. Carleton Sprague Smith, Music Librarian of the New York Public Library, I am indebted for leave to quote a MS in flageolet tablature (Drexel 3909) and the Grainger hectographs; and to the Keeper of Rare Books, Mr. Zoltan Haraszti, of the Boston Public Library, for the use of the Henry Hudson MS. I am obliged to the Duke University Library and the Library of Congress, through the courtesy of Dr. Duncan B. M. Emrich, for the use of photostats of tunes in the Frank C. Brown Folklore Collection;* and to the Rector and Visitors of the University of Virginia, the Alderman Library,

* Volume IV of the Brown Collection, containing "The Music of the Ballads" edited by Jan Philip Schinhan, appeared in December 1957, when the present work was already in page-proof and consequently too late to be of assistance.

and its Curator of MSS, Mr. Francis L. Berkeley, Jr., for the use of Winston Wilkinson's MSS of 1935-1937. I would not leave unmentioned idyllic weeks spent among the Huth and other song collections of the Henry E. Huntington Library, nor the privilege of perusing the Claude Lovat Fraser collection of broadsides at Yale. For similar privileges connected with the Wood, Douce, the Pepys, the Bagford, Roxburghe, Baring-Gould, and other broadside collections, I am indebted to the Bodleian Library, the Cambridge University Library, the Magdalene College Library and its Librarian, Mr. F. McD. C. Turner; and to the Library of the British Museum.

To the Trustees of the John Simon Guggenheim Memorial Foundation and its plenipotent Secretary General, Dr. Henry Allen Moe, I owe grateful acknowledgment for repeated support and encouragement in years when objective approval was morally as well as materially sustaining; and also for their considerable forbearance in not demanding quick returns.

For the accommodating tolerance—or, better, endurance—of the Staff of the Harvard College Library, who through two decades have met my perennial onslaughts with unfailing courtesy and especially of Mr. Robert H. Haynes, Assistant Librarian, who provided working space over months when space was to seek; to Harvard's Librarian, Mr. Keyes D. Metcalf, who readily secured microfilm of the Greig MSS at a visitor's need; to Professor William A. Jackson, Librarian of the Houghton Library, and Mr. William H. McCarthy, Jr., formerly Assistant Librarian, for many courtesies; and to Miss Carolyn E. Jakeman for an amount of trouble-taking, smoothly efficient, and good-natured assistance far beyond my power to reckon or adequately to acknowledge: for all this and other kindness, hospitably extended to one who had no special claims to urge but who, like countless other guests, has learned to accept such treatment there as naturally as he has received the invigorating morning welcome of Houghton's Custodian, I return warm and heartfelt gratitude.

To many nearer home I have equal reason to be grateful: to the President and Regents of the University of California, who, through their duly provident Faculty Research Committee, have made available over a long span of years indispensable annual grants to assist my labors; to Librarian Donald Coney, whose instant grasp of and effective response to scholarly needs is almost anticipatory and who has notably facilitated my research by acquiring for the Library microfilm of the Sharp MSS, the Greig MSS, and the Baring-Gould MSS; to the helpful staff of the Interlibrary Loan Department for much friendly trouble on my behalf; to my colleagues and friends of the Music Department, Professors Albert Elkus, the late Manfred Bukofzer, David Boyden, Joseph Kerman, Edward B. Lawton, for ready help and counsel; and to Dr. Vincent Duckles, Music Librarian, for abundant assistance of various kinds; and to an impressively long procession of graduate students and other assistants who have most cheerfully carried portions of my load and lightened the burden of detail. By some of the latter what began as duty has been transmuted to such a degree of thoughtful, intelligent, and enthusiastic interest as to have earned the entire thanks of friendship. I would here acknowledge an especial debt to Miss Janice Knouse, Miss Madeleine Bond, Mr. Raymond Weil, Miss Constance Nelson, Mrs. Fay Stender, and Mrs. Doris Cooper Powers.

ACKNOWLEDGMENTS

I wish to pay particular acknowledgment to my colleague, Professor Archer Taylor. Among his multifarious activities, he has never been too busy to give me the benefit of his encyclopedic knowledge, his careful consideration, and his valuable advice on any query or problem that was troubling me. He has looked at my proofs with an expert eye; and that he has scanned the headnotes and introduction of this work without disapprobation is reassuring to me now.

To the efficient and considerate personnel of the Princeton University Press I acknowledge an abiding sense of indebtedness, most especially to Mr. Datus Smith, its former Director, who of his own volition revived my expiring hopes at a time when these unprinted sheets gave promise of turning eventually into a winding sheet; to Mr. Herbert S. Bailey, Jr., its active Director; to Miss R. Miriam Brokaw, who has borne the brunt of editorial responsibility with a prompt and unflagging helpfulness, a courteous forbearance, and thoughtful efficiency. I would not omit appreciation of the lynx-eyed vigilance and good judgment of Miss Jean MacLachlan, who gave what formal consistency was possible to the wayward referential practices of copy assembled by fits and starts, at distant times and places. And lastly, to the musical knowledge and calligraphic genius of Mr. Gordon Mapes, whose hand and brain have designed artifacts of beauty for nearly every page of this work, I pay a grateful and admiring homage which is certain to be echoed by every reader.

I am conscious of a further obligation, the magnitude of which will be best appreciated by those who have devoted the labor of many years to a single end. Not to refer to it here would be culpable in the extreme, for without it all other favors would have availed me little. Yet how can I verbally acknowledge, or even appraise, the debt to her whose unstinted contribution to this work, over all the years, has been made out of life itself, and made in charity, and hope, and sustaining faith?

B. H. B.

Berkeley, California
November, 1957

The Traditional Tunes
of the
Child Ballads

Riddles Wisely Expounded

CHILD NO. 1

THE first hint of an air for this ballad comes with the Restoration broadsides, which are directed to be sung to the tune of "Lay the bent to the bonny broom." There is no equally early copy of the tune itself, but we may suppose that it appears in D'Urfey in a form substantially unchanged. The words of the refrain, however, from which the tune gets its name, appear better suited to a ballad of pastoral character, and may probably have been borrowed, along with the melody, from some earlier song. Their "fa la" fashion seems late Elizabethan.

Doubtless also the suggestion, in the broadside text, of rival daughters is taken over from a context where it was once of some use: it will be noted that they are absent from the fifteenth-century text (Child's A*), and that they tend to drop out in later tradition. The knight was not originally of the marrying kind, and sounder tradition makes him out a fiend—even Clootie himself—to be checkmated, rather than confirmed in his election, by the maid's ability to guess his riddles. It is noteworthy that even A*, early as it is, is already confused, in that the fiend first offers the maid all the wisdom of the world if she will be his leman, and abruptly passes to riddles with the threat that she must answer them or belong to him. The contradiction demonstrates a still earlier life for the ballad, and arises from homiletic rehandling, out of memories of Christ's temptation. Yet, though inappropriately, the element is thus early introduced of amorous appeal, which was later to refashion the plot as in the broadsides. (Cf. also P. Barry's article in *BFSSNE*, No. 10 [1935], pp. 8-10.) The earliest text unfortunately lacks a refrain, but it is in rhyming couplets which would admit, and generally do admit, of an interlaced refrain, and so of a four-phrased tune.

D'Urfey's tune, with its hint of Dorian modality, its narrow compass, and its almost complete avoidance of intervals wider than a single step of the scale, suggests an antiquity far higher than that of the accompanying verbal text. Its habit is even earlier than that of "The Three Ravens" (26), one of the first ballad-tunes to be recorded: but atavism is a common phenomenon in folk-music, and one cannot determine the age of an individual by fixing the era when his ancestors flourished. We can assert, however, that the tune is rooted in a common idiom with Gregorian Chant. And if specific parallels be demanded, they can be found in so familiar an example as the *Benedictus qui venit* from the *Sanctus* of the mass *Orbis Factor* (eleventh century). Note-for-note comparison is revealing:

Or we may compare the *Agnus Dei* from the mass *Kyrie Magnae Deus Potentiae*; or, again, the ad libitum *Kyrie Salve*,

with cadences not greatly dissimilar to the more famous ones of the *Dies Irae*. (Cf. also *Western Folklore*, XI, pp. 236-38.)

After D'Urfey, tunes for the ballad appear in the record about once every half-century up to the present time, from scattered localities in England—Northumbria to Cornwall—and from the Appalachian region. Between all the English tunes it is possible to make out a tenuous thread of connection, but this appears to be broken in the Appalachian tradition.

Received from tradition, Miss Mason's Northumbrian tune (1878) in its first two phrases is a major form of the D'Urfey tune with altered rhythm. The second part of the refrain is related, both in words and notes, to a version of the ballad used by John O'Keefe and William Shield in their ballad-opera, *The Highland Reel*, printed c. 1790, oblong quarto, p. 14. Since the tune was here employed dialogue-wise, with text newly composed, little reliance can be placed on its conforming to tradition; but the refrain, with cadential resemblances to Mason, is "Twang Lango Tillo Lang Twango dillo day." It is a major tune, in ¾ time, and has no convincing relation to D'Urfey. It seems less likely that this rewritten piece, with words belonging to the opera and not to the ballad, should have contributed its refrain to tradition than that it should have preserved a piece of earlier tradition in the refrain. The soundness of the Mason variant is thus confirmed and carried well back into the preceding century. But the "dillo, dee" refrain is itself probably not much older than that era, when this style was much affected.

The Gilbert tune (1823), rhythmically, and melodically in its first and third phrases, is related to the Mason tune. But, in spite of its earlier date, it would appear to be more abraded by tradition, both because the second phrase has been attracted to the first, and because of the conventional ending.

Verbally, it derives from the broadside text through tradition, or from the tradition upon which that text was modeled; but substitutes a refrain with a different plant motif. Lucy Broadwood has argued interestingly that such "plant-burdens" are especially proper to riddling-ballads like the present, where they may be "the survival of an incantation used against the demon-suitor." (Cf. *JEFSS*, III, p. 14.) The bent and the broom are said to be potent against witchcraft; and juniper, gentle (i.e., hawthorne), and rosemary are similarly endowed with beneficent powers. But this style in ballad-refrains is not often favored before the beginning of the nineteenth century.

It would be very difficult to make out a connection between the Virginia tune and the foregoing airs. Up to this point, however, the melodic tradition for this ballad, so far as the scanty record reveals it, has been remarkably single-tracked for the span of time which it covers. If the tune was dropped overboard when the ballad came west, we might reasonably surmise that the ballad was transported on paper, rather than in the head, for the Bell Robertsons who remember only the words are black swans in balladry. It is possible, however, that the Davis tune represents an unrecorded, but genuine, tradition, for which the refrain may provide a clue. The connection of the ballad-text and refrain is not at all clear. The new air is of stuff familiar in the Appalachians, and perhaps the song was inundated by a more vigorous melodic tradition, such as that of "Barbara Allan" (84) or "Geordie" (209), both of which often begin similarly and have the characteristic feminine upward swing at the middle and final cadence. Such a case is doubtless of frequent occurrence, and probably one of the chief ways in which ballads acquire a new melodic direction. Nowhere today is the present ballad known to be strongly rooted.

There remains to be noticed the oddity found by Barry in Maine, in 1936, and printed in *BFSSNE*, No. 10 (1935), p. 8,

and No. 12 (1937), p. 8. The text of this version, as Barry demonstrates, is a traditional variant of Aytoun's translation of Herder's free translation into German of the D'Urfey text above. It is difficult to perceive in the tune anything more than an anomaly resulting from imperfect recollection or faulty rendition—*pace* the *rubato-parlando* habit of the singer.

LIST OF VARIANTS

GROUP A

1. "A Riddle Wittily Expounded." Thomas D'Urfey, *Wit and Mirth; or, Pills to Purge Melancholy*, 1719-20, IV, pp. 129-32.
a. "Lay the bent to the bonny broom." William Chappell, *Popular Music of the Olden Time*, II [1859], p. 531. (Probably D'Urfey edited by Chappell.)
b. "Lay the bent to the bonny broom." J. Collingwood Bruce and John Stokoe, *Northumbrian Minstrelsy*, 1882, pp. 76-78. ("The melody is from D'Urfey's words" . . . but not identical with the copy above.)
2. (Dialogue, words by O'Keefe) J. O'Keefe and William Shield, *The Highland Reel*, oblong quarto, engraved by Longman and Broderip, n.d. [c. 1790], p. 14.
3. "There was a Lady in the West." M. H. Mason, *Nursery Rhymes and Country Songs*, 1878, (reprinted 1908), p. 31. Also in Lucy E. Broadwood and J. A. Fuller Maitland, *English County Songs*, [1893], pp. 6-7.
4. "The Three Sisters." Davies Gilbert, *Some Ancient Christmas Carols*, 1823, pp. 65-67. Also in Francis James Child, *The English and Scottish Popular Ballads*, 1882-98, I, p.

4(B); and Sir Richard Terry, *Gilbert and Sandys' Christmas Carols*, 1931, p. xix.

GROUP B

5. "The Devil's Nine Questions." Arthur Kyle Davis, Jr., *Traditional Ballads of Virginia*, 1929, pp. 549 and 59-60.
c. "The Devil's Questions." Richard Chase, *Songs of All Time*, 1946, p. 11. Also in Evelyn Kendrick Wells, *The Ballad Tree*, 1950, p. 169.
6. "The Devil's Nine Questions." Alan and Elizabeth Lomax, LC Archive of American Folk Song, Album I, rec. 4A1. (Mrs. Texas Gladden.)
d. "The Devil's Ten Questions." John Jacob Niles, *Ballads, Carols, and Tragic Legends from the Southern Appalachian Mountains*, Schirmer's American Folk-Song Series, Set 18, 1937, pp. 2-3.

APPENDIX

7. "The Three Riddles." Phillips Barry and S. P. Bayard, *BFSSNE*, No. 10 (1935), p. 8, and No. 12 (1937), p. 8.

TUNES WITH TEXTS

GROUP A

1. [A Riddle Wittily Expounded]

D'Urfey, 1719-20, IV, pp. 129-32 (emended).

a D if e♮ (but –VII)

D'Urfey prints the tune in ₵ time throughout; Chappell, in his revision of it (II [1859], p. 531), regularizes in ¾, giving two beats to the last note of the first and third phrases, and changing the signature to G minor. Bruce and Stokoe (1882, pp. 76-78) profess to print from D'Urfey, but again in two flats, regularizing the timing in ¾, and with four alterations in notes: D for initial A, e raised to f in the third bar, the third d in the same bar lowered to c, and the first A in the penultimate bar raised to c.

1. There was a Lady in the North-Country,
   Lay the Bent to the Bonny Broom,
   And she had lovely Daughters three,
   Fa, la la la, fa, la la ra re.

2. There was a Knight of Noble worth,
   Lay the Bent, &c.
   Which also lived in the North,
   Fa, la, &c.

3. The Knight of Courage stout and brave,
   Lay the Bent, &c.
   A Wife he did desire to have,
   Fa la, &c.

4. He knocked at the Lady's Gate,
   Lay the Bent, &c.
   One Evening when it was late,
   Fa la, &c.

5. The youngest Sister let him in,
   Lay the Bent, &c.
   And pinn'd the Door with a Silver Pin,
   Fa la, &c.

6. The second Sister she made his Bed,
   Lay the Bent, &c.
   And laid soft Pillows under his Head,
   Fa la, &c.

7. The Youngest [Sister] that same Night,
   Lay the Bent, &c.
   She went to Bed to this young Knight,
   Fa la, &c.

8. And in the Morning when it was Day,
   Lay the Bent, &c.
   These words unto him she did say,
   Fa la, &c.

9. Now you have had your will (quoth she)
    Lay the Bent, &c.
  I pray Sir Knight you Marry me,
    Fa la, &c.

10. The young brave Knight to her reply'd,
    Lay the Bent, &c.
  Thy Suit, Fair Maid shall not be deny'd,
    Fa la, &c.

11. If thou can'st answer me Questions three,
    Lay the Bent, &c.
  This very Day I will Marry thee,
    Fa la, &c.

12. Kind Sir, in Love, O then quoth she,
    Lay the Bent, &c.
  Tell me what your three Questions be,
    Fa la, &c.

13. O what is longer than the Way?
    Lay the Bent, &c.
  Or what is deeper than the Sea?
    Fa la, &c.

14. Or what is louder than a Horn?
    Lay the Bent, &c.
  Or what is sharper than a Thorn?
    Fa la, &c.

15. Or what is greener than the Grass?
    Lay the Bent, &c.
  Or what is worse than a Woman was?
    Fa la, &c.

The Damsel's Answer to the Three Questions

16. O Love is longer than the way,
    Lay the Bent, &c.
  And Hell is deeper than the Sea,
    Fa la, &c.

17. And Thunder's louder than the Horn,
    Lay the Bent, &c.
  And Hunger's sharper than a Thorn,
    Fa la, &c.

18. And Poyson's greener than the Grass,
    Lay the Bent, &c.
  And the Devil's worse than the Woman was,
    Fa la, &c.

19. When she these Questions answered had,
    Lay the Bent, &c.
  The Knight became exceeding glad,
    Fa la, &c.

20. And having truly try'd her Wit,
    Lay the Bent, &c.
  He much commended her for it,
    Fa la, &c.

21. And after as 'tis verifi'd,
    Lay the Bent, &c.
  He made of her his lovely Bride,
    Fa la, &c.

22. So now fair Maidens all adieu,
    Lay the Bent, &c.
  This Song I dedicate to you,
    Fa la, &c.

23. I wish that you may Constant prove,
    Lay the Bent to the bonny Broom,
  Unto the Man that you do love,
    Fa, la la la, fa, la la ra re.

2. [Dialogue, words by O'Keefe]

O'Keefe and Shield, *The Highland Reel*, n.d., p. 14. The play was produced in 1788, and the book was engraved by Longman and Broderip soon afterward.

p I

Twang Lang - o Til - lo Lang Twang-o dil - lo day

This tune is admitted, partly on internal evidence, and partly by reason of its being identified as "Lay the bent to the bonny broom" by Thomas Dibdin, who may have received the information from Shield or O'Keefe. Cf. Chappell, *Popular Music*, II [1859], p. 531. The last phrase carries the traditional refrain.

3. "There was a Lady in the West"

Mason, 1878, p. 31. Also in Broadwood and Maitland, 1893, pp. 6-7. Sung in Northumberland.

p I (but inflected IV)

Reprinted again in the 1908 ed. of Mason, where Miss Mason adds that the song was traditional in her mother's family, the Mitfords, of Mitford, Northumberland. As said above, the D'Urfey tune can be discerned behind the first half of this one.

1. There was a lady in the West,
    Lay the bank with the bonny broom,
  She had three daughters of the best,
    Fa lang the dillo,
      Fa lang the dillo, dillo, dee.

2. There came a stranger to the gate,
    Lay the bank with the bonny broom,
  And he three days and nights did wait,
    Fa lang the dillo,
      Fa lang the dillo, dillo, dee.

3. The eldest daughter did ope the door,
     Lay the bank, &c.
   The second set him on the floor.
     Fa lang, &c.

4. The third daughter she brought a chair,
     Lay the bank, &c.
   And placed it that he might sit there,
     Fa lang, &c.

(To first daughter)

5. "Now answer me these questions three,"
     Lay the bank, &c.
   "Or you shall surely go with me."
     Fa lang, &c.

(To second daughter)

6. "Now answer me these questions six,"
     Lay the bank, &c.,
   "Or you shall surely be Old Nick's."
     Fa lang, &c.

(To all three)

7. "Now answer me these questions nine,"
     Lay the bank, &c.,
   "Or you shall surely all be mine."
     Fa lang, &c.

8. "What is greener than the grass?"
     Lay the bank, &c.
   "What is smoother than crystal glass?"
     Fa lang, &c.

9. "What is louder than a horn?"
     Lay the bank, &c.
   "What is sharper than a thorn?"
     Fa lang, &c.

10. "What is brighter than the light?"
      Lay the bank, &c.
    "What is darker than the night?"
      Fa lang, &c.

11. "What is keener than an axe?"
      Lay the bank, &c.
    "What is softer than melting wax?"
      Fa lang, &c.

12. "What is rounder than a ring?"
      Lay the bank, &c.
    "To you we thus our answers bring."
      Fa lang, &c.

13. "Envy is greener than the grass,"
      Lay the bank, &c.,
    "Flattery, smoother than crystal glass."
      Fa lang, &c.

14. "Rumour is louder than a horn,"
      Lay the bank, &c.
    "Hunger is sharper than a thorn."
      Fa lang, &c.

15. "Truth is brighter than the light,"
      Lay the bank, &c.
    "Falsehood is darker than the night."
      Fa lang, &c.

16. "Revenge is keener than an axe,"
      Lay the bank, &c.
    "Love is softer than melting wax."
      Fa lang, &c.

17. "The world is rounder than a ring,"
      Lay the bank, &c.
    "To you we thus our answers bring."
      Fa lang, &c.

18. "Thus you have our answers nine,"
      Lay the bank, &c.
    "And we never shall be thine."
      Fa lang, &c.

By permission of Messrs. J. B. Cramer & Co., Ltd., London.

4. [The Three Sisters]

Gilbert, 1823, pp. 65-67. From editor's recollection; Cornish tradition.

Also in Child, 1882-98, I, p. 4(B).

p I

The tune and first stanza are reproduced in facsimile in Sir Richard Terry, *Gilbert and Sandy's Christmas Carols*, 1931, p. xix. It may be observed that the first refrain-line appears under the notes as "Juniper Gentle and Rosemary," not as given in the text below.

1. There were three Sisters fair and bright,
     Jennifer gentle and Rosemaree,
   And they three loved one valiant Knight,
     As the dew flies over the Mulberry tree.

2. The eldest Sister let him in,
     Jennifer gentle and Rosemaree,
   And barred the door with a silver pin,
     As the dew flies over the Mulberry tree.

3. The second Sister made his bed,
     Jennifer gentle and Rosemaree,
   And placed soft pillows under his head,
     As the dew flies over the Mulberry tree.

4. The youngest Sister fair and bright,
     Jennifer gentle and Rosemaree,
   Was resolved for to wed with this valiant Knight,
     As the dew flies over the Mulberry tree.

5. And if you can answer questions three,
     Jennifer gentle and Rosemaree,
   Oh! then, fair Maid, I will marry with thee,
     As the dew flies over the Mulberry tree.

6. What is louder than an horn?
   Jennifer gentle and Rosemaree,
   And what is sharper than a thorn?
   As the dew flies over the Mulberry tree.

7. Thunder is louder than an horn,
   Jennifer gentle and Rosemaree,
   And hunger is sharper than a thorn,
   As the dew flies over the Mulberry tree.

8. What is broader than the way?
   Jennifer gentle and Rosemaree,
   And what is deeper than the sea?
   As the dew flies over the Mulberry tree.

9. Love is broader than the way,
   Jennifer gentle and Rosemaree,
   And hell is deeper than the sea,
   As the dew flies over the Mulberry tree.

10. . . . .
    Jennifer gentle and Rosemaree,
    And now, fair Maid, I will marry with thee,
    As the dew flies over the Mulberry tree.

GROUP B

5. "The Devil's Nine Questions"

Davis, 1929, p. 549; text, pp. 59-60. Sung by Mrs. Rill
Martin, Giles County, Va., September 11, 1922; noted by
Evelyn Rex. Collected by Alfreda M. Peel.

p π[1]

1. "If you don't answer me questions nine,
      Sing ninety-nine and ninety,
   I'll take you off to hell alive,
      And you are the weaver's bonny.

2. "What is whiter than milk?
      Sing ninety-nine and ninety;
   What is softer than silk?
      Say you're the weaver's bonny."

3. "Snow is whiter than milk,
      Sing ninety-nine and ninety;
   Down is softer than silk,
      And I'm the weaver's bonny."

4. "What is louder than a horn?
      Sing ninety-nine and ninety;
   What is sharper than a thorn?
      Sing I am the weaver's bonny."

5. "Thunder's louder than a horn,
      Sing ninety-nine and ninety;
   Death is sharper than a thorn,
      Sing I'm the weaver's bonny."

6. "What is higher than a tree?
      Sing ninety-nine and ninety;
   What is deeper than the sea?
      Sing I'm the weaver's bonny."

7. "Heaven's higher than a tree,
      Sing ninety-nine and ninety;
   And hell is deeper than the sea,
      Sing I'm the weaver's bonny."

8. "What is innocenter than a lamb?
      Sing ninety-nine and ninety;
   What is worse than woman kind?
      Say I'm the weaver's bonny."

9. "A babe is innocenter than a lamb,
      Sing ninety-nine and ninety;
   The devil's worse than woman kind,
      Sing I'm the weaver's bonny."

10. "You have answered me questions nine,
       Sing ninety-nine and ninety;
    You are God's, you're not my own,
       And you're the weaver's bonny."

6. "The Devil's Nine Questions"

A. and E. Lomax, LC/AAFS, Album I, rec. 4A1. Sung by
Mrs. Texas Gladden, Salem, Va., 1941.

p π[1]

1. "Oh, you must answer my questions nine,
      Sing, ninety-nine and ninety,
   Or you're not God's, you're one of mine,
      And you are the weaver's bonny."

2. "What is whiter than the milk?
      Sing, ninety-nine and ninety,
   And what is softer than the silk?
      And you are the weaver's bonny."

3. "Snow is whiter than the milk,
      Sing, ninety-nine and ninety,
   And down is softer than the silk,
      And I am the weaver's bonny."

4. "Oh what is higher than a tree?
   And what is deeper than the sea?"

5. "Heaven's higher than a tree,
   And Hell is deeper than the sea."

6. "What is louder than a horn?
   And what is sharper than a thorn?"

7. "Thunder's louder than a horn,
   And death is sharper than a thorn."

8. "What's more innocent than a lamb,
   And what is meaner than womankind?"

9. "A babe's more innocent than a lamb,
   And the devil is meaner than womankind."

10. "O you have answered my questions nine,
    And you are God's, you're none of mine."

APPENDIX

7. "The Three Riddles"

Barry and Bayard, *BFSSNE*, No. 10 (1935), p. 8, and No. 12 (1937), p. 8. Sung by Florence Mixer, Stonington, Maine, 1936; learned from her father.

Anomalous

If this be a genuine tune, and no mere singsong, it may bear some comparison with "Newmill" in the Greig MSS., Tune-book I, p. 91. As Barry explains, the text derives from Aytoun's translation of Herder's translation of D'Urfey's broadside version.

1. 'Twas of a gay young cavalier,
     of honor and renown;
   All for to seek a lady fair,
     He rode from town to town.

2. 'Twas at a widow woman's door,
     He drew his rein so free;
   For by her side the knight espied
     Her comely daughters three.

3. Small marvel if his gallant heart
     Beat quick within his breast;
   'Twas hard to choose, yet hard to lose,
     Which might he wed the best.

4. "Come, maidens, pretty maidens,
     Come read my riddles three;
   And she who reads the best of all,
     My loving bride shall be;

5. "Oh, tell me what is longer
     Than the longest path there be;
   And tell me what is deeper
     Than is the deepest sea.

6. "And tell me what is louder
     Than is the loudest horn;
   And tell me what is sharper
     Than is the sharpest thorn.

7. "And tell me what is greener
     Than the grass on yonder hill,
   And tell me what is crueller
     Than a wicked woman's will."

8. The eldest and the second maid,
     They sat and thought a while;
   The youngest she looked up to him,
     And said with a merry smile;

9. "Love, surely it is longer
     Than the longest path there be;
   And Hell, they say is deeper
     Than is the deepest sea;

10. "Thunder, I know is louder
      Than is the loudest horn;
    And hunger it is sharper
      Than is the sharpest thorn;

11. "I know a deadly poison, greener
      Than the grass on yonder hill;
    And a foul fiend is crueller
      Than a wicked woman's will."

12. Now scarcely had she spoke those words,
      When the youth was at her side;
    'Twas all for what she answered him
      He claimed her for his bride.

13. The eldest and the second maid,
      They pondered and were dumb;
    And they, perchance, are waiting yet,
      Some other one to come.

14. Now maidens, pretty maidens,
      Be neither coy nor shy
    But always, when a lover speaks,
      Look kindly and reply.

The Elfin Knight

CHILD NO. 2

THE musical records of this ballad fall into three main groups, each with its own style of verbal refrain. The oldest of these is inseparable from a broadside graft upon earlier tradition, and it is hard to determine what degree of credit should be assigned to its earlier history. Child's A text has no indication of tune, but the relation of B to it is close, and B is directed to be sung to "its own proper tune." B's title—and hence the title of its "proper tune"—is "The Wind hath blawn my Plaid awa"— a form of its last refrain-line. It is provided also with a four-line burden, which begins:

> My Plaid awa, my plaid awa,
> And oure the hills and far awa . . .

The copy is altered from a black-letter broadside, perhaps A, which is nearly identical in these respects, and tentatively dated c. 1670. Tunes, therefore, called either "My plaid awa," or "Oure the hills and far awa," or "The Wind hath blawn my Plaid awa" would, we may suppose, be related to the tune sought; and in fact variants of one and the same tune are found under all three names, in MS. or print, about the turn of the seventeenth century to early eighteenth. There is, however, no occurrence anywhere of this tune mated with the words of this ballad. The tune is familiar today as the setting of Gay's song in *The Beggar's Opera*, "Were I laid on Greenland's Coast." It is called by Stenhouse (*Illustrations of the Lyric Poetry and Music of Scotland*, 1853, p. 62) an old pipe tune, and it has surely very little of the character of a traditional ballad air. Possibly it was attached arbitrarily to the broadside version: its second strain accommodates the burden, which is lacking in all forms of the ballad picked up in later tradition. Yet the maker of the broadside was obviously close to tradition in this case, and may have had the traditional tune in mind. At any rate, the Scottish version, though not much more ballad-like, has possibly the more folkish flavor.

Although the relationship of this tune with the ballad is very dubious, we cannot dismiss the traditional connection of the interlaced refrain, irrelevant though its content now appears. At a comparatively early period, in Scotland, the ballad was being sung in a form in which the second and fourth phrases were some variation of "Ba, ba, lilly ba" and "The wind has blawn my plaid awa"; and this tradition has persisted into the present century, the tune appearing always in duple rhythm—not triple, as elsewhere. But in this duple-rhythm group, the refrain has tended in America to be supplanted by some kind of nonsense syllables—which, after all, is no sharp decline in meaningful statement.

At about the end of the eighteenth century a different form of the ballad becomes dominant, in which the interlaced refrain-lines are "Parsley, sage, rosemary, and thyme" (or a similar jingle) and "Once she (he) was a true lover of mine." All variants of this group are in a triple rhythm (including 6/8). This is, so far as the record shows, the central and leading tradition for the ballad, and is still in comparatively vigorous life.

Before the middle of the last century, however, a third pattern makes its appearance, with a refrain on the order of "Ivy, sing Ivy," and "Holly, go whistle and Ivy" [query if "go whistle" came in when *mistletoe* departed?]. The text of this branch starts with the bequest of an acre of land, the riddle-exchange is altered into a straight catalogue of impossible things performed: the dramatic element descends into simple narrative. A common differentiating feature of the tunes, which in the main are not sharply distinguished from the central group, is that the shorter second verbal phrase forces a compensating lengthening of the accented notes, generally coinciding with the initial vowel of "Ivy."

It may be said here that the second tune in Greig (identified by S. P. Bayard as Thomas Moore's "The Young May Moon" [*Irish Melodies*]), set to a stanza out of Scott's *Heart of Midlothian*, appears to lie too far outside the singing tradition of this ballad, both in text and tune, to be accounted other than a "sport." And again: a text printed by A. S. Harvey, *Ballads, Songs and Rhymes of East Anglia*, London, 1936, p. 113, is directed to be sung to the tune of "Robin Cook's Wife." This tune I have not met; the following poem in Harvey, however, begins "Robin Cook's wife she had a grey mare," with a title "The Old Grey Mare," alternatively known as "Roger the Miller" and "Beautiful Kate."

Of our first group, variants have survived from Scotland, New England, and Texas. The Scottish form is darker (plagal Æ/D), and a favorite type in Northern tradition. It is found with a number of other texts: Child 10, 20, 209, 212, 235, 240, "The Bonnie Lass of Fyvie," and doubtless elsewhere. The other members of the group are all American, all in a major tonality (I/Ly, I, I/M), and all authentic. There is no consistency at the mid-pause, but the first phrase usually ends on V.

For reasons already given, the "O'er the hills and far away" family is not regarded here as authenticated for this ballad, but examples are appended to the first group on account of the association of refrains. The time-values of the Drexel copy are all conjectural, not being indicated in the flageolet tablature whence the tune was transcribed. All the variants appear to me to be I or I/M tunes with an ending on the supertonic. The sole exception is Maver's "Will he no come back again?", which is rather more distantly related. It is a π^1 tune ending on the tonic.

The sturdiest branch of tradition lies with Group B, which might be called "True Lover of Mine." All refrains of this class *end* with these words, although varying elsewhere. I have regarded the melodic clues as more significant than the verbal within this group, and have subdivided somewhat arbitrarily into five types. The first is mainly Northumbrian, and has a mid-cadence on lower *V*, a first cadence on II. It is composed of plagal major tunes. The second type, with variants from England, Ireland, and the United States, is either plagal or authentic, inconsistent as to cadences, but modally ranges from Æ to D. Three variants with ambiguous finals have been placed together, although they come from points far asunder (Northumbria, Ireland, Kentucky). All are of major tonality. Four other variants, authentic, with mid-cadence on V, and coming from Ireland, Cornwall, British Columbia, and Michigan, are also major (I, π^1, I/M). A fifth sub-class, all American, and with mid-cadence on the octave, the fifth, or the tonic, contains I/Ly, π^1, I, and I/M tunes. Most of these are authentic. The group as a whole displays fascinating variety within its unity. Nearly all the tunes are in genuinely triple time (though often 6/8), and very few are extended beyond four phrases.

The third main group—"Acre of Land," with an "Ivy" refrain—is wholly English. The variants mostly have mid-cadence on V, first cadence on I. Four are plagal major tunes (I, I/Ly) and two are Æolian and authentic. So far as concerns the words,

this group has pretty completely descended to the nursery: the riddles have lost their dramatic function, and the story is a straightforward recounting of impossibles, with no challenge from opponents. Here there is little to bolster a theory of evolution from simple to complex.

LIST OF VARIANTS

GROUP A

1. "The Laird o' Elfin." Greig MSS., III, p. 139; text. Bk. 739, XXIX, pp. 6off., King's College Library, Aberdeen. Also in Gavin Greig and Alexander Keith, *Last Leaves of Traditional Ballads and Ballad Airs*, 1925, p. 2(1); and *Rymour Club Miscellanea*, I (1910), p. 201. (Robb)
2. "Blow, Ye Winds, Blow." Phillips Barry, *JAF*, XVIII (1905), pp. 212 and 49-50. Also in Eloise Hubbard Linscott, *Folk Songs of Old New England*, 1939, pp. 170-71.
3. "Redio-Tedio." Phillips Barry, Fanny H. Eckstorm, and Mary W. Smyth, *British Ballads from Maine*, 1929, pp. 3-4.
4. "Oh, say, do you know the way to Selin?" L. R. Ring, *New England Folk Songs*, 1937, pp. 12-13 (E. C. Schirmer, Choral Songs No. 1596, Series No. 1057).
5. "The Cambric Shirt." Mabel Major, *Publications of the Texas Folk-Lore Society*, X (1932), pp. 137-38.
6. "Scarborough Fair." Helen Hartness Flanders and George Brown, *Vermont Folk-Songs & Ballads*, 1931, pp. 194-96.

APPENDIX A

7. "Jockey's Lamentation." Thomas D'Urfey, *Wit and Mirth; or, Pills to Purge Melancholy*, [1706, 1707, 1709], 1719-20, V, pp. 316ff.
8. "My Plaid away." Margaret Sinkler's MS., 1710, National Library of Scotland.
9. "The wind has blown my plaid away." Drexel MS. 3909, [c. 1700-50], New York Public Library.
10. "O'er the Hills and far awa." William McGibbon, *Collection of Scots Tunes*, n.d. [c. 1742-55], Bk. IV, p. 97. Also in James Johnson, *The Scots Musical Museum*, I, [1787], No. 62, pp. 62-63.
11. "'Twas in that year" (O'er the hills & far awa'). Greig MSS., II, p. 25. (Robb)
12. "Oure the Hills and Far Awa." Robert Maver, *Genuine Scottish Ballads*, 1866, No. 418, p. 209.
13. "Will he no come back again?" Maver, 1866, No. 372, p. 186.

GROUP B

14. "The Tasks." Sabine Baring-Gould MSS., CXXVIII(2) and (A), Plymouth Public Library.
15. "The Tasks." Baring-Gould MSS., CXXVIII(3).
16. "The Lover's Tasks." Sharp MSS., 219/306, Clare College Library, Cambridge. (Gilbert)
17. "Scarbro Fair." Child MSS., XXI, No. 18, Harvard College Library.
18. "Scarborough Fair." Frank Kidson, *Traditional Tunes*, 1891, pp. 43-44. Also in Frank Kidson, Ethel Kidson, and Alfred Moffat, *Folk-Songs of the North-Countrie*, 1927, p. 30.
19. "Scarbro Fair." Child MSS., XXI, No. 18.
20. "Scarborough Fair." Lucy E. Broadwood and J. A. Fuller Maitland, *English County Songs*, 1893, pp. 12-13.
21. "Scarborough Fair." Sharp MSS., 2868/. (Hutton). Also in

Sharp, *One Hundred English Folksongs*, 1916, p. 167; and in Sharp, *English Folksongs*, Novello & Co., 1920.
22. "Whittingham Fair." J. Collingwood Bruce and John Stokoe, *Northumbrian Minstrelsy*, 1882, pp. 79-80.
23. "Strawberry Lane." George Lyman Kittredge, *JAF*, XXX (1917), pp. 284-85. Also in Barry, Eckstorm, and Smyth, *British Ballads from Maine*, 1929, p. 10.
24. "Go and make me a cambric shirt." Asher E. Treat, *JAF*, LII (1939), pp. 15-16.
25. "The Six Questions." Barry MSS., I, vn. E, Harvard College Library. Also transcribed in Barry MSS., IV, No. 123.
26. "The Elfin Knight." Phillips Barry, *JAF*, XVIII (1905), pp. 213 and 50-51.
27. "Then you shall be a true lover of mine." Patrick Weston Joyce, *Old Irish Folk Music and Songs*, 1909, No. 117, pp. 59-60.
28. "Every Rose is bonny in time." Mrs. Houston, *JIFSS*, VIII (1910), p. 17.
29. "Scarborough Fair." Kidson, *Traditional Tunes*, 1891, p. 172.
30. "The Elfin Knight." Sharp MSS., 3908/2847. Also in Cecil J. Sharp and Maud Karpeles, *English Folk Songs from the Southern Appalachians*, 1932, I, p. 1. (Jones)
31. "The Sea Side; or, The Elfin Knight." Lucy E. Broadwood, *JFSS*, III (1907), p. 12.
32. "A true lover of mine." Marius Barbeau, Arthur Lismer, and Arthur Bourinot, *Come a Singing*, 1947, p. 33 (National Museum of Canada, Bulletin No. 107). Also in Edith Fulton Fowke and Richard Johnston, *Folk Songs of Canada*, 1954, pp. 138-39.
33. "The Tasks." Baring-Gould MSS., CXXVIII(1) and (B). Also, as "The Lover's Tasks," in S. Baring-Gould, H. Fleetwood Sheppard, and F. W. Bussell, *Songs of the West*, 1905, p. 96.
34. "The Tasks." Baring-Gould MSS., CXXVIII(4).
35. "Strawberry Lane." Elmore Vincent, *Lumber Jack Songs*, [1932], p. 19.
36. "The Lover's Tasks." Sharp MSS., 763/826. Also in Cecil J. Sharp and Charles L. Marson, *Folk Songs from Somerset*, 3rd series, 1906, pp. 26-27. (Huxtable) Also on English Columbia, rec. WA 10685 (DB 335) (Clive Carey); and in *Novello's School Songs*, Set II, No. 960.
37. "The Lover's Tasks." Sharp MSS., 3996/. (Carter)
38. "A True Lover of Mine." Emelyn Elizabeth Gardner and Geraldine Jencks Chickering, *Ballads and Songs of Southern Michigan*, 1939, pp. 137-38.
39. "Rosemary and Thyme." Mary O. Eddy, *Ballads and Songs from Ohio*, 1939, p. 3-4.
40. "The Cambric Shirt." Vance Randolph, *Ozark Folksongs*, 1946, I, pp. 38(A)-39.
41. "Rose de Marian Time." F. C. Brown MS., 16 a 12, Library of Congress, photostat. (Mrs. Norton) Partial text, *The Frank C. Brown Collection of North Carolina Folklore*, II, 1952, p. 14(B). Also in Richard Chase, *Old Songs and Singing Games*, 1938, p. 18; and Winston Wilkinson MSS., 1935-36, pp. 1-2, University of Virginia.

42. "Save Rosemary and Thyme." Alton C. Morris, *Folksongs of Florida*, 1950, pp. 235-36.

43. "The Elfin Knight." Eddy, *Ballads and Songs from Ohio*, 1939, pp. 4-5.

44. "Scarborough Fair." Clive Carey, *Ten English Folk-Songs*, 1915, pp. 20ff. Also in Evelyn K. Wells, *The Ballad Tree*, 1950, p. 171.

45. "The Cambric Shirt." Helen Hartness Flanders, *A Garland of Green Mountain Song*, 1934, pp. 58-59.

46. "The Elfin Knight." W. W. Newell, *JAF*, VII (1894), p. 228.

47. "The Cambric Shirt." Helen Hartness Flanders, and others, *The New Green Mountain Songster*, 1939, pp. 8-10.

48. "The Elfin Knight." Sharp MSS., 4661/3244. Also in Sharp and Karpeles, *Appalachians*, 1932, I, p. 2. (Mitchell)

49. "True Lover of Mine." Sidney Robertson, LC Archive of American Folk Song, rec. 3812 A1. (George Vinton Graham)

APPENDIX B

50. "The Elfin Knight." Greig and Keith, *Last Leaves*, 1925, p. 2(2). (Calder)

GROUP C

51. "The Lover's Tasks." Sharp MSS., 4933/. (Singer unknown)

52. "Sing Ivy." W. Percy Merrick, *JFSS*, I (1901), p. 83.

53. "An Acre of Land." R. Vaughan Williams, *JFSS*, II (1906), p. 212.

54. "Sing Ivy." A. Moffat and Frank Kidson, *Children's Songs of Long Ago*, n.d., p. 48. Tune also in *JFSS*, II (1906), p. 213.

55. "Sing Ivy." H. B. Gardiner, *JFSS*, III (1907), pp. 274-75. Also in H. B. Gardiner, *Folk Songs of Hampshire*, 1909, p. 21 (Vol. III of Cecil J. Sharp and Gustav Holst, *Folk Songs of England*, 1908-12).

TUNES WITH TEXTS

GROUP A

1. "The Laird o' Elfin"

Greig MSS., III, p. 139; text, Bk. 739, XXIX, pp. 6off. Also in Greig and Keith, 1925, p. 2(1). Sung by Alexander Robb, New Deer, Aberdeenshire, 1908.

p Æ/D

The tune as printed in the *Rymour Club Miscellanea*, I (1910), p. 201, gives the initial upbeat as D (i.e., C transposed).

1. The Laird o' Elfin stands on yon hill
   Ba-ba-ba leelie ba
 And he blows his trumpet loud & shrill
   And the wind blaws aye my plaid awa.

2. O gin I'd that horn in my kist
   Ba &c.
 And then get wedded wi' him next
   And the wind &c.

3. But afore that I do that to thee
   Ba &c.
 A weel-sewed sark ye maun sew to me
   And the wind &c.

4. And ye maun sew it needle-thread free
   Ba &c.
 And a weel-sewed sark ye maun sew to me
   And the wind &c.

5. But afore that I do this to thee
   Ba &c.

I'll gie ye some wark to do to me
   And the wind &c.

6. I have a little wee acre o' lan'
   Ba &c.
 That's atween the salt seas & the san'
   And the wind &c.

7. And ye maun ploo't wi your bugle horn
   Ba &c.
 And ye maun saw't wi' Indian Corn
   And the wind &c.

8. And ye maun cut it wi' your pen knife
   [Ba &c.]
 And bind it up just as your life
   And the wind &c.

9. And ye maun thrasht in your shee-sole
   Ba &c.
 And ye maun riddle't in yonder moose hole
   And the wind &c.

10. And ye maun winny't in your nieves
   Ba, &c
 And ye maun seek it in your gloves
   And the wind &c.

11. And ye maun stook it on the sea
   Ba &c.
 And a dry sheaf ye maun bring to me
   And the wind &c.

12. Robin Redbreast and the wran
   Ba &c.
 They'll bring me my corn hame
   And the wind &c.

13. And when ye have done a' this wark
   Ba &c.
 Come ye to me & ye'll get your sark
   And the wind &c.

2. "Blow, Ye Winds, Blow"

Barry, *JAF*, XVIII (1905), pp. 212 and 49-50, as from "Family Songs compiled by Rosa Allen," 1899, p. 14, in whose family, of Medfield, Mass., it had long been traditional. Also in Linscott, 1939, pp. 170-71.

a I/Ly

The Linscott copy was sung by Lucy Allen, West Newton, Mass.; learned from her uncle, c. 1870.

Barry connects this tune with "Donocht Head" (R. A. Smith, *The Scotish Minstrel*, III, p. 96), but if perhaps there is a resemblance in first and last phrases, this does not hold true of the earlier copy in the *SMM*, No. 375.

1. You must make me a fine Holland shirt,
    Blow, blow, blow, ye winds, blow,
    And not have in it a stitch of needlework,
    Blow, ye winds that arise, blow, blow.

2. You must wash it in yonder spring,
    Blow, blow, blow, ye winds, blow,
    Where there's never a drop of water in,
    Blow, ye winds that arise, blow, blow.

3. You must dry it on yonder thorn,
    Blow, blow, blow, ye winds, blow,
    Where the sun never yet shone on,
    Blow, ye winds that arise, blow, blow.

4. My father's got an acre of land,
    Blow, blow, blow, ye winds, blow,
    You must dig it with a goose quill,
    Blow, ye winds that arise, blow, blow.

5. You must sow it with one seed,
    Blow, blow, blow, ye winds, blow,
    You must reap it with your thumb nail,
    Blow, ye winds that arise, blow, blow.

6. You must thrash it on yonder sea,
    Blow, blow, blow, ye winds, blow,
    And not get it wet, or let a kernel be,
    Blow, ye winds that arise, blow, blow.

7. You must grind it on yonder hill,
    Blow, blow, blow, ye winds, blow,
    Where there yet has ne'er stood a mill,
    Blow, ye winds that arise, blow, blow.

8. When you've done, and finished your work,
    Blow, blow, blow, ye winds, blow,

Bring it unto me and you shall have your shirt,
    Blow, ye winds that arise, blow, blow.

3. "Redio-Tedio"

Barry, Eckstorm, and Smyth, 1929, pp. 3-4. Sung by Mrs. Susie Carr Young, Brewer, Maine; learned from Sybil Emery in 1882. Melody recorded by George Herzog.

a I/M (– VI)

N.B. that Herzog noted this air in 4/4, but in notes of only half the values given above.

1. (*He*) "I want you to make me a cambric shirt,
    Fum-a-lum-a-link, sup-a-loo-my-nee,
    With neither seam or needle-work,
    Redio-tedio, toddle-bod-bedio,
    Fum-a-lum-a-link, sup-a-loo-my-nee."

2. (*She*) "I want you to buy me an acre of land,
    Fum-a-lum-a-link, sup-a-loo-my-nee,
    Between salt water and the sea-sand,
    Redio-tedio, toddle-bod-bedio,
    Fum-a-lum-a-link, sup-a-loo-my-nee.

3. "Plow it o'er with an old buck's horn,
    Fum-a-lum-a-link, sup-a-loo-my-nee,
    Plant it o'er with one peppercorn,
    Redio-tedio, toddle-bod-bedio,
    Fum-a-lum-a-link, sup-a-loo-my-nee.

4. "Reap it down with a peacock's feather,
    Fum-a-lum-a-link, sup-a-loo-my-nee,
    Bind it up with the sting of an adder,
    Redio-tedio, toddle-bod-bedio,
    Fum-a-lum-a-link, sup-a-loo-my-nee.

5. "Thrash it out with a mouse's tail,
    Fum-a-lum-a-link, sup-a-loo-my-nee,
    Cart it in on the back of a snail,
    Redio-tedio, toddle-bod-bedio,
    Fum-a-lum-a-link, sup-a-loo-my-nee.

6. "When you have completed your work,
    Fum-a-lum-a-link, sup-a-loo-my-nee,
    Come to me, you shall have your shirt,
    Redio-tedio, toddle-bod-bedio,
    Fum-a-lum-a-link, sup-a-loo-my-nee."

4. "Oh, say, do you know the way to Selin?"

Ring, 1937, pp. 12-13. Sung by "Aunt Fannie" Parker, Carthage, Maine.

a π[1]

1. Oh, say, do you know the way to Selin?
    (Hickalack, tickalack, farmalack-a-day.)
   Remember me to a young lady therein.
    (Hickalack, tickalack, farmalack-a-day,
     Just below my knee.)

2. If she will buy one inch of cloth,
    (Hickalack, tickalack, farmalack-a-day.)
   To make me a shirt to wear thereof.
    (Hickalack, tickalack, farmalack-a-day,
     Just below my knee.)

3. Tell her to sew it up without any seam,
    (Hickalack, tickalack, farmalack-a-day.)
   And wash it in water that never was seen.
    (Hickalack, tickalack, farmalack-a-day,
     Just below my knee.)

4. Tell her to wring it out of a dry well,
    (Hickalack, tickalack, farmalack-a-day.)
   Where never a drop of rain water fell.
    (Hickalack, tickalack, farmalack-a-day,
     Just below my knee.)

5. And hang it out on a bush of thorn,
    (Hickalack, tickalack, farmalack-a-day.)
   Which never bore a bud since Adam was born.
    (Hickalack, tickalack, farmalack-a-day,
     Just below my knee.)

6. Oh, say, do you know the way back again?
    (Hickalack, tickalack, farmalack-a-day.)
   Remember me to a young man therein.
    (Hickalack, tickalack, farmalack-a-day,
     Just below my knee.)

7. If he will buy one acre of land;
    (Hickalack, tickalack, farmalack-a-day.)
   Between the salt water and the sea sand.
    (Hickalack, tickalack, farmalack-a-day,
     Just below my knee.)

8. Tell him to plow it up with one turtle's horn;
    (Hickalack, tickalack, farmalack-a-day.)
   And plant it all over with one pepper-corn.
    (Hickalack, tickalack, farmalack-a-day,
     Just below my knee.)

9. Tell him to reap it down with a goose quill;
    (Hickalack, tickalack, farmalack-a-day.)
   And winnow it up into an egg shell.
    (Hickalack, tickalack, farmalack-a-day,
     Just below my knee.)

10. Tell him to reap it down into a trice;
     (Hickalack, tickalack, farmalack-a-day.)
    And haul it home with a yoke of mice.
     (Hickalack, tickalack, farmalack-a-day,
      Just below my knee.)

11. Tell him to put it into a dry barn;
     (Hickalack, tickalack, farmalack-a-day.)
    Which never's been boarded since Adam was born.
     (Hickalack, tickalack, farmalack-a-day,
      Just below my knee.)

12. Tell the man when he's done his work,
     (Hickalack, tickalack, farmalack-a-day.)
    To come to me and he shall have his shirt.
     (Hickalack, tickalack, farmalack-a-day,
      Just below my knee.)

5. "The Cambric Shirt"

Major, *PTFLS*, X (1932), pp. 137-38. Sung by Mrs. J. C. Marshall, Quanah, Texas.

a I/M

1. "Madam, will you make me a cambric shirt
   With not one stitch of needle work?"

Chorus:
   Keedle up, a keedle up, a-turp, turp tay,
   Tum-a-lum a do, Castle-on-my nay.

2. "Wash it out in an old dry well
   Where never a drop of water fell."

3. "Hang it out on an old dry thorn
   Where the sun never shone since Adam was born."

4. "Kind sir, will you buy me an acre of land
   Between salt waters and sea sand?"

5. "Plow it up with an old ram's horn,
   And seed it down with one grain of corn."

6. "Cut it down with an old case knife
   And haul it in with a yoke of mice."

7. "Then when you've done and finished your work,
   You can come and get your cambric shirt."

6. "Scarborough Fair"

Flanders and Brown, 1931, pp. 194-96. Sung by Ola Leonard (Mrs. Ivan W.) Gray, East Calais, Vt., from family tradition. Collected by Sylvia Bliss, Plainfield, Vt. From *Vermont Folk-Songs and Ballads*, edited by Helen Hartness Flanders and George Brown; copyright 1931 by Arthur Wallace Peach.

a I (–VI)

1. "Oh, where are you going?" "I'm going to Lynn,"
   Fellow ma la cus lomely.
   "Give my respects to the lady therein,
      Ma-ke-ta-lo, ke-ta-lo, tam-pa-lo, tam-pa-lo,
      Fellow ma la cus lomely.

2. "Tell her to buy me a yard of cloth,
   Fellow ma la cus lomely.
   And make me a cambric shirt thereof,
      Ma-ke-ta-lo, ke-ta-lo, tam-pa-lo, tam-pa-lo,
      Fellow ma la cus lomely.

3. "Tell her to make it with a gold ring,
   Fellow ma la cus lomely.
   Stitch it and sew it without a seam,
      Ma-ke-ta-lo, ke-ta-lo, tam-pa-lo, tam-pa-lo,
      Fellow ma la cus lomely.

4. "Tell her to wash it in yonder well,
   Fellow ma la cus lomely.
   Where never a drop of water yet fell,
      Ma-ke-ta-lo, ke-ta-lo, tam-pa-lo, tam-pa-lo,
      Fellow ma la cus lomely.

5. "Tell her to dry it on yonder thorn,
   Fellow ma la cus lomely.
   That never was rooted since Adam was born,
      Ma-ke-ta-lo, ke-ta-lo, tam-pa-lo, tam-pa-lo,
      Fellow ma la cus lomely."

6. "Oh, where are you going?" "I'm going to Japan,"
   Fellow ma la cus lomely.
   "Give my respects to this same young man,
      Ma-ke-ta-lo, ke-ta-lo, tam-pa-lo, tam-pa-lo,
      Fellow ma la cus lomely.

7. "Tell him to buy me an acre of land,
   Fellow ma la cus lomely.
   Between the salt sea and the sea sand,
      Ma-ke-ta-lo, ke-ta-lo, tam-pa-lo, tam-pa-lo,
      Fellow ma la cus lomely.

8. "Tell him to plow it with a deer's horn,
   Fellow ma la cus lomely.
   Sow it all over with one pepper corn,
      Ma-ke-ta-lo, ke-ta-lo, tam-pa-lo, tam-pa-lo,
      Fellow ma la cus lomely.

9. "Tell him to reap it with a sea fowl's quill,
   Fellow ma la cus lomely.
   Tan it all up into an eggshell,
      Ma-ke-ta-lo, ke-ta-lo, tam-pa-lo, tam-pa-lo,
      Fellow ma la cus lomely.

10. "And when he has completed his work,
    Fellow ma la cus lomely.
    Come unto me and he shall have his shirt,
      Ma-ke-ta-lo, ke-ta-lo, tam-pa-lo, tam-pa-lo,
      Fellow ma la cus lomely."

APPENDIX A

7. [Jockey's Lamentation]

D'Urfey, 1719-20, V, pp. 316ff. Related to Child versions A-E by refrain.

p I/M, ending on II

And, 'Tis o'er the Hills, and far away, 'Tis o'er the Hills, and far away, 'Tis o'er the Hills, and far a-way, The Wind has blown my Plad away.

With this copy, compare that in the *SMM*, No. 62 ("O'er the hills, and far away"). John Glen, in a note on the latter, *Early Scottish Melodies*, 1900, p. 77, adds further comment. Stenhouse, in his free way, says (*Illustrations*, p. 62) that of "this old pipe tune" he is possessed of a manuscript copy "of considerable antiquity."

8. "My Plaid away"

Margaret Sinkler's MS., 1710.

p I/M, ending on II

9a. "The wind has blown my plaid away"

Drexel MS. 3909, [c. 1700-50].

p I/M, ending on II

9b. "The wind has blown my plaid away"

Drexel MS. 3909.

p I

9c. "Out over the hills and far away" [Another copy]

Drexel MS. 3909.

p I [?]

These three copies are from different parts of the same MS., written in flageolet tablature. There are no time-values indicated in the original, and the note-values here are therefore entirely conjectural. The superior letters, D and C♯, mean that the lower notes of the decorations are these. Trills are to begin a note above the notes written. In the second tune, the last note of the third bar may be intended to trill on C♯. My transcriptions, unchecked by an expert, are not advanced with much conviction.

10. [O'er the Hills and far awa]

McGibbon, n.d. [c. 1742-55], Bk. IV, p. 97. Also in Johnson, [1787], I, No. 62, pp. 62-63.

p I/M, ending on II

The variant readings are from the *SMM* copy.

11. "'Twas in that year" [O'er the hills & far awa']

Greig MSS., II, p. 25. Sung by Alexander Robb, New Deer, Aberdeenshire, June 1906.

p I/M, ending on II

We'll o-ver the hills and far a-wa'.

12. [Oure the Hills and Far Awa]

Maver, 1866, No. 418, p. 209 (with other words by Burns: "How can my poor heart be glad?").

p I/M, ending on II

13. [Will he no come back again?]

Maver, 1866, No. 372, p. 186 ("First time published").

m π[1]

This copy, possibly somewhat edited, shows a striking transformation of mood. Maver says the first stanza (containing the "owre the hills and far awa" phrase) and the chorus are old; the other verses are by Burns.

GROUP B

14. [The Tasks]

Baring-Gould MSS., CXXVIII(2); text, (A), apparently composite. Sung by Joseph Dyer, Mawgan-in-Pyder, Cornwall, July 6, 1891. Noted by F. W. Bussell.

p I

1. Thou must buy me my lady, a cambrick shirt
   Whilst every grove rings with a merry antine.*
   And stitch it without any needle work
   O and then thou shalt be a true love of mine.

2. And thou must wash it in yonder well,
   Whilst every grove &c.
   Where never a drop of water in fell,
   O and then &c.

3. And thou must hang it upon a white thorn,
   Whilst every, &c.
   That never has blossomed since Adam was born,
   O and then &c.

4. And when that these tasks are finished & done
   Whilst every, &c.
   I'll take thee & marry thee under the sun
   O and then &c.

5. Or ever I do these two and three
   Whilst every, &c.
   I will set of tasks as many to thee
   O and then shall I be a true love of thine.

6. Thou must buy for me an acre of land
   Whilst every, &c.
   Between the salt ocean & the yellow sand,
   O and then &c.

7. Thou must plough it o'er with a horse's horn
   Whilst every, &c.
   And sow it over with one pepper corn
   O and then &c.

8. Thou must reap it, too, with a piece of leather
   Whilst every grove &c.
   And bind it all up with a peacock's feather
   And then, &c.

9. And when these tasks are finished & done
   Whilst every, &c.
   O then I will marry thee under the sun
   And then, &c.

An extra verse from John Dyer:

Pray take it up in a bottomless sack
   And every leaf grows many-in-time,
And bear it to the mill on a butterfly's back
   O then you shall be a true love of mine.

MS. note: "Sent me from Cornwall . . . enacted in farm houses."
* antienne=antiphon (Baring-Gould)

15. [The Tasks]

Baring-Gould MSS., CXXVIII(3). Sung by S. Lobb, Mawgan-in-Pyder, Cornwall, April 1893. Noted by F. W. Bussell.

p I

In the MS., the 10th and 8th notes from the end (D and d) are inadvertently written as quarters instead of eighths.

This version commences like "Jog on" (*Dancing Master*, 1650, p. 53, and later), which is the Elizabethan "Hanskin" (Fitzwilliam Book, 1899, II, pp. 494ff.). Also cf. D'Urfey, *Pills*, 1719, IV, p. 32 ("The Catholick Ballad") and IV, p. 37 ("Sir Francis Drake; or, Eighty Eight"); and Chappell, I, pp. 211-13.

16. [The Lover's Tasks]

Sharp MSS., 219/306. Sent by Mr. Gilbert, June 2, 1904; from his collection.

p I

O, can you make me a cambric shirt?
　　Every leaf grows many a time
Without any needle or any fine work
　　And you shall be true lover of mine.

And wash it down in yonder well
Where neither spring water nor rain ever fell.

And dry it off on yonder thorn
Where there grew no leaf since Adam was born.

O, can you buy me an acre of land
Betwixt the salt water and the sea sand?

And plough it all over with a snail's horn
And sow it throughout with one barleycorn.

Then gather the crop in a no-bottom sack
And send it to mill on a butterfly's back.

17. "Scarbro Fair"

Child MSS., XXI, No. 18. Sent by Frank Kidson, 1884; from oral tradition (? Yorkshire).

p I

1. "Oh where are you going"? "To Scarbro fair,
　　Savoury sage rosemary & thyme
Remember me to a lass who lives there
　　For once she was a true lover of mine

2. "And tell her to make me a cambric shirt
　　Savoury sage &c
Without a needle or thread or ought else
　　And then she shall be a true lover of mine

3. "And tell her to wash it in yonder well
　　Savoury sage &c
Where water ne'er sprung nor a drop of rain fell
　　And then she shall be a true lover of mine

4. "And tell her to hang it on yonder stone
　　Savoury sage &c
Where moss never grew since Adam was born
　　And then she shall &c

5. And when she has finished & done her I'll repay
She can come unto me & married we'll be

———

The Reply

6. Oh where are you going? To Scarbro' fair
　　Savoury sage rosemary & thyme
Remember me to a lad who lives there
　　For once he was a true lover of mine

7. And tell him to buy me an acre of land
　　Savoury &c
Between the wide ocean & the sea sand
　　And then he shall be

8. And tell him to plough it with a ram's horn
　　Savoury sage &c
And sow it all over with one pepper corn
　　And then &c

9. And tell him to reap't with a sickle of leather
　　Savoury sage &c
And bind it up with a peacock's feather
　　And then he shall be &c

10. And when he has finished & done his work
He can come unto me for his cambric shirt

———

Fragments of the same ballad
remembered by another person

11. Oh are you going to Scarbro Fair
　　Remember me to a lass that lives there
　　For once she was a true lover of mine
　　　　* * * * * *

12. Tell her to buy me an acre of land
    Sow it all over with [—] sand
       * * * * * *
13. Reap it with a sickle of leather
    And tie it up with a peacock's feather
    And then she shall be a true lover of mine
       * * * * * *
14. And tell her to wash it in yonder dry well
       Where no water spring* nor a drop of rain fell
    And tell her to wash it in yonder dry well
       Or never be a true lover of mine

    * [sprung?]

18. "Scarborough Fair"

Kidson, 1891, pp. 43-44. Also, with piano accompaniment, in Kidson, Kidson, and Moffat, 1927, p. 30. Sung by a street-singer, Whitby, Yorkshire, c. 1860.

p I/M

1. "O, where are you going?" "To Scarborough fair,"
       Savoury sage, rosemary, and thyme;
   "Remember me to a lass who lives there,
       For once she was a true love of mine.

2. "And tell her to make me a cambric shirt,
       Savoury sage, rosemary, and thyme,
   Without any seam or needlework,
       And then she shall be a true love of mine.

3. "And tell her to wash it in yonder dry well,
       Savoury sage, rosemary, and thyme,
   Where no water sprung, nor a drop of rain fell,
       And then she shall be a true love of mine.

4. "Tell her to dry it on yonder thorn,
       Savoury sage, rosemary, and thyme,
   Which never bore blossom since Adam was born,
       And then she shall be a true love of [mine]."*

5. "O, will you find me an acre of land,
       Savoury sage, rosemary, and thyme,
   Between the sea foam, the sea sand,
       Or never be a true lover of mine.

6. "O, will you plough it with a ram's horn,
       Savoury sage, rosemary, and thyme,
   And sow it all over with one peppercorn,
       Or never be a true lover of mine.

7. "O, will you reap it with a sickle of leather,
       Savoury sage, rosemary, and thyme,
   And tie it all up with a peacock's feather,
       Or never be a true lover of mine.

8. "And when you have done and finished your work,
       Savoury sage, rosemary, and thyme,
   You may come to me for your cambric shirt,
       And then you shall be a true lover of mine."

   * 1891: *thine*.

19. "Scarbro Fair"

Child MSS., XXI, No. 18. Sent by Frank Kidson, 1884; from oral tradition.

p I

20. [Scarborough Fair]

Broadwood and Maitland, 1893, pp. 12-13. Sung by William Moat, a Whitby fisherman, North Riding, Yorkshire, December, 1891. Noted by H. M. Bower.

p I and p Æ

The editors note that this tune is related to a Sussex song, "The Seasons of the Year" (*op.cit.*, p. 143); and the latter in turn to a Wiltshire "Sheep-shearing Song" (*ibid.*, p. 149). With the second half, above, cf. "Over Yonder's a Park" (*JEFSS*, IV [1910], p. 63). This singer, say the editors, insisted on the long pauses.

1. Is any of you going to Scarborough Fair?
   Remember me to a lad as lives there,
   Remember me to a lad as lives there;
       For once he was a true lover of mine.

2. Tell him to bring me an acre of land
   Betwixt the wild ocean and yonder sea sand; (*bis*)
       And then he shall be a true lover of mine.

3. Tell him to plough it with one ram's horn,
   And sow it all over with one peppercorn; *(bis)*
       And then he shall be a true lover of mine.

4. Tell him to reap it with sickle of leather,
   And bind it together with one peacock feather: *(bis)*
       And then he shall be a true lover of mine.

5. And now I have answered your questions three,
   I hope you'll answer as many for me; *(bis)*
       And then thou shalt be a true lover of mine.

6. Is any of you going to Scarborough Fair?
   Remember me to a lass as lives there; *(bis)*
       For once she was a true lover of mine.

7. Tell her to make me a cambric shirt,
   Without any needles or thread or owt through't: *(bis)*
       And then she shall be a true lover of mine.

8. Tell her to wash it by yonder wall
   Where water ne'er sprung, nor a drop o' rain fall; *(bis)*
       And then she shall be a true lover of mine.

9. Tell her to dry it on yonder thorn,
   Where blossom ne'er grew sin' Adam was born; *(bis)*
       And then she shall be a true lover of mine.

10. And now I have answered your questions three,
    And I hope you'll answer as many for me, *(bis)*
        And then thou shalt be a true lover of mine.

By permission of Messrs. J. B. Cramer & Co., Ltd., London.

21. [Scarborough Fair]

Sharp MSS., 2868/. Sung by Richard Hutton (65), Goathland, July 14, 1913.

p D (inflected VII)

Where are you going to Scarboro Fair
Parsley Sage Rosemary and thyme,
Remember me to a bonny lass there
For once she was a true lover of mine.

Tell her to make me a cambric shirt
Without either needle or thread worked in it
And tell her to wash it in yonder spring
Where water never sprung nor a drop ran through.

22. [Whittingham Fair]

Bruce and Stokoe, 1882, pp. 79-80.

a Æ

1. Are you going to Whittingham fair,
       Parsley, sage, rosemary, and thyme;
   Remember me to one who lives there,
       For once she was a true love of mine.

2. Tell her to make me a cambric shirt,
       Parsley, sage, rosemary, and thyme;
   Without any seam or needlework,
       For once she was a true love of mine.

3. Tell her to wash it in yonder well,
       Parsley, sage, rosemary, and thyme;
   Where never spring water nor rain ever fell,
       For once she was a true love of mine.

4. Tell her to dry it on yonder thorn,
       Parsley, sage, rosemary, and thyme;
   Which never bore blossom since Adam was born,
       For once she was a true love of mine.

5. Now he has asked me questions three,
       Parsley, sage, rosemary, and thyme;
   I hope he will answer as many for me,
       For once he was a true love of mine.

6. Tell him to find me an acre of land,
       Parsley, sage, rosemary, and thyme;
   Betwixt the salt water and the sea sand,
       For once he was a true love of mine.

7. Tell him to plough it with a ram's horn,
       Parsley, sage, rosemary, and thyme;
   And sow it all over with one pepper corn,
       For once he was a true love of mine.

8. Tell him to reap it with a sickle of leather,
       Parsley, sage, rosemary, and thyme;
   And bind it up with a peacock's feather,
       For once he was a true love of mine.

9. When he has done and finished his work,
       Parsley, sage, rosemary, and thyme;
   O tell him to come and he'll have his shirt,
       For once he was a true love of mine.

23. "Strawberry Lane"

Kittredge, *JAF*, XXX (1917), pp. 284-85. Also in Barry, Eckstorm, and Smyth, 1929, p. 10. Sung by Mr. E. R. Davis, 1914, as remembered from his grandfather, William Henry Banks (born 1834) of Maine.

a Æ/D

1. As I was a-walking up Strawberry Lane,—
    Every rose grows merry and fine,—
I chanced for to meet a pretty, fair maid,
    Who said she would be* a true-lover of mine.

2. "You'll have for to make me a cambric shirt,—
    Every rose grows merry and fine,—
And every stitch must be finicle work,
    Before you can be a true-lover of mine.

3. "You'll have for to wash it in a deep well,—
    Every rose grows merry and fine,—
Where water never was nor rain ever fell,
    Before you can be a true-lover of mine."

(*The man goes on to make several more conditions. Finally the girl turns on him thus:*)

4. "Now, since you have been so hard with me,—
    Every rose grows merry and fine,—
Perhaps I can be as hard with thee,
    Before you can be a true-lover of mine.

5. "You'll have for to buy me an acre of ground,—
    Every rose grows merry and fine,—
.   .   .   .
    Before you can be a true-lover of mine.

6. "You'll have for to plough it with a deer's horn,—
    Every rose grows merry and fine,—
And plant it all over with one grain of corn,
    Before you can be a true-lover of mine.

7 "You'll have for to thrash it in an eggshell,—
    Every rose grows merry and fine,—
And bring it to market in a thimble,†
    Before you can be a true-lover of mine."

* Or, "wanted to be."
† Or, "And take it to market where man never dwelled."

24. "Go and make me a cambric shirt"

Treat, *JAF*, LII (1939), pp. 15-16. Sung by Pearl Jacobs Borusky and Maud Jacobs, Bryant, Wisc., September 11, 1938; learned in Kentucky.

a Æ/D

Go and make me a cambric shirt
Without any needle or any needle work.
Then you can be that true lover of mine,
Then you can be that true lover of mine.

Go and wash it in yonders stream.
.   .   .   .
Then you can be that true lover of mine,
Then you can be that true lover of mine.

Go and hang it on yonders thorn
That hasn't borne leaves since Adam was born.
Then you can be that true lover of mine,
Then you can be that true lover of mine.

25. "The Six Questions"

Barry MSS., I, vn. E; also transcribed in IV, No. 123. Sung by O. F. A. Conner.

a Æ/D

The original notation as sent by the singer is musically illiterate. The timing here is highly conjectural.

1. I want you to make me a cambric Shirt
Every Rose grows merry in time
Without any seam or any needle work
And then you can be a true lover of mine.

2. I want you to wash it in yonder well
Every Rose grows merry in time
Where there never was water nor never none fell
And then you shall be a true lover of mine.

3. I want you to dry it on yonder thorn
Every Rose grows merry in time
Where there never was a thorn since Adam was born
And then you shall be a true lover of mine.

4. Questions you have asked me three
Every Rose grows merry in time
I hope you can answer as many for me
And then you can be a true lover of mine.

5. I want you to plough me an acre of land
Every Rose grows merry in time
Between the salt water & the sea sand
And then you shall be a true lover of mine.

6. I want you to plough it with a ram's horn
Every Rose grows merry in time
And sow it all over with one grain of corn
And then you shall be a true lover of mine.

7. I want you to reap it with a Pea Fowel's (*sic*) feather
Every Rose grows merry in time
And thrash it all out with the sting of an arrow
And then you shall be a true lover of mine.

8. And when you are done & completed your work
Every Rose grows merry in time
Then come to me & you shall have your Shirt
And then you shall be a true lover of mine.

26. [The Elfin Knight]

Barry, *JAF,* XVIII (1905), p. 213; text, pp. 50-51. Sung by Mrs. S. A. Flint, Providence, R.I., 1904.

If tonic G, p D (but inflected VII); if tonic D, a Æ

According to Barry (p. 213), Mrs. Flint learned (c. 1875) this song from a man born about 1800. The tune seems to shift from an anchorage on G to one on F, after the mid-cadence: that is, from Dorian to F major. Something has probably gone amiss. Cf. Joyce's tune immediately following.

1. I want you to make me a cambric shirt,
    Parsley and sage, rosemary and thyme,
  Without any needle, or any fine work,
    And then you shall be a true lover of mine.

2. Go wash it out in yonder well,
    Parsley and sage, rosemary and thyme,
  Where there's never no water nor drop of rain fell,
    And then you shall be a true lover of mine.

3. Go hang it out on yonder thorn,
    Parsley and sage, rosemary and thyme,
  Where there's never no blossom, since Adam was born,
    And then you shall be a true lover of mine.

4. Now, since you have asked me questions three,
    Parsley and sage, rosemary and thyme,
  I pray you would grant me the same liberty,
    And then you shall be a true lover of mine.

5. I want you to buy me an acre of land,
    Parsley and sage, rosemary and thyme,
  Between the salt water and the sea sand,
    And then you shall be a true lover of mine.

6. Go plough it all up with one cuckold's horn,
    Parsley and sage, rosemary and thyme,
  Go sow it all down with one pepper corn,
    And then you shall be a true lover of mine.

7. Go reap it all up with a sickle of leather,
    Parsley and sage, rosemary and thyme,
  And bind it all up with one cock's feather,
    And then you shall be a true lover of mine.

27. "Then you shall be a true lover of mine"

Joyce, 1909, No. 117, pp. 59-60. Learned in childhood from Biddy Hickey.

a D

Choose when you can an acre of land—
    As every plant grows merry in time—
  Between the salt water and the sea strand,
    And then you shall be a truelover of mine.

Plough it up with an old ram's horn,
    As every plant grows merry in time;
  Sow it all over with one grain of corn—
    And then you shall be a truelover of mine.

28. "Every Rose is bonny in time"

Houston, *JIFSS,* VIII (1910), p. 17. From Coleraine, Ulster.

a M (– II); if tonic G, p I (– VI)

The original is given in bars of 12/8 (two), 6/8 (two), and 12/8 (three). The last line of text would seem to have been repeated.

1. As I went over Bonny Moor Hill—
    Every rose grows bonny in time—
  I met a wee lass, and they ca'ed her Nell;
    She was longing to be a sweet lover of mine.

2. It's questions three I'll ask of thee—
    Every rose grows bonny in time—
  And it's questions three you must answer me
    Before you're a sweet lover of mine.

3. You must get unto me a cambric shirt,
  Without one stitch of your needlework.

4. You must wash it in yonder well,
  Where water ne'er wet and rain never fell.

5. You must bleach it on yonder green,
  Where'er flowers ne'er blossomed nor grass seen.

6. You must dry it on yonder thorn springs,
  Where it ne'er budded since Adam was born.

7. It is questions three you have asked of me,
  And it's questions three you must answer me.

8. You must get unto me an acre of land,
Betwixt the salt sea and the sea water strand.

9. You must plough it with Adam's horn,
And then sow it over with one hub of corn.

10. You must sheer it with one peacock's feather,
And then bind it up in the song of another.

11. You must stock it on yonder sea,
And bring the shell sheaf dry unto me.

12. It is when you have done and finished your work,
Every rose grows bonny in time—
You may call unto me for your cambric shirt.
A then I will be a sweet lover of thine.

Mrs. Houston's note: "In singing this ballad the lines in italics are inserted and varied according to the sense, to come in as second and fourth of each stanza."

29. "Scarborough Fair"

Kidson, 1891, p. 172. Sung by A. Wardill, Goathland.

a M; or on G, p I (with fallen close)

"O where are you going?" "To Scarborough Fair!"
Rue, parsley, rosemary, and thyme!
"Remember me to a lass who lives there:
For once she was a true love of mine."

30. [The Elfin Knight]

Sharp MSS., 3908/2847. Also in Sharp and Karpeles, 1932, I, p. 1. Sung by Mrs. Cis Jones, Manchester, Ky., August 24, 1917.

a π²; or p π¹ (with fallen close)

1. Go tell him to clear me one acre of ground,
    Sether wood, sale, rosemary and thyme,
Betwixt the sea and the sea-land side,
    And then he'll be a true lover of mine.

2. Tell him to plough it all up with an old leather plough,
    Sether wood, etc.

And hoe it all over with a pea-fowl's feather,
    And then he'll be, etc.

3. Go tell him to plant it all over with one grain of corn,
    Sether wood, etc.
And reap it all down with an old ram's horn,
    And then he'll be, etc.

4. Go tell him to shock it in yonder sea,
    (Betwixt the sea and the sea-land side)
    Sether wood, etc.
And return it back to me all dry,
    And then he'll be, etc.

5. Go tell her to make me a cambric shirt,
    Sether wood, etc.
Without any needle or needle's work,
    And then she'll be a true lover of mine.

6. Go tell her to wash it in yonders well,
    Sether wood, etc.
Where rain nor water never fell,
    And then she'll be, etc.

7. Go tell her to hang it on yonders thorn,
    Sether wood, etc.
Where man nor thorn was never seen born,
    And then she'll be a true lover of mine.

31. "The Sea Side; or, The Elfin Knight"

Broadwood, *JFSS*, III (1907), p. 12. Sung by Bridget Geary at Camphire Cappoquin, County Waterford, Ireland, August 1906.

a I/M

1. As I roved out by the sea side,
    (*Ev'ry rose grows merry in time*),
I met a little girl,
And I gave her my hand,
And I says, "Will you be a true lover of mine?

2. If you are to be a true lover of mine
    (*Every rose grows merry in time*),
You must make me a shirt without needle or seam,
And it's then you will be a true lover of mine.

3. You must wash it in a spring well,
    (*Every rose grows merry in time*),
Where the water never ran or the rain never fell,
And it's then you will be a true lover of mine.

4. You must dry it in a hawthorn tree,
   (*Every rose grows merry in time*),
   That never was blossomed since Adam was born,
   And then you will be a true lover of mine."

5. "Now, Sir, you have questioned me three times three,
   (*Every rose grows merry in time*),
   But I might question as many as thee,
   And it's then you will be a true lover of mine.

6. You must get me a farm of the best land
   (*Every rose grows merry in time*),
   Between the salt water and the sea strand,
   And it's then you will be a true lover of mine.

7. You must plough it with a goat's horn,
   (*Every rose grows merry in time*),
   And sow it all over with one grain of corn,
   And it's then you will be a true lover of mine.

8. You must thrash it in a sparrow's nest,
   (*Every rose grows merry in time*),
   And shake it all out with a cobbler's awl,
   And it's then you will be a true lover of mine.

9. And when you are done, and finished your work
   (*Every rose grows merry in time*),
   You can come back to me, and I'll give you your shirt,
   And it's then you will be a true lover of mine!"

32. "A true lover of mine"

Barbeau, Lismer, and Bourinot, 1947, p. 33. Also in Fowke
and Johnston, 1954, pp. 138-39. From Hazelton, British
Columbia, 1920.

a I

1. Pray, can you buy me an acre or more,
   Savory, sage, rosemary and thyme,
   Between the wide ocean and the sea shore,
   And then can you be a true lover of mine.

2. Pray, can you plough it with one ram's horn, . . .
   And sow it all over with one pepper corn? . . .

3. Pray, can you reap it with a sickle of leather, . . .
   And tie it all up with one peacock's feather? . . .

4. —Now, you have asked me of these questions three . . .
   It is my turn to ask three of thee . . .

5. Pray, can you make me a fine cambric shirt . . .
   Without any seam and all needle work? . . .

6. Pray, in your brook, can you wash it and wade . . .
   Where water ne'er flowed since earth it was made? . . .

7. Pray, can you dry it on yonder sweet thorn . . .
   Where blossoms ne'er bloomed since Adam was born? . . .

33. [The Tasks]

Baring-Gould MSS., CXXVIII(1); text, (B) coinciding
with (A) except in the concluding stanzas. Sung by John
Hext, Post Bridge, October 1890. Noted by F. W. Bussell.

a I/M

This form, almost identical, appears in Baring-Gould, Sheppard,
and Bussell, *Songs of the West*, ed. 1905, p. 96, as from P. Symonds,
Jacobstow, John Hext, and James Dyer of Mawgan.
The original copy is in straight 6/8 time throughout.

1. Thou must buy me my lady, a cambrick shirt
      Whilst every grove rings with a merry antine.*
   And stitch it without any needle work
      O and then thou shalt be a true love of mine.

2. And thou must wash it in yonder well,
      Whilst every grove &c.
   Where never a drop of water in fell,
      O and then, &c.

3. And thou must hang it upon a white thorn,
      Whilst every, &c.
   That never has blossomed since Adam was born,
      O and then, &c.

4. And when that these tasks are finished & done
      Whilst every, &c.
   I'll take thee & marry thee under the sun
      O and then, &c.

5. Or ever I do these two and three
      Whilst every, &c.
   I will set of tasks as many to thee
      O and then shall I be a true love of thine.

6. Thou must buy for me an acre of land
      Whilst every, &c.
   Between the salt ocean & the yellow sand,
      O and then, &c.

7. Thou must plough it o'er with a horse's horn
      Whilst every, &c.
   And sow it over with one pepper corn
      O and then, &c.

8. O tell her to bleach it on yonder grass
   Whilst every, &c.
   Where never a foot or a hoof did pass
   [O] and then, &c.

9. O tell him to thrash it in yonder barn
   Whilst every, &c.
   That hangs to the sky by a thread of yarn,
   &c.

* antienne=antiphon (Baring-Gould)

34. [The Tasks]

Baring-Gould MSS., CXXVIII(4). Sung by Mrs. Knapman, Kingsweare, June 30, 1893; as learned from her mother in Northamptonshire. Collected by S. Baring-Gould.

p I

35. "Strawberry Lane"

Vincent, [1932], p. 19.

p I/M

The yodeling "burden" attached to the tune has been omitted as irrelevant to our concern with tradition.

1. One day I was walking in Strawberry Lane, Ev'ry rose
   grows merry and fine
   And there quite by chance a fair maiden I met, Who said
   she would be a true love of mine.
   De yodel layee de O leeoo layee de Ay leeoo layee de layee
   de layee.

2. You'll have for to make me a spiderweb shirt, Ev'ry rose
   grows, merry and fine
   And every stitch must be finicle work, Before you can be a
   true love of mine.
   De yodel layee de O leeoo layee de Ay leeoo layee de layee
   de layee.

3. You'll have for to wash it down deep in a well, Every rose
   grows merry and fine

Where never was water and rain never fell, Before you can
be a true love of mine.
De yodel layee etc.

4. Then up spoke the maid, "Since you're so hard with me,
   Every rose grows merry and fine
   Perhaps I can be even harder with thee, Before you can
   be a true love of mine.
   De yodel layee etc.

5. You'll have for to buy me ten acres of ground, Every rose
   grows merry and fine
   With never a bush nor a rock to be found, Before you can
   be a true love of mine.
   De yodel layee etc.

6. You'll have for to plow it all with a deer's horn, Every
   rose grows merry and fine
   And plant it all over with one grain of corn, Before you can
   be a true love of mine.
   De yodel layee etc.

7. You'll have for to thrash it all in an egg shell, Every rose
   grows merry and fine
   And bring it to market where man never dwell. Before you
   can be a true love of mine.
   De yodel layee etc.

36. [The Lover's Tasks]

Sharp MSS., 763/826. Also in Sharp and Marson, 3rd series, 1906, pp. 26-27. Sung by William Huxtable, Rowbarton, Taunton, January 15, 1906.

a I

The variants are from the singing of Bessie Huxtable, at Minehead, January 12, 1906. She sang the first refrain line as "O yes, she said, Sweet William and time."

This form of the tune is sung by Clive Carey, on a phonograph record (English Columbia, rec. WA 10685 [DB 335]).

1. Say can you make me a cambric shirt
   Sing Ivy Leaf, Sweet William and Thyme,
   Without any needle or needle work?
   And you shall be a true lover of mine.

2. Yes, if you wash it in yonder well
   Sing Ivy Leaf, Sweet William and Thyme,
   Where neither springs water, nor rain ever fell,
   And you shall be a true lover of mine.

3. Say can you plough me an acre of land
   Sing Ivy Leaf, Sweet William and Thyme,
   Between the sea and the salt sea strand?
   And you shall be a true lover of mine.

4. Yes, if you plough it with one ram's horn
   Sing Ivy Leaf, Sweet William and Thyme,
   And sow it all over with one pepper corn,
   And you shall be a true lover of mine.

5. Say can you reap with a sickle of leather
   Sing Ivy Leaf, Sweet William and Thyme,
   And tie it all up with a Tom-tit's feather?
   And you shall be a true lover of mine.

6. Yes if you gather it all in a sack,
   Sing Ivy Leaf, Sweet William and Thyme,
   And carry it home on a butterfly's back,
   And you shall be a true lover of mine.

Sung by Robert Pope, at Rowbarton, Taunton, January 15, 1906:

1. Say can you make me a cambric shirt
        O yes she said Sweet William and time
   Without any needle or needle work
        And then you shall be a true lover of mine.

2. Wash it all up in yonder wink
   Water will never foddle na never know spring.

3. Hang it all out on yonder thorn
   Which never bear leaves since Adam was born.

4. Can you plough me an acre of land
   Between the sea and the sea sand.

5. Plough it all over with a ram's horn
   And sow it all over with one peppercorn.

6. Cut it all down with one strap of leather
   And tie it all up in a tom tit's feather.

7. Put it all in to the bottom of sacks
   And carry it all home on a butterfly's back.

8. Put it all in to a little mouse's hole
   Thrash it all out with a cobbler's awl.

Pope's text appears to be assigned in Sharp's MS. to Bessie Hux-table's and William Huxtable's tune, above. But Pope's name may inadvertently have been written for W. Huxtable's, since Pope belonged to Alcombe, Dunster. Sharp usually tidied up the texts he printed.

37. [The Lover's Tasks]

Sharp MSS., 3996/. Sung by Francis Carter, Proctor, Beatty-ville, Ky., September 8, 1917.

a I/M (– VI)

Sharp MS. note: "The tune imperfectly remembered by the singer." Variant reading (a) suggests confusion with "Lilliburlero."

If you will buy me an acre of land between the salt sea and the sea sand.
Every grave grows merry by time and you shall be a true lover of mine.

38. "A True Lover of Mine"

Gardner and Chickering, 1939, pp. 137-38. Sung by Otis Evilsizer, Alger, Mich., 1935.

a I

1. As I went out walking one morning in May,
   May ev'ry rose bloom merry in time,
   Oh, I met a fair damsel and to her did say,
   "I want you to be a true lover of mine.
   May ev'ry rose bloom merry in time,
   Oh, I want you to be a true lover of mine.

2. "I want you to bring me a new cambric shirt,
   May ev'ry rose bloom merry in time,
   That's made without seam or needle work,
   And then you shall be a true lover of mine.
   May ev'ry rose bloom merry in time,
   And then you shall be a true lover of mine.

(*The second, fourth, fifth, and sixth lines of stanza 2 are repeated in each of the following stanzas.*)

3. "I want you to wash it in yonder well,
   Where water ne'er flew nor dew never fell.

4. "I want you to hang it on yonder thorn,
   Where leaves never grew since Adam was born."

5. " 'Tis three requests you've asked of me,
May now I ask the same of thee?

6. "I want you to buy me ten acres of land,
Between the salt waters and the sea sand.

7. "I want you to plow it with an old sheep's horn,
Then plant it all over with one grain of corn.

8. "I want you to reap it with a sickle of leather,
Then tie it all up with a peacock feather.

9. "Now when you think you've finished your work,
Just come unto me and you shall have your shirt."

39. "Rosemary and Thyme"

Eddy, 1939, pp. 3-4. Sung by Annie Byers, Perrysville,
Ohio; learned from relatives.

m I/Ly

1. "When you go down to yonder town,
Rosemary and thyme,
Send my respects to that young man,
And he shall be a true lover of mine."

She

2. "Go tell him to buy six acres of land
Between salt water and sea sand.

3. "Go tell him to plant ten acres of corn
And harrow it with a mooley cow's horn.

4. "Go tell him to cut it with a sickle of leather,
And haul it in with a pea fowl's feather.

5. "Go tell him to thresh it against the wall,
And do not let one grain of it fall.

6. "Go tell him to take it to yonder mill,
And each kernel of corn shall one bag fill.

7. "Go tell him that when his work is done
To come to me with the kernel of corn."

He

8. "When you go down to yonder town,
Rosemary and thyme,
Send my respects to that young maid,
And she shall be a true lover of mine.

9. "Go tell her to make me a cambric shirt
Without one stitch of needle work.

10. "Go tell her to wash it in yonder well
Where water never rose and rain never fell.

11 "Go tell her that when she has done her work,
To come to me with that cambric shirt."

40. "The Cambric Shirt"

Randolph, I, 1946, pp. 38(A)-39. Sung by Wiley Hembree,
Farmington, Ark., December 29, 1941; learned from his
father in 1896.

a I/Ly (– II)

1. As you go through Yandro's town,
Rozz-marrow and time,
Take my address to this young lady
And tell her to be a true lover of mine.

2. Go tell her to make me a cambric shirt,
Rozz-marrow and time,
Without one stitch of a seamster's work
And then she can be a true lover of mine.

3. Go tell her to wash it in a dry well,
Rozz-marrow and time,
Where water never was nor rain never fell
And then she can be a true lover of mine.

4. Go tell her to dry it on a thorn,
Rozz-marrow and time,
Where a leaf never budded since Adam was born
And then she can be a true lover of mine.

5. Oh it's as you go through Yandro's town,
Rozz-marrow and time,
Take my address to this young man
And tell him to be a true lover of mine.

6. Go tell him to clear me one acre of land,
Rozz-marrow and time,
Between the salt sea and the sea sand
And then he can be a true lover of mine.

7. Go tell him to plough it with a muley-cow's horn,
Rozz-marrow and time,
And plant it all over with one grain of corn,
And then he can be a true lover of mine.

8. Go tell him to reap it with an old stirrup-leather,
Rozz-marrow and time,
And bind it all up in a peafowl's feather
And then he can be a true lover of mine.

9. Go tell him to thresh it against the wall,
Rozz-marrow and time,
And not one grain on the floor shall fall
And then he can be a true lover of mine.

10. Go tell him to take it to the mill,
    Rozz-marrow and time,
    And every grain its bushel shall fill,
    And then he can be a true lover of mine.

11. Go tell this young man when he gets his work done,
    Rozz-marrow and time,
    To come to my house and his shirt'll be done,
    And then he can be a true lover of mine.

41. "Rose de Marian Time"

Brown MS. 16 a 12. Partial text, *North Carolina Folklore*, II, 1952, p. 14(B). Sung by Mrs. [Fannie] Norton, Norton, N.C.

a π¹

Richard Chase, *Old Songs and Singing Games*, 1938, p. 18, gives the same tune as from this singer, with a different, composite text. It is also included, from Chase's singing, in the Winston Wilkinson MSS., 1935-36, pp. 1-2, with four more stanzas than the four below.

As you go through yonder town
    Rose de Marian Time!
Take this dress to that young lady
And tell her she is a true lover of mine.

Tell her to make me a cambric shirt
    Rose de Marian Time!
Without any seam or seamstress work
Then she'll be a true lover of mine.

Tell her to wash it in a dry well
    Rose de Marian Time!
Where water never was nor rain never fell
Then she'll be a true lover of mine.

Tell her to dry it on a thorn
    Rose de Marian Time!
Where leaf never was since Adam was born
Then she'll be a true lover of mine.

42. "Save Rosemary and Thyme"

Morris, 1950, pp. 235-36. Sung by Mrs. G. A. Griffin, Newberry, Fla.; learned from her father.

a I (– VI)

1. Go tell her to make me a cambric shirt,
   Save rosemary and thyme,
   Without any needle or seamster's work,
   And she shall be a true lover of mine.

2. Go tell her to wash it all in a dry well,
   Save rosemary and thyme,
   Where water never sprung, or rain never fell,
   And she shall be a true lover of mine.

3. Go tell her to hang it out on a thorn bush,
   Save rosemary and thyme,
   A bush that never growed since Old Adam was born,
   And she shall be a true lover of mine.

4. Go tell her to iron it against the house back,
   Save rosemary and thyme,
   Without looking down or letting it get black,
   And she shall be a true lover of mine.

5. Go tell him to get him an acre of ground,
   Save rosemary and thyme,
   Betwixt the sea water and the sea sand,
   And he shall be a true lover of mine.

6. Go tell him to plant it in little grain corn,
   Save rosemary and thyme,
   Tell him to plough it in with a horse's horn,
   And he shall be a true lover of mine.

7. Go tell him to reap it with a shickle of leather,
   Save rosemary and thyme,
   Tell him to haul it home on a peafowl's feather,
   And he shall be a true lover of mine.

8. Go tell him to thresh it against the house wall,
   Save rosemary and thyme,
   Without looking down or letting a grain fall,
   And he shall be a true lover of mine.

9. Go tell him when he gets all this work done,
   Save rosemary and thyme,
   Tell him to come to me for his cambric shirt,
   And he shall be a true lover of mine.

43. [The Elfin Knight]

Eddy, 1939, pp. 4-5. Sung by Mary E. Lux, Canton, Ohio; learned from family tradition.

p I/M (– VI)

1. "As you go down to yonder town,
   Rose Mary in time,
   Give my respects to that young lady,
   And tell her she is a true lover of mine."
   (*Repeat the last two lines.*)

He

2. "Go tell her to buy me a cambric shirt,
   Rose Mary in time,
   Without either seam or needle work,
   And then she shall be a true lover of mine."

She

3. "As you go down to yonder town,
   Rose Mary in time,
   Give my respects to that young man,
   And tell him he is a true lover of mine.

4. "Go tell him to buy me one acre of land,
   Rose Mary in time,
   Betwixt salt water and an acre of sand,
   And then he shall be a true lover of mine.

5. "Go tell him to plow it with one big thorn,
   Rose Mary in time,
   Where never has blossomed since Adam was born,
   And then he shall be a true lover of mine.

6. "Go tell him to plant it with one grain of wheat,
   Rose Mary in time,
   And cover it all over with one big sheet,
   And then he shall be a true lover of mine.

7. "Go tell him to reap it with a sickle of leather,
   Rose Mary in time,
   And bind it all up with one humming-bird's feather,
   And then he shall be a true lover of mine.

8. "Go tell him to thresh it against the wall,
   Rose Mary in time,
   And not for his life leave one grain fall,
   And then he shall be a true lover of mine.

9. "Go tell him to take it to yonder mill,
   Rose Mary in time,
   And every grain one barrel to fill,
   And then he shall be a true lover of mine.

10. "Go tell him that when he's through with his work,
    Rose Mary in time,
    To come to me for his cambric shirt,
    And then he shall be a true lover of mine."

44. "Scarborough Fair"

Carey, 1915, pp. 20ff. Also, without accompaniment, in Wells, 1950, p. 171.

p I

1. To Scarborough Fair are you going?
   Parsley, sage, rosemary and thyme,
   Oh give my love to a girl who lives there,
   For once she was a true lover of mine.

2. Oh, tell her to make me a cambric shirt,
   Parsley, sage, rosemary and thyme,
   Without any needle or thread worked in it,
   And she shall be a true lover of mine.

3. Tell her to wash it in yonder well
   Where never spring water nor rain ever fell.

4. Tell her to hang it on yonder thorn
   Which never bore blossom since Adam was born.

5. And when she has answered these questions three,
   If he can answer as many for me,
   Then he shall be a true lover of mine.

6. Tell him to find me an acre of land
   Betwixt the salt water all on the sea sand.

7. And tell him to plough it with a ram's horn
   And all over sow it with one pepper corn.

8. And tell him to cut it with a sickle of leather,
   And bind it all up in a peacock's feather.

9. And when he has done and finished his work,
   He can come unto me for his cambric shirt.

45. "The Cambric Shirt"

Flanders, 1934, pp. 58-59. Sung by H. Luce; learned from E. A. Luce, Vermont. From *A Garland of Green Mountain Song*, edited by Helen Hartness Flanders; copyright 1934 by Helen Hartness Flanders.

a I (– II)

1. As I walked out in a shady grove,
   Every rose grows merry in time,
   Twas there I spied a lovely fair maid
   And once she was a true lover of mine.

2. "Say, will you make me a cambric shirt, etc.
　　Without any stitches or needlework
　　Then you shall be a true lover of mine?

3. "Say, will you wash it out in a dry well, etc.
　　Where water never stood nor rain never fell
　　Then you shall be a true lover of mine?

4. "Say, will you hang it out on a green thorn, etc.
　　That never bore leaves since Adam was born
　　Then, etc."

5. "Now you have asked me questions three, etc.
　　Then answer these questions for me.
　　Then, etc.

6. "Say will you buy me an acre of land, etc.
　　Between the salt water and the sea sand
　　Then, etc.

7. "Say will you plow it up with a hog's horn, etc.
　　And sow it all down with one peppercorn?
　　Then, etc.

8. "Say will you harrow it with a scroll (scrawl), etc.
　　And reap it with a shoemaker's awl,
　　Then, etc.

9. "Say will you draw it in on a shoe sole, etc.
　　And house it all up within a mouse hole?
　　Then, etc.

10. "Say will you thresh it out with a goose quill, etc.
　　And winnow it up within an egg shell?
　　Then, etc.

11. "And when you've done and finished your work, etc.
　　Then call upon me for your cambric shirt,
　　Then you shall be a true lover of mine."

46. [The Elfin Knight]

Newell, *JAF*, VII (1894), p. 228. Sung by Gertrude De-
crow, Boston, Mass.; from family tradition.

a I

1. As I walked out in yonder dell,
　　Let ev'ry rose grow merry in time;
　I met a fair damsel, her name it was Nell;
　　I said, "Will you be a true lover of mine?

2. "I want you to make me a cambric shirt,
　　Let ev'ry rose grow merry in time;
　Without any seam or needlework,
　　And then you shall be a true lover of mine.

3. "I want you to wash it on yonder hill,
　　Let ev'ry rose grow merry in time;
　Where dew never was nor rain never fell,
　　And then you shall be a true lover of mine.

4. "I want you to dry it on yonder thorn,
　　Let ev'ry rose grow merry in time;
　Where tree never blossomed since Adam was born,
　　And then you shall be a true lover of mine."

5. "And since you have asked three questions of me,
　　Let ev'ry rose grow merry in time;
　And now I will ask as many of thee,
　　And then I will be a true lover of thine.

6. "I want you to buy me an acre of land,
　　Let ev'ry rose grow merry in time;
　Between the salt sea and the sea sand
　　And then I will be a true lover of thine.

7. "I want you to plough it with an ox's horn,
　　Let ev'ry rose grow merry in time;
　And plant it all over with one kernel of corn,
　　And then I will be a true lover of thine.

8. "I want you to hoe it with a peacock's feather,
　　Let ev'ry rose grow merry in time;
　And thrash it all out with the sting of an adder,
　　And then I will be a true lover of thine."

47. "The Cambric Shirt"

Flanders, and others, 1939, pp. 8-10. Sung by Amy Perkins;
learned from Emery R. Fisher, Rutland, Vt. Transcribed
by George Brown. From *The New Green Mountain Songster*, edited by Helen Hartness Flanders, Elizabeth Flanders
Ballard, George Brown, and Phillips Barry; copyright 1939
by Helen Hartness Flanders.

a I/M

1. "Oh, where are you going?" "I'm going to Lynn."
　　Every globe goes merry in time,
　"Give my love to the lady within
　　And tell her she's worth a true lover of mine.

2. "Oh, tell her to buy her a yard of tow cloth,"
　　Every globe goes merry in time,
　"For to make me a fine shirt,
　　And she shall be a true lover of mine.

3. "Oh, tell her to stitch it without any needle,"
Every globe goes merry in time.
"Stitch it and sew it without any seam,
And she shall be a true lover of mine.

4. "Oh, tell her to wash it in yonder dry well,"
Every globe goes merry in time,
"Where water ne'er stood nor rain ne'er fell,
And she shall be a true lover of mine.

5. "Oh, tell her to hang it on yonder high thorn,"
Every globe goes merry in time,
"One that had stood since Adam was born,
And she shall be a true lover of mine.

6. "Oh, tell her to iron it with a flat rock,"
Every globe goes merry in time,
"One that's ne'er cold and one that's ne'er hot,
And she shall be a true lover of mine.

7. "Oh, tell this young lady when she's finished her work,"
Every globe goes merry in time,
"Come to me and I'll give her a kiss,
And she shall be a true lover of mine."

Answer

8. "Oh, where are you going?" "I'm going to Cape Ann."
Every globe goes merry in time.
"Give my love to this same young man,
And tell him he's worthy this true love of mine.

9. "Oh, tell him to buy him an acre of land,"
Every globe goes merry in time,
" 'Twixt the sea shore and the sea sand,
And he shall be a true lover of mine.

10. "Oh, tell him to plow it with an old horse's horn,"
Every globe goes merry in time,
"Sow it all over with one peppercorn,
And he shall be a true lover of mine.

11. "Oh, tell him to reap it with a sickle of leather,"
Every globe goes merry in time,
"Bind it up with a peacock's feather,
And he shall be a true lover of mine.

12. "Oh, tell him to cart it on a cake of ice,"
Every globe goes merry in time.
"Cart it in with a yoke of mice,
And he shall be a true lover of mine.

13. "Oh, tell him to stack it in yonder high barn,"
Every globe goes merry in time,
"One that ne'er stood since Adam was born,
And he shall be a true lover of mine.

14. "Oh, tell him to thresh it with his wooden leg,"
Every globe goes merry in time.
"Fan it up in the skin of an egg,
And he shall be a true lover of mine.

15. "Oh, tell this young man when he's finished his work,"
Every globe goes merry in time,
"Come to me and I'll give him a kiss,
And he shall be a true lover of mine."

48. [The Elfin Knight]

Sharp MSS., 4661/3244. Also in Sharp and Karpeles, 1932,
I, p. 2. Sung by Mrs. Polly Mitchell, Burnsville, N.C.,
September 22, 1918.

a π[1]

1. I saw a young lady a-walking all out,
A-walking all out in the yonders green field,
So sav'ry was said come marry in time,
And she shall be a true lover of mine.

2. So tell that young lady to buy me a new cambric shirt
And make it without needles or yet needles' work.
So sav'ry, etc.

3. So tell that young lady to wash it all out
And wash it all out in yonders well,
Where never was water nor rain never fell.

4. So tell that young lady to deemens (*sic*) her work
And bring on my new cambric shirt.

5. I saw a young man a-walking all out,
A-walking all out in the yonders green field,
So sav'ry was said come marry in time,
And he shall be a true lover of mine.

6. So tell that young man to but [*sic*] me an acre of land,
Betwixt the sea and the sun.
So sav'ry, etc.
And he shall be, etc.

7. So tell that young man to sow it all down,
And sow it all down in pepper and corn.

8. So tell that young man to plough it all in,
And plough it all in with that little ram's horn.

9. So tell that young man to haul it all in,
And haul it all in on a chee-chicken feather.

10. So tell that young man to crib it all in,
And crib it all in a little mouse's hole.

11. So tell that young man to thresh it all out,
And thrash it all out in the corner of the house,
On the peril of his life to not lose a grain.

12. So tell that young man to deemens his work
For to bring on the pepper and corn.

49. "True Lover of Mine"

Robertson, LC/AAFS, rec. 3812 A1. Sung by George Vinton Graham, San Jose, Calif., December 3, 1938.

p I/M

not for the life of her let one stick of it burn

1. Where are you going? to Cadrian?
    Green grows the merry antine
And if you see that nice young man
    I want him for a true lover of mine

2. Tell him to plow me one acre of ground
    Green grows the merry antine
And plant it all over with one grain of corn
    And he shall be a true lover of mine

3. Tell him to thrash it 'gainst yonders barn
    Green grows the merry antine
That never was built since Adam was born
    And he shall be a true lover of mine

4. Tell her to make me one cambric shirt
    Green grows the merry antine
And not for the life of her let one stitch of it
                        be needlework
    And she shall be a true lover of mine

5. Tell her to iron it with a red-hot iron
    Green grows the merry antine
And not for the life of her let one stitch of it burn
    And she shall be a true lover of mine

APPENDIX B

50. "The Elfin Knight"

Greig and Keith, 1925, p. 2(2). Sung by Rev. J. Calder, Crimond, Aberdeenshire, 1907.

a I/M

This tune, as S. P. Bayard has observed, is that of "The Young May Moon" (tune, "The Dandy O'") in Thomas Moore's *Irish Melodies*. The words are sung by Effie Deans in *The Heart of Midlothian*; it is undetermined whether they are traditional or by Scott.

The Elfin Knight sat on the brae,
    The broom grows bonnie, the broom grows fair,
And by there cam' liltin' a lady so gay,
    And we daurna gang doon to the broom nae mair.

GROUP C

51. [The Lover's Tasks]

Sharp MSS., 4933/. Singer unidentified, December 1922.

p I/Ly (—VI)

My father gave me an acre of land
Sing Hey sing Ho sing ivy
My father gave me an acre of land
A bunch of green holly a* ivy

* Probably *and* (&).

52. "Sing Ivy"

Merrick, *JFSS*, I (1901), p. 83. Sung by Henry Hills, Shepperton, 1899; learned in Petworth, Sussex, c. 1840-50.

p I (– VI)

1. My mother she gave me an acre of land,
    Sing ivy, sing ivy.
My mother she gave me an acre of land,
    Shall I go whistling ivy?

2. I ploughed it with a ram's horn,
    Sing ivy, sing ivy.
I ploughed it with a ram's horn,
    Shall I go whistling ivy?

3. I sowed it with a peppercorn, &c

4. I harrowed it in with a bramble, &c

5. I harrowed it in with a bramble bush, &c

6. I reaped it with my penknife, &c

7. I housed it in a mouse's hole, &c

8. I threshed it with a beanstalk, &c

9. I wimm'd it with a fly's wing, &c

10. I measured it with my thimble, &c

11. I put it on the cat's back, &c

12. The cat she carried it to the mill, &c

13. The miller swore he'd take a toll, &c

14. The cat she swore she'd scratch his poll, &c

53. "An Acre of Land"

Vaughan Williams, *JFSS*, II (1906), p. 212. Sung by Frank Bailey, Coombe Bisset, Wiltshire, August 31, 1904.

p I

1. My father left me an acre of land,
   There goes this ivery (?)
   My father left me an acre of land,
   And a bunch of green holly and ivery.

2. I ploughed it with my ram's horn
   There goes this ivery (?)
   I sowed it with my thimble,
   And a bunch of green holly and ivery.

3. I harrowed it with my bramble-bush,
   There goes etc.
   I reaped it with my penknife,
   And a etc.

4. I sent it home in a walnut shell,
        etc.
   I threshed it with my needle and thread,
        etc.

5. I winnowed it with my handkerchief,
        etc.
   I sent it to mill with a team of great rats,
        etc.

6. The carter brought a curly whip,
        etc.
   The whip did pop and the waggon did stop,
        etc.

54. [Sing Ivy]

Moffat and Kidson, *Children's Songs of Long Ago*, n.d., p. 48. Tune also in *JFSS*, II (1906), p. 213.

p I (– VI)

1. My father he left me three acres of land,
        Sing ivy, sing ivy!
   My father he left me three acres of land,
        Sing holly, go whistle and ivy.

2. I ploughed it one morning with a ram's horn,
        Sing ivy, sing ivy!
   And sowed it all over with one pepper corn,
        Sing holly, go whistle and ivy.

3. I harrowed it next with a bramble bush,
        Sing ivy, sing ivy!
   And reapèd it all with my little penknife,
        Sing holly, go whistle and ivy.

4. The mice for me, carried it into the barn,
        Sing ivy, sing ivy!
   And there I threshed it with a goose quill,
        Sing holly, go whistle and ivy.

5. The cat she carried it unto the mill,
        Sing ivy, sing ivy!
   And the miller he said that he'd work with a will,
        Sing holly, go whistle and ivy.

55. "Sing Ivy"

Gardiner, *JFSS*, III (1907), pp. 274-75. Sung by William Mason (60), Easton, near Winchester, November 1906.

a Æ

This copy appears with piano accompaniment, in G minor, in C. J. Sharp and G. Holst, *Folk Songs of England*, III, 1909, p. 21 (*Folk Songs of Hampshire*).

1. My father gave me an acre of land,
        Sing ovy, sing ivy,
   My father gave me an acre of land,
        A bunch of green holly and ivy.

2. I harrowed it with a bramble bush,
        Sing ovy, sing ivy,
   I harrowed it with a bramble bush,
        A bunch of green holly and ivy.

3. I sowed it with two peppering corns,
   Sing ovy, sing ivy,
I sowed it with two pepper corns,
   A bunch of green holly and ivy.

4. I rolled it with a rolling-pin,
   Sing ovy, sing ivy,
I rolled it with a rolling-pin,
   A bunch of green holly and ivy.

5. I reaped with my little pen-knife,
   Sing ovy, sing ivy,
I reaped it with my little pen-knife,
   A bunch of green holly and ivy.

6. I stowed it in a mouse's hole,
   Sing ovy, sing ivy,
I stowed it in a mouse's hole.
   A bunch of green holly and ivy.

7. I threshed it out with two beanstalks,
   Sing ovy, sing ivy,
I threshed it out with two beanstalks,
   A bunch of green holly and ivy.

8. I sent my rats to market with that,
   Sing ovy, sing ivy,
I sent my rats to market with that,
   A bunch of green holly and ivy.

9. My team o' rats came rattling back,
   Sing ovy, sing ivy,
My team o' rats came rattling back
With fifty bright guineas and an empty sack,
   A bunch of green holly and ivy.

The Fause Knight upon the Road

CHILD NO. 3

MOTHERWELL was the first to make this odd little song known in print. It is rooted in Scottish tradition, but has been brought thence to Nova Scotia and to the Appalachians and Indiana, and might still appear wherever the Scot carries recollections of home. The tunes that are recorded all seem to have the same ancestry, yet they have developed into surprisingly diversified variants. Perhaps the basic rhythmical pattern of them all is that of a reel. It is interesting to see what a mountain soloist can do with such intractable stuff, in the way of bestowing solemnity, even dignity.

Motherwell printed his text in a confusing manner, in which Child follows him. That text may have been accommodated to a tune of the usual four-phrase type, like the one given by Blaikie in Motherwell's Musical Appendix. (Cf. the first of the following series.) Motherwell prints the second part of lines 1 and 3 of stanza 1 as the first part of lines 2 and 4, which makes the first and third lines unduly short. But when he abbreviates in stanza 2, he prints his "quo etc." on the same line as 1 and 3. This leaves an uncertainty where to divide. It is possible, in spite of the second and fourth lines' having a right to be shorter, that there was some phrasal repetition in those lines as sung, just as there is in the variant printed in his Appendix. The puzzle would not have arisen, of course, if he had concerned himself to capture the ballad *as song*. Yet the Macmath tune, it is to be observed, is rhythmically the exact counterpart of Motherwell's text (i.e., Child's A), which ought therefore pretty certainly to have been printed in couplets. (On this matter, cf. the discussion in *CFQ*, III [1944], pp. 187-89.)

The variant from North Carolina has acquired—or has not lost—a second half, with a too modern-sounding last phrase. But its general movement, its tendency to stay within the same limits, the resemblance of its phrasal contours to Motherwell's first and third, are enough to relate it to the Scottish tune.

In movement, phrasal correspondence, and range, the stanza-part of the second Nova Scotia tune defines its relationship to the tune from North Carolina with distinctness. Miss Creighton's own indication of tempo is "Very quickly in jig time," and she notes that the singer danced the chorus, as was fitting. Motherwell's variant would have gained by a similar increment, and possibly had it in life. The text of this copy is a curious but natural amalgamation of Child 1 and 2.

It is to be observed that Miss Macmath's tune, which as it stands is a circular tune on the pattern ABAB, carries undeniable hints of Miss Creighton's refrain phrases. The sequences c-d-c-d-e-f and f-d-c-a-g occur prominently in both. Indeed, Miss Macmath's tune makes a perfect refrain by itself, and if it were united as such to Motherwell's, both would gain in charm.

The effect of the Tennessee variant is quite different from that of its fellows; yet if it be reduced to a quick 2/4 rhythm throughout, it will be seen that the same melodic material underlies it. The introductory phrase is highly unusual, but is of course made out of phrase 4. The original duple-time tries to reassert itself with the second strain or chorus, but loses heart in the pervading melancholy. The first half of the chorus should be compared with the corresponding part of the North Carolina tune.

The copies from Virginia and Indiana, respectively, seem fairly close to each other, and show vaguer likeness to the rest of the family, rather more distinctly to North Carolina than to the others. Neither record, however, inspires much confidence in its accuracy. The Indiana variant is at best a sadly worn-down affair.

LIST OF VARIANTS

1. "The False Knight." William Motherwell, *Minstrelsy: Ancient and Modern*, 1827, App'x No. 32 and p. xxiv.
a. "The False Knight and the Wee Boy." Alfred Moffat, *Fifty Traditional Scottish Nursery Rhymes* [1933], p. 24.
2. "False Knight upon the Road." Helen Creighton and Doreen H. Senior, *Traditional Songs from Nova Scotia*, 1950, p. 1.
3. "The False Fidee." Paul G. Brewster, *Ballads and Songs of Indiana*, 1940, pp. 29-30.
4. "The False Knight on the Road." Arthur Kyle Davis, Jr., *Traditional Ballads of Virginia*, 1929, pp. 549 and 61.
5. "The False Knight upon the Road." Sharp MSS., 3369/2466, Clare College Library, Cambridge. Also in Cecil J. Sharp and Maud Karpeles, *English Folk Songs from the Southern Appalachians*, 1932, I, p. 3(A); and Cecil J.

Sharp, *American-English Folk-Ballads*, 1918, p. 20.
6. "The False Knight upon the Road." Sharp MSS., 3426/2516. Also in Sharp and Karpeles, 1932, I, p. 4(B).
7. "The False Knight upon the Road." Duncan B. M. Emrich, LC Archive of American Folk Song, Album XXI, rec. 104A-2. (Mrs. Maud Long.)
8. "The Fause Knight upon the Road." Francis James Child, *The English and Scottish Popular Ballads*, 1882-98, V, p. 411, and I, p. 485.
9. "False Knight upon the Road." Helen Creighton, *Songs and Ballads from Nova Scotia*, 1932, pp. 1-2.
10. "The False Knight on the Road." Helen Hartness Flanders and Marguerite Olney, *Ballads Migrant in New England*, 1953, pp. 46-47.

1. [The False Knight]

Motherwell, 1827, App'x No. 32 and p. xxiv.

a M

O whare are ye gaun, quo' the false knight,
    And false false was his rede,
I'm gaun to the scule, says the pretty little boy,
    And still still he stude.

a. [The False Knight and the Wee Boy]

Moffat [1933], p. 24.

Same tune as No. 1 above. But, as printed by Moffat, probably from Motherwell, to the words below, the note-lengths
are doubled, and the third and penultimate bars are composed of even quarter-notes. Also, the cadence of the second
phrase is a half-note on A, followed by a quarter on B (if
transposed to the pitch above).

1. "O where are ye gaun to, my wee lad?"
    (Quo' the False Knight on the road,)
"I'm gaun to the schule," said the bonnie, bonnie boy,
    (And still, still he stood.)

2. "And what is't ye have upon your back?"
    (Quo' the False Knight on the road).
"Atweel, it's my books," said the bonnie, bonnie boy,
    (And still, still he stood.)

3. "And what is that ye've in your arm?"
    (Quo' the False Knight on the road).
"Atweel, it's my peat," said the bonnie, bonnie boy,
    (And still, still he stood.)

4. "Wha owns thae sheep upon the hill?"
    (Quo' the False Knight on the road).
"They're mine and my mither's," said the bonnie, bonnie boy,
    (And still, still he stood.)

5. "How many o' them are mine, my lad?"
    (Quo' the False Knight on the road).
"A' they wi' blue tails," said the bonnie, bonnie boy,
    (And still, still he stood.)

6. "I wish that ye were on yonder tree,"
    (Quo' the False Knight on the road).
"Wi' a ladder under me," said the bonnie, bonnie boy,
    (And still, still he stood.)

7. "And the ladder to break below ye,"
    (Quo' the False Knight on the road).

"And you to fa' down," said the bonnie, bonnie boy,
    (And still, still he stood.)

8. "I wish ye were now in yonder sea,"
    (Quo' the False Knight on the road).
"Wi' a guid ship under me," said the bonnie, bonnie boy,
    (And still, still he stood.)

9. "And the ship for to break and sink wi' ye,"
    (Quo' the False Knight on the road).
"And ye to be drowned!" said the bonnie, bonnie boy,
    (And still, still he stood.)

2. "False Knight upon the Road"

Creighton and Senior, 1950, p. 1. Sung by Evelyn Richardson and Anne Wickens. Melody transcribed by Margaret
Sargent.

p π¹ (with added sharped *IV*)

"Oh where are you going," said the False Knight
    to the child in the road,
"I'm going to school," said the pretty little girl,
But still she stood in the road.

"What do you go to school for?" said the False Knight,
    to the child in the road.
"To learn to read," said the pretty little girl,
But still she stood in the road.

"What do you learn to read for?" said the False Knight,
    to the child in the road.
To keep me from hell," said the pretty little girl,
But still she stood in the road.

"There is no hell," said the False Knight,
    to the child in the road.
"I believe you lie," said the pretty little girl,
But still she stood in the road.

In the 1950 copy, the first two lines of each stanza are printed
as one.

3. "The False Fidee"

Brewster, 1940, pp. 29-30. Sung by Lucile Wilkin, Connersville, Ind., 1935; learned from Mrs. Chester A. Porter.

a I/M (− VI) (compass of fifth)

1. "Where are you going?"
    Said the False, fie, the False Fidee;
"I'm going to my school,"
    Said the child, and there still she stood.

2. "Whose sheep are those?"
    Said the False, fie, the False Fidee;
"They're mine and my mother's,"
    Said the child, and there still she stood.

3. "Which one is mine?"
    Said the False, fie, the False Fidee;
"The one with the blue tail,"
    Said the child, and there still she stood.

4. "There's nary a one with a blue tail,"
    Said the False, fie, the False Fidee;
"And nary a one shall you have,"
    Said the child, and there still she stood.

5. "I wish you were in the bottom of the sea,"
    Said the False, fie, the False Fidee;
"With a good ship under me,"
    Said the child, and there still she stood.

6. "I wish you were in the bottom of the well,"
    Said the False, fie, the False Fidee;
"And you in the lowest depths of Hell,"
    Said the child, and there still she stood.

4. "The False Knight on the Road"

Davis, 1929, p. 549; text, p. 61. Sung by Mrs. Sarah
Finchum, Elkton, Va., November 23, 1918. Collected by
Martha M. Davis.

p I (−VI)

"Where are you going?" said the false, false knight,
    Said the false so rude.
"I am going to school," said the child;
    And still it stood.

"What have you got there?" said the false, false knight,
    Said the false so rude.
"I have good books in my hand," said the child;
    And still it stood.

"Are you a child of God?" said the false, false knight,
    Said the false so rude.
"I say my prayers at night," said the child;
    And still it stood.

"I wish you were in the well," said the false, false knight,
    Said the false so rude.

"And you as deep in hell," said the child;
    And still it stood.

5. [The False Knight upon the Road]

Sharp MSS., 3369/2466. Also in Sharp and Karpeles, 1932,
I, p. 3(A); and, with piano accompaniment, in Sharp, 1918,
p. 20. Sung by Mrs. T. G. Coates, Flag Pond, Tenn., September 1, 1916.

a M (−VI; inflected VII)

1932 gives F♮ (*i.e.*, transposed D♮) in the antepenultimate bar.

1. The knight met a child in the road.
    O where are you going to? said the knight
        in the road.
    I'm a-going to my school, said the child
        as he stood.
        He stood and he stood and it's well because
        he stood.
        I'm a-going to my school, said the child
        as he stood.

2. O what are you going there for?
    For to learn the Word of God.

3. O what have you got there?
    I have got my bread and cheese.

4. O won't you give me some?
    No, ne'er a bite nor crumb.

5. I wish you was on the sands.
    Yes, and a good staff in my hands.

6. I wish you was in the sea.
    Yes, and a good boat under me.

7. I think I hear a bell.
    Yes, and it's ringing you to hell.

6. [The False Knight upon the Road]

Sharp MSS., 3426/2516. Also in Sharp and Karpeles, 1932,
I, p. 4(B). Sung by Mrs. Jane Gentry, Hot Springs, N.C.,
September 12, 1916.

a I/M (−VI)

Where are you going?
Says the knight in the road.
I'm a-going to my school,
Said the child as he stood.
He stood and he stood,
He well thought on he stood.
I'm a-going to my school
Said the child as he stood.

What are you eating?
I'm a-eating bread and cheese.

I wish'd you was in the sea.
A good boat under me.

I wish'd you was in the well.
And you that deep in hell.

7. "The False Knight upon the Road"

Emrich, LC/AAFS, Album XXI, rec. 104A-2. Sung by Mrs. Maud Long of Hot Springs, N.C.; recorded in Washington, D.C., 1947.

m I

Mrs. Long is the daughter of Mrs. Jane Gentry, and learned this ballad from her mother. Cf. the preceding variant.

1. "Where are you going?" said the knight in the road.
   "I'm going to my school," said the child as he stood.
   He stood and he stood, he well thought on, he stood,
   "I'm going to my school," said the child as he stood.

2. "Oh, what do you study there?" said the knight in the road.
   "We learn the word of God," said the child as he stood.
   He stood and he stood, he well thought on, he stood,
   "We learn the word of God," said the child as he stood.

3. "Oh, what are you eating there?" said the knight in the road.
   "I'm eating bread and cheese," said the child as he stood.

4. "Oh, won't you give me some?" said the knight in the road.
   "No, nare a bite nor crumb," said the child as he stood.

5. "I wish you were in the sea," said the knight in the road.
   "A good boat under me," said the child as he stood.

6. "I wish you were in the sand," said the knight in the road.
   "A good staff in my hand," said the child as he stood.

7. "I wish you were in a well," said the knight in the road.
   "And you that deep in Hell," said the child as he stood.

8. [The Fause Knight upon the Road]

Child, 1882-98, V, p. 411; text, I, p. 485. Sung by Miss M. Macmath; learned from Jane Webster, Airds of Kells, Galloway.

a I/Ly (ending on VIII)

"O whare are ye gaun?"
Says the false knight upon the road:
"I am gaun to the schule,"
Says the wee boy, and still he stood.

"Wha's aught the sheep on yonder hill?"
"They are my papa's and mine."

"How many of them's mine?"
"A' them that has blue tails."

"I wish you were in yonder well:"
"And you were down in hell."

9. "False Knight Upon the Road"

Creighton, 1932, pp. 1-2. Sung by Mr. Faulkner and Mr. Ben Henneberry, Devil's Island, Nova Scotia.

m I/Ly

1. "Oh, what have you in your bag? O, what have you
   in your pack?"
Cried the false knight to the child on the road.
"I have a little primer and a bit of bread for dinner,"
Cried the pretty little child only seven years old.

Chorus

Hi diddle deedle dum, deedle diddle deedle dum,
Deedle deedle deedle diddle, deedle deedle dum,
Diddle diddle diddle dee, deedle deedle deedle dum,
Diddle diddle diddle deedle diddle dee de dum.

2. "What is rounder than a ring? What is higher than
   a king?"
Cried the false knight to the child on the road.
"The sun is rounder than a ring. God is higher than
   a king,"
Cried the pretty little child only seven years old.
Chorus

3. "What is whiter than the milk? What is softer than
   the silk?"
Cried the false knight to the child on the road.
"Snow is whiter than the milk. Down is softer than
   the silk,"
Cried the pretty little child only seven years old.
Chorus

4. "What is greener than the grass? What is worse than
   women coarse?"
Cried the false knight to the child on the road.
"Poison is greener than the grass. The devil's worse
   than women coarse,"
Cried the pretty little child only seven years old.
Chorus

5. "What is longer than the wave?* What is deeper than
   the sea?"
Cried the false knight to the child on the road.
"Love is longer than the wave. Hell is deeper than
   the sea,"
Cried the pretty little child only seven years old.
Chorus

6. "Oh, a curse upon your father and a curse upon your
   mother,"
Cried the false knight to the child on the road.
"Oh, a blessing on my father, and a blessing on my
   mother,"
Cried the pretty little child only seven years old.
Chorus

* Or, "way."
Mrs. Creighton's note: "The singer dances to the chorus."

10. "The False Knight on the Road"

Flanders and Olney, 1953, pp. 46-47. Sung by Mrs. E. M.
Sullivan, Springfield, Vt., September 21, 1932; learned in
childhood in Ireland. From *Ballads Migrant in New England*, edited by Helen Hartness Flanders and Marguerite
Olney; copyright 1953 by Helen Hartness Flanders.

a I/Ly

How the last two stanzas are adjusted in the singing is not made
clear by the editors.

1. "O where are you going?"
   Said the false, false knight to the child on the road.
   "I'm going to my school,"
   Said the pretty boy seven years old.

2. "What have you got in your woolen?" (school bag)
   Said the false, false knight to the child on the road,
   "My books and my dinner,"
   Said the pretty boy seven years old.

3. "Who owns all those cows on the hill?" etc.
   "Me and my mamma," etc.

4. "How many of them are mine?" etc.
   "As many as have no tail," etc.

5. "Who taught you so well?" etc.
   "My teachers and my mamma," etc.

6. "What did they teach you so well for?" etc.
   "To keep me from you and from your wicked Hell,"
   And he bowed seven times on the road.

7. "Bad luck to your teacher that taught you so well,"
   Said the false, false knight to the child on the road.
   "Good luck to the teacher that kept me from you
   And from your wicked Hell,"
   Said the pretty boy seven years old.

Lady Isabel and the Elf Knight

CHILD NO. 4

THIS ballad, one of the most impressive of all ballads for the geographical sweep of its popularity and vital tenacity, nevertheless makes no appearance in our musical records until the end of the first quarter of the nineteenth century; and in fact Child's earliest verbal text is not much more venerable. Motherwell observed that the nineteenth song in the third edition (1682) of Forbes' *Songs & Fancies* had a burden much like Buchan's copy (Child's A)*: "The gowans are gay." ... "The first morning in May";—but we learn nothing from Forbes of the earlier tune to our ballad, and the high antiquity of the song has to be deduced from its continental analogues.†

The earliest tunes to appear are Scottish, and give no clear indication of the main melodic traditions as they have since been defined in a very large number of variants collected mostly within the present century, in England and the United States. These traditions display a remarkable unity in their variety, and on the English side, at least, a variety in unity, highly interesting to anyone who wants material on which to base conclusions about a tune's irreducible essence. The dominant English and American patterns tend to divide both rhythmically and in characteristic contour, the English generally preferring a 6/8 triple, the American a duple, measure, and the American showing much greater uniformity of melodic line. The rhythmical bifurcation is present, however, from the very beginning of the musical record; for R. A. Smith and Motherwell, printing in the same decade and both from Scottish sources, give, the one a tune in common time, the other a tune in 6/8. The characteristic Appalachian tune for this ballad is so extraordinarily favored by folk-singers as to turn up everywhere, a hardy perennial of American folk-song, its outlines usually so indelible as to be readily spotted. Much the same holds true of the English pattern, one of the basic British archetypes: cf., e.g., Child 73, 74, 75. The latter usually contrives, however, to differentiate itself characteristically for each ballad with which it is habitually mated.

It would be very easy to divide Group A into a number of sub-classes. The Devon tradition produces a different impression from that of Somerset, and Scottish copies are much more melancholy than English. Yet familiarity will probably conclude that there is a common denominator, and it seems unnecessary to multiply types. Taking the mid-cadence as our essential point of reference, we find few variants resting there on the tonic. Two of those that do are Devonian copies, one is from Somerset, one is Scottish (Motherwell's), and one from Cambridge, Mass. All but the Somerset copy are major in tonality. The great bulk of the English tradition, including the North Atlantic seaboard, comes to a mid-pause on the dominant. First-phrase cadences are nearly always, in these cases, on the tonic: infrequently on the lower dominant and the octave. Initial accents are on I, V, IV, and III. A much smaller number of variants has a mid-cadence on the supertonic, with greater variety at the other two points. There are a few abnormal variants with mid-cadence on III, lower VI, VII, and flattened VII. That on lower VI is Christie's copy from Aberdeen; one on VII is Kidson's Yorkshire variant, another on VII is Irish and early. The copy on flat VII is J. J. Niles', from North Carolina, closely related to his now well-known carol, "Lulle Lullay," and Æ/D rather than the usual major.

Considering the frequency and English feeling of this familiar melodic pattern, it is at least a striking coincidence that a variant of it appears in the tenth century, in the *Sanctus* of the Easter Mass, *Lux et Origo*. How close the parallel is may be easily seen if the notes are given a 6/8 rhythm and written below the original, as follows:

If the parallel here exhibited is only a coincidence, it at least shows how indigenous to the Western mind is this general conformation of phrasal contours.

For the American melodic tradition of this ballad, not shared by England, but probably imported from Scotland, there is also early precedent, though not nearly so ancient as that just cited. The pattern first appears in written record, so far as I am aware, in the Skene MS., dated about the end of the first quarter of the seventeenth century: "Ladie Cassilles Lilt," later "The Gipsy Laddy" tune (200). The odd thing is that only the second strain of the earlier tune has been used, and this fact accounts in part for the tune's present lack of modal decisiveness, the first two phrases seeming to establish a tonic on what later is treated as the fourth. It is arguable that the final is a false Mixolydian (or rather, π^2) ending to a genuine π^1 tune; but in view of the fact that originally this was but the second, or downward, half of a complete arch that began as it ended, I prefer to regard the tune as having established its right, both historically and on grounds of accepted and current traditional use, to be treated as a π^2 tune. Wherever it is used, it is surprisingly steady and consistent; but it may be confused by the unwary with an-

* [This song, incidentally, appears to have passed into tradition: it was found in the Appalachians in the present century, but in a form almost suspiciously close to printed texts. Cf. J. H. Combs, *Folk-Songs du Midi*, 1925, p. 163.]

† See H. O. Nygard, "Narrative Change in the European Tradition of the 'Lady Isabel and the Elf Knight' Ballad," *JAF*, Vol. 65 (Jan.-Mch., 1952), pp. 1-12.

other ancient family almost as generally favored: that of "Boyne Water," which will be frequently met in later connections. Cf., e.g., "Barbara Allen" (84). In fact, the two types occasionally become confused in traditional use, owing to their over-all resemblance of phrasal contour. But the "Boyne Water" tune is usually Æ/D, and its mid-cadence, a feminine one, is easily distinguishable from "Lady Cassilis."

Various distortions of the melodic idea of the latter will be visible at either end of Group B. But typically, the mid-cadence is on the dominant, the first accent on the same, and the cadence of the first phrase—an unemphatic note—on the fourth. This is, to repeat, if one takes the final as tonic, the tune then being regarded as an authentic π^2 tune.

LIST OF VARIANTS

GROUP A

1. "The Outlandish Knight." Sabine Baring-Gould MSS., CXIV(1) and (A), Plymouth Public Library. Also in S. Baring-Gould and Cecil J. Sharp, *English Folk-Songs for Schools*, n.d., p. 26. (Parsons)
2. "The Seven King's Daughters." Arthur Kyle Davis, Jr., *Traditional Ballads of Virginia*, 1929, pp. 551(Q) and 84. (Maxie)
3. "May Collean." William Motherwell, *Minstrelsy: Ancient and Modern*, 1827, App'x No. 24.
a. "Lord Robert and fair Ellen." George Petrie, *The Complete Petrie Collection of Irish Music*, edited by Charles Villiers Stanford, 1902-5, No. 795.
4. "The Outlandish Knight." Sharp MSS., 1226/, Clare College Library, Cambridge. Also in Cecil J. Sharp, *JFSS*, IV (1910), p. 120(6). (Ware)
5. "Lady Isabel and the Elf Knight." Phillips Barry, *JAF*, XVIII (1905), pp. 132-33. Also in Phillips Barry, Fannie H. Eckstorm, and Mary W. Smyth, *British Ballads from Maine*, 1929, p. 24(F). (Hopkinson)
6. "The Outlandish Knight." Lucy E. Broadwood, *JFSS*, IV (1910), p. 119(3). Also in Baring-Gould MSS., CXIV(5).
7. "The Outlandish Knight." Baring-Gould MSS., CXIV(3). (Singer unknown)
8. "The Outlandish Knight." Sharp MSS., 1557/. (Jarrett)
9. "Lady Isabel and the Elf Knight." Sharp MSS., 3140/?. Also in Cecil J. Sharp and Maud Karpeles, *English Folk Songs from the Southern Appalachians*, 1932, I, pp. 7(C)-8. (Moore)
10. "The Outlandish Knight." Sharp MSS., 1822/. (Neville)
11. "The Outlandish Knight." Sharp MSS., 2471/. (Hartwell)
12. "An Outlandish Rover." R. Vaughan Williams, *JFSS*, IV (1910), p. 121(8). (Verrall)
13. "The False-Hearted Knight." Barry, Eckstorm, and Smyth, *British Ballads from Maine*, 1929, pp. 26(G)-28. (Hathaway)
14. "The Outlandish Knight." Frank Kidson, *Traditional Tunes*, 1891, p. 172.
15. "The Outlandish Knight." Sharp MSS., 736/. (Southwood)
16. "The King's Daughter." George W. Boswell, *Tennessee Folk Song Bulletin*, XVII, No. 4 (December 1951), pp. 86-87.
17. "The Outlandish Knight." Sharp MSS., 345/. (Hutchings)
18. "Lady Isabel." Barry MSS., I, No. 4, B, Harvard College Library. (Ravois)
19. "The False Hearted Knight." Davis, *Traditional Ballads of Virginia*, 1929, pp. 551(R) and 84-85. (Harrington)
20a. "The Outlandish Knight." Sharp MSS., 356/. Also in Cecil J. Sharp, *JFSS*, IV (1910), p. 121(7). (Chapman)
20b. "The Outlandish Gentleman." Sharp MSS., 1084/. (Chapman)
21. "The Outlandish Knight." Sharp MSS., 4861/. (Barnard)
22. "The False-hearted Knight." Barry, Eckstorm, and Smyth,

British Ballads from Maine, 1929, pp. 19(C)-20. (Lindenberg)
23. "The Seven King's Daughters." Davis, *Traditional Ballads of Virginia*, 1929, pp. 550(F) and 71-72. (Roop)
24. "Lady Isabel and the Elf Knight." Davis, 1929, pp. 551(S) and 85. (Noel)
25. "Tell-tale Polly." *Charley Fox's Minstrel's Companion*, n.d., p. 52 (photostat copy, Phillips Barry Collection, Harvard College Library).
26. "The Outlandish Knight." Sharp MSS., 751/. (Pike)
27. "The Outlandish Knight." Sharp MSS., 1342/. (Callow)
28a. "The Outlandish Knight." Sharp MSS., 1405/1290. Also in Cecil J. Sharp, *Folk Songs from Somerset*, 4th series, 1908, No. 84; in Cecil J. Sharp, *One Hundred English Folksongs*, 1916, p. 29. (Laver); and in Sharp, *English Folksongs*, Selected Ed., Novello & Co., 1920.
28b. "The Outlandish Knight." Sharp MSS., 1002/. (Laver)
29. "The Outlandish Knight." J. Collingwood Bruce and John Stokoe, *Northumbrian Minstrelsy*, 1882, pp. 48-50. Also in John Stokoe and Samuel Reay, *Songs of Northern England*, [1892], p. 130.
30. "The Outlandish Knight." Frank Kidson, *JFSS*, II (1906), p. 282(2).
31. "The Robber and the Lady." Alice E. Gillington, *Eight Hampshire Folk Songs*, [1907], pp. 4-5.
32. "The Outlandish Knight." Sharp MSS., 2382/. (Hedges)
33. "The Outlandish Knight." Sharp MSS., 2598/. (Bradley)
34. "The Outlandish Knight." Frank Kidson, *JFSS*, II (1906), p. 282(3).
35. "The False-Hearted Knight." Barry, Eckstorm, and Smyth, *British Ballads from Maine*, 1929, p. 21(D). (Brockway)
36. "The Outlandish Knight." Sharp MSS., 2130/. (Gibbs)
37. "The Outlandish Knight." Sharp MSS., 818/. (Crossman)
38. "The Outlandish Knight." Sharp MSS., 1873/. (Callow)
39. "She borrowed some of her father's gold." R. Vaughan Williams, *JFSS*, IV (1910), p. 123(10).
40. "The Outlandish Knight." Sharp MSS., 235/327. Also in Cecil J. Sharp, *JFSS*, IV (1910), p. 120(5). (Richards)
41. "The Outlandish Knight." Baring-Gould MSS., CXIV(2) and (C). Also in John Goss, *Ballads of Britain*, 1937, p. 4(B). (Gregory)
42. "Lady Isabel and the Elf Knight." Helen Creighton and Doreen H. Senior, *Traditional Songs from Nova Scotia*, 1950, p. 8(E).
43. "Lady Isabel and the Elf Knight." Creighton and Senior, 1950, p. 8(F).
44. "Lady Isabel and the Elf Knight." Creighton and Senior, 1950, pp. 4(B)-5.
45. "Lady Isabel and the Elf Knight." Barry MSS., I, M. (Conners)
46. "The Outlandish Knight." Sharp MSS., 2777/2241-43. (Webb)
47. "The Outlandish Knight." Sharp MSS., 1166/. (Wedlock)

48. "The Outlandish Knight." Sharp MSS., 371/502. Also in Cecil J. Sharp, *JFSS*, IV (1910), p. 119(4). (Squires)
49. "Lady Isabel and the Elf Knight." Mary O. Eddy, *Ballads and Songs from Ohio*, 1939, p. 6(A).
50. "Pretty Nancy." Barry, Eckstorm, and Smyth, *British Ballads from Maine*, 1929, pp. 16(B)-18. (Young)
51. "The Outlandish Knight." Sharp MSS., 1070/. (Stokes)
52a. "The Outlandish Knight." Sharp MSS., 679/749-52. (Vincent)
52b. "The Outlandish Knight." Sharp MSS., 942/. (Vincent)
53. "The Outlandish Knight." Charlotte S. Burne, ed., *Shropshire Folk-Lore*, 1883, pp. 652 and 549-50.
54. "The Outlandish Knight." Sharp MSS., 902/. (Trump)
55. "Lady Isabel and the Elf Knight." Sharp MSS., 3645/2703-4. Also in Sharp and Karpeles, *Appalachians*, 1932, I, p. 13(J). (Sloan)
56. "The Outlandish Knight." Sharp MSS., 749/. (Glover)
57. "The Castle by the Sea." Helen Hartness Flanders and Marguerite Olney, *Ballads Migrant in New England*, 1953, pp. 109-11.
58. "The Outlandish Knight." Baring-Gould MSS., CXIV(4) and (B). (Masters)
59. "The King's Daughter Fair." Lester A. Hubbard and LeRoy J. Robertson, *JAF*, LXIV (1951), pp. 39-40.
60. "Pretty Polly." Phillips Barry, *BFSSNE*, No. 1 (1930), pp. 3-4. (Lougee)
61. "Pretty Polly." W. Roy Mackenzie, *Ballads and Sea Songs from Nova Scotia*, 1928, pp. 391 and 7-8.
62. "Mary Goldan." Phillips Barry, *JAF*, XXII (1909), pp. 374-75. (Carson)
63. "The Outlandish Knight." Kidson, *Traditional Tunes*, 1891, p. 27.
64. "Pretty Polly." Carl Sandburg, *The American Songbag*, 1927, pp. 60-61.
65. "The Outlandish Knight." Sharp MSS., 983/. (Coles)
66. "The Highway Robber." R. Vaughan Williams, *JFSS*, IV (1910), p. 122(9). (Colcombe)
67. "Lady Isabel and the Elf Knight." Sharp MSS., 3167/2301-2. Also in Olive Dame Campbell and Cecil J. Sharp, *English Folk-Songs from the Southern Appalachians*, 1917, p. 3(A). (Coit)
68. "Oh, Get Me Some of Your Father's Gold." Frank Kidson Collection, *JFSS*, I (1904), p. 246.
69. "The Outlandish Knight." Sharp MSS., 1196/. (Leader)
70. "The Outlandish Knight." Sharp MSS., 2476/. (Heyhes)
71. "The Outlandish Knight." Sharp MSS., 519/. (White)
72. "The Outlandish Knight." Sharp MSS., 931/. (Chapman)
73. "Lady Isabel and the Elf Knight." Elisabeth B. Greenleaf and Grace Y. Mansfield, *Ballads and Sea Songs of Newfoundland*, 1933, pp. 3-4.
74. "Lady Isabel and the Elf Knight." Creighton and Senior, *Traditional Songs from Nova Scotia*, 1950, pp. 2(A)-3.
75. "If I take off my silken stay." Asher E. Treat, *JAF*, LII (1939), pp. 20-21.
76. "Pretty Polly." William A. Owens, *Texas Folk Songs*, 1950, pp. 35-36.
77. "Pretty Polly." Alton C. Morris, *Folksongs of Florida*, 1950, pp. 239-41.
78. "Lady Isabel and the Elf-Knight." Phillips Barry, *JAF*, XXIV (1911), pp. 333-34. (Smith)
79. "The Outlandish Knight." Ada R. Broadwood, *JFSS*, IV (1910), p. 118.
80. "The Outlandish Knight." Sharp MSS., 1811/. (Say)
81. (Unnamed) Barry, Eckstorm, and Smyth, *British Ballads from Maine*, 1929, pp. 22(E)-23. (Black)

82. (Unnamed) Blaikie MS., No. 45, p. 16, National Library of Scotland.
83. "May Colvin." Robert Archibald Smith, *The Scotish Minstrel*, [1820-24], III, p. 92. Also in Robert Maver, *Genuine Scottish Ballads*, 1866, No. 472, p. 236; and George Eyre-Todd, *Ancient Scots Ballads*, n.d., p. 90.
84. "The Outlandish Knight." Lucy E. Broadwood and J. A. Fuller Maitland, *English County Songs*, 1893, pp. 164-65.
85. "Mey Guldinn." Anne G. Gilchrist, *JEFDSS*, III (1938), p. 189.
86. "Sweet Nellie." Vance Randolph, *Ozark Folksongs*, 1946, I, p. 45(C).
87a. "The Outlandish Knight." Sharp MSS., 2648/. (Porter)
87b. "The Outlandish Knight." Sharp MSS., 2721/. (Porter)
88. "The Outlandish Knight." Sharp MSS., 2582/. (Gardiner)
89. "My Pretty Colinn." Eddy, *Ballads and Songs from Ohio*, 1939, pp. 11(D)-12.
90. "Six Pretty Maidens." C. S. Parsonson, *JFSS*, IV (1910), pp. 116-17.
91. "The Outlandish Knight." Sharp MSS., 1683/. (Monnery)
92. "Lady Isabel and the Elf Knight." Emelyn Elizabeth Gardner and Geraldine Jencks Chickering, *Ballads and Songs of Southern Michigan*, 1939, p. 31.
93. "May Colvine, and Fause Sir John." W. Christie, *Traditional Ballad Airs*, II, 1881, p. 236.
94. "The Outlandish Knight." Frank Kidson, *JFSS*, II (1906), p. 282(1).
95. "The Knight and the Chief's Daughter." Child MSS. XXI, Nos. 51-55, Harvard College Library; British Museum Add. MSS. 20,094, fols. 21-23.
96. "Lady Ishbel and the Elfin-Knight." John Jacob Niles, *Ballads, Love-Songs, and Tragic Legends from the Southern Appalachian Mountains*, Schirmer's American Folk-Song Series, Set 20, 1938, pp. 4-5.
97. "Lady Isabel and the Elf Knight." Sharp MSS., 3141/?. (Campbell)
b. (Unnamed) Barry MSS., Harvard College Library. (Eunice M. Macauslan, Isleford, Maine)

GROUP B

98. "Pretty Polly." Arthur Palmer Hudson, *Folk Tunes from Mississippi*, 1937, No. 11.
99. "Lady Isabel and the Elf Knight." Sharp MSS., 3702/2754. Also in Sharp and Karpeles, *Appalachians*, 1932, I, pp. 10(F)-11. (Vanhook)
100. "Lady Isabel and the Elf Knight." Sharp MSS., 4204/. Also in Sharp and Karpeles, 1932, I, p. 12(H). (Wheeler)
101. "Pretty Polly." Barry, Eckstorm, and Smyth, *British Ballads from Maine*, 1929, p. xxvii. Text, Barry MSS., IV, No. 206. (Osborn)
102. "False Sir John." *Kentucky Mountain Songs*, Elektra, LP rec. 25. (Jean Ritchie)
103. "Pretty Polly." Davis, *Traditional Ballads of Virginia*, 1929, pp. 549(B) and 65-67. (Jackson)
104. "Pretty Polly." Davis, 1929, pp. 550(P) and 83-84. (Singer unknown)
105. "Lady Isabel and the Elf Knight." Sharp MSS., 4585/3208-9. (McCormick)
106. "Lady Isabel and the Elf Knight." Sharp MSS., 3142/? Also in Sharp and Karpeles, *Appalachians*, 1932, I, p. 6(B). (Bishop)
107. "The Six Kings' Daughters." George Korson, *Pennsylvania Songs and Legends*, 1949, pp. 30-32.

108. "Lady Isabel and the Elf Knight." Sharp MSS., 4261/. (Berry)

109. "Six Kings Daughters." Loraine Wyman and Howard Brockway, *Lonesome Tunes*, [1916], pp. 82-87.

110. "Lady Isabel and the Elf Knight." Sharp MSS., 3197/2341. Also in Sharp and Karpeles, *Appalachians*, 1932, I, p. 5(A). (Sands)

111. "Lady Isabel and the Elf Knight." Sharp MSS., 3221/. Also in Sharp and Karpeles, 1932, I, p. 8(D). (Shelton)

112. "The Outlandish Knight." Sharp MSS., 3250/. (Hensley)

113. "The Outlandish Knight." Sharp MSS., 3774/. (Kilburn)

114. "Lady Isabel and the Elf Knight." Sharp MSS., 3777/. (Townsley, Wilson)

115. "Lady Isabel and the Elf Knight." Sharp MSS., 4319/ 3085-86. (Bowyer)

116. "Lady Isabel and the Elf Knight." Sharp MSS., 4331/3092. Also in Sharp and Karpeles, *Appalachians*, 1932, I, pp. 9(E)-10. (Donald)

117. "Lady Isabel and the Elf Knight." Sharp MSS., 4348/. (Dooley)

118. "Lady Isabel and the Elf Knight." Sharp MSS., 4508/3171. Also in Sharp and Karpeles, *Appalachians*, 1932, I, p. 12(G). (Cannady)

119. "Lady Isabel and the Elf Knight." Sharp MSS., 4729/3296. (Boone)

120. "Lady Isabel and the Elf Knight." Dorothy Scarborough, *On the Trail of Negro Folk-Songs*, 1925, pp. 43-45.

121. "Pretty Polly Ann." Randolph, *Ozark Folksongs*, 1946, I, pp. 41(A)-43.

122. "Lady Isabel and the Elf-Knight." Winston Wilkinson MSS., 1935-36, p. 6(B), University of Virginia.

123. "Lady Isabel and the Elf-Knight." Wilkinson MSS., 1935-36, pp. 3-5(A).

124. "The King's Seven Daughters." Herbert Halpert, LC Archive of American Folk Song, rec. 2954 B1. (Mrs. Theodosia Bonnett Long)

c. "The King's Seven Daughters." Hudson, *Folk Tunes from Mississippi*, 1937, No. 10.

d. "Purty Polly." Vance Randolph, *Ozark Mountain Folks*, 1932, pp. 216-19.

e. "Six Kings' Daughters." Paul G. Brewster, *Ballads and Songs of Indiana*, 1940, p. 35.

125. "Six Fair Maids." F. C. Brown MS, 17-XI (16 a 4?), Library of Congress, photostat.

126. "Six Kings' Daughters." John Harrington Cox, *Folk-Songs of the South*, 1925, pp. 521 and 6-7.

127. "Six Kings' Daughters." John Harrington Cox, *Traditional Ballads Mainly from West Virginia*, 1939, pp. 4-5.

128. "The False Sir John." Cox, *Traditional Ballads Mainly from West Virginia*, 1939, pp. 1-3.

129. "The Six Fair Maids." Brown MS, 16 a 4. Text, *The Frank C. Brown Collection of North Carolina Folklore*, II, 1952, pp. 24-25.

130. "The Outlandish Knight." Helen Hartness Flanders and George Brown, *Vermont Folk-Songs & Ballads*, 1931, pp. 190-92.

131. "Willie Came over the Ocean." Randolph, *Ozark Folksongs*, I, 1946, p. 47(E).

132. "Billy Came over the Main White Ocean." Byron Arnold, *Folksongs of Alabama*, 1950, pp. 54-55.

133. "King's Daughter; or, Six Fair Maids." Brown MS, 16 a 4. Text, *North Carolina Folklore*, II, 1952, pp. 15-17.

134. "Pretty Polly." Mabel Major, *Publications of the Texas Folk-Lore Society*, X (1932), pp. 138-40.

135. "Lady Isabel and the Elf Knight." Sharp MSS., 3612/. Also in Sharp and Karpeles, *Appalachians*, 1932, I, p. 13(I). (Ray)

f. "The Six Kings Daughters." Barry MSS., (4C), IV, p. 121.

136. "The King's Daughter; or, Come a Link, Come a Long." Davis, *Traditional Ballads of Virginia*, 1929, pp. 550(D) and 68-69. (Stinnet, Wildman)

137. "Lady Isabel and the Elf Knight." Sharp MSS., 3211/. (Gasnell)

138. "The False-hearted Knight." Flanders and Olney, *Ballads Migrant in New England*, 1953, pp. 4-7.

139. "The King's Daughter." Phillips Barry, *JAF*, XXII (1909), p. 76. (Carter)

140. "Lady Isabel and the Elf Knight." David Seneff McIntosh, *Some Representative Southern Illinois Folk-Songs* (Iowa State University, M.A. thesis in music), 1935, pp. 4-6. Also in LC Archive of American Folk Song, rec. 3250 A1. (David S. McIntosh)

141. "The Outlandish Knight." Flanders and Olney, *Ballads Migrant in New England*, 1953, pp. 129-31.

TUNES WITH TEXTS

GROUP A

1. [The Outlandish Knight]

Baring-Gould MSS., CXIV(1); text, (A). Also, with harmonization, in Baring-Gould and Sharp, *English Folk-Songs for Schools*, n.d., p. 26 (in A♭ major). Sung by James Parsons, Lew Down, 1888. Collected by S. Baring-Gould.

p I

1. An outlandish Knight from the Northern land,
    He said he would marry me.
  He said he would take me to the far, far land,
    And there he would wed with me.

2. O fetch me some of your father's gold,
    And some of your mother's fee.
  And two of the best of your father's nags,
    That stand by thirty & three.

3. Then up & she mounts on her milk white steed
    And he on his dapple grey.
  They rode till they came to the sea, sea side
    Three hours before the day.

4. Light off, light off thy milk white steed,
   And deliver it unto me.
   For six pretty maids have I drowned here
   And the seventh thou shalt be.

5. Pull off, pull off thy silken gown,
   And deliver it unto me,
   For I reckon it be too fine & gay
   To rot in the salt, salt sea.

6. Pull off, pull off thy holland smock
   And deliver it unto me,
   For I reckon it be too fair & fine
   To rot in the salt, salt sea.

7. Pull off, pull off thy silken stays
   And deliver them unto me,
   For I reckon they be too fine & gay
   To rot in the salt, salt sea.

8. If I must pull off my holland smock,
   Pray turn your back to me,
   For it is not fit for a lady like me
   A naked woman to be.

9. If I must pull off my holland smock,
   Pray turn your back to me,
   For it is not fit an outlandish thief
   A naked, me should see.

10. O then he turned his back on her
    And looked upon green tree
    That she might pull off her holland smock
    And that her he might not see.

11. As he turned his back on the fair lady
    A viewing the leaves so green,
    Then she caught him about his middle small
    And she thrust him into the stream.

12. He droppèd high, he droppèd low,
    Until he came to the side,
    Catch hold of my hand, my lady dear
    I'll make thee my lawful bride.

13. Lie there, lie there, thou false hearted man,
    Lie there instead of me.
    Six pretty maids hast thou drowned here,
    And the seventh hath drowned thee.

14. Then up she mounted her milk white steed
    And she led the dapple grey,
    She rode till she came to her father's house,
    Two hours before the day.

15. The parrot was up in the window high,
    And laughed so shrill & did say,
    I'm afraid some ruffian here has been,
    And led my sweet lady away.

16. Don't prittle & prattle my pretty parrot
    Nor tell any tales of me.
    Your cage shall be made of the glittering gold
    Although it was made of a tree
    Your cage shall be made of the glittering gold
    And the door of ivory.

2. "The Seven King's Daughters"

Davis, 1929, p. 551 (Q); text, p. 84. Sung by Mrs. Dan Maxie (*née* Holland), Altavista, Va., March 23, 1914; learned from her mother. Collected by Juliet Fauntleroy.

She picked him up so shyly,
She hauled him in the sea,
"Lie there, lie there, you false-eyed vilyun
Instead of me.
Six of the king's daughters you've drownded,
And the seventh one *you* shall be."

3. [May Collean]

Motherwell, 1827, App'x No. 24.

O heard ye e'er o' a bloody knight
That liv'd in the west Countrie?
For he has stown seven ladies fair
And drown'd them a' in the sea.

This tune appears to have a close kinship with "Lord Robert and fair Ellen," in the Petrie Collection, No. 795, from Dr. Kelly, County Mayo.

4. [The Outlandish Knight]

Sharp MSS., 1226/. Also in Sharp, *JFSS*, IV (1910), p. 120(6). Sung by Mrs. Ware, Over Stowey, January 23, 1907.

This tune may be related to minor forms of "The Miller of the Dee," for which cf. Moffat, and Kidson, *The Minstrelsy of England*, 1901, p. 44, and particularly Kidson's valuable note.

5. [Lady Isabel and the Elf Knight]

Barry, *JAF*, XVIII (1905), pp. 132-33. Also in Barry, Eckstorm, and Smyth, 1929, p. 24(F). Sung by Miss Leslie W. Hopkinson, Cambridge, Mass., May 31, 1904; from family tradition.

a I

1. Pretty Polly, she mounted her milk-white steed,
    And he the ambling gray,
  And they came to the broad water side,
    Full an hour before it was day, day, day,
    Full an hour before it was day.

2. "Now light you down, Pretty Polly," he said,
    "Now light you down," said he,
  "For six Pretty Pollies have I drownded here,
    And the seventh you shall be."

3. "Take off your clothes, so costly, so fine,
    And eke your velvet shoon,
  For I do think your clothing is too good,
    For to lie in a watery tomb."

4. "Won't you stoop down to pick that brier,
    That grows so near the brim?
  For I am afraid it will tangle my hair,
    And rumple my lily-white skin."

5. So he stooped down to pick that brier,
    That grew so near the brim,
  And with all the might that the Pretty Polly had,
    She did tumble the false knight in.

6. "Lie there, lie there false knight," she said,
    "Lie there all in my room,
  For I do not think your clothing is too good,
    For to lie in a watery tomb!"

7. Pretty Polly, she mounted her milk-white steed,
    And led the ambling gray,
  And she came to her father's stable door,
    Full an hour before it was day.

8. Then up and spoke her pretty parrot,
    And unto her did say,
  "Oh, where have you been, my Pretty Polly,
    So long before it was day?"

9. "Oh, hold your tongue, you prattling bird,
    And tell no tales of me,

And you shall have a cage of the finest beaten gold,
    That shall hang on the front willow-tree!"

10. Then up and spoke her father dear,
    And unto the bird did say,
  "Oh, what makes you talk, my pretty parrot,
    So long before it is day?"

11. "The old cat came to my cage door,
    And fain would have eaten me,
  And I was a-calling to Pretty Polly,
    To drive the old cat away."

6. [The Outlandish Knight]

Broadwood, *JFSS*, IV (1910), p. 119(3). Also in Baring-Gould MSS., CXIV(5); sent by Miss Broadwood. Sung by Mrs. Fletcher, near Liston, North Devon, September, 1893.

a I

7. [The Outlandish Knight]

Baring-Gould MSS., CXIV(3). Sung by an unidentified man, March 1891. Noted by F. W. Bussell.

a I

8. [The Outlandish Knight]

Sharp MSS., 1557/. Sung by Mrs. Jarrett, Bridgwater, January 7, 1908.

a I

9. [Lady Isabel and the Elf Knight]

Sharp MSS., 3140/?. Also in Sharp and Karpeles, 1932, I, pp. 7(C)-8. Sung by Mrs. Moore, Rabun Gap, Ga., May 1, 1910. Collected by Olive Dame Campbell.

m I

1. There was a proper tall young man,
   And William was his name;
   He came away over the raging sea,
   He came a-courting me, O me,
   He came a-courting me.

2. He followed me up, he followed me down,
   He followed me in my room.
   I had no wings for to fly away,
   No tongue to say him nay.

3. He took part of my father's gold,
   Half of my mother's fee;
   He took two of my father's stable steeds,
   For there stood thirty and three.

4. The lady rode the milk-white steed,
   The gentleman rode the grey.
   They rode all down by the north green land
   All on one summer's day.

5. Light off, light off, my pretty fair miss,
   I tell you now my mind.
   Six pretty fair maids I've drownded here,
   The seventh one you shall be.

6. Hush up, hush up, you old vilyun,
   That hain't what you promised me.
   You promised to carry me over the raging sea,
   And then for to marry me.

7. Turn your back and trim those nettles
   That grow so near the brim;
   They'll tangle in my golden hair
   And tear my lily-white skin.

8. He turned his back to trim those nettles
   That growed so near the brim;
   This young lady with her skilfulness
   She tripped her false love in.

9. Lie there, lie there, you old vilyun,
   Lie there in the place for me.
   You have nothing so fine nor costly
   But to rot in the salt water sea.

10. First she rode the milk-white steed
    And then she rode the grey.

She returned back to her father's house
Three long hours before it was day.

10. [The Outlandish Knight]

Sharp MSS., 1822/. Sung by Charles Neville, East Coker, September 2, 1908.

a M (inflected VII)

Sharp's MS. note: "In bar (b) Neville Junior invariably sang C♯ [i.e., B♭ in transposed text above] to his father's C♮ [i.e., B♮] throughout the song. In bar (c) they both varied the last note between E & C♯ [i.e., D and B♮]."

11. [The Outlandish Knight]

Sharp MSS., 2471/. Sung by George Hartwell, Idlicote, April 29, 1910.

a M

12. [An Outlandish Rover]

Vaughan Williams, JFSS, IV (1910), p. 121(8). Sung by Mr. Verrall, Horsham, December 22, 1904.

a M

13. "The False-Hearted Knight"

Barry, Eckstorm, and Smyth, 1929, pp. 26(G)-28. Sung by
Mrs. Guy R. Hathaway, Mattawamkeag, Maine, 1928;
learned from her father.

m D

1. I'll tell you of a false hearted knight
      Who courted a lady gay,
   And all that he wanted of this pretty fair maid
      Was to take her sweet life away.

2. "Go bring me some of your mamma's gold,
      And some of your daddy's fee,
   And away we'll ride to some foreign country
      And married we shall be."

3. She brought him some of her mamma's gold,
      And some of her daddy's fee,
   And two of the best horses in her father's stable,
      Where there stood thirty and three.

4. She then mounted the milk-white steed,
      And he upon the grey,
   They rode till they came to a fair river side,
      Six hours before it was day.

5. "Alight, alight, my pretty fair maid,
      I have something to tell unto thee;
   For it's six maidens fair I have drownèd here
      And you the seventh shall be."

6. "Some pity, some pity, my own true love,
      Some pity show unto me,
   For of all the gold that I ever gave to thee,
      I will double it over three."

7. "Take off, take off your satin gown,
      And give it unto me,
   For I do think that your clothing is too gay
      To rot in the watery sea."

8. She then took off her satin gown
      And laid it upon the ground,
   And out of this fair lady's pocket
      He took ten thousand pounds.

9. "Go bring me the sickle, that I may crop the nettle
      That grows on the river's brim,
   That it may not entangle my curly, curly locks
      Nor nettle my milk-white skin."

10. He brought the sickle, that she might crop the nettle
       That grew on the river's brim,

And with all of the strength that this fair maid had,
   She pushed the false knight in.

11. "Lie there, lie there, you false hearted knight,
       For I think that you've got your doom,
    And I do not think that your clothing is too gay
       To rot in a watery tomb."

12. "Some pity, some pity, my pretty fair maid,
       Some pity show unto me:
    For of all the vows that I ever made to thee,
       I will double them over three!"

13. "Lie there, lie there, you false hearted knight,
       Lie there instead of me,
    For it's six maidens fair you have drownèd here,
       And the seventh hath drowned thee."

14. She then mounted the milk-white steed,
       And home she led the grey,
    She rode till she came to her father's stable door,
       Three hours before it was day.

15. The parrot being up in the chamber so high,
       Hearing his mistress, did say:
    "What is the matter, my own mistress,
       That you tarry so long before day?"

16. The maid being up in the chamber so high,
       Hearing what the parrot did say:
    "O! What is the matter, you silly parrot,
       That you prattle so long before day?"

17. "The cat she came to my cage door,
       And would not let me be,
    And I was obliged my own mistress to call
       To drive the cat away."

18. "Hold your tongue, my own parrot,
       And tell no tales on me,
    And your cage shall be made of the finest of gold,
       And doors of ivory."

14. [The Outlandish Knight]

Kidson, 1891, p. 172. Noted by Charles Lolley, Leeds.

a Æ (but – VII)

An Outlandish knight from the Northlands came,
   And he came a-woo-ing to me:
He promised he'd take me to the Northlands,
   And there he would marry me.

15. [The Outlandish Knight]

Sharp MSS., 736/. Sung by Mrs. J. Southwood, Bridgwater, January 1, 1906.

p I

The outlandish knight came from the Northlands
He came a wooing of me
He said he would take me unto the North Lands
And there he would marry me
And there he would marry me.

16. "The King's Daughter"

Boswell, *TFSB*, XVII, No. 4 (December 1951), pp. 86-87. Sung by Mrs. Jane Snodgrass Johnson, Nashville, Tenn., June 24, 1950; learned from her father, W. E. Snodgrass, and brought perhaps from the vicinity of Mount Vernon, Va.

m π[1]

1. He was mounted on a milk-white steed,
   And he led a dappled gray,
   And he rode till he came to the old king's house
   Six hours before it was day, day, day,
   Six hours before it was day.

2. He softly called the princess fair,
   "Come ride abroad with me,
   And I will take you to fair Scotland
   And there I'll marry with thee, thee, thee,
   And there I'll marry with thee."

3. He rode upon the milk-white steed
   And she the dappled gray,
   And they rode till they came to the old salt sea
   Three hours before it was day, day, day,
   Three hours before it was day.

4. "Get off your mount, my pretty fair maid,
   And come stand here by me,
   For here I've drownded the sixth king's daughter
   And you the seventh shall be, be, be,
   And you the seventh shall be.

5. "Take off that gown, that Holland gown,
   And lay it here by me,
   For it's too fine and too costly
   To rot in the old salt sea, sea, sea,
   To rot in the old salt sea."

6. "Oh, turn your face away from me
   To the bright green leaves on the trees;
   It never shall be said such a villain as you
   A naked princess did see, see, see,
   A naked princess did see."

7. He turned his eyes away from her
   To the bright green leaves on the trees,
   And she picked him up so strong in her arms
   And flung him into the sea, sea, sea,
   And flung him into the sea.

8. "Come help, come help, my pretty fair maid,
   Forgive and succor me,
   And I'll yet take thee to fair Scotland
   And there I'll marry with thee, thee, thee,
   And there I'll marry with thee."

9. "Lie there, lie there, you false-hearted knave;
   Lie there in room of me.
   You'd have stripped me as naked as e'er I was born,
   And I ne'er took a stitch from thee, thee, thee,
   And I ne'er took a stitch from thee."

10. She mounted on the milk-white steed,
    And she led the dappled gray,
    And she rode till she came to her father's house
    One hour before it was day, day, day,
    One hour before it was day.

11. Up spoke the old parrot from her cage door,
    And loudly did she say:
    "Where've you been, my pretty princess,
    So long before it is day, day, day,
    So long before it is day?"

12. "Hush up, hush up, my pretty Polly;
    Don't tell any tales on me,
    And your cage shall be lined with a wind-beaten gold
    Hung on yon willow tree, tree, tree,
    Hung on yon willow tree."

13. Up spoke the old king from his chamber,
    From his chamber where he lay:
    "Who are you calling, my pretty Polly,
    So long before it is day, day, day,
    So long before it is day?"

14. "The old cat came to my cage door
    For to devour me,
    And I was calling my pretty princess
    To drive the cat away, 'way, 'way,
    To drive the cat away."

17. [The Outlandish Knight]

Sharp MSS., 345/. Sung by Mrs. Eliza Hutchings, Langport, August 22, 1904.

p I

The outlandish knight came from the North Land
He came a wooing of me
He said he would take me to the Northland
And there he would marry me

18. [Lady Isabel]

Barry MSS., I, No. 4, B. Sung by Mrs. George Ravois, Vineland, N.J., January 8, 1907; learned from her father, Robert O'Farrell, County Sligo.

p I

At the end of the fourth phrase, Barry indicates "a flourish," but without musical notation and without abbreviating the last note of that phrase. The "flourish" took care of the words "oh brine."

1. "Take off, take off this dress you have on.
   It is of the silk so fine.—
   It is too good and costly far,
   To lie in the salt-sea brine,
                        oh, brine,
   To lie in the salt-sea brine!"

2. "Take off, take off this petticoat you have on.
   It is of the satin so fine.
   It is too good and costly far,
   To lie in the salt-sea brine."

3. "Take off, take off this chemise you have on,
   It is of the linen so fine,
   It is too good and costly far
   To lie in the salt-sea brine."

4. "Oh, turn around and back about,
   To view the green leaves of the tree,
   It is not becoming for any young man,
   A naked lady to see."

5. He turned him round and backed about,
   To view the green leaves of the tree.
   She picked him up into her arms,
   And plunged him into the deep.

6. "O, give me a hold of your little finger,
   And a fast, fast hold of your thumb,
   There's not a promise that ever I made,
   But I'll roll it in one bun!"

7. "Lie there, lie there, you false young man,
   Lie there instead of me" . . .

8. "Keep secrets, keep secrets, my pretty parrot,
   Keep secrets this night unto me!" . . .

9. "There's nine wild cats at my cage door,

   ·   ·   ·   ·   ·   ·   ·   ·

Notes by Mrs. Ravois: "The first part of the song tells how the young man came to invite the girl to run away with him,—the parrot told her not to go or she would rue it.
   "She rode on a brown horse, and the young man on the 'ambrel gray.'"

19. "The False Hearted Knight"

Davis, 1929, p. 551(R); text, pp. 84-85. Sung by Mrs. Harrington, Roanoke, Va., December 17, 1916. Collected by Alfreda M. Peel.

m I/Ly

The opening of this variant may be compared with the Kidson (1891) and Sandburg (1927) variants, *post*, Nos. 63 and 64.

1. "Now turn your back to me
   And your face to the leaves on the tree;
   Such a wicked man as thou'rt isn't fit
   A naked woman to see."

2. And turning his back to her
   And his face to the leaves on the tree,
   She picked him up in her own strong arms
   And threw him in the sea.

3. "Lie there, lie there, false-hearted knight,
   Lie there instead of me;
   Three king's [sic] daughters you have drowned,
   But I the fourth shan't be."

4. And mounting on her own bay horse
   And leading the dapple gray,
   She then arrived at her father's house
   One hour and a half before day.

5. Her father hearing her come in
   Got up, and thus did say:
   "Who enters here, who enters here,
   When 'tis so near to day?"

6. The pretty parrot began to talk
   And laugh so fitfully:
   "The cat was before my little cage door
   And about to have eaten me."

7. The girl came up and thus did say
   To the pretty parrot blithe and gay:
   "O mistress Polly, you keep still
   And tell no tales on me;
   Your cage shall be made of beaten gold,
   And hang on a willow tree."

20a. [The Outlandish Knight]

Sharp MSS., 356/. Also in Sharp, *JFSS*, IV (1910), p. 121(7). Sung by Mrs. J. Chapman, West Harptree, Somerset, August 25, 1904.

a I/Ly

An outlandish gentleman came from the North South
                                  a-wooing with* me
He told me he would taken† me unto the North Land
                     and then he would marry me.

* *JFSS*, IV, p. 121, has "unto."
† *JFSS* has "take."

20b. "The Outlandish Gentleman"

Sharp MSS., 1084/. Same singer, August 28, 1906.

a I

21. [The Outlandish Knight]

Sharp MSS., 4861/. Sung by Mrs. Barnard (57), Mitcheldean, September 6, 1921.

a I

It was a cold December morning
When he came a wooing of me
He promised he'd take me to the North land
And there he would marry me.

22. "The False-hearted Knight"

Barry, Eckstorm, and Smyth, 1929, pp. 19(C)-20. Sung by Mrs. A. W. (Barry) Lindenberg, Shirley, Mass., 1922.

a I

1. She mounted on her milk-white steed,
   And he on his dapple gray,
   And forth from her father's house they went,
   Before the break of day.

2. They rode and rode and rode away
   Until they came to the sea,
   And here they pulled their horses up
   Hard by a willow tree.

3. "Now get thee down, my pretty Pollee,
   And harken unto me,—
   Six pretty maidens I've drownded here,
   And you the seventh shall be.

4. "Take off, take off that silken gown,
   And give it unto me,—
   A silken gown is much too fine
   To rot in the salt sea."

5. "O turn about, O turn about,
   And face the willow tree,—
   While I take off the silken gown
   And give it unto thee."

6. He turned about, he turned about,
   And faced the willow tree,—
   She took him in her lily-white arms,
   And threw him into the sea.

7. "Lie there, lie there, my false lover,
   Lie there instead of me,—
   If six pretty maidens you've drownded here,
   Go bear them company!"

8. She mounted on her milk-white steed,
   And led the dapple gray,
   And back she went to her father's house,
   Before the break of day.

9. The first she saw was the little parrot,—
   "O where have you been from me?

O where have you been in the early morn,—
O where have you been from me?"

10. "O say no more, my little parrot,—
O say no more to me,
And I'll give thee a golden cage,
To hang on the chestnut tree!"

11. The next to speak was her mother dear,—
"O where have you been from me?"
"I've been to church in the early morn,
To say a prayer for thee."

23. "The Seven King's Daughters"

Davis, 1929, p. 550(F); text, pp. 71-72. Sung by Miss Odell
Roop, Vinton, Va., September 11, 1922. Collected by Alfreda M. Peel.

a I/M

The earlier copy is in straight 6/8 time.

1. There was a man out in the land,
He courted a maiden fair;
He promised to take her to northern lands,
There the marriage should be.

2. "Go get some of your father's gold,
Some of your mother's fee;
Get two of the horses that stand in the stalls,
That stand by forty and three.

3. "Dismount, dismount your milky steed
And deliver it unto me;
For six king's daughters have I drowned,
And the seventh one you shall be.

4. "Pull off, pull off your silky robe
And deliver it unto me;
For I think it is too costly
To roll in the deep blue sea."

5. "If I must pull off my silky robe,
Please turn your back on me;
For I think it's not nice, you know,
A naked maiden to see."

6. He turned his back all unto her;
She wept most bitterly;
She grabbed him round his thin small waist
And tumbled him into the sea.

7. He waved on high, he waved on low,
He waved till he came to her (side?):
"Take hold of my hand, my pretty Pauline,
And you shall be my bride."

24. [Lady Isabel and the Elf Knight]

Davis, 1929, p. 551(S); text, p. 85. Sung by Lucile Noel,
Vinton, Va., November 30, 1923. Noted by Evelyn Rex.
Collected by Alfreda M. Peel.

a I/M

"Go get me of my father's gold,
And some of my mother's feed;
Get two of the horses that stand in the stall,
That stand by forty and three."

25. [Tell-tale Polly]

Charley Fox's Minstrel's Companion, n.d., p. 52.

a I/M

1. She mounted on her bonny, bonny brown,
And she led the dapple gray,
So merrily she rode by the merry greenwood
Till she came to the brink of the sea,
Till she came to the brink of the sea.

2. Lie there, lie there, you false-hearted man,
Lie there instead of me;
'Tis six fair maidens you have drowned in the sea,
And the seventh one you shall be, &c.

3. She mounted on her bonny, bonny brown,
And she led the dapple gray:
So merrily she rode by the merry greenwood,
So long before it was day, &c.

4. The parrot overheard the noise,
And unto her did say,
What was the matter, my pretty little lass,
So long before 'twas day? &c.

5. The father overheard the noise,
And unto her did say,

What is the matter with my darling little child
So long before the broke of day? &c.

6. There is a cat at my cage-door,
    And it swears it will have me;
  And I have come to call my Collin dear,
    To drive the cat away, &c.

7. Oh, hush! oh hush! my pretty, pretty poll,
    And tell no tales on me:
  Your cage shall be made of pure beaten gold,
    And your door of ivory-ee, &c.

26. [The Outlandish Knight]

Sharp MSS., 751/. Sung by Mrs. Pike, Somerton, January
5, 1906; transmitted by Mrs. Snow.

a M (inflected VII)

27. [The Outlandish Knight]

Sharp MSS., 1342/. Sung by Mrs. Emma Callow, Bog-
borough, April 9, 1907.

a M

28a. [The Outlandish Knight]

Sharp MSS., 1405/1290. Also in Sharp, 4th series, 1908,
No. 84; and Sharp, 1916, p. 29, with piano accompaniment.
Sung by Joseph Laver (73), Bridgwater, August 14, 1907.

a D

1. An outlandish knight came from the North Lands,
  And he came wooing to me,
  He told me he'd take me to some foreign lands
  And there he would marry me.

2. Go fetch me some of your mother's gold
  And some of your father's fee
  And two of the best nags out of the stable
  Where there stood thirty and three.

3. She fetched him some of her mother's gold
  And some of her father's fee
  And two of the best nags out of the stable
  Where there stood thirty and three.

4. Now she mounted on her milk white steed
  And he on his dippled grey
  And they rode till they came to the sea side
  Three hours before it was day.

5. Duff off, duff off, your silken things
  And deliver them up to me
  For it looks too rich and too gay
  To rot all in the salt sea.

6. If I must take off my silken things
  Pray turn thy back unto me
  For it's not fitting that such a ruffian
  A naked woman should see.

7. Now he turned his back unto her
  And viewed the watery stream,
  She catched him round the middle so small
  And forced him into the stream.

8. He drooped high, he drooped low,
  Until he came to the side.
  Catch hold of my hand my pretty Polly
  And you shall be my bride.

9. Lay there, lay there you false hearted man,
    Lay there in the stead of me.
    There are six pretty maidens thou hast a [*sic*] drowned there
    But the seventh have drownded thee.

10. Now she mounted on her milk-white steed
    And led the dipple grey
    And she rode till she came to her own father's house
    Three hours before it was day.

28b. [The Outlandish Knight]

Sharp MSS., 1002/. Sung by Joseph Laver (72), Bridg-water, August 13, 1906.

a D

An outlandish knight came from the north lands
He came a-wooing of me
He said he would take me unto the Northlands
And there he would marry me

29. "The Outlandish Knight"

Bruce and Stokoe, 1882, pp. 48-50. Also, with accompaniment, in Stokoe and Reay, [1892], p. 130. Sung by Mrs. Andrews, Newcastle-on-Tyne.

a I

1. An Outlandish knight came from the north lands,
    And he came a wooing to me;
    He told me he'd take me unto the North lands,
    And there he would marry me.

2. "Come, fetch me some of your father's gold,
    And some of your mother's fee;
    And two of the best nags out of the stable,
    Where they stand thirty and three."

3. She fetched him some of her father's gold,
    And some of her mother's fee;
    And two of the best nags out of the stable,
    Where they stood thirty and three.

4. She mounted her on her milk-white steed.
    He on the dapple grey,
    They rode till they came unto the sea side,
    Three hours before it was day.

5. "Light off, light off thy milk-white steed,
    And deliver it unto me;
    Six pretty maids have I drownèd here,
    And thou the seventh shall be.

6. Pull off, pull off thy silken gown,
    And deliver it unto me,
    Methinks it looks too rich and gay,
    To rot in the salt sea.

7. Pull off, pull off, thy silken stays,
    And deliver them unto me,
    Methinks they are too fine and gay
    To rot in the salt sea.

8. Pull off, pull off, thy Holland smock,
    And deliver it unto me,
    Methinks it looks too rich and gay,
    To rot in the salt sea."

9. "If I must pull off my Holland smock,
    Pray turn thy back to me,
    For it is not fitting that such a ruffian,
    A naked woman should see."

10. He's turned his back towards her,
    And viewed the leaves so green,
    She catched him round the middle so small,
    And tumbled him into the stream.

11. He droppèd high, he droppèd low,
    Until he came to the side,—
    "Catch hold of my hand, my pretty maiden,
    And I will make you my bride."

12. "Lie there, lie there, you false-hearted man,
    Lie there instead of me;
    Six pretty maids have you drownèd here,
    And the seventh has drownèd thee."

13. She mounted on her milk-white steed,
    And led the dapple grey;
    She rode till she came to her own father's hall,
    Three hours before it was day.

14. The parrot being in the window so high,
    Hearing the lady, did say;
    "I'm afraid that some ruffian has led you astray,
    That you've tarried so long away."

15. "Don't prittle or prattle, my pretty parrot,
    Nor tell no tales of me;
    Thy cage shall be made of the glittering gold,
    Although it is made of a tree."

16. The king being in the chamber so high,
    And hearing the parrot, did say:
    "What ails you, what ails you, my pretty parrot,
    That you prattle so long before day."

17. "It's no laughing matter," the parrot did say;
    "But so loudly I call unto thee,
For the cats have got into the window so high,
    And I'm afraid they will have me."

18. "Well turned, well turned, my pretty parrot,
    Well turned, well turned for me;
Thy cage shall be made of the glittering gold,
    And the door of the best ivory."

30. [The Outlandish Knight]

Kidson, *JFSS*, II (1906), p. 282(2). Sung at Knaresbro',
Yorkshire.

a I

An outlandish Knight from the northlands,
    And he came a-wooing to me;
He promis'd he'd take me unto the northlands,
    And there he would marry me;
Oh! and there he would marry me.

31. [The Robber and the Lady]

Gillington, [1907], pp. 4-5. "Taken from the mouths of
the peasantry."

a I

1. An outlandish Knight from the North Countrie
    He came a-bowing to me;
He told me he'd take me to the Northlands,
    And there he'd marry me.

2. "Give me some of your father's gold,
    And some of your mother's fee!
And take two of the best nags out of the stable,
    Where there stands thirty and three."

3. She mounted on her milk-white steed,
    And he on the dapper grey;

And they rode till they came to some fair waterside,
    Three hours before it was day.

4. "Light off, light off your milk-white steed,
    And deliver it unto me!
For six pretty maidens I have a-drown'd here,
    And you the seventh will be!"

5. "Pull off, pull off your silken gown,
    And deliver it unto me!
For I think it do look too rich and too gay
    To rot all in the salt sea!"

6. "O, turn, O, turn" the Lady cried;
    "O, turn your back unto me!—
For it is not fit that such a robber
    An innocent woman should see!"

7. Then she took off her silken gown,
    And bitterly did she weep;
And she caught him round the middle so small,
    And tumbled him into the deep.

8. He floated high, he floated low,
    He floated near the sea side,
"Lay hold of my hand, my pretty Lady,
    I will make you my lawful bride!

9. "Lay there, lay there, thou false-hearted man!
    Lay there instead of me!
For six pretty maidens thou hast a-drown'd here,
    And the seventh will now drown thee!"

10. She mounted on her milk-white steed,
    A-leading the dapper grey,
And she rode till she came to her father's door,
    One hour before it was day.

11. And the parrot being up in the window so high
    And hearing the lady pass by;—
"O, I think some false hearted man you have slain,
    You come rambling so long before day!"

12. "Don't prittle nor prattle, my pretty Polly!
    Don't tell little tales on me!
And your cage shall be made of the glittering gold,
    And your door of the best ivory!"

32. [The Outlandish Knight]

Sharp MSS., 2382/. Sung by William Hedges, Chipping
Camden, September 10, 1909.

a I

33. [The Outlandish Knight]

Sharp MSS., 2598/. Sung by John Bradley, Arnescote, April 15, 1911.

a I

34. [The Outlandish Knight]

Kidson, *JFSS*, II (1906), p. 282(3). Noted by G. Rathbone, Westmoreland.

a I (inflected IV and VII)

35. "The False-Hearted Knight"

Barry, Eckstorm, and Smyth, 1929, p. 21(D). Sung by Mrs. Sidney Brockway, Bonny River, Charlotte County, New Brunswick, September 1928. Melody recorded by George Herzog.

a M (or p I, with dropped close)

In London lived a false-hearted knight,
A false-hearted knight was he.

   • • • • • • • •
   • • • • • • • •

"O, give me some of your mother's gold
And some of your father's fee,
And lead me to your father's stable door
Where the horses stand twenty and three."

O, he mounted her on the milk-white steed
And he on the dapple gray,
And so they rode from her father's house
[Three hours before it was day.]

36. [The Outlandish Knight]

Sharp MSS., 2130/. Sung by N. W. Gibbs (74), Evesham, April 7, 1909.

a M (or p I, with dropped close)

37. [The Outlandish Knight]

Sharp MSS., 818/. Sung by Frederick Crossman, Huish, January 23, 1906.

a M (or p I, with dropped close)

38. [The Outlandish Knight]

Sharp MSS., 1873/. Sung by Mrs. Callow (75), Stockham Cross, September 9, 1908.

a M (or p I, with dropped close)

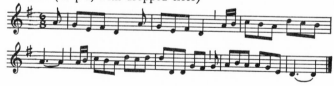

39. "She borrowed some of her father's gold"

Vaughan Williams, *JFSS*, IV (1910), p. 123(10). Sung by Mr. Hilton, South Walsham, Norfolk, April 1908.

a M

40. [The Outlandish Knight]

Sharp MSS., 235/327. Also in Sharp, *JFSS*, IV (1910), p. 120(5). Sung by Harry Richards, Curry Rivell, July 29, 1904.

a M

An outlandish knight came from the North land
As he come a-wooing to me.
He said he would take me unto the North land
And there he would marry me.

Go fetch me some of your father's gold
And some of your mother's fee,
And out in the stable there stands thirty and three.

And she mount on her middle quite speed*
And he on his doublet† gray.
They rode till they came to some broad water's side
Three hours before it was day.

Unlight, unlight, you gay Lady
Unlight of your middle quite speed
Deliver it unto me
For I seems it looks too rich and too gay
To melder all in the salt sea.

Sharp's MS. note: "He sang the song complete once, but on repeating got fuddled in his words. As, however, the words followed the usual versions I did not press him."
* i.e., milk-white steed
† i.e., dapple

41. "The Outlandish Knight"

Baring-Gould MSS., CXIV(2); text, (C). Also in Goss, 1937, p. 4(B). Sung by Richard Gregory, Moor man, Two Bridges, January 1889. Collected by F. W. Bussell.

a M (inflected VII)

Collector's note: "Taken down from Richard Gregory. . . . Will Setter sang the 'Outlandish Knight' & Gregory objected that he had neither words nor tune aright. I missed the first verse, but it did not begin with 'An Outlandish Knight,' I took it down hastily as he sang but so could only get beginning of lines, & catch words & rhymes. The above is as near as I could get it."

1. .   .   .   .
   .   .   .   .
   .   .   .   .

2. He courted her many a long winter's night
   And many a short winter's day
   And he laid in wait both early & late
   To take her sweet life away.

3. Go fetch me some of your father's gold,
   And some of your mother's fee.
   To a land we will go, far, far away
   There shalt thou be my lady.

4. She fetched some of her father's gold
   And some of her mother's fee
   And she went before to the stable door
   Where stood her white palfry.

5. She mounted with speed on her milk white steed
   And he on his iron grey,
   And away they did ride to a clear water side
   Six hours before the day.

6. Unlight, unlight, my lady bright,
   Unlight, unlight! I pray.
   Six pretty maids have I drowned here
   Thou shalt be the seventh today.

7. Take off, take off thy robe of silk
   And lay it upon a stone.
   Thy gay gay gown be all too good,
   To lie in a watery tomb.

8. Then she took off her robe of silk
   And laid it upon a stone,
   And he put his hand in her pocket
   And drew out five hundred crown.

9. Take off, take off, thy Holland smock,
   And lay it upon a stone.
   Thy Holland smock be all too fine
   To lie in a watery tomb.

10. If I must take off my Holland smock,
      Then turn away from me,
   For it ill befits that such as thee
      Should view a stark lady.

11. And never blink, but stoop on the brink
      And pick the thistles away.
   That they may not entangle my curly hair
      Nor my milk white skin may fray.

12. He never did blink, to stoop at the brink,
      And pick the thistles away.
   That they might not entangle her curly hair,
      Nor her lily-white skin might fray.

13. She gave him a push, & a hearty push,
      And the fiend knight pushed in.
   Saying Swim, o swim, thou false-hearted knight,
      Thou never the land shalt win.

14. Saying go, O go .   .   .   .   .
      O go to thine own country
   But I will abide by the clear water side
      And well am I rid of thee.

15. She mounted with speed on her milk white steed
      And she led the iron-grey,
   And away she did ride to the castle side
      Three hours before the day.

16. The parrot he sat in the kitchen window
      And the parrot he did say,
   O where have you been, my pretty fair quean,
      So early before the day.

17. Hush! question me not, thou saucy parrot,
      Hush question me not of me.
   Thy cage shall be made of the glittering gold
      With a door of ivory.

18. Her father he was not so sound asleep
      But he heard what the parrot did say.
   And he called, What waketh my pretty parrot
      So early before the day.

19. The cat was up at the kitchen window,
      And the cat he would me slay.
   So loud did I cry for help to be nigh
      To drive the cat away.

20. Well turn'd, well turn'd, my pretty parrot
      A good turn done unto me.
   Thy cage shall be made of the glittering gold
      And a door of ivory.

42. [Lady Isabel and the Elf Knight]

Creighton and Senior, 1950, p. 8(E). Sung by Mrs. Lottie Dow, Moose River, Nova Scotia.

a M/D

As I rode on a milk white steed
And she rode on the grey,
We rode till we came to her own father's cot
One hour before it was day.
We rode till we came to her own father's cot
One hour before it was day.

Light up, light up my pretty Polly,
I have three words to say.

Oh hush, oh hush my parrot dear
And tell no tales on me,
Your cage shall be made of the best of gold.

43. [Lady Isabel and the Elf Knight]

Creighton and Senior, 1950, p. 8(F). Sung by Lloyd A. Sanford, East Walton, Nova Scotia.

a M/D

Lie there, lie there, you false young man,
Lie there instead of me,
If six pretty maids you have drownded here
You shall the seventh be.

44. [Lady Isabel and the Elf Knight]

Creighton and Senior, 1950, pp. 4(B)-5. Sung by William Nelson, Kinsac, Nova Scotia.

a M/D

1. There was a lord in London Town
   He courted a lady gay,
   And all that he courted this lady for
   Was to take her sweet life away.

2. "Come give to me of your father's gold,
   Likewise your mother's fee,
   And two of the best horses in your father's stable
   For there stands thirty and three."

3. She mounted on her milk white steed
   And he the fast travelling grey,
   They rode till he came to the seashore side
   Three hours before it was day.

4. "Alight, alight my pretty Polly,
   Alight, alight," said he,
   "For six pretty maids I have drownded here
   And you the seventh shall be.

5. "Now take off your silken dress
   Likewise your golden stay,
   For I think your clothing too rich and too gay
   To rot all in the salt sea."

6. "Yes I'll take off my silken dress
   Likewise my golden stay,
   Before I do so, you false young man
   You must face yon willow tree."

7. Then he turnèd his back around
   And faced yon willow tree,
   She caught him around the middle so small
   And throwed him into the sea.

8. And as he rose and as he sank
   And as he rose said he,
   "Oh give me your hand my pretty Polly,
   My bride forever you'll be."

9. "Lie there, lie there you false young man,
   Lie there instead of me,
   For six pretty maids you've drownded here
   And the seventh one has drownded thee."

10. She lighted on her milk white steed
    And led the fast travelling grey,
    And rode till she came to her father's outside
    One hour before it was day.

11. The parrot in the garret so high
    And unto pretty Polly did say,
    "What's the matter my pretty Polly
    You're driving before it is day?"

12. "No tales, no tales, my pretty Polly,
    No tales, no tales," said she,
    "Your cage will be made of the glittering gold
    And yours of ivory.

13. "No tales, no tales, my pretty Polly,
    No tales, no tales," said she,
    "Your cage will be made of the glittering gold
    And hung on yon willow tree."

45. [Lady Isabel and the Elf Knight]

Barry MSS., I, 4 M. Sung by Agnes Conners of Antigonish, Nova Scotia, in Boston, Mass., March 8, 1912.

m I

He mounted on the milk white steed,
   And she on the turbal gray . . .

Lie there, lie there you false hearted lad,
   Lie there in place of me.
For it never was intended for a ruffian like you
   To gaze on a naked lady at sea.

For six pretty maidens you have drowned,
   And the seventh you shall be.

He floated high, he floated low . . .

46. [The Outlandish Knight]

Sharp MSS., 2777/2241-43. Sung by John Webb (72), Pillerton, April 11, 1912.

a I/M (but VII in variants)

middle so small & she huddled him in-to the stream.

1. O the outlandish knight came from the North Land
   He came a wooing to me
   He say he would take her unto the North land
   If she would marry he.

2. But fetch me some of your father's gold
   And some of your mother's fee
   And two of the best nags out of the stable
   Where there stands thirty and three.

3. Then she mounted on her milk white steed
And he on his dapple grey
They rode till they came to the sea water deep
Just three hours before it was day.

4. Pull off, pull off your rich silken gown
Deliver it up to me
For I think it looks too rich and too good
To rot all in the salt sea.

5. Pull off, pull off your pretty petticoat
Deliver it up to me
Etc.

6. If I pull off my rich silken gown
Pray turn your back to me
It is not fitting that such a ruffian as thou
Should see my naked body.

7. If I pull off my pretty petticoat, etc.

8. He turned his back towards her
To view the leaves so green
She caught he round the middle so small
And bundled him into the stream.

9. He gropped high, he gropped low
Until he came to the side
Catch hold of my hand, you pretty lady
And now I will make you my bride.

10. Lie there, lie there, you false hearted knight,
Lie there instead of me
Six pretty maidens you have drowned there
And the seventh has drownded thee.

11. Then she mounted on her milk white steed
And led the dappled grey
Until she came to her father's house
Three hours before it was day.

12. Don't prittle and prattle my pretty Polly
Thy cage shall be of the glistering gold
Although it is made of a tree.

13. Don't prittle and prattle my pretty Polly
Thy cage shall be of the glistering gold,
And the lid of the best ivory.

47. [The Outlandish Knight]

Sharp MSS., 1166/. Sung by John Wedlock, Chew Magna,
January 11, 1907.

a I

48. "The Outlandish Knight"

Sharp MSS., 371/502. Also in Sharp, *JFSS*, IV (1910),
p. 119(4). Sung by Mr. J. Squires, Holford, Somerset,
August 29, 1904.

a I

An outlandish knight came from the North Land,
     And he came a wooing of me
[He] said he would take me to the North Land,
     And there he would marry me,
     And there he would marry me
[He] said he would take me to the North Land,
     And there he would marry me.

49. [Lady Isabel and the Elf Knight]

Eddy, 1939, p. 6(A). Sung by Mrs. Charles Weeks, Canton, Ohio.

a I/M

She brought him a bag of her own father's gold,
     Likewise of her mother's own fee,
And two the best horses that stood in the stall,
     And there stood thirty and three.

She mounted on her milk-white steed,
     And he on the dappled gray,
And quickly they both rode away
     Three hours before it was day.

"Lie there, lie there, you wicked young man,
     Lie there, lie there," said she,
"For six fair maids you've drowned there,
     And I the seventh won't be."

50. "Pretty Nancy"

Barry, Eckstorm, and Smyth, 1929, pp. 16(B)-18. Sung by
Mrs. Susie Carr Young, Maine; learned in 1870. Melody
recorded by George Herzog.

Come, hear what I have to say

1. As I sat down to muse awhile,
     To think what I had done,
   To think that I had placed my mind
     When I a boy so young.

2. As I rode by a farmer's door,
     A beauty did me surprise,
   With rosy blushes on her face
     And diamonds in her eyes.

3. "Come away, come away, my pretty Nancy!
     Come hear what I have to say.
   Tonight we will ride over London Bridge,
     And married there will be.

4. "Go, get some of your father's gold,
     And some of your mother's fee,
   The two best horses in your father's barn,
     Out of the thirty-three."

5. She got some of her father's gold,
     And some of her mother's fee,
   The two best horses in her father's barn,
     Out of the thirty-three.

6. She mounted on the milk-white steed,
     He rode the bonny gray;
   They rode along by the greenwood side
     Till they came to the salt sea.

7. "Take off, take off that gay clothing;
     Take off, take off," said he;
   "For six kings' daughters I've drownèd here
     And you the seventh shall be."

8. "O, turn your back unto the oak,
     Your eyes unto the sea;
   For it is a pity a man like you
     A naked woman should see."

9. He turned his back unto the oak,
     His eyes unto the sea;
   She took him up in her arms so brave,
     And flung him into the sea.

10. "Lie there, lie there, my false lover,
      Lie there instead of me;
    If six kings' daughters you've drownèd there,
      Go keep them company."

11. She mounted on the milk-white steed,
      She led the bonny gray;
    She rode along by the greenwood side
      And got home before it was day.

12. And then upspake the pretty parrot,
      Who in his cage did lay,
    Saying, "Where have you been, my pretty Nancy,
      This long, fine summer day?"

13. "O hold your tongue, you saucy thing,
      Go tell no tales of me,
    And your cage shall be lined with eastern gold,
      With a silver lock and key."

14. And then upspake the old father,
      Who in his bed did lay,
    Saying, "What is the matter, my pretty polly,
      That you are calling so soon for day?"

15. "The cat she lay at my cage door,
      She swore she would me slay;
    And I have been calling for pretty Nancy
      To drive the cat away."

51. [The Outlandish Knight]

Sharp MSS., 1070/. Sung by William Stokes (64), Chew
Stoke, August 27, 1906.

An outlandish knight he came from the North Lands
He came a wooing of me
He said he would take me into the North Lands
And there he would marry me

52a. [The Outlandish Knight]

Sharp MSS., 679/749-52. Sung by John Vincent, Priddy,
December 21, 1905.

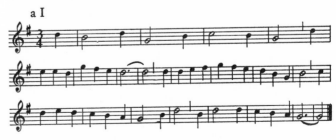

1. From the North lands there came a Northering Knight
   And he came a wooing to me.
   He said he would take me unto the North Lands
   And there for to marry me.

2. Go fetch some of your father's gold
   And some of your mother's fee
   And two of the best nags out of the stable
   Where there stands thirty and three.

3. She fetched some of her father's gold
   And some of her mother's fee
   And two of the best nags out of the stable
   Where there stands thirty and three.

4. She mounted on her middlek* white steed
   And he on the dapper (!) grey.
   They rode till they came to the sea side
   Three hours before it was day.

5. Light off, light off, thy middlek white steed
   And deliver it unto me
   For six pretty maidens have I drowned here
   And thou the seventh shall be.

6. Pull off, pull off, thy silken clothes
   And deliver it unto me;
   I think it looks too rich and gay
   To rot all in the salt sea.

7. Pull off, pull off, thy holland smock
   And deliver it unto me;
   I think it looks too rich and gay
   To rot all in the salt sea.

8. If I must pull off my holland smock
   And deliver it unto thee
   I think it's not fit that such a ruffian
   A naked woman should see.

9. He turn-ed his back towards her
   And viewed the leaves so green.
   She caught him round the middle so small
   And bundled him into the stream.

10. He crop-ped high, he crop-ped low
    Until he came to the side.
    Ketch hold of my hand, my pretty Polly,
    And I will make thee my bride.

11. Lie there, lie there, you false hearted man,
    Lie there in the place of me.
    For six pretty maids have thee drowned here
    And the seventh have drowned thee.

12. She mounted on her middlek white steed
    And ledden the dapper grey.
    She rode till she came to her own father's hall
    Two hours before it was day.

13. The parrot hung on the window so high
    Hearing what the lady did say.
    What ails thee, what ails thee, my pretty lady,
    Thou hast tarried so long away?

14. The king being up in his bedroom so high
    Hearing what the lady did say,
    What ails thee, what ails thee, my pretty Polly,
    Thou hast prattled so long before day.

15. It's no laughing matter, the parrot did say,
    But so loudly I call unto thee,
    The cat has a got in the window so high
    And I'm afraid she'll have I.

16. Well turned, well turn-ed, my pretty Polly,
    Well turn-ed, well turn-ed for me,
    Thy cage shall be made of the glittering gold
    (Although it was made of a tree?)
    And the door of the best ivory.

    * i.e., *midlk*=*milk*. The exclamation point in the next line is Sharp's.

52b. [The Outlandish Knight]

Sharp MSS., 942/. Sung by John Vincent (72), Priddy,
April 25, 1906.

a I

53. [The Outlandish Knight]

Burne, 1883, p. 652; text, pp. 549-50. Sung by Jane Butler,
Edgmond, Shropshire, 1870-80.

a I (inflected IV)

1. [An outlandish knight came from the north lands,]
   A knight from the north countree,
   [He told me he'd take me unto the north lands,
   And there he would marry me.

2. 'Come fetch me some of your father's gold,
                        etc., *as in next verse*]

3. She fetched him some of her father's gold,
   And some of her mother's fee,
   And two of the best nags out of the stable,
   Where they stood thirty and three.

4. She mounted her on the milk-white steed,
    And he on the dapple-grey,
    They rode until they came unto the sea-side
    Three hours before it was day.

5. 'Light off, light off, thy milk-white steed,
    And deliver it unto me;
    Six pretty maidens I've drownded here,
    And thou the seventh shalt be!'

6. 'Doff off, doff off, thy silken gown,
    And deliver it unto me;
    Methinks it looks too rich and too gay,
    All for to rot in the salt sea.

7. 'Doff off, doff off, thy silken stays,
    And deliver them unto me;
    Methinks they look too rich and too gay,
    All for to rot in the salt sea.'

8. 'Doff off, doff off, thy holland smock,
    And deliver it unto me;
    Methinks it looks too rich and too gay,
    All for to rot in the salt sea.'

9. 'If I must doff off my holland smock,
    Pray turn thy back unto me;
    For it is not fitting that such a ruffian
    A naked woman should see.'

10. He turned his back to-wards her,
    And viewed the leaves so green,
    She took him round the middle so small,
    And tumbled him into the stream.

11. He droppéd high, he droppéd low,
    Until he came to the side,
    'Lay hold of my hand, my pretty Pollee,
    And I will make thee my bride.'

12. 'Lie there, lie there, thou false-hearted man!
    Lie there instead of me!
    For six pretty maidens hast thou drownded here,
    And the seventh has drownded thee.'

13. She mounted her on her milk-white steed,
    And led the dapple-grey;
    She rode till she came to her father's hall
    An hour before it was day.

14. O then out spoke the pretty parrot,
    'Thou hast tarried so long away,
    O I greatly fear, my pretty Pollee,
    Some ruffian has led thee astray!'

15. 'Hush, hush! hush, hush! my pretty parrot,
    Don't prittle nor prattle nor tell no tittles of me,
    Thy cage shall be made of the glittering gold,
    And the door of the best ivoree.'

16. [The king being in the chamber so high,
    And hearing the parrot, did say,]
    'O what is the matter, my pretty parrot,
    That you prattle so long before day?'

17. ['It's no laughing matter,' the parrot did say,
    That so loudly I call*ed* unto thee,]
    For the cat was up in the window so high,
    And I fear*ed* she *would* have me.'

18. 'Well turnéd, well turnéd, my pretty parrot!
    Well turnéd, well turnéd for me;
    Thy cage shall be made of the glittering gold,
    And the door of the best ivoree.'

54. [The Outlandish Knight]

Sharp MSS., 902/. Sung by John Trump, North Petherton, April 18, 1906.

a I—M (inflected VII)

In Sharp's MS. the triplets are written, in the penultimate bars of the tune proper—but not in the variants—as eighths instead of quarter-notes. Doubtless this was inadvertent.

There was a knight a Baron knight
A knight of high degree
This knight he came from the North Land
He came a courting me.

55. [Lady Isabel and the Elf Knight]

Sharp MSS., 3645/2703-4. Also in Sharp and Karpeles, 1932, I, p. 13(J). Sung by Mrs. Alice Sloan, Barbourville, Ky., May 7, 1917.

Tonic G: a I (final on V)

1. You promised to take me to the sea-shore
    And there to marry me,
    You promised to take me to the sea-shore
    And there to marry me.*

2. Go steal a bag of your father's gold,
   Perhaps your mother's own fee,
   Two of the finest horses stands in the stall
   For there stands thirty and three.

3. She stole a bag of her father's gold,
   Perhaps her mother's own fee,
   Two of the finest horses stood in the stall
   For there stands thirty and three.

4. They mounted on their pony, pony black,
   She led the dappled grey,
   She rode alone all on the sea shore
   Two hours before it was day.

5. Just mount, just mount (dismount?), my
                              pretty fair maid,
   Just mount, just mount, cried he,
   For six pretty maids I have drowned here
   And the seventh one you must be.

6. Pull off, pull off, your white silk robe,
   And 'liver it up to me.
   It is too fine and costly
   To lie and rot in the sea.

7. If I had to pull off my silk white robe
   And 'liver it up to thee,
   Just turn your eyes to view the blue sky
   And turn your back on me.

8. He turned his eyes to view the blue sky,
   And turned his back on her.
   She clenched him in the waist,
   And splunged him into the sea.

9. O help, O help, you fair pretty maid,
   O help, (O help), cried he.
   If I ever reach the sea-shore,
   Your wedding bride I'll be.

10. Lie there, lie there, false-hearted man,
    Lie there, cried she.
    Six pretty fair maids you have drowned here
    And the seventh one you shall be.

11. She mounted on the pony, pony black
    And led the dappled grey,
    She rode alone all on the sea-shore
    Two hours before it was day.

12. O hold your tongue, you pretty little bird,
    O hold your tongue, cried she,
    Your cage shall be made of the purest gold
    And swung in a willow tree.

* Line repeated in Sharp and Karpeles, 1932, as the tune requires.

56. [The Outlandish Knight]

Sharp MSS., 749/. Sung by Mrs. Glover, Huish, December 5, 1906.

D tonic: a M (final on II)

In Sharp's MS. the last note of the first phrase is a quarter but the next two are eighth-notes.

Hold your tongue my pretty Polly
And tell no tales of me
Your cage shall be made of the glittering gold
And the bars of the best ivory*
And the bars of the best ivory

* Sharp's note: "Ivory should be I'vry."

57. "The Castle by the Sea"

Flanders and Olney, 1953, pp. 109-11. Sung by Mrs. Lena Bourne Fish, East Jaffrey, N.H., May 9, 1940; from family tradition. From *Ballads Migrant in New England*, edited by Helen Hartness Flanders and Marguerite Olney; copyright 1953 by Helen Hartness Flanders.

a I/Ly, ending on II

1. "Arise, O arise, my lady fair,
   For you my bride shall be,
   And we will dwell in a sylvan bower,
   In my castle by the sea.

2. "Then bring along your marriage fee,
   Which you can claim today,
   And also take your swiftest steed,
   The milkwhite and the gray."

3. The lady mounted her milkwhite steed;
   He rode the turban gray,
   They took the path by the wild seashore,
   Or so I've heard them say.

4. As she saw the wall of the castle high,
   They looked so bleak and cold;
   She wished she'd remained in Boston town,
   With her ten thousand pounds in gold.

5. He halted by the wild seashore,
   Saying, "My bride you shall never be,
   For six fair maidens I've drown-ed here;
   The seventh you shall be.

6. "Take off, take off your scarlet robes,
    And lay them down by me;
    They are too fine and too costly
    To rot in the briny sea."

7. "Then turn your face to the water side,
    And your back to yonder tree;
    For it is a disgrace to any man,
    An unclothed woman to see."

8. He turned his face to the waterside,
    And his back to the lofty tree;
    She took him in her arms so bold,
    And flung him into the sea.

9. "Lie there, lie there, you false young man,
    And drown in place of me,
    If six fair maidens you've drown-ed here,
    Go keep them company."

10. She then did mount her milkwhite steed,
    And led the turban gray,
    And rode till she came to Boston town,
    Two hours before it was day.

58. [The Outlandish Knight]

Baring-Gould MSS., CXIV(4); text, (B). Sung by J. Masters (86), Bradstone, June 1891. Collected by H. Fleetwood Sheppard.

On G: a I, ending on *VI*

1. There was a rich nobleman I've heard tell,
    And he came a courting of me.
    And he said, We will ride, & e'er we return
    Then married we will be.

2. She went into her father's stable
    She was gay as gay might be,
    And she mounted upon her milkwhite steed,
    And the dapple grey rode he.

3. Jump off! Jump off! I pray, he said
    And deliver your horse to me,
    Six pretty maids have I drowned here,
    And the seventh thou shalt be.

4. Pull off, pull off, thy silken smock
    And thy silken gown, said he.
    Six pretty maids have I stripped here,
    And the seventh thou shalt be.

5. Take up thy sickle & cut the nettle,
    That grows on the water brim,

For fear it should stick in my gay gold locks,
    And should sting my milkwhite skin.

6. He took the sickle & cut the nettle
    That grew on the water brim,
    And she gave him a most cunning push,
    And she speedily pushed him in.

7. O help! O help! my fair pretty maid,
    And today I will marry thee
    Lie there, lie there thou falsehearted knave,
    Lie there & drown, said she.

8. Lie there, lie there! thou false hearted knave,
    Lie there & drown, said she
    Six pretty maids hast thou drowned here,
    And the seventh drowneth thee.

9. Every leaf was oppress'd(?) & she heard no sound
    Nor to lark nor thrush gave heed.
    Nor the throstle did call in the hold of the tree
    As she mounted her milk white steed.

10. And she mounted her on her milk-white steed
    And she led the dapple grey,
    And she rode till she came to her father's hall
    Just at the break of day.

11. O where have you been my fair pretty quean
    The parrot he did say.
    That you have been out all in the night
    And return before the day.

12. O hush! & O hush! my pretty parrot,
    O say not a word, said she.
    Thy cage it shall be of the beaten gold,
    That was of the timbern tree.

13. Then up & spake her father dear,
    From the bed where on he lay,
    O what is the matter with my parrot
    That he chatters before the day.

14. The cat came to my own cage door,
    And threatenèd to kill me.
    And I called aloud for help to come,
    To come & deliver me.

15. Well turn'd, well turn'd my pretty parrot
    Well turn'd, well turn'd said she.
    Thy cage shall be made of shining gold,
    That was of the timbern tree.

59. "The King's Daughter Fair"

Hubbard and Robertson, *JAF*, LXIV (1951), pp. 39-40.
Sung by Mrs. Lottie Marsh Heed, Ogden, Utah; learned about 1883 from her mother, Jane Marsh, in Willard.

m I

1. There was a noble English lad,
    Who courted a King's daughter fair.
    He promised to take her to the north countree,
    And they would be married there.

2. "Now you must get some of your father's gold
And some of your mother's fee
And two of the finest horses in these stables
Where there are thirty and three."

3. She mounted on her milk-white steed;
He rode the dappled gray.
They rode till they came to the seaside
Two hours before it was day.

4. "Flight off, flight off from your milk-white steed,
Flight off, flight off, I say,
For six pretty fair maids I've drowned here
And the seventh one you shall be."

5. "Now you must take off this silken dress
And give it unto me,
For I think it looks too rich and too rare
To rot in the salty sea."

6. "Well, if I must take off this silken dress,
You must turn your back unto me,
For I don't think it fit for a roughen* like thee
An undressed lady to see."

7. He wheeled himself around about
While bitterly she did weep.
She caught him by the coat collar
And plunged him into the deep.

8. "Take hold, take hold of my finger, love,
Take hold with your lily-white hand,
And I will make you my own true love
And the fairest in the land."

9. "Lie there, lie there, lie there," said she,
"Lie there instead of me,
For if six pretty, fair maids you've drowned here,
The seventh one drownded thee."

10. She mounted on her milk-white steed,
She led the dappled gray.
She rode till she came to her father's house;
The chickens were crowing for day.

11. The parrot rose up in the garret so high
And unto Polly did say,
"Where have you been, my pretty Polly?
You tarry so long before day."

12. "O hush, oh hush, oh hush," said she,
"Don't you tell no tales on me,
And your cage shall be lined with a glittering gold
And hang in the green willow tree."

13. The king rose up in the castle so high
And unto the parrot did say,
"Oh what is the matter, my pretty parrot?
You prattle so long before day."

14. "Nothing's the matter with me, kind sir,
Nothing's the matter, I say,
But there were two white kittens that bothered me so
I called Polly to drive them away."

15. "Well done, well done, well done," said she,
"Well done, well done," said she,
"Now your cage shall be lined with the glittering gold
And hang in the green willow tree."

* i.e., ruffian

60. "Pretty Polly"

Barry, *BFSSNE*, No. 1 (1930), pp. 3-4. Sung by Mrs. Anna W. Lougee, Thornton, N.H., July 16, 1908.

G tonic: m I/M (–VI) (final on III)

1. He mounted on his milk white steed,
And she the turban gray,
And they rode till they came to the river side,
Two hours before it was day.

2. "Light off, light off, my pretty Polly,
And stand by the side of me;
For six pretty maidens I have drownded here,
And you the seventh shall be."

3. "Lie off, lie off, those costly robes,
And lay them down by me;
For they're too rich and costly far,
To rot in this salt sea."

4. He turned him round about to take
A look at the Liberty-tree;
She caught him in her arms so bold,
And threw him into the sea.

5. "Lie there, lie there, you false young man,
Lie there instead of me;
For if six pretty maidens you've drownded here,
Go, keep them company!"

6. She mounted on the milk white steed,
And led the turban gray;
And she rode till she came to her father's house,
Two hours before it was day.

7. Then up spoke her pretty parrot,
Who in his cage did lay;

Saying: "Where have you been, my pretty Polly,
So long before it is day?"

8. "Oh, hold your tongue, you naughty parrot,
And tell no tales of me;
Your cage shall be made of the best of gold,
With a silver lock and key."

9. Then up spoke her father dear,
Who in his bed did lay;
Saying: "What is the matter, my pretty parrot,
So long before it is day?"

10. "The old cat came to my cage door,
And said that she should stay,
And I was calling to pretty Polly,
To drive the old cat away."

61. "Pretty Polly"

Mackenzie, 1928, p. 391; text, pp. 7-8. Sung by Mrs. Levi Langille, Pictou County, Nova Scotia.

a I (final on II)

This variant seems to slip from its major mooring at the mid-cadence and pass into the Dorian mode. Normally, the second half of the tune would have run consistently a step lower; but the Dorian instinct was too strong.

1. There was a lord in Ambertown
Courted a lady fair,
And all he wanted of this pretty fair maid
Was to take her life away.

2. "Go get me some of your father's gold
And some of your mother's fees,
And two of the best horses in your father's stall
Where there stands thirty and three."

3. So she mounted on her steed white milk,
And he on his dappling grey,
And they rode forward to the sea
Two hours before it was day.

4. "Light off, light off thy steed white milk,
And deliver it unto me,
For six pretty maids I have drownded here,
And the seventh one thou shalt be."

5. "Take off, take off thy bonny silk plaid,
And deliver it unto me.
Methinks they are too rich and gay
To rot in the salt salt sea."

6. "If I must take off my bonny silk plaid,
Likewise my golden stays,
You must turn your back around to me
And face yon willow tree."

7. He turned himself around about
To face yon willow tree;
She grasped him by the middle so small,
And she tumbled him into the sea.

8. So he rolléd high and he rolléd low
Till he rolléd to the seaside.
"Stretch forth your hand, my pretty Polly,
And I'll make you my bride."

9. "Lie there, lie there, you false-hearted man,
Lie there instead of me,
For six pretty maids thou has drownded here,
But the seventh hath drownded thee!"

10. She mounted on her steed white milk,
And she led her dappling grey,
And she rode forward to her father's door
An hour before it was day.

11. The old man he, it's being awoke,
And heard all that was said.
"What were you prittling and prattling, my
                                    pretty Polly,
And keeping me awake all night long?"

12. "The old cat had got up to my littock so high,
And I was afraid she was going to eat me,
And I was calling for pretty Polly
To go drive the old cat away."

13. "Don't prittle, don't prattle, my pretty Polly,
Nor tell any tales on me.
Your cage shall be made of the glittering gold
Instead of the greenwood tree."

62. "Mary Goldan"

Barry, *JAF*, XXII (1909), pp. 374-75. Sung by Mrs. Sarah Carson, Boston, Mass., November 30, 1907; learned from her mother, County Tyrone, Ireland.

a π³ (or if on C, a π¹, final on II)

The characteristic final cadence is found also in both English **and** Scottish tradition. Cf. "The Yeoman of Kent" (D'Urfey, 1719, **I,** p. 126), "Queen of Elfan's Nourice" (*post*, Child 40); and Blai**kie** MS., NL Scot., MS. 1578, No. 33 ("There came a maid") and No. 75 ("John the little Scot" [Child 99]).

1. It's false Sir John's a courting gone,
. . . .
. . . .
. . . .

2. "Take off, take off that suit of Holland,
   That suit of Holland so fine,
For it is too rich and too costly,
   To rot in this salt sea brine!"

3. "It's look you round, my false Sir John,
   To view the green leaves on the tree,"
And when he turned him round to view,
   She threw him right into the sea!

4. . . . .

   "Of all the promises ever I made,
      I'll double them every one!"

5. ". . . . .

   It's seven King's daughters you have drowned here,
      And you the eighth shall be."

6. . . . .

   And when she came to her father's gate,
      The clock had just struck one.

7. "It's hold your tongue, my pretty parrot,
   And do not discover on me,
And your cage shall be made of the beaten gold,
   Instead of the chestnut-tree!"

8. Then up and speaks her old father,
   In the chamber where he lay,
"What ails you, what ails you, my pretty parrot,
   You prattle so long before day?"

9. "The cats they have come to devour me,
   And tear me clean away,
And I was calling to Mary Goldan
   To drive those cats away!"

10. Then he speaks, her father,
    In the chamber where he lay,
"Oh, didn't I tell you, Mary Goldan,
   You'd rue your going away!"

63. [The Outlandish Knight]

Kidson, 1891, p. 27. Sung in the North Riding, Yorkshire.

a I—M (inflected VII)

Kidson's words are nearly identical, stanza for stanza, with those given by Bruce and Stokoe (*ante*, no. 29). Cf. this tune with the Davis copy R (*ante*, no. 19).

64. "Pretty Polly"

Sandburg, 1927, pp. 60-61. From the collection of R. W. Gordon.

a M

The barring of the last three measures has been altered by the present editor from regular 6/8 time.

1. "Go get me some of your father's gold
   And some of your mother's too,
And two of the finest horses he has in his stable,
   For he has ten and thirty and two."

2. She got him some of her father's gold,
   And some of her mother's too,
And two of the finest horses he had in his stable,
   For he had ten and thirty and two.

3. Then she jumped on the noble brown,
   And he on the dappled gray,
And they rode till they came to the side of the sea,
   Two long hours before it was day.

4. "Let me help you down, my Pretty Polly;
   Let me help you down," said he.
"For it's six kings' daughters I have drowned here,
   And the seventh you shall be."

5. "Now strip yourself, my Pretty Polly;
   Now strip yourself," said he;
"Your clothing is too fine and over-costly
   To rot in the sand of the sea."

6. "You turn your back to the leaves of the trees,
   And your face to the sands of the sea;
'Tis a pity such a false-hearted man as you
   A naked woman should see!"

7. He turned his back to the leaves of the trees,
   And his face to the sand of the sea;
And with all the strength that Pretty Polly had
   She pushed him into the sea.

8. "Come, lend me your hand, my Pretty Polly;
   Come, lend me your hand," said he,
"And I will be your waiting-boy,
   And will wait upon you night and day."

9. "Lie there, lie there, you false-hearted man!
   Lie there, lie there," said she;
"As six kings' daughters you've drowned here,
   Then the seventh you shall be!"

10. Then she jumped on the noble brown,
    And led the dappled gray,
    And rode till she came to her father's hall,
    Two long hours before it was day.

11. Then up bespoke her Poll Parrot,
    Sitting in his cage so gay,
    "Why do you travel, my Pretty Polly,
    So long before it is day?"

12. Then up bespoke her old father,
    Lying in his room so gay,
    "Why do you chatter, my pretty parrot,
    So long before it is day?"

13. "The cat was around and about my cage,
    And I could not get it away
    So I called unto Miss Pretty Polly
    To drive the cat away."

14. "Well turned, well turned, my pretty parrot,
    Well turned, well turned for me;
    Thy cage shall be made of handbeaten gold,
    Thy door of the finest ivory."

65. [The Outlandish Knight]

Sharp MSS., 983/. Sung by Elizabeth Coles (76), Nether
Stowey, August 10, 1906.

a D (inflected III)

66. "The Highway Robber"

Vaughan Williams, *JFSS*, IV (1910), p. 122(9). Sung by
Mr. W. Colcombe, Weobley, Herefordshire, 1909.

a D

The Æolian variant was sung by the same singer to the words of
"There is an Alehouse."

(O) it's of a noble gentleman, a highwayman was he,
In courting of a lady fair he gained her company.

67. [Lady Isabel and the Elf Knight]

Sharp MSS., 3167/2301-2. Also in Campbell and Sharp,
1917, p. 3(A). Sung by Elizabeth Coit, Amherst, Mass.,
July 1916; learned from her aunt in South Byfield, Mass.

a Æ/D

1. O bring down some of your father's gold
   And more of your mother's money
   And two of the best horses in your father's stable
   That daily are thirty-three.

2. She brought down some of her father's gold
   And more of her mother's money
   And two of the best horses in her father's stable
   That daily are thirty-three.

3. He rode on the milk-white steed
   And she rode on the bay
   And together they came to the North of Scotland
   Three hours before it was day.

4. Light down, light down, my pretty colleen,
   I've something here to tell thee.
   Six kings' daughters lie drowned here
   And thou the seventh shall be.

5. O turn your back to the billowy waves,
   Your face to the leaves of the tree,
   For it ill beseems an outlandish knight
   Should view a stark lady.

6. He turned his back to the billowy waves,
   His face to the leaves of the tree,
   When quickly she threw both her arms round his neck
   And tossed him into the sea.

7. Lie there, lie there, thou false young man,
   Lie there instead of me.
   You promised to take me to the North of Scotland,
   And there you would marry me.

8. O give me hold of your little finger
   And hold of your lily white hand,
   And I'll make you the mistress* of all my estates
   And the ruler of all my land.

9. No, I won't give you hold of my little finger,
   Nor hold of my lily white hand,
   And I won't be the mistress of all your estates
   And the ruler of all your land.

10. She rode on the milk white steed,
    And by her went the bay,
    And together they came to her father's castle
    Three hours before it was day.

11. 'Twas then thet parrot spoke
From his cage upon the wall:
O what is the matter, my pretty colleen,
Why did you not answer my call?

12. O hush, O hush, my pretty parrot,
Don't tell any tales upon me,
And your cage shall be of the beaten gold
And your perch of the almond tree.

13. 'Twas then her father spoke
From the chamber where he lay:
O what is the matter my pretty parrot
That you're calling so long before day.

14. O these rats, these rats are at my cage door;
They're trying to take me away,
So I am just calling my pretty colleen
To drive these rats away.

* 1917: "ruler"
† 1917 adds "pretty."

68. "Oh, Get Me Some of Your Father's Gold"

Kidson Collection, *JFSS*, I (1904), p. 246. From Miss Carr
Moseley; sung by an old lady, born c. 1800, who learned it
from her mother.

a I

Oh, get me some of your father's gold
And some of your mother's clothes,
And into some foreign country we'll go
And married we will be.

69. [The Outlandish Knight]

Sharp MSS., 1196/. Sung by Ben Leader (75), Badgworth,
January 17, 1907.

Tonic G: p I/Ly, ending on *VI*

70. [The Outlandish Knight]

Sharp MSS., 2476/. Sung by Mark Heyhes, Harrington,
April 28, 1910.

p I

71. [The Outlandish Knight]

Sharp MSS., 519/. Sung by Lucy White, Hambridge, August 4, 1905.

p I

72. [The Outlandish Knight]

Sharp MSS., 931/. Sung by Mrs. William Chapman (40),
Ubley, April 23, 1906.

p I

O Hush O Hush my pretty polly
And tell no tales on me
For your cage shall be made of the very best of gold
And your perch of the best ivor[y]

73. [Lady Isabel and the Elf Knight]

Greenleaf and Mansfield, 1933, pp. 3-4. Sung by Mrs. Minnie Payne, Green Point, Newfoundland, 1920.

p I

This variant, both text and tune, appears to be crossed with "The Bailiff's Daughter of Islington" (Child 105). Cf. the Cornish variant published in *JFSS*, IV (1910), p. 116 (*post*, #90). But cf. also the English copy of "Edward" (Child 13) published by Peter Kennedy in *JEFDSS*, VII (1952), p. 38.

1. There was a youth, a well-beloved youth,
    He was a squire's son,
    He courted an innkeeper's daughter,
    . . . .

2. He courted her a long winter's night,
    And many a long summer's day,
    And all he courted his fair lady for
    Was to take her sweet life away.

3. "Now get some of your father's gold," said he,
    "And some of your mother's fee,
    And we will go to a far counteree,
    And married we will be."

4. So she took some of her father's gold,
    And some of her mother's fee,
    And walked till she came to her father's stable door,
    Where lay horses thirty and three.

5. She mounted on a lily-white steed,
    And he on a silvery gray,
    And she rode till they came to a clear riverside
    Six hours before it was day.

6. "Now you pull off your clothes," he said,
    "And prepare for your wat'ry tomb,
    For nine king's daughters I have drownded here,
    And the tenth one you shall be."

7. "Turn, O turn, you false-hearted youth,
    Come turn your back unto me!
    I don't think such a villain as you
    A naked woman should see."

8. He turned himself quite round about;
    In bitter grief she did weep,
    And with all of the strength this fair lady had
    She pushed him into the deep.

9. "O swim, O swim, you false-hearted youth!
    I think you've got your doom;
    For I don't think your clothes too costly
    For to lie in a watery tomb."

10. She mounted on her lily-white steed,
    And led his silvery gray,
    And she got back to her father's stable door
    Three hours before it was day.

11. Her father been so hazily awoke,
    Which caused him to say,

"What makes you prattle, my pretty parrot dear,
    So long before it is day?"

12. "There was two cats came at my cage-door,
    They came for to carry me away,
    And I called upon my young misteress
    To drive those cats away."

13. "Hold your tongue, my pretty parrot dear,
    Now hold your tongue," said she,
    "Your cage shall be made of the yellow beaten gold,
    And shall hang on a willow tree."

74. [Lady Isabel and the Elf Knight]

Creighton and Senior, 1950, pp. 2(A)-3. Sung by Dennis Smith, Chezzetcook, Nova Scotia.

p I

Crossed in text and tune with "The Bailiff's Daughter" (105).

1. 'Twas of a youth and a well bred youth,
    He being a squire's son,
    And he went a-courting an innkeeper's daughter,
    Belonged to North Cumberland.

2. He courted a part of a summer's season
    And part of a winter courted he,
    And all that he courted this fair lady for
    Was to take her sweet life away.

3. "Oh give me half of your father's fee
    And a part of your mother's gold,
    And we will away to some foreign counteree
    And married we will be."

4. Then she went down to her father's stable door
    There stood horses thirty-three,
    Then she mounted a milk white steed
    And him on a silvery grey.

5. She mounted on her milk white steed
    And he rode the fast travelling grey,
    Then they rode till they came to a riverside
    Three hours before it was day.

6. "Alight alight my pretty fair maid,
    Alight alight," cried he,
    "For six pretty maids I have drownded here
    And the seventh you shall be.

7. "Strip off, strip off your silken clothes
    And lie them on the green,
    For I do think your clothing is too gay
    For to lie in that watery stream."

8. "If I strip off my silken clothes
And lie them on the green,
Then I do think it is a great shame
For a naked woman to be seen."

9. Then this young woman turned her back to him
And so bitterlee did weep,
And all the strength that this fair lady had
She shoved him into the brink.

10. "O sink or swim you false hearted man,
I think you have got your doom,
But I do think that your clothing is too gay
For to sink in that watery tomb."

11. Oh then she mounted her milk white steed
And led the silvery grey,
She rode till she came to her father's house
Three hours before it was day.

12. The parrot being up in the window so high,
"Oh where have you been?" cried he,
"I've been away to Scotland's bridge,
Young Henry he lies under the sea.

13. "Don't prittle, don't prattle my pretty Polly dear
And tell no tales on me,
And your cage shall be made of the very best of gold
And hung on an ivory tree."

75. "If I take off my silken stay"

Treat, *JAF*, LII (1939), pp. 20-21. Sung by Pearl Jacobs Borusky, Bryant, Wisc., July 13, 1938; learned in Carter County, Kentucky.

a π¹, ending on VIII

"If I take off my silken stay
And deliver it unto thee,

. . . . . .

A naked woman to see."

. . . .

She grabbed him round the middle so small
And tumbled him into the sea.

"Lie there, lie there, lie there, young man!
Lie there, lie there!" said she.
"If six fair ladies you have drownded here,
The seventh one has drownded thee."

She jumped upon her milk-white steed
And led the dappled-gray,

And came unto her father's house
Three hours before it was day.

"O, where have you been, my pretty fair maid?
O, where have you been, I pray?
I was afraid some ruffian had stold you, my dear,
You tarried so long away."

76. "Pretty Polly"

Owens, 1950, pp. 35-36. Sung by Mrs. Ben Dryden, Sandy Creek, Texas [1941].

p π⁴ (or, if on B♭, a π¹, ending on VI)

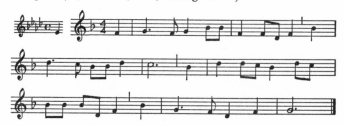

1. "Go bring me some of your father's gold
And bring me your mother's fee.
Oh, come, oh, come my Pretty Polly
And go along with me.

2. "I'll take you by the seashore side,
And there I'll marry thee."
She mounted on her milk white horse
And to some dark she rode.

3. She rode till she came to the salt water sea,
Where there's no one that she could see;
She rode till she came to the salt water sea,
Where there's no one that she could see.

4. "Get down, get down, my Pretty Polly,
And rein your horse to a tree,
For I have killed six of the old Virginny girls
And the seventh one you shall be.

5. "Get down, get down, my Pretty Polly,
And rein your horse to a tree;
Pull off them rings, pull off them pearls,
And lay them on my knee;

6. "For they are too rich and they are too gay
For to lie in the salt water sea;
For they are too rich and they are too gay
For to lie in the salt water sea."

7. "Oh, turn your back and place your eyes
Along the juniper tree;
Oh, turn your back and place your eyes
Along the juniper tree."

8. She pushed him into the salt water sea,
Where there's no one that he could see;
She pushed him into the salt water sea,
Where there's no one that he could see.

9. "Reach down your hand, Pretty Polly, I pray,
   Reach down your hand to me;
   I'll carry you back to your own father's house
   Two long hours 'fore it came day."

10. "Oh, hush, oh, hush, you grand rascal,
    And say no more to me,
    For it's I shall go to my own father's house
    Two long hours 'fore it came day."

11. "Where have you been, my Pretty Polly,
    Where have you been, I pray,
    Where have you been, my Pretty Polly,
    This long summer day."

12. "Oh, hush, oh, hush, my pretty parent,
    And tell no tales on me,
    For your house shall be lined with the finest gold,
    And your doors with ivory."

13. "For I have been to the salt water sea,
    Where there's no one that I can see;
    For that is six of the old Virginny girls
    And the seventh one he shall be."

77. "Pretty Polly"

Morris, 1950, pp. 239-41. Sung by Mrs. W. B. Thornton,
West Palm Beach, Fla.; learned from Mr. J. Allison, Live
Oak, who learned it in the Suwannee River region long ago.

p I/M (–VI)

1. "O rise you up, my pretty Polly,
   And go along with me;
   We'll go away to some broad waters
   Some hours before it comes day."

2. "Go rob your father of his gold,
   Likewise your mother's fees,
   And take two horses out of the stable,
   Where there stand thirty and three."

3. She bounced upon the milk-white steed,
   And he the dapple-gray;
   And they stole away to some broad waters,
   Some hours before it came day.

4. "O, light you down, my pretty Polly,
   O, light you down," said he,
   "This year I've drowned six king's daughters,
   The seventh one you shall be.

5. "Pull off, pull off, that fine silk gown,
   And put it into my hand;

It is too costly and too fine
To rot in the salt sea sand."

6. He turned his back along the sea,
   And then turned to the tree.
   She picked him up in her strong arms
   And throwed him into the sea.

7. "O, hold my hand, my pretty Polly,
   O, hold my hand," said he;
   "And every promise that I have made
   I'll double it thirty times three."

8. "Lie there, lie there, you false-hearted villain,
   Lie there, lie there," said she;
   "For there you have drowned six king's daughters,
   The seventh one you shall be."

9. She bounced upon the milk-white steed
   And led the dapple-gray;
   She rode home to her father's bars
   Two hours before it came day.

10. She put away her father's gold,
    Likewise her mother's fees;
    She put the two horses into the stable,
    Where there stood thirty and three.

11. Up spake, up spake, the pretty parrot,
    And to Miss Polly said,
    "O, what is the matter, my pretty Polly,
    You stir before it comes day?"

12. "O, hold your tongue, my pretty parrot,
    "O, hold your tongue," said she:
    "Your cage shall be made with the gilded gold,
    Instead of the bare oak tree."

13. Up spake, up spake, the old, old man,
    And to the parrot said,
    "O, what is the matter, my pretty parrot,
    You talk before it comes day?"

14. "There's a cat that comes to my cage door,
    To wrestle awhile with me;
    I called to my pretty Polly,
    To drive the cat away."

78. [Lady Isabel and the Elf Knight]

Barry, *JAF*, XXIV (1911), pp. 333-34. Sung by Elizabeth
A. Smith, of Boston, Mass., a native of County Down, Ireland, March 14, 1911.

a I/Ly

Barry notes that the tune was also sung in 3/4 time. The last
phrase suggests "Believe me if all those endearing young charms."

She cast him about the middle so small,
    She threw him into the salt, salt sea.

She mounted on her milk-white steed,
    And led the bonny gray,
And she reached her father's lofty tower,
    Three hours before it was day.

"Oh, where have you been, pretty Polly,
    So long before it was day?"

"Oh, hold your tongue, you prattling bird,
    And tell no tales on me,
And your cage shall be of the beaten gold,
    Instead of the ivory!"

79. [The Outlandish Knight]

Broadwood, *JFSS*, IV (1910), p. 118. Sung by an old woman, St. Stephen's, Hertfordshire, c. 1895.

a I

"Don't prittle, don't prattle, my pretty Polly,
    Nor tell no tales of me,
Your cage shall be made of the glittering gold,
    And your perch of the best ivory."

80. [The Outlandish Knight]

Sharp MSS., 1811/. Sung by George Say, Axbridge, August 28, 1908.

a I/M

Lie there lie there you false hearted man
Lie there instead of me
For its six pretty maidens you have drowned
And the seventh have drownded thee.

81. (Unnamed)

Barry, Eckstorm, and Smyth, 1929, pp. 22(E)-23. Sung by Mrs. Sarah Robinson Black, Southwest Harbor, Maine, September 1928. Melody recorded by George Herzog.

p Æ (inflected VI)

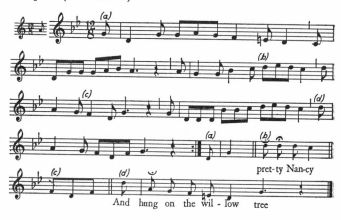

And hung on the wil-low tree

"Go get me some of your mother's gold,
    Some of your father's fee,
And we will ride side by side,

She mounted on her milk-white steed,
    And led the dapple gray,
When she arrived at her father's house
    Three hours before it was day.

The parrot he began to talk
    And unto her did say:
"O Nancy, O Nancy, where have you been
    All on this long summer's day?"

"O parrot, O parrot, hold your tongue,
    Don't tell no tales of me,
Your cage shall be covered all over with gold,
    And hung on the willow tree."

The old folks heard the parrot talk
    And unto him did say:
"O parrot, O parrot, what makes you talk
    So long before it is day?"

"The old cat stands at my cage door
    And threatens [me to slay]*
I'm only calling the pretty Nancy
    To drive the pussy away."

* Sung, "my cage door."

82. (Unnamed)

Blaikie MS., No. 45, p. 16.

p Æ/D (or a Æ/D, ending on VIII)

This variant should be compared with the R. A. Smith copy which follows.

83. [May Colvin]

Smith [1820-24], III, p. 92. Also in Eyre-Todd, *Ancient Scots Ballads*, n.d., p. 90; and Maver, 1866, No. 472, p. 236 (with one alteration at the beginning of the last phrase).

p Æ/D (or a Æ/D, ending on VIII)

The tune appears in *The Scots Musical Museum* with a version of "Cowdenknowes" (Child 217) called "Bonnie May" (No. 110). It is also virtually the same as "The Bonnie Mermaid" in Motherwell, 1827, App'x p. xxx, as Barry has observed in a MS. note. The tune is given by G. P. Jackson, *Spiritual Folk Songs of Early America*, 1937, p. 100, as from *Missouri Harmony*, 1820, with a text attributed to Isaac Watts, and with half a dozen other references, of which the most interesting is that to a copy of "Little Musgrave" (Child 81) collected by Sharp (ed. 1932, I, p. 182[P]; MSS., 4171/), a tune in the major. Smith's text is apparently from David Herd, 1776, I, 93-95, omitting the last five stanzas.

1. O! false Sir John a wooing came
   To a maid of beauty rare;
   May Colvin was this Lady's name,
   Her Father's only heir.

2. He woo'd her butt, he woo'd her ben,
   He woo'd her in the ha',
   Untill he got this Lady's consent
   To mount, and to ride awa.

3. He went down to her Father's bower,
   Where a' the steeds did stand,
   And he's tane ane o' the best steeds
   That was in her Father's hand.

4. And he's got on, and she's got on,
   And fast as they could flee,
   Untill they came to a lonesome part,
   A rock by the side of the sea.

5. "Loup aff the steed," says false Sir John;
   "Your bridal here you see;
   For I have drowned seven young Ladies,
   The eight ane you shall be.

6. "Cast aff, cast aff, my May Colvin,
   All, and your silken gown;
   For 'tis o'er good, and o'er costly,
   To rot in the salt sea foam.

7. "Cast aff, cast aff, my May Colvin,
   All, and your embroidered shune;
   For they are o'er good, and o'er costly,
   To rot in the salt sea foam."

8. 'O, turn ye about, O false Sir John,
   And luik to the leaf o' the tree;
   For it never became a gentleman
   A naked woman to see.'

9. He turn'd himself straight round about,
   To luik to the leaf o' the tree;
   So swift as May Colvin was
   To throw him into the sea.

10. "O help! O help! my May Colvin;
    O help! or else I'll drown;
    I'll tak ye hame to your Father's bower,
    And set you down safe and sound."

11. 'Nae help, nae help, you false Sir John;
    Nae help, tho' I pity thee,
    Tho' seven knights daughters you have drown'd,
    But the eight shall not be me.'

12. So she went on her Father's steed,
    As swift as she could flee;
    And she came hame to her Father's bow'r
    Afore the break o' day.

84. [The Outlandish Knight]

Broadwood and Maitland, 1893, pp. 164-65. Noted by Heywood Sumner, Somerset.

p I/M (–VI)

1. An outlandish knight came from the north lands,
   And he came a wooing to me;

He told me he'd take me unto the north lands,
    And there he would marry me.
"Go get me some of thy father's gold,
    And some of thy mother's fee,
And two of the best nags out of the stable,
    Where there stand thirty and three."

2. She got him some of her father's gold,
    And some of her mother's fee;
And two of the best nags out of the stable,
    Where there stood thirty and three.
She mounted her on the milk-white steed
    And he on the dapple grey;
And they both rode till they came unto the salt sea,
    Just two hours before it was day.

3. "Alight, alight, my pretty lady,
    And deliver it all unto me,
For it's six pretty maidens I have drowned here,
    And the seventh thou shalt be.
Pull off, pull off thy holland smock,
    And deliver it up to me,
For I deem that it looks too fine and too gay
    For to rot all in the salt sea.

4. "Pull off, pull off thy milkwhite stays,
    And deliver them up to me,
For it's six pretty maidens I have drowned here,
    And the seventh thou shalt be.
Pull off, pull off thy silken hose,
    And deliver them up to me,
For I deem that they look too fine and too gay
    For to rot all in the salt sea."

5. "If I have to pull off my holland smock,
    Pray turn thy back upon me,
For it is not meet that a ruffian should
    A naked woman see."
He turned his back upon her, oh!
    And bitterly she did weep,
She caught him round the middle so neat,
    And tumbled him into the deep.

6. He dippèd high, he dippèd low,
    And dippèd to the side,
"Lay hold of my hand, my pretty lady,
    And you shall be my bride."
"Lie there, lie there, thou false-hearted man
    Lie there instead of me,
For it's six pretty maidens you have drowned here,
    But the seventh has drownèd thee."

7. She mounted on her milk-white steed,
    And led the dapple grey;
She rode till she came to her own father's hall
    Three hours before it was day.
The parrot being in the window so high,
    Hearing the lady did say:
"I'm afraid that some ruffian has led you astray,
    That you've tarried so long away."

8. "Don't prittle or prattle, my pretty parrot,
    Nor tell no tales of me;
Thy cage shall be made of the glittering gold,
    And thy perch of the best ivorie."

The King being in his chamber so high,
    And hearing the parrot did say:
"What ails you, what ails you, my pretty parrot,
    That you prattle so long before day?"

9. "It's no laughing matter," the parrot did say,
    "But so loudly I call unto thee,
For the cats have got into the window so high,
    And I'm afraid they will have me."
"Well turned, well turned, my pretty parrot,
    Well turnèd up for me;
Thy cage shall be made of the glittering gold,
    And thy perch of the best ivorie."

By permission of Messrs. J. B. Cramer & Co., Ltd., London.

85. "Mey Guldinn"

Gilchrist, *JEFDSS*, III (1938), p. 189. (Balfour Collection.)
Sung in the Orkney Islands.

a π¹

Miss Gilchrist notes this tune as a variant of "Chevy Chase" (i.e.,
the "Oh, Ponder Well" type).

O heard ye o a bluidy knight
Lives in the west countrie?
He has betrayed eight ladies fair
An' he's dround them in the sea.

86. "Sweet Nellie"

Randolph, 1946, I, p. 45(C). Sung by Mrs. Olga Trail,
Farmington, Ark., November 21, 1938.

p I (– VI)

Cf. "Polly-Wolly Doodle": the singer was aware of the relation.

Sweet Nellie rode a milk-white horse,
And he rode the dapple gray,
And away they went from her father's hall
Three hours before it came day, day, day,
Three hours before it came day.

Pull off, pull off that fine silk dress,
And fold it on my knee,
For it's too fine and too costlee
To rot in the bottom of the sea, sea, sea,
To rot in the bottom of the sea.

Oh turn your back on me, sweet William,
Oh turn your back on me,
He turned his back and she pushed him in,
Away to the bottom of the sea, sea, sea,
Away to the bottom of the sea.

Sweet Nellie rode the milk-white horse
And led the dapple gray,
And she landed safe at her father's hall
Three hours before it came day, day, day,
Three hours before it came day.

Be still, be still, my pretty polly parrot,
Don't you tell no news on me,
And I'll deck your cage with Californy gold,
With doors of ivoree, -ree, -ree,
With doors of ivoree.

87a. [The Outlandish Knight]

Sharp MSS., 2648/. Sung by William Porter (78), Ely,
September 9, 1911.

p I/Ly (– VI)

87b. [The Outlandish Knight]

Sharp MSS., 2721/. Sung by William Porter, Ely, October
20, 1911.

p I (– VI)

88. [The Outlandish Knight]

Sharp MSS., 2582/. Sung by Charlie Gardiner (73), Oak-
ridge, April 11, 1911.

a I/M (compass of sixth)

89. "My Pretty Colinn"

Eddy, 1939, pp. 11(D)-12. Sung by Mrs. William Stork,
Canton, Ohio; learned from her mother.

a I

Another variant of "Polly-Wolly Doodle."

1. "For here you drownded six king's daughters,
       And the seventh one drownded you."

        ·   ·   ·   ·   ·   ·   ·   ·
             ·   ·   ·   ·   ·   ·   ·

2. "Turn your face around about,
       With your face to the leaves of the tree,
   For it is not fit for a false-hearted lover
       A naked woman for to see, see, see,
   A naked woman for to see."

3. He turned his face around about,
       With his face toward the leaves of the tree,
   And she picked him up so manfully
       And she plunged him into the sea.

4. She mounted on her pony young brown
       And led the dapple gray,
   And she rode, and she rode ..
       Three long hours before day.

5. Then out warbled her pretty little parrot
       From behind the cage where it lay,
   "Oh, what is the matter with my Colinn
       That you ride so long before day?"

6. "Oh, hold your tongue, my pretty little parrot,
       Don't you tell no tales on me,

And your cage shall be made of the bright
                    shining gold,
  And shall hang beneath the willow tree."

7. Out spoke the old king himself,
    From behind the coach where he lay,
  "Oh, what is the matter with my pretty little parrot
    That she warbles so long before day?"

8. "The old tom cat came to my cage door
    And was disturbing me,
  And I only called for my pretty Colinn
    For to drive this here old cat away."

90. "Six Pretty Maidens"

Parsonson, *JFSS*, IV (1910), pp. 116-17. Sung by Mr. Lugg (53), Launceston, Cornwall, February 1905.

p I (or a I, ending on VIII)

Reference to this copy, crossed with "The Bailiff's Daughter," has been made above, in connection with a copy from Newfoundland. Lucy Broadwood refers also to *Sussex Songs* and *JFSS*, I, p. 209, and to "Little Musgrave."

1. 'Twas of a youth and a well-beloved youth,
    'Twas of a squier's son,
  He courted a bailiff's daughter so fair,
    And she was an English one.

2. He courted her for many long winter nights,
    And many a long summer day,
  He courted her both early and late,
    For to take her sweet life away.

3. He says, "Go, get me some of your father's gold,
    And some of your mother's fee;
  And away we will go to some foreign countrie,
    And marry, marry we shall be."

4. She went and got some of her father's gold,
    And some of her mother's fee;
  And away they did go to her father's stable door,
    Where horses stood thirty and three.

5. They took two of the best of the nags,
    And she on her lily-white grey;
  Away they did ride to some fair river's side,
    Six hours before it was day.

6. He says, "Unlight, unlight, my pretty Polly,
    Unlight, unlight," cries he,
  "For six pretty maidens I have drowned here before,
    And a seventh thou art to be."

7. She said, "Go, pick a prickle to keep away the thistle,
    That grows by the river Fee,
  That it may not mingle with my curly, curly locks,
    Nor my lily, milk-white skin."

8. He went to pick a prickle to keep away the thistle,
    Then she pushed the young man in,
  Saying, "Lie there, lie there, thou false-hearted man,
    Lie there instead of me."

9. He says, "Take me by the hand my pretty Polly,
    Take me by the hand," cried he,
  "Take me by the hand, my pretty Polly,
    And a lady you shall be."

10. "Now lie there, lie there, thou false-hearted man,
    Lie there instead of me,
  For six pretty maidens thou has drowned here before,
    And the seventh hath drownèd thee."

11. She mounted on her lily-white grey,
    And away she did ride (away),
  And she arrived at her father's stable door
    Three hours before it was day.

12. Now the parrot, being over the window so high,
    And heard what sweet Polly had said,
  And the master, being in at the window so high,
    Soon jumps out over bed.

13. Saying, "What's the matter with you, my pretty Polly?
    What's the matter with you?" cried he,
  "What's the matter with you, my pretty Polly?
    So many hours before it is day."

Spoken.—"Nothing, master, but the old cat's on the top of my cage, to take my sweet life away, and I'm calling on my young mistress to drive the old puss away."

14. She says, "Hush, hush, my pretty Polly,
    Don't pick no prates on me,
  For thou shalt have a cage of the best of gold
    And a door of the best ivory."

91. [The Outlandish Knight]

Sharp MSS., 1683/. Sung by Mrs. Monnery (61), Shipley April 23, 1908.

p I/Ly

Sharp notes the resemblance to "The Bold Fisherman" (cf. *One Hundred English Folksongs*, 1916, No. 42).

92. "Lady Isabel and the Elf Knight"

Gardner and Chickering, 1939, p. 31. Sung by Mrs. Clara Sheldon, Alger, Mich., 1935; learned from her mother.

p I/Ly

The last phrase suggests the familiar "Mermaid" (289).

"Take off, take off those royal robes
And deliver them unto me,
For methinks they are too beautiful
To lie in the deep, deep sea,
To lie in the deep, deep sea."

93. [May Colvine, and Fause Sir John]

Christie, II, 1881, p. 236. Sung in Aberdeenshire.

m π¹

Very possibly the second half of this tune is Christie's invention. A 4/4 variant of this tune appears as a second tune for "The Bailiff's Daughter," in Greig, 1925, p. 84(2) (Greig MSS., Tunebook I, p. 159).

Heard ye ever of a bluidy knight
    Liv'd in the West Countrie,
Wha did betray eight virgins fair,
    And drown them in the sea?
All ladies of a good account,
    As ever yet were known:
This traitor was a baron knight,
    They call'd him fause Sir John.

The eleven stanzas of Christie's text have no independent traditional standing and appear to be drawn mostly from Peter Buchan's copy (1828, II, pp. 45ff.).

94. [The Outlandish Knight]

Kidson, *JFSS*, II (1906), p. 282(1). Noted by C. Lolley, at Driffield, Yorkshire.

a I (inflected IV)

An outlandish Knight from the northlands came,
And he came awooing me;
He promis'd he'd take me unto the northlands
And there he would marry me.

95. "The Knight and the Chief's Daughter"

Child MSS., XXI, Nos. 51-55; from British Museum Add. MS. 20,094, fols. 21-23. Sent by Miss M. Pigott Rogers to [?T. Crofton] Croker, in two letters, April 28 and December 7, ?1829; learned in childhood from an Irish nurse.

a I (inflected IV)

1. "Now steal me some of your father's gold,
        And some of your mother's fee,
    And steal the best steed in your father's stable
        Where there lie thirty three."

2. She stole him some of her father's gold,
        And some of her mother's fee,
    And she stole the best steed from her father's stable
        Where there lay thirty three.

3. And she rode on the milk white steed,
        And he on the barb so grey,
    Until they came to the green green wood
        Three hours before it was day.

4. "Alight, alight, my pretty Colleen,
        Alight immediately
    For six knight's daughters I drowned here,
        And thou, the seventh shall be."

5. "Oh hold your tongue, you false knight villain,
        Oh hold your tongue" said she,
    " 'Twas you that promised to marry me
        For some of my father's fee."

6. "Strip off, strip off your jewels so rare
    And give them all to me,
I think them too rich and too costly by far
    To rot in the sand with thee."

7. "Oh turn away, thou false knight villain
    Oh turn away from me,
Oh turn away with your back to the cliff
    And your face to the willow tree."

8. He turned about with his back to the cliff,
    And his face to the willow tree,
So sudden she took him up in her arms,
    And threw him into the sea.

9. "Lie there, lie there, thou false knight villain,
    Lie there instead of me,
'Twas you that promised to marry me
    For some of my father's fee."

10. "Oh take me by the arm my dear,
    And hold me by the hand,
And you shall be my gay Lady
    And the queen of all Scotland."

11. "I'll not take you by the arm my dear,
    Nor hold you by the hand,
And I won't be your gay lady
    And the queen of all Scotland."

12. And she rode on the milk white steed
    And led the barb so grey,
Until she came back to her father's castle
    One hour before it was day.

13. And out then spoke her parrot so green
    From the cage wherein she lay,
"Where have you now been my pretty Colleen
    This long long summer's day?"

14. "Oh hold your tongue, my favourite bird
    And tell no tales on me,
Your cage I will make of the beaten gold,
    And hang in the willow tree."

15. Out then spoke her father dear
    From the chamber where he lay.
"Oh what hath befallen my favourite bird
    That she calls so loud for day."

16. "'T is nothing at all, good lord" she said
    'T is nothing at all indeed,
It was only the cat came to my cage door,
    And I called my pretty Colleen."

96. "Lady Ishbel and the Elfin-Knight"

Niles, 1938, pp. 4-5. Sung in Asheville, N.C.

a Æ/D

This is related to the same collector's version of the Coventry Carol, "Lulle-Lullay" (*Ten Christmas Carols*, 1935, p. 8; and sung by him on Victor record 2017-B).

1. He followed her up and he followed her down,
    He followed her where she lay,
And she not havin' the strength to withstand,
    Nor the breath to say him nay.

2. "Go fetch me a sack of the old lord's gold,
    And most of your mamma's fee,
And a pited hoss and an iron-gray,
    From your stable of thirty-and-three."

3. If Ishbel did ride at the villian's side,
    With the gold and her mamma's fee,
She was ridin' far off to the broad seaside,
    Where married she would be.

4. "Get down, get down, my right pretty miss,
    Your hour has come, I see,
For here I've drownded nine young ladies gay,
    And you the tenth one will be.

5. "Pull off, pull off that shiny silk gown,
    And them right pretty rings you own,
For wimmen's clothes cost too much gold
    To rest in the salt sea foam."

6. "It's turn, oh turn, oh turn your head,
    And look at yon green-growin' tree,
For if I doff my shiny silk gown,
    A naked lady you'll see."

7. He turnèd his face around about,
    To look at that green-growin' tree,
And she grabbed him round the middle so small,
    And she flicked him into the sea.

8. "Lay there, false villian, lay cold and dead,
    Lay there in room of me,
For it's nine gay ladies you've drownded here,
    But the tenth one drownded ye."

9. Her pited hoss tuck her right quickly home,
    She led the iron-gray,
And when she entered her father's hall,
    The sky was breakin' day.

10. "Speak none of my pranks, my right pretty poll,
    Else I'll make you out a liar.
But if you be wise, your cage shall be made
    Of pretty golden wire."

97. [Lady Isabel and the Elf Knight]

Sharp MSS., 3141/?. Sung by Mrs. Campbell; learned from Belvia Hampton.

p I

The words of this are lacking in Sharp's MSS. The tune suggests "Maid freed from the Gallows" (95).

GROUP B

98. "Pretty Polly"

Hudson, 1937, No. 11. Sung by Mrs. R. C. Jones, Oxford, Miss., c. 1923-30.

m Æ/D

Oh take some of your father's gold,
Likewise your mother's fee,
And two of your father's finest horses,
Where there stands thirty-three, three, three,
Where there stands thirty-three.

99. [Lady Isabel and the Elf Knight]

Sharp MSS., 3702/2754. Also in Sharp and Karpeles, 1932, I, pp. 10(F)-11. Sung by Mrs. Joe Vanhook, Berea College, Madison County, Ky., May 20, 1917.

m D

Versions of "The House Carpenter" (243) resemble this tune.

1. Come rise you up, my pretty Polly,
   And go along with me.
   I'll take you to the North Scotland,
   And married we will be.

2. Go bring me a bag of your father's gold,
   Likewise your mother's fee,
   And two of the best horses that stand in the stall,
   For there stand thirty and three.

3. She brought him a bag of her father's gold,
   Likewise her mother's fee,
   And two of the best horses that stand in the stall,
   For there stand thirty and three.

4. She lit upon her nimble going brown,
   [He] mounted the dapple grey,
   And when they reached the North Scotland
   Just three hours before the day.

5. Light you down, light you down, my pretty Polly,
   Light you down at my command.
   Six kings' daughters here have I drowned,
   And the seventh you shall be.

6. Pull off, pull off those fine gay clothes,
   And hang on yonder tree,
   For they are too fine and they cost too much
   For to rest in the salt lake sea.

7. Go get those sickles for to cut those nettles
   That grow so close to the brine,
   For they may tangle in my long, yellow hair,
   And stain my snowy white skin.

8. He got those sickles for to cut those nettles
   That grow so close to the brine;
   And poor, kind Polly with a pitifully wish
   And shoved false William in.

9. Lie there, lie there, you low William,
Lie there in the room of me.
Six kings' daughters you here have drowned,
And you the seventh shall be.

10. Hush up, hush up, you pretty parrot bird,
Tell none of your tales on me.
Your cage shall be made of the yellow beating gold,
And your doors of ivory.

11. Up speaks, up speaks that good old man
In his rook wherever he be:
What's the matter, what's the matter with my pretty
                                            parrot bird,
She's talking so long before it is day?

12. Here sits three cats at my cage door,
My life expecting to betray;
I was just calling up my pretty, golden bee
For to drive those cats away.

100. [Lady Isabel and the Elf Knight]

Sharp MSS., 4204/. Also in Sharp and Karpeles, 1932, I,
p. 12(H). Sung by Mrs. Laurel Wheeler, Buena Vista, Va.,
May 2, 1918.

m D

Cf. also variants of "The Daemon Lover" or "The House Carpenter" (243).

Take the most of your father's gold
Likewise your mother's fee
And two of your father's best horses
Come go a-long with me.

101. "Pretty Polly"

Barry, Eckstorm, and Smyth, 1929, p. xxvii. Text, Barry
MSS., IV, No. 206. Sung by Milton H. Osborn, Vineland,
N.J., February 17, 1907; learned from his older sister in
Missouri.

a I/M

1. "Mount up, mount up, my pretty Polly,
And come along with me,
And I'll take thee to the far Scotland,
And there I'll marry thee, thee, thee,
And there I'll marry thee!"

2. Then they went to her father's stable,
And viewed the stalls around,
He chose out the dapple gray,
And she the pony brown.

3. She mounted upon the little pony brown,
And he on the dapple gray,
And they rode and they rode thro' the merry
                                        green woods,
Till they came to the side of the sea.

4. "Light off, light off, my pretty Polly,
Light off, light off," said he,
"For 6 King's daughters I've drownded here,
And the seventh you shall be!"

5. "Take off these costly robes of silk,
And fold them upon your knee,
For it is a shame . . .
To rot in the salt water sea!"

6. "Turn your face quite round about,
With your face to the leaves on the tree . .
(*Something about a naked woman follows—
not recollected.*)

7. . . .
And she picked him up quite manfully,
And threw him into the sea.

8. "Lie there, lie there you false-hearted wretch
Lie there in the place of me!
For 6 King's daughters you've drownded here,
And the seventh has drownded thee!"

9. "O help me out, my pretty Polly,
O help me out!" cried he,
"And I'll take thee to the far Scotland,
And there I'll marry thee!"

10. She mounted upon her little pony brown,
And led the dapple gray.

(*Then followed some lines, not recollected, in
which the parrot asks Polly where she has been.*)

11. "O hold your tongue, my pretty parrot,
And tell no lies on me,
And I'll line your cage with the pure yellow gold,
And hang it on a green willow tree!"

(*Then followed some lines, not recollected, in
which Polly's father asks the parrot what is
the matter.*)

12. "The cat she came to my cage window door,
And threatened to devour me,
And I called up my pretty Polly
To drive the cat away!"

102. "False Sir John"

Kentucky Mountain Songs, Elektra, LP rec. 25. Sung by
Jean Ritchie, 1954; learned from family tradition.

m M (−IV)

1. False Sir John a-wooing came
   To a lady young and fair.
   May Colvin was this lady's name,
   Her father's only heir,
   Her father's only heir.

2. He wooed her while she spun the thread
   And while they made the hay,
   Until he gained her low consent
   To mount and ride away,
   To mount and ride away.

3. "It's bring me some of your father's gold
   And some of your mother's fee.
   I'll take thee to some far-off land
   And there I'll marry thee,
   And there I'll marry thee."

4. She's gone unto her father's coffer,
   Where all of his monies lay;
   She's took the yellow and left the white
   And lightly skipped away,
   And lightly skipped away.

5. She's gone unto her father's stables,
   Where all of his steeds did stand;
   She's took the best and left the worst
   In all her father's land,
   In all her father's land.

6. She's mounted on a milk-white steed
   And he on a dapple gray;
   And they rode till they come to a lonesome spot,
   A cliff by the side of the sea,
   A cliff by the side of the sea.

7. "Light down, light down," said False Sir John;
   "Your bridal bed you'll see:
   It's seven women have I drownded here
   And the eighth one you shall be,
   And the eighth one you shall be.

8. "Have off, have off your Holland smock
   With borders all around,
   For it's too costly to lay down here
   And rot on the cold, cold ground,
   And rot on the cold, cold ground."

9. "Turn around, turn around, thou False Sir John,
   And look at the leaves on the tree.
   It don't become a gentleman
   A naked woman to see,
   A naked woman to see."

10. Oh, False Sir John has turned around
    To gaze at the leaves on the tree;
    She's made a dash with her tender little arms
    And pushed him into the sea,
    And pushed him into the sea.

11. "Oh, help! oh, help! May Colvin!
    Oh, help, or I shall drown!
    I'll take you back to your father's house
    And lightly set you down,
    And lightly set you down."

12. "No help, no help," said May Colvin,
    "No help will you get from me.
    The bed's no colder to you, sir,
    Than you thought to give to me,
    Than you thought to give to me."

13. She mounted on the milk-white steed
    And led the dapple gray,
    And rode till she come to her father's house
    At the breaking of the day,
    At the breaking of the day.

14. Then up and spoke the little parrot,
    Said: "May Colvin, where have you been?
    And what have you done with False Sir John
    That went with you ridin',
    That went with you ridin'?"

15. "Oh, hold your tongue, you little parrot
    And tell no tales on me,
    And I'll buy you a cage of beaten gold
    With spokes of ivory,
    With spokes of ivory."

103. "Pretty Polly"

Davis, 1929, p. 549(B); text, pp. 65-67. Sung by Hill Jackson (Negro), Brown's Cove, Va., June 1, 1917. Collected by Miss D. R. Martin, J. M. McManaway; music noted by John Stone, November 3, 1920.

a I/Ly

1. "He followed me up, he followed me down,
   He followed me all the way;
   I had not the heart to say one word,
   Nor heart to say him nay, nay, nay,
   Nor heart to say him nay."

2. "You get all of your father's gold,
    Likewise your mother's fee,
And two of your father's best horses
    Which are of thirty and three,
    And come along with me."

3. She jumped upon the bonny, bonny, brown,
    And he the piebald bay,
And rode along by the broad water side
    That lonely lazy summer day, day, day,
    That long summer day.

4. "Set you down, set you down, Pretty Polly,
    And chat a while with me;
For here I've drownded six king's daughters,
    And you were the seventh to be, to be,
    And you were the seventh to be."

5. "No, Jimmy, my pretty Jimmy,
    That's not what you promised me;
You promised to take me to the marriage land,
    And there to marry me, me, me,
    And there to marry me."

6. "Pull off, pull off those costly robes,
    And hang them on yonder tree;
They are too costly and fine
    To swim in the salt water sea, sea, sea,
    To swim in the salt water sea."

7. "Turn your face about
    Into the leaves of the tree."
She picked him up in her arms so strong
    And plunged home [sic] into the sea, sea, sea,
    And plunged home into the sea.

8. "Lie there, lie there, you false-hearted wretch,
    Lie there, instead of me;
Six king's daughters you've drownded there,
    And I the seventh was to be, be, be,
    And I the seventh was to be."

9. "Oh no, Polly, oh no, Polly,
    All I want is help from thee,
And if I get to shore again,
    I'm sure to marry thee, thee, thee,
    I'm sure to marry thee."

10. She jumped upon the bonny, bonny, brown,
    And he the piebald bay,
And arrived at her father's house
    Three hours before 't was day, day, day,
    Three hours before 't was day.

11. She put the gold into its place,
    And the horses where its would be,
And arrived into her chamber fair,
    Two hours before 't was day, day, day,
    Two hours before 't was day.

12. Then up rised that pretty parrot

    "Oh, what are you doing up
    So long before 't was day, day, day,
    So long before 't was day?"

13. "Set you down, get you down, Pretty Polly,
    Don't tell no tales on me;
Your cage shall be made of hand-beaten gold,
    The door out of ivory, -ry, -ry,
    The door out of ivory."

14. Then up rose that good old man,
    Then up rose that good old man.
"What are you doing up
    So long before 'tis day, day, day,
    So long before 'tis day?"

15. "There are three cats at my cage door,
    Trying to do violence to me,
And I'm just call (-ing) Miss Polly
    To drive those cats away, -way, -way,
    To drive those cats away."

104. "Pretty Polly"

Davis, 1929, p. 550(P); text, pp. 83-84. Sung by an old lady in Lee County, Va., November 3, 1920. Collected by Olive Flora Bryson.

Apparently a D, if correctly noted

With this variant, cf. "Pretty Peggy O" (Sharp and Karpeles, 1932, II, p. 59(B), a version of the Scottish "Lass o' Fyvie").

"Hush, hush, my pretty Polly dear,
    Don't tell any tales on me.
Your cage shall be made of yellow beaten gold
    And hung in a willow tree, -e, -e,
    And hung in a willow tree."

"She rode away on a milk-white steed
    And led the dapple gray

    Three hours before break of day."

The father hears her go out and questions the parrot, who replies:

"A bold cat came to my cage door
    And threatened to worry me (*or*, threatened war with me)
And I was calling to my pretty Polly dear
    To drive the cat away, away,
    To drive the cat away."

They come to a deep pool, the knight secures her jewels and sings:

"Six king's daughters I've drownded here
    And the seventh one you shall be, -e, -e,
    And the seventh one you shall be."

There is a struggle, the maid frees herself and throws the knight into the pool, then sings:

"Lie there, lie there, you false young man,

. . . .

For six king's daughters you've drownded here
  But the seventh one's drownded you, -u, -u,
  But the seventh one's drownded you."

105. [Lady Isabel and the Elf Knight]

Sharp MSS., 4585/3208-9. Sung by Mrs. George McCormick, Garden City, N.C., September 9, 1918.

a π² (or p π¹)

Sharp's sensitive notation was for the second stanza. How the irregularities of other stanzas were accommodated was not recorded.

1. I'll tell you of a brisk young sailor,
   And Jimmy his name shall be,
   He came across the wide ocean,
   And then he came courting of me.

2. He followed me up, he followed me down,
   He followed me to my father's room;
   I'd not any tongue to say O Nay,
   Nor no wings to fly away.

3. I want part of your father's money,
   I want your mother's key,
   And two of the best horses out of thirty and three.

4. I gave him part of my father's money,
   I gave him my mother's key,
   And two of the best horses out of thirty and three.

5. He set me up on the milk-white steed,
   And himself on the iron grey;
   We rode till we came to the Asia shore
   Just the length of a summer's day.

6. Get down, get down, my pretty fair maid,
   And pull the leaves upon the trees.
   Six fair maids I have drowned here
   And the seventh you shall be.

7. Turn your back, she said to him,
   Pull the leaves of the trees.
   She got him round the middle small
   And tripped him into the sea.

8. Lie there, lie there, you dirty dog,
   Lie there in place of me,
   For six fair maids you've drowned here,
   But the seventh you shall be.

9. She got up on the milk-white steed,
   By her side was the iron-grey;
   She rode till she came to her father's gate
   Three long hours before it was day.

106. [Lady Isabel and the Elf Knight]

Sharp MSS., 3142/?. Also in Sharp and Karpeles, 1932, I, p. 6(B). Sung by Mrs. Bishop, Clay County, Ky., July 16, 1909. Collected by Olive Dame Campbell. Text not included in Sharp's MSS.

a π² (or p π¹)

1. Pull off that silk, my pretty Polly,
   Pull off that silk, said he,
   For it is too fine and too costly
   To rot in the briny, briny sea,
   To rot in the briny sea.

2. Turn your back, sweet Willie, said she,
   O turn your back unto me,
   For you are too bad a rebel
   For a naked woman to see.

3. She picked him up in her arms so strong
   And she threw him into the sea,
   Saying: If you have drowned six kings' daughters here,
   You may lay here in the room of me.

4. Stretch out your hand, O pretty Polly,
   Stretch out your hand for me,

   . . . .

   And help me out of the sea . . .

5. She picked up a rock and threw on him, saying:
   Lay there, lay there, you dirty, dirty dog,
   Lay there in the room of me.
   You're none too good nor too costly
   To rot in the briny, briny sea.

6. Hush up, hush up, my pretty parrot,
   Hush up, hush up, said she.
   You shall have a golden cage with an ivory lid
   Hung in the willow tree.

107. "The Six Kings' Daughters"

Korson, 1949, pp. 30-32. Sung by Mrs. Hannah Sayre, Washington County, Pa., 1933. Recorded by Samuel P. Bayard.

a M/D

1. He follered me up, he follered me down,
      He follered wherever I lay;
   I had no wings to fly from him,
      Nor no tongue to tell him nay, nay, nay,
      Nor no tongue to tell him nay.

2. Take some of your father's beaten gold
      Likewise of your mother's fee,
   And send two of the steeds out of your father's stable
      Where stands thir*ty* and three, three, three,
      Where stands thir*ty* and three.

3. She went and she took of her father's gold,
      And some of her mother's fee,
   And two steeds out of her father's stable
      Where there stands thirty and three.

4. She mounted onto the bony, bony black,
      And him on the di-pole gray,
   And they rode along through the merry green woods
      Till they come to the banks of the sea.

5. Light down, light down, my pretty P*olin*,
      I've something to say to thee:
   Six daughters of the king I've drownded here,
      And the seventh you shall be.

6. Take off, take off, that fine silk gown,
      And hang it on the tree,
   For it is too fine and too costly too
      To rot in the salt water sea.

7. And turn yourself three times around,
      And gaze at the leaves on the tree,
   For God never made sich a rascal as you
      A naked woman to see.

8. He turned hisself three times around,
      To gaze at the leaves on the tree;
   She picked him up so manfully-like,
      And plunged him into the sea.

9. Lie there, lie there, you false-hearted knight,
      Lie there in the stead of me—
   You've promised to take me to old Scotland,
      And there you would marry of me.

10. She jumped onto the bony, bony black,
      And led the di-pole gray,
   And she rode till she come to her father's own house,
      Three long hours before it was day.

11. Up bespoke the little parrot,
      Where in his cage it lay,
   Saying, Where are you going, my pretty P*olin*?
      You're traveling so long before day.

12. Hold your tongue, my pretty parrot,
      Tell none of your tales (lies) on me;
   Your cage shall be made of the yellow, beaten gold,
      And hung on the green willow tree.

13. Up bespoke the old man
      Where in his room he lay,
   Saying, What's the matter, my pretty parrot?
      You're prattling so long before day.

14. The old cat come to my cage door,
      And swore she would worry of me,
   And I had to call on my pretty P*olin*
      To drive the bold pussy cat away, -way, -way,
      To drive the bold pussy cat away!

108. [Lady Isabel and the Elf Knight]

Sharp MSS., 4261/. Sung by Mrs. Elizabeth M. Berry,
Nellysford, Va., May 21, 1908.

a π^2 (or p π^1)

Come sit you down, my pretty Polly,
Come sit you down by me;
I'm all to talk to you, you, you,
I'm all to talk to you, you, you,
I'm all to talk to you
I'm all to talk to you, you, you,
I'm all to talk to you.

109. "Six Kings Daughters"

Wyman and Brockway [1916], pp. 82-87. Sung in Letcher
and Estill Counties, Ky.

a π^2 (or p π^1)

1. "Get up, get up, pretty Polly," he says
   "And go along with me,
   I'll take you away to New Scotland
   And there we'll marry and stay."

2. She stole fifty pounds of her father's gold
   And besides her mother's fee
   And two of the horses in the stall
   Where there were thirty and three.

3. She bound herself on the bonny, bonny black
   And him on the tabbit bay,
   They rode 'til they came to the high sea-side
   One hour before it was day.

4. "Light down, light down, pretty Polly," he says,
   "Light down, light down with me,
   This is the place I've drowned six
   And you the seventh shall be."

5. "Pull off, pull off, that costly gown
   And lay it by yonders tree
   It never shall be said such costly wear
   Shall rot in the salt water sea."

6. "O turn yourself all around and about
   Your face toward the sea,
   It never shall be said such a rascal as you
   A naked lady for to see."

7. He turned himself all around and about
   And his face toward the sea
   And with her little white tender arms
   She shoved him into the sea.

8. "Lie there, lie there, you false-hearted man
   Lie there instead of me,
   If this be the place you drowned six
   The seventh you shall be."

9. She bound herself on the bonny, bonny black
   And she led the tabbit bay,
   She rode 'til she came to her father's house
   One hour before it was day.

10. Up speaks, up speaks that pretty parrot bird
    In her cage where she be,
    "What's the matter, what's the matter with my
                                    pretty Polly
    She's up so long before day."

11. "Hush up, hush up, pretty parrot bird,
    Tell none of your tales on me;
    Your cage shall be made of the yellow beaten gold
    And your doors of ivory."

12. "What's the matter what's the matter pretty Polly"
                                    he said
    "What's the matter what's the matter with thee?
    I thought you had gone to New Scotland
    And there for to marry and stay."

110. [Lady Isabel and the Elf Knight]

Sharp MSS., 3197/2341. Also in Sharp and Karpeles, 1932, I, p. 5(A). Sung by Mrs. Mary Sands, Allanstand, N.C., August 2, 1916.

a π² (or p π¹)

Get down, get down, get down, says he,
Pull off that fine silk gown;
For it is too fine and costly
To rot in the salt-water sea, sea, sea,
To rot in the salt-water sea.

Turn yourself all around and about
With your face turned toward the sea.
And she picked him up so manfully
And over'd him into the sea.

Pray help me out, pray help me out,
Pray help me out, says he,
And I'll take you to the old Scotland
And there I will marry thee.

Lie there, lie there,* you false-hearted knight,
Lie there instead of me,
For you stripped me as naked as ever I was born,
But I'll take nothing from thee.

She jumped upon the milk-white steed
And she led the dapple grey,
And she rode back to her father's dwelling
Three long hours before day.

* 1932 omits the second "lie there."

111. [Lady Isabel and the Elf Knight]

Sharp MSS., 3221/. Also in Sharp and Karpeles, 1932, I, p. 8(D). Sung by Mrs. Nancy E. Shelton, Carmen, N.C., August 8, 1916.

a π² (or p π¹)

She mounted on the milk white steed
And led the dapple grey
And when she got to her father's house
It was one long hour till day till day
It was one long hour till day

It's hold your tongue my Pretty Polly
And tell no tales of me
And your cage shall be made of the beaten gold
And swing in the willow tree.

O go and steal your father's gold,
And part of your mother's fee;
And we'll get on the horses and ride to the Squire's
And married we will be, be, be,
And married we will be.

112. [The Outlandish Knight]

Sharp MSS., 3250/. Sung by Mrs. R. Hensley, Carmen,
N.C., August 11, 1916.

a π² (or p π¹)

Sharp's MS. note: "This appoggiatura Mrs. H. called a 'warble.' "

113. [The Outlandish Knight]

Sharp MSS., 3774/. Sung by Mrs. Maud Kilburn, Berea,
Ky., May 31, 1917.

Probably p I, ending on V

Go bring to me your father's gold
And some of yr. brother's fee,
And the two best horses in your father's stable (stall)
Where now stands thirty and three, three, three,
Where now stands thirty and three.

114. [Lady Isabel and the Elf Knight]

Sharp MSS., 3777/. Sung by Mrs. Townsley and Mrs. Wilson, Pineville, Ky., June 2, 1917.

a π² (or p π¹)

115. [Lady Isabel and the Elf Knight]

Sharp MSS., 4319/3085-86. Sung by Mrs. Bowyer, Villamont, Bedford County, Va., June 4, 1918.

a π² (or p π¹)

1. He followed her up, he followed her down,
   He followed her to the room where she lay.
   She had not the power to flee from his arms,
   Nor the tongue to answer Nay.

2. She got on her little pony brown,
   And he got on his grey.
   They rode till they came to the broad water side,
   The length of a long summer day.

3. Get down, get down, my pretty little Miss,
   Get down, get down, these words I say,
   For there's nine kings' daughters I've drownded here,
   And you the tenth shall be.

4. Pull off, pull off that fine silken gown,
   And lay it on yonders stone,
   For it's cost your father too much money
   To rot in the salt sea foam.

5. Pull off, pull off your silken veil
   And lay it on yonders stone,
   For it's cost your father too much money
   To rot in the salt sea foam.

6. Turn yourself around and about,
   Your face to the leaves of the trees,
   For I don't think that any such a wretch,
   A nice a-lady might see.

7. He turned himself around and about,
   His face to the leaves of the trees.
   She gave him a plunge, she plunged him in
   To lie in the salt water sea.

8. O hand me down your soft silken hands,
   O hand them down to me,
   O hand me down your soft silken hands,
   And married we will be.

9. O no, O no, you false-hearted man,
   It's lie there instead of poor me.
   It's nine kings' daughters are drownded here,
   And you the last shall be.

10. She got on her little pony brown,
    She led the dapple grey;
    She rode till she came to her father's gate,
    It were not two hours before day.

11. Where have you been, my pretty little Miss?
    Where have you been? I say.
    Where have you been, my pretty little Miss,
    So long before day?

12. O hush, O hush, my pretty little parrot,
    Don't tell no tales on me.
    Your cage shall be made of yellow beaten gold
    And hung in yonders willow tree.

116. [Lady Isabel and the Elf Knight]

Sharp MSS., 4331/3092. Also in Sharp and Karpeles, 1932, I, pp. 9(E)-10. Sung by Mrs. Laura Virginia Donald, Dewey, Va., June 6, 1918.

a π² (or p π¹)

1. He followed her up and he followed her down,
   He followed her to the room where she lay,
   [And] she had not the power to flee from his arms,
   Nor the tongue to answer Nay, [Nay, Nay,
   Nor the tongue to answer Nay.]

2. She got on her pony, pony brown,
   He got on the iron-grey.
   They rode till they came to the blue water sea
   In the length of a long summer day.

3. Get down, get down, my pretty little Miss,
   Get down, these words I say.
   Here I've drownded nine kings' daughters,
   And you the tenth shall be.

4. Pull off, pull off that fine silken gown,
   And lie it on yonders stone,
   For it cost your father too much money
   For to rot in the salt sea foam.

5. Turn your face around and about,
   Turn to the green leaves on the tree,
   For I don't think as nice a gentleman as you
   A naked lady should see.

6. She picked him up and she splunged him in,
   She splunged* him in the depths of the sea,
   Lie there, lie there, you false-hearted soul,
   In the place of poor me.

7. Hand me down your soft silk hand,
   O hand it down to me,
   O hand me down your soft silk hand,
   And married we shall be.

8. She got on her pony, pony brown,
   And she led her iron grey.
   She rode till she came to her father's gate,
   'Twas just three hours till day.

9. My pretty little parrot, my pretty little parrot,
   Don't tell no tales on me,
   Your cage shall be made out of yellow beaten gold
   And hung in the willow tree.

* 1932: "plunged"

117. [Lady Isabel and the Elf Knight]

Sharp MSS., 4348/. Sung by Mrs. Tina Dooley, Montvale, Va., June 6, 1918.

a π² (or p π¹)

O get you down, get you down, my pretty Polly,
And talk awhile with me,
It's six king's daughters are drowned here
And the seventh one you will be, will be,
And the seventh one you will be.

118. [Lady Isabel and the Elf Knight]

Sharp MSS., 4508/3171. Also in Sharp and Karpeles, 1932, I, p. 12(G). Sung by Mrs. Sarah V. Cannady, Endicott, Va., August 23, 1918.

a π² (or p π¹)

He followed her up [and] he followed her down,
He followed her where she may.*
He never gave her time to turn herself around,
Nor time to say, O Nay, [O Nay,
Nor time to say, O Nay.]

Pull off, pull off that new silken gown,
And hang it on a thorn.
Some other gay lady will wear this dress
When you are dead and gone.

* 1932: "lay"

119. [Lady Isabel and the Elf Knight]

Sharp MSS., 4729/3296. Sung by Mrs. Sina Boone, Shoal
Creek, Burnsville, N.C., October 1, 1918.

a π² (or p π¹)

Remember, dear, when your heart was mine,
When your arms was across my breast,
You made me believe by the faults of men,
The sun it rose in the West, West, West,
The sun it rose in the West.

Remember the promise that you made to me,
It was between thirty and three,
You promised that you'd take me to old Ingel,
And there you'd be my bride.

If ever I made such a promise as that,
It was more than I intended to do
For one that was so easily found,
So easily found as you.

Hush up, hush up, my pretty crowing chicken,
Don't crow till it comes day,
For your cage shall be made of the yellow beaten gold,
And your wings of the silver so gay.

Hush up, hush up, my pretty Polly parrot,
Don't tell no tales on me,
For your cage shall be made of the yellow beaten gold
And hung in the weeping-willow tree.

Turn round, turn round, my pretty true love,
With your face to the leaves on the trees.
She picked him up so manfully strong
And laid him into the sea.

Lie there, lie there, my pretty true love,
Lie there instead of me,
For the six king's daughters you've drownded there,
And the seventh son you shall be.

120. "Lady Isabel and the Elf Knight"

Scarborough, 1925, pp. 43-45. Sung by an old Negro woman,
South Waco, Texas.

a π² (or p π¹)

The 1925 printing gives 2/4 time throughout.

1. There was a tall an' handsome man,
    Who come a-courtin' me.
  He said, "Steal out atter dark to-night
    An' come a-ridin' with me, with me,
    An' come a-ridin' with me.

2. "An' you may ride your milk-white steed
    An' I my apple bay."
  We rid out from my mother's house
    Three hours befo' de day, de day,
    Three hours befo' de day.

3. I mounted on my milk-white steed
    And he rode his apple bay.
  We rid on til we got to the ocean,
    An' den my lover say, lover say,
    An' den my lover say:

4. "Sit down, sit down, sweetheart," he say,
    "An' listen you to me.
  Pull off dat golden robe you wears
    An' fold hit on yo' knee, yo' knee,
    An' fold hit on yo' knee."

5. I ax him why my golden robe
    Must be folded on his knee.
  "It is too precious to be rotted away
    By the salt water sea, water sea,
    By the salt water sea."

6. I say, "Oh, sweetheart, carry me back home,
    My mother for to see,
  For I'm afeared I'll drownèd be
    In this salt water sea, water sea,
    In this salt water sea."

7. He tuck my hand and drug me in
    . . . .
  I say, "Oh, sweetheart, take me back!
    The water's up to my feet, my feet,
    The water's up to my feet."

8. He smile at me an' draw me on.
   "Come on, sweetheart, sweetheart,
   We soon will be across the stream,
   We've reached the deepest part, deepest part,
   We've reached the deepest part."

9. As I went on I cry an' say,
   "The water's up to my knees!
   Oh, take me home! I'm afeared to be drowned
   In this salt water sea, water sea,
   In this salt water sea."

10. He pull me on an' say, "Sweetheart,
    Lay all your fears aside.
    We soon will be across it now
    We've reached the deepest tide, deepest tide,
    We've reached the deepest tide."

11. I sank down in the stream an' cry,
    "The water's up to my waist."
    He pull at me an' drug me on;
    He say, "Make haste, make haste, make haste."
    He say, "Make haste, make haste."

12. I cry to him, "The water's up to my neck."
    "Lay all your fears aside.
    We soon will be across it now,
    We've reached the deepest tide, deepest tide,
    We've reached the deepest tide."

* * * * * * *

13. I caught hol' of de tail of my milk-white steed,
    He was drowned wid his apple bay.
    I pulled out of de water an' landed at my mother's house
    An hour befo' de day, de day,
    An hour befo' de day.

14. My mother say, "Pretty Polly, who is dat,
    A-movin' softly?"
    An' I say to my Polly, "Pretty Polly,
    Don't you tell no tales on me, on me,
    Don't you tell no tales on me."

15. An' my mother say, "Is dat you, Polly?
    Up so early befo' day?"
    "Oh, dat mus' be a kitty at yo' door,"
    Is all my Polly say, Polly say,
    Is all my Polly say.

121. "Pretty Polly Ann"

Randolph, 1946, I, pp. 41(A)-43. Sung by Mrs. Mary Grant,
Anderson, Mo., September 6, 1927.

a π² (or p π¹)

1. He follered me up, he follered me down,
   He follered me into th' room,
   An' I had not th' power to flee from him,
   Nor th' tongue to tell him nay, nay, nay,
   Nor th' tongue to tell him nay.

A version very close to this in text and tune appears in Vance
Randolph, *Ozark Mountain Folks*, 1932, pp. 216-19, as sung by Bill
Hatfield.

2. She took a part of her father's gold,
   An' likewise her mother's fee,
   An' the two best horses in her father's lot
   Where they stood thirty an' three, three, three,
   Where they stood thirty an' three.

3. She throwed herself on the bony bony brown,
   An' he rid the dapply gray,
   So they rid away to the howlin' sea
   All on a long summer's day, day, day,
   All on a long summer's day.

4. Oh give me your hand, pretty Polly,
   Oh give me your hand, says he,
   I've drownded six pretty fair maids here
   An' you the seventh shall be, be, be,
   An' you the seventh shall be!

5. Turn yourself three times around
   An' your face to the greenleaf tree,
   She picked him up by the middle of the waist
   An' throwed him into the sea, sea, sea,
   An' throwed him into the sea.

6. Oh give me your hand, pretty Polly,
   Oh give me your hand, says he,
   An' I'll take you back to your father's house
   An' married we will be, be, be,
   An' married we will be.

7. Lay there, lay there, you salt-hearted man,
   Lay there in the place of me.
   I can get back to my father's house
   Without help or thanks from thee, thee, thee,
   Without help or thanks from thee.

8. She throwed herself on the bony bony brown,
   An' she led the dapply gray,
   An' then got into her father's house
   Three hours before 'twas day, day, day,
   Three hours before 'twas day.

9. She put the horses right where they stood,
   An' the gold right where it lay,
   An' then she got into her own chamber room
   Between midnight an' day, day, day,
   Between midnight an' day.

10. Fly down, fly down, my pretty Polly Ann,
    An' set on my right knee,
    An' I'll bind your cage with a yaller wisp o' gold,
    An' hang it on a green willow tree, tree, tree,
    An' hang it on a green willow tree.

11. Oh I cain't fly down, an' I won't fly down,
    An' set on your right knee,
    For you have murdered your own true love,
    An' you would murder me, me, me,
    An' you would murder me!

122. [Lady Isabel and the Elf-Knight]

Wilkinson MSS., 1935-36, p. 6(B). Sung by Mrs. Kit Williamson, Evington, Va., October 19, 1935.

a π² (or p π¹)

Go bring me a portion of your father's gold
And some of your mother's fee;
Go bring me your father's choice horse
That stands on sixty-three, my love,
That stands on sixty-three.

123. [Lady Isabel and the Elf-Knight]

Wilkinson MSS., 1935-36, pp. 3-5(A). Sung by Nathaniel Melhorn Morris, Harriston, Va., October 16, 1935.

a π² (or p π¹)

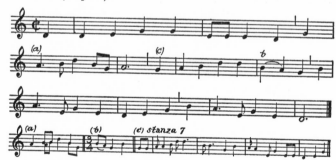

Stanzas 11-14 of this text belong properly to "Young Hunting" (68).

1. Arise you up, my pretty Polly,
    Come go along with me.
    I'll take you to old Scotland
    And there we'll married be, be, be.
    And there we'll married be.

2. Go gather up your father's gold,
    Likewise your mother's fee.
    And two of the best horses in your father's barn,
    Where there were twenty and three, three, three.
    Where there were twenty and three.

3. She gathered up her father's gold,
    Likewise her mother's fee.
    And two of the best of her father's horses
    Where there were twenty and three, three, three.
    Where there were twenty and three.

4. He mounted her on his milk white steed,
    Himself on his tiple gray.
    And they rode, they rode, the livelong night,
    Two hours before it was day. [sic]

5. Get you down, get you down, my pretty Polly,
    Get you down by the help of me.
    For here I have drowned six King's daughters
    And the seventh one you shall be, be, be.
    And the seventh one you shall be.

6. Pull off, pull off, that rich attire,
    And hand it over to me.
    For it cost your father too much gold
    To rot in the salt water sea, sea, sea.
    To rot in the salt water sea.

7. Turn your back, turn your back, my love Henery,
    Cast your eyes upon the leaves of the tree.
    For I think it's a scandal and a shame
    A naked woman you should see, see, see.
    A naked woman you should see.

8. Love Henry turned himself around,
    And cast his eyes upon the leaves of the tree.
    . . . .
    And tripped him into the sea, sea, sea.
    And tripped him into the sea.

9. Lay there, lay there, you false hearted man,
    And there you may lay for me.
    And your flesh may be food for the little insects,
    And your bones may rot in the sea, sea, sea.
    And your bones may rot in the sea.

10. She mounted herself on the milk white steed,
    And she led the tiple gray.
    And she rode, and she rode, to her father's gate
    Two hours before it was day, day, day.
    Two hours before it was day.

11. Come down, come down, my pretty Polly,
    And sit here on my knee.
    Your cage shall be made of pure, pure gold,
    The doors of the ivory-ry-ry.
    The doors of the ivory.

12. I shan't come down, nor I won't come down,
    Nor sit upon your knee.
    For so you killed poor Love Henry
    So now you might kill me, me, me.
    So now you might kill me.

13. I wish I had my bows and spikes,
    And they bent in my hand.
    I'd pierce them through your tender heart
    Where you'd see me no more, more, more.
    Where you'd see me no more.

14. And if you had your bows and spikes,
    And they bent in your hand.
    I'd take a sweet flight and fly from you
    Where you'd see me no more, more, more.
    Where you'd see me no more.

124. "The King's Seven Daughters"

Halpert, LC/AAFS, rec. 2954 B1. Sung by Mrs. Theodosia
Bonnett Long, Saltillo, Miss., 1939.

a π² (compass of sixth)

This variant has been transcribed from the phonograph record. An
earlier performance appears in Arthur P. Hudson, *Folk Tunes from
Mississippi*, 1937, No. 10, where it has a 3/4 meter but no other
melodic differences. The words are mainly the same.

1. "Go bring me some of your father's gold,
    Likewise your mother's keys,
    And bring your father's best horses,
    Where they stand by thirty and three, three, three,
    Where they stand by thirty and three."

2. She got some of her father's gold,
    Likewise her mother's keys,
    And two of her father's best horses,
    Where they stood by thirty and three, three, three,
    Where they stood by thirty and three.

3. She mounted upon the milk-white steed,
    And led the dapple gray,
    She rode and she rode the livelong night,
    Till she come to the salt water sea, sea, sea,
    Till she come to the salt water sea.

4. "Light down, light down, my pretty fair maid,
    Light down in the cause of me,
    For six of the kings' daughters I've drownded here,
    And you the seventh shall be, be, be,
    And you the seventh shall be."

5. "Pull off that costly robe," he said,
    "And fold it on my knee,
    It cost too much of your father's gold,
    To rot in the salt water sea, sea, sea,
    To rot in the salt water sea."

6. "O turn your body around about,
    And view the leaves of the tree,
    You're too much of a gentleman,
    An undressed lady to see, see, see,
    An undressed lady to see."

7. He turned his body around about,
    And viewed the leaves of the tree,

She caught him round his slender waist,
    And tripped him into the sea, sea, sea,
    And tripped him into the sea.

8. "O help me out, my pretty fair maid,
    O help me out," said he,
    "I'll take you to some far off land,
    And married we will be, be, be,
    And married we will be."

9. "Lie there, lie there, you false-hearted man,
    Lie there in the cause of me,
    For six of the kings' daughters you've drownded here,
    And you the seventh shall be, be, be,
    And you the seventh shall be."

10. She mounted upon the milk-white steed,
    And led the dapple grey,
    She rode till she came to her father's cot,
    Two hours before it was day, day, day,
    Two hours before it was day.

11. "Where have you been," my pretty Polly said,
    "O where have you been," said she,
    "I've cried, I've cried the livelong night,
    To be alone with thee, thee, thee,
    To be alone with thee."

12. "Hush up, hush up, my parrot dear,
    Don't tell no tales on me,
    A golden cage that you shall have,
    With doors of ivory, ry, ry,
    With doors of ivory."

125. "Six Fair Maids"

Brown MS., 17-XI (16 a 4?). Sung by Hattie McNeill,
Ashe County, N.C. [?].

a I

The first quarter-note in the second bar may be dotted in the MS.
If so, the next note was probably intended for an eighth, since the
meter is regular throughout.

126. "Six Kings' Daughters"

Cox, 1925, p. 521; text, pp. 6-7. Sung by Mr. Cunningham,
West Virginia. From Professor Walter Barnes, July 1915.
Sung by George W. Cunningham, Elkins, N.C., as learned
shortly after the Civil War.

a I/M (or p I/Ly)

1. He followed me up, he followed me down,
    And he followed me into the room;
I had not the power to speak one word,
    Nor a tongue to answer nay.

2. "Go bring me some of your father's gold
    And some of your mother's fee,
And I will take you to Scotland,
    And there I'll marry thee."

3. She brought him some of her father's gold
    And some of her mother's fee;
She took him to her father's barnyard,
    Where the horses stood thirty and three.

4. "Mount on, mount on that pretty, pretty brown,
    And I on the dapple gray;
And we will ride through some long, lonesome woods,
    Three long hours before it is day."

5. She mounted on the pretty, pretty brown,
    And he on the dapple gray;
They rode on through some long, lonesome woods,
    Till they came to the salt-water sea.

6. "Mount off, mount off your pretty, pretty brown,
    And I off the dapple gray;
For six kings' daughters have I drownèd here,
    And you the seventh shall be."

7. "O hush your tongue, you rag-villain!
    O hush your tongue!" said she;
"You promised to take me to Scotland
    And there to marry me."

8. "Haul off, haul those fine clothing,
    Haul off, haul off," said he;
"For they are too costly and too fine,
    To be rotted all in the sea."

9. "Well, turn your face toward the sea,
    Your back likewise to me,
For it does not become a rag-villain
    A naked woman for to see."

10. He turned his face toward the sea,
    His back likewise to me;
I picked him up all in my arms
    And plunged him into the sea.

11. "O help, come help, my little Aggie!
    Come help, I crave of thee,
And all the vows I've made unto you,
    I will double them twice and three."

12. "Lie there, lie there, thou rag-villain,
    Lie there instead of me;
For six kings' daughters have you drownèd here,
    And yourself the seventh shall be."

13. I mounted on the pretty brown
    And led the dapple gray;
I rode home to my own father's barn,
    Two long hours before it was day.

14. "O what is the matter, my little Aggie,
    That you call so long before day?"
"I've been to drown the false-hearted man
    That strove to drown poor me."

15. "O hold your tongue, my little parrot,
    And tell no tales on me,
And your cage shall be made of the brightest bit of gold,
    And your wings of pure ivory."

16. "O what is the matter, my little parrot,
    That you call so long before day?"
"A cat came to my cage door,
    And strove to weary off* me,
And I called upon my little Aggie
    To come and drive it away."

* worry of

127. "Six Kings' Daughters"

Cox, 1939, pp. 4-5. Sung by Frances Sanders, Morgantown, W.Va., June 1924.

a M (or p I)

1. He followed her up and he followed her down,
    To the bed chamber where she lay . . .

2. She mounted on her bonny, bonny, brown,
    And he on the dappled gray,
And they rode till they came to the salt sea side,
    Four long hours before it was day, day, day,
    Four long hours before it was day.

3. "Six kings' daughters I have drowned here,
    And the seventh one you shall be . . ."

4. · . · . · . · . · . ·
    And tumbled him into the sea, sea, sea,
    And tumbled him into the sea.

5. She mounted on her bonny brown,
   And she led the dappled gray,
And she rode till she came to her father's own door,
   Three long hours before it was day, day, day,
   Three long hours before it was day.

6. . . . .
   "Your cage shall be lined with my father's beaten gold
   And hung on a willow tree, tree, tree,
   And hung on a willow tree."

128. "The False Sir John"

Cox, 1939, pp. 1-3. Sung by Silas A. Lingo, Milan, Ind.,
August 1925.

a I

1. He followed her up and he followed her down,
   And he followed her where she lay;
And she had not the heart to say him nay,
   For the morrow was their wedding day, day, day,
   For the morrow was their wedding day.

2. She told him to go to her father's stables,

   . . . .
   And saddle two of her father's best horses,
   Wherein stood thirty and three, three, three,
   Wherein stood thirty and three.

3. She mounted, she mounted her bonny brown,
   And he the dapple gray;
And away they rode to yon far waterside,
   Three long hours before it was day, day, day,
   Three long hours before it was day.

4. "Light off, light off, my pretty Colleen,
   Light off, light off," says he;
"For six king's daughters I've drowned here,
   And the seventh that you shall be, be, be,
   And the seventh that you shall be.

5. "Take off, take off your fine silk gown,
   Your petticoats of the same;
For they are too rich and costly
   To lie and rot in the main, main, main,
   To lie and rot in the main."

6. "Oh turn yourself all around and about,
   Your face toward the sea,
For it does not become a modest man
   A naked woman for to see, see, see,
   A naked woman for to see."

7. He turned himself all around and about,
   His face toward the sea,
And so manfully she picked him up
   And plunged him into the sea, sea, sea,
   And plunged him into the sea.

8. "Lie there, lie there, you false Sir John,
   Lie there, instead of me;
For six king's daughters you've drowned here,
   But the seventh you never shall see, see, see,
   But the seventh you never shall see."

9. She mounted, she mounted her bonny brown,
   And led the dapple gray,
And away she rode to her father's palace,
   Two long hours before it was day, day, day,
   Two long hours before it was day.

10. Then up bespoke the pretty little parrot,
    Wherein his cage he lay,
Saying, "Where have you been, my pretty Colleen,
    Two long hours before it is day, day, day,
    Two long hours before it is day?"

11. "Hush up, hush up, my pretty little parrot,
    And tell no tales on me,
And your cage shall be made of the yellow beaten gold,
    And hang on a green willow tree, tree, tree,
    And hang on a green willow tree."

12. Then up bespoke the aged old king,
    Wherein his chamber he lay,
Saying, "What is the matter with my pretty little parrot,
    That she chatters so long before day, day, day,
    That she chatters so long before day?"

13. "The cat was in at my cage door,
    My body all for to slay,
And I was calling on Pretty Polly
    To chase the cat away, way, way,
    To chase the cat away."

129. "The Six Fair Maids"

Brown MS., 16 a 4. Text, *North Carolina Folklore*, II, 1952,
pp. 24-25. Sent by Thomas Smith, Zionville, Watauga
County, N.C.; learned from Mrs. Rebecca Icenham, February 1, 1915.

a M

1. He jumped upon the milk-white steed
   And her on the iron gray.
   They rode till they come to the river side,
   Two hours before it was day.

2. 'Light off, light off, my pretty little miss,
   Light you off, I say.
   Six pretty maids have I drowned here,
   And you the seventh shall be.

3. 'Pull off that fine silk dress
   And hang it on my knee.
   It is too fine and costly
   To rot in the sea sandee.'

4. 'Turn your back, you dirty dog,
   Turn your back,' said she;
   'Ain't it a shame and a scandal
   A naked woman for to see!'

5. She picked him up so manfully
   And plunged him into the sea.
   'Six fair maids you have drowned here,
   And you the seventh shall be.'

6. 'Hold your tongue, my pretty parrot,
   Don't tell no tales on me,
   And your cage shall be lined with gold dust
   And your doors with ivoree.'

130. "The Outlandish Knight"

Flanders and Brown, 1931, pp. 190-92. Sung by Mr. Sharon Harrington, Bennington, Vt., September 12, 1930; learned from his mother. Recorded by George Brown. From *Vermont Folk-Songs and Ballads*, edited by Helen Hartness Flanders and George Brown; copyright 1931 by Arthur Wallace Peach.

a M (or p I)

1. He followed me up and he followed me down,
   And he followed [me] where I lie.
   He followed me til I had not a tongue
   To answer "yes" or "no."

2. "Go steal, go steal your mother's gold,
   Likewise your father's fees
   And go and steal two the very best of the steeds
   Where in there stands thirty and three."

3. So she went and she stole her mother's gold
   And likewise her father's fees,
   And she went and she stole the very best of steeds
   Where in there stood thirty and three.

4. Then she jumped onto the milk-white steed
   And she led Nelly Grey.
   She rode till she came to her lover's side
   Four long hours before it was day.

5. Then he jumped onto the milk-white steed
   And she rode Nelly Grey
   And they rode till they came to the broad seashore
   Three long hours before it was day.

6. "Get you down, get you down, my pretty Polly,
   For I've something to tell to thee;
   For six king's daughters I've drownded here
   And you the seventh shall be.

7. "Take off, take off these gay clothing
   And hang 'em on the willow tree.
   For they are too rich and too costly
   To rot with your body in the sea.

8. "Turn yourself around, turn yourself around,
   Around to the limbs of the tree.
   . . . .
   . . . .

9. . . . .
   And she grasped him around the middle so small
   And threw him into the sea.

10. "Lay there, lay there, you false-hearted one,
    Lay there in the room of me.
    For it's six king's daughters you have drownded here
    And the seventh has drownded thee."

11. Then she jumped onto the milk-white steed
    And she led Nelly Grey.
    She rode till she came to her father's barnyard
    Two hours before it was day.

12. Then up speaks the pretty parrot
    Who in his cage did lay.
    Saying, "Why are you calling for pretty Polly,
    So long before 'tis day?"

13. Then up speaks the good old man
    Who in his bed did lie,
    Saying, "Why are you calling for pretty Polly
    So long before it is day?"

14. "There's been a black cat to my cage door
    All for to devour me
    And I've been calling for pretty Polly
    All for to scat that cat away."

15. "Now hark your noise, my pretty parrot,
    And tell no tales on me,
    And your cage will be lined with a yellow beaten gold
    And hung in the willow tree."

131. "Willie Came over the Ocean"

Randolph, I, 1946, p. 47(E). Sung by Lewis Kelley, Cyclone, Mo., August 12, 1931.

a I

Willie come over the mid-wide ocean,
Willie come over the sea,
An' Willie come down to my father's house,
An' Willie come a-courtin' of me, me, me,
An' Willie come courtin' of me.

132. "Billy Came over the Main White Ocean"

Arnold, 1950, pp. 54-55. Sung by Lena Hill, Lexington, Ala.

a π[1]

1. Billy came over the main white ocean,
Billy came over the sea,
Billy came down to my father's house,
Billy came a courtin' of me, me, me,
Billy came a courtin' of me.

2. Go choose your pot of mother's gold
And a pot of father's bees
And to some far country we will go
And it's married we will be, be, be,
And it's married we will be.

3. She went and took a pot of her mother's gold
And down to her father's stable
And there she took a choice of thirty,
And a choice of thirty and three, three, three,
And a choice of thirty and three.

4. She mounted upon a milk white horse,
And Billy on a damsel gray;
They rode up to a sea shore
The length of a long summer day, day, day,
The length of a long summer day.

5. "You mount you down you little pert bird
So lay you down," said he,
"For the six king's daughters I've drowned here
And the seventh you shall be, be, be,
And the seventh you shall be."

6. "Turn your face all around and about
And view the green leaves on the tree
To see what a scandal it will be
To drown me in the sea, sea, sea,
To drown me in the sea."

7. He turned his face all around and about
To view the green leaves on the tree.
She took him by the slender waist
And plunged him in the sea, sea, sea,
And plunged him in the sea.

8. "Reach forth, reach forth, your lily-white hands
And take me out of the sea;
I'll fill all the promises I've made to you
And it's married we will be, be, be.
And it's married we will be."

9. "Lie there, lie there, you false-hearted man
You as well as to lie there as me
For the six kings' daughters you have drowned
And the seventh I won't be, be, be,
And the seventh I won't be."

10. She mounted upon a milk white horse
A leading of a damsel grey;
She rode up to her father's house
About three hours before day, day, day,
Just about three hours before day.

11. "Hush up, hush up, you little pert bird
Don't you tell no tales on me
For I left poor Billy beneath the waves
A looking after me, me, me,
A looking after me."

133. [King's Daughter; or, Six Fair Maids]

Brown MS., 16 a 4. Text, *North Carolina Folklore*, 1952, II, pp. 15-17. Probably sung by Mrs. J. J. Miller (*née* Myra Barnett) and recorded by Mrs. Sutton.

a I/M

1. 'My pretty little crowin' chicken,
It's don't you crow too soon,
And your wing shall be of the yellow beaten gold
And your comb of the silver so gay gay gay
And your comb of the silver so gay.'

2. She stole her father's horses,
And she rode the dappled bay,
And she travelled till she came to the salt-water sea
Six hours before it was day day day,
Six hours before it was day.

3. 'Light down, light down, pretty Polly,
   And stand by the side of me.
   For the six king's daughters that I have drowned here
   And the seventh daughter you shall be, be, be,
   And the seventh daughter you shall be.

4. 'Pull off, pull off those fine, fine clothes
   And give them unto me;
   For I do think that they're too costly and too fine
   To rot in the salt-water sea sea sea,
   To rot in the salt-water sea.'

5. 'Oh turn your back all unto me
   And your face to the leaves on the tree;
   For I do think it's a scandal and a shame
   That a naked woman you should see see see,
   That a naked woman you should see.'

6. He turned his back all unto her
   And his face to the leaves on the tree.
   She picked him up so manly and so strong
   And pitched him into the salt-water sea,
   And pitched him into the sea.

7. 'Lie there, lie there, you false-hearted man,
   Lie there in the place of me.
   For the six king's daughters that you have drowned there,
   And the seventh daughter you shall be be be,
   And the seventh daughter you shall be.'

8. She rode her father's horse
   And she led the dappled bay,
   And she rode till she came to her own father's house
   Three hours before it was day day day,
   Three hours before it was day.

9. 'Oh, where have you been, pretty Polly,
   So long before it is day?'

10. 'Oh, hush, oh, hush, my little parrot,
    And tell no tales on me,
    And your cage it shall be of the yellow beaten gold
    And the doors of the ivory ry ry,
    And the doors of the ivory.'

11. 'Oh, why do you wake, my little parrot,
    So long before it is day?'
    'There came a cat unto my nest to rob me of my rest,
    And I called pretty Polly to drive it away,
    And I called pretty Polly to drive it away.'

134. "Pretty Polly"

Major, *PTFLS*, X (1932), pp. 138-40. Sung by Mrs. J. C.
Marshall, Quanah, Texas.

a I/M

The original printing is in straight 4/4 time.

1. He followed her up, he followed her down;
   He followed her day by day;
   She had no tongue to say no, no,
   No faith to say yea, yea—
   No faith to say yea, yea.

2. "Go bring me all of your father's gold,
   And a part of your mother's fee,
   And two of the best steeds from your father's stalls,
   And married we will be, be, be—
   And married we will be."

3. She mounted on the milk-white steed;
   He rode the dapple gray;
   They rode till they came to the red salt sea
   Three hours before it was day, day, day—
   Three hours before it was day.

4. "Oh, get you down, my pretty Polly;
   Oh, get you down," said he.
   "For six kings' daughters I've drown-ded here,
   And you the seventh shall be, be, be—
   And you the seventh shall be."

5. "Take off, take off those gay, fine clothes,
   And hang on yonders tree;
   They are too costly and too fine,
   To rot in the sea, sea, sea—
   To rot in the sea."

6. "Oh, turn your head, sir, and look around,
   And look on yonders tree."
   She picked him up so manfully,
   And threw him in the sea, sea, sea—
   And threw him in the sea.

7. "Oh, hand me your hand, my pretty Polly,
   Oh, hand me your hand," said he,
   "And I'll fulfill my promise to you,
   And married we will be, be, be—
   And married we will be."

8. "Lie there, lie there, you false young man,
   Lie there in the place of me;
   For six kings' daughters you've drown-ded here,
   And you the seventh shall be, be, be—
   And you the seventh shall be."

9. She mounted on the milk-white steed
   And led the dapple gray;
   She rode till she came to her own father's gate
   One hour before it was day, day, day—
   One hour before it was day.

10. "Oh, what's the matter, my pretty parrot?
    Oh, what's the matter?" said she.
    "Oh, what's the matter, my pretty parrot,
    A-chattering so long before day, day, day—
    A-chattering so long before day?"

11. "The old cat was at my cage door,
    And said she would kill me,
    And I was calling Pretty Polly

To drive the cat away, way, way—
To drive the cat away."

12. "Oh, hold your tongue, my pretty parrot,
   And tell no tales on me;
   Oh, hold your tongue, my pretty parrot
   And tell no tales on me, me, me—
   And tell no tales on me."

135. [Lady Isabel and the Elf Knight]

Sharp MSS., 3612/. Also in Sharp and Karpeles, 1932, I, p. 13(I). Sung by May Ray, Harrogate, Tenn., April 29, 1917.

m M

In 1932, the sixth note is a D; but not in the MS. Sharp's MS. note indicates that the holds are equal to two quarters.

You go and get your father's gold,
Likewise your mother's fee,
And two of the best studs* in yonders Hall,
Where there stand thirty and three.

* 1932: "steeds"

136. "The King's Daughter; or, Come a Link, Come a Long"

Davis, 1929, p. 550(D); text, pp. 68-69. Sung by Edward Stinnet and Mrs. Wildman, Lynch Station, Va., April 11, 1924. Collected by Juliet Fauntleroy.

a π² (or p π¹)

1. "You followed me up, you followed me down,
   You followed me day by day,
   You neither had the tongue for to tell me yea,
   Nor the heart for to turn me away, [-way, -way,
   Nor the heart for to turn me away."]

2. "I followed you up, I followed you down,
   I followed you day by day,
   I neither had the tongue for to tell you yea,
   Nor the heart to turn you away."

3. She got up on the little pony brown,
   He got up on the gray,
   They rode till they came to the blue, salt sea,
   Come a link, come a long summer day.

4. "Get down, get down, my pretty fair Miss,
   And fold your silk veil on my knee,
   For it's cost your father too much money
   To rot in the blue salt sea."

5. He turned his head around and about
   Till he faced to the leaves of the tree,
   [She took him hastily up in her arms]
   And she splunged him into the blue, salt sea.

6. "Oh, hand me down your white lily hand,
   Oh, hand it down to me,
   [Oh, hand me down your white lily hand,]
   And married we shall be."

7. "No, sir, for you have drownded
   Nine of the king's daughters [fair]
   [Bear you them company].
   You lie there in the place of me."

8. She got on the little pony brown,
   And she led the iron gray,
   She rode till she came to her father's gate,
   Just three hours till day.

9. "Wake up, wake up, dear parents,
   And tell no tales on me.
   All the crimes that I have done
   Hangs on a green willow tree."

10. She got on the little pony brown,
    And she started off at full speed.
    The golden rings flew off her fingers,
    And her nose begin to bleed.

11. "And I wish to the Lord I had never been born,
    Or had died when I was young,
    I'd never been here to shed a tear,
    Nor to listen to your lying tongue."

137. [Lady Isabel and the Elf Knight]

Sharp MSS., 3211/. Sung by Mrs. Gasnell, Allanstand, N.C., August 4, 1916.

p I/M

There were a tall young man
And Willie was his name
He followed me up he followed me down
He followed me to my own room

138. "The False-hearted Knight"

Flanders and Olney, 1953, pp. 4-7. Sung by Dr. Temple Burling, Providence, R.I., January 22, 1945. From *Ballads Migrant in New England*, edited by Helen Hartness Flanders and Marguerite Olney; copyright 1953 by Helen Hartness Flanders.

a I

1. Come listen, come listen, my good people all;
Come listen awhile unto me,
Of the false-hearted knight and the little Golden,
The truth unto you I will sing, sing, sing;
The truth unto you I will sing.

2. He followed her up, he followed her down;
He followed her to her bed chamber side.
She had not the wings to fly away from him
Nor the tongue to tell him "O nay!", "O nay!", "O nay!"
Nor the tongue to tell him "O nay!"

3. "Oh, get you up, my little Golden,
And come along with me,
And I'll take you to old Scotland
And there I'll marry thee."

(Follow pattern)

4. "O take of your father's yellow-beating gold,
Likewise of your mother's fee,
And the two best horses in your father's stable,
Where they stand, thirty and three." etc.

5. She took of her father's yellow beating gold,
Likewise of her mother's fee,
And the two best horses in her father's stable,
Where they stand, thirty and three. etc.

6. He mounted on the bonny, bonny brown,
And she on the dappl' and gray,
And they rode till they came to the sea-beating shore,
Three long hours before it was day. etc.

7. "O get you down, my little Golden,
And come along with me.
Six king's daughters have I drownded here,
And the seventh you air for to be. etc.

8. "Take off, take off that gown so fine
And deliver it unto me,
For it is not meet that so costly a thing
Should rot in this wat'ry tomb. etc.

9. "Take off, take off those shoes so fine
And deliver them unto me.
For it is not meet that so costly a thing
Should rot in this wat'ry tomb. etc.

10. "Take off, take off those hose so fine
And deliver them unto me,
For it is not meet that so costly a thing
Should rot in this wat'ry tomb. etc.

11. "Take off, take off that smock so fine
And deliver it unto me,
For it is not meet that so costly a thing
Should rot in this wat'ry tomb." etc.

12. "O turn you all around and about
And gaze on the leaves of the tree,
For it is not meet that a villain like thou
A woman unclad should see." etc.

13. He turned him all around and about
And gazed on the leaves of the tree.
She catched him 'round his middle so small
And tumbled him into the sea. etc.

14. "Lie there, lie there, thou false-hearted knight,
Lie there instead of me.
Six king's daughters have you drownded here,
But the seventh hath drownded thee." etc.

15. She mounted on the bonny, bonny brown,
Led home the dappl' and gray,
And she rode till she came to her father's stable,
Three long hours before it was day. etc.

16. It's up speaks the pirate then
To the Golden and did say,
"O my little Golden, it's where have you been,
So long before it was day?" etc.

17. "Oh, hold your tongue, my pretty pirate,
And tell no tales on me,
And your cage shall be lined with yellow beating gold
And hung on yon willow tree." etc.

18. It's up speaks the father then
To the pirate and did say
"O my pretty pirate, why are you prattling
So long before it is day?" etc.

19. "Oh, I dreamed seven cats came to my cage door
And said that they would eat me,
And I was calling my little Golden
To drive those cats all away." etc.

139. "The King's Daughter"

Barry, *JAF*, XXII (1909), p. 76. Sung by Jonathan Carter, Vineland, N.J., March 18, 1907; learned in Bridgeton, N.J., c. 1860.

a I

140. [Lady Isabel and the Elf Knight]

McIntosh, 1935, pp. 4-6. Sung by Mrs. Lottie Hendrickson, Marion, Ill., June 27, 1934.

p I/Ly, ending on *VI* (or a Æ/D)

This variant, as sung by McIntosh at the National Folk Festival in Chicago in 1937, is LC/AAFS, rec. 3250 A1.

1. I follered her up, and I follered her down
   To the chamber where she lay.
   She neither had the heart for to flee from me,
   Nor the tongue for to tell me nay, nay,
   Nor the tongue for to tell me nay.

2. "Git up, git up, my pretty 'golin',
   Come go along with me.
   Come go with me to old England,
   And there I will marry thee,
   And there I will marry thee."

3. "Go take the best part of your father's gold,
   Likewise of your mother's fee.
   Take two of the best steeds out of your father's stable,
   Where-in there is thirty and three,
   Where-in there is thirty and three."

4. He mounted her on the bonny brown,
   He led the dappled gray.
   And away they rode to the old sea shore,
   Just in the length of a long summer day,
   Just in the length of a long summer day.

5. "Git down, git down, my pretty 'golin';
   Git down, git down, by the sea.
   For here I've drowned six kings daughters,
   And you the seventh shall be,
   And you the seventh shall be."

6. "Turn yourself all around and around,
   With your face to the greenest tree.
   For I never thought it right,
   A naked woman a man for to see,
   A naked woman a man for to see."

7. He turned himself all around and around,
   With his face to the greenest tree.
   She caught him around the middle so small,
   And tripped him into the sea,
   And tripped him into the sea.

8. "Lie there, lie there, you false William;
   Lie there instead of me.
   For you have stripped me as naked as ever I was born,
   Not a thread have I taken from you,
   Not a thread have I taken from you.

9. She mounted herself on the bonny brown;
   She led the dappled gray.
   And away she rode to her father's hall,
   Just three hours before it was day,
   Just three hours before it was day.

10. "Hush up, hush up, my pretty 'golin';
    Don't tell no tales on me.
    I will build you a house with the beating wings of gold,
    And your door shall be silvery,
    And your door shall be silvery."

141. "The Outlandish Knight"

Flanders and Olney, 1953, pp. 129-31. Sung by Hanford Hayes, Staceyville, Maine, September 21, 1940. From *Ballads Migrant in New England*, edited by Helen Hartness Flanders and Marguerite Olney; copyright 1953 by Helen Hartness Flanders.

a I, ending on VIII

The tune settles into the familiar pattern of "Drumdelgie," favorite in the North-East parts of Scotland.

1. There was a knight came from the Northland
   And from the Northland came he.

2. "Bring me some of your father's gold
   And some of your mother's fee;
   Two of the best horses out of the stable
   Where there stands thirty and three."

3. She leaped upon a milk-white steed
   And he took a dapple-gray.
   They rode till they came to the river's side
   Three hours before it was day.

4. "Strip off, strip off your silks and gowns
   And deliver them unto me.
   I'm sure they are too costelee
   To rot in the salt sea."

5. "If I must strip off my silks and gowns
   You must turn your back to me
   For it isn't becoming a robber like you
   A naked woman to see."

6. He turned his back unto her
   A-viewing the leaves so green.
   She caught him by the waist so small
   And plunged him out into the sea.

7. He droop-ed high, he droop-ed low
And turned to the top of the tide.
Saying, "Reach me your hand, my pretty Pollee,
And I will make you my bride."

8. "Lie there, lie there, my false young man,
Lie there, lie there," cried she,
"Six maidens you have drownded here.
The seventh one drownded thee."

9. She leaped upon her milk-white steed
And led her dappled-gray.
She rode till she came to her own father's house
One hour before it was day.

10. The parrot being up in the treetops so high
And hearing the maiden, did say,
"What is the matter, my pretty Pollee,
You tarry so long before day?"

11. "O, hold your tongue, my pretty Polly.
Don't tell no tales upon me.
Your cage shall be made of the glittering gold
And hang upon yonder green tree."

12. The old man being up in the window so high
And hearing the parrot, did say,
"What is the matter, my pretty Pollee,
You prattle so long before day?"

13. "O nothing, O nothing," the parrot replied,
"O nothing, I'm sure it to be.
The cat is up in the window so high
And she is a-watching for thee."

14. "Well turned, well turned, my pretty Pollee,
Well turned, well turned," cried she,
"Your cage shall be made of the glittering gold
And the doors of ivory."

Gil Brenton

CHILD NO. 5

This ballad, of which the non-Continental records are all Scottish, appears to have died out of tradition during the nineteenth century, although Motherwell speaks of it as flourishing in his day. There is little evidence of a strong central current for either text or tune, and the records differ rather widely. It is unfortunate that the earliest record of a tune, sung as it was to the most interesting text, and going back in memory beyond the middle of the eighteenth century, was set down by a confessedly inexpert hand, so that we cannot escape a certain amount of conjecture as to what was intended. There appears, however, to be some melodic affinity between the three extant tunes, on the basis of which one may at least guess with a little more confidence. The records are dated at intervals of about fifty years, but there need not be a distance of more than two generations between the first and the last.

It is noteworthy that both the later records show a triple rhythm and an interlaced refrain,* whilst the first is set down in common time and lacks any indication of a refrain. Also noticeable is the fact that the last has a characteristic (Scottish) feminine cadence, inescapable at the end of the fourth phrase, ambiguous at the other three. These facts may have a bearing upon the first record. All three tunes are in gapped scales (I/M, π^4, Æ/D). The mid-cadences of the Brown and Christie copies are on IV, Motherwell's on the tonic. But the first phrases of Motherwell's and Christie's are alike on the fifth, Mrs. Brown's on the tonic.

The Brown record is from the transcript (now at Harvard) in the hand of Joseph Ritson, made c. 1792-94, from a lost MS. which had belonged to William Tytler, to whom it had been transmitted by Professor Gordon of Aberdeen. It contained the texts of fifteen ballads, taken down from the singing of Mrs. Brown, with their tunes. The tunes were recorded by Mrs. Brown's nephew, "he being then but a meer novice in musick," to give some idea of the "lilts" to which his aunt sang her ballads. Such irregularities as are found in the transcript must be attributed to him: it is certain that Ritson, who had no technical knowledge of music, copied with entire fidelity.

In this MS., it is to be observed that a refrain is present in only one ballad—the elaborate interlaced refrain of "The Two Sisters." (For one other ballad, "Brown Robin," a repetition of, not the last, but the *first*, two lines is indicated by "Repeat to the tune"—a quite unusual proceeding with quatrains.) For a set of ballads taken down from actual singing, this is a very scanty proportion of refrains; and we may reasonably suspect that not everything was put into the record. Moreover, the normal ballad-tune is a tune of not fewer than four phrases, and the rule holds for Mrs. Brown's own tunes. That means that couplets must either be doubled, or provided with refrains. Double couplets are a makeshift unit: tetrameter quatrains normally have an alternate, one-three or two-four, rhyme. It seems possible, therefore, that Mrs. Brown's couplets may actually have been sung, but not dictated, with refrains. One further piece of evidence bearing on the point is that her tune for "Clerk Colven" (42), as we shall see in due time, is too long for a stanza of her text; yet there is no record of a refrain. In the MS., as here, the words of the ballads, with one exception, are not fitted to the notes, but inscribed below.

Whether or not Mrs. Brown sang the present ballad with a refrain interlaced, there are further difficulties in the record before us. The tune is written with six bar-lines. Six bars means twelve accents. Tetrameter couplets, of course, have eight. Even supposing a lost refrain, a six-bar tune would be awkward to accommodate in the straightforward British rhythmical tradition.

It appears, from the evidence of the MS. as a whole, that Mrs. Brown was in the habit of emphasizing certain notes of her phrases by a trill or mordent. There are four trills in the present tune, each at about the point where a cadence might be expected; but all except the third come on unaccented positions as the MS. stands. When the tune is justified by an editor, it seems natural to make the last stress of each phrase coincide with the first beat of a bar; but one might alternatively shift every bar-line one beat ahead of that reading.

Judging by the example of the Christie tune, with which this has demonstrable similarities, it seems possible that Mrs. Brown's tune was really in triple time. Strictly sung, it would be 3/4 throughout, and the time-values of the four notes preceding the first and last phrase-finals would be only half as long as they were set down. It was probably Mrs. Brown's deliberation at these points that threw the recorder off his reckoning. The singer may also have shortened the middle pause by a beat; but I have chosen rather to allow the phrase its full length. The other adjustments are self-explanatory.

Nevertheless, a far easier way, rejected here only after much deliberation, is to accept the 4/4 signature and adjust to regular eight-beat phrases in common time.

* The latter also appears in Child's texts D-H, and a fragment (V, p. 207) printed in 1833. His C-text, said to come from a Galloway peasant woman over ninety years old, and printed c. 1810, is in couplets, but has two stanzas in tetrameter rhymed quatrains and two in ordinary ballad meter. The E-text dates from c. 1730.

LIST OF VARIANTS

1. "Chil' Brenton." Ritson-Tytler-Brown MS., pp. 22-30, Harvard College Library.
2. "Lord Bengwill; or, Lord Bingwell." William Motherwell, *Minstrelsy: Ancient and Modern*, 1827, App'x No. 5.
3. "Aye the Birks a-bowing; or, Lord Dingwall." W. Christie, *Traditional Ballad Airs*, II, 1881, p. 10.

1. "Chil' Brenton"

Ritson-Tytler-Brown MS., pp. 22-30. Sung by Mrs. Brown, Falkland, Aberdeenshire; copied by Joseph Ritson, c. 1792-1794.

Mrs. Brown's tune, conjectural reading

a Æ/D

Chil' Brenton has sent o'er the fame,
Chil' Brenton's brought his lady hame;
An' seven score o' ships came her wi',
The lady by the greenwood tree.
There was twal' and twal' wi' beer and wine,
And twal' and twal' wi' muskadine,
And twal' and twal' wi' bouted flour,
And twal' and twal' wi' the paramour,
And twal' and twal' wi' baken bread,
And twal' and twal' wi' the gou'd sae red.
Sweet Willy was a widows son,
And at her stirrup foot he did run.
An' she was dress'd i' the finest pa',
But ay she loot the tears down fa';
And she was dress'd wi' the finest flow'rs,
But ay she loot the tears down pour.
"O is there water i' your shee?
Or does the wind blaw i' your glee?
Or are you mourning in your meed
That e'er you left your mither gueed?
Or are you mourning i' your tide
That e'er you was Chil' Brentons bride?"
"There is nae water i' my shee,
Nor does the wind blaw i' my glee,
Nor am i mourning i' my tide
That e'er i was Chil' Brentons bride;
But i am mourning i' my meed
That e'er i left my mither gueed.
But, bonny boy, (now) tell to me
What is the customs o' your country."
The customs o' it, my dame, he says,
Will ill a gentle lady please.
Seven kings daughters has our king wedded,
An' seven kings daughters has our king bedded,
But he's cutted the paps frae their breast-bane,
An' sent them mourning hame again.

But whan you come to the palace-yate
His mither a golden chair will set,
An' be you maid or be you nane,
O sit you there till the day be dane;
And gin you're sure that you're a maid,
Ye may gang safely to his bed;
But if o' that ye be nae sure,
Then hire some virgin o' your bower.
O whan she came to the palace-yate
His mither a golden chair did set,
An' was she maid or was she nane,
She sat in it till the day was dane.
An' she's call'd on her bow'r-woman,
That waiting was her bow'r within:
"Five hundred pounds i'll gi to thee
An' sleep this night wi' the king for me."
Whan bells was rung and mess was sung,
And a' man unto bed was gone,
Chil' Brenton and the bonny maid
'Intill' ae chamber they were laid.
"O speak to me, blankets, and speak to me, sheets,
And speak to me, cods, that under me sleeps,
Is this a maid 'at i ha' wedded?
Is this a maid 'at i ha' bedded?"
"It's not a maid that you had wedded,
But it's a maid 'at you ha' bedded;
Your lady lies in her bigly bow'r,
An' for you she drees mony sharp show'r."
O he has ta'en him through the ha',
And on his mother he did ca':
"I am the most unhappy man
That ever was in christen'd lan';
I woo'd a maiden meek and mild,
And i've marry'd a woman great wi' child."
"O stay, my son, into this ha',
An' sport you wi' your merry men a',
And i'll gang to yon painted bow'r,
An' see how't fares wi' yon base whore."
The auld queen she was stark and strang,
She gar'd the door flee off the band;
She gar'd the door lye i' the fleer:
"O is your bairn to laird or loon?
Or is it to your fathers groom?"
"My bairn's nae to laird or loon,
Nor is it to my fathers groom.
But hear me, mither, o' my knee,
'Till my hard wierd i tell to thee.
O we were sisters, sisters seven,
We was the fairest under heaven;
We had nae mair for our seven years wark
But to shape and sew the kings son a sark.
It fell on a Saturdays afternoon,
Whan a' our langsome wark was doone,
We kest the kavels us amang,
To see which should to the green-wood gang.
Ohon! alas! for i was youngest,
An' ay my wierd it was the hardest,
The cavel it on me did fa',
Which was the cause of a' my woe;
For to the green-wood i must gae,
To pu' the nut but an the slae,
To pu' the red rose and the thyme,
To strew my mithers bow'r and mine.

I had nae pu'd a flow'r but ane,
Till by there came a jolly hind-greem,
Wi' high-coll'd hose and laigh-coll'd sheen,
An' he seem'd to be some king his son;
And be i maid or be i nane,
He kept me there till the day was dane;
And be i maid or be i nae,
He kept me there till the close o' day.
He gae me a lock o' yallow hair,
An' bade me keep it for evermair;
He gae me a carket o' gude black beeds,
An' bade me keep them against my needs;
He gae to me a gay gold ring,
An' bade me keep it aboon a' thing;
He gae to me a little penknife,
An' bade me keep it as my life."
"What did you wi' these tokens rare
That ye got frae that young man there?"
"O bring that coffer unto me,
An' a' the tokens ye shall see."
And ay she ra[u]ked and she flang,
Till a' the tokens came till her han'.
"O stay here, daughter, your bow'r within,
Till i gae parly wi' my son."
O she has ta'en her through the ha',
An' on her son began to ca':
"What did you wi' that gay gold ring
I bade you keep aboon a' thing?
What did you wi' that little penknife
I bade ye keep while ye had life?
What did ye wi' that yallow hair
I bade ye keep for evermair?
What did ye wi' that gude black beeds
You should ha' kept against your needs?"
"I gae them till a lady gay
I met i' the green wood on a day;
And i would gie a' my ha's and tow'rs
I had that bright bird i' my bow'rs;
I would gie a' my fathers lan'
I had that lady by the han'."
"O, son, keep still your ha's and tow'rs,
You ha' that lady i' your bow'rs,
An' keep you still your fathers lan',
Youse get that lady by the han'."
Now or a month was come and gone
This lady bare a bonny young son,
An' 'twas well written on his breast-bane,
"Chil' Brenton is my fathers name."

2. "Lord Bengwill; or, Lord Bingwell"

Motherwell, 1827, App'x No. 5. Singer unknown. Collected by Andrew Blaikie, Paisley.

a I/M

It might be better to move all the bars forward one beat, so as to give a feminine ending on the second and fourth phrasal cadences. This would accord with the evidence of Christie's tune, following; and also, we surmise, with Mrs. Brown's.

Seven ladies liv'd in a bower,
Hey down and ho down,
And aye the youngest was the flower,
Hey down and ho down.

3. "Aye the Birks a-bowing; or, Lord Dingwall"

Christie, II, 1881, p. 10. Sung by his paternal grandfather; "arranged." Text "epitomized" from Buchan, 1828, I, p. 204.

a π⁴

The second strain is probably Christie's invention.

O we were sisters, sisters seven,
A-bowing down, a-bowing down;
The fairest women under heav'n,
And aye the birks a-bowing.
And we kiest kevels us amang,
A-bowing down, a-bowing down,
Wha wou'd now to the greenwood gang,
And aye the birks a-bowing. [etc.]

Willie's Lady

CHILD NO. 6

THE preservation of this ballad in the British Isles is owing solely to Mrs. Brown of Falkland, although the Scandinavian record reaches back to the sixteenth century, and the elements of its story in popular legend are widespread and ancient.

Again we are faced with a vexing problem in interpreting the notes purporting to represent Mrs. Brown's tune. Were it not that this is the only record, the monotonous character of the phrases would hardly justify the effort of fitting them to the words.

The question is how to wed tetrameter couplets to five bars of music. The possibility of a missing refrain, discussed in connection with the preceding ballad, will have to be dismissed in the present case. If there had been a refrain, it would naturally have been an interlaced refrain of tetrameter length between the extant couplets. Such a refrain would pose an identical problem for the present tune. Since four tetrameter lines of text could not possibly be cramped into the space of the notes given, we should have to assume full repetition to carry the quatrain. This would not solve the main difficulty, which lies in the inequality of the two halves.*

As it stands, the tune appears to be a sadly *zersungen* thing of the type AB—almost, in fact, AA. The simplest way to solve the puzzle is to start with the final cadence and work backward, fitting typical second lines of couplets to the notes. We thus discover a natural starting-point for the second phrase; and this is confirmed by the fact that the notes immediately preceding constitute a cadence for the first phrase exactly corresponding to—in fact, identical with—the final cadence. Working backward as before, we reach the first accented syllable of a typical iambic tetrameter line without difficulty. It comes on the second B. Hence the note preceding—that is, the held G—must carry the unaccented first syllable. It now appears that the first two notes are unaccommodated to the text: I believe them to be in the nature of opening grace-notes, useful in adjusting hypermetrical lines to the tune, as, for example, in the fortieth couplet. A more natural timing of the tune would be 2/4.

It will, I think, be admitted that to hear the forty-four couplets, even without refrain, sung through to this monotonous chant (plagal I/Ly, lacking its second and fourth) would be less than exhilarating as a musical experience. But doubtless Homer's auditors attended more to the words than to the notes.

* The tune does not allow for an end-refrain, nor can we assume one in the middle.

LIST OF VARIANTS

"Willie's Lady." Ritson-Tytler-Brown MS., pp. 1-5, Harvard College Library.

TUNES WITH TEXTS

"Willie's Lady"

Ritson-Tytler-Brown MS., pp. 1-5. Sung by Mrs. Brown, Falkland, Aberdeenshire; copied by Joseph Ritson, c. 1792-1794.

Mrs. Brown's tune, conjectural reading.

p I/Ly (– II) (compass of sixth)

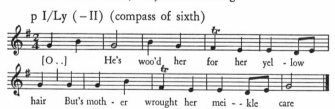

[O..] He's woo'd her for her yel-low hair But's moth-er wrought her mei--kle care

Willie's taen him o'er the fame,*
He's woo'd a wife, and brought her hame;
He's woo'd her for her yallow hair,
But's mother wrought her meickle care,
And meickle dolor gar'd her dree,
For lighter she can never be;
But in her bow'r she sits wi' pain,

And Willie mourns o'er her in vain.
And to his mither he has gane,
That vile rank witch o' vilest kind,
He says, My lady has a cup,
Wi' gold and silver set about,
This goodly gift shall be your ain,
And lat her be lighter o' her young bairn.
"Of her young bairn she's never be lighter,
Nor in her bow'r to shine the brighter,
But she shall die and turn to clay,
And you shall wed another May."
"Another may I'll never wed,
    Another may I'll never bring hame:"
But sighing says that weary wight,
    "I wish my life were at an end."
"Ye doe unto your mother again,
That vile rank witch of viler kind,
And say your lady has a steed,
The like o'm's nae i' the lands of Leed;
For he is golden shod before,
    And he is golden shod behind,
An' at ilka tet of that horse' main
    There's a golden chess and a bell ringing;
This goodly gift shall be her ain,
And lat me be lighter of my young bairn."
"Of her young bairn she's never be lighter,
Nor in her bow'r to shine the brighter,

But she shall die and turn to clay,
And you shall wed another may."
"Another may I'll never wed,
   Another may I'll never bring hame:"
But sighing says that weary wight,
   "I wish my life were at an end."
"Ye doe you to your mother again,
That vile rank witch o' viler kind,
An' say your lady has a girdle,
It's a' red goud unto the middle,
And ay at ilka silver hem
Hings fifty silver bells and ten;
That goodly gift shall be her ain,
An' lat me be lighter o' my young bairn."
"Of her young bairn she's never be lighter,
Nor in her bow'r to shine the brighter,
But she shall die and go to clay,
And you shall wed another may."
   "Another may, etc.
Then out it spake the Belly-blind,†
(He spake ay in a good time)
"Ye doe ye to the market-place,
And there ye buy a loaf o' wax,
You shape it bairn and bairnly like,
And in twa glasen een you pit;
An' bid her come to your boy's christ'ning:
Then notice well what she shall do;

And do you stand a little forbye,
And listen well what she will say."
"O, wha has loos'd the nine witch-knots
That was amo' that lady's locks?
An' wha's ta'en out the kaims o' care,
That hang amo' that lady's hair?
An' wha's taen down the bush o' wood-bine,
That hang atween her bower and mine?
And wha has kill'd the master kid,
That ran beneath that lady's bed?
An' wha has loos'd her left foot shee,
An' latten that lady lighter be?"
O, Willy's loos'd the nine witch-knots
That was amo' his lady's locks;§
And Willy's ta'en out the kaims o' care,
That hang amo' his lady's hair;
And Willy's taen down the bush o' wood-bine,
That hang atween her bower and thine;
And Willy has kill'd the master-kid,
That ran beneath his lady's bed;
And Willy has loos'd her left foot shee;
An' latten his lady lighter be:
And now he's gotten a bonny young son,
And meickle grace be him upon.

* The sea. (So MS., *sc.* "foam"?)
† A good spirit.
§ The 8 following lines were not repeated in the copy. R[itson]

Earl Brand

CHILD NO. 7

THIS impressive ballad exhibits a marked formal cleavage in tradition, the more ancient-looking type having, among several distinguishing traits, an interlaced refrain, the other having none at all. It is fresh evidence of the probability that ballads in tetrameter couplets originally had such a refrain, that although the Abbotsford-Heber copy (Child A* in the abridged edition) lacks it, the copy taken with its tune conforms to the expected pattern.

Although placed late in his series, Child's F-text is actually one hundred and fifty years older, by the record, than any of the others. Had the compiler of Percy's Folio MS., whence it came, but exerted himself with equal diligence to get the proper tunes, he would have doubled and redoubled the debt of posterity, for we might then have had a purchase of utmost value on the earlier ballad-music. Nothing extant can fill this gap— not all the editions of Playford's *Dancing Master*, nor all the earlier instrumental and sophisticated versions of popular tunes.

None of the extant records of a tune is older than the first quarter of last century, and most of them are quite recent. Between the tunes of the two branches of the family there may earlier have been a closer connection: on one side, however, we have to generalize from a solitary instance. It does not appear that the single tune for the older-seeming branch is entitled to anything like the same veneration as its text: some of the records made in Aberdeenshire about the beginning of the present century have a much more antique look.

In the American tunes collected in the present century, there is sufficient evidence of continuity in tradition from the Scottish line of descent. But in the Appalachians, and spreading westward, a strong tendency is noticeable toward a reduction to the "Boyne Water" and "Lady Isabel" (Group B) or "Gypsy Laddie" type of tune. The variants here, however, show greater independence of the norm than heretofore.

The varieties, though presenting points of affiliation, are strongly enough marked to justify division into five groups, if only for convenience of study.

The first group—so-called for courtesy's sake—consists of two Northumbrian copies of about the middle of the last century, deriving from the same source. These are plagal, in one case π^1, in the other I/M: they have an interlaced refrain on the second and fourth phrases. Melodically, as will be obvious, there is

more than a trace of "Loch Lomond" in their later phrases.

Group B is again composed of a few closely related tunes, perhaps likewise deriving from a single (Scottish) source. The two later copies, in fact, may be editorial revisions of the R. A. Smith copy. All are plagal major, of the "progressive" [ABCD] type, and there is no refrain. It is odd that, whereas the tunes of Group A echoed "Loch Lomond" in all but the first phrase, the first phrase of Group B resembles that tune noticeably, but none of the others.

Group C, where the main extant record lies, is a most interesting study in the dissolution of a clear melodic pattern. Variants stretch in time from the early part of the last century (or before) to the present; and in space from Scotland to Newfoundland and the length of the Atlantic seaboard as far south as Georgia. So long as the tune remained in Scotland it was a quite stable, authentic major; but when it reached Western shores it began to experiment. A Maine copy is close enough to the norm, but the Newfoundland copy tries a new attack and never quite recovers. The Appalachian copies seem, as it were, to take this hint and venture on Mixolydian and pentatonic paths, finally going so far afield in melodic contour as to be almost unrecognizable. All, however, remain in the major galaxy.

Group D is a comparatively small gathering of Virginia variants with mid-cadence consistently on the flat seventh. All are authentic Dorian tunes. The group as a whole begins to display marks of the omnipresent "Gypsy Laddie" scheme, which appears much more clearly in the next group.

Group E is composed of variants that squint, having ambiguous finals which might be Mixolydian or plagal Ionian. These are rather distorted forms of the "Gypsy Laddie" tune, but still related to the preceding group.

Group F is composed of variants that, although carrying marks of kinship with the preceding and with one another, are generally speaking so aberrant as to deserve segregation. They come from areas as far asunder as New Brunswick, Indiana, and Tennessee, and are of various modalities which seem unnecessary to specify, since they relate so distantly. The Maine copy is suggestive of Motherwell's "Queen Eleanor's Confession" (156); a Kentucky variant strongly suggests the favorite tune of "The House Carpenter" (243).

LIST OF VARIANTS

GROUP A

1a. "Earl Bran." R. White MSS. (Child MSS., Harvard College Library 25241.51F, p. 49).

1b. "The Brave Earl Brand and the King of England's Daughter." J. Collingwood Bruce and John Stokoe, *Northumbrian Minstrelsy*, 1882, pp. 31-33.

GROUP B

2. "The Douglas Tragedy." Robert Archibald Smith, *The Scotish Minstrel* [1820-24], III, p. 86. Also in George Eyre-Todd, *Ancient Scots Ballads*, n.d., p. 64.

3. "The Douglas Tragedy." Sir Walter Scott, *The Poetical Works of Sir Walter Scott*, 1833-34, III, pp. 1-3 and 6-9.

a. "The Douglas Tragedy." Robert Chambers, *Twelve Romantic Scottish Ballads*, 1844, p. 17.

GROUP C

4. "The Douglas Tragedy." Blaikie MS., National Library of Scotland MS. 1578, No. 44, p. 16.

5. "Lady Margaret and Lord William." W. Christie, *Traditional Ballad Airs*, I, 1876, p. 208 (arbitrarily set to "Prince Robert" [Child 87]).

6. "The Seven Brothers." Phillips Barry, Fannie H. Eck-

storm, and Mary W. Smyth, *British Ballads from Maine,* 1929, pp. 35-37.

7. "The Douglas Tragedy." Greig MSS., I, p. 165; text, Bk. 726, XVI, pp. 97ff., King's College Library, Aberdeen. Also in Gavin Greig and Alexander Keith, *Last Leaves of Traditional Ballads and Ballad Airs,* 1925, p. 7(1c). (Spence)

b. "The Douglas Tragedy." Gavin Greig, *Rymour Club Miscellanea,* I (1910), p. 202.

c. "The Douglas Tragedy." Greig-Duncan MS. 785, p. 2, transcribed by W. Walker, King's College Library, Aberdeen. (Bain)

d. "The Douglas Tragedy." John Ord, *The Bothy Songs & Ballads,* 1930, p. 404.

8. "The Douglas Tragedy." From Duncan MSS., No. 399. Greig and Keith, *Last Leaves,* 1925, p. 7(1a). (Lyall)

9. "Lord Douglas." Greig MSS., IV, p. 27. Also in Greig and Keith, 1925, p. 7(1b). (Dunbar)

10. "Earl Brand." Maud Karpeles, *Folk Songs from Newfoundland,* 1934. II, pp. 83-87.

11. "Earl Brand." Sharp MSS., 4182/3015, Clare College Library, Cambridge. Also in Cecil J. Sharp and Maud Karpeles, *English Folk Songs from the Southern Appalachians,* 1932, I, pp. 21(E)-22. (Gibson)

12. "Earl Brand." Sharp MSS., 3106/? Also in Sharp and Karpeles, 1932, I, pp. 19(D)-20. (Moore)

13. "Earl Brand." Sharp MSS., 3169/2308. Also in Sharp and Karpeles, 1932, I, pp. 14(A)-15. (Shelton)

14. "Earl Brand." Sharp MSS., 3436/2526. Also in Sharp and Karpeles, 1932, I, pp. 17(C)-18. (House)

15. "Earl Brand." Sharp MSS., 3190/2337. Also in Sharp and Karpeles, 1932, I, pp. 16(B)-17. (Sands)

16. "Earl Brand." Sharp MSS., 3897/. Also in Sharp and Karpeles, 1932, I, p. 24(J). (Bishop)

17. "Sweet William." Arthur Palmer Hudson, *Folk Tunes from Mississippi,* 1937, No. 22.

GROUP D

18. "Earl Brand." Sharp MSS., 4287/. Also in Sharp and Karpeles, *Appalachians,* 1932; I, p. 25(L). (Dodd)

19. "Earl Brand." Sharp MSS., 4214/3034. Also in Sharp and Karpeles, 1932, I, pp. 22(F)-23. (Fitzgerald, P.)

20. "Earl Brand." Sharp MSS., 4193/3023. Also in Sharp and Karpeles, 1932, I, p. 23(G). (Fitzgerald, C.)

21. "Earl Brand." Winston Wilkinson MSS., 1936-37, p. 5, University of Virginia.

22. "Earl Brand." Wilkinson MSS., 1935-36, pp. 7-8(A).

23. "Earl Brand." Wilkinson MSS., 1935-36, pp. 9-11(B).

24. "The Seven Brothers; or, The Seven Sleepers." Arthur

Kyle Davis, Jr., *Traditional Ballads of Virginia,* 1929, pp. 552(B) and 88-89.

GROUP E

25. "Lord Douglas." Greig MSS., IV, p. 38; text, Bk. 708, p. 38. Also in Greig and Keith, *Last Leaves,* 1925, p. 7(2). (Robb?)

26. "Earl Brand." Sharp MSS., 3756/. Also in Sharp and Karpeles, *Appalachians,* 1932, I, p. 24(I). (Hayes)

27. "Rise Ye Up." Vance Randolph, *Ozark Folksongs,* 1946, I, pp. 48-49. Also in Vance Randolph, *Ozark Mountain Folks,* 1932, p. 219.

GROUP F

28. "The Seven Brothers." Barry, Eckstorm, and Smyth, *British Ballads from Maine,* 1929, pp. 37-39.

29. "Lord Loving." Mellinger Edward Henry, *Folk-Songs from the Southern Highlands,* 1938, p. 37.

30. "Sweet Willie." Maurice Matteson and Mellinger Edward Henry, *Beech Mountain Folk-Songs and Ballads,* Schirmer's American Folk-Song Series, Set 15, 1936, p. 10.

31. "Sweet Willie." F. C. Brown MS., 16 a 4 H, Library of Congress, photostat. Partial text, *The Frank C. Brown Collection of North Carolina Folklore,* II, 1952, p. 31. (Sutton)

32. "Seven Brothers." Brown MS., 16 a 4 H. Partial text (?), *North Carolina Folklore,* II, 1952, pp. 29-30. (Smith)

33. "Sweet William and Fair Ellen." Brown MS., 16 a 4 H. Partial text, as "Sweet Willie," *North Carolina Folklore,* II, 1952, pp. 31-32. (Sutton 2)

34a. Duncan B. M. Emrich, LC Archive of American Folk Song, Album XII, rec. 60B. (I. G. Greer)

34b. "Sweet William and Fair Ellen." Brown MS., 16 a 4 H. Text, *North Carolina Folklore,* II, 1952, pp. 28-29. (Greer 2)

35. "Lady Margaret." Paul G. Brewster, *Ballads and Songs of Indiana,* 1940, pp. 37-39.

36. "Earl Brand." Sharp MSS., 3946/. Also in Sharp and Karpeles, *Appalachians,* 1932, I, p. 25(K). (Creech)

37. "Sweet William and Fair Ellen." Evelyn K. Wells, *Notes from the Pine Mountain Settlement School,* VII, No. 1 (January 1935), pp. 2-3. Also in Evelyn K. Wells, *The Ballad Tree,* 1950, pp. 147-49.

38. "Lord William and Lady Margaret." Helen Hartness Flanders and Marguerite Olney, *Ballads Migrant in New England,* 1953, pp. 228-29.

39. "Earl Brand." Sharp MSS., 4146/. Also in Sharp and Karpeles, *Appalachians,* 1932, I, p. 24(H). (Dunaway)

40. "The Seven Brothers; or, Lord William." Davis, *Traditional Ballads of Virginia,* 1929, pp. 552(D) and 90-91.

TUNES WITH TEXTS

GROUP A

1a. "Earl Bran"

R. White MSS. (Child MSS., HCL 25241.51F, p. 49). Sung by Mrs. Andrews, Northumberland.

Oh did ye ever hear o' brave Earl Bran
  Ay lally o lilly lally
He courted the king's daughters of fair England
  I') the life o' the one the Randy.
    O')

p π¹

The original is written through in straight 4/4.

1b. [The Brave Earl Brand and the King of England's Daughter]

Bruce and Stokoe, 1882, pp. 31-33. Tune sung by Mrs. Andrews, Claremont Place, Newcastle; text recited by an old Northumberland fiddler.

p I/M

This and the preceding variant (as to tune) came from the same singer. The changes here in the third and fourth phrases may be editorial alterations.

1. O did you ever hear of the brave Earl Brand,
   Hey lillie, ho lillie lallie;
   He's courted the King's daughter o' fair England,
   I' the brave nights so early!

2. She was scarcely fifteen years that tide,
   Hey lillie, &c.
   When sae boldly she came to his bedside,
   I' the brave nights, &c.

3. "O, Earl Brand, how fain wad I see
   A pack of hounds let loose on the lea."

4. "O lady fair, I have no steed but one,
   But thou shalt ride, and I will run."

5. "O, Earl Brand, but my father has two,
   And thou shalt have the best o' tho'."

6. Now they have ridden o'er moss and moor,
   And they have met neither rich nor poor.

7. Till at last they met with old Carl Hood,
   He's aye for ill and never for good.

8. "Now, Earl Brand, an' ye love me,
   Slay this old Carl and gar him dee."

9. "O lady fair, but that would be sair,
   To slay an auld Carl that wears grey hair.

10. "My own lady fair, I'll not do that,
    I'll pay him his fee . . . . ."

11. "O, where have you ridden this lee lang day,
    And where have you stown this fair lady away?"

12. I have not ridden this lee lang day,
    Nor yet have I stown this lady away.

13. "For she is, I trow, my sick sister,
    Whom I have been bringing fra' Winchester."

14. "If she's been sick and nigh to dead,
    What makes her wear the ribbon sae red?

15. "If she's been sick and like to die,
    What makes her wear the gold sae high?"

16. When came the Carl to the lady's yett,
    He rudely, rudely rapped thereat.

17. "Now where is the lady of this hall?"
    "She's out with her maids a-playing at the ball."

18. "Ha, ha, ha! ye are all mista'en,
    Ye may count your maidens owre again.

19. "I met her far beyond the lea,
    With the young Earl Brand his leman to be.

20. His father of his best men armed fifteen—
    And they're ridden after them bidene.

21. The lady looked owre her left shoulder, then
    Says, "O, Earl Brand, we are both of us ta'en."

22. "If they come on me one by one,
    You may stand by me till the fights be done

23. "But if they come on me one and all,
    You may stand by and see me fall."

24. They came upon him one by one,
    Till fourteen battles he has won;

25. And fourteen men he has them slain,
    Each after each upon the plain.

26. But the fifteenth man behind stole round,
    And dealt him a deep and a deadly wound.

27. Though he was wounded to the deid,
    He set his lady on her steed.

28. They rode till they came to the river Doune,
    And there they lighted to wash his wound.

29. "O, Earl Brand, I see your heart's blood."
    "It's nothing but the glent and my scarlet hood."

30. They rode till they came to his mother's yett,
    So faintly and feebly he rapped thereat.

31. "O my son's slain, he is falling to swoon,
    And it's all for the sake of an English loon."

32. "O say not so, my dearest mother,
    But marry her to my youngest brother."

33. "To a maiden true he'll give his hand,
    Hey lillie, ho lillie lallie,
    To the king's daughter o' fair England,
    To a prize that was won by a slain brother's brand,
    I' the brave nights so early."

GROUP B

2. [The Douglas Tragedy]

Smith [1820-24], III, p. 86. Also, with piano accompaniment, in Eyre-Todd, *Ancient Scots Ballads*, n.d., p. 64.

p I

Smith's text appears to follow, with minor verbal differences, Scott's copy in the *Minstrelsy*, omitting stanzas 13, 15, 16, and 19.

3. [The Douglas Tragedy]

Scott, 1833-34, III, pp. 1-3; text, pp. 6-9. Copy from Charles Kirkpatrick Sharpe of Hoddam Castle, Perthshire. Last three stanzas from a stall printing of c. 1792.

p I

R. Chambers, 1844, p. 17, gives Scott's text and a tune sharing traits of this and the R. A. Smith copy.

1. "Rise up, rise up, now, Lord Douglas," she says,
   "And put on your armour so bright;
   Let it never be said that a daughter of thine
   Was married to a lord under night.

2. "Rise up, rise up, my seven bold sons,
   And put on your armour so bright,
   And take better care of your youngest sister,
   For your eldest's awa' the last night."—

3. He's mounted her on a milk-white steed,
   And himself on a dapple grey,
   With a bugelet horn hung down by his side,
   And lightly they rode away.

4. Lord William lookit o'er his left shoulder,
   To see what he could see,
   And there he spy'd her seven brethren bold,
   Come riding over the lee.

5. "Light down, light down, Lady Marg'ret," he said,
   "And hold my steed in your hand,
   Until that against your seven brethren bold,
   And your father, I mak a stand."

6. She held his steed in her milk-white hand,
   And never shed one tear,
   Until that she saw her seven brethren fa',
   And her father hard fighting, who lov'd her so dear.

7. "O hold your hand, Lord William!" she said,
   "For your strokes they are wondrous sair;
   True lovers I can get many a ane,
   But a father I can never get mair."

8. O, she's ta'en out her handkerchief,
   It was o' the holland sae fine,
   And aye she dighted her father's bloody wounds,
   That were redder than the wine.

9. "O chuse, O chuse, Lady Marg'ret," he said,
   "O whether will ye gang or bide?"
   "I'll gang, I'll gang, Lord William," she said,
   "For you have left me no other guide."

10. He's lifted her on a milk-white steed,
    And himself on a dapple grey,
    With a bugelet horn hung down by his side,
    And slowly they baith rade away.

11. O they rade on, and on they rade,
    And a' by the light of the moon,
    Until they came to yon wan water,
    And there they lighted down.

12. They lighted down to tak a drink
    Of the spring that ran sae clear;
    And down the stream ran his gude heart's blood,
    And sair she 'gan to fear.

13. "Hold up, hold up, Lord William," she says,
    "For I fear that you are slain!"—
    "'Tis naething but the shadow of my scarlet cloak,
    That shines in the water sae plain."—

14. O they rade on, and on they rade,
    And a' by the light of the moon,
    Until they cam to his mother's ha' door,
    And there they lighted down.

15. "Get up, get up, lady mother," he says,
    "Get up, and let me in!—
    Get up, get up, lady mother," he says,
    "For this night my fair lady I've win.

16. "O mak my bed, lady mother," he says,
    "O mak it braid and deep!
    And lay Lady Marg'ret close at my back,
    And the sounder I will sleep."—

17. Lord William was dead lang ere midnight,
    Lady Marg'ret lang ere day—
    And all true lovers that go thegither,
    May they have mair luck than they!

18. Lord William was buried in St Marie's kirk,
    Lady Marg'ret in Marie's quire;
    Out o' the lady's grave grew a bonny red rose,
    And out o' the knight's a brier.

19. And they twa met, and they twa plat,
    And fain they wad be near;
    And a' the warld might ken right weel,
    They were twa lovers dear.

20. But bye and rade the Black Douglas,
    And wow but he was rough!
    For he pull'd up the bonny brier,
    And flang'd in St Marie's Loch.

GROUP C

4. [The Douglas Tragedy]

Blaikie MS., NL Scotland MS. 1578, No. 44, p. 16.

a I

5. [Lady Margaret and Lord William]

Christie, I, 1876, p. 208. Sung by an old Buchan woman, before 1850. Christie has arbitrarily mated the tune to Scott's text of "Prince Robert" (87), since his singer had forgotten the right words.

m I

Christie has concocted a second strain, here omitted.

6. "The Seven Brothers"

Barry, Eckstorm, and Smyth, 1929, pp. 35-37. Transmitted by Mrs. Guy R. Hathaway, Mattawamkeag, Maine, September 8, 1928; as remembered by her brother, Harold J. Shedd, of Mattawamkeag.

m I

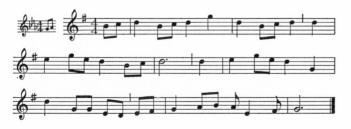

1. "Rise up, rise up, ye seven brothers all,
   And put on your armor so gay,
   And take the care of your elder sister,
   For the younger I'll carry away.

2. "Rise up, rise up, ye seven sons all,
   And put on your armor so fine,—
   For it never shall be said such a saucy young lord
   Ever weds a daughter of mine."

3. She amounted the milk white steed,
   And he upon the grey,
   With his broadsword hanging down by his side,
   This young lord he went riding away.

4. As he looked over his left shoulder
   To see what he could espy,
   'Twas there he saw her seven brothers all
   And her father a-drawing nigh.

5. "Alight, alight, Lady Margaret," he said,
   "And hold my steed in your hand,
   While I fight your seven brothers all,
   And your father near at hand."

6. She stood and she held his steed in her hand,
   And never shed a tear,
   Until she saw her seven brothers fall,
   And her father she loved more dear.

7. "O stay your hand, Lord William!" she cried,
   "Your stripes are wonderous sore,—
   For sweethearts I can many a one have,
   But a father I ne'er can have more."

8. "You can have your choice, Lady Margaret," he said,
   "You can either go or abide."
   "How can I stay, Lord William," she cried,
   "When you've left me no friend nor a guide?"

9. She amounted the milk white steed,
   And he upon the grey,
   With his bugle horn hanging down by his side,
   This young lord he went riding away.

10. He rode on and she rode on,
    All by the light of the moon,
    Until they came to the fair river side,
    Where they both lighted down.

11. "What is the matter, Lord William?" she cried,
    "Your blood flows down the mane!"
    " 'Tis nothing but the shadow of my scarlet robe
    That shines in the watery stream."

12. He rode on and she rode on,
    All by the light of the moon,
    Until they came to his mother's gate,
    Where they both lighted down.

13. "O! Mother dear, pray open your gate
    For to admit your son,
    For I have receivèd my death wound,
    And my true-love and I have come.

14. "O! Mother dear, pray make my bed,
Make it both wide and deep,
And lay Lady Margaret beside of me,
That the sounder I may sleep."

15. Lord William he dièd at midnight,
Lady Margaret she lived till day.
May all true lovers joined in love
Enjoy more comfort than they.

7. [The Douglas Tragedy]

Greig MS., I, p. 165; text, Bk. 726, XVI, pp. 97ff. Also in Greig and Keith, 1925, p. 7(1c). Sung by J. W. Spence, 1906.

m I

This form of the tune appears also in the *Rymour Club Miscellanea*, I (1910), p. 202, with slight differences, probably editorial, in the first stanza of text. Greig is the contributor, but does not there identify his source.

1. "Rise up, rise up, Lord Douglas" she says
And put on your armour sae bright
Let it never be said that a daughter of yours
Was married to a lord or a knight.

2. Rise up, rise up my sons so bold
And put on your armour sae bright
And tak better care o' your youngest sister
For your eldest awa the last night.

3. He's mounted her on a milk-white steed
Himsel' on a dapple gray
With a bright horn hanging down by his side
And sae lightly they both rode away.

4. Lord William looked over his broad shoulder
To see what he could see
And there he spied her seven brothers bold
Come riding over the lea.

5. Light down, light down, Lady Margret, he said
And hold my steed in your hand
Until that against your seven brothers bold
And your father I mak a stand.

6. She held his steed in her milk white hand
And never shed one tear
Until that she saw her seven brothers fa'
And her father still fighting near by.

7. Oh hold your hand Lord William she said
For your strokes they are wondrous sore
True lovers I can get many a one
But a father I'll never get more.

8. Oh choose, oh choose, Lady Margret he said
Choose for to gang or to bide
I'll gang wi' you Lord William she said
For ye've left me no other guide.

9. He's mounted her on a milk white steed
And himself on the dapple gray
With a bugle horn hanging down by his side
And slowly they both rode away.

10. They rode on & on they rode
Twas all by the light of the moon
Until they came to yon bonnie burnie side
And there they both lighted down.

11. They lighted down to take a drink
Of the water that ran there sae clear
And down the stream ran his heart blood
And sair she began to fear.

12. Hold up, hold up, Lord William, she said
For I fear that ye are slain
Tis nothing but the shadow of my scarlet coat
That shines in the water sae plain.

13. They rode on and on they rode
Twas all by the light of the moon
Until they came to his mother's ha' door
And there they both lighted doon.

14. Rise up, rise up, lady mother, he says
Oh rise and let us in
Rise up, rise up, lady mother, he says
For this night my fair lady I've won.

15. Ye'll mak my bed baith lang & wide
Ye'll mak it baith saft & deep
And lay my true love doon by my side
That the sounder we may sleep.

16. Lord William, he died in the middle of the night
Lady Margret she died on the morrow
Lord William he died for the sake of his bride
Lady Margret she died for the sorrow.

17. Lord William was buried in St. Mary's kirk yard
Lady Margret in Mary's quire
And on one the[re]* grew a bonnie myrtle tree
On the other a bonnie sweet brier.

18. They grew & grew & higher they grew
Till they could grow no higher
And they grew together in a true love knot
For true lovers to admire.

* Greig MS. has "their."

8. [The Douglas Tragedy]

Greig and Keith, 1925, p. 7(1a). From Duncan MSS., No. 399. Sung by Mrs. Lyall.

a I

Aye they rode an' on they rode,
'Twas a' by the light o' the moon
Until they cam to his mother's ha' door,
An' 'twas there they both lighted doon.

9. "Lord Douglas"

Greig MSS., IV, p. 27. Also in Greig and Keith, 1925,
p. 7(1b). Sung by Mrs. Dunbar, Longhill of Crimond.

a I/Ly (virtually π¹)

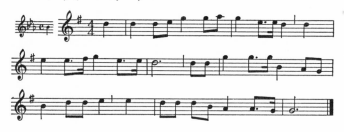

10. [Earl Brand]

Karpeles, 1934, II, pp. 83-87, with original text, transmitted by the collector. Sung by Thomas Ghaney, Colliers,
Conception Bay, Newfoundland, October 22, 1929.

a I

1. Arise, arise, King Henry, he said,
   Or are you not at home?
   Arise and take care of your youngest daughter dear,
   For the eldest are going with me.

2. Arise, arise, my seven sons bold,
   And put on your armour so bright.
   It never shall be said that daughter of mine
   Shall be married to a lord or a knight.

3. Arise, arise, Lady Margaret, he said,
   And hold the white steed in your hand,
   While I go and fight with your seven brothers bold
   And your father in the meadow where he'll stand.

4. Lady Margaret she rose and held the white steed,
   She stood and never shed a tear

Until she had seen her seven brothers fall
And her father that loved her so dear.

5. Ease your hand, ease your hand, Lord Robert, she cries,
   For your blows they are wonderful sore,
   For sweethearts I may get, many's the one,
   But a father dear I never will get more.

6. Choose your choice, choose your choice, Lady Margaret,
                                                  he say,
   Will you come along with me for a bride?
   I must go along with you, Lord Robert, she said,
   For you've left me without any guide.

7. Lord Robert he mounted on a milk-white steed,
   And she on a dapple grey.
   He went sounding of his bugle loud and shrill
   And went bleeding along the highway.

8. He bled till he came to his own mother's door,
   How loud he did rap at the ring.
   Open the door, dear mother, he cries,
   You know my fair lady I have won.

9. Make my bed both deep and wide,
   O make it wide and deep,
   And lay Lady Margaret down by my side
   May the sounder or the better I may sleep.

10. Lord Robert he died about midnight,
    Lady Margaret she died before day.
    I hope every couple that now be together,
    That they may find more enjoyment till day.

11. [Earl Brand]

Sharp MSS., 4182/3015. Also in Sharp and Karpeles, 1932,
I, pp. 21(E)-22. Sung by Mrs. Lizzie Gibson, Crozet, Va.,
April 26, 1918.

a M

In singing the first line of the song, the singer borrowed the first
note of the second phrase for the final syllable, "sleepers," and
slurred the sixteenth and dotted eighth in the same bar for "seven."

1. Wake you up, wake you up, you seven sleepers,
   And do take warning of me;
   O do take care of your oldest daughter dear,
   For your youngest are going with me.

2. He mounted her up on his bonny, bonny brown,
   Himself on the dark apple grey;

He grewn* his buckles down by his side,
And away he went singing away.

3. Get you up, get you up, my seven sons bold,
Get on your arms so bright,
For it never shall be said that a daughter of mine
Shall lie with a lord all night.

4. He rode, he rode that livelong day,
Along with this lady so dear,
Until she saw her seventh brother come
And her father were walking so near.

5. Get you down, get you down, Lady Margaret, he cried,
And hold my horse for a while,
Until I can fight your seventh brother bold,
And your father is walking so nigh.

6. She held, she held, she better, better held,
And never shedded one tear
Until she saw her seventh brother fall
And her father she loved so dear.

7. Do you choose for to go, Lady Margaret, he cried,
Do you choose for to go or to stay?
O I'll go, I'll go, Lord Thomas, she cried,
For you've left me without any guide.

8. He mounted her up on his bonny, bonny brown,
Himself on the dark apple grey;
He grewn* his buckles down by his side,
And away he went bleeding away.

9. He rode, he rode that livelong night
Till he came to his mother's stand.
Get you down, get you down, Lady Margaret, he cried.
So that we can rest for a while.

10. It's mother, mother, make my bed,
And fix it smooth and wide,
And lie my lady down by my side
So that we can rest for a while.

11. Lord Thomas he died by midnight,
Lady Margaret before it were day,
And the old woman for the loss of her son,
And there was several lives lost.

* 1932: "drew"

12. [Earl Brand]

Sharp MSS., 3106/? Also in Sharp and Karpeles, 1932, I,
pp. 19(D)-20. Sung by Mrs. Moore, Rabun County, Ga.,
May 1909.

a π¹

1. He rode up to the old man's gate,
So boldly he did say:
You can keep your youngest daughter at home,
But your oldest I'll take away.

2. O rise you up, you seven brothers all,
And bring your sister down,
It never can be said that a steward's son
Shall take her out of town.

The texts of the variants collected by Olive Dame Campbell and
published in Sharp and Campbell, 1917, are not among the Sharp
MSS.

3. I thank you, kind sir, said he,
I am no steward's son;
My father's of the richest of kings
And my mother's a Quaker's queen.

4. She lit on the milk-white steed,
And he rode on the brown.
. . . . . .
. . . . . .

5. Then they rode about three miles from town,
And then he cast his eyes all around,
And saw her father and seven brothers all
Come trickling down the plain.

6. O, light you off, fair Ellen, said he,
And hold my steed by the rein,
Till I play awhile with your father
And seven brothers all.

7. Fair Ellen she still stood there
And never changed a word
Till she saw her own dear seven brothers all
A-wallowing in their own blood.

8. Fair Ellen she still stood there
And never changed a note,
Till she saw her own dear father's head
Come tumbling by her foot.

9. O hold your hand, sweet William, said she,
Love runs free in every vein,
But father I have no more.
If you are not satisfied with this
I wish you were in your mother's chamberee
And I'se in some house or room.

10. If I was in my mother's chamberee,
You'd be welcome there.
I'll wind you East, I'll wind you West,
I'll trip along with thee.

11. He rode up to his mother's gate
And jangled at the ring:
O mother, dear mother, asleep or awake,
Arise and let me in.

12. O sister, O sister, make my bed,
For my wound is very sore.
O mother, O mother, bind up my head,
For me you'll bind no more.

13. It was about three hours till day,
    And the chickens crowing for day,
    When every wound sweet William received,
    The blood began to pour.

14. Sweet William he died like it was to-day,
    Fair Ellender tomorrow;
    Sweet William died from the wounds he received,
    Fair Ellender died of sorrow.

13. [Earl Brand]

Sharp MSS., 3169/2308. Also in Sharp and Karpeles, 1932,
I, pp. 14(A)-15. Sung by Mrs. Polly Shelton, White Rock,
N.C., July 28, 1916.

a I/Ly

The singer, according to the MS., shortened the mid-cadence to a
half-note's length.

1. O rise you up, ye seven bretherens,
   And bring your sister down;
   It never shall be said that a steward's son
   Had taken her out of town.

2. I thank you kindly, sir, he says,
   I am no steward's son.
   My father is of a regis king,
   My mother's a Quaker's queen.

3. He mound (mounted) her on a milk-white steed,
   He rode the dapple grey.
   He swung a bugle horn all round about his neck
   And so went blowing away.

4. He had not gone three mile out of town
   Till he looked back again,
   And saw her father and seven bretherens
   Come trippling over the plain.

5. Sit you down, fair Ellender, he said,
   And hold this steed by the rein,
   Till I play awhile with your father
   And your seven bretherens.

6. Fair Ellender she sat still.
   It wasn't long till she saw
   Her own dear seven bretherens
   All wallowing in their blood.

7. Fair Ellender she still sat still,
   She never changed a note
   Till she saw her own dear father's head
   Come tumbling by her foot.

8. Saying: Love runs free in every vein,
   But father you have no more,
   If you're not satisfied with this,
   I wish you were in your mother's chamber
   And me in some house or room.

9. If I was in my mother's chamber
   You'd be welcome there.
   I'll wind you east, I'll wind you west,
   I'll wind along with you.

10. He mound her on a milk-white steed,
    He rode the dapple grey,
    He swung a bugle horn all round about his neck
    And so went bleeding away.

11. As he rode up to his father's gate
    He tinkled* at the ring,
    Saying: O dear father, asleep or awake,
    Arise and let me in.

12. O sister, sister, make my bed,
    My wounds are very sore.
    Saying: O dear mother, O bind up my head,
    For me you'll bind no more.

13. It was about three hours till day,
    The cock began to crow.
    From every wound that he received
    His heart blood began to flow.

14. Sweet William he died like it might be to-day,
    Fair Ellender tomorrow.
    Sweet William he died for the wounds he received,
    Fair Ellen died for sorrow.

15. Fair Ellender was buried by the church door,
    Sweet William was buried by her;
    And out of her breast sprung a blood red rose
    And out of his a briar.

16. They growed, they growed to the top of the church
    Till they could grow no higher,
    And there they tied a true love's knot
    And the rose ran round the briar.

* 1932: "tingled"

14. [Earl Brand]

Sharp MSS., 3436/2526. Also in Sharp and Karpeles, 1932,
I, pp. 17(C)-18. Sung by Mrs. Hester House, Hot Springs,
N.C., September 14, 1916.

a I/Ly

1. He rode up to the old man's gate,
   So boldly did he say,
   Saying: Keep your youngest daughter at home,
   For the oldest I'll take away.

7. EARL BRAND

2. He holp her on his milk white steed,
   And he rode the apple grey.
   He swung a bugle horn all around about her neck
   And so went winding away.

3. He hadn't got more than a mile out of town,
   Till he looked back again.
   He saw her own dear seven brothersen
   Come tripping* over the plain.

4. Set you down, fair Ellinor, he said,
   And hold the steed by the rein,
   Till I play awhile with your own dear father
   And your seven brothersen.

5. Fair Ellinor she sat still
   And never changed a word,
   Till she saw her own dear seven brothersen
   All wallowing in their blood.

6. Fair Ellinor she sat still
   And never changed a note,
   Till she saw her own dear father's head
   Come tumbling by her feet.

7. He holp her on her milk white steed
   And he rode the apple grey,
   Till he swung a bugle horn all around about her neck
   And so went winding away.

8. He rode on up to his mother's gate
   And tingled on the ring,
   Saying: O dear mother, asleep or awake,
   Arise and let me in.

9. Sister, sister, fix my bed,
   My wounds are very sore.
   Saying: O dear mother, bind up my head,
   For me you'll bind no more.

10. Sweet William he died with the wounds received,
    Fair Ellinor died with sorrow;
    Sweet William died with the wounds received
    And Ellinor died with sorrow.

11. Sweet William was buried at the upper church yard
    And Ellinor was buried close by.
    Out of William's grave spring a blood red rose
    And out of hers a briar.

12. They grew, they grew to the top of the church
    Where could not grow any higher.
    They wound, they tied in a true love knot,
    The rose wrapped round the briar.

* 1932: "trippling"

15. [Earl Brand]

Sharp MSS., 3190/2337. Also in Sharp and Karpeles, 1932, I, pp. 16(B)-17. Sung by Mrs. Mary Sands, Allanstand, N.C., August 1, 1916.

a π[1]

1. He rode up to her father's gate,
   So boldly he did say:
   You may keep your oldest daughter at home,
   For the youngest I'll take away.

2. He jumped upon the milk-white steed
   And she rode the dapple grey,
   And he hung a bugle horn all round about his neck
   And so went sounding away.

3. He had not got but a mile or two
   Till he looked back over the main,
   And he saw her father and her seven brothers all
   Come trippling over the lane.

4. Get down, get down, get down, says he,
   And hold this steed by the mane,
   Till I play awhile with your father, he says,
   Yes, and your seven brethren.

5. She got down and never spoke,
   Nor never cheeped
   Till she saw her own father's head
   Come trinkling by her feet.

6. Hold your hand, sweet William, she says,
   Pray hold your hand for sure,
   For love runs free in every vein,
   But father I'll have no more.

7. If you hain't pleased at this, he says,
   If you hain't pleased, says he,
   I'll wished you was at home in your mother's chambery
   And me in some house or room.

8. Go wind you East, go wind you West,
   I will go along with you.
   And he hung a bugle all round about his neck,
   And so went bleeding away.

[115]

9. But when he got to his mother's hall,
   He jingled on the ring;
   O dear mother, sleep or awake,
   Rise and let me in.

10. Sister, sister make my bed,
    My wounds are very sore.
    O dear mother, bind my head,
    You'll never bind it no more.

11. It was about three hours before day,
    The chickens begin to crow,
    And every breath that he did draw
    His heart's blood begin to flow.

12. Sweet William died of the wounds he got
    And Barbary died for sorrow,
    And the old woman died for the love of them both
    And was buried on Easter Monday.

16. [Earl Brand]

Sharp MSS., 3897/. Also in Sharp and Karpeles, 1932, I,
p. 24(J). Sung by Mrs. Dan Bishop, Teges, Ky., August 21,
1917.

a I/Ly

Sharp first noted this as straight 2/2, with holds on the quarters
here written as the first, second, and fourth dotted halves.

He rode up to the old man's gate,
So boldly he did say:
Your youngest daughter you can keep at home,
The oldest one I'll take away.

17. "Sweet William"

Hudson, 1937, No. 22. Sung by Mrs. Theodosia B. Long
and Mary Ila Long, Mississippi, between 1923 and 1930.

a I

1. Before the rising of the sun,
   One morning early in sweet May,
   When the tops of the trees were very green,
   And the roots had withered away,
   When the tops of the trees were very green,
   And the roots had withered away.

2. Sweet William mounted the milk-white steed,
   He proudly led the dappled gray,
   He swung his bugles around his neck,
   And he went riding away,
   He swung his bugles around his neck,
   And he went riding away.

3. He rode till he came to fair Eleanor's gate,
   And tingled loudly at the ring,
   "Are you sleeping or not fair Eleanor," he said,
   "Are you sleeping or not within?"
   "Are you sleeping or not fair Eleanor," he said,
   "Are you sleeping or not within?"

4. Fair Eleanor gladly rosed up,
   And quickly slipped on her shoes,
   And straight-way out to her dear sweet William,
   Fair Eleanor she then goes,
   And straight-way out to her dear sweet William,
   Fair Eleanor she then goes.

5. He helped her up on the milk-white steed,
   And proudly rode the dappled gray,
   He swung his bugles around his neck,
   And they went riding away,
   He swung his bugles around his neck,
   And they went riding away.

6. They rode till they came to a distant town,
   And slowly back he looked again,
   He saw her father and seven brothers,
   Come galloping down the lane,
   He saw her father and seven brothers,
   Come galloping down the lane.

7. "Oh, hold these bridles, fair Ellen," he said,
   "And listen to my strong command,
   While I fight your father and seven brothers,
   Upon their own broad land,
   While I fight your father and seven brothers,
   Upon their own broad land."

8. Fair Eleanor there so near she stood,
   And never one single word she said,
   Till she saw her father and seven brothers,
   A-wallowing in their blood,
   Till she saw her father and seven brothers,
   A-wallowing in their blood.

9. "Now hold your tongue sweet William," she said,
   "And listen to all that I have to say,
   Oh, once I had seven brothers and a father,
   And their lives you have taken away,
   Oh, once I had seven brothers and a father,
   And their lives you have taken away."

10. He helped her up on the milk-white steed,
    He quickly mounted the dappled gray,

He swung his bugles around his neck,
And they went riding away,
He swung his bugles around his neck,
And they went riding away.

11. They rode till they came to his mother's gate,
And tingled loudly at the ring,
"Oh tie my head dear mother," he said,
"For you never will tie it again,
Oh make my bed dear sister," he said,
"For you never will make it again."

12. Oh this young man died like today,
And this young lady died like tomorrow,
Oh, this young man died of wounds in the head,
And this young lady of sorrow,
Oh this young man died of wounds in his head,
And this young lady of sorrow.

GROUP D

18. [Earl Brand]

Sharp MSS., 4287/. Also in Sharp and Karpeles, 1932, I,
p. 25(L). Sung by Mrs. Margaret Jack Dodd, Beechgrove,
Va., May 24, 1918.

a M/D

He looked over his left shoulder
To see what he could see,
And there he spied her seven brothers all
Down in yon meadow you see.

19. [Earl Brand]

Sharp MSS., 4214/3034. Also in Sharp and Karpeles, 1932,
I, pp. 22(F)-23. Sung by Philander H. Fitzgerald, Nash,
Va., May 7, 1918.

a D

1. Light off, light off, Lady Margret, he said,
And hold my horse in your hand,
Till I go and fight your seven brothers bold,
And your father by them stand.

2. She held, she held, she bitter, bitter* held,
And she never shed one tear
Until that she saw her last brother fall
And her father she loved more dear.

3. O hold, O hold, Lord William, she cried,
Your strokes are now full sore,
For many a true love I might have had,
But a father I can have no more.

4. She pullèd out her silk handkerchief,
Which was both soft and fine,
And she wipèd off her father's bloody wounds
Till they ran more clearer than wine.

5. Lord William he mounted his milk-white steed,
Lady Margaret mounted her bay,
And he drew his buckler down by his side,
And so they went riding away.

6. They rode, they rode, yes, they bitter, bitter
(or, better) rode,
They rode by the light of the moon,
Until they came to their own mother's door,
Crying: Dear mother, are you at home?

7. O mother, mother, dig my grave,
Dig it both wide and deep,
And lay my true love down by my side,
That the better I may sleep.

8. Lord William died about midnight,
Lady Margaret a while before day.
And I hope that every couple that may every†
come together
They (May?) see more pleasure than they.

* 1932: "better, better"
† 1932: "ever"

20. [Earl Brand]

Sharp MSS., 4193/3023. Also in Sharp and Karpeles, 1932,
I, p. 23(G). Sung by Clinton Fitzgerald, Afton, Va., April
28, 1918.

a D

Lady Margret she mounted her milk-white steed,
Lord William his dapple bay.*
He drew his buckler down by his side,
And so he went riding away.

Light off, light off, Lady Margret, he said,
And hold my reins in your hand,
Till I go fight your seven brothers bold
And your father by them stand.

She held, she held, O she better, better held
(or 'bitter')
And she never shed one tear,
Until she seen her seven brothers fall
And her father she loved so dear.

She pull-ed her silk handkerchief,
Which were both soft and fine,
And she wiped off her father's bloody wounds
Till they ran more clearer than wine.

She lighted on her milk-white steed,
Lord William his dapple bay.
He drew his buckler down by his side,
And so he went riding away.

They rode, they rode, O they better, better† rode
They rode by the light of the moon.
They rode till they came to his own mother's door,
Crying: Mother, are you at home?

Lord William he died about midnight,
Lady Margret just before day.
I hope every couple that may come together
May have more pleasure than they.

* 1932: "dappled grey"
† Editor's MS. query: "bitter?"

21. [Earl Brand]

Wilkinson MSS., 1936-37, p. 5. Sung by Mrs. Nellie M. Lawhorne, Waynesboro, Va., April 23, 1937.

a D

Light off, light off, Lady Margaret, he said,
And hold my horse in your hand,
Till I go and fight your seven brothers bold,
And your father by them stand.

She held, she held, she better, better held,
And she never shed one tear
Until that she saw her last brother fall,
And her father she loved more dear.

O hold, O hold, Lord William, she cried,
Your strokes are now full sore;
For many a true love I might have had,
But a father I can have no more.

She pull-ed out her silk handkerchief,
Which was both soft and fine;
And she wip-ed off her father's bloody wounds
Till they ran more clearer than wine.

Lord William he mounted his milk-white steed,
Lady Margaret mounted her bay;
And he drew his buckler down by his side,
And so they went riding away.

They rode, they rode, yes they better, better rode,
They rode by the light of the moon,
Until they came to their own mother's door,
Crying: Dear mother, are you within?

Lord William died about midnight,
Lady Margaret she died before day.
There never was a couple that ever went together,
But seen more pleasure than they.

22. [Earl Brand]

Wilkinson MSS., 1935-36, pp. 7-8(A). Sung by Nathaniel Melhorn Morris, Harriston, Va., October 9, 1935.

a D

1. Wake up, wake up, you seven sleepers,
   And do beware of thee.
   And take care of your oldest daughter dear,
   For the youngest is going long with me.

2. Wake up, wake up, you seven brothers bold,
   And put on your armor so bright.
   For it never shall be said that a daughter of mine,
   Should stay with Sweet William all night.

3. O they rode, O they rode, they better had a rode,
   And they never delayed no time.

Until she saw her seven brothers bold,
And her father walking so nigh.

4. Git you down, git you down, my pretty Polly,
And hold my steed for awhile.
Until I fight your seven brothers bold,
And your father walking so nigh.

5. She held, O she held, she better had a held,
And she never delayed no time.
Until she saw her seven brothers bold,
And her father she loved so dear.

6. Stop your hand, stop your hand, stop your hand,
she cried.
Stop your hand, stop your hand, stop your hand,
for awhile.
For a many other sweetheart I could have had,
But a father I'll never have no more.

7. You can choose for to go, you can choose for to stay,
You can choose for to go, or to stay.
I'll go, I'll go, Sweet William you know,
For you've left me without any guide.

8. He mounted her on his milk-white steed,
Himself on a (dapple, triple) grey,
And buckled his pistols down by his side,
And away he rode bleeding away.

9. O they rode, they rode, they better had a rode,
And they never delayed no time.
Until he came to his own mother's stile,
And a mother she was to him.

10. O mother, mother, make my bed,
And make it soft and wide.
And lay my lady down by my side,
As I may rest for awhile.

11. Sweet William he died about midnight,
Sweet Polly she died before day.
And the old woman died for the loss of her son,
And there were eleven lives lost.

23. [Earl Brand]

Wilkinson MSS., 1935-36, pp. 9-11(B). Sung by H. B.
Shiflett, Dyke, Va., April 16, 1936.

a D

1. Wake up, wake up, you seven sleepers,
And it's to beware of me;
Take care of your oldest daughter dear,
For the youngest one's a going with me.

2. He mounted her up on a milk white steed,
And himself on a difle grey.
He drew his buckler down by his side,
And away he went singing away.

3. Wake up, wake up, you seven sons dear,
And put on your armor so bright;

I will never have it said that a daughter of mine,
Will be with a lord all night.

4. They rode, they rode, they better had a-rode,
Along with his lady so gay;
Until he saw her seven brothers bold,
And her father a-walking so near.

5. Get you down, get you down, Lady Margaret: he said,
And hold my stakes for awhile;
Until I fight your seven brothers so bold,
And your father a-walking so near.

6. She held, she held, she better had a-held,
And she never shed one tear;
Until she saw her seven brothers fall,
And her father she loved so dear.

7. Stop your hand, stop your hand, Lord William: she cried,
O stop your hand for awhile;
A many sweethearts I once could have had,
But a father dear I'll have no more.

8. You may choose, you may choose, Lady Margaret:
he said,
You may choose to go or stay;
I'll go, I'll go, Lord William: she cried,
For you left me without any guide.

9. He mounted her up on a milk white steed,
And himself on a diple grey;
He drew his buckler down by his side,
And away went bleeding away.

10. He rode, he rode, he better had a-rode,
Along with his lady so gay;
Until he came to his own mother's stile,
Where once he had loved so well.

11. O mother, O mother, make my bed,
And make it soft and wide;
That I may lay my lady by my side,
That I may rest for awhile.

12. Lord William he died about midnight,
Lady Margaret, just before day;
The old woman died for the loss of her son,
And there was eleven lives lost.

24. "The Seven Brothers; or, The Seven Sleepers"

Davis, 1929, p. 552(B); text, pp. 88-89. Sung by Mrs. Rosie Morris, Elkton, Va., August 30, 1922. Collected by Martha M. Davis.

a D (inflected VII)

The timing of the original has had to be drastically overhauled.

1. "Get ye up, get ye up, ye seven sleepers,
   Put on your armor so bright;
   For it never shall be said that a daughter of mine
   Could stay with Sweet William all night."

       *   *   *   *

2. He mounted her on the milk-white steed,
   And himself on the dapple grey;
   He drew his pistol all down by his side,
   And away they went riding away.

3. "Get ye down, get ye down, Lady Margot," he cried,
   "And hold my steed for a while;
   Until I fight your seven brothers bold
   And your father you love so well."

4. She held, she held, she better had held,
   And never delayed any time;
   Until she saw her seven brothers fall
   And her father she loved so well.

5. "Stop your hand, stop your hand, Sweet William,"
                    she cried,
   "Stop your hand, stop your hand for a while;
   It's a many a sweetheart I could have had
   But a father I'll never have again."

6. "You can choose for to go, or to stay alone."

      ·   ·   ·   ·   ·   ·   ·

   "I'll go, I'll go, Sweet William, you know
   You've left me without any guide."

7. He mounted her on the milk-white steed,
   And himself on the dapple grey;
   He drew his pistol down by his side,
   And away he went bleeding away.

8. They rode, they rode, and better they rode,
   And never delayed any time;
   Until they came to his mother's stile,
   And a mother she was to him.

9. "O mother, O mother, go make my bed,
   And make it both soft and wide,
   And lay my lady down by my side
   So I may rest for a while."

10. Sweet William he died before midnight,
    Lady Margot died before day.
    The mother died for loss of her son,
    And eleven lives were lost for one.

GROUP E

25. "Lord Douglas"

Greig MSS., IV, p. 38; text, Bk. 708, p. 38. Also in Greig and Keith, 1925, p. 7(2). Sung by Alexander Robb, New Deer, Aberdeenshire, according to 1925, but unassigned in MS.

a M

He's placed Lady Margret on a milk white steed,
Himself on a dapple gray,
His bugle horn down by his side,
An' slowly they both rode away.

26. [Earl Brand]

Sharp MSS., 3756/. Also in Sharp and Karpeles, 1932, I, p. 24(I). Sung by Mrs. Hayes, Berea, Ky., May 28, 1917.

a M

Rise you up, rise you up, little Marget he did say
Come go along with me
For I can fight your seven brothers bold
Where ever they doth be.

27. "Rise Ye Up"

Randolph, 1946, I, pp. 48-49. Also in Randolph, 1932, p. 219. Sung by Mrs. Lee Stephens, White Rock, Mo., October 5, 1928.

a M

1. Rise ye up, rise ye up, ye drowsy old cheerls,
   Or are you all asleep?
   Arise an' take keer of your oldest daughter dear,
   For th' youngest I'll carry with me.

2. Rise ye up, rise ye up, ye seven sons so bold,
   An' put on your armour so bright,
   For it never shall be said that a daughter of mine
   Was wed to a lord of a night!

3. Light ye down, light ye down, Lady Margaret, he said,
   An' hold my steed's bridle in your hand,
   Till I go an' fight your seven brothers bold,
   For in yonder green meadow they stand.

4. She held his steed's bridle all in her hand,
   An' not one tear did she shed,
   Till she seen her seven bold brothers fall
   An' her father she loved most dear.

5. Light your hand, light your hand, sweet William,
                                              she said,
   For your licks are so wonderful sore,
   An' I can get sweethearts a many a one,
   But a father I can never get more.

6. She pulled out her pocket silk handkerchief
   All made of Holland so fine,
   An' she wiped her father's bleedin' wound
   That bled more redder than wine.

7. You can have your choice, Lady Margaret, he said,
   You can go along with me or stay,
   I will go with you, sweet William, she said,
   For you've left me without any guide.

8. He mounted her up on the milk white steed,
   An' his self on the dapple gray,
   An' he blowed his bugle both loud an' shrill,
   An' bleedin' he rode away.

9. He rode till he come to his mother's coach hall,
   An' he tingled so low at the ring,
   An' who was so ready as the old queen herself
   To rise an' invite them in?

10. Bind my head, bind my head, to his sister he said,
    Which you never shall bind no more;
    For I will die of the wounds I've received,
    An' my face you'll never see no more.

11. Sweet William he died just about midnight,
    Lady Margaret not long before day;
    God send all true lovers that ever gets together
    May see more pleasure than they!

GROUP F

28. "The Seven Brothers"

Barry, Eckstorm, and Smyth, 1929, pp. 37-39. Sung by
Ernest Sprague, Milltown, New Brunswick, 1927; learned
from his father. Melody recorded by George Herzog.

p π[1] (but IV is in variant)

The note-lengths have been doubled in the present copy.
With this tune, cf. Motherwell's "Queen Eleanor's Confession,"
1827, App'x No. 27 (Child 156).

1. "Rise up, rise up, you seven brothers bold,
   .   .   .   .
   Take care of your oldest sister dear,
   For the youngest I will carry away."

2. He mounted on his milk-white steed,
   She upon the grey,
   With his bugle horn hung down by his side,
   And this lord he went riding away.

3. As he rode on and she rode on,
   An' it was by the light of the moon,
   He lookèd over his right shoulder,
   And there he saw them coming.

4. "Li' down, li' down, Lady Marguerite,
   And hold my steed for me,
   Until I go fight your seven brothers bold,
   And your father is at hand."

5. She lighted down, not longer did she stay,
   .   .   .   .
   Until she saw her seven brothers fall
   And her father she loved more dear.

6. "O, hold your hand, Lord William," she cries,
   "Your wounds look wonderful sore,
   For there is many a one I might have had,
   But my father I can't have no more."

7. She takes her pocket handkerchief,
   That was made of the hollan' fine,
   And there she wiped her father's bleeding wounds,
   That run more clear than wine.

8. He mounted on his milk-white steed,
   "O will you go with me, Lady Marguerite,
   Or will you stay with them?"
   "How can I stay, Lord William?" she says,
   "I will go along with thee."

9. As he rode on and she rode on,
   It was by the light of the moon,
   He rode till he came to the broad waterside
   And so manfully laid down.

10. He takes a drink of the water warm,—
  "What's that shines in the main?"
  "It's my scarlet grove I've just put on
  That shines in the watery main."

11. He mounted on his milk-white steed,
  And she was on the grey,
  And his bugle horn hung down by his side,
  And this lord he went riding away.

12. As he rode on and she rode on,
  An' it was by the light of the moon,
  He rode till he came to his own father's gate,
  And so manfully laid down.

13. "Rise up, rise up, dear mother," he says,
  "And let Lord William in;
  For he has received his own death wound
  And his lady he has won.

14. "Oh, make my bed so fine and soft,
  Put soft pillows under my sheets,
  And lay Lady Marguerite down by my side
  That more softly I can sleep."

15. Lord William died in the middle of the night,
  Lady Marguerite before it was day,
  And I hope the next couple that does get wed
  Will be sure to [get] married away.

29. "Lord Loving"

Henry, 1938, p. 37. Sung by Mrs. Samuel Harmon, Cade's Cove, Tenn.

m π¹

The barring of the original copy, which was given 4/4 timing throughout, has been altered, but the note-values are unchanged.

1. "Hold my horse, little Marget," he said,
  "Hold him with your hand,
  Till I go and fight your seven brothers bold
  In the meadow where they stand."

2. She stood and she stood
  And she never shed a tear,
  Till she seed her seven brothers bold fall
  And her father who loved her so dear.

3. She pulled her handkerchief out of her pocket;
  Was of the Holland so fine;
  She tuk and wiped her brother's bloody wounds
  Until the blood run as red as the wine.

4. "Choose you now, little Marget," he says,
  "Go along with me abide."
  "I must go, Lord Loving," she said,
  "Lord, you've left me nary a guide."

5. He mounted himself on a Turkish brown,
  And she on the dapple grey;
  And he blowed his bugle both loud and shrill,
  And he bled as he rode away.

6. He rode by the light of the bright shining moon
  Till he come to his mother's barried* door;
  "Open the door, dear mother," he says,
  "Little Marget, she is won.

7. "Make me a bed, dear mother," he says,
  "Make it wide and deep,
  Lay little Marget in my arms
  That the sounder I may sleep."

8. Lord Loving died before midnight
  And she along 'fore day;
  And if that be the way of all true lovers,
  Who run away together,
  God send them more pleasure than they.

* That is, "barred."

30. "Sweet Willie"

Matteson and Henry, 1936, p. 10. Sung by Mrs. Lloyd Bare Bragg, Elk Park, N.C., August 7, 1933.

a Æ/D

Compare the tunes of this and the next half-dozen variants following with the first tunes in the "Edward" series (13).

1. He rode up to the old man's gate,
  And boldly he did say:
  "You keep your youngest daughter at home,
  But the oldest one I will take away."

2. He got on his milk-white steed
  And she on her dapple gray;
  He swung his bugle-horn around his neck
  And they went riding away.

3. They had not gone more than a mile and a half
  Until they both looked back.
  They saw her father and seven of her brothers
  Come tripping over the slack.

4. "Crawl right down," Sweet Willie cried,
  "And hold my milk-white steed
  Till I fight your father and seven of your brothers,
  Or die in my own life's blood."

5. She got right down without one word,
   And helt the milk-white steed
   Till she saw her father and seven of her brothers
   Go dying in their own hearts' blood.

6. "Oh, slack your hand, Sweet Willie," she cried,
   "Your wounds are deep and sore.
   Oh, slack your hand, Sweet Willie," she cried,
   "For father I can have no more."

7. "If you don't like what I have done,
   You can love some other one;
   I wish you away in your mother's chamberee,
   And me in some house or room."

8. They rode on to his father's gate
   And tapped against the ring.
   "O father, O mother, asleep or awake,
   Arise and let me in."

9. Sweet Willie died like it was today;
   Fair Ellen died tomorrow.
   Sweet Willie died of the wounds that he received;
   Fair Ellen she died of sorrow.

31. "Sweet Willie"

Brown MS., 16 a 4 H. Sent by Mrs. Maude Minish Sutton, who may have learned it from Myra Barnett, in Caldwell County, N.C. First stanza from musical script. Three final stanzas from *North Carolina Folklore*, II, 1952, p. 31; the rest unavailable.

a π⁴

1. As he rode up to the old man's gate
   So boldly did he say,
   'Your oldest daughter you may keep at home
   But your young one I'll take away.'

* * * *

12. 'Oh, mother, mother, come bind my head;
    My wounds they are very sore.
    The blood runs from every wound,
    My head you'll bind no more.

13. 'Oh, mother, mother, make my bed,
    And make it long and wide,
    Lay my good broadsword at my feet,
    Lady Margaret by my side.'

14. Sweet William he died before mid-night,
    Lady Margaret died tomorrow.
    Sweet Willie died of the wounds he received,
    Lady Margaret died of sorrow.

32. "Seven Brothers"

Brown MS., 16 a 4 H. Sung by Mrs. James Miller; obtained from Mrs. Byers and Thomas Smith. One stanza with the music. The rest of the text may be the variant, with the same name, published in *North Carolina Folklore*, II, 1952, pp. 29-30, as from Thomas Smith.

a π⁴

He rode up to the old man's gate
And boldly he did say
'Your oldest daughter you can keep at home
But the youngest I'll take away.'

33. "Sweet William and Fair Ellen"

Brown MS., 16 a 4 H. From Mrs. Maude M. Sutton. One stanza with the music. A second text from Mrs. Sutton appears (in part) as G in *North Carolina Folklore*, II, 1952, pp. 31-32, but with a different title—"Sweet Willie." The present copy, in title, text, and tune, is very close to that of I. G. Greer, below.

a π⁴

Sweet William rode up to the old man's gate
And boldly he did say
'The youngest daughter she may stay at home
But the oldest I'll take away.'

34a. "Sweet William"

Emrich, LC/AAFS, Album XII, rec. 60B. Sung by I. G. Greer of Thomasville, N.C.; recorded in Washington, D.C., 1946.

a π⁴

1. Sweet William rode up to the old man's gate
   And boldly he did say,
   "The youngest daughter she must stay at home,
   But the oldest I'll take away."

2. "Come in, come in, all seven of my sons,
   And guard your sister 'round,
   For never shall it be said that the Stuart's son
   Has taken my daughter out of town."

3. "I thank you, sir, and it's very kind,
   I'm none of the Stuart's son,
   My father was a 'reginers team,*
   My mother a Quaker's queen."

4. So he got on his snow white steed,
   And she on the dapple grey,
   He swung his bugle horn around his neck
   And they went riding away.

5. They hadn't gone more'n a mile out of town
   Till he looked back again,
   And he saw her father and seven of her brothers
   Come trippling over the plain.

6. "Light down, light down, Fair Ellen," said he,
   "And hold my steed by the reins,
   Till I fight your father and seven of your brothers
   Come trippling over the plain."

7. He stood right there and he stood right still,
   Not a word did she return,
   Till she saw her father and seven of her brothers
   A-rolling in their own hearts' blood.

8. "Slack your hand, slack your hand, Sweet William,"
                                              said she,
   "Your wounds are very sore,
   The blood runs free from every vein,
   A father I can have no more."

9. So he got on his snow white steed,
   And she on the dapple grey,
   He swung his bugle horn around his neck
   And they went bleeding away.

10. Soon they rode up to his mother's gate,
    And tingling on the ring,
    "Oh, mother, oh, mother, asleep or awake,
    Arise and let me in.

11. Oh, mother, oh, mother, bind my head,
    My wounds are very sore,
    The blood runs free from every vein,
    For me you will bind them no more."

12. About two hours before it was day,
    The fowls began to crow,
    Sweet William died from the wounds that he received.
    Fair Ellen died for sorrow.

*Editor's query: "king"?

34b. "Sweet William and Fair Ellen"

Brown MS., 16 a 4 H. Sung by I. G. Greer, 1913.

a Æ, ending on VII

The text as given in *North Carolina Folklore*, II, 1952, pp. 28-29, corresponds stanza for stanza with the one just preceding by the same singer, except for an additional stanza at the end, and minor verbal differences, of which the chief are: 3²⁻³ "I'm none of the steward's son;/ My father was a rich Reginer's king." 6¹ "Sight down, sight down." 7¹ "She got right down and she stood right still."

35. "Lady Margaret"

Brewster, 1940, pp. 37-39. Sung by Mrs. A. J. Hopkins, Boonville, Ind., July 20, 1935. Noted by Lucile Wilkin.

m I (impure, with inflected VII and sharped IV)

The timing is problematical, and that of the former editor has not been accepted.

1. Lord William down from the Highlands rode,
   It was all by the light of the moon;
   He rode till he came to my lady's abode,
   And there he lighted down.

2. He mounted her on a milk-white steed
   And himself on his gallant grey,
   And with bugelet horn hung down by his side,
   O how they rode away!

3. O he rode on and she rode on;
   It was all by the light of the moon.
   They rode till he spied her seven brothers bold,
   And then they lighted down.

4. "Light ye down, Lady Margaret," he said,
   "And hold my steed in your hand,
   Until against your seven brothers bold
   And your father I make my stand."

5. She held his steed in her milk-white hand,
   And never shed one tear
   Until her seven brothers fell
   And her father she loved most dear.

6. Then he lifted her on her milk-white steed,
   And himself on his gallant grey,
   And with bugelet horn hung down by his side,
   Slowly they rode away.

7. O he rode on and she rode on;
   It was all by the light of the moon;

They rode till they came to the broad waterside,
And there they lighted down.

8. They lighted down to take a drink,
And the water was a crimson stain;
It was crimson-stained by her truelove's blood,
And she saw that he was slain.

9. He died ere the midnight bell it tolled,
And ere the dawn of day
Lady Margaret died for her truelove bold,
And by his side she lay.

10. They buried them both in the cold, cold tomb;
The grave it was deep, so deep;
And a twin briar rose, twining high overhead,
Only marks where these true lovers sleep.

36. [Earl Brand]

Sharp MSS., 3946/. Also in Sharp and Karpeles, 1932, I,
p. 25(K). Sung by Tilford Creech, Pine Mountain, Ky.,
August 29, 1917.

a π⁴

He mounted her on a milk white steed,
And himself on a iron grey,
He swung his bugle round his neck
And so went riding away
He swung his bugle round his neck
And so went riding away.

37. "Sweet William and Fair Ellen"

Wells, NPMSS, VI, No. 1 (January 1935), pp. 2-3. Sung
by "Singing Willie" Nolan, Harlan County, Ky., 1920. Also
in Wells, 1950, pp. 147-49.

a π⁴

1. Sweet William rode up to Fair Ellen's gate
And he sounded on the ring.
:No one no readier than she was
To arise and let him in.:

2. He mounted her on a milk-white horse
And himself on an iron gray,
:He swung his bugle about his neck
And so went riding away.:

3. He rode till he came in three miles of town,
He turned himself all around;
:He looked and he saw some seven horsemen
Come travelling over the ground.:

4. Get you down, get you down, Fair Ellen, he said,
And take my steed in hand,
:Till I go back to yon little spring,
And I will fight them seven horsemen.:

5. She stood till she saw her six brothers fall,
And her old father she loved so dear;
:Slack your arm, slack your arm, Sweet William,
she said,
For your licks they are wonderful severe.:

6. Are you offended at what I have done,
Or at what's been said before?
:I wish myself in Old England's land,
And you was in the valley so low.:

7. I am not offended at what you have done,
Or at what's been said before,
:I wish myself in Old England's land,
And you was in the valley so low.:

8. She drew her handkerchief from her side,
And wiped Sweet William's wounds,
:The blood kept rolling down his cheeks,
As red as any wine.:

9. He mounted her on her milk-white horse
And himself on his iron grey,
:He swung his bugle around his neck
And so went riding away.:

10. He rode till he came to his mother's hall,
And sounded on the ring.
:Says, Sleeper, awake, Dear Mother, he says,
And arise and let me in.:

11. As she were getting up, a-slipping on her clothes,
To let Sweet William in,
:Bind up my head, sweet sister, he said,
For you never will bind it again.:

38. "Lord William and Lady Margaret"

Flanders and Olney, 1953, pp. 228-29. Sung by Mrs. Lily
Delorme, Cadyville, N.Y., August 16, 1942. Collected by
Marguerite Olney and Marjorie Porter. From *Ballads Migrant in New England*, edited by Helen Hartness Flanders
and Marguerite Olney; copyright 1953 by Helen Hartness
Flanders.

a Æ/D, ending on VIII (inflected VII)

The first half is nearly related to Greig and Keith, 1925, p. 52 (Child 63).

"Lie down, lie down," Lord William cried
"And hold my steed in hand
For betwixt your father and your seven brothers bold
I quicklie make a stand."

"O stop, O stop, Lord William," she cried,
"I fear that you've been slain
And I fear my seven brothers are slain
And my father's been likewise slain."

Then she taen out her handkerchief
That was of the holland so fine
And she did up her father's bloody wounds
That run as red as wine.

"Now make my bed, Lady mother," he said,
"And make it broad and neat
And lay Lady Margaret by my side
That sounder I may sleep."

Lord William died long in the night,
Lady Margaret long in the day
And they took them both home to St. Mary's church
And laid them in the clay.

Out of Lady Margaret's grave there grew a primrose
And out of the knight's a briar
And they linked and they tied in a true lover's knot
And withered away together.

39. [Earl Brand]

Sharp MSS., 4146/. Also in Sharp and Karpeles, 1932, I, p. 24(H). Sung by Mrs. Rebecky Dunaway, St. Helen's, Ky., October 12, 1917.

p M/D

With this form of the tune, cf. variants of Child 243.

He looked over his left shoulder
To see what he could spy
And he saw her seven brothers a coming*
And her father a drowing [sic] nigh†

* 1932: "brotheren coming"
† 1932: "a-drawing nigh"

40. "The Seven Brothers; or, Lord William"

Davis, 1929, p. 552(D); text, pp. 90-91. Sung by Mr. and Mrs. James B. Crawford, near Altavista, Va., May 27, 1915. Collected by Juliet Fauntleroy.

a I/M (– VI) (compass of fifth)

1. Lord William he rose about four o'clock
      And kissed his mother good-bye.
   He drew his sword and pistol down by his side,
      And he went singing away.

(One or more stanzas missing here.)

2. He mounted her upon a milk-white steed,
      And him upon an iron gray.
   He drew his sword and pistol down by his side,
      And they went a-riding away.

3. He rode and he rode, he better had a-rode,
      Along with his lady so dear,
   Until they met her seven brothers bold,
      And her father she loved so dear.

4. "Get you down, get you down, Lady Margaret," says he
      "And hold my horse for a-while,
   That I may fight your seven brothers bold,
      And your father that walks so nigh."

5. She held, she held, she better had have held,
      And she never shedded a tear,
   Until she saw her seven brothers fall,
      And her father she loved so dear.

6. "Hold your hand, hold your hand, Lord William,"
                                        says she
      "Hold your hand, hold your hand for a-while,
   For you have slain my seven brothers bold,
      And my father I loved so dear."

7. "You can choose, you can choose, Lady Margaret,"
                                        said he,
      "You can choose to go or to stay."
   "Oh, yes, Lord William, you know I will go,
      For you've left me without any guide."

8. He mounted her upon a milk-white steed,
      And him upon an iron gray;
   He drew his sword and pistol down by his side,
      And he went bleeding away.

9. He rode, he rode, he better had a-rode,
      Along with his lady so gay;
   For when they reached his own mother's house
      It was just four hours till day.

10. "Oh mother, mother, go make my bed,
    Go make it soft and wide,
That I may lie down for to rest a-while,
    With my new bride by my side."

11. Lord William died before four o'clock,
    Lady Margaret died before day;
The old lady died for the loss of her son,
    And there were eleven lives lost.

The Lady and the Dragoon

CHILD NO. 7, APPENDIX

THIS ballad is plainly of broadside manufacture, and has kept the clear marks of its urban birth throughout its life in tradition. Its age, nevertheless, is impressive enough: the record is much older than anything we possess in English of the preceding ballad, on which it may perhaps have been based. The earliest texts are Restoration broadsides, printed by Thackeray and his confrères, as "The Master-piece of Love Songs," to be sung to the tune of "The Week before [or *after*, in later copies] Easter, the Day's long and clear, &c." [E.g., Brit. Mus. seventeenth-century ballads C. 22. f. 6. fol. 20ᵛ.] A metrical reworking of this is "The Seamans renown in winning his fair Lady," to the same tune—a tune which I have not found.

The melodic tradition, as we have it, belongs entirely to the present century, and appears to be all cut out of the same materials, to which effect, no doubt, the jog-trot of the broadside text in long couplet quatrains has largely contributed. Many of the variants incline to the "Come-all-ye" pattern of ABBA, though it may rather appear as ABCD, C having a good deal of B in its constitution, and D of A. Since it is impossible to determine the earliest shape of the tune, the variants have been grouped according to a logical scheme which in a few cases contraverts geographical distinctions. The first group is comprised of mostly authentic variants, major in tonality (I/Ly, π^1, I, I/M, and M), the majority having a mid-cadence on V, a first cadence on I. All are in duple time.

The second group contains none but plagal tunes, in a major tonality (I/Ly, I, I/M). When the mid-cadence is on I, the first cadence is on V below, with one exception (Nova Scotia); when the mid-cadence is on V below, the first cadence is on III. A Vermont variant (being, like the one from Nova Scotia, in 6/8) has a mid-cadence on V and a first cadence on I.

The third group contains three tunes with debatable finals: perhaps all are p π^1 or p I/M with fallen closes on the lower fifth. They may also be considered to be π^2 and M/D authentic.

The fourth group is composed of variants within the minor galaxy: one is M/D, one a doubtful M/D with a close on V (or else p Æ/D); three are Æ/D, and one π^4. All these are authentic tunes. The mid-cadences are not consistent: on I, IV, V, bVII (in two cases), and the octave. Four first cadences are on the tonic, the other two on IV and bVII. All the variants in this group are Appalachian, but some are strongly reminiscent of the English "High Germany" pattern.

It is tempting to try to find in this very interesting family of tunes an exemplification of the rationale of modal change in folk tradition. But the pendulum will swing in either direction; and it would take a very confident theorist to name the starting-point and the direction of modal drift.

LIST OF VARIANTS

GROUP A

1. "The Lady and the Dragoon." Sharp MSS., 3809/, Clare College Library, Cambridge. (Gentry)
2. "Dragoon and the Lady." Sharp MSS., 1738/. (Lovell)
3. "A Soldier." Mary O. Eddy, *Ballads and Songs from Ohio*, 1939, pp. 14-15. Also in Arthur H. Tolman and Mary O. Eddy, *JAF*, XXXV (1922), p. 414.
4. "The Lady and the Dragoon." Louis E. Chappell, *Folk-Songs of Roanoke and the Albemarle*, 1939, p. 88.
5. "The Dragoon and the Lady." Sharp MSS., 83/143-44. (Nott)
6. "The Soldier's Wooing." Phillips Barry, Fannie H. Eckstorm, and Mary W. Smyth, *British Ballads from Maine*, 1929, pp. 378-79.
7. "The Bold Dragoon and the Lady." Sharp MSS., 1869/-1718-19. (Ash)
8. "The Lady and the Dragoon." Sharp MSS., 3382/2479-80. Also in Cecil J. Sharp and Maud Karpeles, *English Folk Songs from the Southern Appalachians*, 1932, I, p. 334. (Stockton)

GROUP B

9. "Come, all you Maids of Honour." W. Percy Merrick, *JFSS*, I (1900), pp. 108-9.
10. "The Dragoon and the Lady." Sharp MSS., 1667/. (Eldridge)
11. "The Dragoon and the Lady." Sharp MSS., 554/627-28. (Turner)
12. "The Lady and the Dragoon." Sharp MSS., 1090/. (Stokes)

13. "The Dragoon and the Lady." Sharp MSS., 1278/1208. (Sage)
14. "The Poor Soldier." Helen Hartness Flanders and George Brown, *Vermont Folk-Songs & Ballads*, 1931, pp. 232-33.
15. "Song of a Soldier." Helen Creighton, *Songs and Ballads from Nova Scotia*, 1932, pp. 25-26.

GROUP C

16. "A Brave Soldier." Dorothy Scarborough, *A Song Catcher in Southern Mountains*, 1937, pp. 409-10 and 201-2.
17. "The Lady and the Dragoon." Sharp MSS., 4759/. Also in Sharp and Karpeles, *Appalachians*, 1932, I, p. 337(H). (Blankenshipp)
18. "The Poor Soldier." Helen Hartness Flanders, *A Garland of Green Mountain Song*, 1934, pp. 60-61 and 63.

GROUP D

19. "Little Soldier Boy." Sharp MSS., 3188/2334. Also in Sharp and Karpeles, *Appalachians*, 1932, I, p. 333(A). (Sands)
20. "The Lady and the Dragoon." Sharp MSS., 4253/. Also in Sharp and Karpeles, 1932, I, p. 335(E). (Chisholm)
21. "The Soldier Boy." Sharp MSS., 4035/. Also in Sharp and Karpeles, 1932, I, p. 334(C). (Stamper)
22. "The Lady and the Dragoon." Sharp MSS., 4693/. Also in Sharp and Karpeles, 1932, I, p. 337(G). (Boone)
23. "The Lady and the Dragoon." Sharp MSS., 4194/. Also in Sharp and Karpeles, 1932, I, p. 335(D). (Fitzgerald)
24. "The Lady and the Dragoon." Sharp MSS., 4349/3104-5. Also in Sharp and Karpeles, 1932, I, p. 335(F). (Dooley)

GROUP A

1. [The Lady and the Dragoon]

Sharp MSS., 3809/. Sung by Mrs. Jane Gentry, Hot Springs, N.C., July 27, 1917.

a π¹ (compass of sixth)

O daughter O daughter, to be a soldier's wife
Down in this lonesome valley I'll surely take your life.

2. [Dragoon and the Lady]

Sharp MSS., 1738/. Sung by James Lovell, Ball's Caves, Somerset(?), July 31, 1908.

a I, ending on VIII

My father was a Lord
And a Lord of high renown
If ever I wed a soldier
Twill pull his honour down
So it's your birth and my birth
They never will agree
So take it as a warning
Bold Dragoon said she

3. "A Soldier"

Eddy, 1939, pp. 14-15. Sung by Mrs. Galen W. Summer, Canton, Ohio; learned from her mother. Also, with slight differences, in Tolman and Eddy, *JAF*, XXXV (1922), p. 414.

a I/M

1. Soldier, oh soldier, a-coming from the plain,
    He courted a lady through honor and fame;
   Her beauty shined so clear it never could be told,
    And she always loved a soldier because he was so bold.

2. "Soldier, oh soldier, it's I would be your bride,
    But for fear of my father some danger might betide;"
   He pulled out sword and pistol and he hung them by his side,
    And he swore he would be married let what would betide.

3. They had been to the parson, and coming home again
    There they met her father and seven armed men;
   "Let us run," said the lady, "I fear we shall be slain;"
    "Come along," said the soldier, "and never fear again."

4. He then pulled out sword and pistol and caused them to rattle,
    And the lady held the horse while the soldier fought in battle;
   "Oh, stop," said the old man, "and do not be so bold,
    And you shall have my daughter and a thousand pounds of gold."

5. "Fight on," said the lady, "the portion is too small;"
    "Hold your hand," said the old man, "and you shall have it all."
   He then took them home and called them son and dear,
    'Twas not because he loved them, 'twas only through fear.

6. Come, all the ladies, and a pattern take by me,
    And never slight a soldier in any degree;
   For although he may be poor, he is jolly, brisk, and free,
    And so boldly he will fight for his wife and liberty.

4. [The Lady and the Dragoon]

Chappell, 1939, p. 88. Sung by Charles Tillet, Wanchese, N.C., words, 1924; tune, 1935.

p I/M

A soldier, a soldier, a soldier I know I am,
I know I am a soldier and a very feeble man.
He drew his sword and pistol and caused them for to rattle,
And the lady held the horse till the soldier fought the battle.

The first one he came to he pierced him to the brain,
And the next one he came to he served him the same.
O run, cried the others, we all shall be slain,
For to fight that valiant soldier we find it all in vain.

Hold, says the old man, if you will just but hold,
You may have my daughter and a thousand pounds in gold.
No, says the lady, your portion is too small.
Hold your hand, says the old man, and you can have it all.

5. [The Dragoon and the Lady]

Sharp MSS., 83/143-44. Sung by William Nott, Meshaw, Devon, January 8, 1904.

a I (inflected VII)

Come now all you good people,
I pray now lend an ear.
'Tis of a jolly dragoon and soon ye shall hear.
He courted a lady, a lady rich and fair,
So how they got married oh now* you shall hear.

My father was a knight and an honour to the crown,
And if I wed a soldier you'll pull his honour down,
And thy birth and my birth will never agree,
So take it as an answer, dear dragoon, says she.

An answer, an answer, an answer I won't take.
I'd rather lay my life down or of my love forsake.
In hearing of these words wishing the lady's heart to bleed,
Together they went and was married with speed.

Oh when they were married and returning back again
She saw her father coming took by armed men.
O dear, replies the lady, I fear I shall be slain.
O fear not at all, says the valiant dragoon.

So now my dearest Polly no time there is to prattle.
So see how they are armed and fixèd for the battle.
He drawed his sword and pistol the buckles they did rattle,
The lady held the horse while the dragoon fought the battle.

Now all you good people that have got rich in store,
Never disdain a soldier because he is poor.
For he that is poor will fight for his own.
Here's health to the King and the jolly dragoon.

* Sharp Music Bk. has "soon."

6. "The Soldier's Wooing"

Barry, Eckstorm, and Smyth, 1929, pp. 378-79. Sung by Mrs. Susie Carr Young, Brewer, Maine, c. 1927; learned from her uncle, c. 1872. Melody recorded by George Herzog.

a I

1. I will tell you of a soldier who lately came from war;
   He courted a lady, all honor due, by far,
   Her fortune was so great that it scarcely could be told,
   And the lady loved the soldier because he was so bold.

2. As they were a-riding unto the church, 'twas then
   And there they met the old man with seven armèd men.
   "O Dearest," cried the lady, "I fear we shall be slain!"
   "Fear nothing, my charmer!" the soldier said again.

3. Then up spake the old man and unto her did say:
   "Is this your good behavior to me this very day?
   Since you have been so foolish to be a soldier's wife,
   Down in this lonesome valley, I'll quickly take your life."

4. Then upspake the soldier, saying: "I do not like your prattle;
   Although I am a bridegroom, I'm all prepared for battle."
   He took his sword and pistols and caused them to rattle.
   The lady held the horses while the soldier fought the battle.

5. The first man he came to, he quickly had him slain,
   The next man he came to, he usèd him the same.
   "O stay your hand!" the old man cried, "you make my blood run cold!
   And you shall have my daughter with five hundred pounds in gold."

6. "Fight on! Fight on!" the lady cried, "my portion is too small."
   "Stay, stay your hand," the old man cried, "and you shall have it all!"
   The soldiers are the lads that are jolly, brisk and free:
   They will fight for their girls and their rights and liberty.

7. [The Bold Dragoon and the Lady]

Sharp MSS., 1869/1718-19. Sung by Charles Ash (63), Crowcombe, September 9, 1908.

a I/Ly

My father he's a lord and a lord of high renown
If I shall wed a soldier it shall pull his honour down
It's your birth and my birth it never will agree
So take it as a warning, bold dragoon, said she.

A warning, a warning I never intend to take
I'd rather die than leave you it's all for your sweet sake
And then he pressed her hand which made her heart to bleed
To church let us go and get married with speed.

The 1932 printing is in F, in 2/2 time.

Note that this approaches the familiar air of "Villikens and his Dinah" ("Sweet Betsy from Pike," etc.), but in a different meter. Cf. "Lord Randal" (12).

As they was returning from church back again
She met her aged father and seven more armèd men
O now says the lady we both shall be slain
O fear not at all says the jolly light dragoon.

With my broadside and cutlash I'll make their bones to rattle
And the lady hold the horse while the dragoon fought the battle.

Hold up my bold dragoon there is no time to prattle
For don't you see those armèd men all fitted for the battle
Hold up my bold dragoon my portion is but small
Hold up my boldest fellow and you shall have it all.

Hold up you bold dragoon and boldly stand your ground
And you shall have my daughter and thirty thousand pound
And you young ladies who got bright gold in store
Never disdain a soldier for that he is poor.

Although he is poor he will fight for his own
Here's a health to King Edward and the jolly light Dragoon.

8. [The Lady and the Dragoon]

Sharp MSS., 3382/2479-80. Also in Sharp and Karpeles, 1932, I, p. 334. Sung by T. Jeff Stockton, Hogskin Creek, Flag Pond, Tenn., September 4, 1916.

m M

1. Concerning of a soldier who has lately come from war,
   He is courting of my daughter with great riches and a store.

   The lady loved the soldier because he is poor.
   Beyant (beyond) all the gentlemen her soldier goes before.

2. She wrote him a letter was quickly sent by hand.
   No quicker than he got it, to me he returned.
   O soldier, O soldier, this night I'd be your wife.
   I knew that my old parents would freely take my life.

3. O lady, O lady, the soldier is supplied,
   And this night I'll marry you, if you will be my bride.
   It's then they were married returning home again,
   She met her riched parent and seven well-armed men.

4. Go home, my daughter darling. You are the soldier's wife,
   And in this lonesome valley, I'm going to win his life.

5. Now, said the soldier, I'll fight you for that.
   Which caused him to draw off his coat and his hat.

6. He drew his sword and pistols, so loudly made them rattle.
   The lady helt the horse while the soldier fought the battle.

7. The first one he came to he run him through the main,
   The next one he came to he shot him down again.
   Let's run, said the balance, we surely shall be slain,
   For to fight the valiant soldier, we find it's all in vain.

8. Give over, give over, this old man supplied,
   For you shall have my daughter and a thousand pounds beside.

   Fight on, says the lady, the portion is too small.
   Give over to my soldier, for he shall have it all.

GROUP B

9. "Come, all you Maids of Honour"

Merrick, *JFSS*, I (1900), pp. 108-9. Sung by Henry Hills, Shepperton, Sussex.

p I

Come, all you maids of honour,
You maids of high renown,
Oh! never wed a soldier,
'Twould pull your honour down.
Here's your love and my love,
It never can agree.
So take this as a warning,
Bold dràgoon, said she.

My father is a lord,
A lord of high renown;
If I should wed a soldier
'Twould pull his honour down.
Fight on! said the lady;
Fight on! the captain cried,
And you shall have my daughter,
And a thousand pounds beside.

Oh, what's a thousand pounds
Out of my father's purse?
It is but a small trifle
To what my father's worth.
Oh, hold your hand, bold dràgoon, if
That fortune is too small;
Oh, hold your hand, bold dràgoon,
And you shall have it all.

The general he has won the crown,
The honour of King Victory
And the bold light dràgoon.

It is instructive to compare this variant with "The Lark in the Morn," in C. J. Sharp, *One Hundred English Folksongs*, 1916, p. 141.

Her father was a lord, a lord of high renown,
If she should marry a soldier it would pull his honour down,
For it's your birth and my birth I'm sure it won't agree,
So take it as a warning, my light Dragoon, said she.

No warning, love, no warning, no warning intend to take,
I'll either marry or die, love, and it's all for your sweet sake.
Soon as she heard him say those words made her tender heart
to bleed,
Together they went to church and got married by speed.

As they were returning home advancing back again
I'm afraid, says the lady, as they were returning home,
I'm afraid, says the lady, advancing up the hill.
Here comes your father's son and all his armed men.

He drewed his sword and carbine, he made his bones to rattle,
And the lady held the horse while the Dragoon fought the battle.
O stop your hand, O stop your hand, the lady's father cried,
And you shall have my daughter and ten thousand pound besides.

Fight on, fight on, the lady cried, that portion is but small,
O stop your hand, O stop your hand and you shall have it all.
Come all you pretty maidens that have got gold in store,
You should never despise a soldier, although he's low and poor.

10. [The Dragoon and the Lady]

Sharp MSS., 1667/. Sung by Shepherd Eldridge, Shipley, April 21, 1908.

p I

11. [The Dragoon and the Lady]

Sharp MSS., 554/627-28. Sung by Mr. Turner, Bridgwater, August 15, 1905.

p I

It's of a jolly light dragoon so quickly you shall hear,
He married a rich lady and her beauty shone most clear,
He married a rich lady and her beauty shone most clear,
And it was to prove her ruin as you shall quickly hear.

12. [The Lady and the Dragoon]

Sharp MSS., 1090/. Sung by William Stokes, Chew Stoke, August 29, 1906.

p I

With this, cf. Sharp's Somerset copies of "The Knight and Shepherd's Daughter" (110).

My father is a knight
A knight of high renown
If I should marry a soldier
'Twould bring his honour down
For your birth and my birth
It never will agree
So take it as a warning
Bold Dragoon cried she

14. "The Poor Soldier"

Flanders and Brown, 1931, pp. 232-33. Sung by Josiah Kennison, Townshend, Vt., August 29, 1930. Recorded by George Brown. From *Vermont Folk-Songs and Ballads*, edited by Helen Hartness Flanders and George Brown; copyright 1931 by Arthur Wallace Peach.

p I/M

13. [The Dragoon and the Lady]

Sharp MSS., 1278/1208. Sung by Mrs. Sage, Chew Stoke, April 1, 1907.

p I

My father he's a knight and a knight of high renown.
If I would wed a soldier it would bring his honour down.
It's your birth and my birth it never will agree,
So take it as a warning, bold dragoon, cried she.

No warning, no warning, no warning will I take;
I'd rather die than live for my own true lover's sake.
The lady heard these words which it made her heart to bleed.
To church they went together and got married with speed.

In going up to church and in coming back again
The lady spied her father with seven armèd men.
Look yonder, cried the lady, we both shall be slain
For yonder comes my father with seven armèd men.

There is no time to prittle, there is no time to prattle,
The soldier being all armèd prepared for the battle.
The soldier with his broadsword he made their bones to rattle,
And the lady held the horse while the dragoon fought the battle.

Stay your hand, stay your hand, he cried, dragoon, stay your hand,
For you shall have my daughter and ten thousand pound in hand.

Fight on, cried the lady, the portion is too small.
Fight on, my bold Dragoon, you and I will have it all.

Come all you honorèd ladies that have got gold in store
Pray not despise a soldier although he may be poor;
For they are men of honour belonging to the Crown,
Here's a health to Queen Victoria and her jolly light dragoon.

1. I'll tell you of a soldier who lately came from sea.
   He courted a lady of high frisk O free.
   Her riches were so great it scarcely could be told,
   But still she loved the soldier because he was so bold.

2. She said, "My brave soldier, I would be your wife,
   But my father is so cruel, I fear he'd end my life."
   He drew his sword and pistol and he hang them by his side,
   And he swore that he would marry her whatever might betide.

3. As they was going to church one day and on returning home again,
   They met the old man with seven arm-ed men.
   "Oh," then cries the lady, "I fear we shall be slain."
   "Fear nothing, my jewel," the soldier says again.

4. Then up stepped the old man, in form he did say,
   "Is this your behaviour, or is it your wedding day?
   Altho you've been as silly as to be a soldier's wife,
   All in this pleasant valley, I will end your sweet life."

5. Then up stepped the soldier, "I do not like this rattle,
   Altho I am a bridegroom and not prepared for battle."
   He drew his sword and pistol and he caused them for to rattle
   The lady held the horse while the soldier fought the battle.

6. The first man he came to, he soon had him slain.
   The second one he came to, he served him the same.
   "Oh, run," cries the rest, "I fear we shall be slain
   For a fight with a soldier is altogether in vain."

7. "Stay your hand," the old man cries, "Don't carry on so bold
   And you can have my daughter and ten thousand pounds in gold."
   "Fight on," cries the lady, "My portion is too small."
   "Oh, stay your hand," the old man cried, "And you can have it all!"

8. There never was a soldier 'twas fit to carry a gun
   That would flinch or one inch 'til the battle he had won.
   Despise not a soldier because that he is poor
   He's happy at the battlefield as at the barracks door.

15. "Song of a Soldier"

Creighton, 1932, pp. 25-26, Sung by Allan Hartlan, South-East Passage, Nova Scotia.

p I/Ly (compass of sixth)

The original is timed as 3/8. It is not explained how the later stanzas go to the tune; but perhaps the first two phrases were repeated and the third omitted at need.

1. My song is of a soldier just lately came from war,
   Who courted a lady more beautiful and fair,
   And she said she'd have a soldier
   Because they are so bold.

2. He buckled his pistol and sword together
   Which made them for to frattle,
   He laid them by his side, and said that he would marry her
   If she would be his bride.

3. So off they went together. On returning home
   They met her cruel father and seven armed men.
   "Since you are so mean to be a soldier's wife,
   Down in this lonesome valley I will quickly end your life."

4. "Aye, aye," said the soldier, "I do not like your father,
   For I am your bridesmaid and just prepared for battle."
   The lady held the horse
   Till the soldier fought the battle.

5. The first one he came to, he run him through the main,
   Next one he came to, he served him the same,
   "Stay your hand," cries the old man, "you make my blood
                                                run cold,
   You shall have my daughter and £500 in gold."

6. "Fight on, fight on," said the lady, "my fortune is too small,
   "Stay your hand," cries the old man,
   And you shall have it all,
   You shall have my daughter and £50000 in gold."

7. He took him to his house and called him his own,
   And never no more would he let the soldier roam,
   For they are husky lads, the brisky lads a-free,
   They will fight for the pretty girls, the right property.

GROUP C

16. "A Brave Soldier"

Scarborough, 1937, pp. 409-10; text, pp. 201-2. Sung by Aunt Delilah Morris, Yellow Branch, Pirkey, Va., c. 1932. Text written down by Aunt Delilah.

a M/D

1. Oh I'll tell you of a soldier
      who lately came from war,
   Who courted a lady
      with over and great stow.
   Her portion was so great
      It scarcely could be told,
   And yet she loved the soldier
      because he was so bold.

2. Oh, soldier, oh soldier,
      I would freely be your wife,
   But my father is so cruel
      I fear he'll Take your life.
   He took his sode and Pistal,
      He hung them by his side.
   He swore he would get married
      let that would be the tide.

3. Oh they had bin to church
      and returning home again,
   She met her angry father
      and seven army men.
   Oh now, said the lady,
      I fear we will be slain,
   Oh, no, said the soldier,
      Fear nothing again.

4. Oh, daughter, oh daughter,
      what sedence is these?
   What made you bring
      such a scandal on me?
   Oh now you have come to be
      some soldier's wife,
   And here in this valley
      I'll quickly take your life.

5. Oh down jumpted the soldier.
      I have no time to praddle.
   I am a very small man
      intending for a battle.
   He took his sode and Pistal,
      which caused them to ratle,
   And the lady held the horses
      while the soldier Faught the battle.

6. The first one he came to
      He run through the Main;
   The next one he come to
      he run him through again.

Oh, now, said the others,
    Oh, lord, let us run.
To fight a valiant soldier
    for it's all in vain.

7. Oh, you may have my daughter,
        five thousand pounds of gold.
    Come hold your hand, poor soldier,
        It's you may have it all.

17. [The Lady and the Dragoon]

Sharp MSS., 4759/. Also in Sharp and Karpeles, 1932, I, p. 337(H). Sung by Mrs. Mary J. Blankenshipp, Price's Creek, Burnsville, N.C., October 5, 1918.

a π²

Now they were married, returning home again,
They met the lady's father and seven other men;
O run, cried the lady, for fear you will be slain.
Fear nothing, my love, said the soldier again.

18. "The Poor Soldier"

Flanders, 1934, pp. 60-61; text, p. 63. Sung by Elmer George, East Calais, Vt., July 31, 1933. Transcribed by Elisabeth Flanders. From *A Garland of Green Mountain Song*, edited by Helen Hartness Flanders; copyright 1934 by Helen Hartness Flanders.

a π²

1. There was a bold soldier that lately came from sea,
   He courted a lady both honored, rich and free.
   Her fortune was so great that it scarcely could be told
   But still she loved the soldier because he was so bold.

2. As they had been to church one day and was returning
        home,
   They met her old Father with several arm-ed men.
   "O flee," cries the lady, "for fear we shall be slain
   For to fight an angry father is alto-gether vain."

3. "Fear not, my dearest charmer," the soldier says again.
   "As we are on our honeymoon, this insult is a shame
   But I'm brisk and bold and sociable and free
   And I'm willing to fight for my love, as well as liberty."

4. The old man to his daughter, in grieving frowns did say,
   "Is this your behaviour or is it your wedding day
   Since you have been so foolish as to be a soldier's wife
   All in this handsome valley, I'll end your pleasant life."

5. O, then up speaks the soldier, saying "I do not like your
        prattle.
   Although I am a bridegroom, I am prepared for battle."
   With sword and pistol in his hand, he caused them for to
        rattle
   And the lady held the horse while the soldier fought the
        battle.

6. The first man he came to, he quickly had him slain.
   The next man he came to he run him through the same.
   "O, flee," cried the rest, "for fear we shall be slain,
   For to fight an able soldier is altogether vain."

7. O then up speaks the old man, saying "If you'll only spare
        my life,
   I'll give you ten thousand pounds and my daughter for your
        wife."
   "Fight on," cries the lady, "your portion is too small.
   Fight on, fight on, brave soldier, and you shall have it all."

8. The old man took him home with him and treated him as
        an heir.
   'Tis not because he loved him, but it was for dread and fear.
   There never was a soldier twas fit to carry a gun
   That would either flinch or stir an inch til the battle he had
        won.

9. Despise not a soldier because that he is poor.
   He is as happy on the battlefield as at the barracks door.
   H[e']s brave, brisk and bold and sociable and free
   And willing to fight for his love as well as for his liberty.

GROUP D

19. "Little Soldier Boy"

Sharp MSS., 3188/2334. Also in Sharp and Karpeles, 1932, I, p. 333(A). Sung by Mrs. Mary Sands, Allanstand, N.C., August 1, 1916.

a M/D

The 1932 printing is in D.

There was a little soldier boy who lately came from over;
He courted a rich lady who'd money and store;
And her riches was so great that they scarcely could be told,
But yet she loved a soldier boy because he was so bold.

She says: My little soldier, I would freely be your wife
If I knowed my cruel old father would surely spare your life.
He drew his pistol and sword and hung them by his side
And swore he would get married let what would be tried.

As they had been to church and returning home again,
Out slipped her cruel old father and seven armed men.
Say (Easy) sent you intermed that you be the soldier's wife,*
Way down in the valley I will surely take his life.

O says the little soldier, I have no time to tattle
I am here in this world in no fix for battle;
But he drew his pistol and sword and caused them to rattle
And the lady helt the horse while the soldier fought the battle.

The first one he come to he run him through the main,
And the next one he come to he served him the same.
Let's run, says the rest, I'll see we'll all be slain
To fight the valiant soldier I see it all in vain.

Up step (*sic*) this old man, speaking mighty bold,
You shall have my daughter and a thousand pound of gold.
Fight on, says the lady, the pile is too small.
O stop says the old man, and you shall have all.

* Sharp and Karpeles, 1932, have "Saying: Since you are determined to be a soldier's wife."

20. [The Lady and the Dragoon]

Sharp MSS., 4253/. Also in Sharp and Karpeles, 1932, I, p. 335(E). Sung by James H. Chisholm, Nellysford, Va., May 21, 1918.

a M/D, ending on V

I'll tell you of a soldier who lately come from sea,
He courted a lady, both honour, rich, and free;
Her riches was so great that it scarcely could be told
And the reason she loved the soldier because he was so bold.

Sharp's MS. note: "Mr. James Chisholm is the brother of the Woodridge Chisholm who sang me so many songs in September, 1916. They both married Italian wives, descendants of those whom Jefferson brought from France to improve viticulture in America. The Chisholm's themselves have Italian blood being descended from the Genini's. Mr. Jas. Chisholm's wife was a Mullins, i.e. Mullino."

21. "The Soldier Boy"

Sharp MSS., 4035/. Also in Sharp and Karpeles, 1932, I, p. 334(C). Sung by Mrs. Martha Stamper, Hindman, Knott County, Ky., September 18, 1917.

a Æ/D

The 1932 printing is in E minor.

There was a little soldier just lately come from war
He courted a rich lady and money she had in store
Her riches they were so greatly, they scarcely could be told
But yet she loved the soldier, because he were so bold.

22. [The Lady and the Dragoon]

Sharp MSS., 4693/. Also in Sharp and Karpeles, 1932, I, p. 337(G). Sung by Mrs. Julie Boone, Micaville, N.C., September 26, 1918.

a Æ/D

With this form, cf. the familiar "High Germany" (e.g., Sharp, 1916, p. 127).

I knew the little young soldier
Just lately come from war,
He's courting the richest lady
With honour and great store;
But she liked the little soldier,
Because he was so bold.

23. [The Lady and the Dragoon]

Sharp MSS., 4194/. Also in Sharp and Karpeles, 1932, I, p. 335(D). Sung by Clinton Fitzgerald, Royal Orchard, Afton, Va., April 28, 1918.

a Æ/D

'Twas late one Sunday evening, as they rode home from church,
She spied her old father and several* well armed men,
He drew a sword and pistol and caused them to rattle
And this lady held the horse while the soldier fought the battle.

* 1932 "sev'ral"

24. [The Lady and the Dragoon]

Sharp MSS., 4349/3104-5. Also in Sharp and Karpeles, 1932, I, p. 335(F). Sung by Mrs. Tina Dooley, Montvale, Bedford County, Va., June 6, 1918.

a π⁴

1. There was a gallant soldier
   Who* lately came from Spain.
   He courted Miss Sally,
   Great honour and great name.

2. Her riches was so greatly,
   They scarcely could be told,
   Although she loved the soldier
   Because he was so bold.

3. See here, my little Duel,†
   I'd vainly be your wife,
   But my hard-hearted father
   Will shortly end your life.

4. He drew his sword and pistol,
   He placed her by his side,
   He swore that he'd get married
   At their own heart's content.

5. They got on their horses
   And to the church they went,
   And there they got married
   At their own heart's content.

6. They got on their horses,
   Returning home again,
   They met their cruel father
   And seven arm-ed men.

7. See here, my little Duel,
   Do you make this lady your wife,
   Down in some lonesome valley
   I'll shortly take your life.

8. Ride on, ride on, said the lady,
   I have no flatter (?)
   I am but one soldier
   Not fitten for a battle.

9. See here, my little Duel,
   You bring my daughter so low,
   For to marry a soldier,
   And he's so poor.

10. He drew his sword and pistol,
    He caused them to rattle.
    The lady held the horses
    While the soldier fought the battle.

11. The first one he came to
    He pierced him through the main,
    The next one he came to
    He served him the same.

12. Stop, stop, says the old man,
    It's labour all in vain
    To fight this gallant soldier,
    For we will all be slain.

13. See here, my little Duel,
    You must not be so bold.
    O you may have my daughter
    And ten thousand pounds of gold.

* 1932: "just"
† I.e., "jewel"

The Fair Flower of Northumberland

CHILD NO. 9

THIS libel on the Scottish race seems to have had a considerable popularity north of the Border, and six out of the seven recorded tunes for it are Scottish. Scots singers contrived to give it a twist that flattered their nation's sexual vanity; but the compliment still keeps an ugly side. The earliest English text may have been printed before 1600. It is not altogether impossible that the Scottish was the original form, made over by the English for their own purposes. At least, the Deloney text shows much less of a traditional cast and was probably not a little altered by his craftsman's hand. Besides the phraseology, the ingenious alteration of the last refrain line of almost every stanza is a suspicious circumstance, unlikely long to survive the insensitive chances of traditional rendition, and certainly calculated to tax the cooperative powers of a chorus such as Deloney so prettily pictures: "The King and Queene, and all the Nobility heedfully beheld these women, who for the most part were very faire and comely creatures, and were all attired alike from top to toe. Then (after due reuerence) the maidens in dulcet manner chanted out this Song, two of them singing the Ditty, and all the rest bearing the burden." (Quoted from the 10th edition, 1626, of *Iacke of Newberie*, reprinted by F. O. Mann in Deloney's *Works*, Oxford, 1912, p. 33. The book was registered as early as March 7, 1596-97.)

The ballad, perhaps, never had a very wide currency. By the opening of the twentieth century it had almost died out of oral tradition; and all its tunes thus far known belong to the nineteenth century. They all appear to have been cut from the same bolt and maintain the same tripping rhythm; but they nevertheless display a striking variety of melodic outline—so wide, in fact, that it is not easy to account for their appearance at so late

a date and within so comparatively short a span of time unless we posit a fairly long, unbroken, and yet unusually recreative tradition behind them. From Elizabeth's day to the Regency would be long enough; and the predominantly dactylic measure of Deloney's text anticipates the invariably 6/8 rhythm of the extant tunes. Such foreign parallels as Child was able to find are only partial and thematic, and it is not necessary to presume a much longer history for the ballad than has been suggested. Neither is there anything in the character of the tunes to imply a greater age: they lack little of being at home among the dancing-songs of Shakespeare's era and later.

The variants are all in a major tonality (I/Ly, I, π^1, and I/M), and all are authentic except one. (One is mixed.) Two copies, here assigned first place, have finals on the supertonic (as I believe) and mid-cadences above the octave. One is I/Ly, the other π^1. The next two copies, from Northumbria and Buchan, have a mid-cadence on the octave. One is I/Ly, the other Mixolydian. The second strain of Christie's copy is doubtless editorial invention. The next two copies, an unpublished copy from a C. K. Sharpe MS. in the National Library of Scotland and Motherwell's copy from the Paisley region, have the mid-cadence on the dominant. The first is major, and mixed, the second π^1, authentic. The last copy, collected by Duncan, is an I/M plagal tune, with altogether too many echoes in it. Some of these are "Todlin Hame" (cf. *SMM*, No. 275), "My ain Fireside," "Whistle and I'll come to ye, my Lad."

It is odd that Christie refers to his Appendix for another and different air to this ballad, for no such air is discoverable in that place. It seems probable that he forgot his intention.

LIST OF VARIANTS

1. "The Heiress of Northumberland." C. K. Sharpe MS., p. 7, National Library of Scotland. Also in Francis James Child, *The English and Scottish Popular Ballads*, 1882-98, V, pp. 411 and 207-8.
2. "The Provost's Dochter." George R. Kinloch, *Ancient Scottish Ballads*, 1827, pp. 131-34.
3. "The Fair Flower of Northumberland." J. Collingwood Bruce and John Stokoe, *Northumbrian Minstrelsy*, 1882, pp. 51-55. Also in John Stokoe and Samuel Reay, *Songs and Ballads of Northern England* [1892], p. 94; Child MSS., XXI, No. 218, Harvard College Library.

4. "The Flower o' Northumberland." W. Christie, *Traditional Ballad Airs*, II, 1881, p. 46.
5. "The Flower of Northumberland." Lady John Scott's Sharpe MS., National Library of Scotland MS. 843, fol. 17^r.
6. "The Flower of Northumberland." William Motherwell, *Minstrelsy: Ancient and Modern*, 1827, App'x No. 2 and p. xv.
7. "The Fair Flower of Northumberland." Duncan MS., No. 387 (W. Walker). Also in Gavin Greig and Alexander Keith, *Last Leaves of Traditional Ballads and Ballad Airs*, 1925, p. 9.

TUNES WITH TEXTS

1. [The Heiress of Northumberland]

Sharpe MS., p. 7. Also in Child, 1882-98, V, p. 411; text, I, pp. 207-8.

a I/Ly, ending on II

1. "Why, fair maid, have pity on me,"
     Waly's my love wi the life that she wan
 "For I am bound in prison strong,
     And under the heir o Northumberland."

2. "How can I have pity on thee,"
      Waly's my love, etc.
   "When thou hast a wife and children three,
      All dwelling at home in fair Scotland?"

3. Now he has sworn a solemn oath,
      And it was by eternity,
   That wife and children he had none,
      All dwelling at home in fair Scotland.

4. Now she's gone to her father's bedstock,
      Waly's my love, etc.
   And has stolen the key of the dungeon-lock,
      And she the great heir o Northumberland.

5. And she's gone to her father's chest,
   She has stolen away a suit of the best,
      Altho she was heir o Northumberland.

6. Now she's gone to her father's coffer,
   And has taen out gold nane kens how meickle,
      Altho she, etc.

7. She's gane to her father's stable,
   And taen out a steed baith lusty and able,
      For a' she was heir, etc.

8. The rade till they cam to Crafurdmoor,
   He bade her light down for an English whore,
      Altho she, etc.

9. The rade till the came to the water o Clyde,
   He bade her light down, nae farer she should ride,
      "For now I am at hame in fair Scotland."

10. "Yonder view my castle," said he;
    "There I hae a wife and children three,
       All dwelling at home," etc.

11. "O take me by the middle sae sma
    And thro me oer your castle-wa,
       For I darena gang hame to Northumberland."

12. When she came to her father's yett,
    She durst hardly rapp thereat,
       Altho she was, etc.

13. Out then spoke her stepmother sour,
    She bad her pack off for an impudent whore,
       "For thou shalt not be heir o Northumberland."

14. Out then spock her bastard brother;
    "She'll hae nae mair grace than God has gien her,
       And she shall be heir o Northumberland."

15. Out and spoke her father sae mild,
    "She's no the first maid a false Scot has beguild,
       And she shall be," etc.

2. [The Provost's Dochter]

Kinloch, 1827, pp. 131-34.

a π¹, ending on II

1. The Provost's dochter went out a walking—
      A may's love whiles is easie won!
   She heard a puir prisoner making his meane;—
      And she was the fair flow'r o' Northumberland.

2. "Gif onie ladie wad borrow me
      Out into this prison strang,
   I wad mak her a ladie o' hie degree,
      For I am a gret lord in fair Scotland."

3. She has dune her to her father's bed-stock,—
      A may's love whiles is easie won!
   She has stown the keys o' monie braw lock,
      And she has lows'd him out o' prison strang.

4. She has dune her to her father's stable,—
      A may's love whiles is easie won!
   She has tane out a steed, baith swift and able,
      To carry them baith to fair Scotland.

5. Whan they cam to the Scottish corss,—
      A may's love whiles is easie won!
   "Ye brazen-faced hure, licht aff o' my horse;
      And go, get ye back to Northumberland."

6. Whan they cam to the Scottish muir,—
      A may's love whiles is easie won!
   "Get aff o' my horse, ye brazen-fac'd hure,
      So, go, get ye back to Northumberland."

7. "O pity on me! O pity! said she,
      O! that my love was so easie won;
   Have pity on me, as I had upon thee,
      Whan I lows'd ye out o' prison strang."

8. "O how can I hae pity on thee;
      O why was your love sae easie won?
   Whan I hae a wife and children three,
      Mair worthy than a' in Northumberland."

9. "Cook in your kitchen I will be,—
      O that my love was sae easie won!
   And serve your lady maist reverentlie,
      For I darna gang back to Northumberland."

10. "Cook in my kitchen, ye sall not be,—
       Why was your love so easie won?
    For I will hae na sic servants as thee,
       So, get ye back to Northumberland."

11. But laith was he the lassie to tyne,—
       A may's love whiles is easie won!
    He hired an auld horse, and fee'd an auld man,
       To carry her back to Northumberland.

12. Whan she cam her father afore,—
    A may's love whiles is easie won!
She fell at his feet on her knees sae low,—
    She was the fair flow'r o' Northumberland.

13. "O dochter, dochter, why was ye bauld,—
    O why was your love sae easie won!
To be a Scot's hure in your fifteen year auld,
    And ye the fair flow'r o' Northumberland."

14. Her mother on her sae gentlie smil'd,—
    "O that her love was sae easie won!
She's na the first that the Scots hae beguil'd,
    And she's still the fair flow'r o' Northumberland.

15. "She shanna want gowd, she shanna want fee,
    Although her love was easie won;
She shanna want gowd, to gain a man wi',
    And she'll still be the fair flow'r o' Northumberland."

3. [The Fair Flower of Northumberland]

Bruce and Stokoe, 1882, pp. 51-55. Also, with piano accompaniment, in Stokoe and Reay [1892], p. 94; with the difference in bar 4, in Child MSS., XXI, No. 218, from *Newcastle Courant*, n.d., but c. 1880, contributed by Stokoe as collected in Tynedale, Reedwater, and Liddesdale districts.

a I/Ly

1. It was a knight, in Scotland born,
    Follow, my love, come over the strand,
Was taken prisoner and left forlorn,
    Even by the good Earl of Northumberland.

2. Then was he cast in prison strong
    Follow, my love, come over the strand,
Where he could not walk nor lay along,
    Even by the good Earl of Northumberland.

3. And as in sorrow thus he lay,
    Follow, my love, come over the strand,
The Earl's sweet daughter passed that way,
    And she the fair flower of Northumberland.

4. And passing by, like an angel bright,
    Follow, my love, come over the strand,
The prisoner had of her a sight,
    And she the fair flower of Northumberland.

5. And aloud to her this knight did cry,
    Follow, my love, come over the strand,

The salt tears standing in her eye,
    And she the fair flower of Northumberland.

6. "Fair lady," he said, "take pity on me,
    Follow, my love, come over the strand,
And let me not in prison dee,
    And you the fair flower of Northumberland."

7. "Fair sir, how should I take pity on thee,
    Follow, my love, come over the strand,
Thou being a foe to our countree,
    And I the fair flower of Northumberland."

8. "Fair lady, I am no foe," he said,
    Follow, my love, come over the strand,
"Through thy sweet love here was I stayed,
    And thou the fair flower of Northumberland."

9. "Why should'st thou come here for love of me,
    Follow, my love, come over the strand,
Having wife and bairns in thy own countree,
    And I the fair flower of Northumberland.

10. "I swear by the blessed Trinity,
    Follow, my love, come over the strand,
That neither wife nor bairns have I,
    And thou the fair flower of Northumberland.

11. "If courteously thou wilt set me free,
    Follow, my love, come over the strand,
I vow that I will marry thee,
    And thou the fair flower of Northumberland.

12. "Thou shalt be lady of castles and towers,
    Follow, my love, come over the strand,
And sit like a queen in princely bowers,
    Even thou the fair flower of Northumberland."

13. Then parted hence this lady gay,
    Follow, my love, come over the strand,
And got her father's ring away,
    And she the fair flower of Northumberland.

14. Likewise much gold got she by sleight,
    Follow, my love, come over the strand,
And all to help this forlorn knight,
    And she the fair flower of Northumberland.

15. Two gallant steeds, both good and able,
    Follow, my love, come over the strand,
She likewise took out of the stable,
    And she the fair flower of Northumberland.

16. And to the gaoler she sent the ring,
    Follow, my love, come over the strand,
Who the knight from prison forth did bring,
    To meet the fair flower of Northumberland.

17. This token set the prisoner free,
    Follow, my love, come over the strand,
Who straight went to this fair lady,
    And she the fair flower of Northumberland.

18. A gallant steed he did bestride,
    Follow, my love, come over the strand,

And with the lady away did ride,
　　And she the fair flower of Northumberland.

19. They rode till they came to a water clear;
　　Follow, my love, come over the strand,
　　Good sir, how shall I follow you here,
　　And I the fair flower of Northumberland?

20. "The water is rough and wonderful deep,
　　Follow, my love, come over the strand,
　　And on my saddle I shall not keep,
　　And I the fair flower of Northumberland."

21. "Fear not the ford, fair lady!" quoth he,
　　Follow, my love, come over the strand,
　　"For long I cannot stay for thee,
　　Even thou the fair flower of Northumberland."

22. The lady prickt her gallant steed,
　　Follow, my love, come over the strand,
　　And over the water swam with speed,
　　Even she the fair flower of Northumberland.

23. From top to toe all wet was she,
　　Follow, my love, come over the strand,
　　"This have I done for love of thee,
　　Even I the fair flower of Northumberland."

24. Thus rode she all one winter's night,
　　Follow, my love, come over the strand,
　　Till Edinborough they saw in sight—
　　The fairest town in all Scotland.

25. "Now choose," quoth he, "thou wanton flower:
　　Follow, my love, come over the strand,
　　If thou wilt be my paramour,
　　And thou the fair flower of Northumberland.

26. "For I have a wife and children five,
　　Follow, my love, come over the strand,
　　In Edinborough they be alive,
　　And thou the fair flower of Northumberland.

27. "And if thou wilt not give thy hand,
　　Follow, my love, come over the strand,
　　Then get thee home to fair England,
　　And thou the fair flower of Northumberland.

28. "This favour thou shalt have to boot—
　　Follow, my love, come over the strand,
　　I'll have thy horse; go thou on foot,
　　And thou the fair flower of Northumberland.

29. "O false and faithless knight," quoth she;
　　Follow, my love, come over the strand,
　　"And canst thou deal so bad with me,
　　And I the fair flower of Northumberland?

30. "Dishonour not a lady's name,
　　Follow, my love, come over the strand,
　　But draw thy sword and end my shame,
　　And I the fair flower of Northumberland."

31. He took her from her stately steed,
　　Follow, my love, come over the strand,

And left her there in extreme need,
　　And she the fair flower of Northumberland.

32. Then sat she down full heavily,
　　Follow, my love, come over the strand,
　　At length two knights came riding by,
　　And she the fair flower of Northumberland.

33. Two gallant knights of fair England,
　　Follow, my love, come over the strand,
　　And there they found her on the strand
　　Even she the fair flower of Northumberland.

34. She fell down humbly on her knee,
　　Follow, my love, come over the strand,
　　Crying, "Courteous knights take pity on me,
　　Even I the fair flower of Northumberland.

35. "I have offended my father dear,
　　Follow, my love, come over the strand,
　　For a false knight that brought me here,
　　Even I the fair flower of Northumberland."

36. They took her up beside them then,
　　Follow, my love, come over the strand,
　　And brought her to her father again,
　　And she the fair flower of Northumberland.

37. Now all you fair maids be warned by me,
　　Follow no Scotchman over the strand;
　　Scots never were true, nor ever will be,
　　To lord nor lady nor fair England.

4. [The Flower o' Northumberland]

Christie, II, 1881, p. 46. Noted in Buchan. Text apparently refined out of Peter Buchan, *Ancient Ballads and Songs*, 1828, II, pp. 208ff.

a M

A maid pass'd by the prison door,
　　(Maid's love whiles is easy won;)
She saw a prisoner standing there,
　　And wishing to be in fair Scotland. [Etc.]

5. [The Flower of Northumberland]

Lady John Scott's Sharpe MS., NL Scotland MS. 843, fol. 17ʳ.

m I

There was a young lady was walking alone,
  Wat ye, my love, in the life that she wan!
She heard a poor prisoner making his moan;
  And she's the brave heir of Northumberland!

When they came to Scotland brig;
  Wat ye, my love, in the life that she wan!
"Light aff, light aff, from my black steed;
  And hie ye awa' to Northumberland."

6. [The Flower of Northumberland]

Motherwell, 1827, App'x No. 2; text, p. xv. Collected by Andrew Blaikie, Paisley.

a π¹

When they came to Scotland brig,
  O my dear, my love that she wan;
Light off, ye hure, from my black steed,
  And hie ye awa to Northumberland.

7. [The Fair Flower of Northumberland]

Duncan MS., No. 387 (W. Walker). Also in Greig and Keith, 1925, p. 9. Sung by Mrs. Lyall, Lyne of Skene, Aberdeenshire; learned from her mother. Collected by Rev. J. B. Duncan, Lynturk.

p I/M

The rest of the text, eleven stanzas in all, I have not found among the Greig MSS.

O, but your love 'twas easily won,
  O, but your love 'twas easily won,
I'll buy an aul' horse an' I'll hire an aul' man,
  An' I'll hurl ye back to Northumberland.

The Two Sisters

CHILD NO. 10

This ballad still keeps its vitality, at least in the Southern mountains. Its association with dancing is attested by the words of the refrain prevalent where the "play-party game" tradition has been strong, as well as by external evidence (e.g., Jean Thomas, *Devil's Ditties*, 1931). In this connection it has generally kept an elaborate interlaced tripartite refrain, combined with the threefold repetition of the first line of each stanza—a pattern which is ancient, and which has associations also with other ballads, e.g., "The Three Ravens," "Sir Eglamore," "The Wedding of the Frog and the Mouse," "The Friar in the Well," "Mademoiselle from Armentières." The pattern is at least as old as the sixteenth century,* but it does not happen to appear with the present song until almost the middle of the eighteenth. Barry has somewhat rashly asserted that the traditional Scandinavian air of the ballad proves the ballad to have been carried from Scandinavia to Scotland. The course of migration may very probably have moved in that direction,† but one nineteenth-century Swedish tune will hardly clinch the matter. Moreover, the melodic parallel holds only for the "Binnorie" form of the ballad, and takes no account of the British form described above. The latter Barry appears to think borrowed from "The Cruel Mother" (20). [Cf. *BFSSNE*, No. 3 (1931), pp. 11-14. For an attempt to show that all the American variants derive from English, rather than Scottish, tradition, cf. also Archer Taylor, "The English, Scottish, and American Versions of The Two Sisters," *JAF*, XLII (1929), pp. 238-46.]

Musically, the pattern under discussion—that of "The Three Ravens"—implies a two-strained melody, with the middle pause coming after the second element of the refrain; but occasionally a tendency appears in tradition to abbreviate this pattern. At any rate, as the bulk of recent record demonstrates, the two-strain scheme has latterly become the dominant one for the ballad. Yet it may quite possibly be a case of borrowing from a once stronger rival.

So far as the verbal text provides a clue, the earlier scheme would seem to be a simple alternating refrain at the second and fourth phrases of the ballad quatrain. The earliest texts (of mid-seventeenth-century English broadside provenance) are of this type, and it has kept its popularity in Scotland and Ireland. All the variants of the "Binnorie" group belong to it. Rather surprisingly, however, the ballad does not appear in the Herd MSS., nor in the *SMM*, and the currency of the "Binnorie" refrain seems to follow mainly in the wake of its appearance in Scott's *Minstrelsy*, 1802. Scott appears to have had little traditional authority for the combination: further evidence, one may surmise, of the influence of print upon tradition. (The first evidence of "Binnorie" comes from the undependable Pinkerton in 1783—from whom Scott may have caught a hint.)

A group with a refrain involving the use of the name Ann (Annie, Nannie, Nancy), and a swan swimming bonny, seems to have had some slight currency in Celtic communities. There is also a small number of variants built out of the flotsam of tunes and refrains proper to other songs and singing-games, like "London Bridge is falling down," "Mulberry Bush," and the flower-burden of Child 2.

The tune for Child L, which has a unique refrain of "Fal the lal the lal laral lody" on phrases 2 and 4, is not recorded; but the contributor described it as "a slow, quaint strain" that changed to a more lively one when the miller sets about "to make a melodye." Also, it may be worth remark that the refrain of Child Q, "Oh and ohone and ohone and aree!" and "On the banks of the Banna, ohone and aree," has the favored vowel-sounds as well as the rhyme, of the most popular group, and was probably made over for Irish taste out of that series. The rhythm alone would suggest a different tradition and different music from that of the "Binnorie" group.

The first group of tunes, basically four-phrase, with refrains coming on the second and fourth, contains most of the older records, which are Scottish. As a whole, the group moves between the modal limits of Æ to I/M, with variants in most of the intermediate modes (π^4, D, D/M, M). The tunes are all but invariably plagal. The final and mid-cadences are always feminine, but the choice of degree for mid-cadence and first phrase varies a good deal.

Group B is a large and very interesting one which, for convenience, has been subdivided into six parts. A few variants in the group are of English record, but far the greatest portion is American, and recent. The geographical range, as so far displayed, is from the Eastern seaboard (Maine to North Carolina) to Arkansas and Missouri, but it will doubtless be extended as other regions are more thoroughly explored. Typically, the tune is major, two-strained, in 6/8 time. A few variants are authentic only, a few plagal, but most are mixed. There are few pentatonic variants, many hexatonic ones.

The order here has been shifted from the normal sequence in order to exhibit what appears to be an exception to the working hypothesis of the present study, that folk-tunes do not ordinarily pass directly from major to minor. The opposite appears to be true of the tune in question, and one can watch it happen in a succession of variants that put more and more emphasis on the lower VI. This process becomes visible in subgroup Bb, where the cadence note of the first phrase has moved up from lower V of the Ba group, perhaps encouraged by previous Mixolydian emphasis on the flat seventh. After tentative interest on lower VI, we find a growing hesitation to decide on the cadence-note of the first element of the refrain ("Bow down") and then on the final. Nearly throughout Bc, there is genuine ambiguity. In view of the preceding variants, we incline to classify these as mostly I/Ly, with a final on lower VI; but a few of them have clearly made the decision and gone over to Æ/D. Most of class Bd is composed of D/M tunes. Class Be contains lame ducks of various sorts, exhibiting the tune truncated or disordered by loss of its full complement of phrases: there are seven-phrase, six-phrase, five- and four-phrase variants, and increasing reluctance to end on the tonic. The modal range is from major to Æolian. Class Bf contains a few variants which have crossed with the "Two Little Sisters" game-song, with alteration of

---

* It appears in a stanza quoted in William Wager's "The Longer Thou Livest the More Fool Thou," c. 1568:

> There was a mayde cam out of Kent,
> Daintie loue, daintie loue, &c.

On this pattern and the other varieties of refrain found with the present ballad, cf. *CFQ*, III (July 1944), pp. 191-94.
† See the monograph by Paul G. Brewster, *The Two Sisters*, Folklore Fellows Communication No. 147 (Vol. LXII), Helsinki, 1953. See also Harbison Parker's ' "The Twa Sisters"—Going Which Way?' in *JAF*, LXIV (1951), pp. 347-60.

words and refrain. Three of these are π^1 mixed, the other two I/Ly. The time is clearly duple (2/4, 4/4, 2/2).

Group C, with "Edinburgh, Edinburgh" in the refrain, contains some early records, and is entirely Scottish. The tunes are major, I/M, and M, and in 3/4 time. Mrs. Brown's tune, as usual, gives trouble, on account of the inaccuracy of its setting-down: it needs drastic handling as to timing, if any sense is to be made out of it. On the basis of analogues, an attempt has been made here to restore it.

Group D, with the swan-refrain, reverts to the quatrain pattern. It has been found in Scotland, Ireland, and in the United States, but not often. Copies are plagal π^1, I/M, and major.

The last group, E, contains a few anomalies which have occasional tenuous connections with other groups, especially Be, but which for the most part invoke other associations—e.g., "London Bridge," "Mulberry Bush," "Buy a Broom"—or none. We cannot regard any of them as sound exemplars of the melodic tradition for this ballad.

LIST OF VARIANTS

GROUP A

1. "Binnôrie, O Binnôrie; or, The Cruel Sister." W. Christie, *Traditional Ballad Airs*, I, 1876, p. 40.
2. "The bonnie mill-dams o' Balgonie." R. A. Smith, *The Scotish Minstrel* [1824], VI, p. 72.
3. "The Bonny Bows o' London." Christie, *Traditional Ballad Airs*, I, 1876, p. 42.
4. "Binorie." Greig MSS., III, p. 166; text, Bk. 742, XXXII, p. 90, King's College Library, Aberdeen. Also in Gavin Greig and Alexander Keith, *Last Leaves of Traditional Ballads and Ballad Airs*, 1925, p. 12(1b). (Robb)
5. "Binorie." Duncan MS., No. 7 (W. Walker). Also in Greig and Keith, 1925, p. 12(1c). (Gillespie)
6. "Binorie." Greig MSS., II, p. 106. (Littlejohn)
7. "Binnorie; or, The Cruel Sister." J. Collingwood Bruce and John Stokoe, *Northumbrian Minstrelsy*, 1882, pp. 61-63. Also in John Stokoe and Samuel Reay, *Songs of Northern England* [1892], p. 8.
8. "Binorie." Greig MSS., III, p. 40. Also in Greig and Keith, *Last Leaves*, 1925, p. 12(1a). (Unattributed)
9. "Binorie." Greig MSS., IV, p. 21. (Johnstone)
10. "Binorie." Greig MSS., IV, p. 52. (Dunbar)
11. "Binorie." Greig MSS., IV, p. 70. (Sangster)
12. "Norham, down by Norham." Francis James Child, *The English and Scottish Popular Ballads*, 1882-98, V, p. 412, and I, p. 495.
    a. "The Twa Sisters." Robert Ford, *Vagabond Songs and Ballads of Scotland*, 2nd series, 1901, pp. 189-94.
    b. "The Bonnie Mill-Dams o' Binnorie." John Ord, *The Bothy Songs & Ballads*, 1930, p. 430.
13. "Binorie." Greig MSS., II, p. 144. (Fowlie). Also in Greig-Duncan MS. 785, transcribed by W. Walker, King's College Library, Aberdeen.
14. "Benonie." Harris MS., Harvard College Library. Tune also in Child, *The English and Scottish Popular Ballads*, 1882-98, V, p. 412.
15. "The Mill Dams of Binnorie." Blaikie MS., National Library of Scotland MS. 1578, No. 64, p. 21.
16. "Binnorie." Greig MSS., I, p. 122. (Robb). Also in Greig-Duncan MS. 785, p. 11.
17. "Binorie." Greig MSS., III, p. 8. (Reid). Greig-Duncan MS. 785, p. 7.
18. "Binorie." Greig MSS., IV, p. 137. Also in Greig and Keith, *Last Leaves*, 1925, p. 13(2c). (Corbett)
19. "Binnorie." Greig MSS., I, p. 122. Also in Greig-Duncan MS. 785, p. 7, and *Rymour Club Miscellanea*, I (1910), p. 200. (Spence)
20. "Binorie." Duncan MS., No. 30 (W. Walker). Also in Greig and Keith, *Last Leaves*, 1925, p. 12(2a). (Alexander)
21. "Binorie." Duncan MS., No. 7 (W. Walker). Also in Greig and Keith, 1925, p. 13(2b). (Macdonald)
22. "The Two Sisters." Emelyn Elizabeth Gardner and Geraldine Jencks Chickering, *Ballads and Songs of Southern Michigan*, 1939, pp. 32(A)-33.

GROUP Ba

23. "The Old Man in the North Country." Duncan B. M. Emrich, LC Archive of American Folk Song. (Bascom L. Lunsford)
24. "The Two Sisters." Dorothy Horn, *Tennessee Folklore Society Bulletin*, IV (November 1938), p. 74.
25. "The Old Lord of the North Country; or, The Three Sisters." Arthur Kyle Davis, Jr., *Traditional Ballads of Virginia*, 1929, pp. 552(5A) and 93-95.
26. "The Old Man in the North Country." Frank Kidson and Alfred Moffat, *A Garland of English Folk-Songs*, 1926, pp. 24-25. Also, as "The Berkshire Tragedy," in Frank Kidson, *JFSS*, II (1906), pp. 283-84.
27. "The Two Sisters." Sharp MSS., 3524/2600, Clare College Library, Cambridge. Also in Cecil J. Sharp and Maud Karpeles, *English Folk Songs from the Southern Appalachians*, 1932, I, pp. 28(C)-29; and Davis, *Traditional Ballads of Virginia*, 1929, p. 555(G). (Chisholm)
    c. "The Two Sisters; or, The Old Lord by the Northern Sea." John Jacob Niles, *More Songs of the Hill-Folk* [1936], p. 8.
28. "The Two Sisters." Winston Wilkinson MSS., 1935-36, pp. 16-17(D), University of Virginia. (Smith)
29. "The Two Sisters." Sharp MSS., 4170/. (Mayo)
30. "The West Countree." H. M. Belden, *Ballads and Songs*, 1940, pp. 21(E)-23. Also in H. M. Belden, *JAF*, XXX (1917), p. 287.
31. "There was a Man in the West." F. C. Brown MS., 16 b I D, Library of Congress, photostat. Text, *The Frank C. Brown Collection of North Carolina Folklore*, II, 1952, pp. 32-33.
32. (Unnamed) Vance Randolph, *Ozark Folksongs*, I, 1946, pp. 53(C)-55.
33. "The Twa Sisters." Phillips Barry, *JAF*, XVIII (1905), pp. 130-31. Also, as "The Miller and the King's Daughter," in W. Maynard, Barry MSS., IV, No. 198, Harvard College Library.
34. "The Two Sisters." Sharp MSS., 4703/3274. Also in Sharp and Karpeles, *Appalachians*, 1932, I, p. 32(H). (Mitchell)
35. "The Two Sisters." Wilkinson MSS., 1935-36, pp. 12(A)-13.
36. "The Two Sisters." Wilkinson MSS., 1935-36, p. 18(E).
37. "The Two Sisters." Wilkinson MSS., 1935-36, p. 15(C).
38. "The Old Man in the North Countree." Belden, *Ballads and Songs*, 1940, pp. 17(A)-18. Also in H. M. Belden, *JAF*, XIX (1906), pp. 233-34.
39. "The Two Sisters." Sharp MSS., 3535/2608. Also in Sharp and Karpeles, *Appalachians*, 1932, I, p. 29(D); and Davis, *Traditional Ballads of Virginia*, 1929, pp. 556(J) and 103. (Walton)

40. "The Two Sisters; or, Sister Kate; or, The Miller and the Mayor's Daughter." Davis, 1929, pp. 554(5D) and 97-98.

41. "The Two Sisters." Sharp MSS., 3761/. Also in Sharp and Karpeles, *Appalachians*, 1932, I, p. 35(N). (Combs, J.)

GROUP Bb

42. "The Two Sisters." J. N. Smelser, *JAF*, XLIV (1931), pp. 295-96.

d. "The Two Sisters." Reed Smith and Hilton Rufty, *American Anthology of Old-World Ballads*, 1937, pp. 2-3.

e. "The Two Sisters." Columbia, Album M408, rec. 5-6 (WCO 26509-10). (Arthur Rowan Summers)

43. "The Miller's Two Daughters." John Harrington Cox, *Folk-Songs of the South*, 1925, pp. 521 and 20-21.

44. "There was an Old Woman Lived in the West." Paul G. Brewster, *Ballads and Songs of Indiana*, 1940, pp. 46-49.

45. "The Two Sisters." Sharp MSS., 4077/2911. Also in Sharp and Karpeles, *Appalachians*, 1932, I, p. 33(I). (Combs, E.)

46. "The Old Farmer in the Countree." Belden, *Ballads and Songs*, 1940, pp. 18(B)-19.

47. "The Two Sisters." Sharp MSS., 3649/. Also in Sharp and Karpeles, *Appalachians*, 1932, I, p. 34(L). (Franklin)

GROUP BC

48. "The Two Sisters." Jean Thomas, *Devil's Ditties*, 1931, pp. 70-73.

49. "There Was a Squire of High Degree." Frank Kidson, *JFSS*, I (1904), p. 253.

50. "The Two Sisters." Sharp MSS., 3700/. Also in Sharp and Karpeles, *Appalachians*, 1932, I, p. 31(G). (Henry)

f. "The Two Sisters." James Watt Raine, *The Land of Saddle-bags*, 1924, p. 118.

g. "The Two Sisters." E. P. Richardson, *American Mountain Songs*, 1927, p. 27.

51. (Unnamed) Randolph, *Ozark Folksongs*, I, 1946, pp. 60(G)-62.

52. "The Twa Sisters." Mellinger Edward Henry, *Folk-Songs from the Southern Highlands*, 1938, pp. 39(A)-40.

GROUP Bd

53. "The Two Sisters." Wilkinson MSS., 1935-36, p. 23(H).

54. "The Two Sisters," Helen Hartness Flanders, and others, *The New Green Mountain Songster*, 1939, pp. 3-4. Also in Helen Hartness Flanders, *BFSSNE*, No. 6 (1933), pp. 5-6.

h. (Unnamed) Phillips Barry Dictaphone Cylinders, No. 152, cutting 2, Harvard College Library.

55. "The Two Sisters." Sharp MSS., 3518/2597. Also in Sharp and Karpeles, *Appalachians*, 1932, I, pp. 27(B)-28; and Davis, *Traditional Ballads of Virginia*, 1929, p. 554(F) and 99-100. (Batten)

56. "The Two Sisters." Wilkinson MSS., 1935-36, p. 14(B).

57. "The Two Sisters." Wilkinson MSS., 1935-36, p. 19(F).

i. "There was an old man in our town." A. K. Davis Collection, August 4, 1932, aluminum recording, Charlottesville, Va.

58. "The Two Sisters." Wilkinson MSS., 1935-36, pp. 20-22(G).

59. "The Two Sisters." Sharp MSS., 4523/3178. Also in Sharp and Karpeles, *Appalachians*, 1932, I, p. 34(K). (Blackett)

60. "The Two Sisters." Herbert Halpert, LC Archive of American Folk Song, rec. 2737 A1. (Anne Corbin Ball)

GROUP Be

61. "The Barkshire Tragedy." Lucy E. Broadwood and J. A. Fuller Maitland, *English County Songs*, 1893, pp. 118-19.

62. "A Farmer there lived in the North Country." Anne G. Gilchrist, *JFSS*, VIII (1930), p. 247.

63. "The Two Sisters." Sharp MSS., 4175/. Also in Sharp and Karpeles, *Appalachians*, 1932, I, p. 33(J). (Fitzgerald)

64. "The Twa Sisters." Mabel Major, *Publications of the Texas Folk-Lore Society*, X (1932), pp. 141-43.

65. "The Two Sisters." Sharp MSS., 4777/. Also in Sharp and Karpeles, *Appalachians*, 1932, I, p. 35(M). (Hughes)

66. "The Miller's Daughters." Randolph, *Ozark Folksongs*, I, 1946, pp. 50(A)-52.

j. "The Miller's Daughters." Vance Randolph, *Ozark Mountain Folks*, 1932, pp. 211-12.

67. "The Two Sisters." Herbert Halpert, LC Archive of American Folk Song, Album 7, rec. 33A(544). (Horton Barker)

68. "The Two Sisters." Phillips Barry, Fannie H. Eckstorm, and Mary W. Smyth, *British Ballads from Maine*, 1929, p. 42(C).

69. "There was an Old Farmer." John Harrington Cox, *Traditional Ballads Mainly from West Virginia*, 1939, pp. 6-7.

70. "The Old Man in the Old Country." Vance Randolph, LC Archive of American Folk Song, rec. 5244 A. Also in Randolph, *Ozark Folksongs*, I, 1946, pp. 57(E)-58.

71. "The Old Woman of the North Countree." Davis, *Traditional Ballads of Virginia*, 1929, pp. 553(B) and 95-96.

72. "The Sea Shore; or, The Swim Swom Bonny." Samuel P. Bayard, *BFSSNE*, No. 9 (1935), p. 4 (2nd version).

GROUP Bf

73. "The Two Sisters." Sharp MSS., 3689/2749. Also in Sharp and Karpeles, *Appalachians*, 1932, I, p. 31(F). (Knuckles)

74. "The Two Sisters." Sharp MSS., 4641/3234. Also in Sharp and Karpeles, 1932, I, p. 30(E). (Deeton)

75. "The Two Sisters." Sharp MSS., 4627/. (Jones)

76. "The Two Sisters." Arthur Palmer Hudson, *Folk Tunes from Mississippi*, 1937, No. 25.

77. "Two Little Sisters." Theodore Garrison, *Forty-five Folk Songs Collected from Searcy County, Arkansas* (University of Arkansas, M.A. thesis), 1944, pp. 19-20.

k. "The Two Sisters." Henry, *Folk-Songs from the Southern Highlands*, 1938, p. 41(B).

78. "The Two Little Sisters." Mary O. Eddy, *Ballads and Songs from Ohio*, 1939, pp. 17-18.

GROUP C

79. "The Cruel Sister." Ritson-Tytler-Brown MS., No. 15 and pp. 99-102, Harvard College Library. Also in Child, *The English and Scottish Popular Ballads*, 1882-98, V, p. 411.

80. "The Twa Sisters." The Fuller Sisters, Bumpus (London); A. and C. Boni (New York), 1927.

l. "The Twa Sisters." J. M. Diack, *The New Scottish Orpheus*, 1923-24. Also in John Goss, *Ballads of Britain*, 1937, p. 8.

81. "There lived twa Sisters." Lady John Scott's Sharpe MS., National Library of Scotland MS. 843, fol. 11ᵛ. Text, Charles Kirkpatrick Sharpe, *A Ballad Book*, 1824. Ed. of 1891, Part I, pp. 31-34.

GROUP D

82. "The Swan Swims Bonnie O." William Motherwell, *Minstrelsy: Ancient and Modern*, 1827, App'x. No. 20 and p. xx.
83. "The Swan Swims so Bonny, O." Frank Kidson, *JFSS*, II (1906), p. 285. Also in Kidson and Moffat, *A Garland of English Folk-Songs*, 1926, p. 26.
84. "The Two Sisters." Phillips Barry, *BFSSNE*, No. 10 (1935), p. 11. Text, Davis, *Traditional Ballads of Virginia*, 1929, p. 104(K).
85. "The Swim Swom Bonny." Samuel P. Bayard, *BFSSNE*, No. 9 (1935), p. 4 (1st version).
86. "Heigh ho! my Nancy Oh." George Petrie, *The Complete Petrie Collection of Irish Music*, edited by Charles Villiers Stanford, 1902-05, No. 688.
87. "Down by the Waters Rolling." Alton C. Morris, *Folksongs of Florida*, 1950, pp. 243-44.
88. "Two Little Sisters." Morris, *Folksongs of Florida*, 1950, pp. 245-46.

GROUP E

89. "Binorie." Sharp MSS., 2031/. (Overd)
90. "Binorie." Sharp MSS., 2134/. (Bayliss)
91. "The Two Sisters." Sharp MSS., 3419/2509. Also in Sharp and Karpeles, *Appalachians*, 1932, I, p. 26(A). (Gentry)
92. "The Two Sisters." Henry, *Folk-Songs from the Southern Highlands*, 1938, pp. 43(C)-44.
93. "The Two Sisters." Phillips Barry and Annabel M. Buchanan, *BFSSNE*, No. 12 (1937), p. 10.
94. (Unnamed) Randolph, *Ozark Folksongs*, I, 1946, pp. 59(F)-60.
95. "The Two Sisters." Elmore Vincent, *Lumber Jack Songs* [1932], p. 27.
96. "The Youngest Daughter." Helen Hartness Flanders, *BFSSNE*, No. 11 (1936), p. 16.
97. "The Two Sisters." Gardner and Chickering, *Ballads and Songs of Southern Michigan*, 1939, pp. 33(B)-34.

TUNES WITH TEXTS

GROUP A

1. [Binnôrie, O Binnôrie; or, The Cruel Sister]

Christie, I, 1876, p. 40. From a singer in Buchan, ante 1842; "arranged."

p π⁴

Christie notes the presence of eighteenth-century variants of this tune in the *Scots Musical Museum*, V (1796), No. 462, p. 474, and in Neil Gow's *Repository*, Pt. II (1802), p. 3.

There were two sisters liv'd in a bower,
    Binnôrie, O Binnôrie!
There came a knight to be their wooer,
    By the bonny mill-dams o' Binnôrie.

He courted the eldest with glove and ring,
    Binnôrie, O Binnôrie!
But he lovèd the youngest aboon a'thing,
    By the bonny mill-dams o' Binnôrie. [Etc.]

The text has no independent standing, being compounded (with omissions) from Scott and Jamieson.

2. [The bonnie mill-dams o' Balgonie]

Smith [1824], VI, p. 72. To an unrelated text.

p π⁴

3. [The Bonny Bows o' London]

Christie, I, 1876, p. 42. Sung by an old woman in Banffshire. Text "epitomized" from Buchan, 1828, II, p. 128.

p Æ

There were twa sisters in a bower,
    It's hey wi' the gay and the grinding;
And ae king's son has courted them baith,
    At the bonny, bonny bows o' London.

He courted the youngest wi' broach and ring,
    It's hey wi' the gay and the grinding;
And he courted the eldest wi' mony other thing,
    At the bonny, bonny bows o' London. [Etc.]

4. "Binorie"

Greig MSS., III, p. 166; text, Bk. 742, XXXII, p. 90. Also
in Greig and Keith, 1925, p. 12(1b). Sung by Alexander
Robb, New Deer, Aberdeenshire.

p Æ/D

Keith notes the connections of this group of tunes with Johnson,
SMM, No. 462, "The Rantin Laddie" (Child 240), "The Earl of
Aboyne" (Child 235), "The Cruel Mother" (Child 20).

There were twa sisters lived in a ha',
    Binorie, O an' Binorie;
And they had but ae lad between them twa,
    And they ca'd him the bonnie mullart laddie,

O sister, O sister, ye tak' my han'
    Binorie, O an' Binorie;
For I wad like to see my father's fishin' boat come to lan'
    I' the bonnie milldams o' Binorie.

5. "Binorie"

Duncan MS., No. 7 (W. Walker). Also in Greig and
Keith, 1925, p. 12(1c). Sung by Mrs. Gillespie. (Her text,
sixteen stanzas long, has not been found among Greig's
MSS.)

p Æ/D

6. "Binorie"

Greig MSS., II, p. 106. Sung by Miss Littlejohn, Banchory,
January 1907.

p Æ

There were twa sisters lived in a bower,
    Binorie, O and Binorie,
There cam' a knight to be their wooer,
    Bi [norie, O and Binorie.]

7. [Binnorie; or, The Cruel Sister]

Bruce and Stokoe, 1882, pp. 61-63. Also, with piano accompaniment, in Stokoe and Reay [1892], p. 8.

m Æ

The editors of 1882 remark with rash confidence: "The tune is a
true Northumbrian melody, never before published; it differs from
the Scottish tune, which is of modern date" (p. 63).

1. There were twa sisters sat in a bow'r,
        Binnorie, O Binnorie;
   There cam a knight to be their wooer,
        By the bonny mill-dams of Binnorie.

2. He courted the eldest wi' glove and ring,
        Binnorie, &c.
   But he lo'ed the youngest aboon a' thing.
        By the bonny, &c.

3. He courted the eldest wi' broach and knife,
   But he lo'ed the youngest aboon his life.

4. The eldest she was vexed sair,
   And sore envied her sister fair.

5. The eldest said to the youngest ane:
   "Will you go and see our father's ships come in."

6. She's ta'en her by the lily hand,
   And led her down to the river strand.

7. The youngest stude upon a stane,
   The eldest cam' and pushed her in.

8. She took her by the middle sma',
   And dashed her bonny back to the jaw.

9. "O sister, sister, reach your hand,
   And ye shall be heir of half my land."

10. "O sister, I'll not reach my hand,
    And I'll be heir of all your land.

11. "Shame fa' the hand that I should take,
    It's twinèd me, and my world's make."

12. "O sister, reach me but your glove,
    And sweet William shall be your love."

13. "Sink on, nor hope for hand or glove,
    And sweet William shall better be my love.

14. "Your cherry cheeks and your yellow hair
    Garr'd me gang maiden ever mair."

15. Sometimes she sunk, sometimes she swam,
    Until she cam to the miller's dam.

16. The miller's daughter was baking bread,
    And gaed for water as she had need.

17. "O father, father, draw your dam!
    There's either a mermaid or a milk-white swan."

18. The miller hasted and drew his dam,
    And there he found a drown'd woman.

19. Ye couldna see her yellow hair
    For gowd and pearls that were sae rare.

20. Ye couldna see her middle sma',
    Her gowden girdle was sae braw.

21. Ye couldna see her lily feet,
    Her gowden fringes were sae deep.

22. A famous harper passing by,
    The sweet pale face he chanced to spy;

23. And when he looked that lady on,
    He sighed and made a heavy moan.

24. "Sair will they be, whate'er they be,
    The hearts that live to weep for thee."

25. He made a harp o' her breast bone,
    Whose sounds would melt a heart of stone;

26. The strings he framed of her yellow hair
    Their notes made sad the listening ear.

27. He brought it to her father's ha',
    There was the court assembled a'.

28. He laid the harp upon a stane,
    And straight it began to play alane—

29. "O yonder sits my father, the king,
    And yonder sits my mother, the queen;

30. "And yonder stands my brother Hugh,
    And by him my William, sweet and true."

31. But the last tune that the harp played then
    Was—"Woe to my sister, false Helen!"

8. "Binorie"

Greig MSS., III, p. 40. Also in Greig and Keith, 1925, p. 12(1a).

p Æ/D

There wis twa maidens lived in a ha',
    Binorie O, and Binorie;
They had but ae lad atween them twa,
    'Twas the bonnie mullert lad o Binorie.

9. "Binorie"

Greig MSS., IV, p. 21. Sung by J. Johnstone, New Deer, Aberdeenshire.

p Æ/D

Sister, O sister, we'll go to the broom,
    Benorrie, O an' Benorrie,
An' hear the blackbirds changing their tune,
    By the bonnie milldams o' Benorrie.

10. "Binorie"

Greig MSS., IV, p. 52. Sung by Mrs. Dunbar, Crimond.

p Æ/D

11. "Binorie"

Greig MSS., IV, p. 70. Sung by Mrs. Sangster, Cortiecram, Mintlaw.

p Æ/D

12. "Norham, down by Norham"

Child, 1882-98, V, p. 412; text, I, p. 495(W). From Thomas Lugton, Kelso, as sung by an old cotter-woman (c. 1830); learned from her grandfather.

m Æ/D

A copy very close to this is given as from the same source by Robert Ford, *Vagabond Songs and Ballads*, 2nd series, 1901, pp. 189-94 (not included in the one-volume reprint); but his text, in 28 stanzas, appears to be compounded from Scott and others. As given by John Ord, *The Bothy Songs & Ballads*, 1930, p. 430, the tune is identical with the Ford copy, but in the key of F# minor. Ord's text is somewhat different, and in 23 stanzas.

1. Ther were three ladies playing at the ba,
     Norham, down by Norham
   And there cam a knight to view them a'.
     By the bonnie mill-dams o Norham.

2. He courted the aldest wi diamonds and rings,
   But he loved the youngest abune a' things.

   *　*　*　*　*　*　*　*

3. "Oh sister, oh sister, lend me your hand,
   And pull my poor body unto dry land.

4. "Oh sister, oh sister, lend me your glove,
   And you shall have my own true love!"

5. Oot cam the miller's daughter upon Tweed,
   To carry in water to bake her bread.

6. "Oh father, oh father, there's a fish in your dam;
   It either is a lady or a milk-white swan."

7. Oot cam the miller's man upon Tweed,
   And there he spied a lady lying dead.

8. He could not catch her by the waist,
   For her silken stays they were tight laced.

9. But he did catch her by the hand,
   And pulled her poor body unto dry land.

10. He took three taets o her bonnie yellow hair,
    To make harp strings they were so rare.

11. The very first tune that the bonnie harp played
    Was The aldest has cuisten the youngest away.

13. "Binorie"

Greig MSS., II, p. 144. Sung by Mrs. Fowlie, Bonnykelly, September 1907.

p Æ

O sister O sister give to me your hand
      Binorie O and Binorie
And ye'll get the miller for your true love
      Binorie O and Binorie.

14. "Benonie"

Harris MS. Tune also in Child, 1882-98, V, p. 412. Sung by "Mrs. Harris and others."

a D

The timing after the mid-cadence has been altered by the present editor, but the note-values are unchanged.

Oh! Sister, Sister, tak me out agen!
      Nonie, an' Benonie
But wi a sillar cane,*
She shot her farer in,
      To the bonnie mill dam o' Benonie.

* Or, "pin."

15. [The Mill Dams of Binnorie]

Blaikie MS., NL Scotland MS. 1578, No. 64, p. 21. (c. 1825)

a D/M

16. "Binnorie"

Greig MSS., I, p. 122. Sung by A[nnie?] Robb, New
Deer, Aberdeenshire, February 1906.

p I/M

O sister O sister will ye take a walk?
     Binnorie oh Binnorie;
To hear the bonnie blackbirds whistle o'er their tune,
     And we'll maybe see the miller o' Binnorie.

17. "Binorie"

Greig MSS., III, p. 8. Sung by William Reid, Turriff,
September 1907.

p M (inflected VII)

There were twa sisters lived in a bower,
     Binorie oh and Binorie;
And there cam' a knight for to be their wooer
On the bonnie mill-dams o' Binorie.

18. "Binorie"

Greig MSS., IV, p. 137. Also in Greig and Keith, 1925, p.
13(2c). Sung by G. Corbett, New Deer, Aberdeenshire,
1910.

p M

19. "Binnorie"

Greig MSS., I, p. 122. Sung by J. W. Spence, Rosecroft,
Fyvie, April 1906.

p M

Greig seems to have chosen this copy for printing in the *Rymour
Club Miscellanea*, I (1910), p. 200.

There were twa sisters lived in a bower
     Binnorie O Binnorie
There cam' a knight to be their wooer
     By the bonnie Mill Dams o' Binnorie.

20. "Binorie"

Duncan MS., No. 30 (W. Walker). Also in Greig and
Keith, 1925, p. 12(2a). Sung by Robert Alexander, Bourtie,
Aberdeenshire.

p M (inflected VII)

Keith notes association of this form with "The Bonnie Lass of
Fyvie" (e.g., Greig MSS., III, p. 25). Other connections are: "Come
oer frae Pitgair" (Greig MSS., I, p. 189); "Mill o Beenie" (Greig
MSS., II, p. 51); "There cam' a ship" (Greig MSS., III, p. 23).

There was twa young girlies lived in a boo'er,
     Binorie O, Binorie,
An' a bonnie miller laddie a-courtin' them did come
Tae the bonnie mill dams o Binorie, O.

21. "Binorie"

Duncan MS., No. 7 (W. Walker). Also in Greig and
Keith, 1925, p. 13(2b). Sung by Jessie H. Macdonald,
Alford.

p M (inflected VII)

22. "The Two Sisters"

Gardner and Chickering, 1939, pp. 32(A)-33. Sung by Mrs. Charles Muchler, Kalkaska, Mich., 1934.

p I/M

The tune here has lost some, but considerably less, of its patina than has the verbal text.

1. Once there lived two sisters fair,
   Viola and Vinola;
   A young man came a-courting both,
   Down by the waters rolling.

2. The eldest he loved most dearly,
   But the youngest he intended for his bride.

3. The eldest he bought a fine gold chain;
   The youngest he bought a guinea gold ring.

4. These two sisters went out for a walk;
   Of the young man they did talk.

5. They wandered down to the river bank;
   The elder pushed the younger in.

6. "Sister, sister, take my hand,
   And you can have the young man and all of his command."

7. She floated down to the miller's brook;
   The miller caught her with a hook.

8. They hanged the miller on a tree,
   But the cruel sister she went free.

GROUP Ba

23. "The Old Man in the North Country"

Emrich, LC/AAFS, No. 9474 A1. Sung by Bascom L. Lunsford in Washington, D.C., April, 1949; learned in the region around Asheville, N.C.

p π[1]

Was an old man in the North Country,
   Bow down,
Was an old man in the North Country,
   Bow down and balance t' me,

Was an old man in the North Country,
He had daughters one, two, three.
   I'll be true to you, my love,
   If you'll be true to me.

He bought the youngest a silken hat,
   Bow down, bow down,
He bought the youngest a silken hat;
The oldest daughter couldn't stand that.
   I'll be true to you, my love,
   If you'll be true to me.

They walked down by the water's brim,
   Bow down, bow down,
They walked down by the water's brim,
The eldest pushed the youngest in.
   I'll be true to you, my love,
   If you'll be true to me.

She floated down to the miller's dam,
   Bow down, bow down,
She floated down to the miller's dam,
The miller pulled her to dry land.
   I'll be true to you, my love,
   If you'll be true to me.

From her hand he took five rings,
   Bow down, bow down,
From her hand he took five rings,
Then he pushed her in again.
   I'll be true to you, my love,
   If you'll be true to me.

They hung the miller on the gallows high,
   Bow down, bow down,
They hung the miller on the gallows high,
The eldest daughter hung close by.
   I'll be true to you, my love,
   If you'll be true to me.

24. [The Two Sisters]

Horn, *TFSB*, IV (November 1938), p. 74. Sung by John Milmine, Maryville College, Tenn.

m I

There was an old woman lived on the sea-shore.
    Bow down.
There was an old woman lived on the sea-shore.
    Bow and balance to me.
There was an old woman lived on the sea-shore,
    And she had daughters three or four.
I'll be true to my love
    If my love will be true to me.

25. "The Old Lord of the North Country; or, The Three Sisters"

Davis, 1929, p. 552(5A); text, pp. 93-95. Sung by Mr. A. S. Furcron, Fauquier County, Va., November 10, 1919. Collected by John Stone.

p I

1. There lived an old lord in the North Countree,
    Bow down.
There lived an old lord in the North Countree,
    Bow down you bittern to me.
There lived an old lord in the North Countree
And he had daughters, one, two, three.
If this be true, true love, my love, my love, be true to me.

2. There came a young gentle courting there,
    Bow down.

There came a young gentle courting there,
    Bow down you bittern to me.
There came a young gentle courting there,
Courting of the youngest fair.
If this be true, true love, my love, my love, be true to me.

3. The father brought the youngest a beaver hat,
    Bow down.
The father brought the youngest a beaver hat,
    Bow down you bittern to me.
The father brought the youngest a beaver hat,
The elder swore she shouldn't have that.
If this be true, true love, my love, my love, be true to me.

4. "O sister, sister, let's (uh) we walk out,"
    Bow down.
"O sister, sister, let's (uh) we walk out,"
    Bow down you bittern to me.
"O sister, sister, let's (uh) we walk out
And see those ships that sail about."
If this be true, true love, my love, my love, be true to me.

5. They walked till they came to the salt sea brim,
    Bow down.
They walked till they came to the salt sea brim,
    Bow down you bittern to me.
They walked till they came to the salt sea brim,
And the eldest pushed the youngest in.
If this be true, true love, my love, my love, be true to me.

6. "O sister, sister, lend me your hand,"
    Bow down.
"O sister, sister, lend me your hand,"
    Bow down you bittern to me.
"O sister, sister, lend me your hand
And you shall have my house and land."
If this be true, true love, my love, my love, be true to me.

7. "I'll neither lend you my hand nor my glove,"
    Bow down.
"I'll neither lend you my hand nor my glove,"
    Bow down you bittern to me.
"I'll neither lend you my hand nor my glove,
For you shan't have my own true love."
If this be true, true love, my love, my love, be true to me.

8. Oh, the miller he came with his fish hook,
    Bow down.
Oh, the miller he came with his fish hook,
    Bow down you bittern to me.
Oh, the miller he came with his fish hook
And fished that fair maid out of the brook.
If this be true, true love, my love, my love, be true to me.

9. And off of her fingers took five gold rings,
    Bow down.
And off of her fingers took five gold rings,
    Bow down you bittern to me.
And off of her fingers took five gold rings
And pushed her back in the brook again.
If this be true, true love, my love, my love, be true to me.

10. Oh, the miller was hanged at his mill gate,
    Bow down.

Oh, the miller was hanged at his mill gate,
    Bow down you bittern to me.
Oh, the miller was hanged at his mill gate
For the murder of the sister Kate.
If this be true, true love, my love, my love, be true to me.

26. "The Old Man in the North Country"

Kidson and Moffat, 1926, pp. 24-25. Also, as "The Berkshire Tragedy," in Kidson, *JFSS*, II (1906), pp. 283-84, as collected by Charles Lolley in Driffield, Yorkshire. (Text not identical.)

p I (inflected IV)

The variant readings are in the 1906 printing. Doubtless both forms are from the same source.

1. There was an old man in the North Country,
Low down derry down dee,
There was an old man in the North Country,
Valid we ought to be,
There was an old man in the North Country,
He had daughters, one, two, three,
I'll be true to my love if my love will be true to me.

2. There came a young man to the North Country,
Low down derry down dee,
There came a young man to the North Country,
Valid we ought to be.
There came a young man to the North Country,
He came to court the younger dame,
Then I'll be true to my love if my love will be true to me.

3. He bought the younger a beaver hat,
Low down derry down dee,
He bought the younger a beaver hat,
Valid we ought to be.
He bought the younger a beaver hat,
The elder one was not pleased at that,
Then I'll be true to my love if my love will be true to me.

4. He bought the younger a gay gold ring,
Low down derry down dee,
He bought the younger a gay gold ring,
Valid we ought to be.
He bought the younger a gay gold ring,
The elder not being pleased at him,
Then I'll be true to my love if my love will be true to me.

5. "Oh sister let's go to the water brim,
Low down derry down dee.
Oh sister let's go to the water brim,"
Valid we ought to be.
Away they went to the water brim,
The elder pushed the younger in,
I'll be true to my love if my love will be true to me.

6. Away she floated, away she swam,
Low down derry down dee,
Away she floated, away she swam,
Valid we ought to be.
Until she came to the merry mill dam,
She looked so pale and looked so wan,
Then I'll be true to my love if my love will be true to me.

7. The miller's daughter stood at the door,
Low down derry down dee,
The miller's daughter stood at the door,
Valid we ought to be.
She saw this maiden came to shore,
With all the jewels that she wore
Then I'll be true to my love if my love will be true to me.

8. "O Father, O father what's in the mill dam,"
Low down derry down dee,
"O Father, O father what's in the mill dam,"
Valid we ought to be.
"A fish, a fish and a new 'britan,'
Or else it is a snow white swan,"
Then I'll be true to my love if my love will be true to me.

9. Go fetch me out my fishing hook,
Low down derry down dee,
Go fetch me out my fishing hook,
Valid we ought to be.
I'll draw the maiden from the brook,
If I but catch her with my crook,
Then I'll be true to my love if my love will be true to me.

Reprinted by permission of the publishers of "A Garland of English Folk-Songs," Ascherberg, Hopwood & Crew Limited, London.

27. [The Two Sisters]

Sharp MSS., 3524/2600. Also in Sharp and Karpeles, 1932, I, pp. 28(C)-29; and Davis, 1929, p. 555(G). Sung by Louisa Chisholm, Woodridge, Va., September 23, 1916.

p I

The variant of John Jacob Niles, *More Songs of the Hill-Folk* [1936], p. 8, is melodically indistinguishable from the above.

1. There lived an old lord by the northern sea,
   Bow down,
   There lived an old lord by the northern sea,
   The boughs they bent to me.
   There lived an old lord by the northern sea,
   And he had daughters one, two, three.
   That will be true, true to my love,
   Love and my love will be true to me.

2. A young man came a-courting there,
   He took choice of the youngest there.

3. He gave this girl a beaver hat,
   The oldest she thought much of that.

4. O sister, O sister, let's we walk out
   To see the ships a-sailing about.

5. As they walked down the salty brim,
   The oldest pushed the youngest in.

6. O sister, O sister, lend me your hand,
   And I will give you my house and land.

7. I'll neither lend you my hand or glove,
   But I will have your own true love.

8. Down she sank and away she swam,
   And into the miller's mill (or, fish) pond she ran.

9. The miller come out with his fish hook
   And fished the fair maid out of the brook.

10. And it's off of her finger took five gold rings,
    And into the brook he pushed her again.

11. The miller was hung at his mill gate
    For drowning of my sister Kate.

There was a Lord Mayor in our town,
And he had daughters one, two, three.
   Love will be true, true to my love,
   Love will be true to you.

2. There was a young man went courting,
   And he did choose the youngest fair.

3. O Sister, O Sister, let's we walk out,
   And view the ships a-sailing about.

4. The oldest pushed the youngest in,
   And down she sunk and away she swim.

5. O Sister, O Sister, O loan me your hand,
   And you may have my house and land.

6. Sister, O Sister, O loan me your glove,
   And you may have my own true-love.

7. I'll neither loan you my hand nor my glove,
   But I will have your own true-love.

8. Down she sank and away she swum,
   She swum into the miller's mill pond.

9. Miller, O miller, yonder swims a swan,
   Miller, O miller, or a fair maiden one.

10. The miller came out with his fish hook,
    To fish the fair maid from the brook.

11. O miller, O miller, O loan me your hand,
    And you shall have my house and land.

12. O miller, O miller, here's five gold rings,
    If you will turn me home again.

13. And off her fingers he taken her rings,
    And he pushed her in the brook again.

14. The miller was hung at his own mill gate,
    For drowning of my sister Kate.

28. [The Two Sisters]

Wilkinson MSS., 1935-36, pp. 16-17(D). Sung by Mrs. F. S. Smith, Altavista, Va., October 20, 1935.

m I (inflected VII)

1. There was a Lord Mayor in our town,
      Bow down,
   There was a Lord Mayor in our town,
      Bow it's been to me.

29. [The Two Sisters]

Sharp MSS., 4170/. Sung by Mrs. Cleaver Mayo, Greenwood, Va., April 24, 1918.

m I

There lived an old man in the North Countree,
Bow down, Bow down,
There lived an old man in the North Countree,
The boughs they bent to me.
There lived an old man in the North Countree,
And he had daughters, one, two, three
That'll be true,
True to my love,
[?] to my love will be true to me.

30. "The West Countree"

Belden, 1940, pp. 21(E)-23. Also in Belden, *JAF*, XXX
(1917), p. 287. Sung by Mrs. Case; learned during her
childhood in Harrison County, Mo.

p I

1. There was an old man lived in the west,
    Bow down
  There was an old man lived in the west,
    The bow's a-bend o'er me
  There was an old man lived in the west,
  He had two daughters of the best.
    I'll be true, true to my love, if my love will be
                              true to me.

2. The squire he courted the older first,
   But still he loved the younger best.

3. The first that he bought her was a beaver hat;
   The older thought right smart of that.

4. The next that he bought her was a gay gold ring.
   He never bought the older a thing.

5. "Sister, oh sister, let's walk out
   And see the ships all sailing about."

6. They walked all along the salt sea brim;
   The older pushed the younger in.

7. "Sister, oh sister, lend me your hand,
   And then I'll gain the promised land."

8. "It's neither will I lend you my hand nor my glove,
   And then I'll gain your own true love."

9. Sometimes she'd sink, sometimes she'd swim,
   Sometimes she'd grasp a broken limb.

10. Down she sank and off she swam;
    She swam into the miller's dam.

11. The miller went fishing in his own mill-dam,
    And he fished this lady out of the stream.

12. Off of her fingers he pulled three rings
    And dashed her in the brook again.

13. The miller was hanged on his own mill-gate
    For the drowning of my sister Kate.

31. [There was a Man in the West]

Brown MS., 16 b I D. Text, *North Carolina Folklore*, II,
1952, pp. 32-33. Secured by Professor E. L. Starr, Salem
College, from an unnamed source, 1915.

p I

1. There was a man lived in the west
   Bow down, bow down
   There was a man lived in the west
   Bow once to me
   There was a man lived in the west,
   He had two daughters of the best.
   I will be true, true to my love,
   And my love will be true to me.

2. A Squire (Knight) he courted the eldest one,
   But he loved the youngest one.

3. He gave the youngest a gay gold ring
   And to the eldest gave not a thing.

4. He gave the youngest a satin cap;
   The eldest she got mad at that.

5. One day as they walked by the river side
   They sat at the bank and they cried and cried.

6. The eldest she pushed the youngest in;
   The youngest said it was a sin.

7. She swam till she came to the miller's pond,
   And then she swam all around and around.

8. 'O miller, miller, save my life,
   And I will be your loving wife.'

9. The miller threw in his hook and line
   And pulled her out by the hair so fine.

10. The hook and the line were laid on the shelf—
    If you want any more, why, sing it yourself.

32. (Unnamed)

Randolph, 1946, I, pp. 53(C)-55. Sung by Bert Prusser,
Little Rock, Ark., May 3, 1933.

p I (inflected IV)

1. There lived an old man by the Northern Sea,
   Bow down,
   There lived an old man by the Northern Sea,
   The bow has been to me,
   There lived an old man by the Northern Sea,
   He had daughters two and three,
   I will be true, true to my love,
   Yes Lord, and my love will be true to me.

2. There come a young man a-courtin' there,
   Bow down,
   There come a young man a-courtin' there,
   The bow has been to me,
   There come a young man a-courtin' there,
   He took choice to the youngest fair,
   I will be true, true to my love,
   Yes Lord, and my love will be true to me.

3. He bought her a beaver hat,
   Bow down,
   He bought her a beaver hat,
   The bow has been to me,
   He bought her a beaver hat
   The oldest girl did not like that,
   I will be true, true to my love,
   Yes Lord, and my love will be true to me.

4. Sister, oh sister, let's us walk out,
   Bow down,
   Sister, oh sister, let's us walk out,
   The bow has been to me,
   Sister, oh sister, let's us walk out
   And see the ships that sail about,
   I will be true, true to my love,
   Yes Lord, and my love will be true to me.

5. Sister, oh sister, let's us go swim,
   Bow down,
   Sister, oh sister, let's us go swim,
   The bow has been to me,
   Sister, oh sister, let's us go swim
   And hang our clothes on a hickory limb,
   I will be true, true to my love,
   Yes Lord, and my love will be true to me.

6. As they walked by the saucer brim,
   Bow down,
   As they walked by the saucer brim,
   The bow has been to me,
   As they walked by the saucer brim,
   The oldest pushed the youngest in,
   I will be true, true to my love,
   Yes Lord, and my love will be true to me.

7. Down she sunk and away she swum,
   Bow down,
   Down she sunk and away she swum,
   The bow has been to me,
   Down she sunk and away she swum,
   Swum into the miller's pond,
   I will be true, true to my love,
   Yes Lord, and my love will be true to me.

8. The miller come out with his big fish hook,
   Bow down,
   The miller come out with his big fish hook,
   The bow has been to me,
   The miller come out with his big fish hook
   And fished the youngest out of the brook,
   I will be true, true to my love,
   Yes Lord, and my love will be true to me.

33. [The Twa Sisters]

Barry, *JAF*, XVIII (1905), pp. 130-31. From W. Maynard,
USN, June 1904; as sung by midshipmen at Newport, R.I.,
c. 1860. Also, as "The Miller and the King's Daughter," in
Maynard, Barry MSS., Bk. IV, No. 198.

p I

1. There was a man lived in the West,
   Bow down, bow down,
   There was a man lived in the West,
   Bow once to me.

There was a man lived in the West,
And he had two daughters just of the best.
   So it's I'll be true, true to my love,
   And my love will be true to me!

2. The miller, he loved the youngest one.
But he was loved by the eldest one.

3. He gave the youngest a gay gold ring,
But he gave the eldest never a thing.

4. He gave the youngest a satin hat,
But the eldest, she got mad at that.

5. They took a walk by the river side,
Alas! I must tell what did betide.

6. The eldest, she pushed the youngest in,
And all for the sake of the gay gold ring.

7. "Oh, sister, oh, sister, oh, save my life!
And you shall be the miller's wife!"

8. She swam till she came to the miller's pond,
And there she swam around and around.

9. The miller, he took his hook and line,
And caught her by her hair so fine.

2. He gave the youngest a gilbern hat;
The oldest sister didn't much like that.

3. He gave the youngest a gay gold ring;
The oldest sister didn't much like that.

4. It's come, dear sister, and let's take a walk
All down yon green river-side.

5. The oldest sister pushed the youngest in.
She first did float and then did sink.

6. Pull me out, pull me out, I'll give you my cloak.
I won't pull you out unless you give me your love.

7. She swum on down to the miller's gate
  . . . .

8. The miller cast about his hook,
And caught her in her petticoat.

9. He robbed her of her gay gold ring,
And then he pushed her in again.

10. This old miller was hung at the gate,
And the oldest sister was burned at the stake.

* 1932 omits "who."
† 1932 omits "the."

34. [The Two Sisters]

Sharp MSS., 4703/3274. Also in Sharp and Karpeles, 1932,
I, p. 32(H). Sung by Mrs. Effie Mitchell, Burnsville, N.C.,
September 27, 1918.

p I/M

1. There was an old man who lived* in the West,
   Bow down, bow down,
There was an old man who lived* in the West,
   Come bow unto me,
There was an old man who lived* in the West,
He liked the youngest sister the best.†
   True, true, true to my love,
   My love is true to me.

35. [The Two Sisters]

Wilkinson MSS., 1935-36, pp. 12(A)-13. Sung by Mrs. Jane
Morris, Mrs. Lucy McAllister, and Alice Bruce, Harriston,
Va., October 9, 1935.

p M (inflected VII)

1. There was an old woman in Northern 'try,
   Bow her down,
There was an old woman in Northern 'try
   The bough has bent to me.
There was an old woman in Northern 'try
She had some daughters, two or three.
   Love will be true, true to my love,
   Love if my love will be true to me.

2. There went a young man a-courting there,
   He chose the youngest one was there.

3. He gave to her a beaver hat,
   The oldest one thought hard of that.

4. O sister, O sister, let's we walk out,
   To see the ships go (come) sailing about.

5. Across the brook they both did walk,
   The oldest pushed the youngest off.

6. O sister, O sister, lend me your hand,
   You may have my house and land.

7. I neither want your house nor land,
   For your true love I'm going to have.

8. Away she sunk and away she swum,
   She swum on down to the miller's mill-pond.

9. O miller, O miller, yonder swims a swan,
   A-swimming about in your mill-pond.

10. The miller ran out with his fish hook,
    To fish the swan out of the brook.

11. O brother (miller), O brother (miller), here's
    five gold rings,
    If you'll return me home again.

12. Off of her fingers he taken those rings,
    And pushed her in the brook again.

13. The miller was hung at his mill gate,
    For drowning of his sister Kate.

36. [The Two Sisters]

Wilkinson MSS., 1935-36, p. 18(E). Sung by Mrs. Texas Anne Lewis, Mount Crawford, Va., October 31, 1935.

m M (inflected VII)

There was an old woman lived in the Northern 'try,
  Bow'r down,
There was an old woman lived in the Northern 'try,
  The bough has bent to me.

There was an old woman lived in the Northern 'try,
She had some daughters, two or three.
  Love will be true, true to my love,
  Love and my love will be true to me.

37. [The Two Sisters]

Wilkinson MSS., 1935-36, p. 15(C). Sung by Mrs. W. I. Reynolds, Altavista, Va., October 19, 1935.

m M (inflected VII)

There lived an old lord in the North country,
  Bow down,
There lived an old lord in the North country,
  How bough it's been to me.
There lived an old lord in the North country,
He had daughters, one, two, three.
  That'll be true, true to my love,
  Love and my love will be true to you.

38. "The Old Man in the North Countree"

Belden, 1940, pp. 17(A)-18. Also in Belden, *JAF*, XIX (1906), pp. 233-34. Sung by Miss Williams, Clinton County, Mo., 1903; learned in her girlhood in Kentucky.

m I (inflected VII)

The present editor has taken the liberty of writing four quarter-notes in the penultimate bar instead of eighth-notes as in the earlier copy; but the other reading may be the true one.

1. There was an old man in the North Countree,
    Bow down!
There was an old man in the North Countree,
    And a bow 'twas unto me
There was an old man in the North Countree,
And he had daughters one, two, three.
    I'll be true to my love if my love be true to me.

2. There was a young man came a-courting,
And he made choice of the youngest one.

3. He gave his love a beaver cape;
The second she thought much of that.

4. "O sister, O sister, less us go down
And see the ships go sailing by."

5. As they was a-walking by the saucy brimside
The oldest pushed the youngest in.

6. "O sister, O sister, lend me your hand
And I'll give you my house and land."

7. "What care I for house and lands?
All I want is your true love's hand."

8. Down she sank and away she swam
Till she came to the miller's mill-dam.

9. The miller ran out with his fish hook
And fished this maiden out of the brook.

10. "The miller shall be hung on his own mill-gate
For drownding my poor sister Kate."

39. "The Two Sisters"

Sharp MSS., 3535/2608. Also in Sharp and Karpeles, 1932,
I, p. 29(D); and Davis, 1929, p. 556(J) and (text) p. 103.
Sung by Mr. Nuel Walton, Mount Fair, Brown's Cove, Va.,
September 26, 1916.

m I (inflected VII)

Sharp's MS. gives the last three bars as 6/8, 3/8, and 6/8.

There was once an old lady in the North Country,
    The bough were given to me,
There was once an old lady in the North Country,
    The bough were given to me.
There was once an old lady in the North Country,
And she had daughters one, two, three,
    Lover be true, true to my lover,
    Love and my love be true to me.

That young man bought a beaver hat,
The oldest one thought hard of that.

40. "The Two Sisters; or, Sister Kate; or, The Miller and the Mayor's Daughter"

Davis, 1929, p. 554(5D); text, pp. 97-98. Sung by Mrs. L.
L. Arthur and Mrs. Bob Stone (née Taylor), Altavista, Va.,
March 14, 1914. Collected by Juliet Fauntleroy.

m I (inflected VII)

1. There was a Lord Mayor in our town,
    Bow down.
There was a Lord Mayor in our town,
    Bow it's been to me.
There was a Lord Mayor in our town,
And he had daughters, one, two, three.
    Love will be true, true to my love,
    Love will be true to you.

2. There was a young man went courting there,
And he did choose the youngest fair.

3. "O sister, O sister, let's we walk out
And view the ships all sailing about."

4. The oldest pushed the youngest in,
And down she sank and away she swam.

5. "O sister, O sister, Oh, loan me your hand
And you may have my house and land.

6. "Sister, O sister, Oh, loan me your glove,
And you may have my own true love."

7. "I'll neither loan you hand nor glove,
   But I will have your own true love."

8. Down she sank and away she swam,
   She swam into the miller's mill dam.

9. The miller came out with his fish hook,
   To fish the fair maiden from the brook.

10. "O miller, O miller, Oh, loan me your hand,
    And you shall have my house and land.

11. "O miller, O miller, here's five gold rings
    If you will let me home again."

12. And off her fingers he taken her rings,
    And into the brook he pushed her again.

13. The miller was hung at his own mill gate,
    For drowning of my sister Kate.

41. [The Two Sisters]

Sharp MSS., 3761/. Also in Sharp and Karpeles, 1932, I, p. 35(N). Sung by Mrs. Jenny Combs, Berea, Ky., May 30, 1917.

p M

He gave to her a beaver hat,
Bow down,
He gave to her a beaver hat,
These vows were sent to me,
He gave to her a beaver hat
The oldest she thought much of that,
I'll be true true to my love,
If my love will be true to me.

GROUP Bb

42. "The Two Sisters"

Smelser, *JAF*, XLIV (1931), pp. 295-96. Sung by Mrs. Anne Menefee, Missouri.

m π¹

This, with piano accompaniment, is included in Reed Smith and Rufty, *American Anthology of Old-World Ballads*, 1937, pp. 2-3. The variant, text and tune, has been recorded, with dulcimer accompaniment, by Andrew Rowan Summers for Columbia, Album M408, rec. 5-6 (WCO 26509-10).

Sister, dear sister, let's walk the seashore,
Bow ye down, bow ye down,
Sister, dear sister, let's walk the seashore.
Very true to you,
Sister, dear sister, let's walk the seashore,
And watch the ships as they sail o'er,
I'll be true to my love, if my love will be true to me.

As they were walking along the sea brim,
Bow ye down, bow ye down,
As they were walking along the sea brim,
Very true to you,
As they were walking along the sea brim,
The oldest pushed the youngest in.
I'll be true to my love, if my love will be true to me.

She bowed her head and away she swam,
Bow ye down, bow ye down,
She bowed her head and away she swam,
Very true to you,
She bowed her head and away she swam,
She swam unto the Miller's dam.
I'll be true to my love, if my love will be true to me.

The miller he threw out his grab hook,
Bow ye down, bow ye down,
The miller he threw out his grab hook.
Very true to you,
The miller he threw out his grab hook
And brought her safely from the brook.
I'll be true to my love, if my love will be true to me.

I'll give to thee a golden pen,
Bow ye down, bow ye down,
I'll give to thee a golden pen,
Very true to you,
I'll give to thee a golden pen
To push her in the brook again.
I'll be true to my love, if my love will be true to me.

She bowed her head and away she swam,
Bow ye down, bow ye down,

She bowed her head and away she swam,
Very true to you,
She bowed her head and away she swam,
She swam to her eternal home,
I'll be true to my love, if my love will be true to me.

43. "The Miller's Two Daughters"

Cox, 1925, p. 521; text, pp. 20-21. Tune contributed by
A. C. Cowgill, Cold Stream, Va. Text from Marion County,
W.Va., October 1915, from the recollection of Mrs. John
Hood; learned c. 1870.

m π[1]

1. The miller's two daughters brisk and gay,
    Sing lie down, sing lie down;
   The miller's two daughters brisk and gay,
    [The boys are bound for me—
   The miller's two daughters brisk and gay]
   The young one belonged to Johnny Ray,
    And I'll be kind to my true love,
    Because he's kind to me.

2. Johnny bought the young one a gay gold ring,
   The old one swore she hadn't a thing.

3. Johnny bought the young one a beaver hat,
   The old one swore she didn't like that.

4. The miller's two daughters walking along the stream,
   The old one pushed the young one in.

5. "O dear sister, give me your hand,
   And you shall have my house and land.

6. "O dear sister, give me your glove,
   And you shall have my own true love."

7. Sometimes she sank and sometimes she swam,
   And she was drowned in her father's dam.

8. The father drew her near the shore
   And robbed her of her golden ore.

9. The father was hanged on the gallows so high,
   And the sister was burned at the stake near by.

44. "There was an Old Woman Lived in the West"

Brewster, 1940, pp. 46-49. Contributed and noted by Lucile
Wilkin, Connersville, Ind., September 26, 1935.

m π[1]

1. There was an old woman lived in the West,
    Way down, way down;
   There was an old woman lived in the West,
    Way down by the sea.
   There was an old woman lived in the West;
   She had two daughters of the best.
    I'll be true to my love
    If my love'll be true to me.

2. There came a young man a-courting them,
    Way down, way down;
   There came a young man a-courting them,
    Way down by the sea.
   There came a young man a-courting them,
   A-courting for their house and lands;
    I'll be true to my love
    If my love'll be true to me.

3. He gave the young one a beaver hat,
    Way down, way down;
   He gave the young one a beaver hat,
    Way down by the sea.
   He gave the young one a beaver hat,
   And the old one she got mad at that.
    I'll be true to my love
    If my love'll be true to me.

4. He gave the young one a fine gold ring,
    Way down, way down;
   He gave the young one a fine gold ring,
    Way down by the sea.
   He gave the young one a fine gold ring,
   And didn't give the old one anything.
    I'll be true to my love
    If my love'll be true to me.

5. "O Sister, O Sister, let's take a walk,"
    Way down, way down;
    "O Sister, O Sister, let's take a walk,"
    Way down by the sea.
    "O Sister, O Sister, let's take a walk,
    And we will have a quiet talk."
        I'll be true to my love
        If my love'll be true to me.

6. They were walking by a flowing stream,
    Way down, way down;
    They were walking by a flowing stream,
    Way down by the sea.
    They were walking by a flowing stream,
    And the old one pushed the young one in.
        I'll be true to my love
        If my love'll be true to me.

7. "O Sister, O Sister, hand down your hand,"
    Way down, way down;
    "O Sister, O Sister, hand down your hand,"
    Way down by the sea.
    "O Sister, O Sister, hand down your hand,
    And you may have my house and land!"
        I'll be true to my love
        If my love'll be true to me.

8. "I will not hand you down my hand,"
    Way down, way down;
    "I will not hand you down my hand,"
    Way down by the sea.
    "I will not hand you down my hand,
    And I will have your house and land."
        I'll be true to my love
        If my love'll be true to me.

9. "O Sister, O Sister, hand down your glove,"
    Way down, way down;
    "O Sister, O Sister, hand down your glove,"
    Way down by the sea.
    "O Sister, O Sister, hand down your glove
    And you may have my own true love."
        I'll be true to my love
        If my love'll be true to me.

10. "I will not hand you down my glove,"
    Way down, way down;
    "I will not hand you down my glove,"
    Way down by the sea.
    "I will not hand you down my glove,
    And I will have your own true love."
        I'll be true to my love
        If my love'll be true to me.

Sharp and Karpeles give this variant in F, and omit variants b[1] and b[2].

1. There lived a lord in the old country,
        Bow down,
    There lived a lord in the old country,
        Bough* down to me,

2. There lived a lord in the old country,
    He had daughters one, two, three.
        I'll be true to my love
        If my love be true to me.

3. There was a young man in the old country,
    He loved the youngest of the three.

4. The young man bought a beaver hat,
    The oldest she thought much of that.

5. O sister, O sister, let's us walk out
    To see those ships sailing about.

6. They walked on to the river brim;
    The old one pushed the young one in.

7. O sister, O sister, give me your hand
    And you shall have my house and land.

8. You shan't have my hand nor glove,
    But I shall have your old true love.

9. The fisherman up with his fish hook
    And fished the lady from the brook.

* 1932: "bow"

45. [The Two Sisters]

Sharp MSS., 4077/2911. Also in Sharp and Karpeles, 1932, I, p. 33(I). Sung by Elsie Combs, Hindman School, Ky., September 20, 1917.

m π[1]

46. "The Old Farmer in the Countree"

Belden, 1940, pp. 18(B)-19. Sung by Tom Waters, Tuscumbia, Miller County, Mo., 1903. Recorded by W. S. Johnson.

m I (inflected IV)

Sharp and Karpeles, 1932, transpose to F.

1. There was an old farmer lived in the countree,
      Bow down, bow down
   There was an old farmer lived in the countree,
      The bow has been for me
   There was an old farmer lived in the countree;
   He had the charming daughters three.
      If you'll ever be true, truly my love, O lover,
            be true to me.

2. There was a young man went courting there,
   He courted there the oldest fair.

3. He gave the youngest a diamond ring,
   The oldest not a single thing.

4. He gave the youngest a beaver hat;
   The oldest she got mad at that.

5. "O sister, O sister, let us walk out
   And view the boats sailing about."

6. As they went round the river bend
   The oldest shoved the youngest in.

7. "O sister, O sister, lend me your hand
   To help me to the native land."

8. "I will neither loan you my hand nor glove,
   But I'll take from you your own true love."

9. "O miller, O miller, yonder comes a swan
   A-swimming down the old mill pond."

10. The miller threw out his old grab hook
    And brought her safely from the brook.

11. He robbed her of her golden ring
    And plunged her in the brook again.

12. They hung him on his own mill gate
    For drownding of poor sister Kate.

47. [The Two Sisters]

Sharp MSS., 3649/. Also in Sharp and Karpeles, 1932, I,
p. 34(L). Sung by Mrs. Franklin, Barbourville, Ky., May
7, 1917; learned in Ohio.

m I/M

There was an old woman lived on the seashore, bow down,
                                                    bow down,
There was an old woman lived on the seashore and thou hast
                                                    bent to me,
There was an old woman lived on the seashore
She had some daughters some three or four,
And I'll be true to my love, my love will be true to me.

GROUP BC

48. [The Two Sisters]

Thomas, 1931, pp. 70-73. Sung by Rosie Hall, Kentucky.

m I/Ly

1. There lived an old lord by the northern sea,
      Bowee down,
   There lived on old lord by the northern sea,
      Bow and balance to me,
   There lived an old lord by the northern sea
   And he had daughters one, two, three,
      I'll be true to my love
      If my love will be true to me.

2. The youngest one she had a beau
      Bowee down
   The youngest one she had a beau
      Bow and balance to me
   The youngest one she had a beau
   The oldest one she did not have one

I will be true to my love
My love will be true to me.

3. Her beau he bought her a beaver hat
Bowee down
Her beau he bought her a beaver hat
Bow and balance to me
Her beau he bought her a beaver hat
The oldest one she did not like that
I will be true to my love
My love will be true to me.

4. O sister, O sister, let's walk the sea shore
Bowee down
O sister, O sister, let's walk the sea shore
Bow and balance to me
O sister, O sister, let's walk the sea shore
To see the ships a-sailing o'er
I will be true to my love
My love will be true to me.

5. As they were walking along the sea shore
Bowee down
As they were walking along the sea shore
Bow and balance to me
As they were walking along the sea shore
The oldest pushed the youngest one o'er
I will be true to my love
My love will be true to me.

6. O sister, O sister, please lend me your hand
Bowee down
O sister, O sister, please lend me your glove
Bow and balance to me
O sister, O sister, please lend me your hand
And I will bring you to dry land
I will be true to my love
My love will be true to me.

7. I neither will lend you my hand nor my glove
Bowee down
I neither will lend you my hand nor my glove
Bow and balance to me
I neither will lend you my hand nor my glove
For all you want is my own true love
I will be true to my love
My love will be true to me.

8. She bowed her head and away she swam
Bowee down
She bowed her head and away she swam
Bow and balance to me
She bowed her head and away she swam
She swam till she came to the miller's dam
I will be true to my love
My love will be true to me.

9. The miller threw out his drifting hook
Bowee down
The miller threw out his drifting hook
Bow and balance to me
The miller threw out his drifting hook
He drew this maiden to the brook

I will be true to my love
My love will be true to me.

10. The miller was hung at his own mill door
Bowee down
The miller was hung at his own mill door
Bow and balance to me
The miller was hung at his own mill door
For bringing this maiden to the shore
I will be true to my love
My love will be true to me.

11. Her sister was hung at her own yard gate
Bowee down
Her sister was hung at her own yard gate
Bow and balance to me
Her sister was hung at her own yard gate
For drowning of her sister Kate
I will be true to my love
My love will be true to me.

49. "There Was a Squire of High Degree"

Kidson, *JFSS*, I (1904), p. 253. Sung by Miss Carr Moseley; learned from old lady born c. 1800, who learned it from her mother.

Tonic G: m I, ending on *VI* (inflected *V*)

Kidson notes the resemblance to "Greensleeves" in the last two phrases; other readers will note phrases 5 and 6 as identical with "Armentières."

There was a Squire of high degree,
Bow down, Bow down,
There was a Squire of high degree
As the bough doth bend to me.
There was a Squire of high degree,
And he had daughters, one, two, three,
And I'll be true to my true love,
If my love will be true to me.

50. [The Two Sisters]

Sharp MSS., 3700/. Also in Sharp and Karpeles, 1932, I, p. 31(G). Sung by Violet Henry, Berea, Ky., May 21, 1917.

Tonic G: m I/Ly, ending on *VI*

A copy melodically identical is given by J. W. Raine, *The Land of Saddle-Bags*, 1924, p. 118. A third printing is in E. P. Richardson and S. Spaeth, *American Mountain Songs*, 1927, p. 27.

O sister, O sister, there swims a swan,
Bow-ey down,
O sister, O sister, there swims a swan,
Bow and balance to me,
O sister, O sister, there swims a swan,
O no, it's not, it's some fair one.
I'll be true to my love,
If my love'll be true to me.

51. (Unnamed)

Randolph, I, 1946, pp. 60(G)-62. Sung by Mrs. May Kennedy McCord, Springfield, Mo., November 12, 1941; learned from her mother in Galena, Mo., c. 1890.

a Æ/D

1. There was an old lord by the northern sea,
Bow-wee down,
There was an old lord by the northern sea,
Bow and balance to me,
There was an old lord by the northern sea
And he had daughters one, two, three,
I'll be true to my love
If my love will be true to me.

2. There was a beau for the youngest one,
Bow-wee down,
There was a beau for the youngest one,
Bow and balance to me,
There was a beau for the youngest one,

The oldest one she didn't have none,
I'll be true to my love
If my love will be true to me.

3. Her lover he bought her a beaver hat,
Bow-wee down,
Her lover he bought her a beaver hat,
Bow and balance to me,
Her lover he bought her a beaver hat,
The oldest one she didn't like that,
I'll be true to my love
If my love will be true to me.

4. Oh sister, sister come walk the shore,
Bow-wee down,
Oh sister, sister come walk the shore,
Bow and balance to me,
Oh sister, sister come walk the shore,
That we may view the landscape o'er,
I'll be true to my love
If my love will be true to me.

5. As they were walking along the shore,
Bow-wee down,
As they were walking along the shore,
Bow and balance to me,
As they were walking along the shore,
The oldest one pushed the youngest one o'er,
I'll be true to my love
If my love will be true to me.

6. Oh sister, sister please lend me your hand,
Bow-wee down,
Oh sister, sister please lend me your hand,
Bow and balance to me,
Oh sister, sister please lend me your hand
That you may pull me to dry land,
I'll be true to my love
If my love will be true to me.

7. I'll neither lend you my hand nor my glove,
Bow-wee down,
I'll neither lend you my hand nor my glove,
Bow and balance to me,
I'll neither lend you my hand nor my glove
For all you want is my own true love,
I'll be true to my love
If my love will be true to me.

8. She bowed her head and away she swam,
Bow-wee down,
She bowed her head and away she swam,
Bow and balance to me,
She bowed her head and away she swam,
She swum till she come to the miller's dam,
I'll be true to my love
If my love will be true to me.

9. The miller throwed out his drifting oar,
Bow-wee down,
The miller throwed out his drifting oar,
Bow and balance to me,
The miller throwed out his drifting oar
And pulled the maiden to the shore,
I'll be true to my love
If my love will be true to me.

10. The miller was hung at his own mill door,
    Bow-wee down,
    The miller was hung at his own mill door,
    Bow and balance to me,
    The miller was hung at his own mill door,
    For pulling the maiden to the shore,
    I'll be true to my love
    If my love will be true to me.

11. The sister was hung at her own yard gate,
    Bow-wee down,
    The sister was hung at her own yard gate,
    Bow and balance to me,
    The sister was hung at her own yard gate,
    For drownding of her sister Kate,
    I'll be true to my love
    If my love will be true to me.

52. [The Twa Sisters]

Henry, 1938, pp. 39(A)-40. Sung by Cora Clark, Cross-nore, Avery County, N.C., July 12, 1929.

If tonic G, m I/Ly, ending on *VI*

1. There lived an old lord by the Northern Sea,
    Bow'e down!
    There lived an old lord by the Northern Sea,
    Bow and balance to me!
    There lived an old lord by the Northern Sea
    And he had daughters, one, two, three.
        I'll be true to my love,
        If my love will be true to me.

2. A young man came a-courtin' there,
    Bow'e down!
    A young man came a-courtin' there,
    Bow and balance to me!
    A young man came a-courtin' there
    And fell in love with the youngest fair.
        I'll be true to my love,
        If my love will be true to me.

3. He bought the youngest a beaver hat,
    Bow'e down!
    He bought the youngest a beaver hat,
    Bow and balance to me!
    He bought the youngest a beaver hat;
    The oldest sister didn't like that.
        I'll be true to my love,
        If my love will be true to me.

4. The sisters walked down to the river brim,
    Bow'e down!
    The sisters walked down to the river brim,
    Bow and balance to me!
    The sisters walked down to the river brim;
    The oldest pushed the youngest in.
        I'll be true to my love,
        If my love will be true to me.

5. Sister, O sister, lend me your hand,
    Bow'e down!
    Sister, O sister, lend me your hand,
    Bow and balance to me!
    Sister, O sister, lend me your hand;
    I'll give to you my house and land.
        I'll be true to my love,
        If my love will be true to me.

6. She floated down to the miller's dam,
    Bow'e down!
    She floated down to the miller's dam,
    Bow and balance to me!
    She floated down to the miller's dam;
    The miller pulled her safe to land.
        I'll be true to my love,
        If my love will be true to me.

7. From off her finger he took five gold rings,
    Bow'e down!
    From off her finger he took five gold rings,
    Bow and balance to me!
    From off her finger he took five gold rings
    And then he threw her back in.
        I'll be true to my love,
        If my love will be true to me.

8. They hanged the miller on a gallows so high,
    Bow'e down!
    They hanged the miller on a gallows so high,
    Bow and balance to me!
    They hanged the miller on a gallows so high,
    The oldest sister standing close by.
        I'll be true to my love,
        If my love will be true to me.

GROUP B d

53. [The Two Sisters]

Wilkinson MSS., 1935-36, p. 23(H). Sung by Richard Chase, Chapel Hill, N.C., April 4, 1936.

? a Æ/D, ending on IV (inflected III)

Sister, O sister, let's take a walk out,
    Bow down, Bow down,
Sister, O sister, let's take a walk out,
    And the bough has been to me.
Sister, O sister, let's take a walk out
To see those little ships sailing about.
    Be true, true, be true to my love,
    My love will be true to me.

8. First he stripped her from toe to chin,
   And then he threw her in again.

9. First she sank and second she swam
   Until she arrived at her long-lost home.

10. The miller was hang-ed for her sake,
    Her sister burnt up at a stake.

54. "The Two Sisters"

Flanders, and others, 1939, pp. 3-4. Also in Flanders, *BFSSNE*, No. 6 (1933), pp. 5-6. Sung by Susan Montague, Woodstock, Vt., c. 1931; learned from her grandmother in Massachusetts. Transcribed by Marguerite Oiney. From *The New Green Mountain Songster*, edited by Helen Hartness Flanders, Elizabeth Flanders Ballard, George Brown, and Phillips Barry; copyright 1939 by Helen Hartness Flanders.

a D, ending on IV (inflected III)

A copy from the same source is on P. Barry, Dictaphone Cylinder No. 152, cutting 2, in Harvard College Library.

1. Two sisters went down to the river's brim—
    Bow it down, bow it down—
Two sisters went down to the river's brim—
    The boughs are bent with me—
Two sisters went down to the river's brim,
The elder pushed the younger in.
    True, true, to your true love,
    And he'll prove true to thee.

2. "Please, dear sister, give me your hand,
   And you shall have my house and land."

3. "No, I won't give you my hand,
   But I will have your house and land."

4. "Please, dear sister, give me your glove,
   And you shall have my own true love."

5. "No, I won't give you my glove,
   But I will have your own true love."

6. First she sank and second she swam,
   Until she arrived at the miller's dam.

7. The miller threw out his fishing hook,
   And caught her by her petticoat.

55. [The Two Sisters]

Sharp MSS., 3518/2597. Also in Sharp and Karpeles, 1932, I, pp. 27(B)-28; Davis, 1929, p. 554(F); text pp. 99-100. Sung by Welsey Batten, Mount Fair, Va., September 22, 1916.

m D (inflected III)

The notes starred were occasionally sharpened to B♮ and F♯.

1. There lived an old lady in the north country,
    Bow down,
There lived an old lady in the north country,
    The bough has been to me,
There lived an old lady in the north country,
She has daughters one, two, three,
True to my love, love my love be true to thee.*

2. There came a young man a-courting there,
   And he made a† choice of the youngest there.

3. He made her a present of a beaver's hat,
   The oldest thought a heap of that.

4. O sister, O sister, just walk out
   To see those vessels a-sailing about.

5. The oldest pushed the youngest in.
   She did struggle and she did swim.

6. O sister, O sister, give me your hand,
   And I will give you my house and land.

7. I will not give to§ you my hand,
   But I will marry that young man.

8. The miller picked up his drab book (hook?),
   And then he fished her out of the brook.

* 1932: "me"
† 1932: "the"
§ 1932 omits "to."

9. The miller got her golden ring,
   The miller pushed her back again.

10. The miller was hung at his mill gate
    For drownding my poor sister Kate.

And I'll be true to my love
If my love will be true to me.

* The singer pronounced the word with long o.

56. [The Two Sisters]

Wilkinson MSS., 1935-36, p. 14(B). Sung by Mrs. Kit
Williamson, Evington, Va., October 19, 1935.

m D (inflected III)

There was an old man in our town,
     Bow down,
There was an old man in our town,
     And there it's been to me.
There was an old man in our town,
And he had daughters one, two, three.
     That'll be true, true to my love to you.

57. [The Two Sisters]

Wilkinson MSS., 1935-36, p. 19(F). Sung by Z. B. Lam,
Standardsville, Va., November 3, 1935.

m Æ/D

There was an old man who lived in the North,
     Bow down,
There was an old man who lived in the North,
     The bow* is bent to me.
There was an old man who lived in the North,
He had some daughters, one, two, three.

58. [The Two Sisters]

Wilkinson MSS., 1935-36, pp. 20-22(G). Sung by T. Henry
Lam, Elkton, Va., November 6, 1935.

m Æ/D

1. There was an old lady lived in the North,
        Bow down.
   There was an old lady lived in the North,
        They both were bent to me.
   There was an old lady lived in the North,
   And she had daughters, one, two, three,
        And I'll be true to my love,
        If my love will be true to me.

2. There was a young man who came to see them,
   He fell in love with the youngest one.

3. He brought the youngest one a beaver hat,
   The oldest she made much of that.

4. Sister, O sister, let's walk out,
   And see the ships a-sailing about.

5. As they were walking the salt sea brim,
   The oldest shoved the youngest in.

6. Sister, O sister, give me your hand,
   And you may have my house and land.

7. I'll neither give you my hand nor glove,
   Nor you can't have your own true love.

8. O down she sank and away she swam,
   Till she came to the miller's mill dam.

9. Miller, O miller, O yonder's a swan,
   Unless it is some dead woman.

10. The miller ran out with his fish hook,
    To fish the fair maid out of the brook.

11. The miller got hung at his mill gate,
    A-fishing for poor sister Kate.

59. [The Two Sisters]

Sharp MSS., 4523/3178. Also in Sharp and Karpeles, 1932, I, p. 34(K). Sung by Joe Blackett, Meadows of Dan, Patrick County, Va., August 28, 1918.

m Æ/D

There was an old woman who lived by the sea,
    Bow down,
There was an old woman who lived by the sea,
    The vows she made to me,
There was an old woman who* lived by the sea,
And daughters she had one, two, three.
    I'll be true to my love,
    If my love'll be true to me.

There was a young sailor to see them come,
And he chose for his love the youngest one.

He gave to the youngest a beaver hat,
And the oldest she thought hard of that.

O sister, O sister, come to the shore,
And see the ships come sailing o'er.

As they were walking the salty brim,
The oldest pushed the youngest in.

O sister, O sister, give me your hand
And I will give you my house and land.

I will not give you my hand nor glove,
For all I want is your true love.

* 1932 omits "who."

60. [The Two Sisters]

Halpert, LC/AAFS, rec. 2737 A1. Sung by Anne Corbin Ball, Richmond, Va., 1939.

m Æ/D (VI in variants)

Miller, O miller, there swims a swan
    Bow down
Miller, O miller, there swims a swan
    The bough is bent to me
Miller, O miller, there swims a swan
But maybe it was the other one
    And I'll be true to my love
    And my love will be true to me
    And I'll be true to my love
    And my love will be true to me.

GROUP Be

61. [The Barkshire Tragedy]

Broadwood and Maitland, 1893, pp. 118-19. Tune from G. K. Fortescue, Berkshire; text from Thomas Hughes, *The Scouring of the White Horse*, 1859, by permission of Messrs. J. B. Cramer & Co., Ltd., London.

p I

1. A varmer he lived in the West Countree,
    (With a hey down, bow down:)
   [A varmer he lived in the West Countree,]
   And he had daughters, one, two, and three,
    (And I'll be true to my love, if my love'll be true to me).

2. As they were walking by the river's brim
    (With a hey down, bow down:)
   The eldest pushed the youngest in,
    (And I'll be true to my love, if my love'll be true to me).

3. "O sister, O sister, pray gee me thy hand,
    (With a hey down, bow down:)
   And I'll gee thee both house and land,"
    (And I'll be true to my love, if my love'll be true to me).

4. "I'll neither gee thee hand nor glove,
    (With a hey down, bow down:)
  Unless thou'lt gee me thine own true love,"
    (And I'll be true to my love, if my love'll be true to me).

5. So down she sank, and away she swam,
    (With a hey down, bow down:)
  Until she came to the miller's dam,
    (And I'll be true to my love, if my love'll be true to me).

6. The miller's daughter stood by the door,
    (With a hey down, bow down:)
  As fair as any gilly-flower,
    (And I'll be true to my love, if my love'll be true to me).

7. "O vather, O vather, here swims a swan,
    (With a hey down, bow down:)
  Very much like a drownded gentlewoman,"
    (And I'll be true to my love, if my love'll be true to me).

8. The miller he fot his pole and hook,
    (With a hey down, bow down:)
  And he fished the fair maid out of the brook,
    (And I'll be true to my love, if my love'll be true to me).

9. "O miller, I'll gee thee guineas ten,
    (With a hey down, bow down:)
  If thou'lt fetch me back to my vather again,"
    (And I'll be true to my love, if my love'll be true to me).

10. The miller he took her guineas ten,
    (With a hey down, bow down:)
  And he pushed the fair maid in again,
    (And I'll be true to my love, if my love'll be true to me).

11. But the Crowner he came, and the Justice too,
    (With a hey down, bow down:)
  With a hue and a cry and a hullabaloo,
    (And I'll be true to my love, if my love'll be true to me).

12. They hanged the miller beside his own gate,
    (With a hey down, bow down:)
  For drowning the varmer's daughter Kate,
    (And I'll be true to my love, if my love'll be true to me).

13. The sister she fled beyond the seas,
    (With a hey down, bow down:)
  And died an old maid among black savagees,
    (And I'll be true to my love, if my love'll be true to me).

14. So I've ended my tale of the West Countree,
    (With a hey down, bow down:)
  And they calls it the Barkshire Tragedee,
    (And I'll be true to my love, if my love'll be true to me).

62. "A Farmer there lived in the North Country"

Gilchrist, *JFSS*, VIII (1930), p. 247. Sung by Rev. F. D. Cremer, February 12, 1909.

p I

A farmer there lived in the north countree,
Baa, bo, bee, bo (*or,* Bow down, bow down)
A farmer there lived in the north countree,
And he had daughters, one-un, two, three,
Singing I'll be true unto my true love,
And my love'll be true to me.

63. [The Two Sisters]

Sharp MSS., 4175/. Also in Sharp and Karpeles, 1932, I, p. 33(J). Sung by Mrs. Florence Fitzgerald, Royal Orchard, Afton, Va., April 25, 1918.

p I

There was an old man in the North Countree
And he had daughters one, two, three,
Says I'll be true to my love,
My love'll be true to me.

64. [The Twa Sisters]

Major, *PTFLS*, X (1932), pp. 141-43. Sung by A. B. Nelson, Fort Worth, Texas; learned from his grandmother, Maysville, Ky.

p I/M

There was an old woman lived by the sea shore—
    So bow down.
She had some daughters some three or four—
    So bow your bends to me,
    So bow your bends to me.
Oh, she had some daughters, some three or four—
    So bow your bends to me.

2. The youngest one she caught a beau—
    So bow down.
The oldest one she wanted one too—
    So bow your bends to me,
    So bow your bends to me.
Oh, the oldest one she wanted one too—
    So bow your bends to me.

3. The youngest one's bought her a beaver hat—
    So bow down.
The oldest one got mad at that—
    So bow your bends to me,
    So bow your bends to me.
Oh, the oldest one she got mad at that—
    So bow your bends to me.

4. "O sister, O sister, come walk the sea shore"—
    So bow down.
"And watch the ships come sailing o'er"—
    So bow your bends to me,
    So bow your bends to me.
"And watch the ships come sailing o'er"—
    So bow your bends to me.

5. And sister and sister they walked the sea shore—
    So bow down.
The oldest one pushed the youngest one o'er—
    So bow your bends to me,
    So bow your bends to me.
The oldest one pushed the youngest one o'er—
    So bow your bends to me.

6. "O sister, O sister, pray lend me your glove"—
    So bow down.
"O sister, O sister, pray lend me your glove"—
    So bow your bends to me,
    So bow your bends to me.
"O sister, O sister, pray lend me your glove"—
    So bow your bends to me.

7. "I'll neither lend you my hand nor my glove"—
    So bow down.
"But I'll go home and I'll marry your love"—
    So bow your bends to me,
    So bow your bends to me.
"But I'll go home and I'll marry your love"—
    So bow your bends to me.

65. [The Two Sisters]

Sharp MSS., 4777/. Also in Sharp and Karpeles, 1932, I,
p. 35(M). Sung by Mrs. Delie Hughes, Cane River, Burnsville, N.C., October 9, 1918.

p I/M

Instead of the central portion, this variant and the next seem to
have dropped the first two phrases.

       O come, dear sister, and let's take a walk,
       Bow unto me,
       O come, dear sister, and let's take a walk
       All on the green riverside.
       True, true, true to my love,
       And my love is true to me.

66. "The Miller's Daughters"

Randolph, I, 1946, pp. 50(A)-52. Sung by F. M. Goodhue,
Mena, Ark., June 29, 1930; learned from a woman in the
hills near Mena.

a I/Ly

Randolph printed the same tune and a text with slight differences,
in *Ozark Mountain Folks*, 1932, pp. 211-12, as from Carrie Langley.

1. First he bought her was a beaver hat,
    Bow she bent to me,
    First he bought her was a beaver hat,
    The oldest sister did not like that,
    I'll be kind to my true love
    If you'll be kind to me.

2. An' next he bought her was a gay gold ring,
    Bow she bent to me,
    An' next he bought her was a gay gold ring,
    The oldest sister not a thing,
    I'll be kind to my true love
    If you'll be kind to me.

3. Sis, oh sis, let us walk out,
    Bow she bent to me,
    Sis, oh sis, let us walk out
    An' see the ships a-sailin' about,
    I'll be kind to my true love
    If you'll be kind to me.

4. They walked till they come to the salt-cellar brim,
   Bow she bent to me,
   They walked till they come to the salt-cellar brim,
   The oldest pushed the youngest in,
   I'll be kind to my true love
   If you'll be kind to me.

5. Sis, oh sis, hold down your hand,
   Bow she bent to me,
   Sis, oh sis, hold down your hand,
   An' I'll give you my house an' land,
   I'll be kind to my true love
   If you'll be kind to me.

6. Sis, oh sis, hold down your glove,
   Bow she bent to me,
   Sis, oh sis, hold down your glove,
   An' I'll give you my own true love,
   I'll be kind to my true love
   If you'll be kind to me.

7. Miller, oh miller, yonder swims a swan,
   Bow she bent to me,
   Miller, oh miller, yonder swims a swan,
   A-swimmin' down in your mill pond,
   I'll be kind to my true love
   If you'll be kind to me.

8. The miller run out with his fish-hook,
   Bow she bent to me,
   The miller run out with his fish-hook
   An' he drawed her out of that big brook,
   I'll be kind to my true love
   If you'll be kind to me.

9. He took five gold rings off her fingers,
   Bow she bent to me,
   He took five gold rings off her fingers,
   An' pushed her back in that big river,
   I'll be kind to my true love
   If you'll be kind to me.

10. The miller was hung by his mill gate,
    Bow she bent to me,
    The miller was hung by his mill gate,
    For drowndin' of my sister Kate,
    I'll be kind to my true love
    If you'll be kind to me.

11. The miller was hung on a limb so high,
    Bow she bent to me,
    The miller was hung on a limb so high,
    The oldest sister was burnt close by,
    I'll be kind to my true love
    If you'll be kind to me.

1. There was an old woman lived on the seashore,
   Bow and balance to me.
   There was an old woman lived on the seashore,
   Her number of daughters one, two, three, four,
   And I'll be true to my love if my love'll be
                                    true to me.

2. There was a young man came by to see them,
   And the oldest one got struck on him.

3. He bought the youngest a beaver hat,
   And the oldest one got mad at that.

4. "Oh, sister, oh, sister, let's walk the seashore,
   And see the ships as they sail o'er."

5. While these two sisters were walking the shore,
   The oldest pushed the youngest o'er.

6. "Oh, sister, oh, sister, please lend me your hand,
   And you may have Willie and all of his land."

7. "I never, I never will lend you my hand,
   But I'll have Willie and all of his land."

8. Sometime she sank and sometime she swam,
   Until she came to the old mill dam.

9. The miller he got his fishing hook,
   And fished the maiden out of the brook.

10. "Oh, miller, oh, miller, here's five gold rings,
    To push the maiden in again."

11. The miller received those five gold rings,
    And pushed the maiden in again.

12. The miller was hung at his own mill gate,
    For drowning little sister Kate.

67. "The Two Sisters"

Halpert, LC/AAFS, Album 7, rec. 33A(544). Sung by
Horton Barker, Chilhowie, Va., 1939.

p π¹

68. "The Two Sisters"

Barry, Eckstorm, and Smyth, 1929, p. 42(C). Sung by Mrs.
Rose Robbins, Northeast Harbor, Maine, September 1928.
Melody recorded by George Herzog.

p I, ending on V

The alternative readings (d) signify an occasional variable up-beat.

Two sisters crossing the river bend,
The oldest pushed the youngest in,
　　True, true,
　　True to my love,
　　My love so true to me.

The miller he put out his hook
And caught her by the petticoat.

The miller he was hung for her sake,
They burned her sister at the stake,
　　True, true,
　　True to my love,
　　My love so true to me.

69. "There was an Old Farmer"

Cox, 1939, pp. 6-7. Sung by Jessie McCue, Hookersville,
W.Va., November 10, 1925; learned from a family named
Hamricks.

p I/Ly, ending on *VI*

1. There was an old farmer lived out in the West,
　　Oh dear to me,
There was an old farmer lived out in the West,
He had two daughters and one was the best.
　　Tum a la lee, tum a la lee.

2. There was a rich merchant went courting there,
He chose the youngest for his share.

3. The first thing he bought her was a beaver hat,
And the older she thought hard of that.

4. And the next thing he bought her was a diamond ring,
The older, she got not a thing.

5. The older says, "Sister, let's walk out,
And see the ships as they go tossing about."

6. As they were walking on salt sea brim,
The older shoved the younger in.

7. "Sister, oh, sister, reach down your hand,
And you may have my house and land."

8. "I'll neither reach down my hand nor glove,
But I'll go back home and take your love."

9. As she was floating down the stream,
She floated into the old mill dam.

10. "Miller, oh, miller, here's five gold rings,
If you'll only take me home again."

11. The miller took those five gold rings,
And pushed her back into the stream again.

12. The older was hung for her sister's sake,
The miller was hung on the old mill gate.

70. "The Old Man in the Old Country"

Randolph, LC/AAFS, rec. 5244 A. Also, with metrical
differences, in Randolph, 1946, I, pp. 57(E)-58. Sung by
Charles Ingenthron, Walnut Shade, Mo., September 4,
1941; learned in Taney County, Mo., c. 1890.

a M/D

1. There was an old man in the old country
Most gentily,
There was an old man in the old country
And he had daughters one, two, three,
Oh, dear me.

2. There was a young scarf went a-courting there,
Most gentily,
There was a young scarf went a-courting there,
And he courted the younger of the fair,
Oh dear me.

3. He bought for the younger a fine gold ring,
Most gentily,
He bought for the younger a fine gold ring,
And for the older not one thing,
Oh dear me.

4. He bought for the younger a beavers hat,
Most gentily,
He bought for the younger a beavers hat,
And the older she got mad at that,
Oh dear me.

5. Oh sister, will you take a walk with me?
Most gentily,
Oh sister, will you take a walk with me?
And we will see the greenwood tree,
Oh dear me.

6. As they went crossing the salt sea brim,
Most gentily,
As they went crossing the salt sea brim,
The older shoved the younger in,
Oh dear me.

7. Oh sister, will you reach me down your hand?
Most gentily,
Oh sister, will you reach me down your hand,
And you may have my house and land,
Oh dear me.

8. I will not reach you down my hand,
Most gentily,
I will not reach you down my hand
And I will not have your house and land,
Oh dear me.

9. Oh sister, will you reach me down your glove?
Most gentily,
Oh sister, will you reach me down your glove,
And you may have my own true love,
Oh dear me.

10. I will not reach you down my glove,
Most gentily,
I will not reach you down my glove,
And I will not have your own true love,
Oh dear me.

11. As she went a-floating down the mill pond,
Most gentily,
As she went a-floating down the mill pond,
The miller he took her to be a swan,
Oh dear me.

12. The miller throwed out his hook and line,
Most gentily,
The miller throwed out his hook and line
And caught her in the dress so fine,
Oh dear me.

13. The miller was hung in his own mill gate,
Most gentily,
The miller was hung in his own mill gate,
For the drowning of my sister Kate,
Oh dear me.

The timing has here been drastically revised. The earlier copy gives bars 3, 4, and 6 to the end, in notes of double length, i.e., in 3/4 bars of halves and quarters.

1. There was an old woman lived North Countree,
    I'll sing to thee.
There was an old woman lived North Countree,
And she had daughters one, two, three.
    I'll be true to my love and my love will be true to me.

2. There was a young man came courting there,
And he did love the youngest fair.

3. He gave the youngest a beaver hat
And the oldest sister she mashed it flat.

4. Said, "Sister, O sister, let's walk by the shore
And watch the ships as they sail o'er."

5. And so they walked by the salty brim
And the oldest pushed the youngest in.

6. "O sister, O sister, come reach me your hand
And you shall have my houses and land."

7. "No, I'll not reach you my hand nor my glove,
For you shan't have my own true love."

8. She bowed her head and she swam away;
She swam into the miller's bay.

9. The miller he took his old grab-hook,
And fished the girl out of the brook.

10. Said, "Miller, I'll give you these ten gold chains
To bring me to my home again."

11. The ten gold chains the miller took
And pushed the girl back in the brook.

12. They hanged the miller on yonder gate
For the murder of the sister Kate.

71. "The Old Woman of the North Countree"

Davis, 1929, p. 553(B); text, pp. 95-96. Sung by Sam Pritt, Alleghany County, Va., November 28, 1924. Recorded by B. C. Moomaw, Jr.

a Æ/D ending on IV (inflected VII)

72. "The Sea Shore; or, The Swim Swom Bonny"

Bayard, *BFSSNE*, No. 9 (1935), p. 4 (2nd version). Sung by N. W. Butcher, Hundred, West Virginia.

a Æ

Refrain on phrases 2, 4, 5:
Always true to my love!

. . . .
And I'll be true to my love,
If my love'll be true to me!

The following text is stated to be the same as what was sung to the tune above, with the exception of its refrain:

1. "Dear Sister, dear Sister, let's take a walk—
   Hey oh, my Nanny!
   "To see the ships a-sailing o'er—
   And the swim swom bonny!

2. As they were walking along the sea shore,
   The oldest pushed the youngest in.

3. She bowed her head and away she swam,
   And she swum till she come to the miller's dam.

4. (Crying) "Miller, oh miller, it's stop your mill,
   For yonder comes a swan or a milk white maid."

5. The miller threw out his old grab hook;
   He fetched her safely from the brook.

6. The miller got her pretty gold ring,
   And pushed her back in the brook again.

7. She bowed her head and away she swum,
   Till she came to her eternal home.

8. The miller was hung in his own mill-gate,
   For drowning of my sister Kate.

GROUP B f

73. [The Two Sisters]

Sharp MSS., 3689/2749. Also in Sharp and Karpeles, 1932, I, p. 31(F). Sung by Mrs. Delie Knuckles, Barbourville, Ky., May 16, 1917.

m π[1]

1. Two little sisters side and side,
   Sing dow down, sing dow dee,
   Two little sisters side and side,
   The boys all bound for me,
   Two little sisters side and side,
   Johnny chose the youngest for to be his bride.
   So I'll be kind to my true love,
   Because he's kind to me.

2. Johnny bought the youngest a gay gold ring,
   Never bought the oldest a single thing.

3. Johnny bought the youngest a beaver hat,
   The oldest she thought hard of that.

4. They went walking down the stream,
   The oldest pushed the youngest in.

5. Sister, O sister, give me your hand
   And you can have my house and land.

6. Sister, O sister, give [me]* your glove,
   And you can have my own true love.

7. She floated down to the miller's dam,
   The miller drew her safe and sound.

8. The miller he robbed her of her gold
   And splunged her back into that hole.

9. The miller was hung on a gallows so high,
   The oldest sister there close by.

* MS. my.

74. [The Two Sisters]

Sharp MSS., 4641/3234. Also in Sharp and Karpeles, 1932, I, p. 30(E). Sung by Mrs. Clercy Deeton, Mine Fork, Burnsville, N.C., September 19, 1918.

m π[1]

Sharp and Karpeles, 1932, print the tune in F.

1. Two little sisters side by side,*
   Sing I dum, sing I day.
   Two little sisters side by side,*
   The boys are bound for me.
   Two little sisters side by side,*
   The oldest one for Jo[h]nny cried.
   I'll be kind to my true love
   If he'll be kind to me.

2. Johnny bought the old one a beaver hat,
   The youngest one thought hard of that.

3. Johnny bought the young one a gay gold ring,
   He never bought the old one a single thing.

4. Two little sisters a-going down the† stream;
   The oldest one put the young one in.

5. She floated on down to the miller's dam;
   The miller brought her safe and sound.

6. The miller was hung on the gallows so high;
   The oldest one was hung close by.

* 1932: "side and side"
† 1932 omits "the."

Two little sisters walking by the stream,
Sing ay dum, sing ay day.
Two little sisters walking by the stream,
The boys all bound for me.
Two little sisters walking by the stream,
The oldest pushed the youngest in.
I'll be kind to my true love,
Because he's kind to me.

Johnny gave the youngest a gay gold ring,
Sing ay dum, sing ay day.
Johnny gave the youngest a gay gold ring,
The boys all bound for me.
Johnny gave the youngest a gay gold ring,
He didn't give the oldest a single thing.
I'll be kind to my true love,
Because he's kind to me.

75. [The Two Sisters]

Sharp MSS., 4627/. Sung by Mrs. Laurel Jones, Burnsville,
N.C., September 17, 1918.

m π¹

Johnny bought the young one a beaver hat,
Sing I die, sing I day,
Johnny bought the young one a beaver hat,
The boys are bound to me,
Johnny bought the young one a beaver hat,
The old one thought so hard of that,
I'll be kind to my true love
If he be kind to me.

76. "The Two Sisters"

Hudson, 1937, No. 25. Sung by Mrs. R. C. Jones and
Frank Harmon, Oxford, Miss., 1923-30.

m I/Ly

77. "Two Little Sisters"

Garrison, 1944, pp. 19-20. Sung by Mrs. Martha Garrison,
Marshall, Ark., July 1942.

a I/Ly

The original copy is in 4/4 time.

Two little sisters walked down the stream.
    Sing hi dum, sing hi day.
Two little sisters walked down the stream.
    The boys all bound for me.
Two little sisters walked down the stream,
And the old one shoved the young one in.
    I'll be true to my true love,
    If he'll be true to me.

Sister, O Sister, oh hand me your hand;
You may have my house and land.

Sister, O Sister, oh loan me your glove,
And you may have my own true love.

She floated down to the miller's dam;
The miller drew her safe to land.

The miller robbed her of her gold,
And threw her in that big deep hole.

78. "The Two Little Sisters"

Eddy, 1939, pp. 17-18. Sung by Edna and Lena Jennings,
Loudonville, Ohio; learned from school friends.

m I/Ly

Johnny bought the youngest a gay gold ring,
　　Sing hi down, sing hi down,
Johnny bought the youngest a gay gold ring,
　　The oldest she had not one thing,
So I'll be kind to my true love
　　Because she's kind to me.

Johnny bought the youngest a beaver hat,
　　Sing hi down, sing hi down,
Johnny bought the youngest a beaver hat,
　　The oldest she thought hard of that,
So I'll be kind to my true love
　　Because she's kind to me.

Two little sisters walking by the stream,
　　Sing hi down, sing hi down,
Two little sisters walking by the stream,
　　The oldest pushed the youngest in,
So I'll be kind to my true love
　　Because she's kind to me.

Sometimes she sank, sometimes she swam,
　　Sing hi down, sing hi down,
Sometimes she sank, sometimes she swam,
　　She swam till she reached the old mill dam,
So I'll be kind to my true love
　　Because she's kind to me.

GROUP C

79. [The Cruel Sister]

Ritson-Tytler-Brown MS., No. 15; text, pp. 99-102. Also in
Child, 1882-98, V, p. 411. Sung by Mrs. Brown, Falkland,
Aberdeenshire.

Mrs. Brown's tune, conjectural reading.

m M

There was twa sisters in ae bow'r,
　　Edinbrough, Edinbrough;
There was twa sisters in ae bow'r,
　　Stirling for ay;
There was twa sisters in ae bow'r,
There came a knight to be their wooer,
　　Bonny Saint Johnston stands upon Tay.
He courted the eldest wi' glove and ring,
But lov'd the youngest aboon a' thing.
He courted the eldest wi' broach and knife,
But lov'd the youngest as his life,
The eldest she was vexed sair,
And sair envy'd her sister fair.
Into the bow'r she could nae rest,
Wi' grief and spite she almost brest.
Upon a morning fair and clear
She cry'd upon her sister dear,
"O sister, go to yon sea strand,
And see our fathers ships come in."
She's ta'en her by the milk-white hand,
An' led her down to yon sea strand.
The youngest stood upon a stane,
The eldest came and threw her in.
She took her by the middle sma',
And dash'd her bonny back to the jaw.
"O sister, sister, take my hand,

An' ise mak' you heir to a' my land.
O sister, sister, tak' my middle,
An' yese get my goud and gouden girdle.
O sister, sister, save my life,
An' i swear ise never be no mans wife."
"Foul fa' the hand that i should take,
It twin'd me and my warlds make:
Your cherry cheeks and your yallow hair
Gars me gang maiden for evermair."
Sometimes she sank, and sometimes swam,
Til she came down yon bonny mill-dam.
O, out it came the millers son,
And saw the fair maid swimming in.
"O father, haste and draw your dam,
Here's either a mermaid or a swan."
The miller quickly drew his dam,
And there he found a drown'd woman.
You could nae see her yallow hair,
For goud and pearl that was sae rare.
You could nae see her middle sma',
Her gouden girdle it was sae braw.
You could nae see her fingers white,
For the gou'd rings that were sae gryte.
O, by there came a harper fine,
That harped to the king at dine.
When he did look that lady upon,
He sigh'd and made a heavy moan.
He's ta'en three locks o' her yallow hair,
An' wi' them strung his harp sae fair.
The first tune he did play and sing
Was Farewel to my father the king.
The next tune that he played seen
Was Farewel to my mother the queen.
The last tune that he played then
Was Woe to my sister fair Ellen.

80. "The Twa Sisters"

Collected and sung by the Fuller Sisters, 1927 (Bumpus,
London; A. and C. Boni, New York). "Traditional."

a I/M

A copy very nearly the same is printed by J. M. Diack, *The New
Scottish Orpheus*, 1923-24, and thence in J. Goss, *Ballads of Britain*,
1937, p. 8.

There were twa sisters sat in a bow'r,
Edinbro Edinbro.
There were twa sisters sat in a bow'r,
Stirling for aye.

There were twa sisters sat in a bow'r,
There came a Knight to be their wooer,
Bonnie St. Johnston stands on Tay.

81. [There Lived Twa Sisters]

Lady John Scott's Sharpe MS., NL Scotland MS. 843, fol.
11ᵛ. Text, Sharpe, 1824, repr. 1891, I, pp. 31-34. Sung by
Sharpe's mother.

m I

1. There liv'd twa sisters in a bower,
    Hey Edinbruch, how Edinbruch,
  There liv'd twa sisters in a bower,
    Stirling for aye;
  The youngest o' them, O, she was a flower!
  Bonny Sanct Johnstoune that stands upon Tay.

2. There cam a squire frae the west,
    Hey Edinbruch, how Edinbruch,
  There cam a squire frae the west,
    Stirling for aye;
  He lo'ed them baith, but the youngest best,
  Bonny Sanct Johnstoune that stands upon Tay.

3. He gied the eldest a gay gold ring,
    Hey Edinbruch, how Edinbruch,
  He gied the eldest a gay gold ring,
    Stirling for aye;
  But he lo'ed the youngest aboon a' thing,
  Bonny Sanct Johnstoune that stands upon Tay.

4. "Oh, sister, sister, will ye go to the sea?
    Hey Edinbruch, how Edinbruch,
  Oh, sister, sister, will ye go to the sea?
    Stirling for aye;
  Our father's ships sail bonnilie,
  Bonny Sanct Johnstoune that stands upon Tay."

5. The youngest sat down upon a stane,
    Hey Edinbruch, how Edinbruch,
  The youngest sat down upon a stane,
    Stirling for aye;
  The eldest shot the youngest in,
  Bonny Sanct Johnstoune that stands upon Tay.

6. "Oh, sister, sister, lend me your hand,
    Hey Edinbruch, how Edinbruch,
  Oh, sister, sister, lend me your hand,
    Stirling for aye;
  And you shall hae my gouden fan,
  Bonny Sanct Johnstoune that stands upon Tay.

7. "Oh, sister, sister, save my life,
   Hey Edinbruch, how Edinbruch,
Oh, sister, sister, save my life,
   Stirling for aye;
And ye shall be the squire's wife,
   Bonny Sanct Johnstoune that stands upon Tay."

8. First she sank, and then she swam,
   Hey Edinbruch, how Edinbruch,
First she sank, and then she swam,
   Stirling for aye;
Until she cam to Tweed mill dam,
   Bonny Sanct Johnstoune that stands upon Tay.

9. The millar's daughter was baking bread,
   Hey Edinbruch, how Edinbruch,
The millar's daughter was baking bread,
   Stirling for aye;
She went for water, as she had need,
   Bonny Sanct Johnstoune that stands upon Tay.

10. "Oh, father, father, in our mill dam,
   Hey Edinbruch, how Edinbruch,
Oh, father, father, in our mill dam,
   Stirling for aye;
There's either a lady, or a milk-white swan,
   Bonny Sanct Johnstoune that stands upon Tay."

11. They could nae see her fingers small,
   Hey Edinbruch, how Edinbruch,
They could nae see her fingers small,
   Stirling for aye;
Wi' diamond rings they were cover'd all,
   Bonny Sanct Johnstoune that stands upon Tay.

12. They could nae see her yellow hair,
   Hey Edinbruch, how Edinbruch,
They could nae see her yellow hair,
   Stirling for aye;
Sae mony knotts and platts war there,
   Bonny Sanct Johnstoune that stands upon Tay.

13. They could nae see her lily feet,
   Hey Edinbruch, how Edinbruch,
They could nae see her lilly feet,
   Stirling for aye;
Her gowden fringes war sae deep,
   Bonny Sanct Johnstoune that stands upon Tay.

14. Bye there cam a fiddler fair,
   Hey Edinbruch, how Edinbruch,
Bye there cam a fiddler fair,
   Stirling for aye;
And he's taen three taits o' her yellow hair,
   Bonny Sanct Johnstoune that stands upon Tay.

* * *

GROUP D

82. "The Swan Swims Bonnie O"

Motherwell, 1827, App'x No. 20; text, p. xx. Collected by
Andrew Blaikie, Paisley.

a I

There liv'd twa sisters in a bower,
   Hey my bonnie Annie O,
There cam a lover them to woo,
   And the Swan swims bonnie O.
   And the swan swims bonnie O.

83. "The Swan Swims so Bonny, O"

Kidson, *JFSS*, II (1906), p. 285. Sung by an Irishman in
Liverpool. Also in Kidson and Moffat, 1926, p. 26.

p I/Ly

1. The miller's daughter being dress'd in red,
   Hey ho, my Nanny, O,
Oh, she went for some water to make her bread,
   Where the swan swims so bonny, O.

2. And there does sit my false sister Anne,
   Hey ho, my Nanny, O,
Who drowned me for the sake of a man,
   Where the swan swims so bonny, O.

3. The miller's (or, farmer's) daughter being
                              dressed in red,
   Hey ho, my Nanny, O,
She went for some water to make her bread,
   Where the swan swims so bonny, O.

4. They laid her on the bank to dry,
   Hey ho, my Nanny, O,
There came a harper passing by,
   Where the swan swims so bonny, O.

5. He made a harp of her breast-bone,
   Hey ho, my Nanny, O,
And the harp began to play alone,
   Where the swan swims so bonny, O.

6. He made harp-pins of her fingers so fair,
   Hey ho, my Nanny, O,
He made his harp-strings of her golden hair,
   Where the swan swims so bonny, O.

Kidson and Moffat, 1926, give a fourteen-stanza text incorporating some of "The Swan Swims So Bonny, O," but constructed apparently by the editors themselves. In 1906, the first stanza, above, was printed with the notes. Since it duplicates stanza 3, perhaps the fragment actually began with 2.

84. [The Two Sisters]

Barry, *BFSSNE*, No. 10 (1935), p. 11. Text, Davis, 1929, p. 104(K). Collected by Martha M. Davis, Virginia; sung by her grandmother.

p π[1]

The first phrase was originally written a third higher, apparently by mistake.

The miller's daughter went out one day,
   Hey ho, my honey, O,
To get some water to make her bread,
   And the swan swam so bonny, O.
   *   *   *   *   *
The miller went and stopped his dam,
   Hey ho, my honey, O,
And placed the king's daughter on dry land,
   And the swan swam so bonny, O.

85. "The Swim Swom Bonny"

Bayard, *BFSSNE*, No. 9 (1935), p. 4 (1st version). Sung by Nicholas W. Butcher, Hundred, Wetzel County, W.Va.

p I

The reader should be notified of Barry's extensive comment in *BFSSNE*, No. 9 (1935), pp. 5-6, with the positiveness of which one may safely disagree.

[There was an old woman lived on the sea shore,
   Hey oh, my Nanny!
She had some daughters, some three or four,
   And the swim swom bonny (*or* bony)!

He gave to her a guinea gold ring,
And to the other, much nicer thing.]

1. "Dear Sister, dear Sister, let's take a walk—
      Hey oh, my Nanny!
"To see the ships a-sailing o'er—
   And the swim swom bonny!

2. As they were walking along the sea shore,
The oldest pushed the youngest in.*

3. She bowed her head and away she swam,
And she swum till she come to the miller's dam.
[The miller's daughter a-being at need
For to get some water to mix her bread.]

4. (Crying) "Miller, oh miller, it's stop your mill,
For yonder comes a swan or a milk white maid."

5. The miller threw out his old grab hook;
He fetched her safely from the brook.

6. The miller got her pretty gold ring,
And pushed her back in the brook again.

7. She bowed her head and away she swum,†
Till she came to her eternal home.

8. The miller was hung in his own mill-gate,
For drowning of my sister Kate.

* *or*, o'er; *or*, off.
† *or*, It's first she sank and then she swam.
   The bracketed stanzas were sung by the same singer on another occasion, as were also the variant lines in stanzas 2, 3, and 7. Cf. Bayard, *BFSSNE*, No. 10 (1935), p. 10.

86. [Heigh ho! my Nancy Oh]

Petrie, 1902-5, No. 688. Contributed by T. B.; as sung by James Moylan, a gardener.

p I/M

Heigh ho my Nancy oh!
Heigh ho my Nancy oh!
Yonder there's my mother the Queen
And the swan she swims so bonny oh!

87. "Down by the Waters Rolling"

Morris, 1950, pp. 243-44. Sung by Mrs. G. A. Griffin, Newberry, Fla., 1937; learned as a girl in Dooly County, Ga.

p I

There was two sisters living in the East,
By rolling, by rolling;
There was two sisters living in the East
Down by the waters rolling.

They were both courted by the young landlord,
By rolling, by rolling;
They were both courted by the young landlord,
Down by the waters rolling.

He gave the oldest a gay gold ring,
By rolling, by rolling;
He gave the oldest a gay gold ring,
Down by the waters rolling.

He gave the youngest a gay gold pin,
By rolling, by rolling;
He gave the youngest a gay gold pin,
Down by the waters rolling.

The eldest one shoved the youngest one in,
By rolling, by rolling;
"Sister, oh Sister, oh hand me your hand,
Down by the waters rolling."

"You can have the landlord and all his land,"
By rolling, by rolling;
"You can have the landlord and all his land,
Down by the waters rolling."

88. "Two Little Sisters"

Morris, 1950, pp. 245-46. Sung by Mrs. Martha L. Sistrunk,
White Springs, Fla., 1936; learned from a schoolmate in
Hamilton County.

p π[1]

Two little sisters living in the East,
Oleander yolling;
Two little sisters living in the East
Down by the waters rolling.

There was a young man he loved them both,
Oleander yolling;
There was a young man he loved them both
Down by the waters rolling.

He gave the oldest a gay gold ring,
Oleander yolling;
He gave the youngest a gold breast pin
Down by the waters rolling.

Two little sisters crossing of the stream,
Oleander yolling;
Two little sisters crossing of the stream
Down by the waters rolling.

The oldest shoved the youngest in,
Oleander yolling;
The oldest shoved the youngest in
Down by the waters rolling.

"Sister, Sister, hand me your hand,"
Oleander yolling;
"Sister, Sister, hand me your hand,"
Down by the waters rolling.

First she'd sink and then she'd swim,
Oleander yolling;
First she'd sink and then she'd swim
Down by the waters rolling.

GROUP E

89. [Binorie]

Sharp MSS., 2031/. Sung by Mrs. Overd, Langport, January 4, 1909.

a I

90. [Binorie]

Sharp MSS., 2134/. Sung by William Bayliss (63), Buck-
land, April 7, 1909.

a I

The relation of this and the preceding copy to Child 10 seems
very dubious, both words and tune.

One day as Johnny was walking
Down by the river side
He saw his maid come floating
Come floating down the tide.

91. [The Two Sisters]

Sharp MSS., 3419/2509. Also in Sharp and Karpeles, 1932, I, p. 26(A). Sung by Mrs. Jane Gentry, Hot Springs, N.C., September 11, 1916.

p π¹ (VII in variant)

1. O sister, O sister, come go with me,
   Go with me down to the sea.
      Jury flower gent the rose-berry,
      The jury hangs over the rose-berry.

2. She picked her up all in her strong arms
   And threwed her sister into the sea.

3. O sister, O sister, give me your glove
   And you may have my own true love.

4. O sister, O sister, I'll not give you my glove
   And I will have your own true love.

5. O sister, O sister, give me your hand
   And you may have my house and land.

6. O sister, O sister, I'll not give you my hand
   And I will have your house and land.

7. O the farmer's wife was sitting on a rock,
   Tying and a-sewing of a black silk knot.

8. O farmer, O farmer, run here and see,
   What's this a-floating here by me.

9. It's no fish and it's no swan,
   For the water's drowned a gay lady.

10. The farmer run with his great hook
    And hooked this fair lady out of the sea.

11. O what will we do with her finger[s] so small?
    We'll take them and we'll make harp screws.

12. O what will we do with her hair so long?
    We'll take it and we'll make harp strings.

13. O the farmer was hung by the gallows so high,
    And the sister was burned by the stake close by.

92. "The Two Sisters"

Henry, 1938, pp. 43(C)-44. Sung by Mrs. Samuel Harmon, Cade's Cove, Blount County, Tenn., August 13, 1930.

a I/M (– VI) (compass of a fifth)

The timing of the original is in quarters and halves, straight 2/4 throughout.

1. Was two sisters loved one man,
   Jelly flower jan;
   The rose marie;
   The jury hangs o'er
   The rose marie.

2. He loved the youngest a little the best,
   Jelly flower jan;
   The rose marie;
   The jury hangs o'er
   The rose marie.

3. Them two sisters going down stream,
   Jelly flower jan;
   The rose marie;
   The jury hangs o'er
   The rose marie.

4. The oldest pushed the youngest in,
   Jelly flower jan;
   The rose marie;
   The jury hangs o'er
   The rose marie.

5. She made a fiddle out of her bones,
   Jelly flower jan;
   The rose marie;
   The jury hangs o'er
   The rose marie.

6. She made the screws out of her fingers,
   Jelly flower jan;
   The rose marie;
   The jury hangs o'er
   The rose marie.

7. She made the strings out of her hair,
   Jelly flower jan;
   The rose marie;
   The jury hangs o'er
   The rose marie.

8. The first string says, "Yonder sets my sister
      on a rock tying of a true-love's knot."
   Jelly flower jan;
   The rose marie;
   The jury hangs o'er
   The rose marie.

9. The next string says, "She pushed me in
         the deep so far."
   Jelly flower jan;
   The rose marie;
   The jury hangs o'er
   The rose marie.

93. "The Two Sisters"

Barry and Buchanan, *BFSSNE*, No. 12 (1937), p. 10. Sung by Rev. J. L. Sims, Pageton, West Virginia. Collected by Mrs. Buchanan, October 13, 1931.

a D/M

1. Two little girls in a boat one day—
    Oh, the wind and rain—
    Two little girls in a boat one day,
        Crying, oh, the wind and rain.

2. They floated down on the old mill dam—
    Oh, the wind and rain—
    They floated down on the old mill dam,
        Crying, oh, the wind and rain.

3. Charles Miller came out with his long hook and line, etc.

4. He hooked her out by the long yellow hair, etc.

5. He made fiddle strings of her long yellow hair, etc.

6. He made fiddle screws of her long finger bones, etc.

7. And the only tune the fiddle would play, etc.

94. (Unnamed)

Randolph, I, 1946, pp. 59(F)-60. Sung by Mrs. Irene Carlisle, Fayetteville, Ark., October 26, 1941; learned from her grandmother in 1912.

p π¹ (–VI)

1. There was two sisters in their tower,
    Bonnery O, bonnery O,
    Sir Hugh he came to court them there,
    Saying bonnery, bonnery O.

2. He courted the eldest with a brooch and a knife,
    Bonnery O, bonnery O,
    But he loved the youngest one better than life,
    Saying bonnery, bonnery O.

3. The eldest to the young one said,
    Bonnery O, bonnery O,
    Come see our father's boats come in,
    Saying bonnery, bonnery O.

4. She taken the youngest by the hand,
    Bonnery O, bonnery O,
    She led her down to the river bank
    Saying bonnery, bonnery O.

5. The youngest stood upon a stone,
    Bonnery O, bonnery O,
    The eldest come and throwed her in,
    Saying bonnery, bonnery O.

6. Oh sister, sister, reach your hand,
    Bonnery O, bonnery O,
    And you shall have the half of my land,
    Saying bonnery, bonnery O.

7. Oh sister, sister, reach your glove,
    Bonnery O, bonnery O,
    Sir Hugh shall be your own true love,
    Saying bonnery, bonnery O.

8. Sometimes she sunk, sometimes she swam,
    Bonnery O, bonnery O,
    Till down she come to the miller's dam,
    Saying bonnery, bonnery O.

9. Oh miller, miller, dreen your dam,
    Bonnery O, bonnery O,
    And there you'll find a drownded woman,
    Saying bonnery, bonnery O.

95. "The Two Sisters"

Vincent, [1932], p. 27. Arranged by "Nick" Manoloff.

a I/M

(yodeling chorus)

There was a man lived in the west, Bow down, bow down,
He loved his youngest daughter best, Bow down to me
One day he gave her a beaver hat
Her older sister she didn't like that
Prove true, prove true, my love prove true to me.
    O de yodel layee O layee O layee

As they were walking on the green, Bow down, bow down
To see their father's ship come in, Bow down to me
As they were walking upon the wharf
Her older sister she pushed her right off
Prove true, prove true, my love prove true to me.
    O de yodel layee O layee O layee

"Oh sister dear give me your hand, Bow down, bow down,
And you shall have my house and land," Bow down to me
Her sister said "You'll not have my hand
But I will have both your house and your land
Prove true, prove true, my love prove true to me.

Sometimes she sank, sometimes she swam, Bow down, bow down
Until she reached a miller's dam, Bow down to me.
The miller put in a long iron hook
And fished her out by her silk petticoat
Prove true, prove true, my love prove true to me.

He stripped her off from toe to chin, Bow down, bow down
And then he threw her in again, Bow down to me
Sometimes she sank and sometimes she swam
Until she reached her own home once again
Prove true, prove true, my love prove true to me.

They hanged her sister for her sake, Bow down, bow down,.
Because her life she sought to take, Bow down to me
They hanged her sister all for her sake
The horrid miller they burned at the stake
Prove true, prove true, my love prove true to me.

96. "The Youngest Daughter"

Flanders, *BFSSNE*, No. 11 (1936), p. 16. Sung by Amos Easton, South Royalton, Vt.; learned from his mother in Sutton, Vt. From *Bulletin of the Folk-Song Society of the Northeast*, No. 11 (1936), edited by Phillips Barry; copyright 1936 by the Folk-Song Society of the Northeast.

p π¹ (– VI)

Echoes of "Buy a Broom" ("Ach du lieber Augustine") and "Here we go round the Mulberry Bush" seem to be present here.

1. There was a man who lived out west—
   Lived out west, lived out west;
   There was a man who lived out west;
   He loved his youngest daughter best.

2. He bought for his youngest a gay gold ring;
   The oldest she hadn't anything.

3. He bought for his youngest a beaver hat;
   The oldest, she was mad at that.

4. One day these girls went down to swim;
   The oldest pushed her sister in.

5. First she sank and then she swam,
   Until she reached the miller's dam.

6. The miller put out his line and hook,
   And caught her by the petticoat.

7. The miller took off her gay gold ring,
   And threw her into the stream again.

8. The king and his son were riding by;
   They heard the youngest daughter cry.

9. And so the riders pulled her out
   To see what she was crying about.

10. Next day the old miller was hung for her sake,
    And the eldest daughter was burned at the stake.

97. "The Two Sisters"

Gardner and Chickering, 1939, pp. 33(B)-34. Sung by Mrs. Lillian Ammerman, Detroit, Mich., 1931; learned from her mother in Nebraska, c. 1900.

a I/M (– VI, inflected II) (compass of a fifth)

Is this perhaps out of "London Bridge is falling down"?

1. Peter and I went down the lane,
   Down the lane, down the lane;
   Peter and I went down the lane,
   And sister came behind.

2. Both of us sisters loved him well,
   As only I can tell.

3. Peter could love but one of us then,
   So sister must go away.

4. Sister was bending over the well,
   When splash, splash, in she fell.

5. Sister did scream with all her might,
   But I did not help her plight.

6. Out of the well they dragged her then,
   And laid her on the lawn.

7. In the black hearse we carried her then,
   And buried her on the hill.

8. Peter and I were wed one day,
   And oh, what people did say!

9. Sorrow and pain were in my heart,
   Sharp as an arrow could be.

10. Peter then left for foreign parts,
    And I'll die of a broken heart.

The Cruel Brother

CHILD NO. 11

FORMERLY, Child informs us, this ballad was very popular in Scotland, and its central idea, the murderous pride of an offended brother, was familiar also in Scandinavian analogues. Folk-singers, however, as we have of late been reminded, do not cherish ballads in the literal truth of which they no longer believe. The present narrative turns not so much on a permanent trait of human nature as on a system of manners; and it was probably inevitable that with the dying-out of a family code which could rate the forgetting to ask a brother's assent to his sister's marriage as a mortal affront, the ballad would wither from tradition. Although Aytoun and Dixon indicate that the ballad was still current about 1850, its condition since then has been desperate. In Cornwall, the memory of it lingered until the present century, but Greig did not pick it up in Scotland. (Miss Karpeles' references to Kidson's versions are in error: they are intended for "The Two Sisters." Sharp and Karpeles, 1932, I, p. 412.) It has been found in our own day in the United States; but the text now implies, instead of forgetfulness as the fault, a deliberate, willful insult such as would naturally set an already smouldering hatred aflame.

I can grant little credence to Barry's notion (*BFSSNE*, VII [1934], p. 8) of a veiled incest-motive behind the murder, not so much because of the repugnance of the idea as because the "folk" would have felt little need to veil it, if that had been the point, and formerly would have found the motive sufficient without it.

Except for the Appalachian copies, it is next to impossible to discern any clear family resemblance between the extant tunes for this ballad. Perhaps, if we had David Herd's tune and those of the texts that from time to time in the last century were printed in *Notes and Queries*, we should be more inclined to relate the present tunes; for the present refrain-texts are homogeneous by comparison with those others. Nevertheless, all the refrains known are interlaced in pattern, coming on lines 2 and 4; and therefore do not necessitate a different melodic vehicle. Child's E (Scottish) and the Cornish copies of Baring-Gould and Sharp are distinct from the rest in having, besides, a burden of two or more additional lines.

Mrs. Harris' tune, corrected from the MS., has been given first place: a clear Mixolydian with a wide range on account of its commencement. After the opening notes, it remains authentic. Barry's Boston tune may be distantly related, but I have no confidence in the connection. This tune is plagal I/M. Sharp's two North Carolina tunes, both authentic I/M, are obviously close together. The "B" copy is interesting for variation within its own body. The Virginia and third North Carolina copy likewise have points in common.

The earliest copy printed (Davies Gilbert's) looks very undependable, with inflected III and VII, and a dubious final. The notation was probably inexpert, the tune perhaps having been originally a plagal Dorian. There is behind it a vague suggestion of the favorite scheme exemplified in "Searching for Lambs."* The three other exemplars of the Cornish tradition seem to have nothing in common with Gilbert's tune, but are close to one another. It is at least an odd series of coincidences that Baring-Gould's and Sharp's copies derive from one Thomas Williams, through two members of a family named Gilbert, and that one of Sharp's two Appalachian singers to know the song was named Williams (by marriage). Gilbert, incidentally, was the family name of Davies Gilbert's wife, and assumed by him in 1817.

It is proper to mention that Christie's tune for this ballad (1876, I, p. 108) is acknowledged by him to belong to "The Cruel Mother." He has arbitrarily set it to Jamieson's text of "The Cruel Brother."

---

*Lucy Broadwood (*JFSS*, IV [1910], p. 16) has pointed out some of the members of this clan. They include Child 20, 56, 78, 289, a number of carols, and "How should I your true love know?" See also the family survey in *Journal of the American Musicological Society*, III (1950), pp. 126-34.

LIST OF VARIANTS

1. "There waur three Ladies in a Ha'." Harris MS., No. 13, Harvard College Library. Also in Francis James Child, *The English and Scottish Popular Ballads*, 1882-98, V, p. 412, and I, p. 147(C).
2. "The Cruel Brother." Barry MSS., IV, No. 340, Harvard College Library. Also in Phillips Barry, *JAF*, XXVIII (1915), pp. 300-1; and Phillips Barry, Fannie H. Eckstorm, and Mary W. Smyth, *British Ballads from Maine*, 1929, p. 431.
3. "The Cruel Brother." Sharp MSS., 3463/2550, Clare College Library, Cambridge. Also in Cecil J. Sharp and Maud Karpeles, *English Folk Songs from the Southern Appalachians*, 1932, I, pp. 36(A)-37. (House) Also on Folkways LP rec. FP64(1951). (Andrew Rowan Summers)
4. "The Cruel Brother." Sharp MSS., 3814/2802. Also in Sharp and Karpeles, 1932, I, p. 37(B). (Williams)
5. "Oh Lilly O." F. C. Brown MS., 16 a 4 H, Library of Congress, photostat. Text, *The Frank C. Brown Collection of North Carolina Folklore*, II, 1952, pp. 36-37(A).
6. "The Three Maids." Herbert Halpert, LC Archive of American Folk Song, rec. 2758 A2. (Mrs. Polly Johnson)
7. "The Three Knights." Davies Gilbert, *Some Ancient Christmas Carols*, 1823, pp. 68-71. Text also in Child, *The English and Scottish Popular Ballads*, 1882-98, I, p. 148(F).
8. "Flowers of the Valley." Sabine Baring-Gould MSS., CXCI(1) and (A), Plymouth Public Library.
9. "Flowers of the Valley." Sharp MSS., 217/. (Williams, *per* Gilbert)
10. "Flowers of the Valley." Baring-Gould MSS., CXCI(2) and (B).

1. "There waur three Ladies in a Ha'"

Harris MS., No. 13. Also in Child, 1882-98, V, p. 412;
text, I, p. 147(C).

m M

The MS. is very inexpertly noted: the quarter-notes are written
as halves, but most of the eighths as eighths, and the time-signature
is 2/4. In the Child printing, the up-beat of the second phrase is
given as G.

1. There waur three ladies in a ha,
     Hech hey an the lily gey
   By cam a knicht, an he wooed them a'.
     An the rose is aye the redder aye.

2. The first ane she was cled in green;
   "Will you fancy me, an be my queen?"

3. "You may seek me frae my father dear,
   An frae my mither, wha did me bear.

4. "You may seek me frae my sister Anne,
   But no, no, no frae my brither John."

5. The niest ane she was cled in yellow;
   "Will you fancy me, an be my marrow?"

6. "Ye may seek me frae my father dear,
   An frae my mither, wha did me bear.

7. "Ye may seek me frae my sister Anne,
   But no, no, no frae my brither John."

8. The niest ane she was cled in red:
   "Will ye fancy me, an be my bride?"

9. "Ye may seek me frae my father dear,
   An frae my mither wha did me bear.

10. "Ye may seek me frae my sister Anne,
    An dinna forget my brither John."

11. He socht her frae her father, the king,
    An he socht her frae her mither, the queen.

12. He socht her frae her sister Anne,
    But he forgot her brither John.

13. Her mither she put on her goun,
    An her sister Anne preened the ribbons doun.

14. Her father led her doon the close,
    An her brither John set her on her horse.

        *   *   *   *   *   *   *

15. Up an spak our foremost man:
    "I think our bonnie bride's pale an wan."

        *   *   *   *   *   *   *

16. "What will ye leave to your father dear?"
    "My . . . . . an my . . . . . chair."

17. "What will ye leave to your mither dear?"
    "My silken screen I was wont to wear."

18. "What will ye leave to your sister Anne?"
    "My silken snood an my golden fan."

19. "What will you leave to your brither John?"
    "The gallows tree to hang him on."

2. [The Cruel Brother]

Barry MSS., IV, No. 340. Also in Barry, *JAF*, XXVIII
(1915), pp. 300-1; and Barry, Eckstorm, and Smyth, 1929,
p. 431. Noted by Rosalind Fuller of Dorset in Boston, Mass.,
June 17, 1913; traditional in family for three generations.
Text from a Miss E. S. Porter's MS., borrowed from Mrs.
Dorothy Fuller Irving of Sturminster, Dorset.

p I/M

1. Three Ladies played at cup and ball,—
     (With a hey! and my lily gay!)
   Three Knights there came along with them* all.
     (The rose it smells so sweetly!)

2. And one of them was dressed in green,—
   He asked me to be his queen.

3. And one of them was dressed in yellow,—
   He asked me to be his fellow.

4. And one of them was dressed in red,—
   He asked me with him to wed.

5. "But you must ask my father the King,
   And you must ask my mother the Queen,—

6. "And you must ask my sister Anne,
   And you must ask my brother John."

7. "Oh, I have asked your father the King,
   And I have asked your mother the Queen,—

8. "And I have asked your sister Anne,
   And I have asked your brother John."

9. Her father led her down the stairs,
   Her mother led her down the hall.

10. Her sister Anne led her down the walk,
    Her brother John put her on her horse.

11. And as she stooped to give him a kiss,
    He stuck a penknife into her breast.

12. "Ride up, ride up, my foremost man!
    Methinks my lady looks pale and wan!"

13. "Oh what will you leave to your father the King?"
    "The golden coach that I ride in."

14. "And what will you leave to your mother the Queen?"
    "The golden chair that I sat in."

15. "And what will you leave to your sister Anne?"
    "My silver brooch and golden fan."

16. "And what will you leave to your brother John?"
    "A pair of gallows to hang him on."

17. "And what will you leave to your brother John's wife?"
    "Grief and misfortune all her life."†

    * Barry, Eckstorm, and Smyth have "came among them."
    † Barry, Eckstorm, and Smyth have "all of her life."

3. [The Cruel Brother]

Sharp MSS., 3463/2550. Also in Sharp and Karpeles, 1932,
I, pp. 36(A)-37. Sung by Mrs. Hester House, Hot Springs,
N.C., September 15, 1916.

a I/M

Sharp and Karpeles, 1932, transpose to F.
Andrew Rowan Summers sings this variant to his own dulcimer
accompaniment on Folkways LP rec. FP64(1951).

1. There's three fair maids went out to play at ball,
       I-o the lily gay,
   There's three landlords come court them all,
       And the rose smells so sweet I know.

2. The first landlord was dressed in blue.
   He asked his maid if she would be his true.

3. The next landlord was dressed in green.
   He asked his maid if she'd be his queen.

4. The next landlord was dressed in white.
   He asked his maid if she'd be his wife.

5. It's you may ask my old father dear,
   And you may ask my mother too.

6. It's I have asked your old father dear,
   And I have asked your mother too.

7. Your sister Anne I've asked her not,
   Your brother John and I had forgot.

8. Her old father dear was to lead her to the yard,
   Her mother too was to lead her to the step.

9. Her brother John was to help her up.
   As he holp her up he stabbed her deep.

10. Go ride me out on that green hill,
    And lay me down and let me bleed.

11. Go haul me up on that green hill,
    And lay me down till I make my will.

12. It's what will you will to your old father dear?
    This house and land that I have here.

13. It's what will you will to your mother, too?
    This bloody clothing that I have wear.

14. Go tell her to take them to yonders stream,
    For my heart's blood is in every seam.

15. It's what will you will to your sister Anne?
    My new gold ring and my silver fan.

16. It's what will you will to your brother John's wife?
    In grief and sorrow the balance of her life.

17. It's what will you will to your brother John's son?
    It's God for to bless and to make him a man.

18. It's what will you will to your brother John?
    A rope and a gallows for to hang him on.

4. [The Cruel Brother]

Sharp MSS., 3814/2802. Also in Sharp and Karpeles, 1932,
I, p. 37(B). Sung by Mrs. Julie Williams, Hot Springs,
N.C., July 27, 1917.

a I/M

The first landlord was dressed in white,
        I am the lil-i-no,
He asked her would she be his wife,
        And the roses smell so sweet I know.

        *   *   *   *   *   *   *

O what will you will to your mother dear?
        I-o the lil-i-you,
This robe of gold (or silk) that I have here,
        And the roses so sweet I know.

        *   *   *   *   *   *   *

The rest of the stanzas were not noted as they were similar to those sung
by Mrs. House on a former occasion (see preceding variant).

5. "Oh Lilly O"

Brown MS., 16 a 4 H. Collected by Mrs. Sutton. Text,
North Carolina Folklore, II, 1952, pp. 36-37(A). Sung by
"Granny" Houston, Bushy Creek, Avery County, N.C.

p π¹

1. There were three sisters playing at ball
        Oh Lily O
   There were three lawyers courting them all,
        Lily O, sweet hi O

2. The first to come was dressed in red,
        Oh Lily O
   He asked if she would be his bride,
        Lily O, sweet hi O

3. The next to come was dressed in blue,
        Oh Lily O
   Saying 'Oh my sweet, I've come for you,'
        Lily O, sweet hi O

4. 'Oh, you must ask my father dear,'
        Oh Lily O
   'And you must ask my mother, too,'
        Lily O, sweet hi O

5. 'Oh, I have asked your father dear,'
        Oh Lily O
   'And I have asked your mother, too,'
        Lily O, sweet hi O

6. 'Oh, you must ask my sister Ann,'
        Oh Lily O
   'And you must ask my brother, John,'
        Lily O, sweet hi O

7. 'Oh, I have asked your sister Ann,'
        Oh Lily O
   'Your brother John I did forget,'
        Lily O, sweet hi O

8. Her father led her down the steps,
        Oh Lily O
   Her mother led her to the gate,
        Lily O, sweet hi O

9. Her sister led her through the close,
        Oh Lily O
   Her brother put her on the horse,
        Lily O, sweet hi O

10. He took a pen knife long and sharp,
        Oh Lily O
    He stabbed his sister through the heart,
        Lily O, sweet hi O

11. 'Oh, lead me gently up the hill,'
        Oh Lily O
    'And I'll sit down and make my will,'
        Lily O, sweet hi O

12. 'Oh, what will you leave to your mother dear?'
        Oh Lily O
    'My velvet dress and golden gear,'
        Lily O, sweet hi O

13. 'What will you leave to your sister Ann?'
        Oh Lily O
    'My silver ring and golden fan,'
        Lily O, sweet hi O

14. 'What will you leave to your brother John?'
        Oh Lily O
    'The gallows tree to hang him on,'
        Lily O, sweet hi O

6. "The Three Maids"

Halpert, LC/AAFS, rec. 2758 A2. Sung by Mrs. Polly Johnson (73), Wise, Va., 1939.

p I/Ly

1. There was three maids a-playing ball
        I lily O
   There was three maids a-playing ball
   There come three lords for to court them all
        For the rose is sweet I know.

2. The foremost one was dressed in red
   [*Repeat as before, throughout*]
   'And this is the one I make my wed'
   For the rose is sweet I know.

3. The middle one was dressed in green
   'And this is the one I make my queen'

4. The foremost [*sic*] one was dressed in white
   'O this is the one I make my wife'

5. Her brother John was standing by
   He wounded his sister with a knife

6. 'Ride on, ride on to yonder stile
   Till I get down and bleed awhile

7. 'Ride on, ride on to yonder hill
   Till I get down 'n' I make my will'

8. 'What do you will your sister Ann?'
   'My trunk of gold and silver pan'

9. 'What do you will your true-love dear?'
   'This snow-white horse that I rode here'

10. 'What do you will your mother dear?'
    'My snow-white dress that I wore here'

11. 'Tell her to wash it nice and clean
    I lily O
    Tell her to wash it nice and clean
    So my heart's blood can never be seen
    For the rose is sweet I know.'

7. [The Three Knights]

Gilbert, 1823, pp. 68-71. Also in Child, 1882-98, I, p. 148(F).
Sung in Cornwall.

a Harmonic Minor (perhaps originally a Æ) (inflected III
and VII)

1. There did three Knights come from the West,
   With the high and the lily oh!
   And these three Knights courted one Lady,
   As the rose was so sweetly blown.

2. The first Knight came was all in white,
   With the high and the lily oh!
   And asked of her if she'd be his delight,
   As the rose was so sweetly blown.

3. The next Knight came was all in green,
   With the high and the lily oh!
   And asked of her, if she'd be his Queen,
   As the rose was so sweetly blown.

4. The third Knight came was all in red,
   With the high and the lily oh!
   And asked of her, if she would wed,
   As the rose was so sweetly blown.

5. Then have you asked of my Father dear,
   With the high and the lily oh!
   Likewise of her who did me bear?
   As the rose was so sweetly blown.

6. And have you asked of my brother John?
   With the high and the lily oh!
   And also of my sister Anne?
   As the rose was so sweetly blown.

7. Yes, I have asked of your Father dear,
   With the high and the lily oh!
   Likewise of her who did you bear,
   As the rose was so sweetly blown.

8. And I have asked of your sister Anne,
   With the high and the lily oh!
   But I've not asked of your brother John,
   As the rose was so sweetly blown.

9. For on the road as they rode along,
   With the high and the lily oh!
   There did they meet with her brother John,
   As the rose was so sweetly blown.

10. She stooped low to kiss him sweet,
    With the high and the lily oh!
    He to her heart did a dagger meet,
    As the rose was so sweetly blown.

11. Ride ride on, cried the serving man,
    With the high and the lily oh!
    Methinks your bride she looks wond'rous wan,
    As the rose was so sweetly blown.

12. I wish I were on yonder stile,
    With the high and the lily oh!
    For there I would sit and bleed awhile,
    As the rose was so sweetly blown.

13. I wish I were on yonder hill,
    With the high and the lily oh!
    There I'd alight and make my will,
    As the rose was so sweetly blown.

14. What would you give to your Father dear,
    With the high and the lily oh!
    The gallant steed which doth me bear,
    As the rose was so sweetly blown.

15. What would you give to your Mother dear,
    With the high and the lily oh!
    My wedding shift which I do wear,
    As the rose was so sweetly blown.

16. But she must wash it very clean,
    With the high and the lily oh!
    For my heart's blood sticks in ev'ry seam,
    As the rose was so sweetly blown.

17. What would you give to your sister Anne,
       With the high and the lily oh!
     My gay gold ring, and my feathered fan,
       As the rose was so sweetly blown.

18. What would you give to your brother John,
       With the high and the lily oh!
     A rope and gallows to hang him on,
       As the rose was so sweetly blown.

19. What would you give to your brother John's wife,
       With the high and the lily oh!
     A widow's weeds, and a quiet life,
       As the rose was so sweetly blown.

8. "Flowers of the Valley"

Baring-Gould MSS., CXCI(1); text, (A). Sung by Mary
Gilbert, Falcon Inn, Mawgan-in-Pyder, Cornwall; learned
from Thomas Williams, d. 1881. Collected by F. W. Bussell.

a M

The first repeat mark is probably a slip in the MS.

There was a woman & she was a widow
    The flowers that were in the valley.
A daughter had she. . . . . . .
    O the red, the green & the yellow
The harp, the lute, the fife, the flute & the cymbal
    Sweet goes the treble violin
    The flowers that were in the valley.

No more remembered except these lines:—

Three of them were seamen so brave
    The flowers that were in the valley
Three of them were soldiers so bold
    O the red, the green & the yellow
The harp, &c.

and the end was:—

"There was an end of nine brave boys."

Miss Gilbert's brother William remembers another line:

"Nine brave boys of her body were born."

9. "Flowers of the Valley"

Sharp MSS., 217/. Sung by Thomas Williams, St. Mawgan
East, Cornwall. Noted by Mr. W. Gilbert.

a M

There was a widow all forlorn
Nine brave boys from her body were borne [*sic*]
Flowers that were in the Valley
The harp the lute the fife the flute & the cymbal
Sweet goes the treble violin
Flowers that were in the Vally

10. "Flowers of the Valley"

Baring-Gould MSS., CXCI(2); text, (B). Sung by Mr. Old,
"at the same time as the other variant" (i.e., A above).

a M (inflected VI)

There was a Knight all clothed in red
    The Flowers that were in the valley
O & wilt thou be my bride? he said
    O the red, the green & the yellow.
The harp, the lute, &c.

There came a second all clothed in green
    The Flowers that were in the valley.
And he said, My Fair, wilt thou be my queen
    O the red, the green & the yellow.
The harp, the lute, &c.

There came a third, in yellow was he
    The flowers that were in the valley,
And he said, 'My bride for sure thou'lt be,
    O the red, the green & the yellow,
The harp, the lute, &c.

Lord Randal

CHILD NO. 12

THIS ballad now known as "Lord Randal" has held with extraordinary tenacity to its stanzaic pattern, wherever and whenever it has been found—in Italy in the early seventeenth century or in the Appalachians in our own day: the first half of the stanza a question repeated with only a change of address; the second half an answer, addressed to the questioner, and a premonitory assertion of desperate illness. The name of the protagonist, meanwhile, has changed with kaleidoscopic variety: a page could be filled with his aliases. Of a number of rather strange trisyllabic appellatives, beginning with T and D—Tar(r)anty, Tyranty, Tyranting, Tyranna, Terencè, Teronto, Durango, Dorendo—it does not appear to have been suggested that they may probably have arisen from a perversion of one form of the preliminary question: "Oh, where have you been *to, Randal, my son?*"—*to* having slipped off the verb and adhered to the name, with consequent havoc in nomenclature. Those who balk at this hypothesis may prefer Barry's, that all these names are corruptions of *Tyrannus*, and have nothing to do with *Randal*. [Barry, 1929, p. 67—"The name," he says, "is rare," but he finds it once in the *New England Genealogical Register*!]

In an interesting note (*JFSS*, III [1907], p. 44), Annie Gilchrist suggests a connection between this ballad and Piers Plowman's rimes of Randolf, Earl of Chester. The historical Ranulf, or Randall III, sixth Earl of Chester, who died in 1232, was divorced and left no heir, but was succeeded by his nephew John, whose wife was supposed to have tried to poison her husband. This Randall was also associated with minstrelsy in another sort, for which cf. Chappell, earlier ed., p. 10.

Most of the divisions suggesting themselves within the large body of tunes are subdivisions rather than actual cleavages. Thus, for example, the group of tunes that identify themselves with more or less distinctness as variants of the well-known "Villikens and his Dinah" tune—an air that has had enormous vogue for the last hundred years and lent itself to a great variety of contexts—will be felt here rather as a family within the larger clan than as a separate class. What may be called the nursery branch of the ballad, however—the "Croodin Dow" variety in which the hero has retrogressed from young manhood into pre-adolescence—appears not to subscribe to the main melodic tradition; and the same may be said of the consciously comic rifacimento, "Billy Boy," the stanzaic form of which is too closely modeled on the older pattern for its text to be unrelated. Such, incidentally, appears to be the destined end of too many fine old tragic ballads: they are not to be permitted a dignified demise, but we must madly play with our forefathers' relics and make a mock of their calamities. The high seriousness of the parents is the children's favorite joke. So it has been with "Earl Brand," "Young Beichan," "Lord Lovel," "Lady Alice," "The Mermaid," "Bessie Bell and Mary Gray," "Queen Jane," and "The Three Ravens," to name but the most familiar examples; and, in a different sort, Robin Hood dwindled to the stature of a custard-pie farce before he was finally tossed out for daws to peck at. It is a fact—but what to do with it I know not—that all the recovered variants in which the name Henry is used instead of Randal (or its perversions) have a clear duple rhythm. Elsewhere the triple rhythm is the rule.

There is, in addition, a very small number of serious versions of "Lord Randal" which have either acquired a new increment of refrain or burden, or put on an entirely alien melodic dress. These will be duly noted in their turn. In *JAF*, XXIII (1910), pp. 440-45, Phillips Barry makes the confident statement that "Lord Randal" "is in all probability unique as being the only old ballad which has retained its original melody." This assertion appears to me to derive mainly from some transcendental source of information to which I have been denied access. But I am not disposed to cavil over his further declaration that "Lochaber No More," "King James's March to Ireland," "Limerick's Lamentation," and "Reeve's Maggot" are related tunes. Cf., on these, Moffat's *Minstrelsy of Ireland*, 1897, pp. 300, 352.

The main melodic tradition for the ballad lies in Group A, here subdivided into four main varieties, with an appendix containing a few anomalies in which the tune has submitted so thoroughly to contamination by other familiar airs as to lose its identity. The oldest copy with the ballad text is that recovered by Burns in Ayrshire, and sent to Johnson's *Museum*. Melodically, it is one of the comeliest, and closely allied to "Lochaber No More." In kindred versions, this tune can be followed back, as Moffat, *loc.cit.*, has noted, to the latter part of the seventeenth century. Taking Burns's copy as representative of earlier—and richer—forms of the tradition, it will be observed that the tune is typically in the major area, in triple time, with a mid-cadence on the tonic, a first cadence on the supertonic, and considerable emphasis at the beginning on the mediant. As this pattern is passed on, its compass tends to shrink to the limits of a sixth or even a fifth (tonic to dominant), and the cadence of the first phrase shifts to the tonic, the mediant, and, infrequently, to other points. In a few variants, early rather than late, it inclines toward the minor range. *Vid.* the last four tunes in subgroup Aa.

Subgroup Ab is typically of the familiar "Villikens and his Dinah" pattern. With one exception, it stays within the ambit I/Ly to M. The exception is an Æ Irish variant printed by Petrie, which was obtained from Joyce, though Joyce himself later printed the same tune as a major. With two Appalachian exceptions, all the tunes in this subgroup have a mid-cadence on the fifth, a first cadence on the tonic. The first stress is commonly on III or I. The variants are consistently in some form of triple time.

Subgroup Ac is small, and is distinguished by having a mid-cadence on the supertonic. Its first phrase is either on I or II, its first stress on the tonic in four cases out of five. Examples are from Virginia, Massachusetts, and County Mayo.

Subgroup Ad is less stable, and has perhaps less justification as a group. Its members have varying cadence-points, and do not fall readily into the preceding groups: mid-cadences fall on lower V, on III, upper and lower VI, flat VII, and the octave; but the first cadence is usually on I. First stresses are on I, III, and V. The variants come from different regions in every case. The copy from Kentucky, from J. J. Niles, is unique in its Dorian modality: the rest are I, M, π^1, and I/M.

Group B, the "Henry" group, is mainly English, but copies have been found in the west of Scotland and in America. With the exception of two or three doubtful copies, all variants are in duple time. Most of the copies have a fifth or even a sixth phrase. All but two have a mid-cadence on the supertonic. The first cadence varies, but is on the fifth in the majority of cases.

The copies fall fairly easily into three sub-types, of which the first two are major (I, π^1, I/M). The third is Æolian, and so different that it ought perhaps to be classified separately. The two copies composing it come from Cumberland and Carlisle: they are close variants, four-phrase, with first and second cadences on the tonic, and the first stress on the fifth. Both are plagal. Two copies of the second sub-variety, it might be added, seem not to end on the tonic, but on lower V and III.

Group C, the "Croodin' Doo," is of two varieties, to judge by the scanty evidence. One is Scottish and Æolian, with first and second cadences on the tonic. The other is English, and major (I, I/M, M) in tonality, with first and second cadences on the dominant, the whole tune being of the familiar "Lord Lovel" type.

It should be mentioned that the tune printed in Child, V, p. 412, for ballad 12(D) is a spurious air for this ballad. It was sent to Child from the singing of J. F. Campbell, 1883, to words which Child properly rejected. The first stanza is enough to clinch the matter:

O Randal was a bonnie lad When he gaed awa,
A bonnie, bonnie lad was he When he gaed awa.
'Twas in the sixteen year O' grace, and thretty twa
That Randal, the laird's youngest son gaed awa.

[Child MSS., II, p. 130.]

LIST OF VARIANTS

GROUP Aa

1. "Lord Ronald my son." James Johnson, *The Scots Musical Museum* [1792], repr. 1853, IV, No. 327, p. 337.
2. "Lord Randall; or, Fair Elson." Phillips Barry, *JAF*, XVIII (1905), pp. 197(C)-98. Also in Barry, *JAF*, XVI (1903), p. 263; and Barry, *JAF*, XXIII (1910), p. 444(6th). (A.M.)
3. "Lord Randal." Sharp MSS., 3130/?, Clare College Library, Cambridge. Also in Cecil J. Sharp and Maud Karpeles, *English Folk Songs from the Southern Appalachians*, 1932, I, p. 41(E). (McKinney)
4. "Lord Randall; or, Orlando." Phillips Barry, *JAF*, XVIII (1905), p. 204(L). Also in Barry, *JAF*, XXIII (1910), p. 443(3rd). (Utter)
5. "Lord Randall." Phillips Barry, *JAF*, XVIII (1905), pp. 203(K)-4. Also in Barry, *JAF*, XXIII (1910), p. 443(2nd). (Krehbiel)
6. "Durango." C. A. Smith, *Musical Quarterly*, II (January 1916), p. 127. Text, Barry MSS., III, Harvard College Library.
7. "Lord Rendal." Sharp MSS., 4276/. (Harris)
   a. "Wrentham, my Son." Phillips Barry, *JAF*, XXIII (1910), p. 444(5th). (Mrs. Emily W. Hastings, West Campton, N.H., July 31, 1906)
8. "Lorendo." Louis W. Chappell, *Folk-Songs of Roanoke and the Albemarle*, 1939, p. 14.
9. "Tarranty, My Son." Phillips Barry, *BFSSNE*, No. 1 (1930), p. 4. (Hussey)
10. "Lord Randall." Phillips Barry, *JAF*, XVIII (1905), p. 199(E). (Johnson)
11. "Tyranty, My Son." Phillips Barry, Fannie H. Eckstorm, and Mary W. Smyth, *British Ballads from Maine*, 1929, pp. 69(O)-70. (Turner)
12. "Lord Randall." Phillips Barry, *JAF*, XVIII (1905), pp. 201(I)-2. Also, as "Dirante, My Son," in Eloise Hubbard Linscott, *Folk Songs of Old New England*, 1939, p. 191. (J.E.W.)
   b. "Lord Randall." Phillips Barry, *JAF*, XXIII (1910), p. 443(1st). Also in Barry, *JAF*, XVIII (1905), p. 201; and Gelett Burgess, *The Lark*, No. 2 (1895). (G. Burgess)
   c. "Lord Randall." Phillips Barry, *JAF*, XXIII (1910), p. 444(4th). Also in Barry, *JAF*, XVIII (1905), p. 205(N). (Ayer)
13. "Lord Randal." Sharp MSS., 3200/2344. Also in Sharp and Karpeles, *Appalachians*, 1932, I, p. 38(A). (Shelton)
14. "Lord Randal." Sharp MSS., 3205/2350. Also in Sharp and Karpeles, 1932, I, p. 38(B). (Sands)
15. "Lord Rendle." Sharp MSS., 335/465. (Hutchings)
16. "Lord Randall." Barry, Eckstorm, and Smyth, *British Ballads from Maine*, 1929, p. 53(F). (Young)
17. "Lord Randall." Sharp MSS., 3331/2438. Also in Sharp and Karpeles, *Appalachians*, 1932, I, pp. 39(C)-40. (Hensley)
18. "Lord Rendal." Sharp MSS., 420/545. Also in Cecil J. Sharp, *JFSS*, II (1905), p. 31(5). (Brown)
19. "William, my Son." Editor, from E. S. McLellan, Jr., Berkeley, Calif., 1933.
20. "Lord Rendal." Sharp MSS., 4315/. (Long)
21. "Johnny Randolph." Vance Randolph, *Ozark Folksongs*, 1946, I, p. 64(A). Also in Vance Randolph, *Ozark Mountain Folks*, 1932, p. 215.
22. "Lord Rendal." Sharp MSS., 1883/1710. (Gulliford)
23. "Sweet Nelson." Phillips Barry, *JAF*, XVIII (1905), 198(D). Also in Barry, Eckstorm, and Smyth, *British Ballads from Maine*, 1932, pp. 57(I)-58. (Collins)
24. "Lord Ronald." P. N. Shuldham-Shaw, *JEFDSS*, VI (December 1949), p. 15.
25. "Three Drops of Poison." Walter Ford, *JFSS*, V (1918), p. 122.
26. "Johnny Randall." Randolph, *Ozark Folksongs*, 1946, I, p. 64(B).
27. "Terence, My Son." Phillips Barry, *JAF*, XVI (1903), pp. 262-63. Also in Barry, *JAF*, XVIII (1905), p. 202(J); and Barry, *JAF*, XXII (1909), p. 75. (Martin)
28. "Johnny Rillus." Arthur Kyle Davis, Jr., *Traditional Ballads of Virginia*, 1929, pp. 557(B) and 107-8.
   d. "Johnny Rilla." Davis, 1929, p. 557(F). (Wood)
29. "Lord Ronald." Greig MSS., III, p. 62, King's College Library, Aberdeen. Also in Gavin Greig and Alexander Keith, *Last Leaves of Traditional Ballads and Ballad Airs*, 1925, p. 15(2); and *Rymour Club Miscellanea*, I (1910), p. 200. (Robb)
30. "Mother, Make my Bed Soon." Helen Hartness Flanders and George Brown, *Vermont Folk-Songs & Ballads*, 1931, pp. 197-98.
31. "Lord Ronald." Alexander Campbell, *Albyn's Anthology*, II [1818], p. 45. Also in Francis James Child, *The English and Scottish Popular Ballads*, 1882-98, I, p. 160(D).
32. "Where Hast Thou Been Today?" S. Baring-Gould and H. F. Sheppard, *A Garland of Country Song*, 1895, pp. 82-83.
33. "Lord Ronald, my Son." Macmath MS., Harvard College Library. Also in Child, *The English and Scottish Popular Ballads*, 1882-98, V, p. 413, and I, pp. 499-500(P).
34. "Oh mak' my Bed easy." Greig MSS., I, p. 190. Also in George Riddell MS., No. 53, National Library of Scotland. (Riddell)

GROUP Ab

35. "Lord Rendal." Sharp MSS., 322/445. Also in Cecil J. Sharp, *JFSS*, II (1905), p. 29(1); and S. Baring-Gould and Cecil J. Sharp, *English Folk-Songs for Schools*, n.d., No. 2, p. 4. (Hooper)
36. "Where were you all day, my own purtee boy?" A. Martin Freeman, *JFSS*, V (1918), p. 245.
37. "Lord Randall." Barry, Eckstorm, and Smyth, *British Ballads from Maine*, 1929, p. 51(D). (Robbins)
38. "The Jealous Lover." John Harrington Cox, *Traditional Ballads Mainly from West Virginia*, 1939, pp. 9-10.
39. "Lord Rendal." Sharp MSS., 792/. (Coles)
40. "Lord Ronald." Greig MSS., III, p. 63. Also in Greig and Keith, *Last Leaves*, 1925, p. 14(1b). (Barron, Roger)
41. "Lord Randal." George Lyman Kittredge (from H. M. Belden), *JAF*, XXX (1917), p. 290. Also in H. M. Belden, *Ballads and Songs*, 1940, pp. 26(C)-27.
42. "Lord Randall." Barry, Eckstorm, and Smyth, *British Ballads from Maine*, 1929, pp. 46-48. (Black)
43. "Lord Ronald." Greig MSS., III, p. 37. Also in Greig and Keith, *Last Leaves*, 1925, p. 14(1c). (Greig)
e. "Firandal." Phillips Barry Dictaphone Cylinders, No. 84, Harvard College Library. (Tracy)
44. "Lord Ronald." Duncan MS., No. 216 (W. Walker). Also in Greig and Keith, 1925, p. 14(1a). (Alexander)
45. "Lord Rendal." Sharp MSS., 452/. (Lock)
46. "Johnny Randolph." David Seneff McIntosh, *Some Representative Southern Illinois Folk-Songs* (Iowa State University, M.A. thesis in music), 1935, pp. 27-29.
47. "Lord Randal." Sharp MSS., 3561/. Also in Sharp and Karpeles, *Appalachians*, 1932, I, p. 43(G). (Maples)
48. "Lord Randal." Creighton and Senior, *Traditional Songs from Nova Scotia*, 1950, pp. 9-10.
49. "Lord Randal." Sharp MSS., 4710/. Also in Sharp and Karpeles, *Appalachians*, 1932, I, p. 44(J). (Boone)
50. "Lord Randal." Sharp MSS., 4093/. (Smith)
51. "Lord Randal." Winston Wilkinson MSS., 1935-36, pp. 24-25(A), University of Virginia.
52. "Lord Randal." Josephine McGill, *Folk-Songs of the Kentucky Mountains*, 1917, pp. 18-22.
53. "Lord Randal." Sharp MSS., 4198/. Also in Sharp and Karpeles, *Appalachians*, 1932, I, p. 43(H). (Maddox)
54. "Lord Randal." Sharp MSS., 4206/3026. Also in Sharp and Karpeles, 1932, I, pp. 43(I)-44. (Wheeler)
55. "Uriar, My Son." McIntosh, *Some Representative Southern Illinois Folk-Songs*, 1935, pp. 30-32.
56. "Lord Randal." Sharp MSS., 4008/2890. Also in Sharp and Karpeles, *Appalachians*, 1932, I, p. 42(F). (Dunagan)
57. "Lord Rendle." Sharp MSS., 363/. Also in Cecil J. Sharp, *JFSS*, II (1905), p. 31(4). (Wyatt)
58. "Lord Randal." Davis, *Traditional Ballads of Virginia*, 1929, pp. 557(N) and 118.
59. "Lord Randal." Sharp MSS., 4592/. (Mitchell)
60. "Where were you all the day, my own pretty boy?" Patrick Weston Joyce, *Old Irish Folk Music and Songs*, 1909, No. 812, pp. 394-95.
61. "Where were you all the day my own pretty boy?" George Petrie, *The Complete Petrie Collection of Irish Music*, edited by Charles Villiers Stanford, 1902-5, No. 330.

GROUP AC

62. "Lord Randal." Sharp MSS., 4463/. Also in Sharp and Karpeles, *Appalachians*, 1932, I, p. 45(M). (Richards)

63. "Lord Randal." Sharp MSS., 4200/. Also in Sharp and Karpeles, 1932, I, p. 44(K). (Campbell)
64. "John Willow, My Son." Davis, *Traditional Ballads of Virginia*, 1929, pp. 556(A) and 106-7.
65. "Air to an old English Ballad." Petrie, *The Complete Petrie Collection of Irish Music*, 1902-5, No. 794.
66. "Sweet William, My Son." Barry MSS., IV, No. 178. Also in Phillips Barry, *JAF*, XVI (1903), p. 260; and Barry, *JAF*, XVIII (1905), pp. 196(B)-97. (Lincoln)

GROUP Ad

67. "Lord Rendal." Sharp MSS., 2646/. (Darling)
68. "Lord Rendal." Sharp MSS., 4258/. Also in Sharp and Karpeles, *Appalachians*, 1932, I, p. 45(L). (Chisholm)
69. "Lord Randal." Wilkinson MSS., 1935-36, p. 26(B).
70. "Lord Randall." Phillips Barry, *JAF*, XXII (1909), pp. 376-77. Also in Barry, Eckstorm, and Smyth, *British Ballads from Maine*, 1929, pp. 58-59. (Welch)
71. "Jo Reynard my Son." Barry Dictaphone Cylinders, No. 95. (Patterson)
72. "Lord Ronald my Son." Barry, Eckstorm, and Smyth, *British Ballads from Maine*, 1929, pp. 55(H)-56. (McGill)
73. "Lord Ronald." Mary O. Eddy, *Ballads and Songs from Ohio*, 1939, p. 19(A).
74. "Lord Randal." Sharp MSS., 3413/2504. Also in Sharp and Karpeles, *Appalachians*, 1932, I, pp. 40(D)-41. (Wells)
75. "Tiranti, My Son." F. C. Brown MS., 16 a 6, Library of Congress, photostat. Text, *The Frank C. Brown Collection of North Carolina Folklore*, II, 1952, p. 39(A).
76. "Lord Randall." Brown MS., 16 a 6. Text, *North Carolina Folklore*, II, 1952, p. 40(B).
77. "Willie Ransome." Brown MS., 16 a 6. Text, *North Carolina Folklore*, II, 1952, p. 40(C).
78. "Ramble, My Son." Barry MSS., IV, No. 105. Also in Phillips Barry, *JAF*, XXII (1909), p. 77. (Conner)
f. "Jimmy Randal." John Jacob Niles, *Ballads, Love-Songs, and Tragic Legends from the Southern Appalachian Mountains*, Schirmer's American Folk-Song Series, Set 20, 1938, pp. 14-15.

APPENDIX A

79. "Lord Rendal." Sharp MSS., 458/. (Hill)
g. "Lord Randall." Phillips Barry, *JAF*, XVI (1903), p. 264; and Barry, *JAF*, XVIII (1905), p. 206(O). (Hopkinson)
80. "Jimmy Randal." Barry Dictaphone Cylinders, No. 163, cutting 4. (Daniels)
81. "Dear Adel my Son." Sidney Robertson, LC Archive of California Folk Songs, rec. 3814 B2 and B3. (George Vinton Graham)

GROUP Ba

82. "Lord Rendal." Sharp MSS., 2873/. (Buchanan)
83. "Lord Rendal." Sharp MSS., 1584/1430-31. (Davy)
84. "Lord Rendal." Sharp MSS., 755/. (Pike)
85. "Lord Ronald." Duncan MS., No. 375 (W. Walker). Also in Greig and Keith, *Last Leaves*, 1925, p. 15(3).
86. "Lord Randal." Helen Creighton and Doreen H. Senior, *Traditional Songs from Nova Scotia*, 1950, pp. 10-11.
87. "Fair Nelson." Barry MSS., IV, No. 90. Also in Phillips Barry, *JAF*, XVIII (1905), pp. 303(R)-4. (Cobleigh)
88. "Lord Ronald." Lucy E. Broadwood, *JFSS*, V (1915), p. 119.

GROUP Bb

89. "Henry My Son." Francis M. Collinson, *JEFDSS*, V (December 1946), pp. 15-16. Also in F. M. Collinson and F. Dillon, *Folk Songs from "Country Magazine,"* 1952, p. 20.

90. "Lord Rendal." Sharp MSS., 350/. Also in Cecil J. Sharp, *JFSS*, II (1905), pp. 29(2)-30 (Perry); in Sharp, *One Hundred English Folksongs*, 1916, p. 44; and in Sharp, *English Folksongs*, Selected Ed., Novello & Co., 1920.

91. "Lord Rendal." Sharp MSS., 393/524. Also in Cecil J. Sharp, *JFSS*, II (1905), p. 30(3). (Pond)

92. "Lord Rendal." Sharp MSS., 353/480-81. (Bond)

93. "Henry my Son." Barry MSS., IV, Nos. 329, 333(BB). (Wedgwood)

94. "Henry, My Son." Eddy, *Ballads and Songs from Ohio*, 1939, p. 21(C).

95. "Henry, My Son." Eddy, 1939, p. 20(B).

96. "Jimmy Randall." Randolph, *Ozark Folksongs*, 1946, I, pp. 66(D)-67.

GROUP BC

97. "King Henry, my Son." Sydney Nicholson, *JFSS*, III (1907), p. 43.

h. "King Henry, my Son." Lucy E. Broadwood, *English Traditional Songs and Carols*, 1908, p. 96.

GROUP C

98. "Willie Doo." Alfred Moffat, *Fifty Traditional Scottish Nursery Rhymes* [1933], p. 5.

99. "The Wee Little Croodin' Doo." Lucy E. Broadwood, *JFSS*, V (1915), p. 118(2).

100. "The Little Wee Croodin' Doo." Anne G. Gilchrist, *JFSS*, V (1915), p. 117(1).

i. "The Poisoned Child." Alton C. Morris, *Folksongs of Florida*, 1950, pp. 247-48.

101. "Croodin' Doo." Sam Eskin, Sierra Record FMI, 7 (Staff Music Corporation, Berkeley, Calif.). (Des Powell)

102. "Lord Rendal; or, Cruden Doo." Sharp MSS., 2412/2191. (Aylmin)

103. "The Croodin Doo." Norah and William Montgomerie, *Scottish Nursery Rhymes*, 1946, pp. 140-41.

TUNES WITH TEXTS

GROUP Aa

1. [Lord Ronald my son]

Johnson [1792], repr. 1853, IV, No. 327, p. 337. Collected by Robert Burns, as sung in Ayrshire.

p I/M

This is the copy transmitted by Robert Burns as from Ayrshire tradition. It has been fairly frequently reprinted (e.g., R. A. Smith [1820-24], III, p. 58; R. Chambers, 1844, p. 21; G. F. Graham, *Songs of Scotland*, 1848 and subsequently [e.g., 1887, p. 47]; Maver, 1866, p. 18 [No. 35, with a second strain]); and it has received abundant but inconclusive annotation (e.g., especially, Graham, *loc.cit.*, and J. Glen, *Early Scottish Melodies*, 1900, pp. 87-89, 165). The gist of Glen's argument, which catches up previous discussion, is that "Lochaber" may be older than "Lord Ronald" and therefore that Burns may well be wrong in thinking the latter the original tune; and that both derive from "King James March to Ireland" (*sic*), which he prints from the Blaikie MS. of 1692.

O where hae ye been Lord Ronald, my son?
O where hae ye been, Lord Ronald my son?
I hae been wi' my sweetheart, mother, make my bed soon,
For I'm weary wi' the hunting and fain wad lie down.

What got ye frae your sweetheart Lord Ronald, my son.
What got ye frae your sweetheart Lord Ronald, my son.

I hae got deadly poison, mother, make my bed soon;
For life is a burden that soon I'll lay down.

2. [Lord Randall; or, "Fair Elson"]

Barry, *JAF*, XVIII (1905), pp. 197(C)-98. Also in Barry, *JAF*, XVI (1903), p. 263; and *ibid.*, XXIII (1910), p. 444(6th). From A. M., 1903; "as sung by my mother, who would be more than one hundred years old, if living."

a I/M (compass of sixth)

Barry's copy came through "Notes and Queries" in the *Boston Transcript*, July 11, 1903. The contributor's name was withheld.

1. "Oh, where have you been, Fair Elson, my son?
   Oh, where have you been, my own dearest one?"
   "I've been out a-courting, mother make my bed soon,
   For I'm poisoned to my heart, and I fain would lie down."

2. "Oh, what have you been eating, Fair Elson, my son?
   Oh, what have you been eating, my own dearest one?"
   "I've been eating eels, mother make my bed soon,
   For I'm poisoned to my heart, and I fain would lie down."

3. "What color were those eels, Fair Elson, my son?
   What color were those eels, my own dearest one?"

"They were black, white, and yellow, mother make my bed soon,
For I'm poisoned to my heart, and I fain would lie down."

4. "What you will to your father, Fair Elson, my son?
What you will to your father, my own dearest one?"
"A black suit of mourning, mother make my bed soon,
For I'm poisoned to my heart, and I fain would lie down."

5. "What you will to your brother, Fair Elson, my son?
What you will to your brother, my own dearest one?"
"A black yoke of oxen, mother make my bed soon,
For I'm poisoned to my heart, and I fain would lie down."

3. [Lord Randal]

Sharp MSS., 3130/?. Also in Sharp and Karpeles, 1932, I,
p. 41(E). Sung by Florence McKinney, Habersham County,
Ga., June 2, 1910. Collected by Olive Dame Campbell.

m π¹

Sharp and Karpeles, 1932, transpose to F.

1. O where have you been, Lord Randal my son?
O where have you been, my only son?
I've been a-courting, mother, O make my bed soon,
For I'm sick at the heart and fain would lie down.

2. What did you have for your supper . . .
A cup of cold poison.

3. What would you leave your father . . .
My wagon and oxen. . . .

4. What would you leave your mother . . .
My coach and six horses. . . .

5. What would you leave your sweetheart . . .
Ten thousand weights of brimstone to burn her bones brown,
For she was the cause of my lying down.

4. [Lord Randall; or, "Orlando"]

Barry, *JAF*, XVIII (1905), p. 204(L). Also in Barry, *JAF*,
XXIII (1910), p. 443(3rd). Sung by R. P. U(tter), Cambridge, Mass., May 6, 1904; learned in Charlestown, N.H.

m I/M

"What had you for supper, Orlando, my son?
What had you for supper, my sweet little one?"

"Striped eels, fried in batter, mother make my bed soon,
For I am so weary, I fain would lie down."

In JAF, XXIII (1910), p. 443 (3rd), Barry prints this variant in
3/4. The second half is made out of the same stuff as the carol,
"Bethlehem."

"You're pizened, you're pizened, Orlando, my son!
You're pizened, you're pizened, my sweet little one!"
. . . .
. . . .

5. [Lord Randall]

Barry, *JAF*, XVIII (1905), pp. 203(K)-4. Also in Barry,
JAF, XXIII (1910), p. 443 (2nd). Sung by H. E. Krehbiel,
New York, 1905; learned in Pomfret, Conn.

a I/M (compass of sixth)

1. "Oh, where have you been, Taranty, my son?
Oh, where have you been, my dear little one?"
"To see my grandmother, mother make my bed soon,
For I'm sick at the heart, and faint to lie down."

2. "What had you for supper, Taranty, my son?
What had you for supper, my dear little one?"
Eels, fried in batter, mother make my bed soon,
For I'm sick at the heart, and faint to lie down."

3. "What was their color, Taranty, my son?
What was their color, my dear little one?"
"Green striped with yellow, mother make my bed soon,
For I'm sick at the heart, and faint to lie down."

4. "What will you leave your mother, Taranty, my son?
What will you leave your mother, my dear little one?"
"A coach and six horses, mother make my bed soon,
For I'm sick at the heart, and faint to lie down."

5. "What will you leave your sister, Taranty, my son?
What will you leave your sister, my dear little one?"
"A box of rich jewels, mother make my bed soon,
For I'm sick at the heart, and faint to lie down."

6. "What will you leave your brother, Taranty, my son?
What will you leave your brother, my dear little one?"
"A suit of fine clothes, mother make my bed soon,
For I'm sick at the heart, and faint to lie down."

7. "What will you leave your grandmother, Taranty, my son?
What will you leave your grandmother, my dear little one?"
"A rope for to hang her, mother make my bed soon,
For I'm sick at the heart, and faint to lie down."

8. "Where shall I make it, Taranty, my son?
Where shall I make it, my dear little one?"
"In a corner of the churchyard, mother make my bed soon,
For I'm so sick at the heart, and faint to lie down."

6. "Durango"

Smith, *Musical Quarterly*, II (January 1916), p. 127. Text,
The Crimson Rambler, Tonkawa, Okla., December 1913;
transcribed in Barry MSS., III.

a I/M (compass of sixth)

What had you for supper, Durango, my son?
What had you for supper, my darling one?
An eel fried in butter, mother make my bed soon,
For I'm faint and I'm weary, and I want to lie down.

What will you leave mother, Durango, my son?
What will you leave mother, my darling one?
A coach and fine horses, mother make my bed soon,
For I'm faint and I'm weary, and I want to lie down.

What will you leave sister, Durango, my son?
What will you leave sister, my darling one?
A box of fine jewels, mother make my bed soon,
For I'm faint and I'm weary, and I'm almost gone.

What will you leave grandmother, Durango, my son?
What will you leave grandmother, my darling one?
A rope for to hang her, mother make my bed soon,
For I'm faint and I'm weary, and I'm gone, gone, gone.

7. [Lord Rendal]

Sharp MSS., 4276/. Sung by Mrs. Lola Harris, Nellysford,
Va., May 23, 1918.

p I/M

O where have you been, John Willie my son?
O where have you been, my own little one?
I've been out courting, Mother make my bed soon,
Have a pain at my heart and want to lie down.

8. "Lorendo"

Chappell, 1939, p. 14. Sung by Charles Tillett, Wanchese,
N.C., text, 1934; tune, 1935.

a π¹

1. Where have you been, Lorendo, Lorendo, my son?
Where have you been, Lorendo, my dear little one?
I've been to see my sweetheart, mother, make my bed soon,
I am sick to my heart and I wish to lie down.

2. What did you eat for supper, Lorendo, my son?
What did you eat for supper, my dear little one?
A dish of fried eels, mother, pray make my bed soon,
I am sick to my heart and I wish to lie down.

3. What do you will your mother, Lorendo, my son?
What do you will your mother, my dear little one?
My house and plantation, mother, make my bed soon,
I am sick to my heart and I wish to lie down.

4. What do you will your brother, Lorendo, my son?
What do you will your brother, my dear little one?
My horse, bridle, and saddle, mother, make my bed soon,
I am sick to my heart and I wish to lie down.

5. What do you will your sister, Lorendo, my son?
What do you will your sister, my dear little one?
My gold watch and bracelet, mother, make my bed soon,
I am sick to my heart and I wish to lie down.

6. What do you will your sweetheart, Lorendo, my son?
What do you will your sweetheart, my dear little one?
The keys of hell's gate, mother, pray make my bed soon,
For she was the cause of my sad lying down.

9. "Tarranty, My Son"

Barry, *BFSSNE*, No. 1 (1930), p. 4. Sung by Miss S. H.
Hussey, Vineland, N.J., May 8, 1907; learned in Duchess
County, N.Y., sixty years earlier.

a I/Ly

"Oh, where have you been, Tarranty, my son?
Oh, where have you been, my dear little one?"
"I have been to see granny, mother make my bed soon,
For I'm sick to the heart and I fain would lie down."

"Oh, what did she give you, Tarranty, my son?
Oh, what did she give you, my dear little one?"
"Striped eels, fried in butter, mother, make my bed soon,
For I'm sick to the heart and I fain would lie down."

10. [Lord Randall]

Barry, *JAF*, XVIII (1905), p. 199(E). Sung by M. L. J.
(Maria L. Johnson), Lynn, Mass., November 5, 1904.

a π[1] (−VI) (compass of fifth)

"Oh, where have you been to, Teronto, my son?
Oh, where have you been to, my own darling one?"
"I've been to see Mary, mother make my bed soon,
For I'm sick in the heart, and I long to lie down."

"What d' she give you for supper, Teronto, my son?
What d' she give you for supper, my own darling one?"
"Eels, fried in batter, mother make my bed soon,
For I'm sick in the heart, and I long to lie down."

"You're pizened, you're pizened, Teronto, my son!
You're pizened, you're pizened, my own darling one!"

. . . .
. . . .

"What'll you give to your Mary, Teronto, my son?
What'll you give to your Mary, my own darling one?"
"A halter to hang her, mother make my bed soon,
For I'm sick in the heart, and I long to lie down."

11. "Tyranty, My Son"

Barry, Eckstorm, and Smyth, 1929, pp. 69(O)-70. Sung by
George Turner, Malden, Mass., March 12, 1929; learned
from his mother and grandmother eighty years earlier.

a I/M (−VI) (compass of fifth)

"Oh, where have you been, Tyranty, my son?
Oh, where have you been, my dear little one?"
"I've been to see grandmother, mother, make my bed soon,
For I'm sick at my heart, and I'm faint to lie down."

"What did you have for dinner, Tyranty, my son?
What did you have for dinner, my dear little one?"
"I had eels, fried in butter, mother, make my bed soon,
For I'm sick at my heart, and I'm faint to lie down."

"Where did she get the eels, Tyranty, my son?
Where did she get them, my dear little one?"
"Under the haystack, mother, make my bed soon,
For I'm sick at my heart, and I'm faint to lie down."

12. [Lord Randall]

Barry, *JAF*, XVIII (1905), pp. 201(I)-2. Sung by J. E. W.,
Boston, Mass., September 16, 1904.

a I/M (compass of sixth)

The identical tune, with other words, is given by Linscott (*Folk
Songs of Old New England*, 1939, p. 191: "Dirante, My Son") as
traditional in the Kelley family of West Harwich, Mass., who brought
it from Ireland. The tune has escaped my search in Barry's MSS. at
Harvard, and his singer is unidentified.

"Oh, where have you been Tyrante, my son?
Oh, where have you been, my dear little one?" (poor?)
                                               (sweet?)
"I have been to my grandmother's, mother make my bed
                                                     soon,
For I'm sick at the heart, and would fain lay me doon."

"Oh, what gat you to eat, Tyrante, my son?
Oh, what gat you to eat, my dear little one?"
"Striped eels, fried in batter, mother make my bed soon,
For I'm sick at the heart, and would fain lay me doon."

Oh, where are your blood-hounds, Tyrante, my son?
Oh, where are your blood-hounds, my dear little one?"

"Oh, they swelled up and burst, mother make my bed soon,
For I'm sick at the heart, and would fain lay me doon."

"Oh, I fear you are poisoned, Tyrante, my son!
Oh, I fear you are poisoned, my dear little one!"
"Oh, yes! I am poisoned, mother make my bed soon,
For I'm sick at the heart, and would fain lay me doon."

"Oh, where shall I make your bed, Tyrante, my son?
Where shall I make your bed, my dear little one?"
"Make my bed in the kirkyard, mother make my bed soon,
For I'm sick at the heart, and would fain lay me doon."

13. [Lord Randal]

Sharp MSS., 3200/2344. Also in Sharp and Karpeles, 1932,
I, p. 38(A). Sung by Mrs. Dora Shelton, Allanstand, N.C.,
August 2, 1916.

a π¹

Sharp and Karpeles, 1932, transpose to E major.

What you will to your father, Jimmy Randolph my son?
What you will to your father, my oldest, dearest one?
My horses, my buggies, Mother, make my bed soon,
For I am sick-hearted and I want to lie down.

What you will to your brothers . . .
My mules and waggons.

What you will to your sisters . . .
My gold and my silver.

14. [Lord Randal]

Sharp MSS., 3205/2350. Also in Sharp and Karpeles, 1932,
I, p. 38(B). Sung by Mrs. Mary Sands, Allanstand, N.C.,
August 3, 1916.

a π¹

This is transposed to E major in the 1932 printing.

1. What did you eat for your supper, Jimmy Randal my son?
   What did you eat for your supper, my own dearest one?
   Cold poison, cold poultry. Mother, make my bed soon,
   For I am sick-hearted and I want to lie down.

2. What will you will to your mother . . .
   My gold and my silver.

3. What will you will to your father . . .
   My mules and my wagons.

4. What will you will to your sister . . .
   My land and my houses.

5. What will you will to your brothers . . .
   My trunks and my clothing.

6. What will you will to your sweetheart . . .
   Two tushes bullrushes and them both parched brown,
   For she is the cause of my lying down.

15. "Lord Rendle"

Sharp MSS., 335/465. Sung by Mrs. Eliza Hutchings, Langport, Somerset, August 19, 1904.

a I

Where have you been, my fair pretty one?
Where have you been, Rendle, my son?
I've been a fishing, mother make my bed soon.
I am sick to my heart and I fain would lie down.

Where have you been fishing to, my pretty one?
Where have you been fishing to, Rendle my son?
Down on the Scilly banks, mother, make my bed soon,
I am sick to my heart and I fain would lie down.

What have you been eating, etc.
Eels and eels' broth, etc.

16. [Lord Randall]

Barry, Eckstorm, and Smyth, 1929, p. 53(F). Sung by Mrs.
Susie C. Young, Brewer, Me., 1896; traditional in her family. Melody recorded by George Herzog.

a I/M

"O where have you been, O Billy my son?
O where have you been, my own darling one?"
"A-hunting and fishing, mother; make my bed soon,
For I'm sick to the heart and I fain would lie down."

The copy is as noted by Herzog, except that his signature, "4/4," has been altered to 6/8, and the pitch is raised.

"What have you been eating, O Billy my son?
What have you been eating, my own darling one?"
"Fried eels and a serpent, mother; make my bed soon,
For I'm sick to the heart and I fain would lie down."

"What's willed to your brother, O Billy my son?
What's willed to your brother, my own darling one?"
"A suit of fine clothing; mother, make my bed soon,
For I'm sick to the heart and I fain would lie down."

"What's willed to your sister, O Billy my son?
What's willed to your sister, my own darling one?"
"A rope for to hang her; mother, make my bed soon,
For I'm sick to the heart and I fain would lie down."

17. [Lord Randal]

Sharp MSS., 3331/2438. Also in Sharp and Karpeles, 1932, I, pp. 39(C)-40. Sung by Emma Hensley (13), Carmen, N.C., August 28, 1916.

m π[1]

Sharp and Karpeles, 1932, transpose to E major.

1. It's what did you eat for your breakfast, Jimmy Randal my son?

It's what did you eat for your breakfast, my own dearest son?
It's cold pie and cold coffee. Mother, make my bed soon,
For I'm sick at the heart and I want to lie down.

2. It's what will you will to your father . . .
My mules and my wagons.

3. It's what will you will to your brother . . .
My house and plantation.

4. It's what will you will to your sister . . .
My gold and my silver.

5. It's what will you will to your mother . . .
My trunk and my clothing.

6. It's what will you will to your sweetheart . . .
Bulrushes, bulrushes, and them half parched brown,
For she's the whole cause of my lying down.

7. Where do you want to be buried . . .
By my little baby.

18. [Lord Rendal]

Sharp MSS., 420/545. Also in Sharp, *JFSS*, II (1905), p. 31(5). Sung by Miss Doveton Brown, Clevedon, September 11, 1904.

m π[1]

O where have you been to, Rendal my son?
O where have you been to, my handsome young man?
Hunting, mother, hunting, O make my bed soon,
For I'm sick at the heart and I fain would lie down.

Where had you your dinner, Rendal my son?
I dined with my love, O make, etc.

What had you for dinner, Rendal my son?
Eels boiled in broth, O make, etc.

O where are your blood hounds, Rendal my son?
They swelled and they died, O make, etc.

I fear you are poisoned, Rendal my son?
Yes, yes, I am poisoned, O make, etc.

Sharp's MS. note: "Sung by Miss Doveton Brown of Clevedon, who learned it when a child from her mother, who had it from *her* grandmother, Elizabeth Grossman, who was born in 1784."

19. "William, my Son"

Editor, from E. S. McLellan, Jr., Berkeley, Calif., 1933; learned from his mother, who learned it from her uncle, Captain John Wilson, a Confederate soldier, of Roane County, W.Va.

p I/M

"O what did you have for supper, William my son?
O what did you have for supper, my pretty sweet one?"
"Fried eel and fresh butter, Mother, make my bed soon,
For I'm sick to the heart and could freely lie down."

20. [Lord Rendal]

Sharp MSS., 4315/. Sung by Mrs. J. L. Long, Villamont, Va., June 4, 1918.

p π¹

Cf. with Sharp, *One Hundred English Folksongs*, 1916, p. 62, No. 27: "Lamkin" (Child 93).

Jim Riley, Jim Riley, Jim Riley my son
Where have you been wand'ring, my dear little one?
Through bushes, through briers, I'll make my bed down,
So sick in my heart I wants to lie down.

21. "Johnny Randolph"

Randolph, I, 1946, p. 64(A). Sung by Lisbeth Hayes, Fayetteville, Ark., January 12, 1920.

p I/Ly (compass of sixth)

A copy nearly identical was printed by Randolph, *Ozark Mountain Folks*, 1932, p. 215, as from Zeke Langley.

Oh where have you been, Johnny Randolph, my son?
Oh where have you wandered, my dear little one?
I et at my true love's, oh make my bed soon,
I am sick to my heart, an' I want to lay down.

Oh what did she give you, Johnny Randolph, my son?
Oh what did she give you, my dear little one?
She give me black pizen, oh make my bed soon,
I think I will die, an' I want to lay down.

Oh what do you will to your sweetheart, my son,
Oh what do you will her, my dear little one?
Hell's fire an' hot brimstone, oh make my bed soon,
For I'm sick to my heart, an' I want to lay down.

22. [Lord Rendal]

Sharp MSS., 1883/1710. Sung by Mrs. Jane Gulliford, Combe Florey, September 10, 1908.

p I

Where have you been a-roving my only one?
Where have you been a-roving Henry my son?
I've been roving for my sweetheart
Mother make my bed soon
For I'm sick to my heart and I need to lie down.

What did you have for supper my only one?
What did you have for supper Henry my son?
I had spickle-belly fishes mother
Make my bed soon
For I'm sick to my heart and I need to lie down.

23. "Sweet Nelson"

Barry, *JAF*, XVIII (1905), p. 198(D). Also in Barry, Eckstorm, and Smyth, 1929, pp. 57(I)-58. Sung by H. J. C. (Mrs. W. Josephine Collins), Concord, N.H., December 3, 1904; "as sung half a century ago at neighborly gatherings in Hebron, Maine."

1. "Oh, where d'ye go courting, Sweet Nelson, my son?
   Oh, where d'ye go courting, my sweet pretty one?"
   "I went to see Polly, mother, make my bed soon,
   For I'm sick at my heart, and I long to lie down."

2. "What d'ye have for your supper, Sweet Nelson, my son?
   What d'ye have for your supper, my sweet pretty one?"
   "Speckled eels fried in fat, mother, make my bed soon,
   For I'm sick at my heart, and I long to lie down."

a π¹

3. "What d'ye leave to your father, Sweet Nelson, my son?
What d'ye leave to your father, my sweet pretty one?"
"My farm and farming tools, mother, make my bed soon,
For I'm sick at my heart, and I long to lie down."

4. "What d'ye leave to your sister, Sweet Nelson, my son?
What d'ye leave to your sister, my sweet pretty one?"
"My purse and my jewels, mother, make my bed soon,
For I'm sick at my heart, and I long to lie down."

5. "What d'ye leave to your Polly, Sweet Nelson, my son?
What d'ye leave to your Polly, my sweet pretty one?"
"The rope and the gallows. Oh, make my bed soon!
For I'm sick at my heart, and I long to lie down."

6. "Oh, where shall I make it, Sweet Nelson, my son?
Oh, where shall I make it, my sweet pretty one?"
"Yonder in the churchyard, mother, make my bed soon,
For I'm sick at my heart, and I long to lie down."

24. "Lord Ronald"

Shuldham-Shaw, *JEFDSS*, VI (December 1949), p. 15.
Sung by James Laurenson, Fetlar, Shetland Islands, September 4, 1947.

p π¹

What had you for supper Lord Ronald my son,
What had you for supper, my jolly young man?
I had fishes for supper, go make my bed soon,
Sick at the heart, and fain would lie doon.

What leave to your mother, Lord Ronald, my son,
What leave to your mother, my jolly young man,
My watch and my chain, go make my bed soon,
Sick at the heart and fain would lie doon.

What leave to your sweetheart, Lord Ronald, my son
What leave to your sweetheart, my jolly young man.
A rope and a tree, and hanged she shall be
And all for the sake of poisoning me.

25. "Three Drops of Poison"

Ford, *JFSS*, V (1918), p. 122. Sung by Mr. Kemp (c. 75),
an agricultural laborer, Elstead, Surrey, 1907.

a I

"Where are you a-going, my own darling boy?
Where are you a-going, my comfort and joy?"
"Down in yonder meadow, where the violets do grow,
I've a trouble down there, where the violets do grow."

"What will you have for breakfast, my own darling boy?
What will you have for breakfast, my comfort and joy?"
"Three drops of strong poison; go make my bed soon,
I've a pain in my heart, and want to lie down."

"What will you have for foot-stool, my own darling boy?
What will you have for foot-stool, my comfort and joy?"
"A stone at my head, and a stone at my feet,
That I might lie, and take a long sleep."

26. "Johnny Randall"

Randolph, I, 1946, p. 64(B). Sung by William Lewis, Anderson, Mo., October 4, 1927.

a π¹

Oh where have you been, Johnny Randall, my son?
Oh where have you wandered, my dear little one?
I've been with my true love, oh make my bed soon,
I've a pain at my heart and I want to lie down.

27. "Terence, My Son"

Barry, *JAF*, XVI (1903), pp. 262-63. Sung by Mrs. Mary R.
Martin, Newtonville, Mass.; traditional in her family.

a I/M (compass of sixth)

Barry reprints this variant in *JAF*, XVIII (1905), p. 202(J), and XXII (1909), p. 75, but in 3/4 time and with a final on III.

1. "Oh, where have you been to-day, Terence, my son?
Oh, where have you been to-day, my pretty little one?"
"I've been to see my grandame, mother, make my bed soon,
For I'm sick at the heart, and I fain would lie down."

2. "Oh, what did she give you to eat, Terence, my son?
Oh, what did she give you to eat, my pretty little one?"
"Fresh-water potted eels, mother, make my bed soon,
For I'm sick at the heart, and I fain would lie down."

3. "Oh, what will you give your father, Terence, my son?
Oh, what will you give your father, my pretty little one?"
"One half of my fortune, mother, make my bed soon,
For I'm sick at the heart, and I fain would lie down."

4. "And what will you give your mother, Terence, my son?
And what will you give your mother, my pretty little one?"
"Ten thousand sweet kisses, mother, make my bed soon,
For I'm sick at the heart, and I fain would lie down."

5. "And what will you give your brother, Terence, my son?
And what will you give your brother, my pretty little one?"
"'T' other half of my fortune, mother, make my bed soon,
For I'm sick at the heart, and I fain would lie down."

6. "And what will you give your sister, Terence, my son?
And what will you give your sister, my pretty little one?"
"A thousand kind wishes, mother, make my bed soon,
For I'm sick at the heart, and I fain would lie down."

7. "And what will you give your grandame, Terence, my son?
And what will you give your grandame, my pretty little one?"
"A rope for to hang her, mother, make my bed soon,
For I'm sick at the heart, and I fain would lie down."

28. "Johnny Rillus"

Davis, 1929, p. 557(B); text, pp. 107-8. Sung by Mrs. Emily
Via, Stage Junction, Va., November 3, 1920. Collected by
John Stone.

a I/M (compass of sixth)

1. "Where have you been, Johnny Rillus, my son,
Where have you been, my dearest little one?"
"I've been out a-courting, mother, make my bed soon;
I've a pain in my heart and I want to lie down."

2. "Have you been to your supper, Johnny Rillus, my son,
Have you been to your supper, my dearest little one?"
"Yes, been to my supper, mother, make my bed soon;
I've a pain in my heart and I want to lie down."

3. "What did you have for your supper, Johnny Rillus, my son,
What did you have for your supper, my dearest little one?"
"Fresh eel and butter, mother, make my bed soon;
I've a pain in my heart and I want to lie down."

4. "What color were your eels, Johnny Rillus, my son,
What color were your eels, my dearest little one?"
"White and black spotted, mother, make my bed soon;
I've a pain in my heart and I want to lie down."

5. "You are dying, Johnny Rillus, my dearest little son,
You are dying, Johnny Rillus, my dearest little one."
"Yes, dying, mother; mother, make my bed soon;
I've a pain in my heart and I want to lie down."

6. "What will you leave to your sister, Johnny Rillus, my son,
What will you leave to your sister, my dearest little one?"
"A fine horse and saddle, mother, make my bed soon;
I've a pain in my heart and I want to lie down."

7. "What will you leave to your mother, Johnny Rillus, my son,
What will you leave to your mother, my dearest little one?"
"Sweet fields in heaven, mother, make my bed soon;
I've a pain in my heart and I want to lie down."

8. "What will you leave to your sweetheart, Johnny Rillus, my
son,
What will you leave to your sweetheart, my dearest little
one?"
"Brimstone and fire, mother, make my bed soon;
I've a pain in my heart and I want to lie down."

9. "Where do you want to be buried, Johnny Rillus, my son,
Where do you want to be buried, my dearest little one?"
"Down in the green meadow where the grass grows so tall,
Where my sweetheart can see me, for she was the cause of
it all."

29. [Lord Ronald]

Greig MSS., III, p. 62. Also in Greig and Keith, 1925,
p. 15(2); and *Rymour Club Miscellanea*, I (1910), p. 200.
Sung by Alexander Robb, New Deer, Aberdeenshire, 1907.

m π¹

In *Rymour Club Miscellanea*, Keith notes that it is related to the
second strain of "The Braes o' Strathblane," popular in Aberdeenshire.

O whare hae ye been, Lord Ronald my son?
O whare hae ye been, my handsome young man?

30. "Mother, Make my Bed Soon"

Flanders and Brown, 1931, pp. 197-98. Sung by Paul Lorette, Manchester Centre, Vt., 1930. From *Vermont Folk-Songs and Ballads*, edited by Helen Hartness Flanders and George Brown; copyright 1931 by Arthur Wallace Peach.

p I, ending on *V*

1. "Where have you been, my sweet, my love?
   Oh, where have you been, my sweet loving one?"
   "I've been to see Polly, Mother.
   Make my bed soon, for I'm sick to my heart
   And fain to lie down."

2. "What will you give to your sister, my son?
   What will you give to your sweet loving one?"
   "My black mourning gown, Mother.
   Make my bed soon, for I'm sick to my heart
   And fain to lie down."

3. "What will you give to your father, my son?
   Oh, what will you give him, my sweet loving one?"
   "I will give him my farm, Mother.
   Make my bed soon, for I'm sick to my heart
   And fain to lie down."

4. "What will you give to your brother, my son?
   Oh, what will you give him, my sweet loving one?"
   "My black horse and bride,* Mother.
   Make my bed soon, for I'm sick to my heart
   And fain to lie down."

5. "What will you give to your mother, my son?
   Oh, what will you give to her, my sweet loving one?"
   "I'll give nothing at all Mother.
   Make my bed soon, for I'm sick to my heart
   And fain to lie down."

6. "What will you give to your Polly, my son?
   Oh, what will you give her, my sweet loving one?"
   "Hell and banish, Mother.
   Make my bed soon, for I'm sick to my heart
   And fain to lie down."

7. "Where will I make your bed, my son?
   Oh, where will I make it, my sweet loving one?"
   "In the barren ground, Mother.
   Make my bed soon, for I'm sick to my heart
   And fain to lie down."

* *or* bridle.

31. [Lord Ronald]

Campbell, II, [1818], p. 45. Also in Child, 1882-98, I, p. 160(D), as from Scott, 1803, p. 292. Sung by Sophia Scott, the daughter of Sir Walter Scott.

a D/M

1. "O where hae ye been, Lord Randal, my son?
   O where hae ye been, my handsome young man?"
   "I hae been to the wild wood; mother, make my bed soon,
   For I'm weary wi hunting, and fain wald lie down."

2. "Where gat ye your dinner, Lord Randal, my son?
   Where gat ye your dinner, my handsome young man?"
   "I din'd wi my true-love; mother, make my bed soon,
   For I'm weary wi hunting, and fain wald lie down."

3. "What gat ye to your dinner, Lord Randal, my son?
   What gat ye to your dinner, my handsome young man?"
   "I gat eels boild in broo; mother, make my bed soon,
   For I'm weary wi hunting, and fain wald lie down."

4. "What became of your bloodhounds, Lord Randal, my son?
   What became of your bloodhounds, my handsome young man?"
   "O they swelld and they died; mother, make my bed soon,
   For I'm weary wi hunting, and fain wald lie down."

5. "Oh I fear ye are poisond, Lord Randal, my son!
   O I fear ye are poisond, my handsome young man!"
   "O yes! I am poisond; mother, make my bed soon,
   For I'm sick at the heart, and I fain wald lie down."

32. [Where Hast Thou Been Today?]

Baring-Gould and Sheppard, 1895, pp. 82-83. Sung by Miss F. J. Adams; learned from her Devonshire nurse, near Kingsbridge, c. 1825.

p Min. (inflected *VI* and *VII*)

The accidentals may be editorial in this copy. The original timing was 6/8.

1. Where hast thou been to-day,
      Jacky, my son?
   Where hast thou been to-day,
      My honey man?
   I have been a-courting, mother,
      O make my bed soon;
   For that I'm sick to heart, mother,
      Fain would lie down.

2. Where shall I make it to, etc.
   Lowly in the churchyard, mother, etc.

3. What didst thou eat this day, etc.
   Nothing but a little fish, etc.

4. Who gave the fish to thee, etc.
   'Twas my pretty sweetheart, mother, etc.

5. What wilt thou leave thy mother, etc.
   All my money I leave thee, mother, etc.

6. What wilt thou leave thy father, etc.
   All my land I leave him, mother, etc.

7. What wilt thou leave thy sweetheart, etc.
   Hempen rope to hang her, mother, etc.

33. "Lord Ronald, my Son"

Macmath MS. Also in Child, 1882-98, V, p. 413; text, I,
pp. 499-500(P). From William Macmath of Edinburgh;
learned from his aunt, Jane Webster, formerly of Airds of
Kells, who learned it from a nursemaid at Airds, c. 1830.

m Æ/D

1. "Where hae ye been a' day, Lord Ronald, my son?
   Where hae ye been a'day, my handsome young one?"
   "I've been in the wood hunting; mother, make my bed soon,
   For I am weary, weary hunting, and fain would lie doun."

2. "O where did you dine, Lord Ronald, my son?
   O where did you dine, my handsome young one?"
   "I dined with my sweetheart; mother, make my bed soon,
   For I am weary, weary hunting, and fain would lie doun."

3. "What got you to dine on, Lord Ronald, my son?
   What got you to dine on, my handsome young one?"
   "I got eels boiled in water that in heather doth run,
   And I am weary, weary hunting, and fain would lie doun."

4. "What did she wi the broo o them, Lord Ronald, my son?
   What did she wi the broo o them, my handsome young one?"

"She gave it to my hounds for to live upon,
And I am weary, weary hunting, and fain would lie doun."

5. "Where are your hounds now, Lord Ronald, my son?
   Where are your hounds now, my handsome young one?"
   'They are a' swelled and bursted, and sae will I soon,
   And I am weary, weary hunting, and fain would lie doun."

6. "What will you leave your father, Lord Ronald, my son?
   What will you leave your father, my handsome young one?"
   "I'll leave him my lands for to live upon,
   And I am weary, weary hunting, and fain would lie doun."

7. "What will you leave your brother, Lord Ronald, my son?
   What will you leave your brother, my handsome young
      one?"
   "I'll leave him my gallant steed for to ride upon,
   And I am weary, weary hunting, and fain would lie doun."

8. "What will you leave your sister, Lord Ronald, my son?
   What will you leave your sister, my handsome young one?"
   "I'll leave her my gold watch for to look upon,
   And I am weary, weary hunting, and fain would lie doun."

9. "What will you leave your mother, Lord Ronald, my son?
   What will you leave your mother, my handsome young
      one?"
   "I'll leave her my Bible for to read upon,
   And I am weary, weary hunting, and fain would lie doun."

10. "What will you leave your sweetheart, Lord Ronald, my
       son?
    What will you leave your sweetheart, my handsome young
       one?"
    "I'll leave her the gallows-tree for to hang upon,
    It was her that poisoned me;" and so he fell doun.

34. "Oh mak' my Bed easy"

Greig MSS., I, p. 190. Also in Riddell MS., No. 53. Sung by
George Riddell, Rosehearty.

p Æ/D

Oh mak' my bed easy
Oh mak' my bed soon
For oh but I'm weary
And fain wad lie down.

GROUP Ab

35. [Lord Rendal]

Sharp MSS., 322/445-46. Also in Sharp, JFSS, II (1905),
p. 29(1); and Baring-Gould and Sharp, English Folk Songs
for Schools, n.d., No. 2, p. 4. Sung by Mrs. Louie Hooper,
Hambridge, August 18, 1904.

a I/Ly

1. "Where were you all day, my own purtee boy?
   Where were you all day, my true loving joy?"
   "I was fishing and fowling, mother, dress my bed soon;
   I am sick in my heart, and I'd want to lie down."

2. "What did you get from your wife, my own purtee boy?
   What did you get from your wife, my true loving joy?"
   "I got bread and cold poison, mother, dress my bed soon;
   I am sick in my heart, and I'd want to lie down."

3. "What'll you lave your wife?" [as before]
   "The gates of Hell opened."

4. "What'll you lave your father?"
   "My coach and four horses."

5. "What'll you lave your brother?"
   "The keys of my stores."

6. "What'll you lave your sister?"
   "My cows and farm."

7. "What'll you lave your mother?"
   "The world is wide."

8. "Where will you be buried?"
   "In the church of Kilkenny, and make my hole deep,
   A stone to my head and a flag to my feet,
   And lave me down easy, and I'll take a long sleep."

O where have you been, Rendal my son,
O where have you been, my sweet pretty one?
I've been to my sweetheart's, O make my bed soon, ⎫
I'm sick to my heart and fain would lay down.   ⎬ bis
                                                 ⎭

O what should she give you, Rendal, my son,
O what should she give you, my pretty one
She give me some eels, O make my bed soon,   ⎫
I'm sick to my heart and fain would lay down. ⎬ bis
                                              ⎭

O what colour was them,* Rendal my son,
O what colour was them, my sweet pretty one?
They was spickèd and sparkèd,† O make my bed soon,
I'm sick to my heart and fain would lay down.

O where did she get them, Rendal my son,
O where did she get them, my sweet pretty one?
From hedges and ditches, O make, etc.
I'm sick to my heart and fain would lay down.

O they was strong poison, Rendal my son,
O where did she get them, my sweet pretty one?
You'll die, you'll die, Rendal my son.
You'll die, you'll die, my sweet pretty one.

* Sharp, *JFSS*, has "they."
† Sharp, *JFSS*, has "spick-it and spark-it."

36. "Where were you all day, my own purtee boy?"

Freeman, *JFSS*, V (1915), p. 245. Sung by Conchubhar Ó Cochláin, a laborer, Ballyvourney, County Cork, October 5, 1914.

a I

37. [Lord Randall]

Barry, Eckstorm, and Smyth, 1929, p. 51(D). Sung by Mrs. Rose Robbins, Northeast Harbor, Maine, September 1928. Melody recorded by George Herzog.

a I

"Oh, where have you been, fair Randall, my son?
O where have you been my own loving one?"
". . . . ; mother, make my bed soon,
For I'm poisoned to the heart and I fain would lie down."

38. "The Jealous Lover"

Cox, 1939, pp. 9-10. Sung by Elizabeth Aileen Hatfield, Logan, W.Va., January 18, 1928; learned from Nell Caldwell.

a I/M

The timing of the original copy is straight 4/4, beginning on the first beat of the bar.

1. "What do you want for your breakfast, O Willie, my dear?
What do you want for your breakfast, O Willie, my dear?"
    "I don't want nothing; mother, fix my bed soon,
    I'm sick at my heart, I want to lie down."

2. "What do you will to your mother, O Willie, my dear?
What do you will to your mother, O Willie, my dear?"
    "My silver, my gold; mother, fix my bed soon,
    I'm sick at my heart, I want to lie down."

3. "What do you will to your father, O Willie, my dear?
What do you will to your father, O Willie, my dear?"
    "My horse and my saddle; mother, fix my bed soon,
    I'm sick at my heart, I want to lie down."

4. "What do you will to your brother, O Willie, my dear?
What do you will to your brother, O Willie, my dear?"
    "My watch and my chain; mother, fix my bed soon,
    I'm sick at my heart, I want to lie down."

5. "What do you will to your sister, O Willie, my dear?
What do you will to your sister, O Willie, my dear?"
    "My fiddle, my bow; mother, fix my bed soon,
    I'm sick at my heart, I want to lie down."

6. "What do you will to your sweetheart, O Willie, my dear?
What do you will to your sweetheart, my dear one?"
    "A rake and a scaffold for her to be hung; fix my bed
    soon,
    I'm sick at my heart, I want to lie down."

39. [Lord Rendal]

Sharp MSS., 792/. Sung by Mrs. Grace Coles, Enmore, January 17, 1906.

a I/M

Where will you be buried my own darling boy
Where will you be buried my comfort and joy
Under the green mountains mother make my bed soon
I've a pain in my heart and I want to lie down

40. [Lord Ronald]

Greig MSS., III, p. 63. Also in Greig and Keith, 1925, p. 14(1b). Sung by A. Barron and T. Roger, 1908.

a I

41. "Lord Randal"

Kittredge (from Belden), *JAF*, XXX (1917), p. 290. Also in Belden, 1940, pp. 26(C)-27. Sung by Mrs. Eva Warner Case (now Mrs. J. B. Lichtenberg), Harrison County, Mo., 1916. Text from Belden.

a I/M (inflected IV)

1. "Oh, where have you been, Lord Randal, my son?
Oh, where have you been, my handsome young man?"
    "Oh, I've been to the wildwood; mother, make my bed soon,
    I'm weary of hunting and I fain would lie down."

2. "And whom did you meet there, Lord Randal, my son?
And whom did you meet there, my handsome young man?"
    "Oh, I met with my true love; mother, make my bed soon,
    I'm weary of hunting and I fain would lie down."

3. "What got you for supper, Lord Randal, my son?
What got you for supper, my handsome young man?"
    "I got eels boiled in broth; mother, make my bed soon,
    I'm weary of hunting and I fain would lie down."

4. "And who got your leavings, Lord Randal, my son?
And who got your leavings, my handsome young man?"
    "I gave them to my dogs; mother, make my bed soon,
    I'm weary of hunting and I fain would lie down."

5. "And what did your dogs do, Lord Randal, my son?
And what did your dogs do, my handsome young man?"
"Oh, they stretched out and died; mother, make my bed
soon,
I'm weary of hunting and I fain would lie down."

6. "Oh, I fear you are poisoned, Lord Randal, my son,
Oh, I fear you are poisoned, my handsome young man."
"Oh, yes, I am poisoned; mother, make my bed soon,
For I'm sick at my heart and I fain would lie down."

7. "What will you leave your mother, Lord Randal, my son?
What will you leave your mother, my handsome young
man?"
"My house and my lands; mother, make my bed soon,
For I'm sick at my heart and I fain would lie down."

8. "What will you leave your sister, Lord Randal, my son?
What will you leave your sister, my handsome young man?"
"My gold and my silver; mother, make my bed soon,
For I'm sick at my heart and I fain would lie down."

9. "What will you leave your brother, Lord Randal, my son?
What will you leave your brother, my handsome young
man?"
"My horse and my saddle; mother, make my bed soon,
For I'm sick at my heart and I fain would lie down."

10. "What will you leave your true-love, Lord Randal, my son?
What will you leave your true-love, my handsome young
man?"
"A halter to hang her; mother, make my bed soon,
For I'm sick at my heart and I want to lie down."

This is a good example of the freedom with which a singer may
treat a traditional tune, even in a single continuous rendition. It may
remind us of what never should be forgotten: that our written records are for the most part but summary abstracts for an identity that
cannot be set upon a page. Even the present instance, refined and
sensitive though Herzog's notation undoubtedly is, is inevitably conditioned by arbitrary and subjective decisions and simplifications.

42. [Lord Randall]

Barry, Eckstorm, and Smyth, 1929, pp. 46-48. Sung by Mrs.
Sarah Robinson Black, Southwest Harbor, Maine, Septem-
ber 1928; learned from her mother. Melody recorded by
George Herzog.

a I

1. "O where have you been, fair Randall, my son?
O where have you been, my fair pretty one?"
"I've been to see pretty Betsy; mother, make my bed soon,
For I'm poisoned to my heart, and I want to lie down."

2. "What did you have for your supper, fair Randall, my son?
What did you have for supper, my fair pretty one?"
"I had eels fried in butter; mother, make my bed soon,
For I'm poisoned to my heart, and I want to lie down."

3. "Where will you have your bed made, fair Randall, my son?
Where will you have your bed made, my fair pretty one?"
"In the north corner of the churchyard; mother, make my
bed soon,
For I'm poisoned to my heart, and I want to lie down."

4. "What will you will to your father, fair Randall, my son?
What will you will to your father, my fair pretty one?"
"O, horses and oxen; mother, make my bed soon,
For I'm poisoned to my heart, and I want to lie down."

5. "What will you will to your brother, fair Randall, my son?
What will you will to your brother, my fair pretty one?"
"O, land and houses; mother, make my bed soon,
For I'm poisoned to my heart, and I want to lie down."

6. "What will you will to your sister, fair Randall, my son?
What will you will to your sister, my fair pretty one?"
"O, horses and carriages; mother, make my bed soon,
For I'm poisoned to my heart, and I want to lie down."

7. "What will you will to your mother, fair Randall, my son?
What will you will to your mother, my fair pretty one?"
"Gold rings and gold watches; mother, make my bed soon,
For I'm poisoned to my heart, and I want to lie down."

8. "What will you will to your sweetheart, fair Randall, my son?
What will you will to your sweetheart, my fair pretty one?"
"Hell fire and brimstone; mother, make my bed soon,
For I'm poisoned to my heart, and I want to lie down."

43. [Lord Ronald]

Greig MSS., III, p. 37. Also in Greig and Keith, 1925, p. 14(1c). Sung by A. Greig, Oldwhat, 1907.

a I/M

Oh whaur hae ye been to Lord Ronald my son?
Oh whaur hae ye been to my handsome young man?
I've been to the wild wood, mother mak' my bed soon;
For I'm weary, weary wand'ring and fain wad lie doon.

44. [Lord Ronald]

Duncan MS., No. 216 (W. Walker). Also in Greig and Keith, 1925, p. 14(1a). Sung by Beatrice Alexander, Udny, Aberdeenshire.

m I/M

What had ye for supper, Lord Ronald my son?
What had ye for supper, my handsome young man?
A plate o black fishes, mother, mak my bed soon,
For I'm weary, weary wand'rin, an' fain wad lie doon.

45. [Lord Rendal]

Sharp MSS., 452/. Sung by Mrs. Lock, Muchelney Ham, December 23, 1904.

a I

Where did you catch the eels my pretty one
Where did you catch the eels Rendal my son?
Out on the sunny banks Mother make my bed soon
For I'm sick to my heart and fain would lay down

46. "Johnny Randolph"

McIntosh, 1935, pp. 27-29. Sung by Myrtle Brewer, Stonefort, Ill., 1932.

p I

O, what will you have for supper, Johnny Randolph, my son?
O, what will you have for supper, my dear little one?
A cup of cold poison, Mother; make my bed soon.
A cup of cold poison, Mother; make my bed soon.
There's a pain at my heart, and I want to lie down.

Ah, what will you leave your brother, Johnny Randolph, my son?
Ah, what will you leave your brother, my dear little one?
My coach and six horses, Mother; make my bed soon.
My coach and six horses, Mother; make my bed soon.
There's a pain at my heart, and I want to lie down.

Oh, what will you leave your sister, Johnny Randolph, my son?
Oh, what will you leave your sister, my dear little one?
My gold and my silver, Mother; make my bed soon.
My gold and my silver, Mother; make my bed soon.
There's a pain at my heart, and I want to lie down.

Oh, what will you leave your sweetheart, Johnny Randolph, my son?
Oh, what will you leave your sweetheart, my dear little one?
The gates of hell are open, Mother; make my bed soon.
The gates of hell are open, Mother; make my bed soon.
There's a pain at my heart, and I want to lie down.

Ah, what will you leave your mother, Johnny Randolph, my son?
Ah, what will you leave your mother, my dear little one?
A dead boy to bury, Mother; make my bed soon.
A dead boy to bury, Mother; make my bed soon.
There's a pain at my heart, and I want to lie down.

47. [Lord Randal]

Sharp MSS., 3561/. Also in Sharp and Karpeles, 1932, I, p. 43(G). Sung by Mr. and Mrs. James A. Maples, Bird's Creek, Sevierville, Tenn., April 17, 1917.

m π¹

What you will to your mother, my rambling young son?
What you will to your mother, my dearest, fair one?
My horses and cattle, mother, make my bed soon,
I am sick to the heart and I fain would lie down.

48. [Lord Randal]

Creighton and Senior, 1950, pp. 9-10. Sung by Ben Henne-berry, Devil's Island, Nova Scotia.

a I

1. "O what is the matter Henery my son,
   O what is the matter my own dearest one,"
   I've been to my sweetheart mother, make my bed soon,
   I feel sick at the heart, and fain would lie down.

2. "What did she give you, Henery my son,
   O what did she give you, my own dearest one?"
   "She gave me golden fishes, mother, make my bed soon,
   I feel sick at heart and fain would lie down."

3. "What will you will your mother, Henery my son,
   What will you will your mother, my own dearest one?"
   "I will will you my money, mother, make my bed soon,
   I feel sick at the heart and I fain would lie down."

4. "What will you will your father, Henery my son,
   What will you will your father, my own dearest one?"
   "I will him my land and houses, mother, make my bed soon,
   I feel sick at heart and I fain would lie down."

5. "What will you will your sister, Henery my son,
   What will you will your sister, my own dearest one?"
   "I'll will her my sheep and cattle, mother, make my bed soon,
   I feel sick at heart and I fain would lie down."

6. "What will you will your brother, Henery my son,
   What will you will your brother, my own dearest one?"
   "I'll will him my horse and saddle, mother, make my bed soon,
   I feel sick at the heart and I fain would lie down."

7. "What will you will your sweetheart, Henery my son,
   What will you will your sweetheart, my own dearest one?"
   "I'll will her a rope to hang herself on yonder green tree,
   It was poison she gave me and she has you and me."

49. [Lord Randal]

Sharp MSS., 4710/. Also in Sharp and Karpeles, 1932, I, p. 44(J). Sung by Mrs. Sina Boone, Shoal Creek, Burnsville, N.C., September 28, 1918.

a I/Ly (– VI)

In the sixth bar from the end, the 1932 reading, B as the second note, is not according to the MS.

What did you have for supper, Jimmy Randolph, my son?
What did you have for supper, my lost* man?
Fried eels and fresh butter, mother fix my bed soon,
For I am faint-hearted and I can no longer stand.

* 1932. "last"

50. [Lord Rendal]

Sharp MSS., 4093/. Sung by Mr(s?). Hillard Smith, Hindman, Ky., September 23, 1917. (Words not recalled.)

a π²

This variant more than suggests another folk favorite, "The Wagoner's Lad" (e.g., Sharp and Karpeles, 1932, II, p. 126).

51. [Lord Randal]

Wilkinson MSS., 1935-36, pp. 24-25(A). Sung by Mrs. Lucy McAllister, Harriston, Va., October 10, 1935.

a π²

2. "What did you have for your supper, it's Randal my son,
What did you have for your supper, my pretty sweet one?"
"Fried eels and fresh butter, mother make my bed soon,
For I'm sick at the heart, and I fain would lie down."

3. "What will you leave to your father, it's Randal my son,
What will you leave to your father, my pretty sweet one?"
"A chest of fine clothing, mother make my bed soon,
For I'm sick at the heart, and I fain would lie down."

4. "What will you leave to your brother, it's Randal my son,
What will you leave to your brother, my pretty sweet one?"
"My horse and fine saddle, mother make my bed soon,
For I'm sick at the heart, and I fain would lie down."

5. "What will you leave to your sister, it's Randal my son,
What will you leave to your sister, my pretty sweet one?"
"My land and fine buildings, mother make my bed soon,
For I'm sick at the heart, and I fain would lie down."

6. "What will you leave to your sweetheart, it's Randal my son,
What will you leave to your sweetheart, my pretty sweet one?"
"A rope and a gallows, mother make my bed soon,
For I'm sick at the heart, and I fain would lie down."

7. "What will you leave to your mother, it's Randal my son,
What will you leave to your mother, my pretty sweet one?"
"A dead son to bury, mother make my bed soon,
For I'm sick at the heart, and I fain would lie down."*

* Copyright 1917 by Messrs. Boosey & Co. Renewed 1944. Reprinted by permission of Boosey & Hawkes Inc.

1. What did you have for your supper, Jimmy Randal, my son?
What did you have for your supper, my fair and pretty one?
Fried eels and fried onions, Mother fix my bed soon.
I'm sick at my heart and I want to lie down.

2. What you going to will your father, Jimmy Randal, my son?
What you going to will your father, my fair and pretty one?
My farm and fine buildings, Mother fix my bed soon.
I'm sick at my heart and I want to lie down.

3. What you going to will your brother, Jimmy Randal, my son?
What you going to will your brother, my fair and pretty one?
My horse whip and saddle, Mother, make my bed soon.
I'm sick at my heart and I want to lie down.

4. What you going to will your sister, Jimmy Randal, my son?
What you going to will your sister, my fair and pretty one?
My chest and my money, Mother, make my bed soon.
I'm sick at my heart and I want to lie down.

5. What you going to will your mother, Jimmy Randal, my son?
What you going to will your mother, my fair and pretty one?
My dead body to bury, Mother, make my bed soon.
I'm sick at my heart and I want to lie down.

6. What you going to will your true-love, Jimmy Randal, my son?
What you going to will your true-love, my fair and pretty one?
Brimstone and fire to parch her bones brown, Mother, make my bed soon.
I'm sick at my heart and I want to lie down.

53. [Lord Randal]

Sharp MSS., 4198/. Also in Sharp and Karpeles, 1932, I, p. 43(H). Sung by Mrs. Ada Maddox, Buena Vista, Va., April 30, 1918.

a M

Sharp's MS. note to the second bar: "Bars of this rhythm, which occur constantly in this tune, were sung so that the first two notes were given each rather more than their face value, i.e. the first note was nearly a crotchet, the second nearly a minim. The whole melody was sung quite slowly."

What for your supper? John Randolph, my son
What for your supper? my darling one.
Eel soup and vin'gar has made my bed soon, Mother,
I'm sick at the heart and want to lie down.

52. [Lord Randal]

McGill, 1917, pp. 18-22.

a π²

1. "Where have you been, Randal, it's Randal my son,
Where have you been, Randal, my pretty sweet one?"
"O I've been a-courting, mother make my bed soon,
For I'm sick at the heart, and I fain would lie down."

54. [Lord Randal]

Sharp MSS., 4206/3026. Also in Sharp and Karpeles, 1932, I, pp. 43(I)-44. Sung by Mrs. Laura Wheeler, Buena Vista, Va., May 2, 1918.

a M

What for your supper, John Randolph, my son,
What for your supper, pray tell me, little one.
Eel soup and vinegar; go make my bed sound.
I'm sick at the poor heart and want to lie down.

Where were you last night, etc.
I stayed at my love's house, etc.

What you will to your father, etc.
My six hounds and musket, etc.

What you will to your sweetheart, etc.
It's hot lead and brimstone for to parch her soul brown, etc.

55. "Uriar, My Son"

McIntosh, 1935, pp. 30-32. Sung by Raymond Johnson, 1934.

a I/M (compass of sixth)

Oh, where have you been, Uriar, my son?
Oh, where have you been, Uriar, my son?
Oh, where have you been, Uriar, my son?
For you're weak and you're weary,
And you need to lie down.

I've been to grandmother's, Mother;
Make my bed soon.
I've been to grandmother's, Mother;
Make my bed soon.
I've been to grandmother's, Mother;
Make my bed soon.
For I'm weak, and I'm weary,
And I want to lie down.

Wha' ja have for your supper, Uriar, my son?
Wha' ja have for your supper, Uriar, my son?
Wha' ja have for your supper, Uriar, my son?
For you're weak and you're weary,
And you need to lie down.

An eel fried in butter, Mother;
Make my bed soon.
An eel fried in butter, Mother;
Make my bed soon.
An eel fried in butter, Mother;
Make my bed soon.
For I'm weak, and I'm weary,
And I need to lie down.

56. [Lord Randal]

Sharp MSS., 4008/2890. Also in Sharp and Karpeles, 1932, I, p. 42(F). Sung by Mrs. Margaret Dunagan, St. Helens, Lee County, Ky., September 9, 1917.

m M/D

The catch-signature here is that of 1932. Sharp's MS. is in G major. The first note of the sixth bar from the end is wrongly printed a degree too high in 1932.

Where* did you stay last night, O Randal, my son?
Where* did you stay last night, my sweet darling one?
I stayed with my sweetheart. Mother, make my bed soon,
For I'm sick to the heart, and I want to lie down.

What did you eat for your supper, O Randal, my son?
What did you eat for your supper, my sweet darling one?
It was dill and dill broth. Mother, make my bed soon,
For I'm sick to the heart and I want to lie down.

What colour was it, etc.
It was brown and brown-speckled,† etc.

What'll you give to your sister, etc.
My coach and my horses, etc.

What'll you give to your sweetheart, etc.
Fire out of yon burning kiln for to burn her bones brown,
For she is the occasion of my lying down;
Fire out of yon burning kiln for to burn her bones brown,
For she is the occasion of my lying down.

* 1932: "O where"
† 1932: "brown and speckled"

57. [Lord Rendle]

Sharp MSS., 363/. Also in Sharp, JFSS, II (1905), p. 31(4). Sung by George Wyatt, West Harptree, August 26, 1904.

a M

What colour was the fish Rendle my son
What colour was the fish Rendle my son
He was spotted on the back Mother make my bed soon
I am sick to my heart and I fain would lay down

58. "Lord Randal"

Davis, 1929, p. 557(N); text, p. 118. From Alfreda M. Peel, Salem, Va., November 30, 1923.

a π¹

"What will you will to your father, Lord Randal, my son?
What will you will to your father, my dearest sweet one?"
"My horse and my buggy. Mother, make my bed soon,
For I'm sick to the heart, and would freely lie down."

59. [Lord Rendal]

Sharp MSS., 4592/. Sung by Mrs. Effie Mitchell, Burnsville, N.C., September 18, 1918.

a π²

Sharp's MS. note: "Probably incorrectly remembered, but interesting as it stands."
If the last phrase be sung first also, "The Wagoner's Lad" tune is outlined here.

What did you eat for your supper, Jim Randolph my son,
A cup of cold poison, Mother, fix my bed soon,
For I'm sick at my heart and I think to lie down.

60. "Where were you all the day, my own pretty boy?"

Joyce, 1909, No. 812, pp. 394-95. Sung by Peggy Cudmore, c. 1848.

a I

"Where were you all the day, my own pretty boy?
Where were you all the day, my truelove and joy?"
"I was fishing and fowling: mother, dress my bed soon;
There's a pain in my heart, and I want to lie down."

"What did you get for dinner, my own pretty boy?
What did you get for dinner, my truelove and joy?"
"Bread, mutton, and poison: mother, dress my bed soon;
There's a pain in my heart, and I want to lie down."

"What will you leave your mother, my own pretty boy?
What will you leave your mother, my truelove and joy?"
"A coach and four horses: mother, dress my bed soon;
There's a pain in my heart, and I want to lie down."

*   *   *   *   *

"What will you leave your married wife, my own pretty boy?
What will you leave your married wife, my truelove and joy?"
"A long rope to hang her: mother, dress my bed soon;
There's a pain in my heart, and I want to lie down."

61. "Where were you all the day, my own pretty boy"

Petrie, 1902-5, No. 330. From P. W. Joyce.

a Æ (inflected III)

It seems odd that this copy, so similar to Peggy Cudmore's in all but mode, also came from Dr. Joyce. We may perhaps suspect editorial revision by Petrie or Stanford.

GROUP AC

62. [Lord Randal]

Sharp MSS., 4463/. Also in Sharp and Karpeles, 1932, I, p. 45(M). Sung by Mr. Francis Richards, St. Peter's School, Callaway, Va., August 16, 1918.

p I/Ly

O what did you have for your supper, my son?
O what did you have for your supper, my beloved sweet one?
Sweet milk and parsnips, Mother, make my bed soon,
For I'm sick at my poor heart and fain would lie down.

63. [Lord Randal]

Sharp MSS., 4200/. Also in Sharp and Karpeles, 1932, I, p. 44(K). Sung by Mrs. Ella Campbell, Buena Vista, Va., May 1, 1918.

p π¹

What you will to your father, Jimmy Randal, my son?
What you will to your father my own darling one?
My farms* in the country go make my bed down,†
For I'm sick at my heart and be till I die.

* 1932: "farm"
† 1932: "soon"

64. "John Willow, My Son"

Davis, 1929, p. 556(A); text, pp. 106-7. Sung by Mrs. James B. Crawford, Altavista, Va., September 9, 1915. Collected by Juliet Fauntleroy.

a I

1. "Oh, where have you been, John Willow, my son,
Oh, where have you been, my dear little one?"
"I've been to my sweetheart's. Mother, make my bed soon;
There's a pain in my heart, and I want to lie down."

This will suggest "The Campbells are comin'" to most readers.

2. "What did you have for your supper, John Willow, my son,
What did you have for your supper, my dear little one?"
"Eels fried in batter. Mother, make my bed soon;
There's a pain in my heart, and I want to lie down."

3. "What did you do with your leavings, John Willow, my son,
What did you do with your leavings, my dear little one?"
"I gave them to my dogs. Mother, make my bed soon;
There's a pain in my heart, and I want to lie down."

4. "Where are your dogs, John Willow, my son,
Where are your dogs, my dear little one?"
"They lay down and died. Mother, make my bed soon;
There's a pain in my heart, and I want to lie down."

5. "I'm afraid you are poisoned, John Willow, my son,
I'm afraid you are poisoned, my dear little one."
"Oh yes, I am poisoned. Mother, make my bed soon;
There's a pain in my heart, and I want to lie down."

6. "What do you will to your father, John Willow, my son,
What do you will to your father, my dear little one?"
"My house and my land. Mother, make my bed soon;
There's a pain in my heart, and I want to lie down."

7. "What do you will to your mother, John Willow, my son,
What do you will to your mother, my dear little one?"
"I wish you a home in heaven. Mother, make my bed soon;
There's a pain in my heart, and I want to lie down."

8. "What do you will to your sister, John Willow, my son,
What do you will to your sister, my dear little one?"
"My horse, saddle, and bridle. Mother, make my bed soon;
There's a pain in my heart, and I want to lie down."

9. "What do you will to your sweetheart, John Willow, my son,
What do you will to your sweetheart, my dear little one?
"Hell-fire and brimstone, to scorch her so brown;
She's the cause of this pain, and I want to lie down."

65. [Air to an old English Ballad]

Petrie, 1902-5, No. 794. From Dr. Kelly; learned in County Mayo.

p π¹

66. "Sweet William, My Son"

Barry MSS., IV, No. 178. Also, with variant in second phrase, in Barry, *JAF*, XVI (1903), p. 260; and *ibid.*, XVIII (1905), pp. 196(B)-97. Sung by Mrs. Julia M. Lincoln, Springfield, Mass., September 21, 1903, as sung eighty years earlier.

p I (– VI)

1. "Oh, where have you been, Sweet William, my son?
   Oh, where have you been, my own dearest one?"
   "Oh, I've been a-hunting, mother make the bed soon,
   For I'm poisoned to the heart, and I fain would lie down."

2. "Oh, what have you been a-drinking, Sweet William, my son?
   Oh, what have you been a-drinking, my own dearest one?"
   "Oh, 't is ale I've been a-drinking, mother make the bed soon,
   For I'm poisoned to the heart, and I fain would lie down."

3. "Oh, who gave it you, Sweet William, my son?
   Oh, who gave it you, my own dearest one?"
   "My Sweetheart, she gave it me, mother make the bed soon,
   For I'm poisoned to the heart, and I fain would lie down."

4. "Oh, what will you give Father, Sweet William, my son?
   Oh, what will you give Father, my own dearest one?"
   "My horses and cattle, mother make the bed soon,
   For I'm poisoned to the heart, and I fain would lie down."

5. "Oh, what will you give Mother, Sweet William, my son?
   Oh, what will you give Mother, my own dearest one?"
   "My love and my blessing, mother make the bed soon,
   For I'm poisoned to the heart, and I fain would lie down."

6. "Oh, what will you give Brother, Sweet William, my son?
   Oh, what will you give Brother, my own dearest one?"
   "My sword and my pistol, mother make the bed soon,
   For I'm poisoned to the heart, and I fain would lie down."

7. "Oh, what will you give Sister, Sweet William, my son?
   Oh, what will you give Sister, my own dearest one?"
   "My gold and my jewels, mother make the bed soon,
   For I'm poisoned to the heart, and I fain would lie down."

8. "Oh, what will you give Sweetheart, Sweet William, my son?
   Oh, what will you give Sweetheart, my own dearest one?"
   "Give her Hell and damnation, mother make the bed soon,
   For I'm poisoned to the heart, and I fain would lie down."

GROUP A d

67. [Lord Rendal]

Sharp MSS., 2646/. Sung by John Darling (43), Ely, September 8, 1911.

p I

What will you have for supper John Riley my son
What will you have for supper my fair pretty one
Stewed eels bread and butter mother make my bed soon
For I feel sick and weary I fain would lay down

What will you leave your father?
   My watch and chain

What will you leave your mother
   My purse and money

What will you leave your lover
A rope to hang her!

Sharp's MS. note: "All he could remember."

68. [Lord Randal]

Sharp MSS., 4258/. Also in Sharp and Karpeles, 1932, I, p. 45(L). Sung by Mrs. Emma Chisholm, Nellysford, Va., May 21, 1918.

a I, ending on VIII

What did you have for your supper Jimmy Randolph my son?
What did you have for your supper, my dear little one?
Eggs fried in butter, Mother, make my bed soon,
There's a pain in my heart, and I want to lie down.

69. [Lord Randal]

Wilkinson MSS., 1935-36, p. 26(B). Sung by Mrs. Rosa Meadows Lam, Standardsville, Va., November 3, 1935.

a I, ending on VIII

What d'you have for your supper, Johnny Rillow, my son?
What d'you have for your supper, my dear little one?
Fresh eels fried in butter, Mother, make my bed soon.
There's a pain at my heart, I want to lie down.

70. [Lord Randall]

Barry, *JAF*, XXII (1909), pp. 376-77. Also in Barry, Eckstorm, and Smyth, 1929, pp. 58-59. Sung by A. W. (Mrs. Ann Welch), Brunswick, Maine, September 4, 1907; learned in County Clare.

m π¹

"Where were you all day, my own pretty boy?
Where were you all day, my heart's loving joy?"
"I was fishing and fowling, mother, make my bed soon,
I'm sick to my heart, and I want to lie down."

"What had you for dinner, my own pretty boy?
What had you for dinner, my heart's loving joy?"
"I had salt eels and pizen, mother, make my bed soon,
I'm sick to my heart, and I want to lie down."

"What will you leave your brother, my own pretty boy,
What will you leave your brother, my heart's loving joy?"
"I leave him my horse and my hounds, mother, make my bed
    soon,
I'm sick to my heart, and I want to lie down."

"What will you leave your sister, my own pretty boy?
What will you leave your sister, my heart's loving joy?"
"I leave her a fortune, mother, make my bed soon,
I'm sick to my heart, and I want to lie down."

"What will you leave your father, my own pretty boy?
What will you leave your father, my heart's loving joy?"
"I leave him my blessing, mother, make my bed soon,
I'm sick to my heart, and I want to lie down."

"What will you leave your girl, my own pretty boy?
What will you leave your girl, my heart's loving joy?"
"I leave her a barrel of powder, to blow her up high!
For I'm sick to the heart, and I want to lie down."

71. "Jo Reynard my Son"

Barry Dict. Cyl., No. 95. From L. H. Patterson, tr. Barry-Bayard MS., p. 35. Transcribed by Samuel P. Bayard.

a I (inflected II and VII)

Some of Bayard's refinements of notation have been omitted.

72. "Lord Ronald my Son"

Barry, Eckstorm, and Smyth, 1929, pp. 55(H)-56. Sung by Mrs. James McGill, Chamcook, New Brunswick, April 1928; learned from her mother in Galloway, Scotland. Melody recorded by George Herzog.

a M

1. "Whaur hae ye been a' day, Lord Ronald my son?
   Whaur hae ye been a' day, my jolly young man?"
   "I've been awa huntin', mither mak my bed sune,
   For I'm weary wi' huntin' an' fain wad lie doon."

2. "What'll ye hae tae yer supper, Lord Ronald my son?
   What'll ye hae tae yer supper, my jolly young man?"
   "I've gotten my supper, mither mak my bed sune,
   For I'm weary wi' huntin' an' fain wad lie doon."

3. "What did ye get tae yer supper, Lord Ronald my son?
   What did ye get tae yer supper, my jolly young man?"
   "A dish o' gold fishes, mither mak my bed sune,
   For I'm weary wi' huntin' an' fain wad lie doon."

4. "Where got ye the fishes, Lord Ronald my son?
   Where got ye the fishes, my jolly young man?"
   "In my faither's black ditches, mither mak my bed sune,
   For I'm weary wi' huntin' an' fain wad lie doon."

5. "They hae poisoned Lord Ronald, they hae poisoned my son,
"They hae poisoned Lord Ronald, my jolly young man."
"O my heart it is weary, mither mak my bed sune,
For I'm weary wi' huntin' an' fain wad lie doon."

6. "What'll ye leave tae yer faither, Lord Ronald my son?
What'll ye leave tae yer faither, my jolly young man?"
"My lands an' my houses, mither mak my bed sune,
For I'm weary wi' huntin' an' fain wad lie doon."

7. "What'll ye leave tae yer brother, Lord Ronald my son?
What'll ye leave tae yer brother, my jolly young man?"
"My horse an' my saddle, mither mak my bed sune,
For I'm weary wi' huntin' an' fain wad lie doon."

8. "What'll ye leave tae yer sister, Lord Ronald my son?
What'll ye leave tae yer sister, my jolly young man?"
"My box of gold rings, mither mak my bed sune,
For I'm weary wi' huntin' an' fain wad lie doon."

9. "What'll ye leave tae yer sweetheart, Lord Ronald my son?
What'll ye leave tae yer sweetheart, my jolly young man?"
"A rope for to hang her on yon gallows tree,
For it's her this night that has poisonèd me."

73. "Lord Ronald"

Eddy, 1939, p. 19(A). Sung by Mrs. Jane Small, Canton,
Ohio; learned in Scotland from her mother, who was born
in Ireland.

a M

"Where hae ye been huntin', Lord Ronald my son,
  Where hae ye been huntin', my jolly young man?"
"In yon green woods, mother, go make my bed soon,
  For I'm weary, weary huntin', and fain would lie doon."

"What got ye from your sweetheart, Lord Ronald, my son,
  What got ye from your sweetheart, my jolly young man?"
"I got deadly poison, mother, make my bed soon,
  For life it is a burden, and soon I'll lay't doon."

74. [Lord Randal]

Sharp MSS., 3413/2504. Also in Sharp and Karpeles, 1932,
I, pp. 40(D)-41. Sung by William F. Wells, Swannanoa,
N.C., September 9, 1916.

a π[1] (but IV occurs in variant)

1. Where have you been a-roving, Jimmy Randal my son?
   Where have you been a-roving, my oldest dear one?
   I've been out a-courting, mother, make my bed soon,
   I'm sick to the heart and I want to lie down.

2. What did you will to your mother . . .
   My houses and my lands.

3. What did you will to your father . . .
   My waggon and my team.

4. What did you will to your brother . . .
   My horn and my hounds.

5. What did you will to your sister . . .
   My rings off my finger.

6. What did you will to your sweetheart . . .
   A cup of strong poison.

7. What is your reason . . .
   Because she poisoned me.

75. "Tiranti, My Son"

Brown MS., 16 a 6. Text, *North Carolina Folklore*, II,
1952, p. 39(A). Collected by Amy Henderson, Worry,
Burke County, N.C., 1914.

p I

The original copy is barred erroneously in 4/4.

'Where have you been to, Tiranti, my son?
Where have you been to, my sweet little one?'
'I've been to grandmother's; mother, make my bed soon,
I am sick at my heart and faint to lie down.

'What did you have for your supper, Tiranti, my son?
What did you have for your supper, my sweet little one?'
'Eels fried in soap-grease; mother, make my bed soon,
I'm sick at my heart and faint to lie down.'

'What'll you leave to your father, Tiranti, my son?
What'll you leave to your father, my sweet little one?'
'My houses and land; mother, make my bed soon,
I'm sick at my heart and faint to lie down.'

'What'll you leave to your mother, Tiranti, my son?
What'll you leave to your mother, my sweet little one?'
'My jewels and silver; mother, make my bed soon,
I'm sick at my heart and faint to lie down.'

'What will you leave to your grandmother, Tiranti, my son?
What will you leave to your grandmother, my sweet little
one?'
'A halter to hang her; mother, make my bed soon,
I am sick at my heart and am faint to lie down.'

76. [Lord Randall]

Brown MS., 16 a 6. Text, *North Carolina Folklore*, II, 1952,
p. 40(B). Collected by Mrs. Sutton; source unidentified.

p π[1]

1. 'Oh, where have you been, Lord Randall, my son?
Oh, where have you been, my handsome young man?'
'I have been to the greenwood; mother, make my bed soon,
For I'm weary with hunting and I want to lie down.'

2. 'Who cooked you your dinner, Lord Randall, my son?
Who cooked you your dinner, my handsome young man?'
'My true love she cooked it; mother, make my bed soon,
For I'm weary with hunting and I want to lie down.'

3. 'What had you for dinner, Lord Randall, my son?
What had you for dinner, my handsome young man?'
'Eels fried in fresh butter; mother, make my bed soon,
For I'm weary with hunting and I want to lie down.'

4. 'She's fed you snake poison, Lord Randall, my son,
She's fed you snake poison, my handsome young man.'
'Oh, yes, I am dyin'; mother, make my bed soon,
For I'm weary with hunting and I want to lie down.'

5. 'What leave you your mother, Lord Randall, my son?
What leave you your mother, my handsome young man?'
'My lands and my houses; mother, make my bed soon,
For I'm weary with hunting and I want to lie down.'

6. 'What leave you your brother, Lord Randall, my son?
What leave you your brother, my handsome young man?'
'My hounds and my horses; mother, make my bed soon,
For I'm weary with hunting and I want to lie down.'

7. 'What leave you your true love, Lord Randall, my son?
What leave you your true love, my handsome young man?'
'A rope for to hang her; mother, make my bed soon,
For I'm weary with hunting and I want to lie down.'

77. "Willie Ransome"

Brown MS., 16 a 6. Text, *North Carolina Folklore*, II
(1952), p. 40(C). Collected by Mrs. Sutton; from singing
of Myra Barnett (Mrs. J. J. Miller), Caldwell County, N.C.,
1928.

p π[1]

1. 'Where you been, Willie Ransome, Willie Ransome, my son?
Where you been, Willie Ransome, my own darling one?'
'Been a-ramblin' and a-gamblin'; mother, make my bed down,
For I'm sick at the heart and I'd fancy lie down.'

2. 'What'd you have for your supper, Willie Ransome, my son?
What'd you have for your supper, my own darling one?'
'Eels and eel broth; mother, make my bed down,
For I'm sick at the heart and I'd fancy lie down.'

3. 'What d'you will to your father, Willie Ransome, my son?
What d'you will to your father, my own darling one?'
'My house and my home; mother make my bed down,
For I'm sick at the heart and I'd fancy lie down.'

4. 'What d'you will to your sister, Willie Ransome, my son?
What d'you will to your sister, my own darling one?'
'My trunk and trunk keys; mother, make my bed down,
For I'm sick at the heart and I'd fancy lie down.'

5. 'What d'you will to your brother, Willie Ransome, my son?
What d'you will to your brother, my own darling one?'
'My horn and my hounds; mother, make my bed down,
For I'm sick at the heart and I'd fancy lie down.'

6. 'What d'you will to your sweetheart, Willie Ransome, my son?
What d'you will to your sweetheart, my own darling one?'
'A cup of cold p'isen; mother, make my bed down,
For I'm sick at the heart and I'd fancy lie down.'

78. "Ramble, My Son"

Barry MSS., IV, No. 105. Also in Barry, *JAF*, XXII (1909),
p. 77. Sung by O. F. A. Conner, Harrisburg, Pa., March 27,
1907.

p I/M

This form of the tune is very close to "The Little Brown Bulls," as
sung by Emery DeNoyer on LC/AAFS, Album 1, rec. 5. Cf. also
"Whistle and I'll come to ye, my lad."

79. [Lord Rendal]

Sharp MSS., 458/. Sung by Caroline Hill, Huish Episcopi, December 27, 1904.

a I, ending on VIII

This tune has traces of "Death and the Lady," beloved of Goldsmith. Cf., e.g., Sharp, 1916, No. 22.

Where have you been Rendal my fair one
I've been a-fishing mother make my bed soon
For I am sick to the heart fain would lay down

80. "Jimmy Randal"

Barry Dict. Cyl., No. 163, cutting 4. Sung by Mrs. Myra Daniels, East Calais, Vt.

a M

'Where have you been, Jimmy Randal, my son?
Where have you been, my own lovely one?'
'I have a-been [*not understood*], Mother, make my bed soon,
For I'm sick at my heart and I want to lie down.
    Down derry down, down derry down,
For I'm sick at my heart and I want to lie down.'

'What had you for your breakfast, Jimmy Randal, my son?
What had you for your breakfast, my own lovely one?'
'I had eels fried in butter, Mother, make my bed soon,
For I'm sick at my heart and I want to lie down,
    Down derry down, down derry down,
For I'm sick at my heart and I want to lie down.'

'What color were they, Jimmy Randal, my son?
What color were they, my own lovely one?'
'They were green, white, and speck-lèd, Mother, make my bed soon,
For I'm sick at my heart and I want to lie down.
    Down derry down, down derry down,
For I'm sick at my heart and I want to lie down.'

[*No more transcribed*]

81. "Dear Adel my Son"

Robertson, LC/AAFS, rec. 3814 B2 and B3. Sung by George Vinton Graham, San Jose, Calif., 1938.

a M

'Where have you been, dear Adel my son?
Where have you been, my darling sweet one?'
'O I've been courting, mother, make my bed soon,
For I'm sick at my heart, and I wish (want) to lie down.'

82. [Lord Rendal]

Sharp MSS., 2873/. From Kate Buchanan, 2 The Groves, Stockton on Tees, February 6, 1913.

p I

O where have you been roaming 'Enery my son
O where have you been roaming such a pretty one
I've been a roaming mother O mother make my bed soon
For I feel sick at heart and inclined to lay down.

83. [Lord Rendal]

Sharp MSS., 1584/1430-31. Sung by Alice Davy, Colombe Lodge, Dunster, February 12, 1908; noted by Miss Wyatt Edgell.

p I

1. Where have you been courting, Henry my son?
   Where have you been courting, my charming one?
   Only with my sweetheart mother make my bed soon
   I'm sick to the heart and faint to lie down.

2. What have you been eating, etc.
   Only little fishes mother, etc.

3. What colour was those fishes?
   They were speckled and sparkled.

4. How did she cook those fishes?
   She cooked them in the frying-pan.

5. What have you been drinking?
   Only a little wine.

6. What colour was that wine?
   It was as red as a cherry.

7. What will you leave your mother?
   I will leave her purse and money.

8. What will you leave your father?
   I will leave him house and farm.

9. What will you leave your brother?
   I will leave him horse and coach.

10. What will you leave your sister?
    I will leave her watch and chain.

11. What will you leave your sweetheart?
    I will leave her a rope to hang herself, mother.

84. [Lord Rendal]

Sharp MSS., 755/. Sung by Mrs. Pike, Somerton; transmitted by Mrs. Snow, January 5, 1906.

p I

Where have you been to day Henery my son
Where have you been to day Henery my one
Courting mother courting mother make my bed soon
For I'm sick to my heart and I want to lie down.

85. [Lord Ronald]

Duncan MS., No. 375 (W. Walker). Also in Greig and Keith, 1925, p. 15(3). Sung by James M. Brown, Glasgow; learned in Aberdeen.

p I

There is a resemblance, perhaps coincidental only, between this and "Admiral Benbow" (cf. C. J. Sharp, *Folk Songs from Somerset*, 3rd series, 1906, pp. 51-52).

What'll ye leave to your mother, Henry my son?
What'll ye leave to your mother, my pretty one?
I'll leave her all my jewels, mother, mak my bed soon,
For I'm sick to the heart, an' I fain wad lie doon
For I'm sick to the heart, an' I fain wad lie doon.

86. [Lord Randal]

Creighton and Senior, 1950, pp. 10-11. Sung by Mrs. William McNab, Halifax, Nova Scotia.

p π[1]

"What did your sweetheart give you,
Henery my son,
What did your sweetheart give you,
My own dearest one?"

"She gave me little fishes, mother,
Make my bed soon
For I'm sick unto the heart
And I fain would lie down."

"What like unto were the fishes,
Oh Henery my son?
What like unto were the fishes,
My own dearest one?"

"Oh they had speckled bellies,
Mother make my bed soon,
For I'm sick unto the heart
And I fain would lie down."

"What will you give your father,
Oh Henery my son?

What will you give your father,
My own dearest one?"

"My purse and my money,
Mother make my bed soon,
For I'm sick unto the heart
And I fain would lie down."

87. "Fair Nelson"

Barry MSS., IV, No. 90. Also in Barry, *JAF*, XVIII (1905), pp. 303(R)-4. Sung by R. B. C. (Mrs. R. B. Cobleigh), Newbury, Vt., October 10, 1905; traditional in her family for a century.

p I/Ly (– VI)

1. "Oh, where have you been a-courting, Fair Nelson, my son?
Oh, where have you been a-courting, my fair,—
you are a pretty one!"
"I've been courting my Julia, mother make my bed soon,
For I'm sick to my heart, and I long to lie down."

2. "What did you have for your breakfast, Fair Nelson, my son?
What did you have for your breakfast, my fair,—
you are a pretty one!"
"Eels, fried in batter, mother make my bed soon,
For I'm sick to my heart, and I long to lie down."

3. "What will you will to your father, Fair Nelson, my son?
What will you will to your father, my fair,—
you are a pretty one!"
"My land and my houses, mother make my bed soon,
For I'm sick to my heart, and I long to lie down."

4. "What will you will to your mother, Fair Nelson, my son?
What will you will to your mother, my fair,—
you are a pretty one!"
"My gold and my silver, mother make my bed soon,
For I'm sick to my heart, and I long to lie down."

5. "What will you will to your Julia, Fair Nelson, my son?
What will you will to your Julia, my fair,—
you are a pretty one!"
"Hell-fire and brimstone, mother make my bed soon,
For I'm sick to my heart, and I long to lie down."

88. "Lord Ronald"

Broadwood, *JFSS*, V (1915), p. 119. Sung by Dr. Farquhar MacRae, Island of Lewis and Ross-shire, in London, May 14, 1908.

a π[1]

Miss Broadwood has noted that this is related to a favorite West Highland air, "Cuir a nall duinn am botal" (*JFSS*, IV [1910], p. 154) and thinks Burns may have got his "A Hieland Lad my Love was born" from the same air. Cf. also "The Campbells are comin'."

"What will ye leave for your brother, Lord Ronald, my son?
What will ye leave for your brother, my handsome young man?"
"My greyhound to cherish, mother, make my bed soon,
For I'm weary of hunting, and fain would lie doon."

"What will ye leave for your sister, Lord Ronald, my son?
What will ye leave for your sister, my handsome young man?"
"A Bible to read, mother, make my bed soon,
For I'm weary of hunting, and fain would lie down."

"What will ye leave for your sweetheart, Lord Ronald, my son?
What will ye leave for your sweetheart, my handsome young man?"
"A gallows to hang her, mother, make my bed soon,
For I'm weary of hunting, and fain would lie down."

GROUP Bb

89. "Henry My Son"

Collinson, *JEFDSS*, V (December 1946), pp. 15-16, and F. M. Collinson and F. Dillon, *Folk Songs from "Country Magazine,"* 1952, p. 20. Sung by Phyllis Johnson, Coventry; learned c. 1926.

p I

Where have you been all day Henry my son?
Where have you been all day my beloved one?
"In the green fields, in the green fields;
Oh make my bed, I've a pain in my head,
And I want to lie down."

What have you had to eat, Henry my son?
What have you had to eat, my beloved one?
"Oh poisoned berries; oh poisoned berries.
Oh make my bed, I've a pain in my head,
And I want to lie down."

Who gave you those to eat, Henry my son?
Who gave you those to eat, my beloved one?
"Father, dear mother; father, dear mother.
Oh make my bed, etc."

How shall I make your bed, Henry my son?
How shall I make your bed, my beloved one?
"Deep, long and narrow; deep, long and narrow.
Oh make my bed, etc."

5. "What will you leave your brother, Henery, my son?
   What will you leave your brother? You're a pretty one."
   "Ham and chicken, mother,
   Ham and chicken, mother;
   Make my bed quick, I've a pain in my heart
      And I wants to lie down."

6. "What will you leave your sister, Henery, my son?
   What will you leave your sister? You're a pretty one."
   "A rope to hang her, mother,
   A rope to hang her, mother;
   Make my bed quick, I've a pain in my heart
      And I wants to lie down."

Only the first stanza appears in Sharp's MSS.

90. [Lord Rendal]

Sharp MSS., 350/. Also in Sharp, *JFSS*, II (1905), pp. 29
(2)-30, and Sharp, *One Hundred English Folksongs*, 1916,
p. 44. Sung by Mrs. Perry, Langport, August 23, 1904.

a I

This is doubtless the set altered for use in *One Hundred English Folk Songs*, 1916, No. 18, p. 44.

1. "Where have you been to all the day, Henery my son?
   Where have you been to all the day? You're a pretty one."
   "Out in the green fields, mother,
   Out in the green fields, mother;
   Make my bed quick, I've a pain in my heart
      And I wants to lie down."

2. "What have you been eating of, Henery, my son?
   What have you been eating of? You're a pretty one."
   "Eels, mother,
   Eels, mother;
   Make my bed quick, I've a pain in my heart
      And I wants to lie down."

3. "What will you leave your father, Henery, my son?
   What will you leave your father? You're a pretty one."
   "Land and houses, mother,
   Land and houses, mother;
   Make my bed quick, I've a pain in my heart
      And I wants to lie down."

4. "What will you leave your mother, Henery, my son?
   What will you leave your mother? You're a pretty one."
   "Coals and horses, mother,
   Coals and horses, mother;
   Make my bed quick, I've a pain in my heart
      And I wants to lie down."

91. [Lord Rendal]

Sharp MSS., 393/524. Also in Sharp, *JFSS*, II (1905), p.
30(3). Sung by Mrs. Anna Pond, Shepton Beauchamp,
September 3, 1904.

a I

1. Where have you been to all this day, Henry my son?
   Where have you been to all this day, my pretty one?
   In the green fields, in the green fields, make my bed quick,
   There's a pain in my heart and I want to lay down,
   And I want to lay down.

2. What have [you] been eating of, etc.
   Eels, dear mother, etc.

3. What colour was those eels?
   Green and yellow.

4. What will you leave your mother?
   Gold and silver.

5. What will you leave your father?
   Land and houses.

6. What will you leave your brother?
   Cows and horses.

7. What will you leave your lover?
   A rope to hang her with.

8. Where shall I make your bed?
   In the green fields.

9. How shall I make your bed?
   Long and narrow.

92. [Lord Rendal]

Sharp MSS., 353/480-81. Sung by Mrs. Bond, Barrington, August 23, 1904.

a I

Where have you been to all the day, Henery my son?
Where have you been to all the day, you're a pretty one.
Out in the green fields, mother (bis)
Make my bed quick I've a pain in my heart
And I wants to lie down, I wants to lie down.

What have you been eating of Henery my son?
What have you been eating of, my pretty one?
Eels mother, eels mother,
Make my bed quick, etc.

What will you leave your father, etc.
Land and houses, mother, etc.

What will you leave your mother, etc.
Goals and horses, mother, etc.

What will you leave your brother, etc.
Hen and chicken, etc.

What will you leave your sister, etc.
A rope to hang her, etc.

93. "Henry my Son"

Barry MSS., IV, Nos. 329, 333(BB). Sung by Harriet L. Wedgwood, Boston, Mass., October 14, 1912, and January 10, 1913; learned from an Irish girl, Mary L. McDonald, who learned it from a book.

a I (-VI) (compass of a sixth)

The original is in 2/4 time.

1. Where have you been, Henry my son,
   Where have you been, my pretty one?
   Down to sister's Down to sister's;
   I've a pain in my side and I want to lay right down.

2. What have you ating (sic), Henry my son,
   What have you ating, my pretty one?
   Bread and poison Bread and poison;
   I've a pain in my side and I want to lay right down.

3. What will you leave your mother, Henry my son,
   What will you leave your mother, my pretty one?
   Gold and silver Gold and silver;
   I've a pain in my side and I want to lay right down.

4. What will you leave your father, Henry my son,
   What will you leave your father, my pretty one?
   A gold watch A gold watch;
   I've a pain in my side and I want to lay right down.

5. What will you leave your brother, Henry my son,
   What will you leave your brother, my pretty one?
   A diamond ring A diamond ring;
   I've a pain in my side and I want to lay right down.

6. What will you leave the baby, Henry my son,
   What will you leave the baby, my pretty one?
   Kisses from heaven Kisses from heaven;
   I've a pain in my side and I want to lay right down.

7. What will you leave your sister, Henry my son,
   What will you leave your sister, my pretty one?
   Ropes to hang her Ropes to hang her;
   I've a pain in my side and I want to lay right down.

94. "Henry, My Son"

Eddy, 1939, p. 21(C). Sung by William Lavey, Canton, Ohio; learned from Russian Jewish children in Winnipeg.

a I/M (compass of sixth)

The original is in 2/4 time.

1. "Where have you been, Henry, my son,
      Where have you been, my beloved one?"
   "At sister's, at sister's,
      Make my bed for the pain at my side,
   For I want to lie down and die."

2. "What did she give you, Henry, my son,
      What did she give you, my beloved one?"
   "Poison to drink, poison to drink;
      Make my bed for the pain at my side,
   For I want to lie down and die."

3. "What will you give your father, Henry, my son,
      What will you give your father, my beloved one?"
   "Golden watches, golden watches;
      Make my bed for the pain at my side,
   For I want to lie down and die."

4. "What will you give your mother, Henry, my son,
      What will you give your mother, my beloved one?"
   "Gold and silver, gold and silver;
      Make my bed for the pain at my side,
   For I want to lie down and die."

5. "What will you give your brother, Henry, my son,
    What will you give your brother, my beloved one?"
  "Heavenly kisses, heavenly kisses;
    Make my bed for the pain at my side,
  For I want to lie down and die."

6. "What will you give your sister, Henry, my son,
    What will you give your sister, my beloved one?"
  "Knives to kill her, ropes to hang her;
    Make my bed for the pain at my side,
  For I want to lie down and die."

95. "Henry, My Son"

Eddy, 1939, p. 20(B). Sung by Jennie Mirkin, Canton, Ohio; learned from an English girl in Springfield, Mass.

p I/M (–VI), ending on V. Tonic G

The original is in 2/4 time.

1. "Where have you been all day, Henry, my son,
    Where have you been all day, my sweet loving one?"
  "Up to grandma's, up to grandma's; Make my bed soon,
    I've a pain in my side, and I want to lay right down."

2. "What did you do there, Henry, my son,
    What did you do there," *etc.*
  "Mind the baby, wash the dishes,
    Make my bed soon," *etc.*

3. "What did she give you, Henry, my son?"
  "A glass of poison, a glass of poison."

4. "What will you leave your father, Henry, my son?"
  "Suits to wear, suits to wear."

5. "What will you leave your mother, Henry, my son?"
  "Kisses from heaven, kisses from heaven."

6. "What will you leave your brother, Henry, my son?"
  "Shoes and stockings, shoes and stockings."

7. "What will you leave to your sister, Henry, my son?"
  "Dresses to wear, dresses to wear."

8. "What will you leave the baby, Henry, my son?"
  "Toys to play with, toys to play with."

9. "What will you leave your Grandma, Henry, my son?"
  "Ropes to hang her, knives to kill her."

96. "Jimmy Randall"

Randolph, 1946, I, pp. 66(D)-67. Sung by Mrs. Lillian Short, Cabool, Mo., April 25, 1941.

a π¹ (–VI), ending on III

Where have you been, Jimmy Randall, my son?
Where have you been, my handsome young one?
I've been to my true love, Mamma,
I've been to my true love, Mamma.
Oh make my bed soon, Mamma,
'Cause I'm sick to the heart,
I want to lay down.

Where are your hounds, Jimmy Randall, my son?
Where are your hounds, my handsome young one?
They swelled up and died, Mamma,
They swelled up and died, Mamma.
Oh make my bed soon, Mamma,
'Cause I'm sick to the heart,
I want to lay down.

What did you eat, Jimmy Randall, my son?
What did you eat, my handsome young one?
Some fried eels and onions, Mamma,
Some fried eels and onions, Mamma.
Oh make my bed soon, Mamma,
'Cause I'm sick to the heart,
I want to lay down.

I'm feared you're pizened, Jimmy Randall, my son,
I'm feared you're pizened, my handsome young one.
Oh, I'm feared I'm pizened, Mamma,
Yes, I'm feared I'm pizened, Mamma.
Oh make my bed soon, Mamma,
'Cause I'm sick to the heart,
I want to lay down.

GROUP BC

97. "King Henry, my Son"

Nicholson, *JFSS*, III (1907), p. 43. Sung by Mr. Lattimer, Carlisle; learned as a boy in Cumberland.

p Æ

Lucy Broadwood, *English Traditional Songs and Carols*, 1908, pp. 96-99, prints an almost identical copy (with accompaniment) as from

Margaret Scott, Cumberland, who sang it, in a fuller version, before 1868.

Miss Broadwood refers to the cognate tune, "The trees they do grow high," collected by Vaughan Williams in Sussex (JFSS, II [1906], p. 206).

"Oh, where have you been wandering, King Henery, my son,
[Oh,] where have you been wandering, my pretty one?"
"I've been to my sweetheart's, mother, make my bed soon,
For I'm sick to the heart, and would fain lay me down."

"And what did your sweetheart give you, King Henery, my son,
What did your sweetheart give you, my pretty one?"
"She fried me some paddocks, mother, make my bed soon,
For I'm sick at the heart, and would fain lay me down."

"And what will you leave your sweetheart, King Henery, my son?
What will you leave your sweetheart, my pretty one?"
"My garter to hang her, mother, make my bed soon,
For I'm sick at the heart, and would fain lay me down."

GROUP C

98. "Willie Doo"

Moffat, [1933], p. 5.

a Æ

O where hae ye been a' the day,
(Willie Doo,* Willie Doo?)
I've been to see my stepmither,
(Die shall I now!)

What got ye frae your stepmither,
(Willie Doo, Willie Doo?)
She gaed to me a speckled trout,
(Die shall I now!)

Where got she you the speckled trout,
(Willie Doo, Willie Doo?)
'Twas caught amang the heather hills,
(Die shall I now!)

What gaed she you there for to drink,
(Willie Doo, Willie Doo?)
She brewed some deadly hemlock stocks,
(Die shall I now!)

They made his bed, then laid him down
Puir Willie, Willie Doo!
He turned his wee face to the wa',
Willie's died now!

* Doo: dove.

99. "The Wee Little Croodin' Doo"

Broadwood, JFSS, V (1915), p. 118(2). Sung by Henry Fowler Broadwood (b. 1811, d. 1893), Lyne, Sussex.

a I

"Where hae ye been the live-long day,
My wee little croodin' doo?"*
"I've been to see my step-mother,
Mammy, mak' my bed noo."

"And what did your step-mother give ye to eat,
My wee little croodin' doo?"
"She gave me a wee, wee blue fish.
Mammy, mak' my bed noo."

"And what did ye do with the bones of the fish,
My wee little croodin' doo?"
"I gave them to my wee, wee dog,
Mammy, mak' my bed noo."

"And what did your dog when he'd eat of the bones,
My wee little croodin' doo?"
"He stretched his wee leggies and died,
Mammy, as I do noo."

* Cooing dove.

100. "The Little Wee Croodin' Doo"

Gilchrist, JFSS, V (1915), p. 117(1). Sung by Mrs. F. D. Cremer, Eccles, Lancashire, February 12, 1909.

m I/M

The version in Alton C. Morris, *Folksongs of Florida*, 1950, pp. 247-48, was learned from this copy, but minorized by the singer. There may be a connection with the following version by this means.

"Oh, where have you been this live-long day,
My little wee croodin' doo?"
"I've been to see my step-mother,
Marmee, oh, make my bed noo!"

"And what did your step-mother give you to eat,
    My little wee croodin' doo?"
"She gave me but a wee, wee fish
    All covered with green and blue."

"And what did you do with the bones of the fish,
    My little wee croodin' doo?"
"I gave them to my wee, wee dog—
    Marmee, oh, make my bed noo!"

"And what did your dog when he'd ate up the fish,
    My little wee croodin' doo?"
"He stretched his wee, wee limbs and died—
    Marmee, as I do noo—
    Marmee, as I do noo!"

101. "Croodin Doo"

Eskin, Sierra Record FMI, 7. Sung by Desmond Powell,
University of Arizona, Tucson, Ariz.

a Æ (–VII)

O where have you been all the livelong day
My little wee croodin doo?
I've been to see my grandmother,
Mammy, come make my bed soon.

And what did your grandmother give you to eat
My little wee croodin doo?
She gave to me a little fish,
Mammy, come make my bed soon.

And what did you do with the bones of the fish
My little wee croodin doo?
I gave them to my wee, wee dog,
Mammy, come make my bed soon.

And what did your dog when he ate o' the bones
My little wee croodin doo?
He laid his wee self down and died;
Mammy, come make my bed soon.

102. [Lord Rendal; or, Cruden Doo]

Sharp MSS., 2412/2191. Sung by Fanny S. Aylmin, Farnham, Surrey, June 11, 1909.

a M

O where have you been this livelong day,
    My little wee Cruden Doo?
I've been to see my godmother,
    O mammy mak my bed noo.

103. [The Croodin Doo]

N. and W. Montgomerie, 1946, pp. 140-41.

p I

The text appears to be copied from Motherwell.

"Whaur hae ye been a the day,
Ma bonny wee croodin doo?"
    "O, I hae been at ma stepmither's hoose;
Mak ma bed, mammie, noo, noo, noo!
Mak ma bed, mammie, noo!"

"Whaur did ye get yer dinner,
Ma bonny wee croodin doo?"
    "I got it in ma stepmither's;
Mak ma bed, mammie, noo, noo, noo!
Mak ma bed, mammie, noo!"

"Whit did she gie ye tae yer dinner,
Ma bonny wee croodin doo?"
    "She gae me a wee fower-fitted fish;
Mak ma bed, mammie, noo, noo, noo!
Mak ma bed, mammie, noo!"

"Whaur got she the fower-fitted fish,
Ma bonny wee croodin doo?"
    "She got it doon in yon well-strand;
Mak ma bed, mammie, noo, noo, noo!
Mak ma bed, mammie, noo!"

"Whit did she dae wi the banes o't,
Ma bonny wee croodin doo?"
    "She gae them tae the wee dog;
Mak ma bed, mammie, noo, noo, noo!
Mak ma bed, mammie, noo!"

"O, whit becam o the wee dog,
Ma bonny wee croodin doo?"
    O, it shot oot its feet an deed!
O, mak ma bed, mammie, noo, noo, noo!
O mak ma bed, mammie, noo!"

Billie Boy

CHILD NO. 12, APPENDIX

OUR earliest record of this spirited parody of "Lord Randal" comes from the final volume of the *Scots Musical Museum*, where, however, the words used are the pretty ones of Hector Macneill, themselves based on the parody. For evidence of age, cf. Stenhouse, *Illustrations*, p. 440, note to *SMM*, No. 502, where two stanzas of the old song are quoted. But see also Glen, *Early Scottish Melodies*, 1900, p. 216, where it is reported that the first appearance of the song was in *The Bee*, an Edinburgh magazine, in May 1791, and thereafter in Napier, G. Thomson, and Urbani, all before the *SMM* copy.

This tune, as Glen rightly notices, is cut from the same cloth as "Muirland Willie," which he discusses elsewhere at length (*op.cit.*, pp. 37-39), animadverting with some asperity on Chappell's claims (*PM*, pp. 559-61, 786) that the tune is English. Chappell, at least, prints a form of the tune from *Apollo's Banquet*, 1669.

It is clear, at any rate, that the records of the parody are of approximately equal age with those of the serious ballad; and that the existence of the tunes can be carried back another century in both cases.

It seems likely that all the tune-families for the present ballad are at least distantly related, but they diverge in characteristic and vigorous ways. The Celtic form stands apart; the English shows two varieties hard to disentangle; and the American form is again characteristic, quite consistent, and very widely known.

The Celtic variants, although scarce, have been set first. They swing between Æolian and Dorian. Miss Gilchrist has pointed out the relation of one of them to "When Johnny comes marching home," calling attention also to analogy with "John Anderson, my Jo" and another tune in the *Museum*, "The Maid gaed to the Mill," No. 481. She also quotes a partial text of an earlier version from Herd's MSS. Cf. H. Hecht, *Songs from David Herd's Manuscripts*, 1904, p. 105.

The English and American variants, on the contrary, are without exception in major tonality (I, π^1, I/M). Three Somerset variants stand together with a Northumbrian capstan chanty as particularly related, both words and music, although varying considerably in contour. These form our group B. Group C comes half from Somerset, half from American singers, Appalachian and Canadian. All these variants have a mid-cadence on the fifth, and all have noticeable traits in common with one another, but again with considerable variety. Much the same may be said of Group D, which is, however, all English, all plagal major. Group E contains the main stream of tradition in America. Its melodic contour changes too seldom to be very interesting; but the last few variants display shifts of octave-emphasis and finally a tendency to level out in a lazier line, which point toward deterioration.

LIST OF VARIANTS

GROUP A

1. "My boy Tammy." James Johnson, *The Scots Musical Museum*, VI, [1803], No. 502, p. 518.
2. "My Boy Tommy, O!" D. J. O'Sullivan, *JIFSS*, XVIII (1921), p. 33.
3. "Bonny Lad, Highland Lad." H. E. D. Hammond, *JFSS*, VIII (1930), p. 210. Also in *Novello's School Songs*, 1922, Set VIII, No. 1331.

GROUP B

4. "Billy Boy." Sharp MSS., 184/271, Clare College Library, Cambridge. (Welch)
5. "Billy Boy." Sharp MSS., 520/591. (White)
6. "Billy Boy." Richard Runciman Terry, *The Shanty Book*, 1921, Pt. I, pp. 2-3.
7. "Billy Boy." Sharp MSS., 1102/. (Adams)

GROUP C

8. "My Boy Billy." Sharp MSS., 4341/3099. Also in Cecil J. Sharp and Maud Karpeles, *English Folk Songs from the Southern Appalachians*, 1932, I, p. 39(C). (Grey)
9. "Oh, where are you going, Billy, Billy boy?" F. W. Waugh, *JAF*, XXXI (1918), p. 78.
10. "Billy Boy." F. C. Brown MS., 16 b IV, Library of Congress, photostat.
11. "Billy Boy." Mellinger Edward Henry, *Folk-Songs from the Southern Highlands*, 1938, pp. 383-84.
12. "Billy boy." Sharp MSS., 653/. ("Ginger Jack")
13. "My boy Billy." Sharp MSS., 775/. (Milton)
14. "My Boy Billy." Sharp MSS., 3377/2471. (Crane)

GROUP D

15. "My boy Willy." Sharp MSS., 2618/. Also in Cecil J. Sharp, *Folk-Songs of England* (Worcestershire), 1912, IV, p. 6 (Bradley); and in *Novello's School Songs*, Set IX, No. 1413.
16. "My Boy Billy." English Columbia, rec. WA 10685 (DB 335). (Clive Carey). Also in R. Vaughan Williams, *Folk-Songs for Schools*, Novello & Co., Ltd., 1912, Set VI, No. 1134.
17. "Lord Rendal; or, Billy Boy." Sharp MSS., 482/. (Fook)
18. "My Boy, Billy Boy." Edward F. Rimbault, *Nursery Rhymes*, n.d., p. 32. Also in Edward F. Rimbault, *Old Nursery Rhymes*, n.d., p. 34.

GROUP E

19. "Billy Boy." Eloise Hubbard Linscott, *Folk Songs of Old New England*, 1939, pp. 166-67.
   a. "Billy Boy." Mary O. Eddy, *Ballads and Songs from Ohio*, 1939, p. 117.
   b. "Billy Boy." John Harrington Cox, *Folk-Songs of the South*, 1925, p. 532.
   c. "Billy Boy." Brown MS., 16 b IV.
20. "Billy Boy." Helen Creighton and Doreen H. Senior, *Traditional Songs from Nova Scotia*, 1950, pp. 246-47.
21. "Billy Boy." Brown MS., 16 b IV.
22. "My boy Billy." Sharp MSS., 3483/2568. Also in Sharp and Karpeles, *Appalachians*, 1932, I, p. 38. (Gentry)
23. "Billy Boy." F. Eileen Bleakney, *JAF*, XXXI (1918), p. 161.
24. "Billy Boy." Emelyn E. Gardner, *JAF*, XXXIII (1920), p. 92.
25. "Billy Boy." Sharp MSS., 3762/. (Combs)

26. "Billie Boy." Loraine Wyman and Howard Brockway, *Lonesome Tunes*, [1916], pp. 14 and 17.
27. "Billy Boy." Dorothy Scarborough, *A Song Catcher in Southern Mountains*, 1937, pp. 435 and 297-98.
28. "Billy Boy." John A. and Alan Lomax, *American Ballads and Folk Songs*, 1934, p. 320.
29. "Billy Boy." Helen Hartness Flanders and George Brown, *Vermont Folk-Songs & Ballads*, 1931, pp. 162-63.

TUNES WITH TEXTS

GROUP A

1. [My boy Tammy]

Johnson, VI, [1803], No. 502, p. 518.

a Minor (inflected VI)

On the connection with "Muirland Willie," see the variant next following. See the headnote reference for four copies earlier than the above, but unseen by the present editor. Three date from the 1790's, the fourth, 1800.

1. Whar hae ye been a' day, my boy Tammy
   [W]har hae ye been a' day my boy Tammy.
   I've been by burn and flow'ry brae
   Meadow green and mountain grey
   Courting o' this young thing just come frae her mammy.

2. ||: And whar gat ye that young thing my boy Tammy? :||
   (Bis)
   I gat her down in yonder how,
   Smiling on a broomy know,
   Herding ae wee Lamb and Ewe for her poor Mammy.

3. ||: What said ye to the bonny bairn my boy Tammy? :||
   I prais'd her een sae lovely blue,
   Her dimpled cheek, and cherry mou;—
   I pree'd it aft as ye may true—She said, she'd tell her Mammy.

4. ||: I held her to my beating heart "—my young my smiling Lammy! :||
   "I hae a house—it cost me dear,
   "I've walth o' plenishan and geer;
   "Ye'se get it a' war't ten times mair, gin ye will leave your Mammy."

5. ||: The smile gade aff her bonny face—"I manna leave my Mammy. :||
   "She's ge'en me meat; she ge'en me claise;
   "She's been my comfort a' my days—
   "My Father's death brought mony waes—I canna leave my Mammy.

6. ||: "We'll tak her hame and mak her fain, my ain kind hearted Lammy! :||

"We'll gee her meat; we'll gee her claise,
"We'll be her comfort a' her days:"—
The wee thing gi'es her hand and says "There! gang and ask my Mammy."

7. ||: Has she been to Kirk wi' thee my boy Tammy? :||
   She has been to Kirk wi' me,
   And the tear was in her ee,—
   But Oh! she's but a young thing just come frae her Mammy!

2. "My Boy Tommy, O!"

O'Sullivan, *JIFSS*, XVIII (1921), p. 33. Sung by Bat Riordan, Kilnanare, County Kerry.

a Æ/D

As O'Sullivan remarks, this tune (like the preceding) appears related to "Muirland Willie," for which cf., e.g., A. Moffat, *Minstrelsy of Scotland*, n.d., p. 150. Moffat notes that "Muirland Willie" was printed in *Orpheus Caledonius*, 1725, and in *Musick for Allan Ramsay's Collection*, 1726, and that "Lord Frog," in *Apollo's Banquet*, London, 1669, "seems to be an early version."

1. "Where have you been all the day,
   My boy Tommy, O?
   Where have you been all the day,
   My bonny blue-eyed Tommy, O?"
   "I've been rolling in the hay,
   With a lassie young and gay."
   "Wasn't she the young thing
   That lately left her mammy, O?"

2. "What did she give you to eat?
   My boy Tommy, O?
   What did she give you to eat,
   My bonny blue-eyed Tommy, O?"
   "She gave me bread, she gave me meat,
   And that's what she gave me to eat."
   "Wasn't she the young thing
   That lately left her mammy, O?"

3. "What did she give you to drink,
   My boy Tommy, O?
   What did she give you to drink,
   My bonny blue-eyed Tommy, O?"

"She gave me wine as black as ink,
And that's what she gave me to drink."
"Wasn't she the young thing
    That lately left her mammy, O?"

4. "Can she mend and can she make,
    My boy Tommy, O?
Can she mend and can she make,
    My bonny blue-eyed Tommy, O?"
"She can mend and she can make,
She can give and she can take."
"Wasn't she the young thing
    That lately left her mammy, O?"

5. "Can she bake a corn-cake,
    My boy Tommy, O?
Can she bake a corn-cake,
    My bonny blue-eyed Tommy, O?"
"She can bake a corn-cake
Fit for any man to eat."
"Wasn't she the young thing
    That lately left her mammy, O?"

6. "Can she make a feather bed,
    My boy Tommy, O?
Can she make a feather bed,
    My bonny blue-eyed Tommy, O?"
"She can make a feather bed
Fit for any man to rest."
"Wasn't she the young thing
    That lately left her mammy, O?"

7. "What age is this young thing,
    My boy Tommy, O?
What age is this young thing,
    My bonny blue-eyed Tommy, O?"
"Twice two, twice four,
Twice seven and eleven more."
"Wasn't she the young thing
    That lately left her mammy, O?"

O'Sullivan's editorial note: "Noted some years ago from the singing of my friend Bat Riordan, of Kilnanare. Both words and air are undoubtedly of Scottish origin, and the song appears in Johnson's *Museum* (see *Popular Songs of Scotland*, Balmoral Edition, page 270). The air is probably an altered form of 'Muirland Willie.' I have not seen any other version in which the surprise concerning the lady's age is given, and this may be a piece of Irish humour. As regards the manner of singing this last verse, it may be remarked that in Kerry, as in other parts of Munster, the word *twice* is pronounced very nearly as disyllable, even in ordinary speech, thus: *two-ice*."

3. "Bonny Lad, Highland Lad"

Hammond, *JFSS*, VIII (1930), p. 210. Sung by Mrs. Russell, Upwey.

p D

Do you wish to know her age, bonny lad, Highland lad,
Do you wish to know her age my brave Highland laddy O?
She is twice six seven, twice twenty and eleven,
Isn't she a young thing, lately from her mammy O!

Miss Gilchrist finds a connection here with "Johnny comes marching home," and notes an early variant of the tune of "John Anderson, my Jo" (*SMM*, No. 481), which she believes related.

GROUP B

4. [Billy Boy]

Sharp MSS., 184/271. Sung by Mrs. Lizzie Welch, Hambridge, April 4, 1904.

m I/M

This tune may be compared with "Admiral Byng and Brave West," in Christie, 1881, II, p. 260; and with "Johnny Hall," Petrie, 1902-5, No. 747.

Is she fitting for your wife, Billy B'y,
    Billy B'y,
Is she fitted for your wife, Billy B'y?
She's fitted to my wife
As the haft is to the knife.
    She's my Nancy, please my fancy,
    I'm her charming Billy B'y.

Did she ask you to sit down, Billy [B'y],*
    Billy [B'y]?
Did she ask you to sit down, Billy [B'y]?
Yes, she asked me to sit down
And she cruchèd† to the ground.

Did she light you up to bed, Billy [B'y], etc.
Yes she light me up to bed
With the bowing of her head.

Did she lay so close to you, Billy [B'y], etc.
Yes, she lay so close to me
As the [r]ind unto the tree.

* The MS. reads "Bie" (for Boy) throughout the remaining stanzas.
† For "curtsied."

5. [Billy Boy]

Sharp MSS., 520/591. Sung by Lucy White, Hambridge,
August 4, 1905.

a I

The second phrase of this tune seems to have been dropped in
transcription, as the text demands its presence.

Did she ask you to sit down, Billy boy, Billy boy,
Did she ask you to sit down, Billy boy?
Did she ask me to sit down
But to curtsy on the ground.*
She's my Nancy please my fancy,
She's my charming Billy boy.

Did she ask you to have meat Billy boy, etc.
With neither knife nor fork to eat.
She's my Nancy, etc.

* The music-book gives:
Yes she asked me to sit down
But to curtsy to the ground.

6. [Billy Boy]

Terry, 1921, Pt. I, pp. 2-3. A Northumbrian capstan shanty.

a I (inflected IV)

The timing of this variant seems debatable: if it is to conform to
the prevailing pattern, the bar-lines of the first two phrases might
better be moved forward three beats, with a 9/8 bar at the junction
of the second and third phrases (bars 7 and 8 above).

Where hev ye been åål the day,
Billy Boy, Billy Boy?
Where hev ye been åål the day, me Billy Boy?
I've been walkin' åål the day
With me charmin' Nancy Grey.
And me Nancy kittl'd me fancy
Oh me charmin' Billy Boy.

Is she fit to be yor wife
Billy Boy, Billy Boy?
Is she fit to be yor wife, me Billy Boy?
She's as fit to be me wife
As the fork is to the knife
And me Nancy, etc.

Can she cook a bit o' steak
Billy Boy, Billy Boy?
Can she cook a bit o' steak, me Billy Boy?
She can cook a bit o' steak,
Aye, and myek a gairdle cake
And me Nancy, etc.

Can she myek an Irish Stew
Billy Boy, Billy Boy?
Can she myek an Irish Stew, me Billy Boy?
She can myek an Irish Stew
Aye, and "Singin' Hinnies" too.
And me Nancy, etc.

7. [Billy Boy]

Sharp MSS., 1102/. Sung by Richard Adams, East Harptree, August 30, 1906.

a I

Did she ask you to come in Billy Boy Billy boy
Yes she ask me to come in with her nose above her chin
And its [N]ancy pancy please my fancy charming Billy boy
Billy boy Billy boy
And its Nancy Pancy please my fancy charming Billy boy

GROUP C

8. [My Boy Billy]

Sharp MSS., 4341/3099. Also in Sharp and Karpeles, 1932,
I, p. 39(C). Sung by Mrs. Lawson Grey, Montvale, Bedford County, Va., June 6, 1918.

a I/M

O where have you been, Billy boy, Billy boy?
O where have you been charming Billy?
I've been out to-night to seek my wife (she's the joy of my life)
She's a young thing and cannot leave her mother.

Does she ever go to church, etc.
Yes she goes to church with a bonnet white as perch,
She's a young thing, etc.

Can she bake a cherry pie, etc.
She can bake a cherry pie by the time a cat can wink his eye,
She's a young thing, etc.

How old is she, etc.
Twice six, twice seven, twice forty and eleven,
She's a young thing, etc.

How tall is she, etc.
She's tall as any pine and slim as any line,
She's a young thing, etc.

9. "Oh, where are you going, Billy, Billy boy?"

Waugh, *JAF*, XXXI (1918), p. 78. From Ontario, Canada.

p I/Ly

"Oh, where are you going,
    Billy, Billy boy?
Oh, where are you going,
    my darling Billy?"
"To marry me a wife
    for the comfort of my life.
But she was too young,
    and she couldn't leave her mammy."

10. [Billy Boy]

Brown MS., 16 b IV. Sung by Mrs. Ada Wilson, Silverton, June 22, 1926.

p π[1]

O where have you been, Billy Boy, Billy Boy?
O where have you been, charming Billy?
I have been to seek a wife, She's the joy of my life
But she's a young thing and can't leave her mother.

11. "Billy Boy"

Henry, 1938, pp. 383-84. Sung by Mrs. C. L. Franklin, Crossnore, N.C., August 1931.

p π[1]

1. Oh, where have you been, Billy Boy, Billy Boy?
   Oh, where have you been, charming Billy?
   I've been to see my wife; she's the joy of my life;
   But the young thing can't leave her mammy.

2. How old is she, Billy Boy, Billy Boy?
   How old is she, charming Billy?
   Six, seven, twice forty-five-eleven;
   But the young thing can't leave her mammy.

3. Does she bid you come in, Billy Boy, Billy Boy?
   Does she bid you come in, charming Billy?
   She bids me come in with a dimple in her chin;
   But the young thing can't leave her mammy.

4. Can she bake a cherry pie, Billy Boy, Billy Boy?
   Can she bake a cherry pie, charming Billy?
   She can bake a cherry pie in the twinkle of her eye;
   But the young thing can't leave her mammy.

5. Can she hoe? Can she plow, Billy Boy, Billy Boy?
   Can she hoe? Can she plow, charming Billy?
   She can hoe; she can plow; she can milk a muley cow;
   But the young thing can't leave her mammy.

6. Can she whistle? Can she sing, Billy Boy, Billy Boy?
   Can she whistle? Can she sing, charming Billy?
   She can whistle; she can sing; she can do most anything;
   But the young thing can't leave her mammy.

12. [Billy boy]

Sharp MSS., 653/. Sung by "Ginger Jack," Lew Trenchard, September 12, 1905.

p I

For the sake of consistency, this might be rebarred at the halves of the present bars; but there are no words to help a decision.

13. [My boy Billy]

Sharp MSS., 775/. Sung by Mary Anne Milton (80), Washford, January 13, 1906.

p I

Can you lie close to me my boy Billy
Can you lie close to me Billy boy Tommy
I can lie close to thee as the bark unto the tree
Yes oh yes too young to be taken from her mammy
Twice 6 twice 7 twice twenty and eleven
Yes oh yes too young to be taken from her mammy

14. [My Boy Billy]

Sharp MSS., 3377/2471. Sung by Hezekiah Crane, Flag Pond, Tenn., September 3, 1916.

p I/M

Where are you going, Billy, Billy boy,
Where are you going, charm Billy?
I'm going to see my wife
For the rest of my life.
She's a young thing can't leave her mama.

Is she fit for a wife, Billy, Billy boy,
Is she fit for a wife, charm Billy?
She's as fit for a wife
As my pocket is my knife.
She's a young thing etc.

Can she bake a cherry pie etc.
She can bake a cherry pie
As quick as a cat can blink its eye.
She's a young thing etc.

Can she make a bed etc.
She can make a bed
Six foot over her head.
She's a young thing etc.

How old is she etc.
How old etc.
She's twice six, twice seven,
Twice twenty and eleven.
She's a young thing etc.

GROUP D

15. [My boy Willy]

Sharp MSS., 2618/. Also, with piano accompaniment, in Sharp, 1912, IV, p. 6. Sung by John Bradley, Shiperton Union, August 22, 1911.

p I

MS. note by Sharp: "Time oscillated between compound time and compound 6/8."

O where have you been all the day my boy Willy
O where have you been all the day
O Willie wont you tell me now
I've been all the day courting of a lady gay
But she is too young to be taken from her mammy.

Can she brew and can she bake, my boy Willie (2)
Oh Willy wont you tell me now?
She can brew & she can bake, she can make a wedding cake
But she is too young to be taken from her mammy.

Can she knit & can she spin my boy Willie (2)
    Etc.
She can knit & she can spin, she can do most anything
But she is etc.

O how old is she now, my boy Willie (2)
    Etc.
Twice six, twice seven, twice twenty & eleven
But she is too young to be taken from her mammy.

16. "My Boy Billy"

English Columbia, rec. WA 10685 (DB 335). Sung by
Clive Carey, c. 1935.

p I

Where have you been all this day, my boy Billy?
Where have you been all this day, pretty Billy, tell me?
    I have been all this day
    Courting with a lady gay
But she is too young to be taken from her mammy,
But she is too young to be taken from her mammy.

Can she bake or can she brew, my boy Billy?
Can etc.
    She can brew and she can bake
    She can make a wedding-cake,
But etc.

Can she cook a plate of fish, my boy Billy?
Can etc.
    She can cook a plate of fish,
    Put her fingers in the dish,
But etc.

Can she make a feather-bed, my boy Billy?
Can etc.
    She can make a feather-bed
    Fit for any lady's head
But etc.

How old might she be, my boy Billy?
How old might she be, pretty Billy, tell me?
    She is one, she is two,
    Twice eleven are twenty-two,
But she is too young to be taken from her mammy,
But she is too young to be taken from her mammy.*

* Carey sings a version collected and set by R. Vaughan Williams
and printed by Novello & Co., *Folk-Songs for Schools*, No. 1134.

17. [Lord Rendal; or, Billy Boy]

Sharp MSS., 482/. Sung by Mrs. Fook, Rockenford, January 6, 1905.

p I

Sharp named this "Lord Rendal" in his MS., but took down only
the words of the first half-line:
            Where have you been all this day.
The tune seems to relate it rather to the "Billy Boy" tradition.
    This copy has echoes of "Derby Ram" in it—another song of
humorous exaggeration.

18. [My Boy, Billy Boy]

Rimbault, *Nursery Rhymes*, n.d., p. 32. Also in Rimbault,.
Old Nursery Rhymes, n.d., p. 34.

m I (inflected IV)

Where have you been all the day,
    My boy, Billy boy?
Where have you been all the day?
    Pretty Billy, tell me.
I have been all the day
    Courting of a lady gay;
Though she's but a young thing,
    Just come from her mammy.

Did she ask you to sit down,
    My boy, Billy boy?
Did she ask you to sit down?
    Pretty Billy, tell me.
She did ask me to sit down
In a chair that cost a crown;
Tho' she's but a young thing,
Just come from her mammy.

Did she ask you for to eat,
    My boy, Billy boy?
Did she ask you for to eat?
    Pretty Billy, tell me.
She did ask me for to eat
Of a fowl and dish of meat;
Tho' she's but a young thing,
Just come from her mammy.

Pray how old then might she be,
My boy, Billy boy?
Pray how old then might she be?
Pretty Billy, tell me.
Thrice six, twice seven,
Twice twenty and eleven;
Tho' she's but a young thing,
Just come from her mammy.

GROUP E

19. "Billy Boy"

Linscott, 1939, pp. 166-67. Sung by Mrs. Elizabeth W.
Hubbard, Taunton, Mass.; learned from her father.

a I

1. Oh, where have you been, Billy Boy, Billy Boy,
   Oh, where have you been, charming Billy?
      I have been to seek a wife,
      She's the joy of my life,
   She's a young thing and cannot leave her mother.

2. Did she bid you to come in, Billy Boy, Billy Boy,
   Did she bid you to come in, charming Billy?
      She did bid me to come in,
      She's a dimple in her chin,
   She's a young thing and cannot leave her mother.

3. Did she set for you a chair, Billy Boy, Billy Boy,
   Did she set for you a chair, charming Billy?
      She did set for me a chair,
      She had ringlets in her hair,
   She's a young thing and cannot leave her mother.

4. Can she make a cherry pie, Billy Boy, Billy Boy,
   Can she make a cherry pie, charming Billy?
      She can make a cherry pie,
      Quick's a cat can wink her eye,
   She's a young thing and cannot leave her mother.

5. Can she make a feather bed, Billy Boy, Billy Boy,
   Can she make a feather bed, charming Billy?
      She can make a feather bed,
      Put the pillows at the head,
   She's a young thing and cannot leave her mother.

6. How old is she, Billy Boy, Billy Boy,
   How old is she, charming Billy?
      Three times six, four times seven,
      Twice twenty and eleven,
   She's a young thing and cannot leave her mother.

20. "Billy Boy"

Creighton and Senior, 1950, pp. 246-47. Sung by Mrs.
Dennis Greenough, West Petpeswick, Nova Scotia.

a I/M

1. Where have you been all the day Billy Boy, Billy Boy,
   Where are you going charming Billy?
   I've been gone to seek a wife, she's the joy of my life,
   She's a young thing and cannot leave her mammy.

2. Can she bake a cherry pie, Billy Boy, Billy Boy,
   Can she bake a cherry pie, charming Billy?
   She can bake a cherry pie, quick as a cat can wink her eye,
   She's a young thing and cannot leave her mammy.

3. Can she make a feather bed, Billy Boy, Billy Boy,
   Can she make a feather bed, charming Billy?
   She can make a feather bed, with good pillows at the head,
   But she's a young thing and cannot leave her mammy.

4. Is she fit to be your wife, Billy Boy, Billy Boy,
   Is she fit to be your wife, charming Billy?
   She's as fit to be my wife, as the fork is to the knife,
   She's a young thing and cannot leave her mammy.

5. Can she knit, can she spin, Billy Boy, Billy Boy,
   Can she knit and can she spin, charming Billy?
   She can knit and she can spin, she can spin most anything,
   She's a young thing and cannot leave her mammy.

6. How old is she, Billy Boy, Billy Boy,
   How old is she, charming Billy?
   She is one, she is two, twice eleven and twenty-two,
   She's a young thing and cannot leave her mammy.

21. [Billy Boy]

Brown MS., 16 b IV. Sung by G. W. Murphy; collected by
Mrs. C. R. Westwood, Wallace, N.C.

a I/M (– VI)

22. [My boy Billy]

Sharp MSS., 3483/2568. Also in Sharp and Karpeles, 1932, I, p. 38. Sung by Mrs. Jane Gentry, Hot Springs, N.C., September 16, 1916.

a I/M

O where have you been, Billy boy, Billy boy,
O where have you been, charming Billy?
I have been to seek a wife
For the pleasures of my life;
She's a young girl and cannot leave her mammy.

How old is she, Billy boy, Billy boy,
How old is she, charming Billy?
She's a hundred like and nine
And I hope she will be mine.
She's a young girl, etc.

How tall is she, etc.
She's as tall as any pine
And as slim as a pumpkin vine.
She's a young girl, etc.

Can she make a chicken pie, etc.
She can make a chicken pie
Till it make the preachers cry.
She's a young girl, etc.

Can she roll a boat ashore, etc.
She can roll a boat ashore
And make her own door.
She's a young girl, etc.

23. [Billy Boy]

Bleakney, *JAF*, XXXI (1918), p. 161. A child's game-song, from Ottawa, Canada.

a I

"Can you make a cherry-pie,
Billy boy, Billy boy?

Can you make a cherry-pie,
Charming Billy?"
"I can make a cherry-pie
Quick as a cat can wink its eye,
I can make a cherry-pie,
Charming Billy."

24. "Billy Boy"

Gardner, *JAF*, XXXIII (1920), p. 92. Sung by Edna Hardie, Hudson, Mich.; a play-party game.

a I

Where are you going, Billy Boy, Billy Boy?
Where are you going, charming Billy?
I'm going to see my wife; she's the pride of my life;
She's a young thing and can't leave her mother.

Did you knock on the door, Billy Boy, Billy Boy?
Did you knock on the door, charming Billy?
Yes, I knocked on the door till my knuckles were sore;
She's a young thing and can't leave her mother.

Did she ask you to come in, Billy Boy, Billy Boy?
Did she ask you to come in, charming Billy?
Yes, she asked me to come in, with a dimple in her chin;
She's a young thing and can't leave her mother.

Did she take your hat, Billy Boy, Billy Boy?
Did she take your hat, charming Billy?
Yes, she took my hat, but she fed it to the cat;
She's a young thing and can't leave her mother.

Did she offer you a chair, Billy Boy, Billy Boy?
Did she offer you a chair, charming Billy?
Yes, she offered me a chair, but the bottom wasn't there;
She's a young thing and can't leave her mother.

25. [Billy Boy]

Sharp MSS., 3762/. Sung by Mrs. Jenny L. Combs, Berea, Ky., May 30, 1917.

a I/M

O where have you been? Billy boy, Billy boy,
O where have you been, charming Billy?
I've been to see my wife, She's the joy of my life,
She's a young thing and cannot leave her mammy.

26. [Billie Boy]

Wyman and Brockway, [1916], p. 14; text, p. 17. Sung in
Jackson County, Ky.

a I/M

1. "Where are you going, Billie Boy, Billie Boy
   Where are you going charming Billie?"
   "I am going to see my wife
   At the pleasure of my life,
   She's a young thing cannot leave her mother."

2. "Can she bake a cherry pie Billy Boy, Billie Boy
   Can she bake a cherry pie charming Billie?"
   "She can bake a cherry pie
   As quick as a cat can wink her eye,
   She's a young thing cannot leave her mother."

3. "Can she sweep up a house Billie Boy, Billie Boy
   Can she sweep up a house charming Billie?"
   "She can sweep up a house
   As quick as a cat can catch a mouse,
   She's a young thing cannot leave her mother."

4. "Can she bake a pone of bread Billie Boy, Billie Boy
   Can she bake a pone of bread charming Billie?"
   "She can bake a pone of bread
   Between the oven and the lid,
   She's a young thing cannot leave her mother."

5. "Can she make up a bed Billie Boy, Billie Boy
   Can she make up a bed charming Billie?"
   "She can make up a bed
   Seven feet above her head,
   She's a young thing cannot leave her mother."

6. "How tall is she Billie Boy, Billie Boy
   How tall is she charming Billie?"
   "She's as tall as any pine
   And as straight as pumpkin vine,
   She's a young thing cannot leave her mother."

7. "How old is she Billie Boy, Billie Boy
   How old is she charming Billie?"
   "Twice six, twice seven
   Twice twenty and eleven,
   She's a young thing cannot leave her mother."

27. "Billy Boy"

Scarborough, 1937, p. 435; text, pp. 297-98. Sung by Ed
Bostwick, Russell Fork, Council, Va.

a I/M

1. Where are you going, Billy Boy, Billy boy?
   Where are you going, charming Billy?
   I'm going to see my girl she's the darling of the world;
   She's a young thing and cannot leave her mamma.

2. How old is she, Billy Boy, Billy Boy?
   How old is she, charming Billy?
   She's twice six, twice seven,
   Forty-eight and eleven.
   She's a young thing and cannot leave her mamma.

3. How tall is she, Billy Boy, Billy Boy?
   How tall is she, charming Billy?
   She's as tall as a pine
   And wears a number nine.
   She's a young thing and cannot leave her mamma.

4. How much does she weigh, Billy Boy, Billy Boy?
   How much does she weigh, charming Billy?
   She's forty feet around,
   And weighs a thousand pound.
   She's a young thing and cannot leave her mamma.

5. Can she make up a bed, Billy Boy, Billy Boy?
   Can she make up a bed, charming Billy?
   She can make up a bed
   From the foot to the head.
   She's a young thing and can't leave her mamma.

6. Can she bake a cherry pie, Billy Boy, Billy Boy?
   Can she bake a cherry pie, charming Billy?
   She can bake a cherry pie
   Before a cat can lick its eye.
   She's a young thing and can't leave her mamma.

7. Can she knit, can she sew, Billy Boy, Billy Boy?
   Can she knit and sew, charming Billy?
   She can back-stitch a thread,
   She can throw it over her head.
   She's a young thing and can't leave her mamma.

8. Can she milk a cow, Billy Boy, Billy Boy?
   Can she milk a cow, charming Billy?
   She can milk a cow
   When her mamma show her how.
   She's a young thing and can't leave her mamma.

28. [Billy Boy]

J. A. and A. Lomax, 1934, p. 320.

a I/M

The text is composite, and is therefore not given here.

29. [Billy Boy]

Flanders and Brown, 1931, pp. 162-63. Sung by Mrs. George Tatro, Springfield, Vt., November 17, 1930. From *Vermont Folk-Songs and Ballads*, edited by Helen Hartness Flanders and George Brown; copyright 1931 by Arthur Wallace Peach.

a I

1. "O where have you been, Billy Boy, Billy Boy?
   O where have you been, charming Billy?"
   "I have been to see my wife, she's the joy of my life; [but]
   She's a young thing and cannot leave her mother."

2. "Did she offer you a chair, Billy Boy, Billy Boy?
   Did she offer you a chair, charming Billy?"
   "Yes, she offered me a chair with the ringlets in her hair;
   She's a young thing and cannot leave her mother."

3. "Did she take your hat, Billy Boy, Billy Boy?
   Did she take your hat, charming Billy?"
   "Yes, she took my hat, but what of that?
   She's a young thing and cannot leave her mother."

4. "Can she fry a dish of meat, Billy Boy, Billy Boy?
   Can she fry a dish of meat, charming Billy?"
   "She can fry a dish of meat, and do it all complete,
   She's a young thing and cannot leave her mother."

5. "Can she make a loaf of bread, Billy Boy, Billy Boy?
   Can she make a loaf of bread, charming Billy?"
   "She can make a loaf of bread, but it's heavy as any lead,
   She's a young thing and cannot leave her mother."

6. "Can she make a cherry pie, Billy Boy, Billy Boy?
   Can she make a cherry pie, charming Billy?"
   "She can make a cherry pie quick as a cat can wink her eye.
   She's a young thing and cannot leave her mother."

7. "Can she row a boat to shore, Billy Boy, Billy Boy?
   Can she row a boat to shore, charming Billy?"
   "She can row a boat to shore without a paddle or an oar.
   She's a young thing and cannot leave her mother."

8. "Did she light you to bed, Billy Boy, Billy Boy?
   Did she light you to bed, charming Billy?"
   "Yes, she lit me to bed with the candle on her head.
   She's a young thing and cannot leave her mother."

9. "Did she kiss you good-night, Billy Boy, Billy Boy?
   Did she kiss you good-night, charming Billy?"
   "Yes, she kissed me good-night and hugged me very tight,
   She's a young thing and cannot leave her mother."

10. "How old is she, Billy Boy, Billy Boy?
    How old is she, charming Billy?"
    "Twice six, twice seven, twenty-three, and eleven,
    She's a young thing and cannot leave her mother."

Edward

CHILD NO. 13

THIS ballad has mainly been confined in European traditional singing to the Scandinavian countries, to Finland, and to Scotland, whence it has traveled to take fresh root in the Appalachian regions. Archer Taylor has argued convincingly that the ballad passed from Britain to Scandinavia. ("*Edward*" *and* "*Sven i Rosengård*," Chicago, 1931.) It appears to me that the most artistic and best-known version, first given to the world in Percy's *Reliques*, is a literary rehandling of the traditional song. (Cf. *SFQ*, IV [1940], pp. 1-13, 159-61.) None of the traditional variants except Motherwell's, which was possibly influenced by Percy, implicates the mother in the son's guilt.

Although Motherwell says he prints his text chiefly with the intention of introducing the traditional melody, he curiously fails to give us any tune; so that all the tunes that have been found for this ballad, save one or two, come from the Appalachians, and all have been recovered only in the present century. The ballad would seem to have died out of tradition in Scotland before Greig began his labors. Very recently, a copy has been found in Hampshire, at Aldershot.

Three tunes associated particularly with other ballads are also employed traditionally with this one—evidence, perhaps, of the slender hold maintained upon tradition by the present ballad. All three have points in common and have been grouped together (B). Our last group (C) is composed of tunes having little or nothing in common with the other groups or with one another. They are probably vehicles borrowed for present use by individual singers. The first three, however, from North Carolina, Virginia, and Texas, may be related; and they bespeak kinship with the American branch of "Gypsy Davy" (200). The fourth, from Arkansas, appears to have "Camptown Races" as its closest relative. These four tunes are in major tonalities (I/Ly, I, π^1, authentic). The fifth, taken from the artful singing of G. Marston Haddock to a lute accompaniment,

may be suspected to be untraditional for this ballad. The tune, however, is perfectly sound as folk-melody: a variant of "Come all you worthy Christian men." It is barely possible that there is some melodic connection between this and Group A. The text used by Haddock is Percy's. A fifth tune, from J. J. Niles, appears to have been worked over from traditional stock.

Group A is composed of Appalachian variants and their derivatives. The type is defined in the first four variants (π^4, Æ/D, and authentic). The skeletal outline is identical as far as the mid-cadence (on the fifth). The other three variants show the identity of the tune in a state of rapid dissolution. Although the meter of all is ¾, cadences are unstable and modes differ (p Æ/D, M, π^1).

Group B falls into three distinct and familiar patterns. The first is that of "Gypsy Laddie" (the Cassilis type: cf. No. 200) or "Lady Isabel." The final is ambiguous, and the variants, all but one pentatonic, may be regarded as either a π^2 or p π^1. The second pattern is that of "Boyne Water."* Again the final squints: the two pentatonic variants may be either a π^3 or p π^2 with fallen closes. The heptatonic variant is pretty clearly Mixolydian. The third pattern—if pattern it may be called—employs the "House Carpenter" (243) idea at starting, in a Mixolydian plagal form. But it falls away rapidly, seduced by other memories. There is no constancy in either cadences or modes, one copy being π^3, another M/D, and a third p I, without its sixth. A fourth is p I/Ly, but far gone in the direction of "Ain't goin' to rain no more."

It is arbitrary to distinguish these latter variants of Group B from those of Group C; but I have felt that the drift from the archetypal pattern of "House Carpenter" could be made out through the first two or three variants; and after that, connections appear from tune to tune.

* Cf., e.g., 209, 213, 214, 233, for its use with other ballads.

LIST OF VARIANTS

GROUP A

1. "Edward." Sharp MSS., 3558/2628, Clare College Library, Cambridge. Also in Cecil J. Sharp and Maud Karpeles, *English Folk Songs from the Southern Appalachians*, 1932, I, p. 47(D); and Cecil J. Sharp, *American-English Folk-Ballads*, Schirmer's American Folk-Song Series, Set 22, 1918, No. 1. (Gann)

a. "Edward." John Harrington Cox, *Traditional Ballads Mainly from West Virginia*, 1939, p. 11.

b. "Edward." Dorothy Scarborough, *A Song Catcher in Southern Mountains*, 1937, p. 405(B).

2. "Edward." Helen Hartness Flanders and Marguerite Olney, *Ballads Migrant in New England*, 1953, pp. 100-1.

3. "The Murdered Brother." Scarborough, *A Song Catcher in Southern Mountains*, 1937, pp. 406(C) and 183-84.

4. "How came that blood on your shirt sleeve?" William A. Owens, *Texas Folk Songs*, 1950, pp. 62-63.

5. "Edward." Scarborough, *A Song Catcher in Southern Mountains*, 1937, pp. 404(A) and 181-82.

6a. "The Little Yellow Dog." Vance Randolph, *Ozark Folksongs*, I, 1946, p. 71(D).

6b. "The Little Yellow Dog." Vance Randolph, LC Archive of American Folk Song 1393, Album XII, rec. 57B. (Charles Ingenthron)

GROUP B

7. "Edward." Sharp MSS., 3823/2805. Also in Sharp and Karpeles, *Appalachians*, 1932, I, p. 49(E). (Shook, Haynes)

8. "Edward." Sharp MSS., 4552/3185. Also in Sharp and Karpeles, 1932, I, p. 53(J). (Gibson)

c. "Blood on th' Pint o' your Knife." Vance Randolph, *Ozark Mountain Folks*, 1932, p. 207.

9. "What blood on the point of your knife?" Randolph, *Ozark Folksongs*, I, 1946, pp. 67(A)-68.

10. "The Blood of Fair Lucy." Herbert Halpert, LC Archive of American Folk Song 2863, rec. B2. (Mrs. Ewart Wilson)

11. "Edward." Sharp MSS., 3821/2804. Also in Sharp and Karpeles, *Appalachians*, 1932, I, p. 47(C). (Medford)

12. "Edward." Sharp MSS., 4527/3173. Also in Sharp and Karpeles, 1932, I, p. 52(I). (Weaver)

13. "Edward." Sharp MSS., 3316/2421. Also in Sharp and Karpeles, 1932, I, p. 46(A). (Gentry)

14. "Edward." Sharp MSS., 4475/3153. Also in Sharp and Karpeles, 1932, I, p. 50(G). (Richards)

15. "Edward." Sharp MSS., 4502/3165. Also in Sharp and Karpeles, 1932, I, pp. 51(H)-52. (Cannady)

16. "Edward." Sharp MSS., 4314/3083. Also in Sharp and Karpeles, 1932, I, p. 50(F). (Long)

17. "Edward." Sharp MSS., 4534/. (Plegné)

18. "What Blood is this." Peter Kennedy, *JEFDSS*, VI (December 1951), p. 99. Corrected reading, Peter Kennedy, *JEFDSS*, VII (1952), p. 38.

19. "What is that on the end of your sword?" Arthur Kyle Davis, Jr., *Traditional Ballads of Virginia*, 1929, pp. 558(C) and 123.

GROUP C

20. "Edward." Sharp MSS., 3332/. Also in Sharp and Karpeles, *Appalachians*, 1932, I, p. 47(B). (Hensley)

21. "How come that blood on your shirt sleeve?" Owens, *Texas Folk Songs*, 1950, pp. 60-62.

22. "Edward." Davis, *Traditional Ballads of Virginia*, 1929, pp. 558(D) and 124.

23. "Ronald." Randolph, *Ozark Folksongs*, I, 1946, p. 71(D).

24. "Edward, Edward." Musicraft, Album 55, rec. 263AB. (G. Marston Haddock)

d. "Edward." John Jacob Niles, *Anglo-American Ballad Study Book*, Schirmer's American Folk-Song Series, Set 24, 1945, pp. 10-11.

TUNES WITH TEXTS

GROUP A

1. [Edward]

Sharp MSS., 3558/2628. Also in Sharp and Karpeles, 1932, p. 47(D); and Sharp, 1918, No. 1. Sung by Trotter Gann, Sevierville, Sevier County, Tenn., April 13, 1917.

a π⁴ (II in variant b)

In Sharp's MS., the first two notes are also written as a dotted quarter and an eighth, with no hold.

1. What has came* this blood on your shirt sleeve?
O dear love, tell me.
This is the blood of the old grey horse
That ploughed that field for me, me, me,
That ploughed that field for me.

2. It does look too pale for the old grey horse
That ploughed that field for you, you, you,
That ploughed that field for you.

3. What has came* this blood on your shirt sleeve?
O dear love, tell me.
This is the blood of the old grey hound
That traced that fox for me, me, me,
That traced that fox for me.

4. It does look too pale for the old grey hound
That traced that fox for you, you, you,
That traced that fox for you.

5. What has come [*sic*] this blood on your shirt sleeve?
O dear love, tell me.
This is the blood of my brother-in-law

That went away with me, me, me,
That went away with me.

6. And it's what did you fall out about?
O dear love, tell me.
About a little bit of bush
That soon would have made a tree, etc.

7. And it's what will you do now, my love?
O dear love, tell me.
I'll set my foot in yanders ship,
And I'll sail across the sea, etc.

8. And it's when will you come back, my love?
O dear love, tell me.
When the sun sets into yanders sycamore tree,
And it's that will never be, be, be,
And it's that will never be.

* 1932: "come"

2. [Edward]

Flanders and Olney, 1953, pp. 100-1. Sung by Edith Ballenger Price, Newport, R.I., October 8, 1945; learned in Amherst, Mass., c. 1910. From *Ballads Migrant in New England*, edited by Helen Hartness Flanders and Marguerite Olney; copyright 1953 by Helen Hartness Flanders.

a π⁴

The 1953 copy has been corrected in the first note of line 4—from A to G—by authority of Miss Olney.

1. "How came this blood on your shirt sleeve,
O dear love, tell me, me, me?"
"It is the blood of my old gray hound
That traced that fox for me, me, me,
that traced that fox for me."

2. "It does look too pale for the old gray hound,
    O dear love, tell me, me, me—
It does look too pale for the old gray hound
That traced that fox for thee, thee, thee,
    that traced that fox for thee."

3. "How came this blood on your shirt sleeve,
    O dear love, tell me, me, me?"
"It is the blood of my old gray mare
That ploughed that field for me, me, me,
    that ploughed that field for me."

4. "It does look too pale for the old gray mare,
    O dear love, tell me, me, me—
It does look too pale for the old gray mare
That ploughed that field for thee, thee, thee,
    that ploughed that field for thee."

5. "How came this blood on your shirt sleeve,
    O dear love, tell me, me, me?"
"It is the blood of my brother-in-law
That went away with me, me, me,
    that went away with me."

6. "And it's what did you fall out about,
    O dear love, tell me, me, me?"
"About a little bit of bush
That never would have growed to a tree, tree, tree,
    that never would have growed to a tree."

7. "And it's what will you do now, my love,
    O dear love, tell me, me, me?"
"I'll set my foot into yonders ship
And sail across the sea, sea, sea—
    and sail across the sea!"

8. "And it's when will you come back again,
    O dear love, tell me, me, me?"
"When the sun sets into yonders sycamore tree
And that will never be, be, be—
    and that will never be!"

3. [The Murdered Brother]

Scarborough, 1937, p. 406(C); text, pp. 183-84. Sung by
Ora Keene Bowerman, Russell Fork, Council, Va., c. 1932.

p Æ/D (inflected VII)

1. What is that blood all on your hand?
    My son, please tell to me.
It is the blood of my guinea greyhound
    That chased the fox for me.

2. I never saw hound's blood so red,
    My son, please tell to me.
It is the blood of my guinea grey mare
    That ploughed in the fields with me.

3. There never was mare's blood so red,
    My son, please tell to me.
It is the blood of my dear brother
    That worked in the fields with me.

This tune appears corrupt: the F♯ can hardly be traditional.

4. What did you and your brother fall out about?
    My son, please tell to me.
Fell out about a hazel-nut bush,
    Although it was a tree.

5. Oh, what will you do when your papa comes home?
    My son, please tell to me.
I'll step my foot on yonder steam-boat,
    I'll sail across the sea.

6. What will you do with your wife and child?
    My son, please tell to me.
I'll leave them here with you, dear mother,
    For to keep you company.

7. Oh, what will you do with your house and land?
    My son, please tell to me.
I'll leave it here with you, mother,
    For you to sell for me.

8. When will you be back again?
    My son, please tell to me.
When the sun sets on yonder hill forever,
    And you know that will never be.

4. "How come that blood on your shirt sleeve?"

Owens, 1950, pp. 62-63. Sung by Mrs. T. H. Burke, Silsbee,
Texas.

p π[1]

"How come that blood on your shirt sleeve,
My son, come telling to me?"
"It is the blood of my own brother dear
Who worked in the fields with me."

"What have you killed your own brother for,
My son, come telling to me?"
"I killed him for cutting yonders bush
That might have made a tree."

"What will you do when your father comes home,
My son, come telling to me?"
"I'll set my foot in a sailing ship
And sail across the sea."

"What will you do with your pretty little wife,
My son, come telling to me?"
"I'll take her by the lily-white hand
To sail along with me."

"What will you do with your children three,
My son, come telling to me?"
"I'll leave them here with my own mother dear
To keep her company."

"When you coming home to see your children three,
My son, come telling to me?"
"Whene'er the sun sets on yonders green hill,
Which you know will never be."

5. [Edward]

Scarborough, 1937, p. 404(A); text, pp. 181-82. Sung by
Clara Callahan, near Saluda, N.C., c. 1932.

a M

1. How come that blood on your shirt sleeve,
    My son, come tell to me.
  It is the blood of the old greyhound
    That chased the fox for me.
  It does look too pale for the old greyhound
    That chased the fox for thee, thee, thee,
    That chased the fox for thee.

2. How come that blood on your shirt sleeve,
    My son, come tell to me.
  It is the blood of the old gray mare
    That ploughed the field for me.
  It does look too pale for the old gray mare
    That ploughed the field for thee, thee, thee,
      That ploughed the field for thee.

3. How came the blood on your shirt sleeve,
    My son, come tell to me.
  It is the blood of my brother-in-law
    That went away with me, me, me,
    That went away with me.

4. And it's what did you fall out about,
    My son, come tell to me.
  About a little bit of a bush
    That soon would have made a tree, tree, tree,
    That soon would have made a tree.

5. And it's what will you do now, my son,
    My son, come tell to me.
  I'll set my foot in yonder ship
    And I'll sail across yonder sea, sea, sea,
    And I'll sail across the sea.

6. And it's when will you be back, my son?
    My son, come tell to me.
  When the sun sets yonder in the sycamore tree, tree, tree,
    And that will never be.

6a. "The Little Yellow Dog"

Randolph, I, 1946, pp. 69(B)-70. Sung by Charles Ingenthron, Walnut Shade, Mo., February 1, 1941; learned near Day, Mo., c. 1895-1900. (For the words, see below, no. 6b.)

a π^1

6b. "The Little Yellow Dog"

Randolph, LC/AAFS 1393, Album XII, rec. 57B. Sung by Charles Ingenthron, Walnut Shade, Mo., 1941.

a π^1

1. "Oh, what's that stain on your shirt sleeve?
    Son, please come tell me."
  "It is the blood of my little yellow dog
    That followed after me."

2. "It is too pale for your little yellow dog,
    Son, please come tell me."
  "It is the blood of my little yellow horse
    That I rode to town today."

3. "It is too pale for your little yellow horse,
 Son, please come tell me."
 "It is the blood of my own brother dear
 That rode by the side of me."

4. "Oh, what did you fall out about?
 Son, please come tell me."
 "We fell out about a sprout
 That might have made a tree."

5. "Oh, what will you do when your father comes home?
 Son, please come tell me."
 "I'll step on board of yondo (yonder) ship
 And sail across the sea."

6. "Oh, what will you do with Katie dear?
 Son, please come tell me."
 "I'll take her on board of yondo ship
 To bear me company."

7. "Oh, when will you come back, my dear?
 Son, please come tell me."
 "When the sun rises never to set,
 And you know that'll never be."

7. [Edward]

Sharp MSS., 3823/2805. Also in Sharp and Karpeles, 1932,
I, p. 49(E). Sung by Mrs. Meg Shook and Mrs. Haynes,
Clyde, Hayward County, N.C., August 2, 1917.

a π²

The printed copy in 1932 mistakenly reads G instead of A at the
mid-cadence.
 Mr. Sharp and Miss Karpeles judged the tonic to be G. For reasons
elsewhere stated (of historical derivation and widespread tradition),
I prefer to regard the final as tonic.

1. How come that blood on the point of your knife?
 My son, come tell to me.
 It is the blood of my old coon dog
 That chased the [fox*] for me, me, me,
 That chased the [fox*] for me.

2. How come that blood, etc.
 It is the blood of that old horse
 That ploughed the† field for me, etc.

3. How come that blood, etc.
 It is the blood of one of my brothers (or, of Edward)§
 Which fell out with me, etc.

4. What did you fall out about?
 My son, etc.
 We fell out about a holly-bush
 That would have made a tree, etc.

5. What will you do when your father comes home?
 I'll put my foot in a bunkum boat
 And sail across the sea.

6. What will you do with your dear little wife?
 I'll put her foot in a bunkum boat
 And sail across the sea.

7. What will you do with your dear little babe?
 I'll leave it here in this lone world
 To dandle on your knee.

8. And what will you do with your old gobbler?
 I'll leave it here with you when I'm gone
 To gobble after me.

 * Sharp MS.: "dog"
 † 1932: "that"
 § 1932 omits "(or, of Edward)"

8. [Edward]

Sharp MSS., 4552/3185. Also in Sharp and Karpeles, 1932,
I, p. 53(J). Sung by Mrs. Mary Gibson, Marion, N.C.,
September 3, 1918.

a π²

1. What blood is that all on your shirt?
 O son, come tell to me.
 It is the blood of the old grey mare
 That ploughed the corn for me, O me,
 That ploughed the corn for me.

2. It is too red for the old grey mare.
 O son, etc.
 It is the blood of the old grey hound
 That run the deer for me, etc.

3. It is too red for the old grey hound.
 It is the blood of the little guinea-pig
 That eat the corn for me.

4. It is too red for the little guinea-pig.
 It is the blood of my oldest brother
 That travelled along with me.

5. What did you fall all* out about?
 About a little holly bush
 That might have made a tree.

6. What will you do when your father comes home?
   I'll set my foot in a bunkum boat
   And sail all on the sea.

7. What will you do with your pretty little wife?
   I'll take her on a bunkum boat
   And sail along with me.

8. What will you do with your oldest son?
   I'll leave him here for you to raise
   And dance around your knees.

9. What will you do with your oldest daughter?
   I'll leave her here for you to raise
   For to remember me.

   * 1932 omits "all."

9. "What blood on the point of your knife?"

Randolph I, 1946, pp. 67(A)-68. Sung by Mrs. Emma L.
Dusenbury, Mena, Ark., January 4, 1931.

a π² (tonic D)

A dialect printing of this is given in Mr. Randolph's earlier book
as from Carrie Langley (*Ozark Mountain Folks*, 1932, p. 207).

1. What blood? What blood on th' p'int of your knife?
   Dear son, come tell to me.
   It's th' blood of my old gray horse
   That plowed th' corn for me, me, me,
   That plowed the corn for me.

2. What blood? What blood on the p'int of your knife?
   Dear son, come tell to me.
   It's the blood of my old Guinea sow
   That ate the corn for me, me, me,
   That ate the corn for me.

3. What blood? What blood on the p'int of your knife?
   Dear son, come tell to me.
   It's the blood of my oldest brother
   That fought the battle with me, me, me,
   That fought the battle with me.

4. What did you an' your dear brother fight about?
   Dear son, come tell to me.
   We fit about the holly bush
   That grows by the mary tree, tree, tree,
   That grows by the mary tree.

5. What will you do when your father comes home?
   Dear son, come tell to me.
   I'll put my foot in a bumken boat
   An' sail across the sea, sea, sea,
   An' sail across the sea.

6. What will you do with your pretty little wife?
   Dear son, come tell to me.
   I'll put her in the bumken boat
   To sail along with me, me, me,
   To sail along with me.

7. What will you do with your pretty little babe?
   Dear son, come tell to me.
   I'll leave it all along with you
   To dandle on your knee, knee, knee,
   To dandle on your knee.

10. "The Blood of Fair Lucy"

Halpert, LC/AAFS 2863, rec. B2. Sung by Mrs. Ewart
Wilson, Pensacola, N.C., 1939.

a I/M

'What caused this blood on your shirt sleeve,
   O son, pray tell to me?'
'That blood it came from my gross hog
   But, Mama, it'll follow me.'

'That looks too bright for your gross hog,
   O son, pray tell to me?'
'This blood it came from fair Lucy
   And, Mama, it'll follow me.'

'O what will you do with your children three,
   O son, pray tell to me?'
'I'll leave them with you to keep you sweet company.'

'O what will you do when your father comes home,
   O son, pray tell to me?'
'I'll put my foot in yon little boat
   And sail over the sea.'

11. [Edward]

Sharp MSS., 3821/2804. Also in Sharp and Karpeles, 1932,
I, p. 47(C). Sung by Strauder Medford, Balsam, N.C.,
July 31, 1917.

a π³

How came that blood on the point of your knife?
My son, come tell to me.
It is the blood of my old coon dog

This is the "Boyne Water" type.

The 1932 printing is transposed to C final (with B♭ throughout).

That chased the fox for me, O me,
That chased the fox for me.

How came that blood, etc.
It is the blood of the olive bush
Which would have made a tree, etc.

How came that blood, etc.
It is the blood of my oldest brother
Who raised a row with me, etc.

O what are you going to do with your little children?
O son, come tell to me.
I'll leave them here to stand around you
And cry after me when I'm gone.

12. [Edward]

Sharp MSS., 4527/3173. Also in Sharp and Karpeles, 1932,
I, p. 52(I). Sung by Mrs. Nannie Weaver, Woolwine, Va.,
August 25, 1918.

a π³

How came that blood on your shirt-sleeve?
My son, come tell it to me.
It is my own brother's blood
That fled the show for me.

* * * * * * *

When will you return again?
My son, come tell it to me.
When the sun and moon shall set in yonders east,
Which you know will never be.

13. [Edward]

Sharp MSS., 3316/2421. Also in Sharp and Karpeles, 1932,
I, p. 46(A). Sung by Mrs. Jane Gentry, Hot Springs, N.C.,
August 24, 1916.

a M

1. How come that blood on your shirt sleeve?
   Pray, son, now tell to me.
   It is the blood of the old greyhound
   That run young fox for [me].*

2. It is too pale for that old greyhound.
   Pray, son, now tell to me.
   It is the blood of the old grey mare
   That ploughed that corn for me.

3. It is too pale for that old grey mare.
   Pray, son, now tell to me.
   It is the blood of my youngest brother
   That hoed that corn for me.

4. What did you fall out about?
   Pray, son, now tell to me.
   Because he cut yon holly bush
   Whigh might have made a tree.

5. O what will you tell to your father dear
   When he comes home from town?
   I'll set my foot in yonder ship
   And sail the ocean round.

6. † O what will you do with your three little babes?
   Pray, son, now tell to me.
   I'll leave them here in the care of you
   For to keep you company.

7. O what will you do with your sweet little wife?
   Pray, son, now tell to me.
   I'll set her foot in yonder ship
   To keep me company.

8. O what will you do with your house and land?
   Pray, son, now tell to me.
   I'll leave it here in the§ care of you
   For to set my children free.

* Sharp MS. has "(you?)."
† 1932 gives stanzas 6 and 7 in reverse order.
§ 1932 omits "the."

14. [Edward]

Sharp MSS., 4475/3153. Also in Sharp and Karpeles, 1932,
I, p. 50(G). Sung by Mr. Ebe Richards, St. Peter's School,
Callaway, Va., August 18, 1918.

m M

Where did you get that* little blood red?
My son, come tell to me.
I got it out of the little grey hawk
That sets† on yonders tree.

The first note of the 5/4 bar is mistakenly G in 1932.
This form has been largely appropriated by the Appalachian variants of "The House Carpenter" (cf. 243).

That little grey hawk's blood was never so red.
My son, come tell to me.
I got it out on that little red (*sometimes*, grey) colt
That ploughed on yonders field.

That little grey (*or*, red) colt's blood was never so red.
My son, come tell to me.
I got it out of my poor little brother
That rode away with me.

What are you going to do when your papa comes home?
My son, come tell to me.
I'll set my foot in the bottomless ship,
And sail across the sea.

When are you coming back, my son?
My son, come tell to me.
When the moon and the§ sun sets in yonders hill,
And that will never be.

    * 1932: "your"
    † 1932: "sits"
    § 1932 omits "the."

15. [Edward]

Sharp MSS., 4502/3165. Also in Sharp and Karpeles, 1932, I, pp. 51(H)-52. Sung by Mrs. S. V. Cannady, Endicott, Va., August 23, 1918.

a π³

The 1932 printing mistakenly gives the last note of the second bar one degree higher than the MS. reading.
This variant has much in common with "Little Marget" (74) in B. L. Lunsford and L. Stringfield, *30 and 1 Folksongs* [1929], p. 2.

1. O what is this the blood of?
    Son, pray tell it to me.
    It is the blood of my good old horse
    That ploughed the fields for me.

2. It is too red for your good old horse.
    Son, pray tell it to me.
    It is the blood of my good old cow
    That gave the milk for me.

3. It is too red for your good old cow.
    Son, pray tell it to me.
    It is the blood of my good old dog
    That ran the deer for me.

4. It is too red for your good old dog.
    Son, pray tell it to me.
    It is the blood of my good old brother
    That walked the road with me.

5. O what did you and your brother fall out about?
    Son, pray tell it to me.
    We fell out about a hazel-nut bush
    Which might have made a hazel-nut tree.

6. O what are you going to do?
    Son, pray tell it to me.
    I'll set my foot on yonders shore,
    And I'll sail across the sea.

7. What are you going to do with your pretty little wife?
    Son, pray tell it to me.
    I'll set her foot on yonders shore,
    And she'll sail by the side of me.

8. What are you going to do with your sweet little babe?
    Son, pray tell it to me.
    I'll leave it here with my papa
    Till I come home again.

9. O when will that be?
    Son, pray tell it to me.
    When the sun rises in the West and sets in the East
    And that can never be.

16. [Edward]

Sharp MSS., 4314/3083. Also in Sharp and Karpeles, 1932, I, p. 50(F). Sung by Mrs. J. L. Long, Villamont, Bedford County, Va., June 4, 1918.

a D/M

Compare with this the text and tune of "Lizzie Wan" (51) in Sharp MSS., 3838/2810, and Sharp and Karpeles, 1932, I, p. 89.

O what are you going to do when your father comes home?
O son, come and tell to me.
I'll put my foot in yonders boat,
And sail across the sea.

O when will you return, O when will you return?
O son, come and tell to me.
When the moon and the sun sets in yonders hills,
And that will never be.

17. [Edward]

Sharp MSS., 4534/. Sung by Mrs. Clara Plegné, Winston-Salem, N.C., September 1, 1918.

p I (–VI)

O when will you return again,
My son come tell it to me,
When the sun shall set in yonders East,
Which you know shall never be.

18. [What Blood is This]

Kennedy, *JEFDSS*, VI (December 1951), p. 99. Corrected reading, *JEFDSS*, VII (1952), p. 38. Sung by Mrs. Day, Aldershot, Hants, August 1950, and Miss Adcock, Watton, Norfolk, August 1951.

p I

Compare "Lady Isabel and the Elf Knight," in E. B. Greenleaf and G. Y. Mansfield, *Ballads and Sea Songs of Newfoundland*, 1933, p. 3.

What blood is this lies sprinkled on the ground
My son come tell unto me:—
Is it the blood of the old grey mare
Or the sins of the mother of three?

It's not the blood of the old grey mare,
For she's in the stable, I know.
It is the blood of the mother of three
Whose sins God and man did o'erthrow.

What will your father say when he come to know?
My son come tell unto me.
I'll dress myself in a new suit of blue
And sail straight to New Germany.

19. "What is that on the end of your sword?"

Davis, 1929, p. 558(C); text, p. 123. Sung by Mrs. Archibald Cummins, Berryville, Va., April 23, 1913; traditional in her family. Collected by Martha M. Davis.

p I/Ly

This suggests "Ain't goin' to rain no mo'" in its first half.

1. "What is that on the end of your sword,
      My dear son, tell to me?"
   " 'Tis the blood of an English crow
      And I wish it had never been."

2. "Crow's blood was ne'er so red as that,
      My dear son, tell to me."
   " 'Tis the blood of my dear little brother,
      And I wish it had never been."

3. "How did it happen,
      My dear son, tell to me?"
   " 'Twas digging round the hollow tree,
      And I wish it had never been."

4. "What will you do with your dear little son,
      My dear son, tell to me?"
   "I will leave him with his grandpapa
      To make him think of me."

5. "What will you do with your dear little daughter,
      My dear son, tell to me?"
   "I will leave her with her grandmama
      To make her think of me."

6. "What will you do with your dear little wife,
      My dear son, tell to me?"
   "She will put her foot on yonder boat
      And sail away with me."

7. "When will you come back,
      My dear son, tell to me?"
   "When the sun and moon set on yonder hill
      And that will never be."

GROUP C

20. [Edward]

Sharp MSS., 3332/. Also in Sharp and Karpeles, 1932, I, p. 47(B). Sung by Mrs. Rosa Hensley, Carmen, N.C., August 28, 1916; learned from her father.

p I/Ly

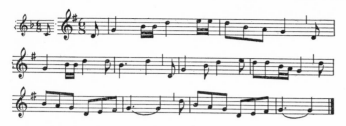

The MS. is in G; 1932 transposes to F.
Cf. the American variants of "Gypsy Davy" (200) and "Camptown Races."

O what will you say when your father comes back
O what will you say to me?
I'll set my foot on yonder little boat
I'll sail away over the sea
I'll sail away over the sea

Sharp's MS. note: "This is apparently the last verse of Edward. It was the only one Mrs. Hensley ever heard her father George Washington Shelton sing and he sang it to one of his children who had put her foot into a puddle. Mrs. Shelton is still living 8 miles from Del Rio, Tennessee, in the 15th District on the West Prong of the Big Creek."

21. [How come that blood on your shirt sleeve?]

Owens, 1950, pp. 60-62. Sung by Mrs. Ben Dryden, Sandy Creek, Texas.

a I, ending on II

1. How come that blood on your shirt sleeve,
My son, come tell to me?
How come that blood on your shirt sleeve,
My son, come tell to me?

2. It is the blood of the old grey mare
That pulled the plow for me;
It is the blood of the old grey mare
That pulled the plow for me.

3. That blood's too red for that,
My son, come tell to me,
How come that blood on your shirt sleeve,
My son, come tell to me?

4. It is the blood of the old grey goose
That flew by the side of me;
It is the blood of the old grey goose
That flew by the side of me.

5. That blood's too red for that,
My son, come tell to me,

How come that blood on your shirt sleeve,
My son, come tell to me?

6. It is the blood of my own dear brother
That plowed by the side of me;
It is the blood of my own dear brother
That plowed by the side of me.

7. What did you and your brother fall out about,
My son, come tell to me?
We fell out about that little juniper tree
That grows under yander tree.

8. What you gonna do when your father comes home,
My son, come tell to me?
I'll set my foot in a sailing boat
And I'll sail across the sea.

9. What you gonna do with your pretty little wife,
My son, come tell to me?
I'll set her foot by the side of my side,
To sail across the sea.

10. What you gonna do with your pretty little children,
My son, come tell to me?
I'll leave them here in youry care
Till I return to thee.

11. When you coming back
My son, come tell to me?
I'm coming back when the sun goes east and west
And that shall never be.

22. [Edward]

Davis, 1929, p. 558(D); text, p. 124. Sung by Mrs. Travers D. Moncure, Aylett, Va., September 13, 1917; learned from her mother, who learned it from *her* mother. Collected by John Stone.

a π¹ (compass of sixth)

The original copy is written straight through in 6/8 time.

"What is that on your sword so red?
Dear son, pray tell unto me."
"'Tis the blood of a gay gilleon.
Dear mother, pity me.
'Tis the blood of a gay gilleon.
Dear mother, pity me."

"No gilleon's blood was e'er so red.
Dear son, pray tell unto me."
"'Tis the blood of my dear brother.
O mother, pity me.
'Tis the blood of my dear brother.
O mother, pity me."

"What will you do when your father comes home?
  Dear son, tell unto me."
"I'll get aboard of yonder ship
  And sail away to sea.
  I'll get aboard of yonder ship
  And sail away to sea."

"When will you return, my son?
  Dear son, pray tell unto me."
"When the sun and the moon set on yonder hill,
  And that will never be.
  When the sun and the moon set on yonder hill,
  And that will never be."

Oh what's that red upon your blade?
Ronald, Ronald,
Oh what's that red upon your blade?
My dear son, now tell me O.

Oh I have killed my little gray hawk,
Mother, mother.
Oh I have killed my little gray hawk
That used to hunt with me O.

23. "Ronald"

Randolph, I, 1946, p. 71(D). Sung by Mrs. Irene Carlisle, Fayetteville, Ark., October 26, 1941; learned from her grandmother in 1912.

a π¹ (compass of sixth)

"Camptown Races" is strongly suggested by this variant.

24. [Edward, Edward]

Musicraft, Album 55, rec. 262AB. Sung by G. Marston Haddock. (Perhaps arbitrary.)

m Æ

For this tune, cf. the headnote. Haddock employs the Child A text (from Bishop Percy).

Babylon

CHILD NO. 14

In the English language, this ballad has a recorded history of about a century and a half, and the musical record, as seldom happens, is nearly as old and good. The tradition appears to have held pretty consistently to LM quatrains, rhyming alternately,* with interlaced refrain as the general habit. The words of the refrain vary considerably, as is often true of refrains which are rather musical than meaningful.

It appears to me that there are at most two melodic families in the record for this ballad; but the divergence of copies is considerable. The rhythm seems originally to have been triple in both cases, and in both to have shifted gradually to duple time. It may be that such a shift has occurred much oftener in ballad melody than there is any likelihood of demonstrating. Kinloch's copy, virtually a π^3 tune, but literally D/M, may be allowed to head the larger group, composed of Dorian and Æolian variants, the Bute copy of which is closer to the "Hind Horn" (17) tradition than to the present. Motherwell's copy, Mixolydian but lacking its fourth, may be related—though not proudly!—to the debased π^1 version found in Vermont, "Heckey-Hi Si-Bernio." From "bower" to "barn" is a decline in tradition: whether from a "rank robber" to a "bank robber" is the opposite, who shall say? These last two copies may by courtesy be allowed to stand as a separate group.

[* There is probably a corruption in stanzas 14-17 of Motherwell's version, where the rhyme of lines 1 and 3 disappears. The injury may have occurred by the dropping-out of the true line 3 in stanza 14, so that the actual rhymes come in different stanzas: $14^3 = 15^1$, $15^3 = 16$; then an interpolated and unnecessary line, 17^1, to make up the complement, where $16^3 = 17^3$ are the proper pair. The curious name, "Baby Lon," doubtless a perversion, is not yet accounted for, and awaits some lucky guess.]

LIST OF VARIANTS

GROUP A

1. "The Duke of Perth's Three Daughters." G. R. Kinloch, *Ancient Scottish Ballads*, 1827, App'x to p. 210 and pp. 212-16.
2. "The Duke of Perth's Three Daughters." Robert Maver, *Genuine Scottish Ballads*, 1866, No. 358, p. 179 (to other words).
3. "The Bonny Banks of Virgie-O." Maud Karpeles, *Folk Songs from Newfoundland*, 1934, II, pp. 78-82.
4. "The Bonny Banks of the Virgie, O." Elisabeth Bristol Greenleaf and Grace Yarrow Mansfield, *Ballads and Sea Songs of Newfoundland*, 1933, pp. 10-11.
5. "The Burly, Burly Banks of Barbry-O." Helen Hartness Flanders and Marguerite Olney, *Ballads Migrant in New England*, 1953, pp. 61-63. Also on an LP record, *Eight Traditional British-American Ballads*, New England Folk-Song Series 1, Helen Hartness Flanders Collection, Middlebury College, Middlebury, Vt., 1953. (Elmer Barton)
6. "Doon by the Bonnie Banks o' Airdrie, O." A. Reid, *Rymour Club Miscellanea*, II (1910), p. 78.

GROUP B

7. "The Banks of Fordie." William Motherwell, *Minstrelsy: Ancient and Modern*, 1827, App'x No. 26 and p. xxii.
8. "Heckey-Hi Si-Bernio." Helen Hartness Flanders, *BFSSNE*, No. 7 (1934), p. 6.

TUNES WITH TEXTS

GROUP A

1. [The Duke of Perth's Three Daughters]

Kinloch, 1827, App'x. to p. 210; text, pp. 212-16. Sung in Mearnsshire.

m D/M

1. The Duke o' Perth had three daughters,
     Elizabeth, Margaret, and fair Marie;
   And Elizabeth's to the greenwud gane
     To pu' the rose and the fair lilie.

2. But she hadna pu'd a rose, a rose,
     A double rose, but barely three,
   Whan up and started a Loudon Lord,
     Wi' Loudon hose, and Loudon sheen.

3. "Will ye be called a robber's wife?
   Or will ye be stickit wi' my bloody knife?
   For pu'in the rose and the fair lilie,
   For pu'in them sae fair and free."

4. "Before I'll be called a robber's wife,
   I'll rather be stickit wi' your bloody knife,
   For pu'in the rose and the fair lilie,
   For pu'in them sae fair and free."

5. Then out he's tane his little penknife,
   And he's parted her and her sweet life,
   And thrown her o'er a bank o' brume,
   There never more for to be found.

6. The Duke o' Perth had three daughters,
     Elizabeth, Margaret, and fair Marie;
   And Margaret's to the greenwud gane
     To pu' the rose and the fair lilie.

[248]

7. But she hadna pu'd a rose, a rose,
   A double rose, but barely three,
When up and started a Loudon Lord,
   Wi' Loudon hose, and Loudon sheen.

8. "Will ye be called a robber's wife?
   Or will ye be stickit wi' my bloody knife?
For pu'in the rose and the fair lilie,
For pu'in them sae fair and free."

9. "Before I'll be called a robber's wife,
   I'll rather be stickit wi' your bloody knife,
For pu'in the rose and the fair lilie,
For pu'in them sae fair and free."

10. Then out he's tane his little penknife,
    And he's parted her and her sweet life,
For pu'in the rose and the fair lilie,
For pu'in them sae fair and free.

11. The Duke o' Perth had three daughters,
    Elizabeth, Margaret, and fair Marie;
And Mary's to the greenwud gane
    To pu' the rose and the fair lilie.

12. She hadna pu'd a rose, a rose,
    A double rose, but barely three,
When up and started a Loudon Lord,
    Wi' Loudon hose, and Loudon sheen.

13. "O will ye be called a robber's wife?
    Or will ye be stickit wi' my bloody knife?
For pu'in the rose and the fair lilie,
For pu'in them sae fair and free."

14. "Before I'll be called a robber's wife,
    I'll rather be stickit wi' your bloody knife,
For pu'in the rose and the fair lilie,
For pu'in them sae fair and free."

15. But just as he took out his knife,
    To tak' frae her, her ain sweet life,
Her brother John cam ryding bye,
And this bloody robber he did espy.

16. But when he saw his sister fair,
    He kenn'd her by her yellow hair,
He call'd upon his pages three,
To find this robber speedilie.

17. "My sisters twa that are dead and gane,
    For whom we made a heavy maene,
It's you that's twinn'd them o' their life,
And wi' your cruel bloody knife.

18. Then for their life ye sair shall dree,
    Ye sall be hangit on a tree,
Or thrown into the poison'd lake,
To feed the toads and rattle-snake."

2. [The Duke of Perth's Three Daughters]

Maver, 1866, No. 358, p. 179 (to other words).

a D/M

3. "The Bonny Banks of Virgie-O"

Karpeles, 1934, II, pp. 78-82. Sung by Mr. and Mrs. Kenneth Monks, King's Cove, Bonavista Bay, Newfoundland, September 24, 1929. Text as collected by Miss Karpeles.

m D

1. Three young ladies went out for a walk;
   All a lee and a lonely O
They met a robber on their way,
   On the bonny bonny banks of Vergeo.

2. He took the first one by the hand,
   And whipped her around till he made her stand.

3. O will you be a robber's wife?
   Or will you die by my penknife?

4. I will not be a robber's wife;
   I would rather die by your penknife.

5. He took the penknife in his hand,
   And it's there he took her own sweet life.

6. He took the second one by the hand,
   And whipped her around till he made her stand.

7. O will you be a robber's wife?
   Or will you die by my penknife?

8. I will not be a robber's wife;
   I would rather die by your penknife.

9. He took the penknife in his hand,
   And it's there he took her own sweet life.

10. He took the third one by the hand,
    And whipped her around till he made her stand.

11. O will you be a robber's wife?
    Or will you die by my penknife?

12. I will not be a robber's wife,
    Nor I will not die by your penknife.

13. If my brothers were here to-night
You would not have killed my sisters fair (*or* bright).

14. Where are your brothers, pray now tell?
One of them is a minister.

15. And where is the other, I pray now tell?
He's out a-robbing like yourself.

16. The Lord have mercy on my poor soul,
I've killed my sisters all but one.

17. Then he took his penknife in his hand,
And then he took away his own sweet life.

4. "The Bonny Banks of the Virgie, O"

Greenleaf and Mansfield, 1933, pp. 10-11. Sung by May, Mildred and Victoria White, Sandy Cove, Newfoundland, 1929.

m Æ

1. Three young ladies went for a walk,
Too ra lee, and a lonely O,
And they met a robber on their way,
On the bonny, bonny banks of the Virgie, O.

2. He took the first one by the hand,
He whipped her round till he made her stand.

3. He took the second one by the hand:
"I'd rather die by my penknife."

4. He took the third one by the hand:
"I'd rather my brothers 're here to-night."

5. "What is your brothers, I pray you tell?"
"For one is a robber like yoursel'."

6. "What did the other, I pray you tell?"
"The other is a minister, sir," said she.

7. "Lord have mercy for what I have done!
I have murdered my three sisters all but one!"

8. He took the penknife in his hand,
And 'twas there he took his own sweet life.

5. "The Burly, Burly Banks of Barbry-O"

Flanders and Olney, 1953, pp. 61-63. Sung by Elmer Barton, Quechee, Vt., 1942. From *Ballads Migrant in New England*, edited by Helen Hartness Flanders and Marguerite Olney; copyright 1953 by Helen Hartness Flanders.

m D

The original time-signature is 2/2.

Mr. Barton's singing of this ballad has been recorded on a longplaying record, *Eight Traditional British-American Ballads*, New England Folk-Song Series 1, Helen Hartness Flanders Collection, Middlebury College, Middlebury, Vt., 1953. There are slight differences in the variant as sung, e.g. (a).

1. There were three sisters picking flowers
High in the lea and the lonely O.
They scarce had picked but one or two,
On the burly, burly banks of Barbry-O.

2. It's there they spied a bank-robber bold.
It's there they spied a bank-robber bold.

3. He took the oldest by the hand.
He hurled her round 'n he made her stand,

4. Saying, "Will you be a bank-robber's wife?
Or will you die by my penknife?"

5. "No, I won't be a bank-robber's wife;
I'd rather die by your penknife."

6. Then he took out his penknife;
It's there he ended her sweet life.

7. He took the next one by the hand.
He hurled her round; he made her stand,

8. Saying, "Will you be a bank-robber's wife;
Or will you die by my penknife?"

9. "No, I won't be a bank-robber's wife;
I'd rather die by your penknife."

10. Then he took out his penknife
And it's there he ended her sweet life.

11. He took the youngest by the hand,
He hurled* her round; he made her stand,

12. Saying, "Will you be a bank-robber's wife?
Or will you die by my penknife?"

13. "Yes, I will be a bank-robber's wife
So† I won't die by your penknife.

14. "O dear, O dear, I wish my two brothers were here!"§
"O what would your two brothers do?"

15. "For one is a minister; the other like you
On the burly, burly banks of Barbry-O."

16. Then he took out his penknife,
And it's there he ended his own life.

Between the two final stanzas, Mr. Barton sings:

"Oh God, oh God, oh what have I done!
I've murdered my sisters, all but one!"

* Sung: whirled
† Sung: Then
§ *bis* as sung, the second line beginning the next stanza.

6. [Doon by the Bonnie Banks o' Airdrie, O]

Reid, *Rymour Club Miscellanea*, II (1910), p. 78. Sung by little girls, Kingarth, Bute.

m Æ/D

Three sisters went to gather flow'rs,
Three sisters went to gather flow'rs,
Three sisters went to gather flow'rs,
Down by the bonnie banks o' Airdrie, O.

GROUP B

7. [The Banks of Fordie]

Motherwell, 1827, App'x No. 26; text, p. xxii. Collected by Andrew Blaikie, Paisley.

a M (–IV)

There were three sisters liv'd in a bower,
    Fair Annet, and Margaret, and Marjorie,
And they went out to pu' a flower,
    And the dew draps off the hyndberry tree.

The long version that Motherwell admits as full text (18 stanzas), pp. 88-92, does not go so well to the tune above. It begins:

There were three ladies lived in a bower,
    Eh vow bonnie,
And they went out to pull a flower,
    On the bonnie banks o' Fordie.

The last six stanzas, to which the headnote makes reference, are as follows:

13. "I'll not be a rank robber's wife,
    Eh vow bonnie,
Nor will I die by your wee penknife,
    On the bonnie banks o' Fordie.

14. "For I hae a brother in this wood,
    Eh vow bonnie,
And gin ye kill me, it's he'll kill thee,
    On the bonnie banks o' Fordie."

15. "What's thy brother's name, come tell to me?
    Eh vow bonnie."
"My brother's name is Baby Lon,
    On the bonnie banks o' Fordie."

16. "O sister, sister, what have I done,
    Eh vow bonnie,
O have I done this ill to thee,
    On the bonnie banks o' Fordie?

17. "O since I've done this evil deed,
    Eh vow bonnie,
Good sall never be seen o' me,
    On the bonnie banks o' Fordie."

18. He's taken out his wee penknife,
    Eh vow bonnie,
And he's twyned himsel o' his ain sweet life,
    On the bonnie banks o' Fordie.

8. "Heckey-Hi Si-Bernio"

Flanders, *BFSSNE*, No. 7 (1934), p. 6. Sung by Mrs. Marjorie L. Porter, Plattsburg, N.Y.; learned from family tradition on her mother's side, in Vermont. From *Bulletin of the Folk-Song Society of the Northeast*, No. 7 (1934), edited by Phillips Barry; copyright 1934 by the Folk-Song Society of the Northeast.

p π¹ (–VI)

1. There were three maids lived in a barn;—
    Heckey hi si bernio—
When up there rose a wicked man,
On the bonny banks of Bernio.

2. He took the eldest by the hand,
He whirled her round and made her stand.

3. "Heckry, lass, will you be young Robey's wife?
Or rather would you die by my penknife?"

4. "Never will I be young Robey's wife;
Rather would I die by your penknife."

5. So he took her life and laid it by
To keep the greensward compan-eye.

6. He took the next one by the hand,
He whirled her round and made her stand.

7. Heckry, lass, will you be young Robey's wife?
Or rather would you die by my penknife?"

8. "Never will I be Young Robey's wife,
   Rather would I die by your penknife."

9. So he took her life and laid it by,
   To keep the greensward compan-eye.

10. He took the youngest by the hand,
    He whirled her round and made her stand.

11. "Heckry, lass, will you be Young Robey's wife?
    Or rather would you die by my penknife?"

12. "Never will I be young Robey's wife,
    Neither will I die by your penknife."

13. So she took his life and laid it by,
    To keep her sisters compan-eye.

Sheath and Knife

CHILD NO. 16

THIS ballad has been rarely found in British tradition, never outside Scotland. No new copy has appeared since the first half of the last century; and the only tune known is the plaintive one which Burns salvaged for Johnson's *Museum* in the last decade of the eighteenth century. Of this, a variant was published, with other words, in 1866.

Of this very appropriate tune there is a manuscript copy, with no differences except for holds on the second and third phrase-finals, in Nat. Lib. Scotland MS. 843, fol. 18ᵛ. This MS. is of "Ballads, &c. from the Collection of the late Charles Kirkpatrick Sharpe, Esquire, of Hoddam. Arranged for The Right Honourable Lady John Scott." The words are taken from Jamieson, 1806. There is still another copy, marked "very old,"

in Lady John Scott's MS. (Nat. Lib. Scotland MS. 840). These copies may probably have been taken from Johnson and not directly from tradition. It might be mentioned that the haunting refrain appears in an almost identical form in Child 15 B, a ballad for which, unfortunately, no tune is known.

The melodic variation of the Maver copy (1866) is too considerable to have resulted from mere editorial rehandling, although one can have little confidence in the traditional authenticity of Maver's versions. He has not thought fit to give the proper words—a fact for which the purpose and date of publication are sufficient explanation. The earlier variants are authentic Ionian; Maver's has a wider range (m I).

LIST OF VARIANTS

1. "The broom blooms bonie." James Johnson, *The Scots Musical Museum* V, [1796], No. 461, p. 474.
a. "The broom blooms bonnie." Lady John Scott's Sharpe MS., National Library of Scotland MS. 843, fol. 17ᵛ.

b. "The Broom Blooms Bonnie." Lady John Scott MS., National Library of Scotland MS. 840.
2. "The Broom Blooms Bonnie." Robert Maver, *Genuine Scottish Ballads*, 1866, No. 331, p. 166 (with other words).

TUNES WITH TEXTS

1. [The broom blooms bonie]

Johnson, V [1796], No. 461, p. 474.

a I

It's whisper'd in parlour, it's whisper'd in ha',
    The broom blooms bonie, the broom blooms fair;
Lady Marget's wi' child amang our ladies a',
    And she dare na gae down to the broom nae mair.

One lady whisper'd unto another,
    The broom blooms bonie, the broom blooms fair;

Lady Marget's wi' child to Sir Richard her brother,
    And she dare na gae down to the broom nae mair.
            *   *   *   *   *
O when that you hear my loud loud cry,
    The broom blooms &c.
Then bend your bow and let your arrows fly,
    For I dare na gae down &c.

2. [The Broom Blooms Bonnie]

Maver, 1866, No. 331, p. 166 (with other words).

m I

Hind Horn

CHILD NO. 17

ALL the tunes which have been recorded for this ballad are representatives of a single melodic idea. Save in one or two cases, there has been remarkably little variation, considering that together they span a century and an ocean. The same tune, in one guise or another (usually with greater variation), occurs with a number of alien texts, and especially with a song of which the English *textual* record is a good deal older than that of "Hind Horn"—namely, the "Bird Song" [cf., e.g., Sharp and Karpeles, 1932, II, p. 304], found on Restoration broadsides with the titles, "The Woody Querristers" and "The Birds Lamentation" [printed by (a) Clarke, Thackeray, & Passinger; and (b) P. Brooksby], and there directed to be sung to the tune of "The Bird-catchers Delight"—a tune which I have not found in any early collection. The "Bird Song" is known widely in this country, especially in New England and the Southern mountains, and has recently been given added currency on radio programs and phonograph records as "The Leather-winged Bat." [E.g., by Burl Ives, in Okeh Album K3-No. 8 (6318)]. The persistence of some of the seventeenth-century stanzas is startling, as will be seen from the following, taken from the Clarke, Thackeray, Passinger broadside:

> Then said the Leather-winged Batt,
> Mind but my tale, and I'le tell you what
> Is the cause that I do flye by night,
> Because I lost my hearts delight.

The favorite tune is also very generally known with a cowboy song, "Oh, bury me not on the lone prairie" [cf., e.g., Sharp and Karpeles, 1932, II, pp. 236-37; Sandburg, *American Songbag*, 1927, p. 20, among numerous examples]. Other permutations of the tune may be seen in the collection of Sharp and Karpeles: "The Lost Babe" [*op.cit.*, II, p. 160, in 6/8 time]; "Sally and her Lover" [II, p. 210, in 3/4 time]; "No-e in the Ark" [II, p. 216, in 4/4]; and among the ballads, "The Cruel Ship's Carpenter" [*ibid.*, I, p. 327(U)]. It occurs also as a play-party game tune [cf. "Weevily Wheat," *JAF*, XXIV (1911), p. 302 (Missouri)]. According to Keith [Greig and Keith, 1925, p. 20], it is common in Scottish folk-song, and "is, no doubt, the original of the modern air, 'Logan Braes' [Johnson, *SMM*, No. 42], and often sung to the old words of 'Logan Banks.'" Variants of the tune in Greig's MSS., sung to a great diversity of texts, are: I, 58, 59, 123, 187; II, 1, 19, 64, 65, 72, 113; III, 6, 25, 61, 87, 98, 163; IV, 31, 62, 78, 134. It is proper to call attention here to "The Whummil Bore" (27), which may be related to "Hind Horn."

Variants of this tune-family with a "Hind Horn" text are pretty well confined, so far as the record shows, to Scotland and the Northeastern seaboard of America, taking in Maine, New Brunswick, and Newfoundland. The tune is almost always Æ/D, plagal, and in duple time. Two Scottish copies, with doubtful finals, may be plagal majors (Blaikie's and Miss Macmath's); and the same is true of Miss Karpeles' Newfoundland tune. Characteristically, the mid-cadence is on V, the first-phrase cadence on lower flat VII. Nearly all variants are of the "progressive" type, ABCD, although the later phrases contain elements of the earlier. Second strains, where they occur, may be regarded with suspicion.

LIST OF VARIANTS

1. "Young Hynd Horn." Lady John Scott's Sharpe MS., National Library of Scotland MS. 843, fol. 14ᵛ.
2. "The Beggar Man." Maud Karpeles, *Folk Songs from Newfoundland*, 1934, II, pp. 99-103.
a. "Hind Horn." Helen Creighton and Doreen H. Senior, *Traditional Songs from Nova Scotia*, 1950, pp. 12-13(A).
3. "Hynde Horn." William Motherwell, *Minstrelsy: Ancient and Modern*, 1827, App'x No. 13 and pp. 35-43.
4. "The Old Beggar Man." Phillips Barry, Fannie H. Eckstorm, and Mary W. Smyth, *British Ballads from Maine*, 1929, pp. 73(A)-75.
5. "Hind Horn." Barry, Eckstorm, and Smyth, *British Ballads from Maine*, 1929, pp. xxv and 78(C).
6. "Hynde Horn." W. Christie, *Traditional Ballad Airs*, II, 1881, p. 252.
7. "Hind Horn." Greig MSS., IV, p. 69, King's College Library, Aberdeen. Also in Gavin Greig and Alexander Keith, *Last Leaves of Traditional Ballads and Ballad Airs*, 1925, p. 21(e). (Sangster)
8. "Hynd Horn." Greig MSS., II, p. 13. (Robb)
9. "Hynd Horn." Greig MSS., II, p. 64. (Ewen)
10. "Hind Horn." Greig MSS., II, p. 12. (Rettie)
11. "Hynd Horn." Greig MSS., III, p. 118; text, Bk. 731, XXI, pp. 51-53. (Thain)
12. "Hind Horn." Greig MSS., IV, p. 28. (Dunbar)
13. "Hind Horn." Greig MSS., IV, p. 12; text, Bk. 764, LIV, pp. 59ff. Also in Greig and Keith, *Last Leaves*, 1925, p. 20(a). (Cruickshank)
14. "Hind Horn." Greig MSS., II, p. 64. Also in Greig and Keith, 1925, p. 21(c). (Quirie)
15. "Hind Horn." Greig MSS., III, p. 104. Also in Greig and Keith, 1925, p. 21(d). (Corbet)
16. "Hind Horn." Duncan MS., No. 327. Greig-Duncan MS. 785, transcribed by W. Walker, King's College Library, Aberdeen. Also in Greig and Keith, *Last Leaves*, 1925, p. 20(b). (Garioch)
17. "Hind Horn." Creighton and Senior, *Traditional Songs from Nova Scotia*, 1950, p. 15(C).
18. "Hind Horn." Helen Hartness Flanders and Marguerite Olney, *Ballads Migrant in New England*, 1953, pp. 47-48.
19. "The Begging Weed." Greig MSS., I, p. 133; text, Bk. 713, III, pp. 102ff. (Findley)
20. "The Begging Weed." Greig MSS., I, p. 132. (Milne)
21. "The Beggarman." Elisabeth Bristol Greenleaf and Grace Yarrow Mansfield, *Ballads and Sea Songs of Newfoundland*, 1933, pp. 12-14.
22. "Hind Horn." Creighton and Senior, *Traditional Songs from Nova Scotia*, 1950, p. 17(E).
23. "Hind Horn." Francis James Child, *The English and Scottish Popular Ballads*, 1882-98, V, p. 413, and I, pp. 503-4.

1. [Young Hynd Horn]

Lady John Scott's Sharpe MS., NL Scotland MS. 843, fol. 14ᵛ. (C. K. Sharpe Collection; present tune from Sir Walter Scott, 1825.)

a Harmonic Minor (inflected VII)

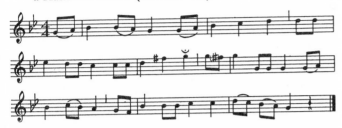

Except the first stanza, the words have not been copied, since they were attributed to Motherwell; but the latter's refrain ends "bonny," not "bonnielie." The present tune was probably sung in a pure Æolian form.

Near Edinbro' was a young child born
With a hay lillelu and a how lo lan;
And his name it was called young Hind Horn,
And the birk and the broom blooms bonnielie.

2. "The Beggar Man"

Karpeles, 1934, II, pp. 99-103. Sung by Jacob Courage, Frenchman's Cove, Garnish, Fortune Bay, Newfoundland, July 15, 1930; text from Collector's MS.

p I

The Nova Scotia variant (listed a above), with a longer text (13 stanzas), is melodically almost identical with the present copy.

1. On board of a ship and away sailed he,
   He sailed right away to a far countrie.
   He looked at the ring, it was pale and dim;
   That showed that his love was false to him.

2. You put on my driving suit,
   And I'll put on your begging rig.
   Your driving suit it won't fit me,
   My begging suit it won't fit thee.

3. Let it be right or let it be wrong,
   The begging suit I will put on.
   When he came to Napoleon's gate,
   He lay on his staff in a weary state.

4. He saw his true love come skipping downstairs,
   Rings on her fingers, gold in her hair,
   And in her hand a glass of wine,
   To treat this little old beggar man.

5. He drink-ed and he drink-ed and he drink-ed so free,
   Into the tumbler the ring slipped he.
   Did you get it by the land, or did you get it by the sea,
   Or did you get it from a drowned man's hand?

6. I neither got it from land, I neither got it from sea,
   Nor neither did I get it from a drowned man's hand.
   But I got it from a true love was courting me so gay,
   And now I return it on her wedding day.

7. Then rings from her fingers she then pulled off
   And gold from her hair it all fell off,
   Saying: I'll follow my true love for ever, ever more,
   And beg my bread from door to door.

8. Between the kitchen and the hall
   The beggar man's suit he then let fall;
   He showed the best and the first of them all,
   He was the best little man in the hall.

3. [Hynd Horn]

Motherwell, 1827, App'x No. 13; text, pp. 35-43. Collected by Andrew Blaikie, Paisley. Motherwell's text is a composite of two traditional copies and another printed by R. H. Cromek.

p I

The first phrase of this copy is like the opening of the old "Ladie Cassilles Lilt" ("Gypsy Laddie") tune in the Skene MS., but not the rest. Keith notes the parallel, and adds the recent "A wee bird cam" for another (cf. A. Moffat, *Minstrelsy of Scotland* [1894], p. 4, for the latter).

1. Near Edinburgh was a young child born,
       With a hey lillelu and a how lo lan;
   And his name it was called Young Hynd Horn,
       And the birk and the brume blooms bonnie.

2. Seven lang years he served the King,
       With a hey lillelu and a how lo lan;
   And it's a' for the sake of his dochter Jean,
       And the birk and the brume blooms bonnie.

3. The King an angry man was he,
    With a hey lillelu and a how lo lan;
He sent young Hynd Horn to the sea,
    And the birk and the brume blooms bonnie.

4. "Oh I never saw my love before,
    With a hey lillelu and a how lo lan;
Till I saw her thro' an augre bore,
    And the birk and the brume blooms bonnie.

5. "And she gave to me a gay gold ring,
    With a hey lillelu and a how lo lan;
With three shining diamonds set therein,
    And the birk and the brume blooms bonnie.

6. "And I gave to her a silver wand,
    With a hey lillelu and a how lo lan;
With three singing laverocks set thereon,
    And the birk and the brume blooms bonnie.

7. "What if those diamonds lose their hue?
    With a hey lillelu and a how lo lan;
Just when my love begins for to rew,
    And the birk and the brume blooms bonnie."

8. "For when your ring turns pale and wan,
    With a hey lillelu and a how lo lan;
Then I'm in love with another man,
    And the birk and the brume blooms bonnie."

9. He's left the land, and he's gone to the sea,
    With a hey lillelu and a how lo lan;
And he's stayed there seven years and a day,
    And the birk and the brume blooms bonnie.

10. Seven lang years he has been on the sea,
    With a hey lillelu and a how lo lan;
And Hynd Horn has looked how his ring may be,
    And the birk and the brume blooms bonnie.

11. But when he looked this ring upon,
    With a hey lillelu and a how lo lan;
The shining diamonds were both pale and wan,
    And the birk and the brume blooms bonnie.

12. Oh! the ring it was both black and blue,
    With a hey lillelu and a how lo lan;
And she's either dead, or she's married,
    And the birk and the brume blooms bonnie.

13. He's left the seas, and he's come to the land,
    With a hey lillelu and a how lo lan;
And the first he met was an auld beggar man,
    And the birk and the brume blooms bonnie.

14. "What news, what news, my silly auld man?
    With a hey lillelu and a how lo lan;
For it's seven years since I have seen land,
    And the birk and the brume blooms bonnie.

15. "What news? what news? thou auld beggar man,
    With a hey lillelu and a how lo lan;
What news? what news? by sea or land?
    And the birk and the brume blooms bonnie."

16. "No news at all, said the auld beggar man,
    With a hey lillelu and a how lo lan;
But there is a wedding in the king's hall,
    And the birk and the brume blooms bonnie.

17. "There is a King's dochter in the west,
    With a hey lillelu and a how lo lan;
And she has been married thir nine nights past,
    And the birk and the brume blooms bonnie.

18. "Into the bride-bed she winna gang,
    With a hey lillelu and a how lo lan;
Till she hears tell of her ain Hynd Horn,
    And the birk and the brume blooms bonnie."

19. "Wilt thou give to me thy begging coat,
    With a hey lillelu and a how lo lan;
And I'll give to thee my scarlet cloak,
    And the birk and the brume blooms bonnie.

20. "Wilt thou give to me thy begging staff,
    With a hey lillelu and a how lo lan;
And I'll give to thee my good gray steed,
    And the birk and the brume blooms bonnie."

21. The auld beggar man cast off his coat,
    With a hey lillelu and a how lo lan;
And he's ta'en up the scarlet cloak,
    And the birk and the brume blooms bonnie.

22. The auld beggar man threw down his staff,
    With a hey lillelu and a how lo lan;
And he has mounted the good gray steed,
    And the birk and the brume blooms bonnie.

23. The auld beggar man was bound for the mill,
    With a hey lillelu and a how lo lan;
But young Hynd Horn for the King's hall,
    And the birk and the brume blooms bonnie.

24. The auld beggar man was bound for to ride,
    With a hey lillelu and a how lo lan;
But young Hynd Horn was bound for the bride,
    And the birk and the brume blooms bonnie.

25. When he came to the King's gate,
    With a hey lillelu and a how lo lan;
He asked a drink for young Hynd Horn's sake,
    And the birk and the brume blooms bonnie.

26. These news unto the bonnie bride came,
    With a hey lillelu and a how lo lan;
That at the yett there stands an auld man,
    And the birk and the brume blooms bonnie.

27. "There stands an auld man at the King's gate,
    With a hey lillelu and a how lo lan;
He asketh a drink for young Hynd Horn's sake,
    And the birk and the brume blooms bonnie."

28. "I'll go through nine fires so hot,
    With a hey lillelu and a how lo lan;
But I'll give him a drink for young Hynd Horn's sake,
    And the birk and the brume blooms bonnie."

29. She went to the gate where the auld man did stand,
    With a hey lillelu and a how lo lan;
And she gave him a drink out of her own hand,
    And the birk and the brume blooms bonnie.

30. She gave him a cup out of her own hand,
     With a hey lillelu and a how lo lan;
   He drunk out the drink, and dropt in the ring,
     And the birk and the brume blooms bonnie.

31. "Got thou it by sea, or got thou it by land?
     With a hey lillelu and a how lo lan;
   Or got thou it off a dead man's hand?
     And the birk and the brume blooms bonnie."

32. "I got it not by sea, but I got it by land,
     With a hey lillelu and a how lo lan;
   For I got it out of thine own hand,
     And the birk and the brume blooms bonnie."

33. "I'll cast off my gowns of brown,
     With a hey lillelu and a how lo lan;
   And I'll follow thee from town to town,
     And the birk and the brume blooms bonnie.

34. "I'll cast off my gowns of red,
     With a hey lillelu and a how lo lan;
   And along with thee I'll beg my bread,
     And the birk and the brume blooms bonnie."

35. "Thou need not cast off thy gowns of brown,
     With a hey lillelu and a how lo lan;
   For I can make thee lady of many a town,
     And the birk and the brume blooms bonnie.

36. "Thou need not cast off thy gowns of red,
     With a hey lillelu and a how lo lan;
   For I can maintain thee with both wine and bread,
     And the birk and the brume blooms bonnie."

37. The bridegroom thought he had the bonnie bride wed,
     With a hey lillelu and a how lo lan;
   But young Hynd Horn took the bride to the bed,
     And the birk and the brume blooms bonnie.

4. "The Old Beggar Man"

Barry, Eckstorm, and Smyth, 1929, pp. 73(A)-75. Sung by
Thomas Edward Nelson, Union Mills, New Brunswick,
September 28, 1928; learned from his mother, who was
born in Ireland. Melody recorded by George Herzog.

m Æ/D

1. "Whence came ye, or from what counteree?
   Whence came ye, or where were you born?"
   "In Ireland I was bred and born
   Until 1 became a hele and his horn.

2. "I gave my love a gay gold watch
   That she might rule in her own counteree,
   And she gave me a gay gold ring,
   And the virtue of this was above all things.

3. "'If this ring bees bright and true,
   Be sure your love is true to you;
   But if this ring bees pale and wan,
   Your true love's in love with some other man.'"

4. He set sail and off went he,
   Until that he came to a strange counteree;
   He looked at the ring, it was pale and wan,
   His true love was in love with some other one.

5. He set sail and back came he,
   Until that he came to his own counteree,
   And as he was riding along the plain,
   Who should he meet but an old beggar man.

6. "What news, what news, you old beggar man?
   What news, what news have you got for me?"
   "No news, no news," said the old beggar man,
   "But tomorrow is your true love's wedding day."

7. You lend me your begging rig,
   And I'll lend you my riding stage."
   "Your riding stage ain't fit for me,
   Nor my begging rig ain't fit for you."

8. "Whether it be right, or whether it be wrong,
   The begging rig they must go on.
   So come, tell to me as fast as you can
   What's to be done with the begging rig."

9. "As you go up to yonder hill,
   You may walk as fast as 'tis your will,
   And when you come to yonder gate,
   You may lean upon your staff with trembling step.

10. "You may beg from Pitt, you may beg from Paul,
    You may beg from the highest to the lowest of them all;
    But from them all you need take none
    Until you come to the bride's own hand."

11. She came trembling down the stairs,
    Rings on her fingers and gold in her hair,
    A glass of wine all in her hand,
    Which she gave to the old beggar man.

12. He took the glass and drank the wine,
    And in the glass he slipped the ring.
    "O, where got you this, by sea or by land,
    Or did you get it off a drowned one's hand?"

13. "Neither got I it by sea or land,
    Neither did I get it off a drowned one's hand;
    I got it in my courting gay,
    And gave it to my love on her wedding day."

14. Rings from her fingers she did pull off,
Gold from her hair she did let fall,
Saying, "I'll go with you forevermore
And beg my bread from door to door."

15. Between the kitchen and the hall
The diner's coat he did let fall,
All a-shining in gold amongst them all,
And he was the fairest in the hall.

5. [Hind Horn]

Barry, Eckstorm, and Smyth, 1929, p. xxv; and, with text,
p. 78(C). Sung by Fred Nesbitt, St. Stephen, New Brunswick, October 1927. Recorded by D. A. Nesbitt.

m Æ/D

She asked him if he got it by sea or by land,
Or if he got it by a drowned man's hand.

He said, "I neither got it by sea or by land,
And neither got it by a drowned man's hand;

"But I got it in my courting gay,
And gave it to my love on her wedding day."

6. [Hynde Horn]

Christie, II, 1881, p. 252. (He prints an unrelated text, but
says this tune is sung to the Horn ballad.)

m Æ/D

Christie notes that "Logan Braes" appears to be a more recent
"set" of this air. Keith (*Last Leaves*, &c., p. 20) agrees with a reference to the *SMM* copy (No. 42). The second part is doubtless Christie's invention.

7. [Hind Horn]

Greig MSS., IV, p. 69. Also in Greig and Keith, 1925, p.
21(e). Sung by Mrs. Sangster, Mintlaw, September 1910.

p Æ/D

8. [Hynd Horn]

Greig MSS., II, p. 13. Sung by Alexander Robb, New Deer,
Aberdeenshire, June 1906.

m Æ/D

"Hey horn bound lovie Hey horn free
Where was ye born and in what counterie?"
"It was in fair Scotland that I was born
And back to fair Scotland I will return."

9. [Hynd Horn]

Greig MSS., II, p. 64. Sung by James Ewen, Loanhead,
New Deer, Aberdeenshire, August 1906.

m Æ/D

It's aye home-bound, love, aye home-free,
Where was you born or in what counterie?
'Twas in fair Scotland that I was born,
And all my friends has me forlorn.

10. [Hind Horn]

Greig MSS., II, p. 12. Sung by Mrs. Rettie, Milbrex, September 1906.

m Æ/D

Hynd Horn fair, Hynd Horn free,
Where was you born or in what counterie?
In good greenwood where I was born
But ah! my friends hae me forlorn.

11. [Hynd Horn]

Greig MSS., III, p. 118; text, Bk. 731, XXI, pp. 51-53.
Sung by Mrs. Thain, New Deer, Aberdeenshire, June 1908.

m Æ/D

1. Hynd Horn fair & Hynd Horn free,
   Where was you born & what counterie?
   In good greenwood where I was born,
   But my friends they hae left me a' forlorn.

2. I gave my love a gay gold wand,
   It was to rule oer fair Scotland,
   And he gave me a gay gold ring
   To me it had the virtue above all thing.

3. As long as that ring does keep its hue
   Unto you I will prove true,
   But when that ring grows pale & wan
   You'll know that I love some other man.

4. So he hoised his sail & away went he,
   Away away to some far counterie;
   But when he looked into his ring
   He knew that she loved some other man.

5. So he hoised his sail & home came he,
   Home home again to his ain counterie;
   The first he met upon dry land
   It was an auld auld beggar man.

6. "What news what news ye auld beggar man,
   What news what news hae ye to gie?"
   "Nae news nae news hae I to gie,
   But the morn is our queen's wedding day."

7. "Oh you'll gie me your begging weed,
   And I'll gie you my riding steed,"
   "It's my begging weed's nae fit for you
   But your riding steed's too high for me."

8. But be it right or be it wrong,
   The begging weed he has put on;
   "Now since I've got the begging weed,
   (Pray) tell to me the begging lead."

9. "Oh you'll gang up to the heid o' yon hill,
   And blaw your trumpet loud & shrill
   And you'll gang crawlin' down yon brae
   As if you could neither step or stray.

10. "You'll seek frae Peter & you'll seek frae Paul
    You'll seek frae the high to the low o' them all,
    But frae nane o' them, tak' ye nae thing
    Unless it comes frae the bride's ain han'."

11. So he socht frae Peter & he socht frae Paul,
    He socht frae the high to the low o' them all,
    But frae nane o' them wad he hae nae thing
    Unless it cam' frae the bride's ain han'.

12. So the bride came tripping down the stair,
    With combs of yellow gold in her hair,
    With a glass o' red wine in her han'
    To gie to the auld auld beggar man.

13. Out o' the glass he drank the wine,
    And into it he dropped the ring,
    "Oh got you it by sea or got you it by lan',
    Or got you it off o' a droont man's hand?"

14. "I got nae it by sea nor yet by lan',
    Nor yet did I on a droont man's han',
    But I got it frae you in my wooin' gay,
    And I'll gie't to you on your wedding day."

15. She tore the gold down frae her heid,
    "I'll follow you & beg my breid;"
    She tore the gold down frae her hair
    Says, "I'll follow you for evermair."

16. So atween the kitchen & the ha'
    And there he loot his duddy cloak fa',
    He shone wi gold aboon them a',
    And the bride frae the bridegroom 's stown awa.

12. [Hind Horn]

Greig MSS., IV, p. 28. Sung by Mrs. Dunbar, Longhill of
Crimond.

m Æ/D

13. [Hind Horn]

Greig MSS., IV, p. 12; text, Bk. 764, LIV, pp. 59ff. Also
in Greig and Keith, 1925, p. 20(a). Sung by Mrs. Cruickshank, New Deer, Aberdeenshire.

m Æ/D

1. Ha ho I am bound love
   And ha ho I'm free
   Where was you born or what country
   In fair Scotland where I was born
   And all my friends they did leave me forlorn.

2. She's gin him a gay gold ring
   And the value of it was above all things.

3. As long as this ring keeps its hue,
   Ye will know my love's aye true
   But when that it grows pale & wan
   You'll know I am in love wi' some other man.

4. He hoist up sails & away went he,
      Away, away to some far country
   But when he looked the ring upon
   He knew she was in love wi' some other man.

5. He hoist up sails & home came he
      Home, home again to his ain countrie
   The first that he met upon dry land
      Was a poor auld beggar man.

6. What news, what news, have ye got to me?
   No news, no news have I got to say
   But the morn is our Queen's wedding day

7. Ye'll give to me your begging weeds
   And I'll give you my riding steed
   My begging weed it is no fit for thee
   And your riding steed it is no fit for me.

8. Be it right or be it wrong
      The begging weeds & he's put on.

9. He seeks first from Peter & seeks next from Paul
   He seeks from the highest & lowest of them all
   But from them & he would take none
   Until that he got it from the bride herself.

10. Down comes the pretty bride a-tripping down the stair
    With the combs of the yellow gold in her hair
    And a glass of the red wine in her hand
    And she gave it to the auld beggar man.

11. Out of the glass & he drunk the wine
    And into the glass he dropped the ring
    Oh got you it by sea, or got you it by land,
    Or got you it off a drowned man's hand?

12. I got not it by sea, I got not it by land,
    Nor I got not it off a drowned man's hand
       But I got it at my wooin',
    And I'll give it you at your wedding.

13. Between the kitchen & the hall,
    He let his dudie great coat fall
    And he shined like the yellow gold ower them a',
    And the bride from the bridegroom he has stolen awa'.

14. [Hind Horn]

Greig MSS., II, p. 64. Also in Greig and Keith, 1925, p. 21(c). Sung by J. Quirie, Turriff, August 1906.

m Æ/D

O hey horn born & hey born free
It's where was ye born or in what counterie?
In fair Scotland that I was born,
And all my friends they've me forlorn.

15. [Hind Horn]

Greig MSS., III, p. 104. Also in Greig and Keith, 1925, p. 21(d). Sung by Mrs. Corbet, New Deer, Aberdeenshire, May 1908.

m Æ/D

16. [Hind Horn]

Duncan MS., No. 327 (W. Walker). Also in Greig and Keith, 1925, p. 20(b). Sung by George Garioch, Leochel-Cushnie, Aberdeenshire.

m Æ

He gaed butt thro' the kitchen, an' ben thro' the ha',
An' in amo' the nobles great an' sma,
He cuttit clootie cloaks an' he let them doon fa',
An' he was the bravest gentleman that was amo' them a'.

17. [Hind Horn]

Creighton and Senior, 1950, p. 15(C). Sung by Lloyd A. Sanford, East Walton, Nova Scotia.

m Æ

"O it's where was you bred or where was you born?"
"In Scotland's town where I was born,
Oh Scotland town being my native land
Until I became a roving lad."

"Where did you get it, by sea or by land,
Or did you get it from a drowned man's hand?"

"I neither got it by sea nor by land
Neither from a drowned man's hand,
But I got this ring from a true love so gay
And I give it back on her wedding day."

18. [Hind Horn]

Flanders and Olney, 1953, pp. 47-48. Sung by Mrs. Harriet Gott Murphy, Rumford Centre, Maine, September 12, 1942; from family tradition. Collected by Marguerite Olney. From *Ballads Migrant in New England*, edited by Helen Hartness Flanders and Marguerite Olney; copyright 1953 by Helen Hartness Flanders.

m Æ

The original time-signature is 2/4. The final, D, in 1953, is a misprint, here corrected on Miss Olney's authority.

The maid came tripping down the stairs,
Rings on her fingers and gold in her hair,
With a glass of wine all into her hands.
She gave it to the poor old beggarman.

Out of a tumbler he drank the wine;
Into the tumbler he slipped the ring.
She said, "Where did you get this by sea or by land,
Where did you get it—off the drowned man's hand?"

"I neither got it by sea or by land,
Neither did I get it from a drowned man's hand;
My ma-ma gave it to me on her courting day
And I'll give it back on her wedding day."

Rings from her fingers she did let fall,
Gold from her hair she did tear off,
Saying, "I'll go with thee forever, ever more,
If I have to beg my bread from door to door."

19. "The Begging Weed"

Greig MSS., I, p. 133; text, Bk. 713, III, pp. 102ff. Sung by Andrew Findley, March 1906.

p Æ/D

1. I know an' fair lovey, I know an' free,
Where come you* from or from what countrie?
In fair Scotland I was bred & born
My friends they all hae me forlorn.

2. I gied to my love a gay gold ring,
The value o' it was above all thing;
She gave to me a silver one,
It was to rule o'er a' the lan',

3. While this ring does keep its hue
You'll know that I prove true to [you]†
But when this ring does grow pale [and wan]
You'll know that I love another m[an]

4. He hysed up sail and away sailed he
Some foreign country for to see,
He looked to the ring & it was pale & wan
And he knew she loved another m[an]

5. He hysed up sail & hame cam' he,
Hame again to his ain countree
And when he cam' to fair Scotlan'
The first that he met was an auld beggar [man]

6. O aul' man, aul' man, aul' man, said [he]
What news, what news hae ye to gie?
Nae news, nae news hae I to gie,
But this is oor Queen's weddin' day.

7. Aul' man, aul' man, aul' man, said he
What is the language that ye beg [wi'?]
I seek meat (mate) frae ane, I seek [meat] frae twa,
I seek meat frae the highest to the lowest o' them a'[.]

8. Ye'll gie me your beggin' weed,
And I'll gie you my ridin' steed[.]
My beggin' weed it wadna suit thee
Your ridin' steed it wadna suit me.

* So in music MS.; text reads, "Where are you come from."
† Here and at the ends of some lines succeeding, the microfilm failed to register; but the bracketed readings seem too evident to require corroboration from the original.

9. But pairt ye be richt or pairt ye be wrong,
   The beggin' weed he has put on,
   An' when he cam' to yonder hall
   He blew his trumpet loud & shrill.

10. I'll seek meat frae ane, I'll seek meat frae twa,
    I'll seek meat frae the highest to the lowest o' them a',
    But I'll tak' nane o' the meat that ye gie,
    Unless it come frae the bride to me.

11. The bride cam' trippin' doon the st[air]
    Wi' the combs o' gay gold in her ha[ir]
    And a glass o' red wine in her han'
    It was to gie to the auld beggar man.

12. He took up the glass & he drank oot the wine
    And into the glass he dropped the ring
    Got ye it by sea or got ye it by la[nd]
    Or got ye it on a drowned man's han[d?]

13. I got na it by sea, I got na it by lan'
    Nor I got na it on a drooned man's han'
    But I got it in my wooin' gay,
    And I'll gie't to you on your weddin' [day]

14. I'll tak' the gold combs frae my heid,
    And follow you in your beggin' weed,
    I'll tak' the gold combs frae my hair,
    And follow you for evermair.

20. "The Begging Weed"

Greig MSS., I, p. 132. Sung by A. M. [Alexander Milne],
Maud, March 1906.

p Æ/D

21. "The Beggarman"

Greenleaf and Mansfield, 1933, pp. 12-14. Sung by Daniel
Endacott, Sally's Cove, Newfoundland, 1921.

m Æ

1. O, 'twas of a young couple they lived in this place,
   They was courting by each other, you may plainly see,
   Until strange news was come to him,
   That he would sail* in a far counteree.

2. When they was a-parting, she gived to him
   A gay gold ring . . .
   "When you looks at the ring and it's bright and clear,
   You know I am constant to my dear.

3. . . . .
   . . . .
   "And when you looks at your ring and 'tis pale and wan,
   You may know I'm engaged with some other young man."

4. Then he took a ship and away sailed he,
   He sailed till he came to a far counteree;
   He looked at his ring and 'twas bright and clear,
   He knowed she was constant to her dear.

5. And then he took a ship and away sailed he,
   He sailed till he came to the Turkish shore;
   He looked at his ring and 'twas pale and wan,
   He knowed she was engaged with some other young man.

6. Then he took a ship and back sailed he,
   He sailed till he came to his own counteree;
   As he was riding along one day,
   And who should he meet but an old beggarman?

7. "What news, beggarman, have you for me?"
   "Bad news, bad news, I have for thee;
   Bad news, bad news, I have for thee,
   For to-morrow is your true-love's wedding day."

8. "O, you'll give to me your bag and rig,
   And I'll give to you my riding steed."
   "My bag and rig is no good for thee,
   Nor your riding steed is no good for me."

9. O let it be so, or let it be not,
   The beggar's rig he then put on.
   "Beggarman, beggarman, come tell me with speed,
   What must I do with your bag and rig?"

10. "You'll walk as fast as is your will
    Until you come to yonder hill,
    And you'll walk as fast as is your rate,
    And you'll lean on your staff in wayward state,

11. "And you'll beg from Peter and you'll beg from Paul,
    You'll beg from the highest to the lowest of them all,
    And from none of them you'll receive nothing
    Until you receives it from the bride's own hand."

12. He walked as fast as was his will,
    Until he came to yonder hill,
    And he walked as fast as was his rate,
    And he leaned on his staff in wayward state.

13. He begged from Peter and he begged from Paul,
    He begged from the highest to the lowest of them all,
    And from none of them he received nothing
    Until he received it from the bride's own hand.

14. As she came trippling down the stairs
    With rings on her fingers, gold bobs on her hairs,
    And a glass of wine in her hand so small,
    And she gave it to the old beggarman.

15. Then out of the glass he drinks the wine,
    And into the glass he slipped a ring.
    "Did you get it by sea, or yet by land,
    Or did you get it from a drownded man's hand?"

16. "I neither got it by sea, nor yet by land,
    Nor yet did I get it from a drowned man's hand;
    But I got it in a courting way,
    And I give it to my true-love on her wedding day."

17. The rings from her fingers they fell on the floor,
    Gold bobs from her hair she throwed against the wall:
    "I will go with you forevermore,
    Supposing I beg my bread from door to door!"

18. Between the kitchen and the hall
    The beggar's rig he then let fall;
    For he shines the blackest among them all,
    He's the richest man that's in the hall.

    * Or, "was sailing."

22. [Hind Horn]

Creighton and Senior, 1950, p. 17(E). Sung by Ralph
Huskins, Cape Sable Island, Nova Scotia.

a M

    I'll beg from Peter and I'll beg from Paul,
    I'll beg from the highest to the lowest of them all
    As for money I will take no toll
    Unless it's received from the bride's own hand.

    O the maid came tripping down the stairs
    With rings on her fingers and jewels on her hair,
    And a glass of wine all in her hand
    For to treat this old beggar man.

    He took the glass and he drank the wine,
    And in the glass he slipped this ring,
    "Oh where did you get it, from sea or land,
    Or did you get it from some dead man's hand?"

    "I neither got it from sea nor land,
    Nor neither did I get it from some dead man,
    This ring I received on my courting days,
    I'll return it back to you on your wedding day."

    The rings from her fingers she did pull off,
    The jewels from her hair she did let fall,
    Saying, "I'll go with you for ever ever more
    If I have to beg my bread from door to door."

Between the kitchen and the hall
The beggar's rig he did let fall,
The gold upon him shone bright on them all,
He was the best looking man that was in the hall.

23. [Hind Horn]

Child, 1882-98, V, p. 413; text, I, pp. 503-4. Sung by Jane
Webster, Stewartry of Kirkcudbright, December 12, 1882,
and by Jessie Jane Macmath and Agnes Macmath, nieces of
Miss Webster, December 11, 1882; learned from an old
nurse. Noted by Minnie Macmath.

p I/M (ending on II)

1. She gave him a gay gold ring,
       Hey lillelu and how lo lan
   But he gave her a far better thing.
       With my hey down and a hey diddle downie.

2. He gave her a silver wan,
   With nine bright laverocks thereupon.

   *   *   *   *   *   *

3. Young Hynd Horn is come to the lan,
   There he met a beggar man.

4. "What news, what news do ye betide?"
   "Na news but Jeanie's the prince's bride."

5. "Wilt thou give me thy begging weed?
   And I'll give thee my good grey steed."

6. "Wilt thou give me thy auld grey hair?
   And I'll give ye mine that is thrice as fair."

7. The beggar he got on for to ride,
   But young Hynd Horn is bound for the bride.

8. First the news came to the ha,
   Then to the room mang the gentles a'.

9. "There stands a beggar at our gate,
   Asking a drink for young Hynd Horn's sake."

10. "I'll ga through nine fires hot
    To give him a drink for young Hynd Horn's sake."

11. She gave him the drink, and he dropt in the ring;
    The lady turned baith pale an wan.

12. "Oh got ye it by sea, or got it by lan?
    Or got ye it off some dead man's han?"

13. "I got it not by sea, nor I got it not by lan,
    But I got it off thy milk-white han."

14. "I'll cast off my dress of red,
    And I'll go with thee and beg my bread.

15. "I'll cast off my dress of brown,
    And follow you from city to town.

16. "I'll cast off my dress of green,
    For I am not ashamed with you to be seen."

17. "You need not cast off your dress of red,
    For I can support thee on both wine and bread.

18. "You need not cast off your dress of brown,
    For I can keep you a lady in any town.

19. "You need not cast off your dress of green,
    For I can maintain you as gay as a queen."

Sir Lionel

CHILD NO. 18

THE only orally traditional form of this ballad which makes any attempt to maintain a dignified romantic tone is that recorded by Christie, in 1850, from an old woman in Buckie, Enzie, Banffshire. Through her, Christie said he could trace the song a hundred years further back. Still another hundred years backward (that is, before 1650) lies the text, without a tune, of the Percy Folio—very defective, and not certainly known to have been sung. The latter is also serious in tone. All other versions of the ballad which have been found, whether in England or in America, are farcical in varying degree. About a half-dozen English texts, or fragments of texts, were recorded in the nineteenth century, all with an interlaced refrain close to the seventeenth-century one of "Blow thy horne, good hunter," and "As I am a gentle hunter," occurring as the second and fourth lines of the quatrain; and one American variant on the same plan has been found in recent tradition. The resemblance of this refrain to the text of a song of Henry VIII's time attracted Child's attention. The old song is easily accessible in Chappell's *Popular Music*, I, p. 58. The stanzaic pattern of it may possibly be regarded as a ballad quatrain with the short lines rhyming, followed by a two-line burden or refrain. The latter is

> Cum, blow thy horne, hunter,
> Cum, blow thy horne, joly hunter.

But the two first lines are a similar exhortation:

> Blow thy horne, hunter,
> Cum, blow thy horne on hye!

and it is impossible to tell without other stanzas whether these are intended as repetitive matter or as introduction—probably the latter, as otherwise the whole poem would be committed to the same rhyme. (The music gives the word "hunter" two accents, to fill out the tetrameter.) The third and fourth lines contain the "epical" matter of the stanza:

> In yonder wode there lyeth a doo,
> In fayth she woll not dye.

There is certainly little in the melody to suggest a ballad air. The doe may or may not be figurative, but Child does not hint that he sees a ballad lurking behind the song, and it seems unlikely that it was ever more narrative than lyric.* The connection with the refrain of our ballad is, then, doubtless fortuitous. But it is odd that the later the survivals of the refrain, the less popular they sound. "Jolly," one would think, is popular enough; "gentle," in the seventeenth century, is more literary; but "jovial," in the nineteenth-century traditional versions of the ballad, sounds furthest of all from actual tradition! If there were a truly traditional descent here, we might expect to find the epithets in the reverse order. The whole thing smacks of literary, or semi-literary, origins never completely worked out by oral transmission.

But in the present century, there appears a change of word and pattern.† Instead of the staid refrain of the older versions, we get, both in England and America, a series of nonsense syllables, fitted into an ancient stanzaic scheme. The pattern is exemplified by a Wiltshire variant, published in 1923, without a tune:

> Bold Sir Rylas a-hunting went—
> I an dan dilly dan
> Bold Sir Rylas a-hunting went,
> Killy koko an.
> Bold Sir Rylas a-hunting went,
> To kill some game was his intent—
> I an dan dilly dan killy koko an.
> [Alfred Williams, *Folk Songs of the
> Upper Thames*, 1923, p. 118.]

This, with occasional shortening, is the nearly universal scheme of the ballad in current tradition. Obviously, there has either been a complete break here with older tradition, or the traditional antecedents are not represented in the examples printed by Child. The latter alternative, I believe, is the true state of the case. What has happened to the narrative will offer support to this hypothesis.

Child pointed out that "Sir Lionel" had much in common with the old metrical romance of "Sir Eglamour of Artois." The relationship is clearest in the Percy Folio text of the ballad, where the narrative element, though much injured by lacunae, is still the fullest. Here we have: a lady sore beset, whose knight has been slain by a wild boar; a fight between Sir Lionel and the boar (lost with leaves missing from the MS.); a rencounter between a giant, the owner of the boar, and Sir Lionel, in which the knight is worsted but granted a forty-day respite against a new contest; his return to fight with the giant and rescue the lady; and finally, in the last [missing] portion (but baldly stated in Christie's version), the defeat of the giant. All these elements appear in the old romance, which Child is careful *not* to call the original of the ballad.

In the nineteenth-century English version, the giant's place has been supplied by a "wild woman" whom the hero treats as unmercifully as he had earlier treated the giant. The central incident, however, is the boar-fight. The lady in distress is scantly mentioned, and easily confounded with the wild woman. In the more recently collected versions, she appears only long enough to tell the knight that a blast of his horn will bring on the boar, or (as usually in the American variants) she makes no appearance at all. The wild woman does double duty in some variants, but also tends to drop out of the story, like her predecessors. What remains is the single episode of the boar-fight, told now as riotous farce.

At some time in the seventeenth century, another ballad on the subject of Sir Eglamore became popularly current, and was perpetuated on broadsides. The first known copy would seem to be that in Samuel Rowlands' *The Melancholie Knight*, 1615; and perhaps Rowlands wrote the ballad. By the last quarter of

---

* Yet the line is not very easy to draw. Cf. the freshly popular two-man song collected by Sharp, "The Keeper" (*One Hundred English Folk Songs*, 1916, pp. 178-79), and its antecedent, "The Huntsmans Delight" (Pepys Broadsides, IV, p. 271). A song modeled hereupon, especially as to refrain, was printed in the *Town and Country Magazine* (November 1782), p. 608, out of O'Keefe's *The Castle of Andalusia*, 1782.

† Family tradition nevertheless carries the memory of some of these variants several generations back, probably at least into the eighteenth century.

the century, it was certainly generally known and circulating independent of print. It had a catchy tune which went about in variant forms, in the manner of popular tunes unchecked by copyright laws. One form of the tune was printed (with other words, but named "Sir Eglamore") in N. Thompson's *180 Loyal Songs*, 1685, p. 276, as follows:

Another was copied into a MS. at approximately the same time, as follows: (Edinburgh Univ. Lib. MS. Dc. 1. 69, No. 1 [at the back])§

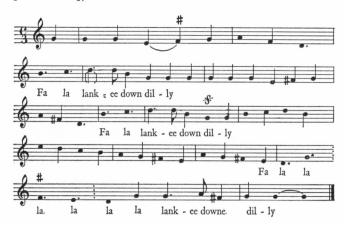

This variant, in almost identical form,** was printed later by D'Urfey, with a text of the "Sir Eglamore" ballad—as given below.

It is at once obvious that here is the stanzaic pattern of the current "Brangywell" or "Bangum and the Boar," and it will presently appear that the tunes sung in our century are variants

of the same melodic idea. We may therefore conclude that the two songs have fallen together in their traditional journeying. The crossing has already been discussed in *CFQ*, III (July, 1944), pp. 199-203.

The stanzaic pattern of "Eglamore" has been widely used from at least the sixteenth century until the present. We have met it already in variants of the riddle song, Child 1, and as the common pattern of "The Two Sisters" (10), and shall meet it soon again with "The Three Ravens" (26) and elsewhere. It is not primarily a ballad-pattern, apparently; and, where it occurs, generally accompanies humorous, playful, or nursery texts. It seems to belong properly to the carol tradition and to have been perpetuated in dances and dancing-games. Many carol-texts fall into it if their first two lines are sung twice—which would perhaps be commonly done when they were danced; and this, with the third repetition of line 1, produces a text which corresponds to a tune of sixteen bars' length. Such a length is especially apt for many of the old country dances, being divisible into two identical fours, balanced against an eight which may also be equally divided or broken into six and two. A large number of well-known Elizabethan and seventeenth-century dance-tunes conform to the type: e.g., "Trenchmore" (Playford, *Dancing Master*, 1653, and on), "The Noble Shirve" (Chappell, I, p. 348), "Confess" (*Dancing Master*, 1650, and on), "Shackley-hay" (Chappell, I, p. 368); and a number of comical songs of that day and later, such as the still favorite "Frog's Wedding," songs made up of impossibilities (e.g., "Ri-fol-lattity-O"), "Duncan Gray"—and "Madamoiselle from Armentières."

"The Frog's Wedding" has obviously become crossed with "Bangum and the Boar" in some of the American texts, such as Belden's Missouri variant, where Bangum starts out a-wooing instead of a-hunting, only to meet with his inevitable boar.

The older, "Eglamore," melodic tradition seems generally major, plagal, in 6/8 time, although collateral tunes branch into minor tonalities. The modern "Bangum," tradition, is also nearly always in a major mode, usually plagal, and in duple time. Christie's tune stands apart from the rest: it is a plagal Æolian, in duple time, and certainly related to tunes used in Scottish tradition for a number of other ballads. Cf. Greig's tunes for "Geordie" (209), "Duke of Athol's Nurse" (212), "Yarrow" (214-215), "The Rantin' Laddie" (240).

§ Printed with the courteous permission of Dr. L. W. Sharp, Librarian.
** A third form, with other titles, is in Playford's *English Dancing Master*, 1650 (reprint, 1933, p. 42), reprinted with grossly unjustifiable majorization of a Dorian tune in Chappell, I, p. 274.

LIST OF VARIANTS

GROUP A

1. "Isaac-a-Bell and Hugh the Graeme." W. Christie, *Traditional Ballad Airs*, I, 1876, pp. 110-11.
2. "Wild Boar." Herbert Halpert, LC Archive of American Folk Song, rec. 2805B. (Samuel Harmon)

GROUP B

3. "Sir Eglamore." Thomas D'Urfey, *Wit and Mirth; or, Pills to Purge Melancholy*, 1719-20, III, pp. 293-94.

GROUP C

4. "Sir Lionel." Kidson MSS. Printed in *JEFDSS*, III (1936), p. 46.
5. "Brangywell." Ella Mary Leather, *The Folk-Lore of Herefordshire*, 1912, pp. 203-4.

6. "Bangum and the Boar." Josephine McGill, *Folk-Songs of the Kentucky Mountains*, 1917, pp. 78-81.
7. "Bangum and the Boar." H. M. Belden, *Ballads and Songs*, 1940, pp. 29-30.
8. "Ole Bangum." Dorothy Scarborough, *A Song Catcher in Southern Mountains*, 1937, pp. 407 and 192-93. Also in Dorothy Scarborough, *On the Trail of Negro Folk-Songs*, 1925, pp. 51-52; and Arthur Kyle Davis, Jr., *Traditional Ballads of Virginia*, 1929, pp. 559(F) and 131-32.
9. "Sir Lionel." Sharp MSS., 3701/, Clare College Library, Cambridge. Also in Cecil J. Sharp and Maud Karpeles, *English Folk Songs from the Southern Appalachians*, 1932, I, p. 55(D). (Henry)
10. "Old Bang 'em." Davis, *Traditional Ballads of Virginia*, 1929, pp. 559(B) and 127-28. Also in Reed Smith and

Hilton Rufty, *American Anthology of Old World Ballads*, 1937, p. 4.

11. "Sir Lionel." Sharp MSS., 3679/2731. Also in Sharp and Karpeles, *Appalachians*, 1932, I, p. 55(C). (Broghton)

12. "Bangum and the Boar." Davis, *Traditional Ballads of Virginia*, 1929, pp. 558(A) and 125-26.

13. "Dilly Dove." Leather, *The Folk-Lore of Herefordshire*, 1912, p. 204.

14. "Old Bangum." Vance Randolph, *Ozark Folksongs*, 1946, I, p. 72.

15. "Sir Lionel." Sharp MSS., 3551/2624. Also in Sharp and Karpeles, *Appalachians*, 1932, I, p. 54(B); and Davis, *Traditional Ballads of Virginia*, 1929, p. 560(G). (Smith, Chisholm)

16. "Sir Lionel." Sharp MSS., 3264/2379. Also in Sharp and Karpeles, *Appalachians*, 1932, I, p. 54(A). (Rice)

17. "Old Bangum." Helen Hartness Flanders and Marguerite Olney, *Ballads Migrant in New England*, 1953, pp. 60-61.

TUNES WITH TEXTS

GROUP A

1. [Isaac-a-Bell and Hugh the Græme]

Christie, I, 1876, pp. 110-11. Sung by an old woman in Buckie, Enzie, Banffshire, about 1850.

p Æ

As usual, the second strain is doubtless Christie's invention.
In this case, Christie states that the text is genuine.
The tune has numerous relations in that region. Cf., e.g., Greig and Keith, 1925, p. 133(2), "Geordie"; p. 136(1), "The Duke of Athole's Nurse"; pp. 143-44, "Yarrow"; p. 194, "The Rantin' Laddie."

1. A knight had two sons o' sma' fame,
        Hey nien nanny,
    Isaac-a-Bell and Hugh the Græme,
        And the Norlan' flowers spring bonny;
    And to the youngest he did say,
        Hey nien nanny,
    "What occupation will you ha'e,
        When the Norlan' flowers spring bonny?

2. "Will you gae fee to pick a mill?
        Hey nien nanny;
    Or will you keep hogs on yon hill,
        While the Norlan' flowers spring bonny?"
    "I winna fee to pick a mill,
        Hey nien nanny;
    Nor will I keep hogs on yon hill,
        While the Norlan' flowers spring bonny.

3. "But it is said, as I do hear,
        Hey nien nanny,
    That war will last for seven year,
        And the Norlan' flowers spring bonny,

    With a giant and a boar,
        Hey nien nanny,
    That range into the wood o' Tore,
        And the Norlan' flowers spring bonny.

4. "You'll horse and armour to me provide,
        Hey nien nanny,
    That through Tore wood I may safely ride,
        When the Norlan' flowers spring bonny."
    The Knicht did horse and armour provide,
        Hey nien nanny;
    That through Tore wood Græme micht safely ride,
        When the Norlan' flowers spring bonny.

5. Then he rode through the wood o' Tore,
        Hey nien nanny;
    And up it started the grisly boar,
        When the Norlan' flowers spring bonny.
    The firsten bout that he did ride,
        Hey nien nanny,
    The boar he wounded in the left side,
        When the Norlan' flowers spring bonny.

6. The nexten bout at the boar he gaed,
        Hey nien nanny,
    He from the boar took aff his head,
        And the Norlan' flowers spring bonny.
    As he rode back through the wood o' Tore,
        Hey nien nanny,
    Up started the giant him before,
        And the Norlan' flowers spring bonny.

7. "Oh, cam' you through the wood o' Tore,
        Hey nien nanny;
    Or did you see my good wild boar,
        And the Norlan' flowers spring bonny?"
    "I cam' now through the wood o' Tore,
        Hey nien nanny;
    But woe be to your grisly boar,
        And the Norlan' flowers spring bonny.

8. "The firsten bout that I did ride,
        Hey nien nanny,
    I wounded your wild boar in the side,
        And the Norlan' flowers spring bonny.
    The nexten bout at him I gaed,
        Hey nien nanny,
    From your wild boar I took aff his head,
        And the Norlan' flowers spring bonny."

9. "Gin you have cut aff the head o' my boar,
    Hey nien nanny,
It's your head shall be ta'en therefore,
    And the Norlan' flowers spring bonny.
I'll gi'e you thirty days and three,
    Hey nien nanny,
To heal your wounds, then come to me,
    While the Norlan' flowers spring bonny."

10. "It's after thirty days and three,
    Hey nien nanny;
When my wounds heal, I'll come to thee,
    When the Norlan' flowers spring bonny."
So Græme is back to the wood o' Tore,
    Hey nien nanny;
And he's kill'd the giant, as he kill'd the boar,
    And the Norlan' flowers spring bonny.

2. "Wild Boar"

Halpert, LC/AAFS, rec. 2805B. Sung by Samuel Harmon,
Maryville, Tenn., 1939; learned from his father.

p π¹

1. Abram Bailey he'd three sons
    Blow your horn center*
And he is through the wildwood gone
    Just like a jovial hunter.

2. As he marched down the greenwood side
    Blow your horn center
A pretty girl O there he spied
    As he was a jovial hunter.

3. There is a wild boar all in this wood
    Blow your horn center
He slew the lord and his forty men
    As he was a jovial hunter.

4. How can I this wild boar see?
    Blow your horn center
Wind up your horn and he'll come to you
    As you are a jovial hunter.

5. He wound his horn unto his mouth
    Blow your horn center
He blew East, North, West, and South
    As he was a jovial hunter.

6. The wild boar heard him unto his den
    Blow your horn center
He made the oak and ash then far to bend
    As he was a jovial hunter.

7. They fit three hours by the day
    Blow your horn center
And at length he this wild boar slay
    As he was a jovial hunter.

8. As he marched by the mouth of the wild boar's den
    Blow your horn center
He saw the bones of five hundred men
    As he was a jovial hunter.

9. He meets the old witch wife on the bridge
    Blow your horn center
Begone you rogue, you've killed my pig
    As you are a jovial hunter.

10. There is three things I crave of thee
    Blow your horn center
Your hawk, your hound, your gay lady
    As you are a jovial hunter.

11. These three things you'll not have of me
    Blow your horn center
Neither hawk nor hound nor gay lady
    As you are a jovial hunter.

12. He split the old witch wife to the chin
    Blow your horn center
And on his way he went ag'in
    Just like a jovial hunter.

* "Center" seems clearly the word sung, but I do not understand it.
Scenter? Centaur? Or is it an adverb in the comparative degree? The
text as a whole resembles Child's C.

GROUP B

3. [Sir Eglamore]

D'Urfey, 1719-20, III, pp. 293-94.

p I

The last two phrases would normally divide evenly, but here the
leading of the words has been respected.

See the headnote above for other members of this branch of the
tribe.

Sir *Eglamore*, that valiant Knight,
    Fa la, lanky down dilly;
He took up his Sword, and he went to fight,
    Fa la, lanky down dilly:
And as he rode o'er Hill and Dale,
All Armed with a Coat of Male,
    Fa, la, la, la, la, la, lanky down dilly.

There leap'd a Dragon out of her Den,
That had slain God knows how many Men;
But when she saw Sir *Eglamore*,
Oh that you had but heard her roar!

Then the Trees began to shake,
Horse did Tremble, Man did quake;
The Birds betook them all to peeping,
Oh! 'twould have made one fall a weeping.

But all in vain it was to fear,
For now they fall to't, fight Dog, fight Bear;
And to't they go, and soundly fight,
A live-long day, from Morn till Night.

This Dragon had on a plaguy Hide,
That cou'd the sharpest steel abide;
No Sword cou'd enter her with cuts,
Which vex'd the Knight unto the Guts.

But as in Choler he did burn,
He watch'd the Dragon a great good turn;
For as a Yawning she did fall,
He thrust his Sword up Hilt and all.

Then like a Coward she did fly,
Unto her Den, which was hard by;
And there she lay all Night and roar'd,
The Knight was sorry for his Sword:
But riding away, he cries, I forsake it,
He that will fetch it, let him take it.

1. Tom and Harry went to plough,
    Dillom down dillom
As Tom and Harry went to plough,
    Quidly quo quam
As Tom and Harry went to plough
They saw a fair maid on a bough,
    Kambery quo, quoddle dam, quidly quo quam.

2. "Why do ye, fair maid, sit so high
That no young man can you come nigh?"

3. The fair maid unto them did say
"If you can fetch me down you may.

4. There is a wild boar in the wood,
If he comes out he'll suck your blood!"

         *   *   *   *   *

5. The wild boar came with such a sound
That rocks and hills and trees fell down.

5. "Brangywell"

Leather, 1912, pp. 203-4. Sung by Mrs. Mellor, Dilwyn, Herefordshire, 1905; noted by R. Hughes Rowlands.

p I

1. As Brangywell went forth to plough,
    Dillum, down dillum;
As Brangywell went forth to plough,
    Kil-ly-co-quam;
As Brangywell went forth to plough,
He spied a lady on a bough,
    Kil-ly-do, cuddle-dame,
    Kil-ly-co-quam.

2. "What makes thee sit so high, lady,
That no one can come nigh to thee?"

3. "There is a wild bear [*sic*] in the wood,
If I come down he'll suck my blood."

4. "If I should kill the boar [*sic*]," said he,
"Wilt thou come down and marry me?"

5. "If thou shouldst kill the boar," said she,
"I will come down and marry thee."

6. Then Brangywell pulled out his dart,
And shot the wild boar through the heart.

GROUP C

4. [Sir Lionel]

Kidson MSS. Printed in *JEFDSS*, III (1936), p. 46. From an unknown source (not in Kidson's hand).

m I (inflected IV)

Miss Gilchrist has a long and interesting note on this song, *JEFDSS*, III, pp. 46-49. She calls attention to the connection with "Duncan Gray," which she says was first printed in Oswald's *Caledonian Pocket Companion*, c. 1750.

7. The wild boar fetched out such a sound
That all the oaks and ash fell down.

8. Then hand in hand they went to the den,
And found the bones of twenty men.

6. "Bangum and the Boar"

McGill, 1917, pp. 78-81. Sung in Kentucky.

m I (inflected IV)

1. There is a wild boar in these woods,
    Dillom dom dillom.
  He eats our flesh and drinks our blood,
    Tum a qui quiddle quo qum.

2. How shall I this wild boar see?
    Dillom dom dillom.
  "Blow your horn and he'll come to thee."
    Tum a qui quiddle quo qum.

3. Bangum blew his horn a blast,
    Dillom dom dillom.
  The wild boar came cutting oak and ash.
    Tum a qui quiddle quo qum.

4. Bangum drew his wooden knife,
    Dillom dom dillom.
  And he worried the wild boar out of his life.
    Tum a qui quiddle quo qum.

5. Bangum rode to the wild boar's den,
    Dillom dom dillom.
  And he found the bones of a thousand men.
    Tum a qui quiddle quo qum.

Copyright 1917 by Boosey & Co. Renewed 1944. Reprinted by permission of Messrs. Boosey & Hawkes, Inc.

7. "Bangum and the Boar"

Belden, 1940, pp. 29-30. Sung by Josephine Casey, Kansas City, Mo., 1916; from Virginia. Collected by Mrs. Eva W. Case.

p I (but modulates with inflected I)

1. Old Bangum would a-wooing ride,
    Dillum, down, dillum down
  Old Bangum would a-wooing ride,
    Dillum down

Belden quotes Miss Casey to the effect that a Danish maid in her family recognized the tune above as one she had danced to in her girlhood in Denmark.

Old Bangum would a-wooing ride
With sword and buckler by his side.
  Cum-e-caw, cud-e-down, kill-e-quo-qum.

2. Old Bangum rode to the greenwood-side
And there a pretty maid he spied.

3. "There is a wild boar in this wood
That'll cut your throat and suck your blood."

4. "Oh, how can I this wild boar see?"
"Blow a blast and he'll come to thee."

5. Old Bangum clapped his horn to his mouth
And blew a blast both loud and stout.

6. The wild boar came in such a rage
He made his way through oak and ash.

7. They fit three hours in the day.
At last the wild boar stole away.

8. Old Bangum rode to the wild boar's den
And spied the bones of a thousand men.

8. "Ole Bangum"

Scarborough, 1937, p. 407; text, pp. 192-93. Also in Scarborough, 1925, pp. 51-52; and Davis, 1929, pp. 559(F) and 131-32(text). Sung by Mrs. Landon R. Dashiell, Richmond, Va., c. 1932; learned from Negroes.

p I

The alternative notes are differences among the three printings, not given as variants.

1. "Ole Bangum, will you hunt an' ride?"
    Dillum down dillum.
  "Ole Bangum, will you hunt an' ride?"
    Dillum down.

"Ole Bangum, will you hunt an' ride,
Sword an' pistol by your side?"
  Cubbi ki, cuddle dum,
   Killi quo quam.

2. There is a wild bo' in these woods,
  Dillum down dillum.
There is a wild bo' in these woods,
  Dillum down.
There is a wild bo' in these woods,
Eats men's bones an' drinks their blood,
  Cubbi ki, cuddle dum,
   Killi quo quam.

3. Ole Bangum drew his wooden knife,
  Dillum down dillum.
Ole Bangum drew his wooden knife,
  Dillum down.
Ole Bangum drew his wooden knife,
An' swore by Jove he'd take his life,
  Cubbi ki, cuddle dum,
   Killi quo quam.

4. Ole Bangum went to the wild bo's den,
  Dillum down dillum.
Ole Bangum went to the wild bo's den,
  Dillum down.
Ole Bangum went to the wild bo's den,
An' found the bones of a thousand men,
  Cubbi ki, cuddle dum,
   Killi quo quam.

5. They fought fo' hours in that day,
  Dillum down dillum.
They fought fo' hours in that day,
  Dillum down.
They fought fo' hours in that day,
The wild bo' fled and flunk away,
  Cubbi ki, cuddle dum,
   Killi quo quam.

6. "Ole Bangum, did you win or lose?"
  Dillum down dillum.
"Ole Bangum, did you win or lose?"
  Dillum down.
"Ole Bangum, did you win or lose?"
He swore by Jove he'd won the shoes,
  Cubbi ki, cuddle dum,
   Killi quo quam.

9. [Sir Lionel]

Sharp MSS., 3701/. Also in Sharp and Karpeles, 1932, I,
p. 55(D). Sung by Violet Henry, Berea, Ky., May 21, 1917.

p I

O Bangum would a-hunting ride, Cubby Kye cuddle,*
O Bangum would a-hunting ride
Cuddle* down. . . .
O Bangum would a-hunting ride
Sword and pistol by his side, Cubby Kye, cuddle*
      down killy quo quam

  * 1932: "cuddal."

10. "Old Bang 'em"

Davis, 1929, p. 559(B); text, pp. 127-28. Also in Smith and
Rufty, 1937, p. 4. Sung by Evelyn Purcell of the Farmville
Ballad Club, Albemarle County, Va., November 20, 1913;
handed down from her great-grandfather, c. 1760.

p I

The third and fourth bars from the end may be mis-timed, as
they upset the verbal rhythm.

1. Old Bang'em would a-hunting ride,
  Dillem, down, dillem.
Old Bang'em would a-hunting ride,
  Dillem down.
Old Bang'em would a-hunting ride,
Sword and pistol by his side.
  Cubby, ki, cuddle down,
   Killi, quo, quam.

2. "There is a wild boar in this wood,"
  Dillem, down, dillem.
"There is a wild boar in this wood,"
  Dillem down.
"There is a wild boar in this wood
Will eat your meat and suck your blood."
  Cubby, ki, cuddle down,
   Killi, quo, quam.

3. "Oh, how shall I this wild boar see?"
  Dillem, down, dillem.
"Oh, how shall I this wild boar see?"
  Dillem down.
"Oh, how shall I this wild boar see?"
"Blow a blast and he'll come to thee."
  Cubby, ki, cuddle down,
   Killi, quo, quam.

4. Old Bang'em blew both loud and shrill,
The wild boar heard on Temple Hill.
  Cubby, ki, cuddle down,
   Killi, quo, quam.

5. The wild boar came with such a rush
He tore down hickory, oak and ash.
  Cubby, ki, cuddle down,
   Killi, quo, quam.

6. Old Bang'em drew his wooden knife
And swore that he would take his life.
Cubby, ki, cuddle down,
Killi, quo, quam.

7. "Old Bang'em, did you win or lose?"
He swore that he had won the shoes.
Cubby, ki, cuddle down,
Killi, quo, quam.

11. [Sir Lionel]

Sharp MSS., 3679/2731. Also in Sharp and Karpeles, 1932, I, p. 55(C). Sung by Mrs. Mollie Broghton, Barbourville, Knox County, Ky., May 10, 1917.

p I (−VI)

I went out a-hunting one day,
Dellum down dillum,
I went out a-hunting one day,
And I found there where a wild boar lay.
Come a call, cut him down,
Quilly quo qua.

I hunted over hills and mountains,
And there I found him on his way.

The wild boar came in such a dash,
He cut his way through oak and ash.

I called up my army of men;
He killed one, two, three score of ten (them?).*

* 1932: "them."

12. "Bangum and the Boar"

Davis, 1929, p. 558(A); text, pp. 125-26. Sung by Mr. H. W. Adams, near Altavista, Va., May 24, 1914. Collected by Juliet Fauntleroy.

p I (−VI)

1. Old Bangum came riding across the glen,
Dillum, down, dillum.
Old Bangum came riding across the glen,
Kimmy-ko.
Old Bangum came riding across the glen,
He was the bravest of all brave men.
Dillum down, kimmy-ko, kwam.

2. A pretty fair maid came riding astride,
Dillum, down, dillum.
A pretty fair maid came riding astride,
Kimmy-ko.
A pretty fair maid came riding astride,
Old Bangum rode up by her side.
Dillum down, kimmy-ko, kwam.

3. "Oh, pretty fair maid, will you marry me?"
Dillum, down, dillum.
"Oh, pretty fair maid, will you marry me?"
Kimmy-ko.
"Oh, pretty fair maid, will you marry me?"
"Oh, yes, kind sir, I do agree."
Dillum down, kimmy-ko, kwam.

4. "There is a wild hog in this wood,"
Dillum, down, dillum.
"There is a wild hog in this wood,"
Kimmy-ko.
"There is a wild hog in this wood
That'll eat your flesh and drink your blood."
Dillum down, kimmy-ko, kwam.

5. The wild hog came in such a rash,
Dillum, down, dillum.
The wild hog came in such a rash,
Kimmy-ko.
The wild hog came in such a rash
He tore his way through oak and ash.
Dillum down, kimmy-ko, kwam.

6. Old Bangum drew his trusty knife,
Dillum, down, dillum.
Old Bangum drew his trusty knife,
Kimmy-ko.
Old Bangum drew his trusty knife
And deprived the wild boar of his life.
Dillum down, kimmy-ko, kwam.

7. Old Bangum rode to the wild boar's den,
Dillum, down, dillum.
Old Bangum rode to the wild boar's den,
Kimmy-ko.
Old Bangum rode to the wild boar's den
And spied the bones of a thousand men.
Dillum down, kimmy-ko, kwam.

13. "Dilly Dove"

Leather, 1912, p. 204. Sung by Mrs. E. Goodwin, Weobley, Herefordshire, 1909. Noted by Ralph Vaughan Williams from phonograph record.

a I/M (compass of sixth)

He said, fair maid what makes you sit so high?
vt. ref. st 3,4,5   vt. sts.3,4

Old Bangum did a-huntin' ride,
Dillium down dillium,
Old Bangum did a-huntin' ride,
Sword an' pistol by his side,
Dillium down dillium,
An' a kwiddle, kwee ho kwo.

The wild boars they run in the woods,
Dillium down dillium,
The wild boars they run in the woods,
An' they seen the bones of a thousand men,
Dillium down dillium,
An' a kwiddle, kwee ho kwo.

1. Dilly-dove he went to plough,
   With those two horses and a plough,
       Collin-dame, cum and go, killy-co-cum.

2. Dilly-dove he went to plough,
   And saw a fair maid on a bough,
       Collin-dame, cum and go, killy-co-cum.

3. He said "Fair maid what makes you sit so high
   That no young man can come anigh?"
       Collin-dame, cum and go, killy-co-cum.

4. "O there's a wild boar in the wood,
   If I come down he'll suck my blood."
       Suck my blood, collin-dame, come and go, killy-co-cum.

5. "If you'll come down and go with me,
   Both you and I will go and see."
       Go and see, collin-dame, come and go, killy-co-cum.

6. Then he went unto the park,
   And shot the wild boar through his heart.
       Through his heart, collin-dame, come and go, killy-co-cum.

7. Then he went unto the den,
   And there were bones of forty men,
       Collin-dame, cum and go, killy-co-cum.

15. [Sir Lionel]

Sharp MSS., 3551/2624. Also in Sharp and Karpeles, 1932, I, p. 54(B); and Davis, 1929, p. 560(G). Sung by Mrs. Betty Smith and Mr. N. B. Chisholm, Woodbridge, Va., September 28, 1916.

p I/M

There is a wild boar in these woods,
Dellum down, dellum down,
There is a wild boar in these woods,
He'll eat your meat and suck your blood.
Dellum down, dellum down.

Bang[r]um drew his wooden knife
And swore he'd take the wild boar's life.

The wild boar came in such a flash,
He broke his way through oak and ash.

14. "Old Bangum"

Randolph, I, 1946, p. 72. Sung by Frank Payne, Galena, Mo., May 14, 1934.

p π¹

One may suspect a basic ¾ rhythm here; or else that some of the quarter-notes were intended for eighths.

16. [Sir Lionel]

Sharp MSS., 3264/2379. Also in Sharp and Karpeles, 1932, I, p. 54(A). Sung by Mrs. Tom Rice, Big Laurel, N.C., August 16, 1916.

a π¹, ending on II

Bangry Rewey a-courting did ride,
His sword and pistol by his side.
Cambo key quiddle down, quill-o-quon.

Bangry rode to the wild boar's den
And there spied the bones of a thousand men.

Then Bangry drew his wooden knife
To spear the wild boar of his life.

17. "Old Bangum"

Flanders and Olney, 1953, pp. 60-61. Sung by Dr. Alfred
Ferguson, Middlebury, Vt., July 14, 1942; learned from his
mother, whose ancestors came from Massachusetts. From
Ballads Migrant in New England, edited by Helen Hart-
ness Flanders and Marguerite Olney; copyright 1953 by
Helen Hartness Flanders.

p D (inflected IV)

1. Old Bangum would a-hunting ride,
   Derrum, derrum, derrum.
   Old Bangum would a-hunting ride,
   Kili-ko
   Old Bangum would a-hunting ride
   With sword and pistol by his side.
   Derrum-kili-ko-ko.

2. He rode unto the riverside.
   Where he a pretty maid espied.

3. "Fair maid," said he, "will you marry me?"
   "Ah no," said she, "for we'd ne'er agree."

4. "There lives a bear in yonder wood,
   He'd eat your bones, he'd drink your blood."

5. Brave Bangum rode to the wild bear's den,
   Where lay the bones of a thousand men.

6. Brave Bangum and the wild bear fought;
   At set of sun the bear was naught.

7. He rode again to the riverside
   To ask that maid to be his bride.

King Orfeo

CHILD NO. 19

THAT a tune should in the midst of the twentieth century be recovered for this whisper from the Middle Ages was as little to be expected as that we should hear "the horns of Elfland faintly blowing." The Shetlands seem to have proved the only and last retreat in traditional recollection of this very charming product of medieval re-creative imagination. Clearly, the fragment before us stems in a direct line from the form printed by Child, from the same utmost isle of Unst. That text was itself fragmentary, but it told a complete story and kept identities straight. The present stanzas correspond to Child's 9-10, 12-13; but King Orfeo has become a nondescript plural—as it were a "noise of musicians"—who (merely) are invited into a hall, enter, and do their office. Only the distance whence it has been transported (by what frail means, against what odds!) makes this freight precious.

The air falls in well enough with the kind of melodic material recovered by Greig in the northeast of Scotland. Cf. "Fair Ellen" (63), *Last Leaves*, 1925, p. 52, and "Sweet William and Fair Annie" (73), p. 56, for parallel examples. It is hardly worth mention that there is a curious resemblance to its outlines in the latter phrases of Josephine McGill's popular modern composition, "Duna," itself perhaps a folk-echo.

LIST OF VARIANTS

"King Orfeo." P. N. Shuldham-Shaw, *JEFDSS*, V (December 1947), p. 77. Also in E. S. Reid Tait, *Shetland Folk Book*, II (1951), pp. 56-57, with the Child text.

TUNE WITH TEXT

"King Orfeo"

Shuldham-Shaw, *JEFDSS*, V (December 1947), p. 77.
Sung by John Stickle, Baltasound, Unst, April 28, 1947.

Then they played the good old gab-ber reel, Scow an Earl

Will ye come in into our Ha',
Scowan Earl grey,
Yes we'll come in into your ha',
For yetter kangra norla

And we'll come in into your ha'
And we'll come in among ye a'

First they played the notes o noy
Then they played the notes o joy

Then they played the good old gabber reel
    Scowan Earl Grey.
Which might a made a sick heart heal,
    For gettar kangra norla.

The Cruel Mother

CHILD NO. 20

For the number of beautiful melodic variations on a basically constant rhythmic pattern this ballad is exceptional. The binding element in the rhythmical design appears to have been the interlaced refrain at the second and fourth lines. This has suffered for the most part only slight variation, and, where variations occur, has been usually able to find metrical equivalents for the supplanted syllables. Thus the majority of variants shows a second phrase closely approximating this meter:

and a fourth phrase like the following:

Such a scheme appears to have been a favorite of this ballad for a century and a half. The melodic record is almost as old as the textual one in England and Scotland, if we exclude a late seventeenth-century broadside text. Between the latter and the first traditional record there is a gap of nearly a century. But the broadside text is very good, in the sense of being unusually close to traditional style; in fact, stanzas 6 to 22 (the ballad has 26) might be almost uncontaminated by the broadside pen. The refrain of the broadside, however, is different from that perpetuated in traditional variants, and would seem to imply a different tune. Although it comes likewise on the second and fourth phrases, the second is apparently a five-stress iambic line and the fourth a tetrameter. Though either might be compressed to a different scheme in singing, neither has the characteristic feminine ending of the traditional variants. It is incidentally to be noted that verbally this older refrain contains a distinct resemblance to the usual one of "The Two Sisters" (10):

> Come bend and bear away the Bows of Yew . . .
> Gentle Hearts be to me true.

There is no clue to the tune of the broadside, unfortunately: the printed direction is merely, "to an excellent new tune"—a stereotyped phrase found on numberless broadsides, and of no significance.

It is further to be observed that certain other favorite traditional ballads consistently exhibit the same rhythmical characteristics in the second and fourth phrase: "Binorie" (10), "Barbara Allen" (84), "Geordie" (209), and the two "Yarrow" ballads (214, 215), as well as a few not generally found out of Scotland, e.g., "Earl of Aboyne" (235) and "Rantin' Laddie" (240). It is not surprising, therefore, to find melodic relationships more or less clearly marked between these and the present ballad. The roots of the pattern, one would consequently guess, are probably Celtic.

Besides the habitual refrain (such as "All alone and alonie . . . Down by the greenwood sidie"), there is another which has seldom appeared outside Scotland, with mention of flowers in the first half (e.g., "Fine flowers in the valley," or "Hey my rose an' my lindsay O," or "Hey for the Rose o' Malindie O"). As this has not modified the shape of the tune, the examples of it have not been segregated. The two manners are coterminous in the record. The earliest traditional copy, Herd's, has a unique refrain: "Oh and alellladay, oh and alellladay," and "Ten thousand times good night and be with you." Two

of Motherwell's copies have numerical refrains: "Three, three, and three by three" and "Three, three, and thirty-three," or "Ah me, some forty-three." It might be supposed from a reading of Child's texts alone that the copies divided on the basis of whether the second and fourth lines have three stresses or four. But an examination of the tunes proves that as the ballad is sung, the two styles are treated alike—that is, as four-stress lines. Two English variants, from Shropshire and Somerset, are perhaps solitary in their employment of ancient nonsense patterns in the first half of the refrain: "Ri fol i diddle i gee wo" and "Fol the dal the di-do." A Banffshire variant, if Christie is to be trusted, shows the Edinburgh-Stirling-St. Johnston on Tay refrain with which we have already met in Mrs. Brown of Falkland's version of "The Twa Sisters"; and this pattern was probably duplicated in a copy in *Albyn's Anthology*, there given with other words. There are several versions exceptional in one way or another, either by accretion of extraneous elements or by abrasion, by failure to achieve definition, or by confusion with other ballads, e.g., "The Wife of Usher's Well" (79). J. J. Niles's copy has been thoroughly sophisticated.

The first four of the following groups appear to me valid and defensible on internal grounds; the fifth is a group only by courtesy. The first group contains some of the oldest copies, as well as recent ones that are Scottish, English, and American. Two-thirds of the group are plagal, the other third authentic without seriously deranging the cast of the melody. Modes are Æ, Æ/D, π^4, D, and D/M. There is not much consistency of cadence, although a mid-cadence on the lower fifth is favored.

The second group, containing some good nineteenth- and twentieth-century copies, is (with one Dorian exception) Mixolydian, I/M, and I in tonal cast. The favored mid-cadence point is on V; the favored first cadence is on the tonic. The variants of this group are all authentic.

The third group is again predominantly major (I/Ly, I, π^1, I/M), but plagal. One worn-down Virginia copy is probably authentic and π^2. Here again the cadences are not consistent, but lower V for the first phrase is relatively common. Mid-cadences are most frequently on II and V.

Group D is composed of two related tunes in triple time, plagal Mixolydian, and of the "Two Sisters" pattern. Both are Scottish.

The last group is hardly entitled to the unifying name, even by our loose definitions. The first tune, from North Carolina, is disconcerting, with an ill-defined tonic and a striking augmented fourth between the first and second phrases. The following tune, from Kentucky, is a full-blown two-strain tune. A variant of this tune is a shape-note hymn. (Cf. G. P. Jackson, *Spiritual Folk-Songs of Early America*, 1937, No. 14, p. 42: "Patton.") The next tune, from Tennessee, is so dilapidated as to be confined to three notes, D, E, G. It is likely that it would have been classified with Group C, had more of it remained. Three copies of an Ozark tune are faultily transcribed. It too appears to have suffered from forgetfulness. If its final is the true tonic, it is a π^2 plagal tune. The following tune, from Georgia, is crossed and confused with "The Wife of Usher's Well" (79), both melodically and textually. The last tune in this group has been too drastically handled to be restored to tradition.

GROUP A

1. "Fine Flowers in the Valley." James Johnson, *The Scots Musical Museum*, [1792], IV, No. 320, p. 331. Also in Lady John Scott's Sharpe MS., National Library of Scotland MS. 843, fol. 19ᵛ; Robert Archibald Smith, *The Scottish Minstrel*, 1820-24, IV, p. 33; and Robert Maver, *Genuine Scottish Ballads*, 1866, No. 365, p. 183.

2. "Hey wi' the rose and the lindie, O." W. Christie, *Traditional Ballad Airs*, I, 1876, p. 106.

3. "The Cruel Mother." Greig MSS., I, p. 174, King's College Library, Aberdeen. Also in Gavin Greig and Alexander Keith, *Last Leaves of Traditional Ballads and Ballad Airs*, 1925, p. 22(1). (Robb)

4. "The Cruel Mother." H. E. D. Hammond, *JFSS*, III (1907), p. 70(2)

5. "The Rose o' Malindie O." Francis James Child, *The English and Scottish Popular Ballads*, 1882-98, App'x to V, p. 413, and I, p. 224.

6. "Down by the Greenwood Side." Phillips Barry, Fannie H. Eckstorm, and Mary W. Smyth, *British Ballads from Maine*, pp. xxii and 80-82.

7. "The Greenwood Siding." John Harrington Cox, *Folk-Songs of the South*, 1925, pp. 522 and 30(C).

8. "The Greenwood Side." Josephine McGill, *Folk-Songs of the Kentucky Mountains*, 1917, pp. 82-86.

9. "The Cruel Mother." H. E. D. Hammond, *JFSS*, III (1907), p. 70(1).

10. "The Cruel Mother." Sharp MSS., 4268/, Clare College Library, Cambridge. Also in Cecil J. Sharp and Maud Karpeles, *English Folk Songs from the Southern Appalachians*, 1932, I, p. 61(J). (Roberts)

11. "The Cruel Mother." Sharp MSS., 4256/. Also in Sharp and Karpeles, 1932, I, p. 61(I). (Chisholm)

12. "The Cruel Mother." Greig MSS., IV, p. 117. Also in Greig and Keith, *Last Leaves*, 1925, p. 23(3). (Johnstone)

13. "The Cruel Mother." Helen Creighton and Doreen H. Senior, *Traditional Songs from Nova Scotia*, 1950, p. 20.

14. "The Cruel Mother." Mary O. Eddy, *Ballads and Songs from Ohio*, 1939, p. 24. Also in Tolman MSS., Harvard College Library.

15. "The Minister of New York's Daughter." Greig MSS., III, p. 41. Also in Greig and Keith, *Last Leaves*, 1925, p. 22(2). (? Mrs. Milne)

16. "The Cruel Mother." H. E. D. Hammond, *JFSS*, III (1907), p. 71(3).

17. "The Cruel Mother." Sharp MSS., 3343/. Also in Sharp and Karpeles, *Appalachians*, 1932, I, p. 58(E). (Shelton)

18. "The Cruel Mother." Creighton and Senior, *Traditional Songs from Nova Scotia*, 1950, pp. 18-19.

19. "The Greenwood Siding." W. Roy Mackenzie, *Ballads and Sea Songs from Nova Scotia*, 1928, pp. 391 and 12-13.

20. "The Cruel Mother." Creighton and Senior, *Traditional Songs from Nova Scotia*, 1950, p. 20.

21. "The Cruel Mother." Helen Hartness Flanders and Marguerite Olney, *Ballads Migrant in New England*, 1953, pp. 66-67.

22. "There was a Lady lived in York." George Korson, *Pennsylvania Songs and Legends*, 1949, pp. 38-39.

GROUP B

23. "The Cruel Mother." George R. Kinloch, *Ancient Scottish Ballads*, 1827, App'x to p. 44 and pp. 46-48.

24. "The Cruel Mother." Charlotte Sophia Burne, *Shropshire Folk-Lore*, 1886, pp. 651 and 540.

25. "The Cruel Mother." Clive Carey, *JEFDSS*, I (December 1934), p. 130.

26. "The Cruel Mother." Maud Karpeles, *Folk Songs from Newfoundland*, 1934, I, pp. 8-12.

27. "The Cruel Mother." G. B. Chambers *JEFDSS*, I (December 1934), pp. 130-31.

28. "Fair Flowers of Helio." Elisabeth Bristol Greenleaf and Grace Yarrow Mansfield, *Ballads and Sea Songs of Newfoundland*, 1933, p. 15.

29. "The Cruel Mother." Phillips Barry Dictaphone Cylinders, No. 110, transcribed by S. P. Bayard, Harvard College Library MS., p. 53.

30. "The Cruel Mother." Sharp MSS., 4681/3257. Also in Sharp and Karpeles, *Appalachians*, 1932, I, p. 62(L). (Boone)

31. "The Cruel Mother." Sharp MSS., 1454/1333-34. Also in Cecil J. Sharp, *One Hundred English Folksongs*, [1916], p. 35 (Woodberry) and in Sharp, *English Folksongs*, Selected Ed., Novello & Co., 1920.

32. "The Cruel Mother." Sharp MSS., 3769/2782. Also in Sharp and Karpeles, *Appalachians*, 1932, I, pp. 58(F)-59. (Kilburn)

33. "Hey wi' the rose and the lindie." Christie, *Traditional Ballad Airs*, I, 1876, p. 108.

GROUP C

34. "Down by the Greenwood Side-e-o." Phillips Barry, *BFSSNE*, No. 8 (1934), p. 7.

35. "The Cruel Mother." Arthur Kyle Davis, Jr., *Traditional Ballads of Virginia*, 1929, pp. 560(A) and 133-34.

36. "The Cruel Mother." Esther White, *JFSS*, II (1905), p. 109.

37. "Cruel Mother." Helen Creighton, *Songs and Ballads from Nova Scotia*, 1932, pp. 3-5.

38. "The Cruel Mother." Winston Wilkinson MSS., 1935-36, p. 30(B), University of Virginia.

39. "The Cruel Mother." Wilkinson MSS., 1935-36, p. 29(A).

40. "The Cruel Mother." Sharp MSS., 4554/3186. Also in Sharp and Karpeles, *Appalachians*, 1932, I, p. 60(H). (Gibson)

41. "The Cruel Mother." Sharp MSS., 4565/. Also in Sharp and Karpeles, 1932, I, p. 62(M). (Snipes)

42. "The Cruel Mother." Sharp MSS., 3394/2492. Also in Sharp and Karpeles, 1932, I, p. 57(C). (Stockton)

43. "The Cruel Mother." Davis, *Traditional Ballads of Virginia*, 1929, pp. 561(C) and 135.

44. "The Cruel Mother." Sharp MSS., 3515/. Also in Sharp and Karpeles, *Appalachians*, 1932, I, p. 57(D); and Davis, 1929, p. 560. (Chisholm)

45. "The Cruel Mother." Creighton and Senior, *Traditional Songs from Nova Scotia*, 1950, pp. 19-20.

46. "The Cruel Mother." Sharp MSS., 4087/2930. Also in Sharp and Karpeles, *Appalachians*, 1932, I, pp. 59(G)-60. (Pratt)

47. "The Cruel Mother." Alton C. Morris, *Folksongs of Florida*, 1950, pp. 251-52.

48. "The Cruel Mother." Davis, *Traditional Ballads of Virginia*, 1929, pp. 560(B) and 134.

GROUP D

49. "Edinbrie, Edinbrie." Alexander Campbell, *Albyn's Anthology*, II, [1818], p. 8. Also in Phillips Barry, *BFSSNE*, No. 3 (1931), p. 13.

50. "Bonny Saint Johnston stands fair upon Tay." Christie, *Traditional Ballad Airs*, I, 1876, p. 104.

GROUP E

51. "The Cruel Mother." Sharp MSS., 3236/2371. Also in Sharp and Karpeles, *Appalachians*, 1932, I, p. 56(A). (Hensley)

52. "The Cruel Mother." Sharp MSS., 3776/. Also in Sharp and Karpeles, 1932, I, p. 61(K). (Huff)

53. "The Cruel Mother." Mellinger Edward Henry, *Folk-Songs from the Southern Highlands*, 1938, pp. 47-48.

54. "Down by the Greenwood Side." Vance Randolph, *Ozark Folksongs*, 1946, I, pp. 73-74. Also in Vance Randolph, *The Ozarks*, 1931, p. 185; and Dorothy Scarborough, *A Song Catcher in Southern Mountains*, 1937, p. 403.

55. "The Cruel Mother." Sharp MSS., 3105/? Text, Sharp and Karpeles, *Appalachians*, 1932, I, pp. 56(B)-57. (Moore)

56. "There was a Lady drest in Green." Anne G. Gilchrist, *JFSS*, VI (1919), p. 80.

a. "The Cruel Mother." John Jacob Niles, *Ballads, Carols, and Tragic Legends from the Southern Appalachian Mountains*, Schirmer's American Folk Song Series, Set 18, 1937, pp. 18-19.

TUNES WITH TEXTS

GROUP A

1. [Fine Flowers in the Valley]

Johnson, [1792], IV, No. 320, p. 331. Also (in nearly identical notes) in Lady John Scott's Sharpe MS., NL Scotland MS. 843, fol. 19ᵛ; Smith, 1820-24, IV, p. 33; and Maver, 1866, No. 365, p. 183.

p Æ/D (but inflected VII)

According to Stenhouse (*Illustrations*, p. 308), Burns was the transmitter of this piece to Johnson's *Museum*.
The variants given are from the R. A. Smith copy. The sharp in the penultimate bar were better away.

1. She sat down below a thorn,
       Fine flowers in the valley
   And there she has her sweet babe born
       And the green leaves they grow rarely.

2. Smile na sae sweet, my bonie babe
       Fine flowers in the valley,
   And ye smile sae sweet, ye'll smile me dead,
       And the green leaves they grow rarely.

3. She's taen out her little penknife
       Fine flowers, &c.
   And twinn'd the sweet babe o' its life.
       And the green, &c.

4. She's howket a grave by the light o' the moon,
       Fine flowers, &c.
   And there she's buried her sweet babe in,
       And the green, &c.

5. As she was going to the church,
       Fine flowers, &c.

She saw a sweet babe in the porch.
       And the green, &c.

6. O sweet babe and thou were mine,
       Fine flowers, &c.
   I wad cleed thee in the silk so fine.
       And the green, &c.

7. O mother dear, when I was thine,
       Fine flowers, &c.
   You did na prove to me sae kind.
       And the green, &c.

2. [Hey wi' the rose and the lindie, O]

Christie, I, 1876, p. 106. Sung in Banffshire.

p Æ

As a lady was looking o'er her castle wa'
       It's hey wi' the rose and the lindie, O,
She spied twa bonny boys at the ba'
       Alone by the green burn sidie, O [Etc.].

Christie's text has no validity in tradition, and is therefore omitted.

3. "The Cruel Mother"

Greig MSS., I, p. 174. Also in Greig and Keith, 1925, p. 22(1). Sung by Alexander Robb, New Deer, Aberdeenshire, 1906.

p Æ/D

The same singer's tune for "Binorie" is very close to this. Cf. Child 10, above.

My father was the noble Duke of York,
  Hey my rose & my lindsay O,
An' I coorted with my father's clerk,
  Down by yon greenwood sidie O.

4. [The Cruel Mother]

Hammond, *JFSS*, III (1907), p. 70(2). Sung by Mrs. Case, Sydling St. Nicholas, Dorset, September 1907.

p Æ

The outlines of this typical tune can be traced, in one meter or another, in scores of folk-tunes, from "How should I your true love know?" onward to the present time. For illustrations of its keeping a recognizable identity through changes of all sorts, cf. the above with Sharp's 5/4 version of "Searching for Lambs" (1916, No. 48, p. 108), and with the Scottish tunes for "Thomas the Rhymer" (*post*, No. 37). Cf. on the type, *Journal of the American Musicological Society*, III, No. 3 (1950), pp. 126-34.

1. She laid herself back against a thorn,
    All aloney, aloney,
  And there she had two pretty babes born,
    Down by the greenwood sidey.

2. She had a penknife long and sharp,
    All aloney, aloney,
  And she pressèd it through their tender hearts
    Down by the greenwood sidey.

3. She diggèd a grave both wide and deep,
    All aloney, aloney,
  And she buried them under the marble stone,
    Down by the greenwood sidey.

4. As she was set in her Father's hall,
    All aloney, aloney,
  Oh! there she saw two pretty babes playing at ball,
    Down by the greenwood sidey.

5. "Oh! babes, Oh! babes if you were mine,
    All aloney, aloney,
  I would dress you up in the scarlet fine,"
    Down by the greenwood sidey.

6. "Oh! Mother, Oh! mother, we once were thine,
    All aloney, aloney,
  You did not dress us in the scarlet fine.
    Down by the greenwood sidey.

7. You digged a grave both wide and deep,
    All aloney, aloney,
  And you buried us under the marble stone."
    Down by the greenwood sidey.

5. "The Rose o' Malindie O"

Child, 1882-98, App'x. to V, p. 413, 20 Ja; text, I, p. 224. From Mrs. Harris "and others."

p Æ/D

1. She leant her back against a thorn,
    Hey for the Rose o' Malindie O
  And there she has twa bonnie babes born.
    Adoon by the green wood sidie O.

2. She's taen the ribbon frae her head,
  An hankit their necks till they waur dead.

3. She luikit outowre her castle wa,
  An saw twa nakit boys, playin at the ba.

4. "O bonnie boys, waur ye but mine,
  I wald feed ye wi flour-bread an wine."

5. "O fause mother, whan we waur thine,
  Ye didna feed us wi flour-bread an wine."

6. "O bonnie boys, gif ye waur mine,
  I wald clied ye wi wilk sae fine."

7. "O fause mother, whan we waur thine,
  You didna clied us in silk sae fine.

8. "Ye tuik the ribbon aff your head,
  An' hankit our necks till we waur dead.

　　*　　*　　*　　*　　*　　*

9. "Ye sall be seven years bird on the tree,
  Ye sall be seven years fish i the sea.

10. "Ye sall be seven years eel i the pule,
  An ye sall be seven years doon into hell."

11. "Welcome, welcome, bird on the tree,
  Welcome, welcome fish i the sea.

12. "Welcome, welcome, eel i the pule,
  But oh for gudesake, keep me frae hell!"

6. "Down by the Greenwood Side"

Barry, Eckstorm, and Smyth, 1929, p. xxii; and, with text, pp. 80-82. Sung by Mrs. Susie Carr Young, Brewer, Maine, c. 1925; learned from her grandmother, c. 1865. Melody recorded by George Herzog.

p D

The timing in the original copy is a queried 5/4, in bars double the length of the above, and notes half their value here.

1. There was a lady lived in York,
    It was all alone and alo-ne;
    She fell in love with her father's clerk,
    Down by the greenwood si-de.

2. She leaned her back against an oak,
    It was all alone and alo-ne;
    First it bent and then it broke,
    Down by the greenwood si-de.

3. She leaned her back against a thorn,
    It was all alone and alo-ne;
    And there those two pretty babes were born,
    Down by the greenwood si-de.

4. She took her penknife out of her pocket,
    It was all alone and alo-ne;
    She pierced those pretty babes to the heart,
    Down by the greenwood si-de.

5. She washed her penkife in the brook,
    It was all alone and alo-ne;
    The more she washed it the redder its look,
    Down by the greenwood si-de.

6. She wiped her penknife on the clay,
    It was all alone and alo-ne;
    And there she wiped the stains away,
    Down by the greenwood si-de.

7. She dug a grave both long and deep,
    It was all alone and alo-ne;
    She lay-ed those pretty babes in for to sleep,
    Down by the greenwood si-de.

8. When she returned to her father's farm,
    It was all alone and alo-ne;
    She spied those pretty babes arm in arm,
    Down by the greenwood si-de.

9. When she returned to her father's hall,
    It was all alone and alo-ne;
    She spied those pretty babes playing ball,
    Down by the greenwood si-de.

10. "Pretty babes! pretty babes, if thou art mine,"
    It was all alone and alo-ne;
    "I'll dress you up in satin so fine,"
    All down by the greenwood si-de.

7. "The Greenwood Siding"

Cox, 1925, p. 522; text, p. 30(C). Sung by G. W. Cunningham, Elkins, West Virginia, about July, 1915.

p D (but inflected IV)

In the original, bars 3 and 4 are printed as one, with holds over the two D's, the first of which is a quarter, the second a dotted eighth. The timing of the former copy is 4/4. One may question the propriety of the C♯.

"O baby, O baby, if you were mine,
    All along and alone-y;
I would dress you up in scarlet so fine,
    All along by the greenwood siding."

"O mother, O mother, when I was yours,
You pierced me through my poor tender heart.

"O mother, O mother, thou hast cut stakes,
You shall be keeper of hell's gates."

8. "The Greenwood Side"

McGill, 1917, pp. 82-86. Sung in Kentucky.

m Æ/D (but inflected VII)

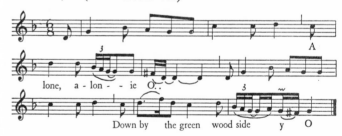

1. There was a lady in yonder town,
    Alone, alonie O;
    She's taken her a walk one day
    Down by the greenwood sidey O.

2. She leaned her back against a thorn,
    Alone, alonie O;
    And there her two little babes were born
    Down by the greenwood sidey O.

3. She drew a penknife from her side,
    Alone, alonie O;
    She took her two little babies' lives
    Down by the greenwood sidey O.

4. She passed along again one day,
   Alone, alonie O;
   She saw her two little babes at play
   Down by the greenwood sidey O.

5. "O babes, O babes, if you were mine,"
   Alone, alonie O;
   "I'd dress you up in silk so fine"
   Down by the greenwood sidey O.

6. "O mother, O mother, when we were yours,"
   Alone, alonie O;
   "You neither allowed us coarse nor fine"
   Down by the greenwood sidey O.

7. "You drew a penknife from your side,"
   Alone, alonie O;
   "You took your two little babies' lives"
   Down by the greenwood sidey O.

8. "Seven long years you've rested well,"
   Alone, alonie O;
   "The rest of your life you'll spend in hell"
   Down by the greenwood sidey O.

9. [The Cruel Mother]

Hammond, *JFSS*, III (1907), p. 70(1). Sung by Mrs. Russell, Upwey, Dorset, February 1907.

p D

She pressed herself against the wall,
   All alone and so lonely,
And there she had two pretty babes born,
   And 'tis down by the greenwood side oh!

Oh! Mother, Oh! Mother, if these were mine,
   All alone and so lonely (*or*, so lone O!)
I would dress them in silks so fine!
   And 'tis down by the greenwood side O!

10. [The Cruel Mother]

Sharp MSS., 4268/. Also in Sharp and Karpeles, 1932, I, p. 61(J). Sung by Mrs. Willie Roberts, Nellysford, Va., May 22, 1918.

p D, ending on V

Babes, O babes, I wish you were mine,
Down by the green wood sidey,
Babes, O babes, I wish you were mine,
Down by the green wood sidey,

I'd dress you all in silk so fine
Down by the green wood sidey,
I'd dress you all in silk so fine,
Down by the green wood sidey.

Sharp's MS. note: "Mrs. Roberts learned this and the other songs she sang me from her mother who died when Mrs. Roberts was quite young. She has not sung these old songs for many years, but sang them, nevertheless, without hesitation and with a very beautiful voice."

11. [The Cruel Mother]

Sharp MSS., 4256/. Also in Sharp and Karpeles, 1932, I, p. 61(I). Sung by James H. Chisholm, Nellysford, Va., May 18, 1918.

p D (but inflected III and VII)

Sharp and Karpeles begin on C.

Baby, O baby if you were mine
All along lum a loby,
I would dress you in the scarlet so fine
Down by the green river sidey.

12. [The Cruel Mother]

Greig MSS., IV, p. 117. Also in Greig and Keith, 1925, p. 23(3). Sung by J. Johnstone, New Deer, Aberdeenshire.

a π⁴

O bonnie boys, gin ye waur mine,
    Hey my rose an' my lindsay O,
I wad feed you upon bread an' wine,
    Down by yon green wood-sidie O.

13. [The Cruel Mother]

Creighton and Senior, 1950, p. 20. Sung by Dennis Smith, Chezzetcook, Nova Scotia.

a I

Oh babes Oh babes if you were mine
All alone and aloney,
I'd feed you up on bread and wine
Down by the greenwood sideyo.

"Oh mother, mother when we were young*
You neither fed us on bread nor wine."

* sc. "yourn"?

14. [The Cruel Mother]

Eddy, 1939, p. 24. Also (differently noted) in Tolman MSS. Sung by Mrs. Virginia Summer, Canton, Ohio; learned from her mother.

a Æ/D

"No, no, dear mother, when we were thine,
    All alone in the lily, oh,
Our victuals were not of the bread and wine,
Our garments were not of the silk so fine,
    Down by the Greenbury side."

15. "The Minister of New York's Daughter"

Greig MSS., III, p. 41. Also in Greig and Keith, 1925, p. 22(2). Singer unspecified; perhaps Mrs. Milne, October 1907?

a D/M

Welcome, welcome calling bells;
    Hey the rose & the linsie O;
But Guid keep me frae the torments o' hell;
    Doon by yon green wood sidie O.

16. [The Cruel Mother]

Hammond, JFSS, III (1907), p. 71(3). Sung by Mrs. Bowring, Cerne Abbas, Dorset, September 1907.

a D

"Oh! babes, oh! babes, if you were mine,
    All alone, and aloney,
I would dress you in scarlet fine."
    Down by the greenwood sidey.

17. [The Cruel Mother]

Sharp MSS., 3343/. Also in Sharp and Karpeles, 1932, I, p. 58(E). Sung by William Riley Shelton (65), Alleghany, N.C., August 29, 1916.

a π⁴ (but II in variant)

O dear mother when we was there
All along along-y*
You'd neither dress us coarse nor fine
Down by the greenwood side-y

* 1932: "alongey"

18. [The Cruel Mother]

Creighton and Senior, 1950, pp. 18-19. Sung by Mrs. John Smith, Chezzetcook, Nova Scotia.

a Æ/D

1. There was a lady came from York
   All alone and aloneyo,
   She fell in love with her father's clerk,
   Down by the greenwood sideyo.

2. She leaned her back against an oak
   When first it bent and then it broke.

3. She leaned herself against a thorn.
   And there her two pretty babes were born.

4. She had nothing to wrap them in
   But her apron, it was thin.

5. She took her penknife keen and sharp
   And she pierced it through their innocent hearts.

6. As she entered her father's hall
   She saw those pretty babes playing ball.

7. "Babes, oh babes, if you were mine
   I would dress you up in silks so fine."

8. "Oh mother, oh mother, when we were thine
   Why didn't you dress us in silks so fine?

9. "But you took your penknife keen and sharp
   And you pierced it through our innocent hearts."

10. "Oh pretty maidens can you tell
    Whether I'll reign in heaven or hell?"

11. "No mother dear we can't tell well
    But your body's here and your soul's in hell.

12. "Oh mother mother for your sin
    Hell's gates will be opened and you shoved in."

19. "The Greenwood Siding"

Mackenzie, 1928, p. 391; text, pp. 12-13. Sung by Mrs. Ellen Bigney, Pictou, Nova Scotia.

a D

1. There was a lady came from York,
       Down alone in the lonely
   She fell in love with her father's clerk,
       Down alone by the greenwood siding.

2. She loved him well, she loved him long,
   Till at length this young maid with child she did prove.

This variant is nearly identical with Kidson's copy, from Eskdale, of "The Dowie Dens of Yarrow" (1891, p. 22, and *post*, No. 214). The original timing is 2/4.

3. She leaned her back against an oak,
   When first it bowed and then it broke.

4. She leaned herself against a thorn,
   And then her two babes they were born.

5. She took her pen-knife keen and sharp,
   And she pierced it through their innocent hearts.

6. She dug a hole seven feet deep,
   She threw them in and bid them sleep.

7. It's when this young maid was returning home,
   She saw two babes a playing ball.

8. "O babes, O babes, if you were mine,
   I would dress you up in silks so fine."

9. "O mother, O mother, when we were thine,
   You did not dress us in silks so fine.

10. "But you took your pen-knife keen and sharp,
    And you pierced it through our innocent hearts.

11. "You dug a hole seven feet deep,
    You threw us in and bid us sleep."

12. "O babes, O babes, what shall I do,
    For the wicked crime I have done unto you?"

13. "O mother, O mother, it's us can tell:
    For seven long years you shall ring a bell.

14. "And seven more like an owl in the woods,
    And seven more like a whale in the sea.

15. "The rest of your time you shall be in hell,
    And it's there you'll be fixed for eternity!"

20. [The Cruel Mother]

Creighton and Senior, 1950, p. 20. Sung by John Roast, Chezzetcook, Nova Scotia.

a Æ

She said "Pretty maids if you were mine
All alone and aloneyo,
I would dress you up in silks so fine
Down by the greenwood siding."

21. [The Cruel Mother]

Flanders and Olney, 1953, pp. 66-67. Sung by Mrs. W. H.
Smith, Houlton, Maine, September 23, 1940. From *Ballads
Migrant in New England*, edited by Helen Hartness Flanders and Marguerite Olney; copyright 1953 by Helen Hartness Flanders.

a D

The original time-signature is 2/2. The G occurring four notes
from the end is a correction of the F in the earlier printing, on the
authority of Miss Marguerite Olney.

In New York lived a lady fair
All alone and alone-y!
There she had two pretty little babes
Down by the greenwood side-y!

"O babes, O babes, if you were mine,
All alone and alone-y,
I would dress you up in silks so fine
Down by the greenwood side-y."

"O mother, dear, we once were thine,
All alone and alone-y.
You neither dressed us coarse or fine,
Down by the greenwood side-y.

"But you had a penknife keen and sharp
All alone and alone-y.
You pierced us both to the tender hearts,
Down by the greenwood side-y.

"You dug a hole both wide and deep,
All alone and alone-y
You laid us down and bade us sleep,
Down by the greenwood side-y."

22. "There was a Lady lived in York"

Korson, 1949, pp. 38-39. Sung by Peter Cole, Greene
County, Pa., 1929. Recorded by Samuel P. Bayard.

a M

1. There was a lady lived in York,
    Tra la lee and a lidey O!
 She fell in love with her father's clerk,
    Down by the greenwood sidey O!

2. She leant herself against an oak,
    Tra la lee and a lidey O!
 And first it bent, and then it broke,
    Down by the greenwood sidey O!

3. She leant herself against a tree,
    And there she had her misery.

4. She leant herself against a thorn,
    And there's where these two babes were born.

5. She pulled out her little penknife;
    She pierced them through their tender hearts.

6. She pulled out her white handkerchief;
    She bound them up both head and foot.

7. She buried them under a marble stone,
    And then returned to her merry maid's home.

8. As she sat in her father's hall,
    She saw these two babes playing ball.

9. Says she, Pretty babes, if you were mine,
    I'd dress you in the silk so fine.

10. Say, dear mother, when we were thine,
    You neither dressed us coarse nor fine.

11. But you pulled out your little penknife;
    You pierced it through our tender hearts.

12. Then you pulled out your white handkerchief;
    You bound us up both head and foot.

13. You buried us under a marble stone,
    And then returned to your merry maid's home.

14. Seven years to wash and wring,
    Seven more to card and spin.

15. Seven more to ring them bells,
    Tra la lee and a lidey O!
 Seven more to serve in hell,
    Down by the greenwood sidey O!

GROUP B

23. [The Cruel Mother]

Kinloch, 1827, App'x to p. 44; text, pp. 46-48.

a I/M

1. There lives a lady in London—
   All alone, and alonie;
   She's gane wi' bairn to the clerk's son—
   Doun by the greenwud sae bonnie.

2. She has tane her mantle her about—
   All alone, and alonie;
   She's gane aff to the gude greenwud,
   Doun by the greenwud sae bonnie.

3. She has set her back until an aik—
   All alone, and alonie;
   First it bowed and syne it brake—
   Doun by the greenwud sae bonnie.

4. She has set her back until a brier—
   All alone, and alonie;
   Bonnie were the twa boys she did bear,
   Doun by the greenwud sae bonnie.

5. But out she's tane a little penknife—
   All alone, and alonie;
   And she's parted them and their sweet life,
   Doun by the greenwud sae bonnie.

6. She's aff unto her father's ha'—
   All alone, and alonie;
   She seem'd the lealest maiden amang them a',
   Doun by the greenwud sae bonnie.

7. As she lookit our the castle wa'—
   All alone, and alonie;
   She spied twa bonnie boys playing at the ba'
   Doun by the greenwud sae bonnie.

8. "O an thae twa babes were mine"—
   All alone, and alonie;
   "They should wear the silk and the sabelline,"
   Doun by the greenwud sae bonnie.

9. "O mother dear, when we were thine"—
   All alone, and alonie;
   "We neither wore the silks nor the sabelline,"
   Doun by the greenwud sae bonnie.

10. "But out ye took a little penknife,—
    All alone, and alonie;
    "An ye parted us and our sweet life,
    Doun by the greenwud sae bonnie.

11. "But now we're in the heavens hie—
    All alone, and alonie;
    And ye have the pains o' hell to dree"—
    Doun by the greenwud sae bonnie.

24. [The Cruel Mother]

Burne, 1886, p. 651; text, p. 540. Sung by Elizabeth Wharton and her brothers, Shropshire gypsies, July 13, 1885. Collected by James Smart.

a I/M

1. There was a lady, a lady of York,
   (Ri fol i diddle i gee wo!)
   She fell a-courting in her own father's park,
   Down by the greenwood side, O!

2. She leaned her back against the stile,*
   (Ri fol i diddle i gee wo!)
   There she had two pretty babes born,
   Down by the greenwood side, O!

3. And she had nothing to lap 'em in (etc.)
   But she had a penknife sharp and keen (etc.)

4. [She did not care if they felt the smart] (etc.),
   There she stabbed them right through the heart (etc.).

5. She wiped the penknife in the sludge,
   The more she wiped it, the more the blood showed.

6. As she was walking in her own father's park,
   She saw two pretty babes playing with a ball.

7. 'Pretty babes, pretty babes, if you were mine,
   I'd dress you up in silks so fine.'

8. 'Dear mother, dear mother [when we were thine],
   You dressed us not in silks so fine!'

9. 'Here we go to the heavens so high,
   (Ri fol i diddle i gee wo!)
   You'll go to bad when you do die!
   Down by the greenwood side, O!

   * Read "thorn."

25. [The Cruel Mother]

Carey, *JEFDSS*, I (December 1934), p. 130. Sung by Mrs. Hollingsworth, Sibley's Green, Thaxted, Essex, October 5, 1911. See variant No. 27 for the same singer's rendition a decade later, with the full text.

a I

The student should consult Miss Gilchrist's interesting note following this copy, in the *Journal, loc.cit.*, with parallel Lake Country dance-tune variants, called "Iron Legs."

There was a lady lived at York
  All alone in a loney,
A farmer's son he courted her,
  All down by the greenwood sidey.

26. [The Cruel Mother]

Karpeles, 1934, I, pp. 8-12. Sung by Mrs. Theresa Corbett,
Conception Harbour, Newfoundland, October 24, 1929.
(Original text restored from Miss Karpeles' MS.)

a I

There is a noticeable connection between this and the usual tune
for "The Bailiff's Daughter" (105).

1. As she was a-walking her father's hall,
     Fair flowers the valley O.
   She saw two babes a-playing ball.
     Down by the greenwood sidey O.

2. She says: Dear babes, if you were mine,
   I would dress you up in silk so fine.

3. O, they said: Dear mother, when we were yours,
   You neither dressed us in silk or coarse.

4. You took a pen-knife from your skirt,
   And you pierced it in our tender hearts.

5. She said: Dear babes, it's you can tell,
   If my poor soul is for heav'n or hell.

6. Yes, dear mother, we can tell,
   Whether your poor soul's for heav'n or hell.

7. You have seven years to roll a stone,
     Seven more to stand alone,
   And the rest of your time you'll walk alone
     Down by the greenwood sidey O.

8. You have seven more to ring a bell,
     Yes, dear mother, we can tell,
   And seven more you'll spend in hell
     Down by the greenwood sidey O.

27. [The Cruel Mother]

Chambers, *JEFDSS*, I (December 1934), pp. 130-31. Sung
by Mrs. Hollingsworth, Thaxted, Essex, July 1921. See No.
25 above.

a I/M

1. There was a lady lived in York
     All alone in a loney,
   A farmer's son he courted her,
     All down by the greenwood sidey.

2. He courted her for seven long years
     All alone in a loney;
   At last she proved in child by him,
     All down by the greenwood sidey.

3. He (she) pitched her knee against a tree,
     All alone, etc. . . . .
   And there she found great misery
     All down, etc. . . . .

4. She pitched her back against a thorn,
     All alone, etc. . . . .
   And there there was a baby born
     All down, etc. . . . .

5. She drew a fillet off her head,
     All alone, etc. . . . .
   She bound the baby's hands and legs,
     All down, etc. . . . .

6. She drew a knife both long and sharp,
     All alone, etc. . . . .
   She pierced the baby's innocent heart,
     All down, etc. . . . .

7. She wiped the knife upon the grass,
     All alone, etc. . . . .
   The more she wiped the blood run fast,
     All down, etc. . . . .

8. She washed her hands all in the spring,
     All alone, etc. . . . .
   Thinking to (re)turn a maid again,
     All down, etc. . . . .

9. As she was going to her father's Hall,
     All alone, etc. . . . .
   She saw three babes aplaying at ball,
     All down, etc. . . . .

10. One dressed in silk the other in satin,
     All alone, etc. . . . .
   The other star(k) naked as ever was born
     All down, etc. . . . .

11. Oh, dear baby, if you was mine
     All alone, etc. . . . .
   I'd dress you in silk and satin so fine,
     All down, etc. . . . .

12. Oh! dear Mother, I once was thine,
    All alone, etc. . . .
    You never would dress me cos or fine,
    All down, etc. . . .

13. There heaven gates stand open wide,
    All alone, etc. . . .
    There's room for me but none for you,
    All down, etc. . . .

14. There is a fire behind hell's gate,
    All alone, etc. . . .
    And there you're burn both early and late,
    All down, etc. . . .

28. "Fair Flowers of Helio"

Greenleaf and Mansfield, 1933, p. 15. Sung by Agatha
Walsh, Fleur de Lys, Newfoundland, 1930.

a M

1. There was a lady lived in New York,
   Fair flowers of Helio,
   She was courted of her father's clerk,
   In the green hills of Helio.

2. She had two babes by this young man,
   She prayed to God it would never be known.

3. She took a penknife long and sharp
   And pierced it through their tender white hearts.

4. Those two babes will never be known;
   And she buried them under a marble stone.

5. As she was walking along one day,
   She saw two babes playing with a ball.

6. "O children dear, if you were mine,
   I'd dress you up in silks so fine."

7. "O mother dear, when we were thine,
   You wouldn't give us time to wear coarse or fine.

8. "Heaven is high and hell is low,
   And when you die, it's to hell you'll go."

29. [The Cruel Mother]

Barry Dict. Cyl., No. 110, transcribed by S. P. Bayard,
Harvard College Library MS., p. 53. Sung by Mrs. Gallant.
Transcription simplified and abridged by present editor.
Text not transcribed.

a D (inflected III)

30. [The Cruel Mother]

Sharp MSS., 4681/3257. Also in Sharp and Karpeles, 1932,
I, p. 62(L). Sung by Mrs. Julie Boone, Micahville, Yancey
County, N.C., September 25, 1918.

a M

Three young ladies was a-taking of a walk,
    All alone and aloney,
Three little babes was a-playing with their ball,
    Down by the Greenwood sidey.

One was Peter, the other was Paul,
The other was as naked as the hour it was born.

O babe, O babe, if you was mine,
Dress you up in silk so fine.

O mammy, O mammy, I once was yourn,
You neither dressed me in silk so fine.*

You took your knife out of your pocket,
Primmed (sic) me of my little sweet knife.†

You buried me under the marble stone,
Then you turned as fair maid home.

Seven long years a-ringing of a bell,
Seven long years you'll prim (sic) us in hell.

Sharp's MS. note: "It was difficult to catch these words, and I am
not sure that they were the same in both cases. It might have been
'twinned' (deprived) in stanza 5, and 'prin' (suffer) in the last
stanza."
  * 1932 omits this stanza.
  † 1932: "life"

31. [The Cruel Mother]

Sharp MSS., 1454/1333-34. Also in Sharp, [1916], p. 35.
Sung by Mrs. Woodberry (80), Ash Priors, August 31,
1907. [The text of 1916 has been filled out.]

a M

There was a lady dwell in York
    Fal the dal the dido
She fell in love with her father's clerk
    Down by the green wood side O.

As she was walking home one day
    Fal the dal the dido
She met those babes all dressed in white
    Down by the green wood side O.

She said dear children where have you been
    Fal the dal the dido
. . . .
    Down by the green wood side O.

O yes Dear Mother we can tell
    Fal the dal the dido
For it's we to Heaven & you to Hell
    Down by the green wood side O.

32. [The Cruel Mother]

Sharp MSS., 3769/2782. Also in Sharp and Karpeles, 1932, I, pp. 58(F)-59. Sung by Mrs. Maud Kilburn, Berea, Madison County, Ky., May 31, 1917.

a I/M

Sharp's MS. note informs us that he took his text from J. W. Raine, who had previously secured it from the same singer.

1. There was a lady near the town,
    Low, so low and so lonely,
  She walked all night and all around,
    Down in the green woods of Iv'ry.

2. She had two pretty little babes,
    Low, so low, etc.
  She thought one day she'd take their lives,
    Down in the green woods, etc.

3. She got a rope so long and neat,
  And tied them down both hands and feet.

4. She got a knife so keen and sharp,
  And pierced it through each tender heart.

5. Then she went out one moonlit night;
  She saw two babes all dressed in white.

6. O babes, O babes, if you were mine,
  I'd dress you up in silk so fine.

7. O mamma, O mamma, when we were yours,
  You dressed us in our own heart's blood.

8. In seven years you'll hear a bell,
  In seven years you'll land in hell.

33. "Hey wi' the rose and the lindie"

Christie, I, 1876, p. 108. Sung in Buchan. (Given arbitrarily with "The Cruel Brother.")

m I/Ly

The second strain is doubtless Christie's invention.

GROUP C

34. "Down by the Greenwood Side-e-o"

Barry, *BFSSNE*, No. 8 (1934), p. 7. Sung by Mrs. F. M. Bradman, Brownville, Maine, January 1934. Collected by Mrs. Susan M. Lewis.

m I/Ly

Cautious reference should be made to Barry's extensive notes on the relations between this and the "Two Sisters" airs, *loc.cit.* and *BFSSNE*, No. 3, p. 13, and No. 7, p. 11.

1. As I was pacing father's hall,
    All alone, aloney-o;
  I saw three infants playing ball,
    Down by the greenwood side-e-o.

2. One's name was Peter, and the other's name
   was Paul,
   And the other little infant had no name
   at all.

3. Said I to this infant, "Will you be mine?
   I'll dress you in silks and satins fine."

4. Then said this infant, "When I was thine,
   You dressed me in neither coarse nor fine."

     *   *   *   *   *

5. Then she took her pen-knife long and sharp,
   And pierced it through his tender heart.

6. And then she dug a little grave,
   And neither sheet nor blanket gave.

7. Then she stuck her pen-knife in the clay,
   And there it sticks to this very day.

35. [The Cruel Mother]

Davis, 1929, p. 560(A); text, pp. 133-34. Sung by Mrs.
James B. Crawford, Altavista, Va., September 11, 1915.
Collected by Juliet Fauntleroy.

p I

1. As I was going to my father's house,
   All along and lonely,
   I saw two babies playing with a ball,
   Down on the green river sidey.

2. "Oh babes, Oh babes, if you were mine,"
   All along and lonely,
   "I'd dress you up in scarlet fine,"
   Down on the green river sidey.

3. "Oh mother, Oh mother, when we were thine,"
   All along and lonely,
   "You would not dress us in scarlet fine,"
   Down on the green river sidey.

4. "You stuck a pen-knife to our tender little heart,"
   All along and lonely,
   "And buried us down in brush in the dark,"
   Down on the green river sidey.

*(One stanza forgotten here about the mother's grief,
Mrs. Crawford says.)*

5. "Oh babes, Oh babes, if you could tell,"
   All along and lonely,
   "How long on earth have I to dwell?"
   Down on the green river sidey.

6. "Seven long years on earth to dwell,"
   All along and lonely,
   "The balance of your time you'll spend in hell,"
   Down on the green river sidey.

36. [The Cruel Mother]

White, *JFSS*, II (1905), p. 109. Sung by Mrs. A. R. Martin,
Anchorage, Ky.

p I

"My dear little children, if you were mine,
All alone, and aloney O!
I'd dress you up in silk so fine
Down by the green-woody sidey, O!"

37. [Cruel Mother]

Creighton, 1932, pp. 3-5. Sung by Ben Henneberry, Devil's
Island, Nova Scotia.

p I (–VI)

1. There was a lady came from York,
   All alone and a-loney,
   She fell in love with her father's clerk
   Down by the greenwood siding.

2. She loved him well, she loved him long,
   All alone and a-loney,
   Till at length this young maid with child she did prove,
   Down by the greenwood siding.

3. She leaned her back against her yoke,
   All alone and a-loney,
   When first it bowed and then it broke,
   Down by the greenwood siding.

4. She leaned herself against a thorn
   All alone and a-loney,
   And there her two pretty babes were born
   Down by the greenwood siding.

5. She had nothing to wrap them in,
   All alone and a-loney,
   But her apron. It was thin,
   Down by the greenwood siding.

6. She took the cap from off her head,
      All alone and a-loney,
   And tied those pretty babes' arms and legs,
      Down by the greenwood siding.

7. She took her penknife keen and sharp,
      All alone and a-loney,
   And she pierced it through their innocent hearts,
      Down by the greenwood siding.

8. She stuck her penknife in the green,
      All alone and a-loney,
   The more she rubbed the blood was seen
      Down by the greenwood siding.

9. Then she threw it far away,
      All alone and a-loney,
   The farther she threw it the nearer it came,
      Down by the greenwood siding.

10. As she entered her father's hall,
      All alone and a-loney,
   She saw those pretty babes playing ball,
      Down by the greenwood siding.

11. "Oh babes, oh babes, if you were mine,
      All alone and a-loney,
   I would dress you up in silks so fine,
      Down by the greenwood siding."

12. "Oh mother, oh mother, when we were thine,
      All alone and a-loney,
   You did not dress us up in silks so fine,
      Down by the greenwood siding.

13. "But you took your penknife, keen and sharp,
      All alone and a-loney,
   And you pierced it through our innocent hearts,
      Down by the greenwood siding."

14. "Oh, pretty maidens, can you tell,
      All alone and a-loney,
   Whether I'll reign in heaven or hell?
      Down by the greenwood siding."

15. "No, mother dear, we can't tell well,
      All alone and a-loney,
   But your body's here, but your soul's in hell,
      Down by the greenwood siding.

16. "Seven years a beast in the woods,
      All alone and a-loney,
   And seven more a fish in the sea,
      Down by the greenwood siding.

17. "And seven more did toll the bell,
      All alone and a-loney,
   Before you can be redeemed from hell,
      Down by the greenwood siding."

38. [The Cruel Mother]

Wilkinson MSS., 1935-36, p. 30(B). Sung by Mrs. Lucy
McAllister, Harriston, Va., October 9, 1935.

p I/M

1. She loved him up and she loved him down,
      Lil, O Lily in the lowly.
   She loved him till he filled her arms,
      Down by the greenwood siding.

2. She placed her foot against an oak,
   First it bent and then it broke.

3. She placed herself against a thorn,
   And there's where those babes were born.

4. When she was sitting in her father's hall,
   She spied those little babes a-playing ball.

5. O little babes if you were mine,
   I'd dress you up in silks so fine.

6. O mother, O mother, when we were born,
   You never dressed me in coarse nor fine.

7. Now we're in Heaven a-doing well,
   Your redeemer is down in hell.

39. [The Cruel Mother]

Wilkinson MSS., 1935-36, p. 29(A). Sung by Jennie Davis,
Harrisonburg, Va., October 5, 1935.

a π¹ (compass of sixth)

As Lily was walking out on the strand,
O Lily of the lowlands,
Out came two babes a-playing in the sand.
Down by the greenwood side.

O little babes if you were mine,
O Lily of the lowlands,
I'd dress you up in silks so fine.
Down by the greenwood side.

O mother, O mother, when we were thine,
O Lily of the lowlands,
You neither gave us coarse or fine.
Down by the greenwood side.

You buried us here beneath the ground,
O Lily of the lowlands,
You buried us without a sheet or gown.
Down by the greenwood side.

40. [The Cruel Mother]

Sharp MSS., 4554/3186. Also in Sharp and Karpeles, 1932,
I, p. 60(H). Sung by Mrs. Mary Gibson, Marion, N.C.,
September 3, 1918.

p π¹

1. There was a lady in New York,
    All along little omey,*
  She fell in love with her father's clerk,
    All down by the greenwood sidey.

2. She was a-going across the bridge,
  She found herself a-growing big.

3. She leant herself against an oak;
  First it bent and then it broke.

4. She leant herself against a thorn;
  And there she had two little babes born.

5. She carried a penknife both keen and sharp;
  She pierced those little babes to the heart.

6. She buried them under a bunch of rue;
  She prayed to the Lord they'd never come to.

7. When she was a-walking across the porch,
  She saw two little babes at play.

8. O babes, O babes, if you were mine,
  I'd dress you up in silk so fine.

9. Mother, O mother, when we were yours
  You neither gave us coarse nor fine.

10. Mother, O mother, for our sakes
  You'll always carry the keys of Hell's gates.

* 1932: "Omy"

41. [The Cruel Mother]

Sharp MSS., 4565/. Also in Sharp and Karpeles, 1932, I,
p. 62(M). Sung by Mrs. Emily J. Snipes, Marion, N.C.,
September 5, 1918.

p I/M

  Mother, mother do so no more,
    All lea* little Oney,
  For this you shall carry the keys of Hell's door,
    All down by the green road† sidey.

* 1932: "lee"
† So the MS. The printed copy has "wad" (for "wood"?).

The second half is the common "Barbara Allen" tune (84). It may
be observed that the oddness of this variant lies partly in the fact
that the first half is pentachordal, and the second half pentatonic.
Emphasis on the fourth in the opening phrases is belied by its
subsequent disappearance.

42. [The Cruel Mother]

Sharp MSS., 3394/2492. Also in Sharp and Karpeles, 1932,
I, p. 57(C). Sung by T. Jeff Stockton, Hogskin Creek,
Flag Pond, Tenn., September 4, 1916.

p π¹

  O babes, O babes, if you was mine,
  I'd dress you up in silk so fine.

  O mother, O mother, when we were thine,
  You neither dressed us up in coarse nor fine.

  O mother, O mother, that surely's you,
    All alone, aloney,
  The gates of hell is open for you to walk [through],*
    All down by the greenwood sidey.

  * MS. reads "in."

43. [The Cruel Mother]

Davis, 1929, p. 561(C); text, p. 135. Sung by a mountain
woman, Rockingham County, Va., May 8, 1916; learned
from her grandmother. Collected by Martha M. Davis.

p π¹

As Lily was walking out on the strand,
　　O, lily of the lowlands!
Out come two babes a-playing in the sand,
　　Down by the greenwood side.

"O, little babes, if you were mine,"
　　O, lily of the lowlands!
"I'd dress you up in silks so fine,"
　　Down by the greenwood side.

"O mother, O mother, when we were thine,"
　　O, lily of the lowlands!
"You neither gave us coarse nor fine,"
　　Down by the greenwood side.

"You buried us here beneath the ground,"
　　O, lily of the lowlands!
"You buried us without a sheet or a gown,"
　　Down by the greenwood side.

44. [The Cruel Mother]

Sharp MSS., 3515/. Also Sharp and Karpeles, 1932, I, p. 57(D); and Davis, 1929, p. 560. Sung by Mr. N. B. Chisholm, Woodridge, Va., September 21, 1916.

p M (inflected VII)

The MS. is in the key of G: the 1932 printing is transposed to A.

O baby O baby if you were mine
All along and aloney
I would dress you in the scarlet so fine
Down by the green river sidey

45. [The Cruel Mother]

Creighton and Senior, 1950, pp. 19-20. Sung by Mrs. R. W. Duncan, Dartmouth, Nova Scotia.

p M (inflected VII)

1. There was a lady came from York
　All alone, alone and aloney,
　She fell in love with her father's clerk
　Down by the greenwood siding.

2. When nine months was gone and past
　Then she had two pretty babes born.

3. She leaned herself against a thorn
　There she had two pretty babes born.

4. Then she cut her topknot from her head
　And tied those babies' hands and legs.

5. She took her penknife keen and sharp
　And pierced those babies' tender hearts.

6. She buried them under a marble stone
　And then she said she would go home.

7. As she was (going through) (a-going in)* her father's hall
　She spied those babes a-playing at a ball.

8. "Oh babes, oh babes if (you were) (thou wast) mine
　I would dress you up in silks so fine."

9. "Oh mother dear when we were thine
　You did not dress us up in silks so fine,

10. "You took your topknot from your head
　And tied us babies' hands and legs.

11. "Then you took your penknife (long) (keen) and sharp
　And pierced us babies' tender hearts.

12. "It's seven years to roll a stone
　And seven years to toll a bell.

13. "It's mother dear oh we can't tell
　Whether your portion is heaven or hell."

*The song was noted twice; parentheses mark the singer's changes.

46. [The Cruel Mother]

Sharp MSS., 4087/2930. Also in Sharp and Karpeles, 1932, I, pp. 59(G)-60. Sung by Mrs. Doc. Pratt, Hindman, Knott County, Ky., September 22, 1917.

p I (− VI)

1. There was a young lady so fair,
　　Down in the loney, oney, O,
　She was courted by the king's son so great,
　　Down by the greenwood sideys, O.

2. He courted her for seven long years,
   Until one evening she went walking.

3. It's first she leaned against an oak;
   First it bent and then it broke.

4. The next she leaned against a pine;
   Two sweet little babes to her was born.

5. She took her garter from her leg,
   And there she tied her sweet little babes.

6. She took her penknife from her side,
   Then she took their sweet little lives.

7. She was sitting one day in her father's hall;
   She saw two sweet little babes playing.

8. Saying: Babes, sweet babes, if you was mine,
   I'd dress you up in silk so fine.

9. O yes, false mother, we once was thine;
   You neither dressed us coarse nor fine.

10. O babes, sweet babes, can you tell me,
    What'll be my fate for killing you?

11. O yes, false mother, we can tell you.
    A false character you will bear.

12. Until your soul is called* away,
    And then will hell scorch your bones.

* 1932: "scorched"

47. [The Cruel Mother]

Morris, 1950, pp. 251-52. Sung by Mrs. G. A. Griffin, Newberry, Fla., 1937; learned from her father.

a M

1. There was a lady lived in New York,
   All de lone and de loney;
   She fell in love with her father's clerk,
   All down by the greeny woodside ny;
   She fell in love with her father's clerk,
   All down by the greeny woodside ny.

2. She leant herself against the oak,
   All de lone and de loney;
   It was it leant and then it broke,
   All down by the greeny woodside ny;
   It was it leant and then it broke,
   All down by the greeny woodside ny.

3. She leaned herself against the thorn,
   All de lone and de loney;
   There she had two pretty babes borned,
   All down by the greeny woodside ny.
   There she had two pretty babes borned,
   All down by the greeny woodside ny.

4. She takened her hairstring offen her hair,
   All de lone and de loney;
   She tied them up both hands and feet,
   All down by the greeny woodside ny;
   She tied them up both hands and feet,
   All down by the greeny woodside ny.

5. She takened her pen knife outen her pocket,
   All de lone and de loney;
   She pierced it to their tender hearts,
   All down by the greeny woodside ny;
   And she buried them both at Marblestone,
   All down by the greeny woodside ny.

6. One even she was sitting in her father's hall,
   All de lone and de loney;
   She saw two pretty babes playing with a ball,
   All down by the greeny woodside ny;
   She saw two pretty babes playing with a ball,
   All down by the greeny woodside ny.

7. "O babes, O babes, if you was mine,
   All de lone and de loney;
   I'd dress you up in silks so fine,
   All down by the greeny woodside ny;
   I'd dress you up in silks so fine,
   All down by the greeny woodside ny.["]

8. "O Mother, O Mother, when we was yours,
   All de lone and de loney;
   You seemed to give us coarse nor fine,
   All down by the greeny woodside ny;
   You seemed to give us coarse nor fine,
   All down by the greeny woodside ny;

9. "You takened your hairstring offen your hair,
   All de lone and de loney;
   You tied us up both hands and feet,
   All down by the greeny woodside ny;
   You tied us up both hands and feet,
   All down by the greeny woodside ny.

10. "You takened your pen knife all outen your pocket,
    All de lone and de loney;
    You pierced it to our tender hearts,
    All down by the greeny woodside ny;
    You buried us both at Marblestone,
    All down by the greeny woodside ny."

48. [The Cruel Mother]

Davis, 1929, p. 560(B); text, p. 134. Sung by Mrs. Virgie Mayhew Keesee, Pittsylvania County, Va., May 26, 1915; learned from her uncle, who learned it in Tennessee. Collected by Juliet Fauntleroy.

a π^2

One day I was setting in my father's hall,
    I saw three babes a-playing ball.
All day long and I love you all,
    Down by the greenwood side-y, Oh!

"Oh, little babes, if you was mine,
    I'd dress you up in scarlet fine."
All day long and I love you all,
    Down by the greenwood side-y, Oh!

"Oh, dear mother, when we was thine
    You neither put on our coarse nor fine."
All day long and I love you all,
    Down by the greenwood side-y, Oh!

"Oh, little babes, if you could tell,
    How long on earth have (am) I to dwell?"
All day long and I love you all,
    Down by the greenwood side-y, Oh!

"Seven long years on earth to dwell,
    The balance of your time you'll spend in hell."
All day long and I love you all,
    Down by the greenwood side-y, Oh!

Cf. C. K. Sharpe's copy of "The Twa Sisters" (10).

It fell ance upon a day, Edinbro', Edinbro',
It fell ance upon a day, Stirling for aye;
It fell ance upon a day, A lady saw babies at their play,
And bonny Saint Johnston stands fair upon Tay. [Etc.]

GROUP E

51. [The Cruel Mother]

Sharp MSS., 3236/2371. Also in Sharp and Karpeles, 1932,
I, p. 56(A). Sung by Mrs. Rosie Hensley, Carmen, N.C.,
August 10, 1916.

p M

1. She laid herself all against the oak,
        All along in the Ludeney
||: And first it bent and then it broke,
        Down by the greenwood side. :||

2. She lent* herself all against the thorn,
    And there she had two fine babes born.

3. She pulled out her snow-white breast,
    And she bid them a-suck for that would be the last.

4. She pulled down her yellow hair,
    And she bound it around their little feet and hands.

5. She pulled out her little penknife,
    And she pierced all in their little tender† hearts.

6. She was setting in her father's hall,
    And she saw her babes a-playing with their ball.

7. O babes, O babes, if you were mine,
    I would dress you in the silk so fine.

GROUP D

49. "Edinbrie, Edinbrie"

Campbell, II, [1818], p. 8. Also in Barry, *BFSSNE*, No. 3
(1931), p. 13. Sung by Thomas Hogg, Thirlstane, 1816.

p M

50. [Bonny Saint Johnston stands fair upon Tay]

Christie, I, 1876, p. 104. Sung in Banffshire.

m M (−IV)

8. O mother, O mother, when we were thine,
   You neither dressed us in the coarse silk nor fine.

* 1932: "leaned"
† 1932: "tender little"

52. [The Cruel Mother]

Sharp MSS., 3776/. Also in Sharp and Karpeles, 1932, I,
p. 61(K). Sung by Mrs. Ollie Huff, Berea, Ky., May 31,
1917.

a I/Ly

This tune, as was suggested in the headnote, reminds one of a
folk-hymn. Cf., e.g., George Pullen Jackson, *Spiritual Folk-Songs of
Early America*, 1939, p. 42 ("Patton"). The line of descent, of course,
might be from secular to sacred.

She had three babes, three pretty little babes,
Down by the green wood side,
She spied those babes those pretty little babes,
Down by the green wood side,
Said: Dear babes if you were mine,
All alone and alone ilee,
I'd dress you up in silk so fine,
Down by the green wood side.

53. [The Cruel Mother]

Henry, 1938, pp. 47-48. Sung by Mrs. Samuel Harmon,
Cade's Cove, Tenn., August 1930.

a π²/π³ (– V) (compass of fourth)

1. A mother had two little babes,
   All along in the lone e o.

2. She carried them down in the greenwood sides,
   All along in the lone e o.

3. She tuk her knife and cut their throats,
   All along in the lone e o.

4. She buried them under a marble stone,
   All along in the lone e o.

5. She covered them up with a marble ball,
   All along in the lone e o.

6. She went to the river for to wash her hands,
   All along in the lone e o.

7. The more she washed the bloodier they got,
   All along in the lone e o.

8. She went to the house for to dry her hands,
   All along in the lone e o.

9. She seen her two little babes under the marble stone,
   All along in the lone e o.

10. Playing with that marble ball,
    All along in the lone e o.

11. "Babes, O babes, if you were mine,
    All along in the lone e o.

12. I'd dress you in the silks so fine,"
    All along in the lone e o.

13. "Mama, O mama, we onct was yourn,
    All along in the lone e o.

14. You neither dressed us coarse nor fine,"
    All along in the lone e o.

54. "Down by the Greenwood Side"

Randolph, I, 1946, pp. 73-74. Sung by Mrs. Emma L.
Dusenbury, Mena, Ark., June 1, 1930.

a π²

This copy, perhaps inaccurately set down, reappears in Randolph,
The Ozarks, 1931, p. 185, and in Scarborough, *A Song Catcher in
Southern Mountains*, 1937, p. 403. The timing of the original is
6/8 throughout.

1. She leaned her back ag'in th' wall,
   All aloney,
   She thought in her heart her back would break,
   Down by th' greenwood side.

2. She leaned her back ag'in the thorns,
   All aloney,
   An' there she had two pretty sons born,
   Down by the greenwood side.

3. She had a little pen knife both keen an' sharp,
   All aloney,
   An' she pierced them tender babies' heart,
   Down by the greenwood side.

4. She washed her knife all in the flood,
   All aloney,
   She turned the river all to blood,
   Down by the greenwood side.

5. As she returned back home again,
   All aloney,
   She seen three pretty babes playin' with a ball,
   Down by the greenwood side.

6. One was dressed in silks so fine,
   All aloney,
   T'other two was naked as they was born,
   Down by the greenwood side.

7. Oh babes, oh babes, if you was mine,
   All aloney,
   I'd take an' dress you in silks so fine,
   Down by the greenwood side.

8. Oh mother, oh mother, when we was yours,
   All aloney,
   You neither dressed us in silks, nor coarse nor fine,
   Down by the greenwood side.

9. You dressed us in our own heart's blood,
   All aloney,
   You turned the river all to blood,
   Down by the greenwood side.

10. Seven years, seven years you shall burn in hell,
    All aloney,
    Seven years you shall never enter heaven,
    Down by the greenwood side.

55. [The Cruel Mother]

Sharp MSS., 3105/? Text, Sharp and Karpeles, 1932, I,
pp. 56(B)-57. Sung to Sharp, March 1916, by Olive Dame
Campbell, who learned it from Mrs. Moore, Rabun County,
Ga., 1909.

a Æ/D (inflected VII)

This is an interesting example of contamination: cf. both text and
tune with Child 79.

1. Christmas time is a rolling on,
   When the nights are long and cool,
   When three little babes come running down
   And run in their mother's room.

2. As she was going to her father's hall,
   All down by the greenwood side,
   She saw three little babes a-playing ball.
   All down by the greenwood side.

3. O babes, O babes, if you were mine,
   I'd dress you in the silks so fine.

4. O mother, O mother, when we were yourn,
   You neither dressed us coarse nor fine.

5. You took your penknife out of your pocket,
   And you pierced it through our tender hearts.

6. You wiped your penknife on your shoe,
   And the more you wiped it the bloodier it grew.

7. You buried it under a marble stone,
   You buried it under a marble stone.

8. The hell gates are open and you must go through,
   The hell gates are open and you must go through.

56. "There was a Lady drest in Green"

Gilchrist, *JFSS*, VI (1919), p. 80. Sung by a little girl,
Saunders St. Orphanage, Southport, 1915.

a π¹

1. There was a lady drest in green,
   Fair a lair a lido,
   There was a lady drest in green
   Down by the greenwood side, O.

2. She had a baby in her arms.

   Refrain and repetition as in verse 1.

3. She had a penknife in her hand.

4. She stuck it in the baby's arm ['eart?].

5. She went to the well to wash it off.

6. The more she washed, the more it bled.

7. She went upstairs to lay it down.

8. There came a rat-tat at the door.

9. She went downstairs to let them in.

10. There came three bobbies rushing in.

11. They asked her what she did last night.

12. She said she killed her only son.

13. Off to prison you must go.

14. That was the end of Mrs. Green.

St. Stephen and Herod

CHILD NO. 22

THE sole text here is closer to the fifteenth-century text in the Sloane MS. than anything yet picked up in recent tradition: indeed, it may be a literary, rather than a traditional, redaction of Sloane, which was in print by the middle of the last century. The Edwards family appears on this and other showing to have been in touch with a peculiarly literate antiquarian tradition. Cf. Mr. Edwards' versions of Child 13, 166, 266, in the same collection. At any rate, until other traditional variants of the ballad are disclosed, we may reserve judgment as to the authenticity of this one.

The tune appears to be an abraded form of familiar melodic outlines, the monotone second and fourth phrases being perhaps withheld from the tell-tale definition which a more varied contour and a final cadence on the tonic would have given them.

The gypsy copy, "King Pharim," collected by Miss Broadwood belongs more properly to Child 55, q.v. Cf. Lucy E. Broadwood, *English Traditional Songs and Carols*, 1908, p. 74; and *JFSS*, I (1902), p. 183.

LIST OF VARIANTS

"St. Stephen and Herod." Helen Hartness Flanders and Marguerite Olney, *Ballads Migrant in New England*, 1953, pp. 217-18.

TUNE WITH TEXT

"St. Stephen and Herod"

Flanders and Olney, 1953, pp. 217-18. Sung by George L. Edwards, Burlington, Vt., October 16, 1934; learned from his grandmother, of Seaton, East Riding, Yorkshire. From *Ballads Migrant in New England*, edited by Helen Hartness Flanders and Marguerite Olney; copyright 1953 by Helen Hartness Flanders.

a I, ending on III, lacking II (compass of sixth)

St. Stephen was a serving-man
In Herod's royal hall.
He serv-ed him with meat and wine
That doth to kings befall.

He was serving him with meat, one day,
With a boar's head in his hand,
When he saw a star come from the East
And over Bethlehem stand.

St. Stephen was a righteous man
And in his faith was bold.
He was waiting for the birth of Christ
As by the prophets told.

He cast the Boar's head on the floor
And let the server fall;
He said, "Behold a child is born
That is better than we all."

Then quickly he went to Herod's room
And unto him did say,
"I am leaving thee, King Herod,
And will proclaim thy wicked ways."

Bonnie Annie

CHILD NO. 24

OF A round dozen of ballads in dactylic measure, this and "Willie Macintosh" (183) are, I believe, the only ones in Child's canon with consistently feminine rhymes, or line-endings. So infrequent a phenomenon calls aloud for an explanation, but I am at a loss to supply one. If the formal influence here be Gaelic, why is it so seldom seen? There is certainly no community of spirit or subject-matter between these two ballads, nor, for that matter, between the members of the larger group in dactyls, including, as it does, things so diverse and far-brought as "Lord Randal," "King John and the Bishop," "The Cherry-Tree Carol," "Lamkin," "The Death of Queen Jane," "Bonnie James Campbell," and "The Farmer's Curst Wife." Any category smaller than Ballad itself would hardly contain them all.

Neither Kinloch nor Motherwell, who provide us with our earliest texts, has preserved a tune for "Bonnie Annie." In fact, Baring-Gould, gathering songs in Devon and Cornwall toward the end of the last century, appears to have been the first collector to secure a tune, and he neglected to print it. (Three variants, under the name "The Undutiful Daughter," and an analogue from *The Baby's Opera*, are preserved in his MSS.) Consequently, all our records are of the present century or close to it. Neither is there anything in any one of them that sounds old. The texts are in much the same case, being, perhaps, for the most part pretty well saturated with nineteenth-century broadside influences. It must, I think, be acknowledged, that if Child, on the strength of the Jonah parallel, intended us to draw inferences of great age for this song, he was himself drawing a very long bow. "Captain Glen," a song popular in the last century and circulating in tradition as well as on broadsides, contains the same idea; but few would draw any inference of age from that fact. Superstitions flourish at sea.

With few exceptions, the tunes for this ballad are closely related. They are plagal, usually major or I/Ly, and habitually in genuine triple time. They are properly two phrases long, the cadence at the first phrase usually balancing the final feminine cadence; e.g., *V III* and II I. All the Somerset variants save one conform to this pattern. The sole Scottish variant, further from the norm, and disguised by 2/4 time, yet seems related. A Hampshire variant, more sophisticated with inflected VI and VII, belongs, I believe, to the same tribe. One Somerset variant (Mrs. Hooper's) is more independent, and suggests five phrases; but declares the allegiance in the last two cadences. A New England copy, derived from Irish antecedents, is pentachordal and too *zersungen* to be trustworthy in any way.

LIST OF VARIANTS

1. "Banks of Green Willow." Sharp MSS., 373/502, Clare College Library, Cambridge. Also in Cecil J. Sharp, *JFSS*, II (1905), p. 35(5). (Mogg)
2. "Banks of Green Willow." Sharp MSS., 346/474. Also in Cecil J. Sharp, *JFSS*, II (1905), p. 34(4). (Overd)
3. "Banks of Green Willow." Sharp MSS., 2914/. (Tarr)
4. "The Undutiful Daughter." Sabine Baring-Gould MSS., CXXV(3) and (C), Plymouth Public Library.
a. "Frog and Crow." Baring-Gould MSS., CXXV(4).
5. "Banks of Green Willow." Sharp MSS., 266/. Also in Cecil J. Sharp, *JFSS*, II (1905), p. 34(3). (Welch)
6. "The Undutiful Daughter." Baring-Gould MSS., CXXV-(2).
7. "The Undutiful Daughter." Baring-Gould MSS., CXXV-(1) and (A).
8. "Banks of Green Willow." Sharp MSS., 846/. (Hector)
9. "Banks of Green Willow." Sharp MSS., 1850/1695. (Gulliford)
10. "Banks of Green Willow." Sharp MSS., 427/. (Vickery)
11. "Banks of Green Willow." Sharp MSS., 433/553. (Nott)
12. "Banks of Green Willow." Sharp MSS., 1909/. (Ash)
13. "Bonnie Annie." Gavin Greig and Alexander Keith, *Last Leaves of Traditional Ballads and Ballad Airs*, 1925, pp. 23(A)-24.
14. "Banks of Green Willow." Sharp MSS., 153/231-32. Also in Cecil J. Sharp, *JFSS*, II (1905), p. 33(2). (Spearing)
15. "The Banks of Green Willow." R. Vaughan Williams, *JFSS*, III (1909), pp. 292-93.
16. "Banks of Green Willow." Sharp MSS., 567/. (Milton)
17. "Banks of Green Willow." Sharp MSS., 103/94. Also in Cecil J. Sharp, *JFSS*, II (1905), p. 33(1). (White, Hooper)
18. "Bonnie Annie." Phillips Barry, *BFSSNE*, No. 10 (1935), p. 11. Revised in Phillips Barry, *BFSSNE*, No. 11 (1936), pp. 9-10.

TUNES WITH TEXTS

1. [Banks of Green Willow]

Sharp MSS., 373/502-3. Also in Sharp, *JFSS*, II (1905), p. 35(5). Sung by Elizabeth Mogg, Holford, August 30, 1904.

p I

1. It's of a sea captain
   Down by the sea-side O,
   He courted a young damsel
   And got her by a child.

2. Go and get your mother's will O
   And all your father's money

To sail across the ocean
Along with your Johnny.

3. I've got my father's will O
And all my mother's money
To sail across the ocean
Along with my Johnny.

4. We had not sailed miles,
No not great many,
Before she was delivered
Of a beautiful baby.

5. Go and get me a white napkin
To tie my head easy
To throw me quite overboard
Both me and my baby.

6. Now see how she totters,
Now see how she tumbles,
Now see how she's rolling
All on the salt water.

7. Go and get me a long boat
To row my love back again,
To row my love back again
Both she and her baby.

8. Now she shall have a coffin,
A coffin shall shine yellow,
And she shall be buried
On the banks of Green Willow.

9. The bells shall ring mournful
O for my dearest Polly
And she shall be buried
For the sake of her money.

O hush your tongue, you silly girl,
O hush your tongue, you huzzy,
For I can do so much for thee
As any woman can for thee.

Go and get a silk napkin
And I'll tie thy head up softly
And I'll throw thee overboard,
Both thee and thy baby.

Look how my love's swimming along,
See how my love swager.
I'm afraid she'll swim to dry land
Which makes my heart quaver.

I'll buy my love a coffin,
And the gold shall shine yellow,
And she shall be buried
By the banks of green willow.

3. [Banks of Green Willow]

Sharp MSS., 2914/. Sung by Sarah Tarr, Dulverton Union,
April 28, 1914.

p I/Ly

4. [The Undutiful Daughter]

Baring-Gould MSS., CXXV(3); text, (C). Sung by Samuel
Fone, February 27, 1893. Collected by F. W. Bussell.

p I (inflected IV)

1. 'Tis of a sea captain down by the sea side O,
He courted a maiden & got her with child O!
. . . .

2. O get a white kerchief about my head bind it!
O get a white kerchief about my feet wind it.
. . . .
. . . .

3. O sea boy! O sea boy! I see her to totter
With the babe at her breast all in the salt water.
Now push off the long boat, now push it off easy
And bring back the lady, both her & her baby.

2. [Banks of Green Willow]

Sharp MSS., 346/474. Also in Sharp, *JFSS*, II (1905), p.
34(4). Sung by Mrs. Overd, Langport, August 22, 1904.

p I/Ly

Go and get your father's good will
And get your mother's money,
And sail right over the ocean
Along with your Johnny.

She had not been sailing
Been sailing many days O.
Before she wanted some woman's help
And could not get any.

4. They pushed out the longboat, so brave & free hearted
   And brought her back safely, both she and her baby.
   On the deck   .   .   .   .
   .   .   .   .

5. A coffin shall be made of the shining gold yellow
   And she shall be buried under the banks of green willow.

5. [Banks of Green Willow]

Sharp MSS., 266/. Also in Sharp, *JFSS*, II (1905), p. 34(3).
Sung by Mrs. Lizzie Welch, Hambridge, August 5, 1904.

p I

Go and get me some of your father's gold
And some of your mother's money
And you shall go aboard with me
And be my dear honey
And you shall go aboard with me
And be my dear honey

6. [The Undutiful Daughter]

Baring-Gould MSS., CXXV(2). Sung by Richard Gregory,
Post Bridge, January 7, 1890. Collected by F. W. Bussell.

p I

The words of this variant seem not to have been preserved, and
would appear to have been in a different meter. The quarter note in
bar 4 may be only the inadvertent omission of an eighth flag, but
since the following sixteenths were attached to the subsequent eighth,
the abnormality has been allowed to stand as perhaps intentional.

7. [The Undutiful Daughter]

Baring-Gould MSS., CXXV(1); text, (A). Sung by J.
Masters, Bradstone, 1888; including verses sung by H.
Smith, Two Bridges, 1889. Collected by H. Fleetwood
Sheppard.

p M, ending on *IV*

The order of phrases stands here as in the MS., but it is hard **not**
to believe that the derangement is scribal instead of as sung.

1. 'Twas of a sea-captain came o'er the salt billow
   He courted a maiden down by the green willow.
   "O take of your father his gold and his treasure,
   O take of your mother her fee without measure."

2. "I've ta'en of my father his gold & his treasure,
   I've ta'en of my mother her fee without measure."
   She has come to the Captain unto the sea side, O
   "We'll sail to lands foreign upon the blue tide, O."

3. And when they had sailed today & tomorrow[,]
   She was wringing her hands, she was crying in sorrow,
   And when she has sailed not many a mile O,
   The maid was delivered of a beautiful child, O.

4. And when she had sailed today & tomorrow,
   She was wringing her hands, she was crying in sorrow,
   And when she had sailed, the days were not many
   The sails were outspread, but of miles made not any.

5. [They cast the black bullets, as they sailed on the water
   The black bullet fell to the undutiful daughter.
   Now, who in the ship must go over the side O
   O none save the maiden, the fair captain's bride O.]

6. "O Captain! O Captain! here's fifty gold crown O!
   I pray thee to spare me, & turn the ship round O!
   O Captain! O Captain! here's fifty gold pound O!
   If thou wilt but set me again on the ground, O!"

7. "O never! O never! the wind it blows stronger,
   O never! O never! the time it grows longer,
   O better it were that thy baby & thou O!
   Should die than the crew of the vessel I vow, O!"

8. "O get me a boat that is narrow & thin O!
   And set me & my sweet little baby therein O!"
   "O no, it were better thy baby & thou O!
   Should drown than the crew of the vessel I vow O!"

9. "O take a white napkin, about my head bind it:
   O take a white napkin, about my feet wind it:
   Alack that I must in the deep salten water
   Alack I must sink, both me and my baby (*sic*)."

10. They got a white napkin, about her head bound it,
    They got a white napkin, about her feet wound it,
    They cast her then overboard, baby & she O!
    Together to sink in the cruel salt sea O!

11. The moon it was shining, the tide it was running
    O what in the wake of the vessel is swimming
    O see, boys, O see! how she floats in the water
    O see, boys, O see! the undutiful daughter.

12. "Why swim in the moonlight, upon the sea swaying
O what art thou seeking, for what art thou playing?"
"O Captain, O captain, I float on the water
For the sea giveth up the undutiful daughter."

13. "O take of my father the gold & the treasure.
O take of my mother the fee without measure.
O make me a coffin of deepest stole (*sic*) yellow,
And bury me under the banks of green willow."

14. "I will make thee a coffin of deepest stole yellow
I will bury thee under the banks of green willow.
I will bury thee there, both thee and thy baby,
I will bury thee there as beseemeth a lady."

15. The sails they were spread, & the wind it was blowing
The sea was so salt, and the tide it was flowing,
They steered for the land, & they reachéd the shore, O
But the mother & Baby had got there before, O!

8. [Banks of Green Willow]

Sharp MSS., 846/. Sung by Mrs. Hector (75), Stathe, Borough Bridge, April 7, 1906.

p I

Tie a napkin round my head and tie it soft and easy
And throw me right overboard
Both me and my baby

9. [Banks of Green Willow]

Sharp MSS., 1850/1695. Sung by Jane Gulliford, Combe Florey, September 8, 1908.

a I (ending on VIII)

Sea captain, sea captain, down by the banks of willow,
He caught a fair damsel and he brought her with child.

She had not sailed miles nor miles nor many
Before she was a mother of a beautiful baby.
You go back and tell them and tell my mother from me
That I'll sail the briny ocean all along with young Johnny.
Sea captain, sea captain, here is fifty bright guineas
To throw me overboard both me and my baby.
O no, said the captain, such things it never can be
For it's better to lose two lives than 'tis to lose many.
You give to me a napkin I'll wrap my head in it.
I'll throw myself overboard both me and my baby.
You give to me a lifeboat I'll fetch my love back in it,
I'll fetch my love back again, both she and her baby.
Do you see how she totters, do you see how she tremble,
Do you see how she totters all on the salt water.
For she shall have a coffin of golden shining yellow
And she shall be buried upon the banks of green willow.

10. [Banks of Green Willow]

Sharp MSS., 427/. Sung by W. Vickery, East Worlington, September 14, 1904.

p I/Ly

Sea Captain Sea Captain down by the seaside O
He court a fair damsel and brought her with child O

11. [Banks of Green Willow]

Sharp MSS., 433/553. Sung by William Nott, Meshaw, September 14, 1904.

p I

It's of a sea captain
Down by the sea-side O
Where he courted a fair damsel
And he brought her with child O.

He had not sailed
Of miles no (*sic*) many
Before she was delivered
Of a beautiful baby.

Oh captain, O captain,
Here's fifty pounds for thee
If thee'll take my love back again
Both she and her baby.

No, no, says the captain,
That never can be
For it's best two lives
Than it is to lost many.

The coffin shall be made
Of the gold that is so yellow
And she shall be buried
On the banks of green willow.

12. [Banks of Green Willow]

Sharp MSS., 1909/. Sung by Charles Ash, Crowcombe,
September 16, 1908.

a I (ending on VIII)

Sharp's MS. note: "Ash not at all sure of this tune, but quite clear
about first phrase."

Go get me a long boat and dont long detain me
And I'll roll my love back again safe and her baby

13. "Bonnie Annie"

(Perhaps Duncan MS.; not located in Greig MSS.) Greig
and Keith, 1925, pp. 23(A)-24. Sung by James M. Brown,
Glasgow; learned in Falkirk district.

a I/M

Keith has noted a fortuitous resemblance here to "Kathleen
Mavourneen."

There was a rich merchant who lived in Strathdinah
And he had a daughter whose name was called Annie.

There was a rich merchant who came from Dumbarton
And he's gat this bonnie lassie big, big wi bairn.

And hey, she sang,* Johnnie, and ho,
  she sang,* Johnnie,
Will ye gang and leave me aleen here to mourn?

* Under the notes, "said."

14. [Banks of Green Willow]

Sharp MSS., 153/231-32. Also in Sharp, *JFSS*, II (1905),
p. 33(2). Sung by William Spearing, Isle Brewers, Somerset, April 6, 1904.

p I

1. It's of a sea captain O
   Lived by the sea-side O.
   He courted a pretty girl
   Till he got her by child O.

2. She went for to sail
   . . . .
   They had not sailed miles many O
   Before she was delivered of a beautiful baby.

3. O take me back again,
   Here's fifty pounds I will to thee
   To row me safe back again
   Both me and my baby.

4. O I cannot turn the ship O
   For to turn it would lose many lives O.
   It's better to lose my* life
   Than so many O.

5. O fetch me a napkin O
   And bind my head so easy
   And overboard throw me
   Both me and my baby.

6. O they fetched him a napkin
   And bound her head so easy,
   And overboard he threw his love
   Both she and her baby.

7. O see how my love's a-rollin'
   O see how my love's a-tumblin'.†
   O fetch to me the life-boat
   And bring my love safe back again,
   Both she and her baby.

8. O make my love a coffin
   Of the gold that shines yellow

And she shall be buried
On the banks of green willow.

* Sharp, *JFSS:* "one"
† Sharp, *JFSS:* "a-tremblin' "

15. [Banks of Green Willow]

Vaughan Williams, *JFSS*, III (1909), pp. 292-93. Sung by
David Clements (80), Basingstoke, Hampshire, 1909.

p Minor (inflected VI and VII)

(a) was almost C♯ once; (b) occasionally almost F♯.

1. It's of a sea captain livéd near the seaside, oh,
   And he courted a lady till she proved by child.

2. "Oh, it's fetch me some of your father's clothes, and some
       of your mother's money,
   That I might go on board of ship with my own dearest
       honey."

3. We hadn't been on board of ship but six weeks or better
   Before she wanted women and could not get any.

4. "Oh, it's hold your tongue, oh you silly girl, oh, it's hold
       your tongue my honey,
   For we cannot get women for love nor for money."

5. He tied a napkin round her head, and he tied it round
       softly,
   And he threw her right over, both she and her baby.

6. I got out upon the deck for to see my love in the water.

7. Seeing how she doth swim, my boys, seeing how she doth
       swagger,
   She will never leave swimming till she come to some
       harbour.

　　　　　*　*　*　*　*　*

8. Oh, she shall have a coffin if ever she is founded,

9. Oh, she shall have a coffin, and the nails shall shine yellow;
   And my love she shall be buried in the banks of green
   willow.

16. [Banks of Green Willow]

Sharp MSS., 567/. Sung by Mrs. Mary Anne Milton (80),
Washford, August 17, 1905.

p I/Ly

I gainèd my fathers good will
Likewise my mother's money
And I roved off to sea
Along with young Johnny.

17. [Banks of Green Willow]

Sharp MSS., 103/94. Also in Sharp, *JFSS*, II (1905), p.
33(1). Sung by Mrs. White and Mrs. Louie Hooper, Hambridge, December 28, 1903.

p I

Contrary to the rest, this is clearly a five-phrase tune. Note also
the textual influence of "Lady Isabel" (4).

Go home and get some of your father's gold
And some of your mother's money
And you shall go and board with me
For to be my dear honey, for to be my dear honey.

He had not sailed many miles,
Not many miles nor scarcely
Before he was troubled
With her and her baby, with her and her baby.

He tied a napkin round her head
And he tied it to the baby,
And then he threw them overboard,
Both her and her baby, both her and her baby.

See how my love she will try to swim,
See how my love she will taver,
See how my love she will try to swim
To the banks of green willow, to the banks of green willow.

I will have the coffin made for my love
And I'll edge it all with yellow.
Then she shall be buried
On the banks of green willow, on the banks of green willow.

18. [Bonnie Annie]

Barry, *BFSSNE*, No. 10 (1935), p. 11. Revised in Barry, *BFSSNE*, No. 11 (1936), pp. 9-10. Sung by Rose Davis, Brewer, Maine, 1935; learned from her mother, who came from Ireland.

a I/M (– VI) Pentachordal I-V

"Captain, take gold, and, captain, take money,
Captain, take gold, but leave me my honey!"

Barry found this copy musically superior to all others for this ballad. I take it to display the vestiges of the omnipresent "Villikens" tune—as being unable, in fact, to escape from the groove of its first phrase. Note, moreover, that in *BFSSNE*, No. 11, pp. 9-10, Miss Davis has bethought her of more words that actually occur in "Villikens." Barry believed the borrowing was the other way round.

Willie's Lyke-Wake

CHILD NO. 25

OF THIS ballad, continental analogues are found in both northern and southern Europe, and the Danish records carry it up into the sixteenth century. But in English it has never (to my knowledge) been found outside Scotland, and no record of it is older than the nineteenth century. That, of course, is no reason for concluding that it did not exist in Scotland centuries before*; but it is perhaps allowable to infer a limited currency for a ballad that was not met by Herd, Scott, or Jamieson, to mention no lesser collectors. It has been recorded, however, by five collectors of the nineteenth century: Kinloch, Motherwell, Buchan, Christie, and Duncan (Greig).

Only four tunes have been noted, all of them so far apart and carrying such marks of alien affiliation as to confirm the suspicion that no steady oral tradition has been upholding the ballad since the record began. Conversely, the comparative steadiness of the text, especially in the refrain, might argue some control from print—*laxis effertur habenis*—and there is extant a broadside of 1810 to support the hypothesis. Nevertheless, Christie's second tune is furthest away from the melodic idea that the other three tunes seem as a group to be suggesting.

* Certainly the enterprising Willie could have given Barbara Allan's lover some pertinent lessons in survival, and seems to date from a happier era, vital, and not sicklied o'er with the introspective habit.

LIST OF VARIANTS

1. "The blue flowers and the yellow." W. Christie, *Traditional Ballad Airs*, I, 1876, p. 120. Text, Peter Buchan, *Ancient Songs and Ballads*, 1828, I, pp. 185-88 (adapted).
2. "Among the Blue Flowers and the Yellow." Duncan MS., No. 56 (W. Walker). Also in Gavin Greig and Alexander Keith, *Last Leaves of Traditional Ballads and Ballad Airs*, 1925, p. 25.

3. "Amang the Blue Flowers and Yellow." William Motherwell, *Minstrelsy: Ancient and Modern*, 1827, App'x No. 17 and p. xix.
4. "Willie's Lyke-Wake." Christie, *Traditional Ballad Airs*, I, 1876, p. 122. Text, Buchan, *Ancient Songs and Ballads*, 1828, II, pp. 51-54.

TUNES WITH TEXTS

1. [The blue flowers and the yellow]

Christie, I, 1876, p. 120. Sung by an old woman in Banffshire. Text adapted from Buchan, 1828, I, pp. 185-88.

a Æ (inflected VI)

Child prints this text as his B b copy. (I, pp. 251-252).

"O Willie my son, what makes you sae sad?
  As the sun shines over the valley."
"I am sarely sick for the love of a maid,
  Amang the blue flowers and the yellow."
"Is she an heiress or lady sae free,
  As the sun shines over the valley;
That she will take no pity on thee,
  Amang the blue flowers and the yellow?

"Ye'll gi'e the principal bellman a groat,
  As the sun shines over the valley;
And ye'll gar him cry your dead lyke-wake,
  Amang the blue flowers and the yellow."
Then he gae the principal bellman a groat,
  As the sun shines over the valley;
And he bade him cry his dead lyke-wake,
  Amang the blue flowers and the yellow.

The maiden stood till she heard it a',
  As the sun shines over the valley;
And down frae her cheeks the tears did fa',
  Amang the blue flowers and the yellow.
And she is hame to her father's ain bower,
  As the sun shines over the valley;
"I'll gang to yon lyke-wake ae single hour,
  Amang the blue flowers and the yellow."

"Ye maun tak' wi' you your ain brither John,
  As the sun shines over the valley;
It's not meet for maidens to venture alone,
  Amang the blue flowers and the yellow."
"I'll not take wi' me my ain brither John,
  As the sun shines over the valley;
But I'll gang along, myself all alone,
  Amang the blue flowers and the yellow."

When she came to young Willie's yate,
  As the sun shines over the valley;
His seven brithers were standing thereat,
  Amang the blue flowers and the yellow.

Then they did conduct her into the ha',
    As the sun shines over the valley;
Amang the weepers and merry mourners a',
    Amang the blue flowers and the yellow.

"Fair maid, ye've come here without a convoy,
    As the sun shines over the valley;
And ye shall return wi' a horse and a boy,
    Amang the blue flowers and the yellow.
Fair maid, I love thee as my life,
    As the sun shines over the valley;
But ye shall gae hame a lov'd wedded wife,
    Amang the blue flowers and the yellow."

2. "Among the Blue Flowers and the Yellow"

Duncan MS., No. 56 (*per* W. Walker). Also in Greig and
Keith, 1925, p. 25. Sung by Mrs. Gillespie, Glasgow;
learned in Buchan from her father's stepmother.

m I/M

Keith notes the coincidence here with "Loch Lomond," and with
other folksongs, as "Be kind to your nainsel, John." It may be also
noted that the scaffolding of the tune is the same as that of "Lord
Lovel" and the English "Lady Isabel" type, to mention no more.

O Willie, my son, what makes ye sae sad,
    As the sun shines over the valley?—
I lie sairly sick for the love o a maid,
    Among the blue flowers an' the yellow.

O is she an heiress or lady fine,
    As the sun shines over the valley,
That she winna tak nae pity on thee,
    Amang the blue flowers an' the yellow?

    *   *   *   *   *

Though a' your kin were aboot yon bower,
    As the sun shines over the valley,
Ye shall not be a maiden one single hour,
    Amang the blue flowers an' the yellow.

For maid ye cam here without a convoy,
    As the sun shines over the valley,
And ye shall return wi a horse and a boy,
    Amang the blue flowers an' the yellow.

Ye cam here a maiden sae meek and mild,
    As the sun shines over the valley,
But ye shall gae hame a wedded wife wi a child,
    Amang the blue flowers an' the yellow.

3. [Amang the Blue Flowers and the Yellow]

Motherwell, 1827, App'x No. 17; text, p. xix. Collected by
Andrew Blaikie, Paisley.

a π⁸

This is a variety of the type we have called "Boyne Water."

O Johnie, dear Johnie, what makes ye sae sad,
    As the sun shines ower the valley;
I think nae music will mak ye glad,
    Amang the blue flowers and the yellow.

4. [Willie's Lyke-Wake]

Christie, I, 1876, p. 122. Text from Buchan, 1828, II, pp.
51-54, "with some changes from the way the Editor has
heard it sung."

p Æ/D

With this tune, cf. "Johnie Cock (114) and "Trooper and Maid"
(299).
    Child prints this text as version E in I, p. 506. It is nearly the same
as Peter Buchan's (1828, II, pp. 51-54).

1. If my love loves me, she lets me not know,
    This is a dowie chance;
  I wish that I the same could do,
    Tho' my love were in France, France,
    Tho' my love were in France.

2. O lang think I, and very lang,
    And lang think I, I trow;
  But langer and langer will I think,
    'Ore my love o' me rue, rue,
    'Ore my love o' me rue.

3. But I will write a broad letter,
    And write it sae perfite;
  That gin she winna o' me rue,
    I'll bid her come to my lyke, lyke,
    I'll bid her come to my lyke.

4. Then he has written a broad letter,
    And seal'd it wi' his hand,
And sent it on to his true love,
    As fast as boy could gang, gang,
    As fast as boy could gang.

5. When she lookèd the letter upon,
    A light laugh then ga'e she;
But ere she read it to an end,
    The tear blinded her e'e, e'e,
    The tear blinded her e'e.

6. "O saddle to me a steed, father,
    O saddle to me a steed;
For word has come to me this night,
    That my true love is dead, dead,
    That my true love is dead.

7. The steeds are in the stable, daughter,
    The keys are casten by;
Ye canna won the night, daughter,
    The morn ye'se won away, away,
    The morn ye'se won away.

8. She has cut aff her yellow locks,
    A little aboon her e'e;
And she is on to Willie's lyke,
    As fast as gang could she, she,
    As fast as gang could she.

9. As she gaed ower yon high hill head,
    She saw a dowie light;

It was the candles at Willie's lyke,
    And torches burning bright, bright,
    And torches burning bright.

10. Three o' Willie's eldest brothers
    Were making for him a bier;
One half o' it was gude red gowd,
    The other silver clear, clear,
    The other silver clear.

11. Three o' Willie's eldest sisters
    Were making for him a sark;
The one half o' it was cambric fine,
    The other needle wark, wark,
    The other needle wark.

12. Out spake the youngest o' his sisters,
    As she stood on the fleer;
"How happy would our brother been,
    If ye'd been sooner here, here,
    If ye'd been sooner here."

13. She lifted up the green covering,
    And ga'e him kisses three;
Then he look'd up into her face,
    The blythe blink in his e'e, e'e,
    The blythe blink in his e'e.

14. O then he started to his feet,
    And thus to her said he:
"Fair Annie, since we're met again,
    Parted nae mair we'se be, be,
    Parted nae mair we'se be."

The Three Ravens

CHILD NO. 26

THE earliest text we possess of this moving elegy comes from Ravenscroft's *Melismata*, 1611, where it is given with the music, arranged for four voices. When Ritson reprinted it in 1790, he remarked that it was obviously much older than the date of first publication. No one who has studied it carefully will be likely to dispute the assertion. There exists a piece of collateral evidence which would move it back into the fifteenth century. That evidence is the now well-known "Corpus Christi" carol, still current, like the ballad, in oral tradition, and of which the oldest extant text was recorded in the first part of the sixteenth century. A good deal has been written by recent scholars about the occult significance of this carol, as to which the student may consult R. L. Greene, *Early English Carols*, 1935, pp. 221-22, 411-12, and the important references there given. For our immediate purpose it is sufficient to note general agreement that the piece is a pious adaptation of an earlier secular folk-song or ballad. My own persuasion is that some prior variant of "The Three Ravens" is that very antecedent. The disjointed introduction making use of birds without regard to the narrative proper; the comparable particularization of place; the knight with his grievous and bloody wounds; the devoted animals attending him, his steed (in a traditional variant), his hawks, his hounds:

> His hounds they lie down at his feete,
> So well they can their master keepe.
> > [Ravenscroft]

> His hounds all standing at his feet,
> Licking his wounds that run so deep.
> > [18th-19th century traditional]

> At that bed side there lies a hound,
> Which is licking the blood as it daily runs down.
> > [Staffordshire variant of carol]

Then the appearance of the knight's love: in Ravenscroft's variant a fallow doe put figuratively for a woman, but perhaps originally—like the white hind of "Leesome Brand" (15) that was "of the woman kind," like the "Biche Blanche" of French folksong, like the hypothetical doe behind "Molly Bawn," and other similar ballad creatures—a case of metensomatosis; her weeping solicitude and tender action:

> She lift up his bloudy hed
> And kist his wounds that were so red:—

all these points of comparison appear too striking to be purely accidental.*

The best copies of the ballad, those that seem to maintain its early form, are themselves in the carol- or dancing-pattern which we have already more than once met, most notably in "The Two Sisters": a couplet with first line thrice repeated, and interlaced with elements of refrain. This seems, I repeat, to have been the original habit of the ballad in its English branch, and we shall note that the habit has persisted down to our own day, even when almost all else has disappeared, whether of ancient dignity or pathetic narrative, and when the air has suffered a strange transmutation.

The Scottish counterpart of the ballad appears to be responsible for sweeping away its former tenderness and suffusing it with an alien and reckless cynicism. It is the Scottish branch which is oftenest met in this country today, and it will doubtless before long have swallowed up all trace of the other in oral tradition—if it has not already effectually done so. It is noteworthy that, while both Motherwell and Chappell spoke in the early and middle part of the last century of the ballad's widespread contemporary currency in Scotland and England, neither Sharp nor Greig at the beginning of the present century ran across it in Britain. All Sharp's copies are Appalachian; but in debased forms it is widely known in America. Kittredge attributed this popularity to its vogue in the old minstrel shows. (*JAF*, XXXI [1918], p. 273, cited by H. M. Belden, *Ballads and Songs*, 1940, p. 31.)

It is of course regrettable that we have so few earlier traditional copies of the tune, but we must consider ourselves lucky to have one so early as 1611. Ravenscroft's is a very fine tune as it stands, but it can hardly be regarded as untouched tradition. It is probable that if we had an earlier traditional copy it would be in a triple time, as indeed are many of the later ones. The interests of harmony seem to have had some effect upon the Dorian modality of the original. No copy of the later seventeenth century has come down, but it may be observed that the phrasal pattern is one of the commonest country dance-tune forms to be found in Playford's collection, of which perhaps two-thirds of the total number are in 6/8 time. There is nothing to show for the eighteenth century; but the nineteenth, so far as it is represented by the scanty record, favors a common-time duple rhythm. When the Scottish influence becomes paramount, the melodic pattern loses its continuity and alien encroachments are everywhere apparent. The proper narrative element drops away, and nothing remains except the raucous fun of the crows. After the relatively dignified involvement with "Johnny comes marching home," and with "Bonnie Doon," there appear noticeable echoes of "Whisky Johnny," "Sweet Adeline," "Little Brown Jug," "Buffalo Gals," "Rig-a-jig." Most of these debased versions are plagal, and in the major galaxy (I/Ly, I/M, π^1, M). The older and better tradition is nearly always in a minor tonality (D, Æ/D), authentic or plagal. The shift to major is in keeping with the change of spirit.

It is proper to note that "The Twa Corbies" published by Niles (in *Ballads, Carols, and Tragic Legends from the Southern Appalachian Mountains*, 1937, p. 10), and related by him to this ballad, has no right to be included in the family, either textually or melodically.

---

* A connection between the two has been suggested before by J. A. Fuller-Maitland, with utmost brevity (*JFSS*, IV, p. 64). He refrains—wisely, no doubt—from drawing any inferences; and probably the question will never be carried as far as to certainty.

LIST OF VARIANTS

TUNES WITH TEXTS

GROUP A

1. [The Three Ravens]

Ravenscroft, 1611, No. 20. Also in Ritson, 1790, pp. 155-56. Text, Child, 1882-98, I, p. 254.

m D (but inflected VII)

Cf. on this also Chappell, 1855, I, p. 59. In the lost lute MS. compiled by Robert Gordon of Straloch, 1627-29, there was a tune, "There wer three Ravns." (Cf. Dauney, *Ancient Scottish Melodies*, 1838, p. 368.) The early copy is unbarred.

To the present editor it seems likely that the tune is built out of plain chant material, perhaps not from a single chant, but from common phrases in the first or second mode. Compare, for example, the phrases of the *Agnus Dei* in the Mass *Orbis Factor* (XI in the Ordinary); or, with the tune's second half, the clauses of the great *Dies Irae*, beginning at "Quaerens me, sedisti lassus" and proceeding through the next five.

1. There were three rauens sat on a tree,
   Downe a downe, hay down, hay downe
   There were three rauens sat on a tree,
   With a downe
   There were three rauens sat on a tree,
   They were as blacke as they might be.
   With a downe derrie, derrie, derrie, downe, downe

2. The one of them said to his mate,
   'Where shall we our breakfast take?'

3. 'Downe in yonder greene field,
   There lies a knight slain vnder his shield.

4. 'His hounds they lie downe at his feete,
   So well they can their master keepe.

5. 'His haukes they flie so eagerly,
   There's no fowle dare him come nie.'

6. Downe there comes a fallow doe,
   As great with yong as she might goe.

7. She lift vp his bloudy hed,
   And kist his wounds that were so red.

8. She got him vp vpon her backe,
   And carried him to earthen lake.

9. She buried him before the prime,
   She was dead herselfe ere euen-song time.

10. God send euery gentleman,
    Such haukes, such hounds, and such a leman.

2. [The Three Ravens]

Motherwell, 1827, App'x No. 12; text, p. xviii. Collected by Andrew Blaikie, Paisley.

a Æ/D

Three ravens sat upon a tree,
    Hey down, hey derry day,
Three ravens sat upon a tree, hey down,
Three ravens sat upon a tree
And they were black as black could be,
    And sing lay doo and la doo and day.

3. [The Three Ravens]

Kidson, 1891, pp. 17-18. Sung by John Holmes, Roundhay; learned from his mother in Derbyshire, c. 1825.

p Æ/D, ending on II (– VII)

The barring of each of the last three measures has been delayed by a note to conform to the verbal accent. Also the present editor has introduced the holds and shortened the written value of the notes over which they stand by a half-beat's length.

There were three ravens on a tree,
    A-down, a-down, a derry down,
There were three ravens on a tree,
    Heigh ho!
The middlemost raven said to me,
"There lies a dead man at yon tree,"
    A-down, a-down, a derry down,
    Heigh ho!

There comes his lady full of woe,
    A-down, a-down, a derry down,
There comes his lady full of woe,
    Heigh ho!
There comes his lady full of woe,
[As great with child?] as she could go,
    A-down, a-down, a derry down,
    Heigh ho!

"Who's this that's killed my own true love,
    A-down, a-down, a derry down,
Who's this that's killed my own true love,
    Heigh ho!
I hope in heaven he'll never rest,
Nor e'er enjoy that blessed place."
    A-down, a-down, a derry down,
    Heigh ho!

GROUP B

4. "Three Black Crows"

Chappell, 1939, p. 15; text, pp. 5-6. Sung by Charles Tillett, Wanchese, N.C., text, 1924; tune, 1935.

p I/Ly

Whillop, Whillop

The connection here with "When Johnny comes marching home"—which itself doubtless has venerable roots—is not so clear in the present copy as in the next two.

Three old crows sat on a tree,
O Billy McGee McGaw,
Three old crows sat on a tree,
And they were black as crows could be,
And they all flapped their wings and cried,
Whillop, whillop,
And they all flapped their wings and cried,
O Billy McGee McGaw.

One old crow said to his mate,
O Billy McGee McGaw,
One old crow said to his mate,
What shall we do for something to eat?
And they all flapped their wings and cried,
Whillop, whillop,
And they all flapped their wings and cried,
O Billy McGee McGaw.

There's an old horse on yonders plain,
O Billy McGee McGaw,
There's an old horse on yonders plain
By some cruel old butcher slain,

And they all flapped their wings and cried,
Whillop, whillop,
And they all flapped their wings and cried,
O Billy McGee McGaw.

They placed themselves on his backbone,
O Billy McGee McGaw,
They placed themselves on his backbone,
And they plucked his eyes out one by one,
And they all flapped their wings and cried,
Whillop, whillop,
And they all flapped their wings and cried,
O Billy McGee McGaw.

5. "The Crow Song"

Cox, 1939, pp. 13-14. Sung by Iris M. McClure, Morgantown, W.Va., November 1927; learned from her uncle, J. F. McClure.

p Æ/D (but inflected VII)

There were three crows sat on a tree,
O Billy Magee Magar!
There were three crows sat on a tree,
O Billy Magee Magar!
There were three crows sat on a tree,
And they were black as crows could be,
And they all flapped their wings and cried,
"Caw! Caw! Caw! Billy Magee Magar!"
And they all flapped their wings and cried,
"Billy Magee Magar!"

Said one old crow unto his mate,
"O Billy Magee Magar!"
Said one old crow unto his mate,
"O Billy Magee Magar!"
Said one old crow unto his mate,
"What shall we do for grub to ate?"
And they [all] flapped their wings and cried,
"Caw! Caw! Caw! Billy Magee Magar!"
And they all flapped their wings and cried,
"Billy Magee Magar!"

6. "Three Black Crows"

Owens, 1950, pp. 43-44. Sung by Samuel Lee Asbury, College Station, Texas; learned in the Carolinas, c. 1880.

p Æ/D

There were three crows sat on a tree,
Sing Billy McGee, McGaw;
There were three crows sat on a tree,
Sing Billy McGee, McGaw;
There were three crows sat on a tree
And they were black as they could be
And they all flopped their wings and cried, "Caw, caw, caw!"

Says one old crow unto his mate,
Sing Billy McGee, McGaw;
Says one old crow unto his mate,
Sing Billy McGee, McGaw;
Says one old crow unto his mate,
Oh, what shall we do for something to eat?
And they all flopped their wings and cried, "Caw, caw, caw!"

There lies a horse on yonders plain,
Sing Billy McGee, McGaw;
There lies a horse on yonders plain,
Sing Billy McGee, McGaw;
There lies a horse on yonders plain,
Who's by some cruel butcher slain;
And they all flopped their wings and cried, "Caw, caw, caw!"

We'll perch ourselves on his backbone,
Sing Billy McGee, McGaw;
We'll perch ourselves on his backbone,
Sing Billy McGee, McGaw;
We'll perch ourselves on his backbone,
And eat his eyeballs one by one;
And they all flopped their wings and cried, "Caw, caw, caw!"

7. [The Three Ravens]

Sharp MSS., 3808/2799. Sung by Mrs. Jane Gentry, Hot Springs, N.C., July 27, 1917.

m Æ/D

There was three crows sat on a tree
    O Billy MacGee MacGore,
There was three crows sat on a tree,
    O Billy MacGee MacGore,
There was three crows sat on a tree
And they were as black as crows could be,
    And they all flapped their wings and cried:
    Caw, caw, caw,
    And they all flapped their wings and cried:
    Billy MacGee MacGore.

Said one old crow unto his mate:
What will we do for grub to eat?

There is a dead horse on yonders plain,
Just by some cruel butcher's slain.

We'll perch ourselves on his back-bone,
And pick his eyes out one by one.

GROUP C

8. [The twa Corbies]

Campbell, II, [1818], pp. 26-27. Sung by Thomas Shortreed, Jedburgh; learned from his mother.

m M

The same, with insignificant differences, is in R. Chambers, 1844, p. 15; there given in 4/4 time.

As I cam' by yon auld house end
I saw twa corbies sittin thereon,
The tane unto the t'other did say,
"O whare sall we gae dine the day?"—-

"Whare but by yon new fa'en birk,
There, there lies a new slain knight;
Nae mortal kens that he lies there
But his hawks and hounds, and his ladye fair.

"We'll sit upon his bonny breast bane,
And we'll pick out his bonny gray een;
We'll set our claws intil' his yellow hair
And big our bow'r,—its a' blawn bare.

My mother clekit me o' an egg,
And brought me up i' the feathers gray,
And bade me flee where'er I wad,
For winter wad be my dying day.

Now winter it is come and past,
And a' the birds are biggin' their nests,

But I'll flee high aboon them a'
And sing a sang for summer's sake.

Campbell's note: "This Edition of the words, and Set of the Air of 'The Twa Corbies,' was taken down by the present Editor from the singing of Mr. Thomas Shortreed of Jedburgh, as sung and recited by his mother, the lady mentioned in a preceding page of this work. The sweetly wild peculiarity of the melody, and correspondent imagery of this Scottish lyric, are very striking."

9. [The Twa Corbies]

Eyre-Todd, n.d., pp. 82-84. From "tradition." Text from Scott's *Minstrelsy*, with insignificant alteration.

a I/M (within a sixth)

This looks like a worn-down version of a very familiar type. Cf. the relatively recent "Buffalo Gals" and "Rig-a-jig."

As I was walking all alane
I heard twa corbies making mane,
The tane unto the tither say,
"Whare sall we gang and dine the day?"

"In behint yon auld fail dyke
I wot there lies a new-slain knight;
Naebody kens that he lies there
But his hawk, his hound, and his lady fair.

"His hound is to the hunting gane,
His hawk to fetch the muirfowl hame,
His lady's tane anither mate,
Sae we may mak' our dinner sweet.

"Ye'll sit on his white hause-bane,
And I'll pyke out his bonnie blue e'en;
Wi' ae lock o' his gowden hair
We'll theek our nest when it grows bare.

"Mony a ane for him mak's mane,
But nane shall ken whare he is gane;
O'er his white banes, when they are bare,
The wind sall blaw for evermair."

GROUP D

10. "The Three Crows"

Cox, 1925, p. 522; text, pp. 31-32(A). From J. H. Cox, Morgantown, Monongalia County, W.Va., 1915; learned from his father in Illinois.

p I/Ly

This is of course a variant of the "Bonny Doon" tune.

There were three crows sat on a tree,
And they were black as black could be.
    Philly McGee McGaw!

One of them said unto his mate,
"What shall we do for meat to ate?"
    Philly McGee McGaw!

"There lies a steed on yonder plain
That by his master has been slain."
    Philly McGee McGaw!

"We'll perch ourselves on his backbone
And pluck his eyes out one by one."
    Philly McGee McGaw!

11. [The Three Ravens]

Creighton and Senior, 1950, p. 21. Sung by William Nelson, Kinsac, Nova Scotia.

p I/Ly

Three black crows sat on a tree
Ca beelya geelya gaw ye,
And they were black as crows could be
Ca beelya geelya gaw ye.

One black crow said unto his mate,
Ca beelya geelya gaw ye,
What shall we do for something to eat?
Ca beelya geelya gaw ye.

An old red horse in yonder lane,
Ca beelya geelya gaw ye,
Who very lately has been slain,
Ca beelya geelya gaw ye.

We'll pick his eyes out one by one,
Ca beelya geelya gaw ye,
And pick the meat from off his bones,*
Ca beelya geelya gaw ye.

* Or, "and eat its flesh until it's gone."

12. [The Three Ravens]

Wilkinson MSS., 1935-36, p. 31(A). Sung by Mrs. Lucy McAllister, Harriston, Va., October 9, 1935.

p I/Ly

There were three crows sat on a tree.
They're just as black as crows can be.
One of them said to the mate:
What shall we do for grub to eat?

There's an old dead horse in yonder's lane,
Whose body has been lately slain.
We'll fly upon his old breast bone,
And pluck his eyes out one by one.

13. [The Three Ravens]

Wilkinson MSS., 1935-36, p. 32(B). Sung by Mrs. Mary McAllister, Grottoes, Va., October 30, 1935.

p π[1]

There were three crows sat on yonder's tree.
They're just as black as crows can be.
One of them said to the mate:
What shall we do for grub to eat?

There's an old dead horse in yonder's lane,
Whose body has been lately slain.
We'll fly upon his old breast bone,
And pluck his eyes out one by one.

Old Satan tried to injure me
By cutting down my apple tree.
He could not injure me at all,
For I had apples all the fall.

GROUP E

14. [The Two Crows]

Sharp MSS., 4208/. Also in Sharp and Karpeles, 1932, I, p. 64(C). Sung by Mrs. Queenie Woods, Buena Vista, Va., May 2, 1918.

p I/Ly (– VI)

This may have kinship with a shanty, "Whisky Johnnie," for which see, e.g., Whall, *Sea Songs and Shanties*, 6th ed., 1927, p. 83; J. C. Colcord, *Songs of American Sailormen*, 1938, p. 49; L. A. Smith, *Music of the Waters*, 1888, p. 28. There is a Negro song, recorded by Huddie Leadbetter (Asch-Stinson, rec. SC 80), called "You can't lose-a me, Cholly," made out of the same materials.

There were three crows sat on a tree
Lordy, Foldy, Ip fie oddy io . . .
And they were as black as crows could be
Lordy Foldy Ip fie oddy io.

15. [The Two Crows]

Sharp MSS., 4211/3028. Also in Sharp and Karpeles, 1932, I, p. 64(B). Sung by Mrs. Ada Maddox, Loch Laird, Buena Vista, Va., May 3, 1918.

p I

There were two crows sat on a tree,
    Lardy, hip tie hardy* ho, ho,
There were two crows sat on a tree,
And they were black as crows could be,
    Lardy, hardy, hip tie hardy* ho, ho.

One old crow said to his mate:
    Lardy, etc.,
One old crow said to his mate:
What shall we have to-day to eat?
    Lardy, etc.

Yonder lies a horse in yonders lane,
Whose body has not been very long slain.

We'll press our feet on his breast-bone,
And pick his eyes out one by one.

    *1932: "hoddy"

GROUP F

16. [The Three Ravens]

Sharp MSS., 3552/. Also in Sharp and Karpeles, 1932, I, p. 63(A); and Davis, 1929, p. 562(I). Sung by Ben Burgess (76), Charlottesville, Va., September 28, 1916.

a M

Three old crows sat on a tree
Just as black as crows could be
Poor old crow
The old he-crow says to his mate
What shall we do for meat to eat.
Poor old crow

The tune suggests the "play-party" song, "Cluck, Old Hen."

Sharp's MS. note: "This fragment was learned by the singer when a boy, from the singing of his great grandfather, an Italian, Genini [*or*, Giannini?] who was brought to America by Thos. Jefferson at the conclusion of the latter's Ambassadorial term at Paris, for the purpose of importing Italian methods of viticulture into America. Mr. Burgess could not remember the refrain which succeeds each couplet, but was pretty sure it began with 'Poor old Crow.'"

17. "[The] Three Crows"

Davis, 1929, p. 562(J) and (K); text, p. 142. Sung by Elizabeth Grubb, Norfolk County, Va., October 15, 1919, and December 2, 1919. Collected by Mrs. J. B. Ferneyhough.

a π^1 (– VI) (compass of fifth)

There were three crows sat on a tree,
And they were black as crows could be.

Said one old crow unto his mate,
"What shall we do for bread* to ate?"

"There lies a horse in yonder shed
That† has been now some three weeks dead.

"We'll perch upon his bare backbone
And pick his eyes out one by one."

* (K): "grub"
† (K): "who"

Said one black crow to the other two,
"I wish we had some gum to chew."

"In yonder field lies an old gray horse,
And we can chew and chew and chew."

GROUP G

18. "The Three Crows"

Randolph, I, 1946, p. 75(A). Sung by Fred Terry, Joplin, Mo., January 30, 1933.

a I(– II, III)

This version relates to "The Little Brown Jug."

There was three crows set on a tree,
    Billy MaGee MaGaw,
There was three crows set on a tree,
They was as black as black could be,
    Billy MaGee MaGaw, MaGaw,
    Billy MaGee MaGaw.

The old crow he said to his mate,
    Billy MaGee MaGaw,
The old crow he said to his mate,
What shall we do for meat to eat?
    Billy MaGee MaGaw, MaGaw,
    Billy MaGee MaGaw.

There lies a horse in Yonder's Town,
    Billy MaGee MaGaw,
There lies a horse in Yonder's Town,
That by the butcher has been slain,
    Billy MaGee MaGaw, MaGaw,
    Billy MaGee MaGaw.

We'll set ourselves on his backbone,
    Billy MaGee MaGaw,
We'll set ourselves on his backbone,
And pick his eyes out one by one,
    Billy MaGee MaGaw, MaGaw,
    Billy MaGee MaGaw.

APPENDIX

19. [The Three Ravens]

Hudson, 1937, No. 1. Probably from Oxford, Miss., 1923-1930.

p I/Ly

This seems composed of "Sweet Adeline," the last half simplified.

There were three crows in a hickory tree,
And they were black as crows could be.

20. (Unnamed)

Sharp MSS., 4254/. Sung by James H. Chisholm, Nellysford, Va., May 21, 1918.

a Æ

This variant begins like the favorite "Wife of Usher's Well," as the Appalachian singers have it, but it soon loses interest.

There were two crows sat on one tree,
They were as black as crows could be.
Some rascal tried to injure me
By cutting down my apple tree.

21. [The Three Ravens]

Wilkinson MSS., 1935-36, p. 33(C). Sung by J. H. Chisholm, Greenwood, Va., March 12, 1936.

a D

This should be compared with Sharp's copy, noted eighteen years earlier from the same singer (cf. preceding variant). Wilkinson refers to the hymn-tune "Windham," for which, with a note on tune and text, see George Pullen Jackson, *Down-East Spirituals and Others*, [1943], p. 120.

There were two crows sat on one tree.
They were just as black as crows could be.
Some rascal tried to injure me
By cutting down my apple tree.
But he did not injure me at all
For I had apples all the fall.

There were two crows sat on one tree.
They were just as black as crows could be.
The old one said unto the cub:
What shall we young crows do for grub?

The Whummil Bore

CHILD NO. 27

SINCE there is but one copy of this ballad, text or tune, and that an imperfect copy, it offers a free field for conjecture. It appears to be a further example of pawky fun at the expense of high romance—such another as "Kempy Kay," "The Twa Corbies," and "Sir Eglamore." There is, of course, high precedent for this kind of thing: witness, "Sir Thopas." My own suspicion is that "The Whummil Bore" is a by-blow of a serious romantic ballad; and the evidence of the tune would suggest "Hind Horn" (17). Miss Macmath's tune for the latter ballad is one of those circular things which has forgotten its proper ending. If the order of the first and second phrases of the tune below be reversed, we have a close enough parallel to the Macmath tune, amounting almost to identity in the third phrase, with an additional fifth phrase supplying a termination equally appropriate to the "Hind Horn" tune as to this.

It is to be noted that the last refrain line of Motherwell's MS. copy (printed in Child) is rhythmically different and longer than the one printed with the tune, and would require some modification of the latter to be sung. The longer refrain, incidentally, is in the same stress-pattern as that of Child 288 ("Earl of Essex's Victory"), and ought probably, like the latter, to be printed in two lines, signifying two musical phrases. Other examples can be found among the versions of "The Two Sisters," e.g.:

> I'll be true, true to my love,
> Love, if my love will be true to me.

It is perhaps not too fanciful to see a connection between this tune and Linscott's "Blow ye Winds" (cf. 2); as also to "The Maid peept out of the window" (cf. 276).

LIST OF VARIANTS

"The Whummil Bore." William Motherwell, *Minstrelsy: Ancient and Modern*, 1827, App'x No. 3 and p. xvi.

TUNE WITH TEXT

[The Whummil Bore]

Motherwell, 1827, App'x. No. 3; text, p. xvi. Collected by Andrew Blaikie, Paisley.

p π¹, ending on V

Seven lang years I have served the king,
Fa, fa, fallilly,
And I ne'er got a sight of his dochter but ane,
With my glimpy, glimpy, glimpy, eedle,
Lillum too a tee too a tally.

The Marriage of Sir Gawain

CHILD NO. 31, APPENDIX

THERE is no doubt that the theme of the bride's transformation from loathly to lovely is very ancient and widespread. It is also altogether likely that if the theme were to survive traditionally in ballad-form, the supernatural element would be rationalized away. Whether, in the absence of intervening stages of transmission, we are justified in regarding this spirited modern piece as a legitimate traditional descendant of the old ballad saved from oblivion by the Percy Folio is certainly open to question. On account of its intrinsic merit and because nothing closer offers as surrogate, it is welcomed here. At least it will be granted that many a Restoration broadside admitted by Child is no more satisfactory on stylistic and other grounds.

LIST OF VARIANTS

"The Half-Hitch." Helen Hartness Flanders and Marguerite Olney, *Ballads Migrant in New England*, 1953, pp. 33-37.

TUNE WITH TEXT

"The Half-Hitch"

Flanders and Olney, 1953, pp. 33-37. Sung by Mrs. W. E. Pierce, Shrewsbury, Vt., July 14, 1932; learned from her father. From *Ballads Migrant in New England*, edited by Helen Hartness Flanders and Marguerite Olney; copyright 1953 by Helen Hartness Flanders.

a M

1. A noble lord in Plymouth did dwell.
   He had a fine daughter, a beautiful gal.
   A young man of fortune, and riches supplied,
   He courted this fair maid to make her his bride,
       To make her his bride,
   He courted this fair maid to make her his bride.

2. He courted her long and he gained her love.
   At length this fair maiden intended him to prove.
   From the time that she owned him, she fairly denied,
   She told him right off, she'd not be his bride,
       She'd not be his bride,
   She told him right off she'd not be his bride.

3. Then he said, "Straight home I will steer,"
   And many an oath under [unto?] her he did swear.
   He swore he would wed the first woman he see
   If she was as mean as a beggar could be,
       As a beggar could be,
   If she was as mean as a beggar could be.

4. She ordered her servants this man to delay.
   Her rings and her jewels she soon laid away.
   She dressed herself in the worst rags she could find.
   She looked like the divil before and behind. Etc.

5. She clapped her hands on the chimney back,
   She crocked her face all over so black,
   Then down to the road she flew like a witch
   With her petticoat hi-sted upon her half-hitch. Etc.

6. Soon this young man came riding along.
   She stumbled before him, she scarcely could stand
   With her old shoes on her feet all tread of askew.
   He soon overtook her and said, "Who be you?" Etc.

   SPOKEN: "I'm a woman, I s'pose."

7. This answer grieved him much to the heart.
   He wished from his very life he might part.
   Then he wished that he had been buried
   And then he did ask her and if she was married. Etc.

   SPOKEN: "No, I ain't."

8. This answer suited him much like the rest.
   It lay very heavy and hard on his breast.
   He found by his oath he must make her his bride.
   Then he did ask her behind him to ride. Etc.

   SPOKEN: "Your horse will throw me, I know he will."

9. "O no, O no, my horse he will not,"
   So on behind him a-straddle she got.
   His heart it did fail him. He dare not go home
   For his parents would say, "I'm surely undone." Etc.

10. So to a neighbor with whom he was great
    The truth of the story he dared to relate.
    He said, "Here with my neighbor you may tarry
    And in a few days with you I will marry." Etc.

    SPOKEN: "You won't. I know you won't."

[317]

11. He vowed that he would and straight home he did go.
    He acquainted his father and mother also
    Of what had befallen him. Now he had sworn.
    His parents said to him, "For that don't you mourn. Etc.

12. "Don't break your vows but bring home your girl
    And we'll fix her up and she'll do very well."
    The day was appointed. They invited the guests
    And then they intended the bride for to dress. Etc.

    SPOKEN: "Be married in my old clothes, I s'pose!"

13. Married they were and sat down to eat.
    With her hands she clawed out the cabbage and meat.
    The pudding it burned her fingers so bad
    She licked 'em, she wiped 'em along on her rags. Etc.

14. Hotter than ever, she at it again.
    Soon they did laugh til their sides were in pain:
    Soon they did say, "My jewel, my bride,
    Come sit yourself down by your true lover's side." Etc.

    SPOKEN: "Sit in the corner, s'pose, where I used ter."

15. Some were glad and very much pleased.
    Others were sorry and very much grieved.
    They asked them to bed the truth to decide
    And then they invited both bridegroom and bride. Etc.

    SPOKEN: "Give me a light and I'll go alone."

16. They gave her a light—what could she want more—
    And showed her the way up to the chamber door.

    SPOKEN: "Husband when you hear my old shoe go
    'klonk' then you may come."

17. Up in the chamber she went klonking about.
    His parents said to him, "What think she's about?"
    "O mother, O mother, say not one word.
    No one bit of comfort to me this world can afford."

18. At length they heard her old shoe go klonk.
    They gave him a light and bade him go along.
    "I choose to go in the dark," he said,
    "For I very well know the way to my bed."

19. He jumped into bed, his back to his bride.
    She rolled and she tumbled from side unto side.
    She rolled and she tumbled. The bed it did squeak.
    He said unto her, "Why can't you lie still?" Etc.

    SPOKEN: "I want a light to unpin my clothes."

20. He ordered a light her clothes to unpin.
    Behold she was dressed in the finest of things.
    When he turned over her face to behold,
    It was fairer to him than silver or gold. Etc.

21. Up they got and the frolic they had,
    For many a heart was merry and glad.
    They looked like two flowers just springing from bloom,
    With many fair lassies who wished them much joy.

King Henry

CHILD NO. 32

Mrs. Brown of Falkland is again the sole preserver of this off-shoot of Arthurian romance. Her tune has been preserved in two manuscripts, the "Abbotsford" manuscript of Scottish songs in Scott's library, and the Ritson transcript of Tytler's manuscript, now at Harvard. There is no difficulty about the reading in the present case. But the student should be warned that, whether from some error in the Abbotsford transcript or for some other reason, the tune is wrongly printed in Child, V, p. 422, as that of "Lady Elspat." It will not sing to the latter text without violent handling, as Spalding's "revised" copy in Child, *loc.cit.*, demonstrates. The matter is put beyond debate by the Ritson transcript, which gives this tune to "King Henry" and another to "Lady Elspat." Cf. also *CFQ*, I (1942), pp. 191-92.

The present variant is Æolian—better Æ/D—and authentic. It will be found again with "Young Benjie" (86); and it should be compared with Kinloch's "Geordie" (209). It also appears to be a variant of the tune Christie prints as "Love Robbie," a version of Child 97 (Christie, I, p. 136).

LIST OF VARIANTS

"King Henry." Ritson-Tytler-Brown MS., pp. 85-90, Harvard College Library.

TUNE WITH TEXT

[King Henry]

Ritson-Tytler-Brown MS., pp. 85-90. Sung by Mrs. Brown, Falkland, Aberdeenshire.

a Æ (+VI in grace note)

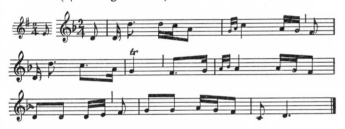

Lat never a man a wooing wend
    That lacketh thingis three,
A routh o' gold, and open heart,
    An' fu' o' charity.

As this i speak o' king Henry,
    (For he lay burd alone,)
And he's ta'en until a jelly hunts ha',
    Was seven miles frae a town.

He chase'd the deer now him before,
    An' the roe down by the den,
Til the fattest buck in a' the flock,
    King Henry he has slain.

O he has ta'en him til his ha',
    To make him beerly cheer,
An' in it came a griesly ghost,
    Stood stapping in the fleer.

Her head hat the reef-tree o' the house,
    An' her middle ye mat well span,
He's thrown to her his gay mantle,
    Says, Lady, hap your lingcan.

Her teeth was a' like taether stakes,
    Her nose like club or mell;
An' i ken nae thing she 'pear'd to be,
    But the fiend that wiends in hell.

"Some meat, some meat, ye king Henry,
    Some meat ye gie to me!"
"An' what meat's i' this house, lady?
    An' fat have i to gie?"
"O ye dee slay your berry-brown steed,
    An' you bring him here to me."
O whan he slew his berry-brown steed,
    Wow but his heart was sair!
She eat him a' up, skin and been,
    Left naething but hide and hair.

"Mair meat, mair meat, ye king Henry,
    Mair meat ye gie to me!"
"An' fat meat's i' this house, lady?
    An' what have i to gie?"
"O ye do kill your good greyhounds,
    An' bring them a' to me."
O whan he slew his good greyhounds,
    Wow but his heart was sair!
She eat them a' up, skin and bane,
    Left naething but hide and hair.

"Mair meat, mair meat, ye king Henry,
    Mair meat ye bring to me!"
"An' what meat's i' this house, lady,
    That ye've nae welcome ti?"
"O ye do fell your gay goss-hawks,
    An' you bring them a' to me."
O whan he fell'd his gay goss-hawks,
    Wow but his heart was sair!
She eat them a' up, bane by bane,
    Left naething but feathers bare.

"Some drink, some drink, ye king Henry,
    Some drink ye bring to me!"
"O what drink's i' this house, lady,
    That you're nae welcome ti?"
"O ye sew up your horses hide,
    An' bring in a drink to me."

"A bed, a bed now, king Henry,
    An' a bed you mak' to me!"
"O what bed's i' this house, lady,
    That you're nae welcome ti?"

"O ye man pu' the green heather,
    An' mak' a bed to me."
O pu'd has he the green green,
    An' made to her a bed,
An' up has he ta'en his gay mantle,
    And o'er it has he spred.
"Tak' aff your claiths now, king Henry,
    An' lye down me beside."
O god forbid, said king Henry,
    That ever the like betide!
That ever the fiend that wons in hell
    Should streak down by my side!

Whan night was gane and day was come,
    An' the sun shone through the ha',
The fairest lady that ever was seen,
    Lay atween him and the wa'.
O well is me! said king Henry,
    How lang will this last wi' me?
An' out it spake that fair lady,
    "Even til the day you dee.
For i've met wi' mony a gentle knight,
    That's gi'n me sic a fill,
But never before wi' a courteous knight
    That gae me a' my will."

Kempy Kay

CHILD NO. 33

OF THIS BALLAD, another piece of gross mockery of high romance, several texts have been preserved, all of the early nineteenth century; but only Motherwell and latterly Moffat have been careful to save the tune. The latter is a high-spirited and characteristically Celtic jig-tune. An Irish jig in the Joyce collection (1909, No. 301, p. 141), "The Devil in Dublin," is very close to it; but two other suggestively named tunes in the same collection seem also to be allied: "The Joys of Wedlock" and "Spla-foot Nance" (*ibid.*, Nos. 130, 132, pp. 66-67). There are also three tunes in the Blaikie MS. that closely resemble it:

Nos. 55, 55a, and 79. The first has the pencil title, "Lord Maxwell's goodnight" (cf. Child 195), and the last is named "Argyle's Courtship," which might relate to Child 199. Moffat's tune seems related to Motherwell's; it also reminds of a handful of characteristic 6/8 tunes ending off the tonic, in Playford's *The English Dancing Master*, 1650 *et seq.*

It may be observed that Motherwell's tune does not suit the CM quatrains of the text, and that they have therefore been tagged with an additional foot on the even lines, the superfluous syllables, "a wee," turning the stanzas into LM.

LIST OF VARIANTS

1. "Kempy Kane." William Motherwell, *Minstrelsy: Ancient and Modern*, 1827, App'x No. 33 and p. xxiv.

2. "Sandy Seaton's Wooing." Alfred Moffat, *Fifty Traditional Scottish Nursery Rhymes*, [1933], p. 31.

TUNES WITH TEXTS

1. [Kempy Kane]

Motherwell, 1827, App'x No. 33; text, p. xxiv. Collected by Andrew Blaikie, Paisley. Child, 1882-98, I, p. 303(C), gives what may be the remainder of this version, from Motherwell's MS., p. 193.

a I/M

Kempy Kane's a wooin' gane
    And far ayont the sea awee;
And there he met wi' Drearylane,
    His gay gude father to be awee.

2. [Sandy Seaton's Wooing]

Moffat, [1933], p. 31. A Fifeshire singing-game.

a M, ending on V

O Sandy Seaton's gane to woo
    Down by Kirka'dy Lea,

And there he met wi' a puir auld man
    His guidfaither to be.

He led his daughter by the hand,
    His daughter ben brought he;
"O, is not she the fairest lass
    That's in great Christendye?"

"I winna marry wi' ony lad
    In a' the land o' Fife;
I winna leave my mammie yet
    And I winna be his wife!"

He's courted her and brocht her hame
    His guidwife for to be;
He's gi'en her jewels and gi'en her gold,
    And he's kissed her three times three.

Moffat's note: "This is an old Fifeshire singing-game. It seems to be a nursery derivative of 'Kempy Kaye' an ancient ballad which C. K. Sharpe considered to be of Scandinavian origin."

Kempion

CHILD NO. 34

AGAIN Mrs. Brown is our only authority for a tune. This one, so far as I know, has never been printed before. The words are not written with the notes in the manuscript, and Gordon's notation leaves one uncertain of the time-values of his grace notes. Instead of borrowing from the end of the preceding bar for his up-beats at the beginning of a phrase, he sometimes writes a grace note before the first beat, sometimes a quaver. It seems wisest to give the reading of the manuscript here, in the face of this uncertainty. I know of no obvious relatives for this striking pentatonic melody (π^4).

LIST OF VARIANTS

"Kempion." Ritson-Tytler-Brown MS., pp. 77-81, Harvard College Library.

TUNE WITH TEXT

[Kempion]

Ritson-Tytler-Brown MS., pp. 77-81. Sung by Mrs. Brown, Falkland, Aberdeenshire.

p π^4

"Come here, come here, ye freely feed,
    An' lay your head low on my knee,
The heaviest wierd i will you read,
    That ever was read til a lady.
O meikle dolour shall you drie,
    An' ay the sa't seas o'er ye swim,
An' far mair dolour shall you drie,
    On East-muir-craigs, ere ye them clim'.
I wot yese be a weary wight,
    An' relieved shall you never be,
Til Kempion the kingis son
    Come to the craig and thrice kiss thee."
O meikle dolour did she drie,
    An' ay the sa't seas o'er she swam,
An' far mair dolour did she drie
    On East-muir-craigs ere she them clam':
An' ay she cry'd for Kempion,
    Gin he would but come til her hand.
Now word has gane to Kempion
    That sic a beast was in his land;
An' a be sure she would gae mad,
    Gin she got nae helping frae his hand.
Now, by my sooth, says Kempion,
    This fiery beast i'll gang and see.
And by my sooth, says Segramour,
    My ae brother, i'll gang you wi'.
O biggit ha' they a bonny boat,
    An' they ha' set her to the sea

An' Kempion and Segramour
    The fiery beast ha' gane to see.
A mile afore they reach'd the shore,
    She gar'd the red fire flee.
"O Segramour, keep my boat afloat,
    An' lat her nae the land sae near,
For the wicked beast shall sure gae mad,
    An' set fire to a' my land and mair."
"O out o' my sty i winna rise,
    And it is not for the awe o' thee,
Til Kempion the kingis son,
    Come to the craig and thrice kiss me."
He's louted him o'er the East-muir-craig,
    An' he has gane her kisses ane;
Awa' she gi'd, and again she came,
    The fieryest beast that ever was seen.
"O out o' my sty i winna rise,
    An' it is not for the awe o' thee,
Till Kempion the kingis son
    Come to the craig and twice kiss me."
He's louted him o'er the East-muir-craig,
    An' he has gien her kisses twa;
Awa' she gi'd and again she came
    The fieryest beast that ever you saw.
"O, out o' my sty i winna rise,
    An' it is not for the awe o' thee,
Till Kempion the kingis son
    Come to the craig and thrice kiss me."
He's louted him o'er the East-muir-craigs,
    And he has gi'n her kisses three;
Awa' she gi'd and again she came
    The bonnyest lady that ever could be.
An' by my sooth, says Kempion,
    My ain true love, (for this is she,)
O was it wolf into the wood,
    Or was it fish into the sea,
Or was it man, or vile woman,
    My ain true love, that misshap'd thee?
"It was not wolf into the wood,
    Nor was it fish into the sea,
But it was my wicked step-mother
    An' wae and weary may she be!
O a heavier wierd light her upon,
Than ever fell on vile woman,

Her hairs' grow rough, and her teeths' grow lang,
And on her four feet shall she gang;
Nane shall take pity her upon,
But in wormes wood she shall ay won;

An' relieved shall she never be
Til Saint Mungo come o'er the sea."
An' sighing said that weary wight,
I fear that day i'll never see.

Thomas Rymer

CHILD NO. 37

THE single tune which has been preserved in two variants for this ballad may well be, as Scott calls it, "ancient." Scott, or his musical editor, writes as if a modern tune was also current in his day; but, if so, it has not been recorded, any more than recent texts that might accompany it. The tune which has survived is a member of a large family, in use with a number of ballads and songs in the south of England as well as the north, many of them very beautiful, and flowering in quite diverse ways both melodically and rhythmically. We have met it already in connection with Nos. 18, 20, and 26; Sharp's "Lord Bateman," and "Searching for Lambs," are also members of this clan, which can be followed back to the sixteenth century with ease, and doubtless a good deal further. Cf. *Journal of the Musicological Society*, III (1950), pp. 126, 132. A study of the variants will provide further evidence in support of the claim, made more fully elsewhere (e.g., "Young Beichan" [53]), that rhythmical developments in English folk-music have occurred through an instinctive tendency on the part of native singers to extend 3/4 into 4/4 time, 4/4 into 5/4 and finally into 6/4 or 3/2.

LIST OF VARIANTS

1. True Thomas; or, Thomas the Rhymer." Sir Walter Scott, *Minstrelsy of the Scottish Border*, 1833, IV, opp. p. 116, and pp. 117-21.

2. "Thomas the Rhymer." Blaikie MS., National Library of Scotland MS. 1578, No. 63, p. 21.

TUNES WITH TEXTS

1. [True Thomas; or, Thomas the Rhymer]

Scott, 1833, IV, opp. p. 116 ("The Ancient Tune"); text, pp. 117-21.

p Æ

1. True Thomas lay on Huntlie bank;
    A ferlie he spied wi' his ee;
And there he saw a ladye bright,
    Come riding down by the Eildon Tree.

2. Her shirt was o' the grass-green silk,
    Her mantle o' the velvet fyne;
At ilka tett of her horse's mane,
    Hung fifty siller bells and nine.

3. True Thomas, he pull'd aff his cap,
    And louted low down to his knee,
"All hail, thou mighty Queen of Heaven!
    For thy peer on earth I never did see."—

4. "O no, O no, Thomas," she said,
    "That name does not belang to me;
I am but the Queen of fair Elfland,
    That am hither come to visit thee.

5. "Harp and carp, Thomas," she said;
    "Harp and carp along wi' me;

And if ye dare to kiss my lips,
    Sure of your bodie I will be."—

6. "Betide me weal, betide me woe,
    That weird shall never daunton me."—
Syne he has kissed her rosy lips,
    All underneath the Eildon Tree.

7. "Now, ye maun go wi' me," she said;
    "True Thomas, ye maun go wi' me;
And ye maun serve me seven years,
    Thro' weal or woe as may chance to be."

8. She mounted on her milk-white steed;
    She's ta'en true Thomas up behind:
And aye, whene'er her bridle rung,
    The steed flew swifter than the wind.

9. O they rade on, and farther on;
    The steed gaed swifter than the wind;
Until they reach'd a desert wide,
    And living land was left behind.

10. "Light down, light down, now, true Thomas,
    And lean your head upon my knee;
Abide and rest a little space,
    And I will shew you ferlies three.

11. "O see ye not yon narrow road,
    So thick beset with thorns and briers?
That is the path of righteousness,
    Though after it but few enquires.

12. "And see ye not that braid braid road,
    That lies across that lily leven?
That is the path of wickedness,
    Though some call it the road to heaven.

13. "And see not ye that bonny road,
　　　That winds about the fernie brae?
　　That is the road to fair Elfland,
　　　Where thou and I this night maun gae.

14. "But, Thomas, ye maun hold your tongue,
　　　Whatever ye may hear or see;
　　For, if you speak word in Elflyn land,
　　　Ye'll ne'er get back to your ain countrie."

15. O they rade on, and farther on,
　　　And they waded through rivers aboon the knee,
　　And they saw neither sun nor moon,
　　　But they heard the roaring of the sea.

16. It was mirk mirk night, and there was nae stern light,
　　　And they waded through red blude to the knee;
　　For a' the blude that's shed on earth
　　　Rins through the springs o' that countrie.

17. Syne they came on to a garden green,
　　　And she pu'd an apple frae a tree—
　　"Take this for thy wages, true Thomas;
　　　It will give thee the tongue that can never lie."—

18. "My tongue is mine ain," true Thomas said;
　　　"A gudely gift ye wad gie to me!

I neither dought to buy nor sell,
　　At fair or tryst where I may be.

19. "I dought neither speak to prince or peer,
　　　Nor ask of grace from fair ladye."—
　　"Now hold thy peace!" the lady said,
　　　"For as I say, so must it be."—

20. He has gotten a coat of the even cloth,
　　　And a pair of shoes of velvet green;
　　And till seven years were gane and past,
　　　True Thomas on earth was never seen.

2. [Thomas the Rhymer]

Blaikie MS., NL Scotland MS. 1578, No. 63, p. 21.

p Æ/D

The Wee Wee Man

CHILD NO. 38

THIS ballad has not been found in oral tradition since the first quarter of the nineteenth century. Herd's text was set to a double-strain jig-tune in Johnson's *Museum*; and thence has been very frequently reprinted with no change except editorial transposition into other keys, an occasional adjustment of detail, and fresh accompaniments for the piano. I see no reason to suppose that the ballad was ever sung to this tune traditionally: the melody, without doubt a fine one, is obviously made for an instrument, pipe or fiddle, and is both unvocal in style and hard to sing. The same tune has been found also in Ireland, where it appears to have had more traditional currency than in Scotland. G. F. Graham thought it to be of the same stock as the Irish "Garryowen," and not much older.

It has been printed in Ritson, *Scotish Songs*, 1794, II, p. 139; R. A. Smith, c. 1824, IV, p. 70; G. F. Graham, 1854-56, III, p.

64, and in later editions; Maver, 1866, No. 98, p. 49; Eyre-Todd, *Ancient Scottish Ballads*, n.d., pp. 132-33; and doubtless elsewhere.

There is an unnamed variant of the tune, with two additional strains or variations, in the Hudson MS., "Collection of Folk Songs of the Irish Peasantry," in the Boston Public Library, tune No. 62. Another occurs in the Pigot collection, printed in Joyce, 1909, No. 692, p. 347, under the title, "Beer and Ale and Brandy." Another, Scottish, called "Bundle and Go," is in the Greig MSS., II, p. 135, and in Robert Ford, *Vagabond Songs and Ballads of Scotland*, 1899, I, pp. 33-35, and 1904, pp. 35-37.

The tune would have to be classed as Dorian, if we adhered to the final-as-tonic rule. But it has, to our ear, nothing of Dorian feeling, and may more plausibly be considered a circular tune in the major, ending on the supertonic.

LIST OF VARIANTS

1. "The Wee Wee Man." James Johnson, *The Scots Musical Museum*, IV, [1794], No. 370, p. 382.
a. "The Wee Wee Man." Robert Maver, *Genuine Scottish*

Ballads, 1866, No. 98, p. 49.
b. "The Wee Man." R. A. Smith, *The Scotish Minstrel*, [c. 1824], IV, p. 61.

TUNE WITH TEXT

1. [The Wee Wee Man]

Johnson, IV, [1794], No. 370, p. 382. His text follows Herd, 1776, I, pp. 95-96.

a I, ending on II

As I was a walking all alone,
    Between a water and a wa',
And there I spy'd a wee wee man,
    And he was the least that e'er I saw.
His legs were scarce a shathmont's* length,
    And thick and thimber was his thighs,
Between his brows there was a span,
    And between his shoulders there was three.

He took up a meikle stane,
    And he flang't as far as I could see,
Though I had been a Wallace wight,
    I couldna liften't to my knee.
O wee wee man, but thou be strong,
    O tell me where thy dwelling be.
My dwelling's down at yon' bonny bower,
    O will you go with me and see.

Oh we lap and awa we rade,
    Till we came to yon bonny green;
We 'lighted down for to bait our horse,
    And out there came a lady fine.
Four and twenty at her back,
    And they were a' clad out in green,
Though the King of Scotland had been there,
    The warst o' them might ha' been his queen.

On we lap and awa we rade,
    Till we came to yon bonny ha',
Where the roof was o' the beaten gould,
    And the floor was o' the crystal a'.
When we came to the stair foot,
    Ladies were dancing jimp and sma',
But in the twinkling of an eye,
    My wee wee man was clean awa'.

* According to a note supplied by Johnson, this means the fist closed with the thumb extended.

Tam Lin

CHILD NO. 39

THIS fine ballad has made infrequent appearances since Robert Burns sent his copy to Johnson's *Museum*, and, so far as the evidence exists to show, each time—as is to be expected when a song occurs so seldom—to a different tune. Of the surviving tunes two appear to be Scottish, one Northern English (via the United States), and one Irish. Two are plagal majors; and two belong to minor modes, Æ, D, but with inflections, and the Irish variant ending, possibly, on V.

The evidence of a singing and dancing tradition, of whatever sort, connected with Tam Lin, or Tamlene, or Thomalyn, or Thom of Lyn, or Thomlin, is frequent enough from the middle of the sixteenth century, but we are in darkness as to the nature of what was sung and danced about him. Some of it, however, must have belonged to the nursery branch of "Tommy a Lynn" or "Brian o' Lynn," which has also had a very wide vogue and often found its way into print. There seems to be no connection beyond the name. A version of the latter song may be found in Baring-Gould, *Songs of the West*, ed. Sharp, 1905, No. 41; and abundant references in the notes,

App'x p. 13, to other occurrences. Cf. also I. and P. Opie, *The Oxford Dictionary of Nursery Rhymes*, 1951, pp. 413-14. In a Scottish medley of the early seventeenth century, printed by Forbes in 1666, but removed from the next edition of his work, certain musical notes are set down to the following words:

> The pypers drone was out of tune,
> sing young Thomlin, be merry,
> be merry, and twise so merry,
> with the light of the Moon,
> hey, hey down, down a down;

but the corresponding notes do not shape a tune, and it is not even certain that so much of the text is consecutive. Other than this, we have nothing in music until the end of the eighteenth century, when Burns, as said above, collected our best text of the ballad. Blaikie's tune, coming soon after, depends for connection on its title. It has not been printed before, so far as I know.

LIST OF VARIANTS

1. "Lord Robinson's Only Child." C. Milligan-Fox, *JIFSS*, I (1904), p. 47.
2. "Tam Lin." James Johnson, *The Scots Musical Museum*, V [1796], No. 411, p. 423.
3. "Janet of Carterhaugh." Blaikie MS., National Library of Scotland MS. 1578, No. 76, p. 24.
4. "Tam Lane." Dorothy Scarborough, *A Song Catcher in Southern Mountains*, 1937, pp. 422 and 251-54.

TUNES WITH TEXTS

1. [Lord Robinson's Only Child]

Milligan-Fox, *JIFSS*, I, (1904), p. 47. Sung by Ann Carter, Belfast, 1904; learned from an old woman in Connemara. Recorded by Mrs. Elizabeth Wheeler.

a D (– II), ending on VIII (inflected VI)

As I went out one evening down by my
　　father's lawn,
A gentleman came up to me; these words
　　to me did say:
"What makes you pull those branches?
　　what makes you pull those boughs?

What makes you walk through these green
　　fields without the leave of me?"

"I have leave from my mother and from
　　my father too.
Why can't I walk through these green fields
　　without the leave of you?
And now, sir, as you prevent me, pray tell
　　me what's your name?
That when I see my father I may tell him
　　the same."

"My name is young Lord Robinson, did you
　　ever hear tell of me?
I was stolen by the Queen of Fairies when
　　I was a young babié.
Tomorrow will be the first of May, we'll all
　　go out to ride;
If you come down to Crickmagh, there we all
　　will pass by.

"Let the black steed pass you by, secondly
　　the brown;
When a milk-white steed appears, pull the
　　rider down.
Then hold me fast and fear me not,
　　I'm Lord Robinson's only child."

Early the next morning to Crickmagh she
    went,
And just as he had told her, she saw them
    as they went.
She let the black steed pass her by, and
    secondly the brown,
But when the milk-white steed appeared,
    she pulled the rider down.
"Hold me fast and fear me not," said Lord
    Robinson's only child.

Out spoke the Queen of the Fairies,
In angry tones said she,
"Had I but known this story
One hour before the day,
I'd take[n] out your false, false heart,
And put in one of clay."
The first that they transformed him to
Was to a worm so long:
"Hold me fast and fear me not, I am a man
    so strong."

The next that they transformed him to
Was to a fiery snake:
"Hold me fast and fear me not,
I'm a child of God's own make."
The last that they transformed him to
Was to a bird so wild:
"You have me now; come, take me home,"
Said Lord Robinson's only child.

2. [Tam Lin]

Johnson, V, [1796], No. 411, p. 423.

a Æ (but inflected VII)

The same, with dotted rhythm in the first two bars, and to other
words, "O raging fortune's withering blast" (Burns's words), but
with an air named "Tam Lin," appears in R. A. Smith, *The Scotish
Minstrel*, (c. 1824), I, p. 2.
The time-values of the notes have been doubled in the present copy.
The division of the stanzas has been readjusted in accordance with the
rhyme. This is Child's A.

1. O I forbid you, maidens a'
       That wear gowd o[n] your hair,
   To come or gae by Carterhaugh,
       For young Tam Lin is there.

2. There's nane that gaes by Carterhaugh
       But they leave him a wad;
   Either their rings, or green mantles,
       Or else their maidenhead.

3. Janet has belted her green kirtle,
       A little aboon her knee,
   And she has broded her yellow hair
       A little aboon her bree;
   And she's awa to Carterhaugh
       As fast as she can hie[.]

4. When she came to Carterhaugh
       Tom-Lin was at the well,
   And there she fand his steed standing
       But away was himsel.

5. She had na pu'd a double rose
       A rose but only twa,
   Till up then started young Tam-Lin,
       Says, Lady, thou's pu' nae mae.

6. Why pu's thou the rose, Janet,
       And why breaks thou the wand!
   Or why comes thou to Carterhaugh
       Withoutten my command?

7. Carterhaugh it is my ain,
       My daddie gave it me;
   I'll come and gang by Carterhaugh
       And ask nae leave at thee.

8. Janet has kilted her green kirtle,
       A little aboon her knee,
   And she has snooded her yellow hair,
       A little aboon her bree,
   And she is to her father's ha,
       As fast as she can hie.

9. Four and twenty ladies fair,
       Were playing at the ba,
   And out then cam the fair Janet,
       Ance the flower amang then a',

10. Four and twenty ladies fair,
        Were playing at the chess,
    And out then cam the fair Janet,
        As green as onie glass.

11. Out then spak an auld grey knight,
        Lay o'er the castle wa',
    And says, Alas, fair Janet for thee,
        But we'll be blamed a'.

12. Haud your tongue, ye auld fac'd knight,
        Some ill death may ye die,
    Father my bairn on whom I will,
        I'll father nane on thee.

13. Out then spak her father dear,
        And he spak meek and mild,
    And ever alas, sweet Janet, he says,
        I think thou gaes wi' child.

14. If that I gae wi' child, father,
        Mysel maun bear the blame;
    There's ne'er a laird about your ha,
        Shall get the bairn's name.

15. If my Love were an earthly knight,
        As he's an elfin grey;
    I wad na gie my ain true-love
        For nae lord that ye hae.

16. The steed that my true-love rides on,
        Is lighter than the wind;
    Wi' siller he is shod before,
        Wi' burning gowd behind.

17. J[a]net has kilted her green kirtle
    A little aboon her knee;
And she has snooded her yellow hair
    A little aboon her brie;
And she's awa to Carterhaugh
    As fast as she can hie[.]

18. When she cam to Carterhaugh,
    Tam-Lin was at the well;
And there she fand his steed standing,
    But away was himsel.

19. She had na pu'd a double rose,
    A rose but only twa,
Till up then started young Tam-Lin,
    Says, Lady thou pu's nae mae.

20. Why pu's thou the rose Janet,
    Amang the groves sae green,
And a' to kill the bonie babe
    That we gat us between.

21. O tell me, tell me, Tam-Lin she says,
    For's sake that died on tree,
If e'er ye was in holy chapel,
    Or Christendom did see.

22. Roxbrugh he was my grandfather,
    Took me with him to bide
And ance it fell upon a day
    That wae did me betide.

23. And ance it fell upon a day,
    A cauld day and a snell.
When we were frae the hunting come
    That frae my horse I fell.
The queen o' Fairies she caught me,
    In yon green hill to dwell[.]

24. And pleasant is the fairy-land;
    But, an eerie tale to tell!
Ay at the end of seven years
    We pay a tiend to hell.
I am sae fair and fu' o' flesh
    I'm fear'd it be mysel.

25. But the night is Halloween, lady,
    The morn is Hallowday;
Then win me, win me, an ye will,
    For weel I wat ye may.

26. Just at the mirk and midnight hour
    The fairy folk will ride;
And they that wad their truelove win,
    At Milescross they maun bide.

27. But how shall I thee ken Tam-Lin,
    Or how my true love know[,]
Amang sae mony unco knights,
    The like I never saw[?]

28. O first let pass the black Lady,
    And syne let pass the brown;
But quickly run to the milk white steed,
    Pu ye his rider down.

29. For I'll ride on the milk-white steed,
    And ay nearest the town.
Because I was an earthly knight
    They gie me that renown.

30. My right hand will be glov'd lady,
    My left hand will be bare.
Cockt up shall my bonnet be,
    And kaim'd down shall my hair,
And thae's the takens I gie thee,
    Nae doubt I will be there.

31. They'll turn me in your arms lady,
    Into an esk and adder,
But hald me fast and fear me not,
    I am your bairn's father.

32. They'll turn me to a bear sae grim,
    And then a lion bold,
But hold me fast and fear me not,
    As ye shall love your child.

33. Again they'll turn me in your arms,
    To a red het gaud of airn.
But hold me fast and fear me not,
    I'll do to you nae harm.

34. And last they'll turn me in your arms,
    Into the burning lead;
Then throw me into well water,
    O throw me in wi' speed.

35. And then I'll be your ain true love,
    I'll turn a naked knight.
Then cover me wi' your green mantle,
    And cover me out o' sight[.]

36. Gloomy, gloomy was the night,
    And eerie was the way,
As fair Jenny in her green mantle
    To Milescross she did gae.

37. About the middle o' the night,
    She heard the bridles ring;
This lady was as glad at that
    As any earthly thing.

38. First she let the black pass by,
    And syne she let the brown;
But quickly she ran to the milk white steed,
    And pu'd the rider down.

39. Sae weel she minded what he did say
    And young Tam Lin did win;
Syne cover'd him wi' her green mantle
    As blythe's a bird in spring.

40. Out then spak the queen o' fairies,
    Out of a bush o broom;
Them that has gotten young Tam Lin,
    Has gotten a stately groom.

41. Out then spak the queen o' fairies,
    And an angry queen was she;
Shame betide her ill-far'd face,
    And an ill death may she die,

For she's ta'en awa the boniest knight
In a' my companie[.]

42. But had I kend Tam Lin, she says,
What now this night I see[,]
I wad hae taen out thy twa grey een,
And put it twa een o' tree.

3. [Janet of Carterhaugh]

Blaikie MS., NL Scotland MS. 1578, No. 76, p. 24.

p I/M

4. "Tam Lane"

Scarborough, 1937, p. 422; text, pp. 251-54. Sung by Margaret Widdemer, c. 1932; the first stanza learned from Elinor Wylie, who learned it from her nurse, a woman "from the northern marshes." The text as a whole appears to be refashioned, perhaps in good part on Child's D.

p I

This tune seems nearly allied to Motherwell's "Lady Jean" (52), though in a different modal area.

1. May Margery sat in her castle tower
Sewing her silken seam;
She looked from out the high window
And she saw the leaves growing green,
My love,
And she saw the leaves growing green.

2. She's let the seam drop to her foot,
The needle to her toe,
And she's away to Cartershay
As fast as she can go,
My love,
As fast as she can go.

3. She hadna pulled a red, red rose,
A rose but barely three,
When up there started a wee, wee man,
Says, Let the roses be,
My love,
Says, Let the roses be.

4. "Oh, I will pull the bush," she says,
"And I will pull the tree,
And I will be at Cartershay
And ask no leave of thee,
My love,
And ask no leave of thee."

5. He took her by the milk-white hand,
Among the leaves so green,
And what they did I darena say,
The green leaves were atween,
My love,
The green leaves were atween.

6. "Now tell to me the truth, Tam Lane,
A truth we will na lee,
If ever you were a human man
And sained in Christendy,
My love,
And sained in Christenty?"

7. "Oh, I will tell the truth, Margaret,
A truth I willna lee.
It's truth I have been in holy chapel
And sained as well as thee,
My love,
And sained as well as thee;

8. But once it fell upon a day
As hunting I did ride,
As I rode east and I rode west,
Strange chance did me betide,
My love,
Strange chance did me betide.

9. There blew a drowsy, drowsy wind,
Dead sleep upon me fell,
The Queen o'Fairies she was there
And she took me to herself,
My love,
And she took me to herself."

10. And never I would tire, Margaret,
In fairyland to dwell,
But aye at every seven years,
They pay the teind to hell,
My love,
And I fear 'twill be myself.

11. The night is Hallowe'en, Margaret,
When fairy folk will ride
And if you would your true love win,
At Miles Cross you must bide,
My love,
At Miles Cross you must bide."

12. "But how shall I thee ken, Tam Lane,
And how shall I thee know,
Among so many unearthly knights
The like I never saw,
My love,
The like I never saw?"

13. "Oh, first let by the black black steed,
   And then let by the brown,
But grip you to the milk-white steed
   And pull the rider down,
      My love,
   And pull the rider down.

14. For I'll be on the milk-white steed,
   With a gold star in my crown,
Because I was a christened knight
   They gave me that renown,
      My love,
   They gave me that renown.["]

15. Gloomy, gloomy was the night
   And eerie was the way
When Margaret in her green mantel
   To Miles Cross she did gae,
      My love,
   To Miles Cross she did gae.

16. And first went by the black, black steed,
   And then went by the brown,
And syne she gripped the milk-white steed
   And pulled the rider down,
      My love,
   And pulled the rider down.

17. Up then spoke the Queen o' Fairies,
   Out of a bush of broom,

She that has gotten young Tam Lane
   Has gotten a stately groom,
      My love,
   Has gotten a stately groom.

18. Up then spoke the Queen o' Fairies
   Out of a bush of rye,
She's taken away the bonniest knight
   In all my company,
      My love,
   In all my company.

19. If I had but kent yestreen, Tam Lane,
   A lady would borrow thee,
I'd taken out thy two grey een
   Put in two of tree,
      My love,
   Put in two of tree.

20. If I had kenned, Tam Lane, she says,
   Before we came from home,
I'd taken out your heart of flesh
   And put in a heart of stone,
      My love,
   And put in a heart of stone.

21. If I had but half the wit yestreen
   That I have bought today
I'd paid my tiend seven times to hell
   Ere ye'd been won away,
      My love,
   Ere ye'd been won away.

The Queen of Elfan's Nourice

CHILD NO. 40

ONLY one tune, and that recorded late in the last century, is known for this ballad, which has all but died out of traditional recollection. Child found only one text, but he got the tune from another source, which should have supplied an independent text, unless it was sung from book. A more recent text was discovered in Wisconsin, with an entirely different stanzaic pattern which could hardly have been used with the other tune. (*JAF*, XX [1907], p. 155.) The later variant was also from Scottish tradition, and the ballad does not appear to have been sung by "outlandish" people, whether southron or others.

William Walker supplied both Greig and Child with copies of the only surviving tune. There are minor differences in Child's copy as printed, which render it less fitted for the words. The fact might suggest that Walker's mother used other words or none at all, and that it was editorially adapted to the Sharpe text with some slight modification of both text and tune. Walker's note in the manuscript copy is: "Perhaps an improvised adaptation of a pibroch tune." Keith does not print this ballad in Greig and Keith, 1925, possibly because the tune had already appeared in Child's work. The only text found in the Greig MSS. for this ballad is that printed by Child, from the Skene MS. (Greig MSS., Bk. 765, LV, pp. 8ff.)

It may be mentioned that the tune appearing with the Wisconsin version of the ballad in Evelyn K. Wells, *The Ballad Tree*, 1950, p. 141, is a happy borrowing from a Gaelic song on the theft of a child by the fairies. Cf. Alfred Moffat, *Minstrelsy of the Scottish Highlands*, n.d., pp. 24-25.

LIST OF VARIANTS

"The Queen of Elfan's Nourice." Greig MSS., III, p. 183. Text, Greig MSS., Bk. 765, LV, pp. 8ff., King's College Library, Aberdeen. Also in Francis James Child, *The English and Scottish Popular Ballads*, 1882-98, V, p. 413.

TUNE WITH TEXT

[The Queen of Elfan's Nourice]

Greig MSS., III, p. 183. Text, Greig MSS., Bk. 765, LV, pp. 8ff. Also, with variations below, in Child, 1882-98, V, p. 413. Noted by W. Walker, Aberdeen; learned from his mother.

a Æ/D

[I heard a coo low and a bonnie coo low
And a coo low doon in yon glen;
But lang lang will my young son greet
Ere his minnie bids him come hame.]

Two tunes in the Blaikie MS., Nos. 33 and 75 (the latter "John the little Scot"—Child 99), have the same final cadence as the above, and it is sometimes found in English tunes—e.g., "The Yeoman of Kent," in D'Urfey, *Pills*, 1719, I, p. 126. Cf. also the variant of "The Cruel Mother" from Mrs. Milne (Greig and Keith, 1925, No. 2, p. 22).

1. I heard a cow low, a bonnie cow low,
    An' a cow low down in yon glen,
Lang, lang will my young son greet
    Or his mither bid him come ben.

2. I heard a cow low, a bonnie cow low,
    An' a cow low down in yon fauld,
Lang, lang will my young son greet
    Or his mither take him frae cauld.

3. Waken, Queen of Elfan,
    An' hear your Nourice moan.
O moan ye for your meat,
    Or moan ye for your fee,
Or moan ye for the ither bounties
    That ladies are wont to gie.

4. I moan na for my meat,
    Nor yet for my fee,
But I moan for Christened land,—
    It's there I fain would be.

5. O nurse my bairn, Nourice, she says,
    Till he stan' at your knee,
An' ye's win hame to Christen land,
    Whar fain it's ye wad be.

6. O keep my bairn, Nourice,
    Till he gang by the hauld,
An' ye's win hame to your young son
    Ye left in four nights auld.

7. O Nourice, lay your head
    Upo' my knee;
See ye na that narrow road
    Up by yon tree?

8. That's the road the righteous goes,
    And that's the road to heaven.
An' see ye na that braid road
    Down by yon sunny fell?
Yon's the road the wicked gae,
    An' that's the road to hell.

Hind Etin

CHILD NO. 41

Many Continental texts of this ballad exist, three Danish records going back to the sixteenth century. The rest are all of the nineteenth century, yet Child observes that the Scandinavian branch derives from the German. To the latter the rare Scottish copies are more closely allied. Two tunes are known, of the later nineteenth, and early twentieth century. They have little in common, save for the concluding phrase, which corresponds closely enough for traditional variants. Both come from the Scottish northeast. Greig's tune shows similarities with several others: Motherwell's "Lady Jean" (52), Greig's "Child Waters" (63) and "Jellon Graeme" (90)—both of the latter from the present singer; and comparison may also be made with the *SMM* tune of "Tam Lin" (39).

LIST OF VARIANTS

1. "Young Akin." W. Christie, *Traditional Ballad Airs*, II, 1881, p. 156. Text from Buchan's concluding stanzas, 1828, I, pp. 6-15.
2. "Hind Etin." Greig MSS., IV, p. 92; text, Bk. 769, LIX, p. 10, King's College Library, Aberdeen. Also in Gavin Greig and Alexander Keith, *Last Leaves of Traditional Ballads and Ballad Airs*, 1925, p. 31.

TUNES WITH TEXTS

1. [Young Akin]

Christie, II, 1881, p. 156. Sung in Banffshire. Text from Buchan's concluding stanzas, 1828, I, pp. 6-15.

a π^3

Christie gives his copy in 2/4, with note-values half the present length.

[Lady Margaret sits in her bower door
Sewing at her silken seam;
She heard a note in Elmond's-wood,
And wished she there had been.

She loot the seam fa' frae her side,
And the needle to her tae;
And she is on to Elmond's-wood
As fast as she cou'd gae.]
Etc.

2. [Hind Etin]

Greig MSS., IV, p. 92; text, Bk. 769, LIX, p. 10. Also in Greig and Keith, 1925, p. 31. Sung by Alexander Robb, New Deer, Aberdeenshire.

a Æ/D

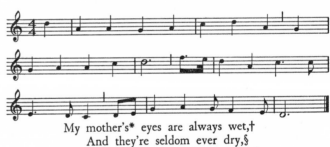

My mother's* eyes are always wet,†
And they're seldom ever dry,§
And^x what can ail my dear mother?—
For she weeps continually.

Your mother was the fairest woman
That ever my eyes did see,—
. . . .
. . . .

* Greig and Keith, 1925: "mithers"
† Greig and Keith, 1925: "weet"
§ Greig and Keith, 1925: "An' they are seldom dry"
x Greig and Keith, 1925: "An'"

Clerk Colvill

CHILD NO. 42

It is disappointing in the extreme that a fine ballad like "Clerk Colvill," whose analogues for upwards of four hundred years have covered the face of Europe from Iceland to Brittany, Spain, and Italy, and from Scotland to Bohemia, should yield, in the British musical record, but one solitary tune—and that through a cloudy glass. For it is again to Mrs. Brown and her nephew that we must resort; and this time they put us to no little trouble to divine a meaning. There are two copies of Gordon's record of his aunt's tune, one in the Abbotsford MS., and one at Harvard, in the Ritson-Tytler-Brown MS. The former is reproduced in Child's Appendix of Tunes, with an alternative reading by Spalding. The Ritson copy shows slight divergences from the printed copy, but no doubt both were taken from a single original. Macmath notes that there is a third copy of the same tune, in Glenriddell's hand, in a copy of Herd's *Scottish Songs*, 1776, in the Signet Library at Edinburgh. This I have not seen. (Cf. Child V, p. 414n.)

The notes themselves look plausible; the problem is to fit them to the words. The first six bars obviously make provision for two lines of text, of equal length. The repeat would thus accommodate a full quatrain. But there are four bars left over, and these are to be repeated. If this be a second strain, to which the second and alternate stanzas are to be sung, it is very odd that it should be two bars shorter than the first: it has to carry the same length of text. There is no indication in the manuscript that the ballad possessed anything in the nature of a refrain, and it would be virtually impossible to eke out something to fill the extra *four* bars by repeating part of the quatrain

for a refrain, even without the indicated repetition of the four bars. The only reasonable alternative appears to be the assumption of an unrecorded refrain or burden of different line-length, probably falling into two equal parts to follow the melodic scheme. Such a pattern would be by no means unprecedented, and is exemplified more than once in Greig's collection of tunes from the same region.

The prevailing iambic meter of the text suggests also a revision of Gordon's barring, so as to provide up-beats for the phrase openings. Spalding's version, which takes unwarranted liberties with the record, is in Child, V, p. 414. Further discussion of the tune may be found in *CFQ*, I (1942), pp. 189-90, where it is noted that a tune in Greig for Child 237 (Greig and Keith, 1925, p. 189, tune 1b) parallels the first two (oddly Brahmsian) phrases. It may be admitted that the temptation to which Spalding succumbed, of changing the triple rhythm of the Gordon record to a dotted one (6/8 or 6/4) corresponding to the iambic meter, is hard to resist. Yet it is equally hard to believe that Gordon would have heard a succession of alternating halves and quarters (or quarters and eighths) as a sequence of notes of even length. And if he did not, he would not have written them so, for his notation is by no means illiterate. In this case, his notation makes reasonable sense, apart from suiting the words or not. Moreover, there is corroborative evidence in the large number of Christie's records from the same region which have a metrical pattern of a triple sort, where the meter of the words would suggest a dotted duple one.

LIST OF VARIANTS

"Clark Colven." Ritson-Tytler-Brown MS., pp. 6-9, Harvard College Library.

TUNE WITH TEXT

[Clark Colven]

Ritson-Tytler-Brown MS., pp. 6-9. Sung by Mrs. Brown, Falkland, Aberdeenshire.

Conjectural reading

p π³

Clark Colven and his gay lady,
    As they walk'd to yon garden green,
A belt about her middle gimp,
    Which cost Clark Colven crowns fifteen.
"O hearken well now, my good lord,

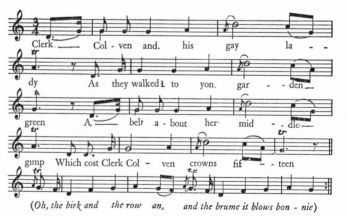

(Oh, the birk and the rowan, and the brume it blows bonnie)

O hearken well to what i say;
When ye gae to the walls o' Stream,
    Be sure ye touch nae well far'd may."
"O had your tongue, my gay lady,
    An' dinna deave me wi' your din;
For i saw never a fair woman
    But wi' her body i cou'd sin."

[334]

He mounted on his berry-brown steed,
    An' merry merry rade he on,
Till he came til the walls o' Stream,
    An' there he saw the mermaiden.
"Ye wash, ye wash, ye bonny may,
    And ay's ye wash your sark o' silk."
"It's a for you, ye gentle knight,
    My skin is whiter than the milk."
He's taen her by the milk-white hand,
    And likewise by the grass-green sleeve,
An' laid her down upon the green,
    Nor of his lady speer'd he leave.
Ohon! alas! says Clark Colven,
    An' ay sae sair's i mean my head.
And merrily leugh the mermaiden:
    "O, even on, till ye be dead.   (Aside.)
But out ye tak' your little pen-knife,
    An' frae my sark ye shear a gare,
Row that about your lovely head,
    And the pain you'll never feel nae mair."
Out has he taen his little pen-knife,
    An' frae her sark he's shorn a gare,

Row'd that about his lovely head;
    But the pain increased mair and mair.
Ohon! alas! says Clark Colven,
    An' ay sae sair's i mean my head.
An' merrily leugh the mermaiden:
    " 'Twill ay be war 'till ye be dead."
Then out he drew his trusty blade,
    An' thought wi' it to be her dead;
But she became a fish again,
    And merrily sprang into the fleed.
He's mounted on his berry-brown steed,
    An' dowy, dowy rade he hame,
'Till he came to his lady's bow'r door,
    An' heavily he lighted down.
"O mither, mither, mak' my bed,
    An', gentle lady, lay me down;
O brither, brither, unbend my bow,
    'Twill never be bent by me again."
His mither she has made his bed,
    His gentle lady laid him down,
His brother he has unbent his bow,
    'Twas never bent by him again.

The Broomfield Hill

CHILD NO. 43

THERE is no evidence to connect this song with any early song-title or burden mentioning the broom in lyrical fashion, as the "Brume, brume on hill" of *The Complaynt of Scotland*, c. 1549, and Wager's "The Longer thou Livest, the More Fool thou art," c. 1568, or "All flowers in brome" in W. Ballet's Lute Book, c. 1600. Setting aside poems and tales on the theme, some of which were recorded as far back as the twelfth century, there are Scandinavian, German, and Italian ballads, Danish copies of the mid-seventeenth century being the earliest that have survived. So far as the British record is known, it begins with broadsides of the earlier (?) eighteenth century (Child's F). The earliest traditional copies were picked up in Scotland in the latter part of the same century, and the ballad was apparently common among the Scots at the beginning of the nineteenth century. Since that time it has nearly died out in the north; but it has been found in the present century occasionally in the Midlands and frequently in the more southern counties, particularly Somerset. It has been discovered also in the United States, but here it is of the utmost rarity, and only one tune appears to have been recorded for any American variant.

Except in the Somerset region, the recorded tunes show considerable variation—so much, in fact, that it is very difficult to make out whether there is actual relationship or not. Between the two oldest Scottish records there seems to be almost nothing in common; but one of them is clearly connected with most of the southwestern variants, and the other is doubtfully related to the recent variants from the Aberdeen region. A third distinct pattern has been found in the south, in several variants; two distant variants of a fourth, in Norfolk and Dorset; and several copies, in scattered counties, which cannot be related with any confidence to the rest, but which seem standard folk-tunes. Most of the tunes are full of charm and interest.

(A) The largest group of related variants comes mostly from Sharp's Somerset collection, but one member of the group is perhaps the oldest of record and is Scottish. All these variants are in major tonality (I, I-M, I/M). The striking feature is the mid-cadence on the octave; but the first phrase is almost as consistently on the tonic. All the tunes of this group are authentic.

(B) The second group is Scottish and too small to be very positive about. It affects a burden with nonsense syllables, and seems to prefer to end on the supertonic. If this analysis be correct, all variants are π^1 or I/M. Variants of the same tune occur with "Earl of Errol" (231) and "Our Goodman" (274).

(C) The third group is again Southern English, and major authentic; the first and mid-cadences are I and (usually) V.

(D) A fourth group contains only two tunes, from Norfolk and Dorset. Both are plagal; one Dorian, with a mixed meter; the other Æ/D, in straight triple measure.

(E) Four tunes, from Lincolnshire, Dorset, Herefordshire, and Somersetshire, have been grouped together, somewhat doubtfully. Two, major and I-M, are plagal; two, Dorian and D-Æ, are authentic. All are in duple time, and may be related to Group A. (The Herefordshire text starts on the Group A pattern.) They have noticeable connections with other songs, especially "The Bailiff's Daughter" (105) and "The Mermaid" (289).

(Appendix) A final group, from Maine, Newfoundland, Nova Scotia, and Ireland, have seemingly little to do with any of the rest, and go to a curious marine adaptation of the text. Three are Mixolydian, authentic, and in 6/8 time; one Irish copy is Ionian; a copy from Newfoundland is Dorian, and another—the only plagal tune and a different melodic type—is Æ/D.

LIST OF VARIANTS

GROUP A

1. "Merry Broomfield." Sharp MSS., 1460/1339, Clare College Library, Cambridge. (Chedgey)
2. "The Broomfield (Bromfield?) Wager." Sharp MSS., 246/344-45. (Overd)
3. "Lord John." George R. Kinloch, *Ancient Scottish Ballads*, 1827, pp. 195-98.
4. "Broomfield Wager." Sharp MSS., 1212/1189-91. Also in Cecil J. Sharp, *JFSS*, IV (1914), p. 112(2). (Briffet)
5. "Broomfield Wager." Sharp MSS., 915/. (Betty)
6. "The Merry Broomfield." Sharp MSS., 1225/. (Ware)
7. "The Broomfield Wager." Sharp MSS., 1848/. Also in H. A. Jeboult and H. E. D. Hammond, *JFSS*, VII (1923), p. 33(2). (Conybeare)
8. "The Broomfield Wager." Sharp MSS., 2013/. (Seeley)
9. "The Merry Broomfield." Sharp MSS., 3092/. Also in Cecil J. Sharp, *JFSS*, VIII (1927), p. 1(2). (Barnett)
10. "The Bromfield Wager." Sharp MSS., 1387/. Also, as "The Bonny (Merry) Broomfield(s)," in Cecil J. Sharp, *JFSS*, VIII (1927), p. 1(1). (Badley)
11. "The Broomfield Hill." Lester A. Hubbard and LeRoy J. Robertson, *JAF*, LXIV (1951), pp. 41-42.

GROUP B

12. "The Broomfield Hill." Gavin Greig and Alexander Keith, *Last Leaves of Traditional Ballads and Ballad Airs*, 1925, p. 32(2).
13. "Leatherum thee thou and a'." Greig MSS., I, p. 266, King's College Library, Aberdeen. Also in Greig and Keith, 1925, p. 32(1).
14. "The Wager." Lady John Scott's Sharpe MS. National Library of Scotland MS. 843, fol. 25ᵛ.

GROUP C

15. "The Bonny Bushy Broom." Alice E. Gillington, *Songs of the Open Road*, 1911, No. 8, p. 18.
16. "The Broomfield Wager." Sharp MSS., 810/. (? Carter)
17. "The Merry Broomfield." Sharp MSS., 1457/. (Cooper)
18. "The Broomfield Wager." Sharp MSS., 602/692. (White)

GROUP D

19. "The Broomfield Hill." H. E. D. Hammond, *JFSS*, III (1907), p. 69.
20. "The Squire who lived in the West." The Hon. M. Amherst, *JFSS*, IV (1911), p. 114(4).

TUNES WITH TEXTS

GROUP A

1. [Merry Broomfield]

Sharp MSS., 1460/1339. Sung by Mrs. Chedgey, Wick, September 4, 1907.

aI/M

There is perhaps a connection between this and the "Mermaid" tunes (287). See, for example, the copy Chappell received from Charles Sloman about 1840 (Chappell, *Popular Music*, II, p. 743).

Stanza with music:
A wager a wager a wager I will lay
I'll bet fifty pounds to your one
O that you don't ride a maid
    to the bonny bush a bloom (*sic*)
And a maid return again.

Stanza in text MS.:
Sleep more in the night Master
Wake more in the day
And then you shall see when your true love comes
And when she goes away.

I'll bet you twenty pounds, master,
And twenty pounds unto your ten,
I'll meet my love in the yon green 'oods)
And a maid return back again.   ) (*bis*)

And when she came to the yon green woods
She found her love asleep.
Nine times she kissed his rosy cheek
As he lay fast asleep.

She took the ring from her finger,
Put it on his right hand,
That he might know when he did awake
That his love been there and gone.

Awake, awake, awake he did
And looked up in the sky,
He turned round all on the ground
And he wept most bitterly.

He called to his servant man,
A man he loved so dear:
Why hadn't thou awakened me
When my true love was here?

And with my voice I called Master,
And with my bell I rung,
Saying: Awake, awake, awake, master,
For thy true love been and gone.

If I'd been awake when my true love were here
I know I'd a-had my will,
Or else these birds in yon green 'ood
On her should have had their fill.

2. [The Broomfield (Bromfield?) Wager]

Sharp MSS., 246/344-45. Sung by Mrs. Overd, Langport, August 2, 1904.

a I

3. [Lord John]

Kinloch, 1827, pp. 195-98.

m M (inflected VII)

1. "I'll wager, I'll wager," says Lord John,
   A hundred merks and ten,
   That ye winna gae to the bonnie broom-fields,
   And a maid return again."—

2. "But I'll lay a wager wi' you, Lord John,
   A' your merks oure again,
   That I'll gae alane to the bonnie broom-fields,
   And a maid return again."

3. Then Lord John mounted his grey steed,
   And his hound wi' his bells sae bricht,
   And swiftly he rade to the bonny broom-fields,
   Wi' his hawks, like a lord or knicht.

4. "Now rest, now rest, my bonnie grey steed,
   My lady will soon be here;
   And I'll lay my head aneath this rose sae red,
   And the bonnie burn sae near."

5. But sound, sound, was the sleep he took,
   For he slept till it was noon;
   And his lady cam at day, left a taiken and away,
   Gaed as licht as a glint o' the moon.

6. She strawed the roses on the ground,
   Threw her mantle on the brier,
   And the belt around her middle sae jimp,
   As a taiken that she'd been there.

7. The rustling leaves flew round his head,
   And rous'd him frae his dream;
   He saw by the roses, and mantle sae green,
   That his love had been there and was gane.

8. "O whare was ye, my gude grey steed,
   That I coft ye sae dear;
   That ye didna waken your master,
   Whan ye ken'd that his love was here."—

9. "I pautit wi' my foot, master,
   Garr'd a' my bridles ring;
   And still I cried, Waken, gude master,
   For now is the hour and time."—

10. "Then whare was ye, my bonnie grey hound,
    That I coft ye sae dear,
    That ye didna waken your master,
    When ye ken'd that his love was here."—

11. "I pautit wi' my foot, master,
    Garr'd a' my bells to ring;
    And still I cried, Waken, gude master,
    For now is the hour and time."—

12. "But whare was ye, my hawks, my hawks,
    That I coft ye sae dear,
    That ye didna waken your master,
    When ye ken'd that his love was here."—

13. "O wyte na me, now, my master dear,
    I garr'd a' my young hawks sing,
    And still I cried, Waken, gude master,
    For now is the hour and time."—

14. "Then be it sae, my wager gane!
    'Twill skaith frae meikle ill;
    For gif I had found her in bonnie broom-fields,
    O' her heart's blude ye'd drunken your fill."

4. [Broomfield Wager]

Sharp MSS., 1212/1189-91. Also in Sharp, *JFSS*, IV (1910), p. 112(2). Sung by William Briffet, Bridgwater, January 19, 1907.

a I

1. A squire, a squire, he lived in the wood,*
   He courted a lady gay,
   A little while and he passed a joke
   And a wager he did lay.

2. A wager, a wager I'll lay to any man,
   A thousand guineas to one
   That a maid won't go to the merry green woods
   And a maid return again.

3. O when she came to the merry green woods
   She found her love asleep
   With a knife in his hand and a sword by his side
   And a greyhound at his feet.

4. Three times she walked all round his head,
   Three times all round his feet,
   Three times she kissed his red rosy cheeks
   As he lay fast asleep.

5. And when she done all what she could
   She walked softly away;
   She hide herself in the merry green wood
   To hear what her love did say.

6. When he waked out from his dream,
   He looked up in the skies;
   He looked round and round and down on the ground
   And he wept most bitterly.

7. Up he called his serving man
   Whom he loved so dear:
   Why hasn't thou awakened me
   When my true love was here?

8. And with my voice I halloed Master
   And with my bells I rung;
   Awake, awake and awake, Master,
   Your true love's been and gone.

9. I wish I had my true love here
   As free as I a got my will

And every bird in the merry green wood
For they should have their fill.

10. Sleep more in the night, master,
And wake more in the day,
And then you will see when your true love come
And when she goes away.

* Sharp, *JFSS*: "woods"

5. [Broomfield Wager]

Sharp MSS., 915/. Sung by Mrs. Elizabeth Betty, Bridg-water, April 18, 1906.

a I/M

A wager a wager to any young man
Five guineas unto one
That a maid she would go to the merry green woods
And a maid she would return

6. [The Merry Broomfield]

Sharp MSS., 1225/. Sung by Mrs. Ware, Eley(?), Over Stowey, January 23, 1907.

a I/M

7. [The Broomfield Wager]

Sharp MSS., 1848/. Also in Jeboult and Hammond, *JFSS*, VII (1923), p. 33(2). Sung by Henry Conybeare (71), Combe Florey, September 8, 1908.

a I

A squire a squire in the merry green wood
He courted a lady gay
It was once on a time as they were passing of a joke
That a wager she would lay

It may be that the singer shortened the mid-cadence, as there appears no dot after that G in the MS. The *JFSS* copy, noted three years earlier, has a dotted rhythm at nine points where Sharp's copy is even.

8. [The Broomfield Wager]

Sharp MSS., 2013/. Sung by Elizabeth Seeley, Bridgwater, December 8, 1908.

a I/M

9. [The Merry Broomfield]

Sharp MSS., 3092/. Also in Sharp, *JFSS*, VIII (1927), p. 1(2). Sung by Jack Barnett, Bridgwater, January 6, 1916.

a I/M

As she went to the merry green wood
Her true love fast a-sleep
Sword by his side and a pistol in hand
And a greyhound at his feet.

Three times she walked around his head
Three times around his feet
Three times she kissed his red ruby lips
As he lay fast asleep.

She took a ring from her middle finger
And put it on his right hand
That he may see when he have awake
His true love been and gone.

When he wake he wept most bitterly
.   .   .   .
.   .   .   .
.   .   .   .   .   .

He called to his servant man
The one he loved so dear
Why havent you a-waked me
When my true love was near

O with my voice I called Master
A- with my bell I rung
Many* person was passing by
They would think you was dead & gone.

Sleep a-more by night Master
And wake a-more by day
That you may see when your true love come
And when she go away.

*Sharp, JFSS: "If any"

10. [The Bromfield Wager]

Sharp MSS., 1387/. Also, as "The Bonny (Merry) Broom-field(s)," in Sharp, JFSS, VIII (1927), p. 1(1). Sung by Martha Badley, North Petherton, August 8, 1907.

a I

A squire a squire lived in a wood
courting a lady gay
He courted her a little while
and a wage a wage was him

11. [The Broomfield Hill]

Hubbard and Robertson, JAF, LXIV (1951), pp. 41-42. Sung by Salley A. Hubbard (86), Salt Lake City, Utah; learned from "Doc" Lish, Willard, in 1871.

a I

"A wage a love a wager, and go along with me,
I'll bet you five hundred to one
That a maiden you may go to the May blooming field
And a maiden you never will return."

"A wage a love a wager and I'll go with thee,
And I'll bet you five hundred to one
That a maiden I may go to the May blooming field
And a maiden I'm sure to return."

Away this young man ran to the May blooming field
His wages all for to win,
He set himself down by a clear purling stream,
And he set till he fell fast asleep.

Nine times she walked around his head,
And nine times she walked around his feet,
And nine times she kissed his ruby, ruby lips
As he lay on the bank fast asleep.

She had a ring on her little finger,
And on his she placed it as his own;
She placed it there as a token of love
That she had been there but was gone.

"If I'd a-been awake when I was asleep
A maiden she never would return,
For her I would have killed and the blood I would have spilled,
And the butcher told the tale of the dead."

"You false-hearted young man, you hard-hearted youth,
Your heart to me is as hard as any stone.
Would you think of killing one who's never harmed you?
I'd a-mourned for the grave you lie in."

GROUP B

12. "The Broomfield Hill"

Greig and Keith, 1925, p. 32(2). Sung by Mrs. Gillespie. (Not in Greig MSS.)

a I/M

Leddrin thee thoo an' a',
Sma' an' nanny hue, O,
Come sell a me my ebrachee,
An' a maiden I see you, O.

13. "Leatherum thee thou and a'"

Greig MSS., I, p. 266. Also in Greig and Keith, 1925, p. 32(1). Sung by Alexander Robb, New Deer, Aberdeen-shire, May 1906.

a π1, ending on II

There was a knicht an' a lady bricht,
  Set trysts amang the broom,
The ane to come at twelve o'clock,
  An' the ither true at noon.
    Leatherum thee thou an' a'
    Madam aye wi' you,
    An' the seal o' me be abrachee,
    Fair maiden I'm for you.

And three times she walked to the sole of his feet;
And three times she walked to the crown of his head;
And three times she kissed of his red and cherry lips,
A-sleeping as he lay all on the ground.

5. She had a ring on her little finger;
   She placed it on her true love's right hand;
   To let him, let him know that a lady had been there,
   That a lady has been here, but she is gone.

14. [The Wager]

Lady John Scott's Sharpe MS., NL Scotland MS. 843, fol. 25ᵛ.

a π¹, ending on II

The words are not given with this variant, Sharpe having set it to verses composed by himself for the use of ladies.

GROUP C

15. "The Bonny Bushy Broom"

Gillington, 1911, No. 8, p. 18. Sung by Hampshire gypsies.

a I

An extra two lines in stanza 4 were accommodated by repeating the phrase between the signs.

1. A wager, a wager, a wager I will lay
   I'll bet you five guineas to your one
   That you won't ride unscathed to the bonny bushy broom,
   And unscathed to return home again

2. "A wager, a wager, a wager I will lay!
   I'll lay you five guineas to your one!
   That you won't ride unharmed to the bonny bushy broom,
   And unharmed to return home again!"

3. Come, saddle me my milk white team;
   Come, bring to me my broad sword and gun!
   That I may ride unharmed to the bonny bushy broom,
   And unharmed to return safe again!

4. And when she got there, her true love lay asleep,
   With a bunch of green broom in his hand;

6. Then when he awoke, and awoken was he,
   And very well awoken was him;
   He stampéd down his foot on the bonny bushy broom,
   Saying, "The lady has been here, but she is gone."

7. O! had I awake, and the lady had been here,
   Sure alive I should her heart's blood spill,
   And every little bird in the bonny bushy broom
   They surely must have drunk their fill!

8. O! what an hard-hearted man must I be!
   My heart must be harder than a stone;
   To murder the girl who so dearly lovéd me
   All alone in the bonny bushy broom!*

  * Reprinted by permission of Joseph Williams Ltd., London, copyright owners.

16. [The Broomfield Wager]

Sharp MSS., 810/. (Source unnoted, but perhaps sung by Lucy Carter, Tintinhall, end of January 1906.)

a I

A wager a wager with you young man I'll lay
I'll lay you ten-thousand pound to one
That the girl she shall go with me to yonder shady trees
And a maid she never shall return

17. [The Merry Broomfield]

Sharp MSS., 1457/. Sung by Mrs. Priscilla Cooper, Stafford Common, September 2, 1907.

a I

A wager a wager a wager I will lay
I'll bet you five and fifty pounds to your one O
That you don't ride a maid to the bonny bush abloom
And a maid to return safe home again

(a) was sometimes a B♭.

18. [The Broomfield Wager]

Sharp MSS., 602/692. Sung by Mrs. Lucy White, Hambridge, August 25, 1905.

a I (inflected IV)

A wager, a wager with you I will lay,
I will lay you five hundred to one
That a maid shall go with me to some may blooming fields
And a maid back again she shan't return.

And they walked till they came to some may blooming field
Where the May looked pleasant all round
As he felt tired and weary he laid himself
As he lay on the grass fast asleep.

Nine times did she walk round the crown of his head,
Nine times round the soles of his feet,
Nine times did she kiss of his ruby, ruby feet
As he lay on the ground fast asleep.

The ring that he wore on his little finger
She tooked it off and placed on her own,
That this may be a token when my false love is awake
That I have been here and have gone.

GROUP D

19. [The Broomfield Hill]

Hammond, JFSS, III (1907), p. 69. Sung by Mrs. Russell, Upwey, Dorset, February 1907.

p D

Why had'st not thou awaked me, my little foot-boy,
That I might have my will?
And all the little birds in the merry greenwood,
Of her should have their fill.
And all the little birds in the merry greenwood,
Of her should have their fill.

20. "The Squire who lived in the West"

Amherst, JFSS, IV (1911), p. 114(4). Sung by George Turvey (77), an agricultural laborer, Foulden, Stoke Ferry, Norfolk.

p Æ/D

1. 'Tis of a young Squire who lived in the West,
   And he courted a lady so fair;
   But my love unto you I never will request,
   For I mean to go merry and free.

2. "A wager, a wager, with you my pretty maid,
   Here's five hundred pounds to your ten,
   That a maid you shall go to yon merry, green broom,
   But a maid you shall no more return."

3. "A wager, a wager, with you kind sir,
   With your hundred pounds to my ten;
   That a maid I will go to yon merry, green broom,
   And a maid I will boldly return."

4. Now when that she came to this merry green broom,
   Found her true love was fast in a sleep,
   With a fine finished rose, and a new suit of clothes,
   And a bunch of green broom at his feet.

5. Then three times she went from the crown of his head,
   And three times from the sole of his feet,

[342]

And three times she kissed his red, rosy cheeks
As he layed fast in a sleep.

6. Then she took a gold ring from off her hand,
And put that on his right thumb,
And that was to let her true love to know
That she had been there and was gone.

7. As soon as he had awoke from his sleep,
Found his true love had been there and was gone;
It was then he remembered upon the cost,
When he thought of the wager he'd lost.

8. Then three times he called for his horse and his man,
The horse that he'd once bought so dear;
Saying, "Why didn't you wake me out of my sleep
When my lady, my true love, was here?"

9. "Three times did I call to you, master,
And three times did I blow with my horn;
But out of your sleep I could not awake,
Till your lady, your true love, was gone."

10. "Had I been awake when my true love was here,
Of her I would had my will;
If not the pretty birds in this merry green broom,
With her blood they should all had their fill."

GROUP E

21. "The Bonny Green Woods"

Robinson, *JFSS*, IV (1911), pp. 110-11. Sung by Anne
Hiles, a servant girl, Kirton in Lindsey, Lincolnshire,
March 1904.

p I

Miss Broadwood compares this with Sussex versions of "The Bailiff's
Daughter" (105); and with "Sweet William's Ghost" (77) and "The
Collier Laddie" in the *SMM* (Nos. 363 and 361); also with "The
Young Maxwell" (Hogg, *Jacobite Relics*, II, 1821, p. 32), and with
"The Seeds of Love" in some variants.

1. A gentleman to a young lady said
"I'll bet you five hundred to one,
That a maid you go down to yon bonny green wood side,
But a maid you'll not return back again."

2. "I'll bet you the same," the young lady said,
"And the money I'll freely lay down,
That a maid I'll go to yon bonny green woods,
And a maid I'll return back again."

3. Then she mixed him a glass of something so strong,
He thought it had been some wine,
And when he got down to yon bonny green woods
The sleep it came into his mind.

4. And when she got down to yon bonny green wood-side,
Her lover he lie fast asleep,
With his hare and his hounds in silk and satin gowns,
And his ribbons hanging down to his feet.

5. Three times she walked round the crown of his head,
And twice around the soles of his feet,
And three times she kissed his cherry, cherry cheeks
As he lied on the ground fast asleep.

6. She pulled off her finger her best diamond ring,
And pressed it in her lover's right hand.
That was to let him know when he awakened out of sleep,
That his lady had been, but was gone.

7. When he awakened out of his sleep
So well a well-awakened was he,
He turned his face towards yon bonny, bonny broom,
And wept most bitterly.

8. "Oh where hast thou been to, my bonny greyhound?
And why did you stay away so long?
And why did you not awaken me out of sleep
Since the maiden has been but she's gone?"

9. "It's three times I tapped at your silk and satin robe,
And twice I groaned so loudly,
But I could not awaken you out of sleep,
Since the lady has been, but she's gone."

10. "If I only had her fast in my arms
And I could but have my will,
All the birds in the wood should drink of her blood
Until they had all had their fill."

22. [The Merry Broomfield]

Hammond, *JFSS*, VII (1923), pp. 31(1)-32. Sung by Mrs.
Perry, Cheddington, Dorset, June 1906.

p M (inflected VII)

1. It's of a Lord in the North Countrie,
He courted a lady gay;
As they were riding side by side
A wager she did lay.

2. "I'll bet to you five hundred pounds,
Five hundred pounds to one,
That a maid I will go to a merry green wood
And a maid I will return."

3. When she arrived to a merry green wood
   Her love lay fast asleep,
   With a grey nag and a silver saddle on
   And a greyhound under his feet.

4. Three times she rode around his head,
   Six times around his feet,
   Nine times she kissed his cherry, cherry cheek
   As he lay fast asleep.

5. She took the ring off her right hand,
   Put it on his left hand,
   To let him know she had a-been there—
   And so quickly gone again.

6. When he woke out of his sleep
   The birds began to sing,
   Saying "Awake, wake, awake, Master!
   Your true love's gone again!"

7. "I wish my love was back again,
   Was back again!" he cried [cried he]
   "Then all the birds of the merry green wood
   Should have their fill of she!"

23. "A Wager, A Wager"

Vaughan Williams, *JFSS*, IV (1911), p. 114(5). Sung by Mrs. Powell, near Weobley, Herefordshire, August 1910.

a D

Miss Broadwood calls attention to "The Pretty Ploughboy" (*JFSS*, II, p. 146; IV, pp. 303-8; VIII, p. 268). Again, it is worth citing "The Mermaid" from Calcott, "The Child's Own Singing Book," 1843 (reprinted in John Goss, *Ballads of Britain*, 1937, p. 136), for an interesting variant.

24. [Broomfield Wager]

Sharp MSS., 568/644. Also, as "The Broomfield Hill," in Sharp, *JFSS*, IV (1910), pp. 112(3). Sung by Mrs. Mary Anne Milton, Washford, August 17, 1905.

a D (inflected VI)

He pulled rings off his fingers
And put 'em on my right hand
To let 'em all to know he had a-been there,
He had a-been there and was gone.

O that will be too long for me,
O that will be too long,
My heart it will [burst and burst?]* it must
If you should stay so long.

This commences with the commonplace but perennially effective formula of "The Bailiff's Daughter" (105) and other favorites.

It's a cold winter's night, it's a cold winter's night,
It's a cold winter's night unto.
I oftentimes wished her in my arms
For fear of the foggy dew.

* brust and give?
The second and third stanzas are scraps of other songs.

APPENDIX

25. "The Sea Captain"

Mackenzie, 1928, p. 394(19A); text, pp. 74-75. Sung by Mrs. James Campbell, River John, Pictou County, Nova Scotia.

m M

1. It was of a sea captain that followed the sea.
      Let the winds blow high or blow low O.
   "I shall die, I shall die," the sea captain did cry,
      "If I don't get that maid on the shore O,
      If I don't get that maid on the shore."

2. This captain had jewels, this captain had gold,
      This captain had costly a ware O.
   And all he would give to this pretty fair maid,
      If she'd please take a sail from the shore O,
      If she'd please take a sail from the shore.

3. With great persuasions they got her on board,
      The weather being fine and clear O.
   She sang so sweet, so neat and complete,
      That she sang all the seamen to sleep O,
      That she sang all the seamen to sleep.

4. She took all his jewels, she took all his gold,
      She took all his costly a ware O.
   She took his broadsword to make her an oar,
      And she paddled her way to the shore O,
      And she paddled her way to the shore.

5. "O were my men mad or were my men drunk,
    Or were my men deep in despair O,
To let her away with her beauty so gay
To roam all alone on the shore O,
To roam all alone on the shore?"

6. "Your men were not mad, your men were not drunk,
    Your men were not deep in despair O.
I deluded your men as well as yourself.
I'm a maid again on the shore O,
I'm a maid again on the shore!"

26. "The Fair Maid by the Seashore"

Barry, 1939, pp. 40-41. Sung by Mrs. Annie V. Marston,
Charlestown, Maine.

a M

See, in this connection, Barry's long note in *BFSSNE*, No. 7 (1934),
pp. 12-13, where are further references.

1. There was a fair lady far crossed in love,
    Far crossed in love, as it were, O;
Nothing could she find,
To ease her fair mind,
    Than to stray all along the sea shore, O,
    Than to stray all along the sea shore!

2. There was a sea captain a-ploughing the deep,
    A-ploughing the deep as it were, O;
Nothing could he find,
To ease his sad mind,
    Than to sail all along the sea shore, O,
    Than to sail all along the sea shore!

3. "I shall die, I shall die," the sea captain he cried,
    "If I don't get that lady so fair, O!
What will I not give
To my jolly seamen,
    If they'll bring that fair damsel on board, O,
    If they'll bring that fair damsel on board!

4. "O, I have got silver, and I have got gold,
    And I have got costly a ware, O;
All these I will give
To my jolly seamen,
    If they'll bring this fair damsel on board, O,
    If they'll bring this fair damsel on board!"

5. With many persuasions she came on board,
    The captain he welcomed her there, O;
He welcomed her down
To the cabin below,
    Saying, "Fare thee well, sorrow and care, O!"
    Saying, "Fare thee well, sorrow and care!"

6. She sang him a song, it was at his request,
    She sang it so sweet and so fair, O,
She sang it so sweet,
So neat and complete,
    That she sang the sea-captain to sleep, O,
    That she sang the sea-captain to sleep!

7. Then she robbed him of silver, she robbed him of gold,
    She robbed him of costly a ware, O;
And the captain's broadsword
She used for an oar,
    And she paddled her boat to the shore, O,
    And she paddled her boat to the shore!

8. "O, were my men sleeping, or were my men mad,
    Or were my men sunk in despair, O,
That the lady so gay
Should thus run away,
    When the captain he welcomed her there, O,
    When the captain he welcomed her there?"

9. "No, your men were not sleeping, your men were not mad,
    Your men were not sunk in despair, O;
I deluded your crew,
And likewise yourself too,
    And again I'm a maid on the shore, O,
    And again I'm a maid on the shore!"

27. [The Sea Captain; or, The Maid on the Shore]

Karpeles, 1934, I, pp. 30-31. Sung by Mrs. Joanie Ryan,
Stock Cove, Bonavista Bay, Newfoundland, September 18,
1918. Text according to collector's MS.

a M

1. 'Twas of a sea captain 'twas deep in love,
He was deep in despair O;
For I shall die, the sea captain, he cried,
If we don't get this maid from the shore, shore,
If we don't get this maid from the shore.

2. I have silver and I have gold,
I have costly wear O,
And I will buy a jolly ship's crew,
If they'll row me this maid from the shore, shore,
If they'll row me this maid from the shore.

3. With long persuaded they got her on boat, [sic]
   The seas rose calm and clear O.
   She sang so neat, so sweet and complete,
   She sent sailors and captain to sleep.

4. She robbed them of silver, she robbed them of gold,
   And robbed them of costly wear O;
   She took a broad sword instead of an oar,
   And paddled away from the shore.

5. When this man woke and found she was gone,
   He was like a man in despair O.
   He called up his men and commanded a boat
   To row me away for the shore.

6. And this man's not drunk,
   He's not deep in despair.
   She saluted the captain as well as the crew,
   Said: I am a maiden once more on the shore.

28. [The Mermaid]

Joyce, 1909, No. 327, p. 152.

a I

O were my men drunk or were my men mad,
   Or were my men drownèd in care—O,
When they let her escape, which made us all sad?
   And the sailors all wished she was there—O, there,
   And the sailors all wished she was there.

29. "The Maiden Who Dwelt by the Shore"

Greenleaf and Mansfield, 1933, pp. 63-64. Sung by Mrs. Annie Walters, Rocky Harbour, Newfoundland, 1929.

a D

1. 'Twas of a young maiden who lived all alone,
      She lived all alone on the shore, O;
   There was nothing she could find to comfort her mind,
      But to roam all alone on the shore, shore, shore,
      But to roam all alone on the shore.

2. It was of a young captain who sailed the salt sea,
      Let the wind blow high or low, O,
   "I will die, I will die," the young captain did cry,
      "If I don't get that maid on the shore, shore, shore,
      If I don't get that maid on the shore.

3. "I have lots of silver, I have lots of gold,
      I have lots of costly wear, O;
   I'll divide, I'll divide with my jolly ship's crew,
      If they'll row me that maid from the shore, shore, shore,
      If they'll row me that maid from the shore."

4. After long persuadence they got her on board,
      Let the winds blow high or low, O,
   Where he placed her a chair in his cabin below;
      "Here's adieu to all sorrows and care, care, care,
      Here's adieu to all sorrows and care."

5. Where he placed her a chair in his cabin below,
      Let the winds blow high or blow low, O,
   She sung charming and sweet, she sung neat and complete,
      She sung captain and sailors to sleep, sleep, sleep,
      She sung captain and sailors to sleep.

6. She robbed him of silver, she robbed him of gold,
      She robbed him of costly wear, O,
   And she stole his broadsword, instead of an oar,
      And she paddled her way to the shore, shore, shore,
      And she paddled her way to the shore.

7. "My men must be crazy, my men must be mad,
      My men must been deep in despair, O,
   To let her go 'way, with her beauty so gay,
      And paddle her way to the shore, shore, shore,
      And paddle her way to the shore."

8. "Your men was not crazy, your men was not mad,
      Your men was not deep in despair, O;
   I deluded the sailors as well as yourself;
      I'm a maiden again on the shore, shore, shore,
      I'm a maiden again on the shore."

30. "The Sea Captain"

Karpeles, 1934, I, p. 36. Sung by James Day, Fortune Harbour, Notre Dame Bay, Newfoundland, 1929-30. Text from Collector's MS.

m Æ/D

1. It's of a sea captain that ploughs the salt seas,
      Where the seas they were calm, fine and clear,
   A beautiful damsel I chanced for to spy,
      A-walking along on the shore, shore,
      A-walking along on the shore.

2. O what will I give to my sailors so bold,
Ten guineas I vow and declare,
If you'll fetch me that lady on board of my ship,
That walks all alone on the shore, etc.

3. The sailors they hoisted out a very long boat
And then to the shore they did steer.
Saying: Ma'am if you please will you enter on board
And view a fine cargo of ware.

4. I have no money, the lady replied,
For to buy such costly ware.
Don't never mind that now, the sailors replied.
We'll trust you till you get on shore.

5. She sat herself down in the stern of the boat
And straight to the ship they did steer,
And when they arrived alongside of the ship,
The captain he ordered a chair, for her,
The captain he ordered a chair.

6. She sat herself down in the stern of the ship
Where the seas they were fine, calm and clear.
She sang the sea captain and his crew asleep,
And her conjuring voice didn't spare, I declare,
And her conjuring voice didn't spare.

7. She loaded herself up with riches so great
And all such costly wear.
The captain's broadsword she took for an oar
And she paddled away to the shore.

The Twa Magicians

CHILD NO. 44

ONLY two British texts of this interesting ballad appear to have been recorded, although it is claimed to have been heard more than once within recent memory (cf. Barry, Eckstorm, and Smyth, 1929, pp. 442ff.). One of the texts is Scottish, of the first quarter of the last century; the other English, picked up at Minehead in 1904. At first glance, the two appear very different. The Northern text is in ordinary ballad quatrains, with a four-line burden that first appears after the sixth quatrain, changes textually after the eleventh, but persists after every stanza to the end. The Southern text appears quite irregular: after a single quatrain there comes a passage of some dozen lines (or fewer, according to personal judgment) in irregular lengths and with very infrequent rhymes. Then follows another quatrain, the first line of which is short by a foot; then the irregular burden (if it may so be termed) recurs entire; then another quatrain, again short in the first line; then the burden; another quatrain, again short; and again the long burden.

In spite of the formal difference, the English song appears to me (contrary to the editors of *British Ballads from Maine*) to have been derived either from Buchan's text or from a very close variant of it; to have been set to a comparatively modern tune which gradually acquired a considerable amount of re-adjustment in accordance with the textual changes in the course of oral transmission. Unfortunately, we lack Buchan's tune, so that no comparisons are possible, except by inference. If Buchan's text was sung as it stands, the burden would have to go to the same tune as the stanza. This it could perfectly well do, since the only metrical difference is that its first line is short by *one foot*—the same difference we have noted between Sharp's first and succeeding stanzas. All that is musically required by way of adaptation is for the last note or syllable of the first phrase to be given extra length, to compensate for the missing foot. Many instances of this practice could be cited.

Assume, then, for Buchan a four-phrase tune of the ordinary ballad sort, with possibly a second strain which was little other than a variant form of the tune, but the first phrase of which was slightly altered, the better to accommodate a three-stress line. Our affair is to determine how Sharp's form of the ballad may have developed from these materials. Before we examine the tune, it will be best to compare the texts. Two observations are in order here. The first is that Buchan's text is in a much sounder state than Sharp's, being fuller, more regular, heedful of rhymes, and generally more resourceful. Sharp's text is much inferior, both logically, technically, and in narrative interest. There is nothing in Sharp that has not appeared already in Buchan, and with greater effectiveness; there is a good deal in Buchan which is not in Sharp, including five additional trans-formations on the part of hero and heroine. Buchan is more than twice as long as Sharp. The second thing to be noted is that Sharp's overgrown burden is not, as to text, properly a burden at all. It contains an essential part of the narrative, coming most fittingly at a particular point in time, and entail-ing some awkwardness in later repetition. Its content finds a place among Buchan's regular stanzas. But it is notable that, after the first occurrence of the so-called burden in Sharp, the regular stanzas fall into the shorter pattern which characterizes the real burden in Buchan. As the song is sung, it almost comes to seem as if the later stanzas were the burden, and the burden the main substance.

The following are the textual parallels, with Sharp's burden treated as stanzaic material, the irregularities lopped off. The position of one stanza in Buchan has been shifted to correspond with Sharp:

Buchan

(1) The lady stands in her bower-door
    As straight as willow wand;
    The blacksmith stood a little forebye,
    Wi hammer in his hand.

(3) 'Awa, awa, ye coal-black smith,
    Woud ye do me the wrang
    To think to gain my maidenhead,
    That I hae kept sae lang!

(5) 'I'd rather I were dead and gone,
    And my body laid in grave,
    Ere a rusty stock o coal-black smith
    My maidenhead shoud have.'

(Burden)
    O bide, lady, bide,
    And aye he bade her bide;
    The rusty smith your leman shall be,
    For a' your muckle pride.

Sharp

(1) O she look'd out of the window,
    As white as any milk,
    But he look'd into the window,
    As black as any silk.

(Burden)
    'Hulloa, hulloa . . . you coal-black smith,
    You have done me no harm;
    You never shall have my maiden-name
    That I have kept so long:

(Burden)
    I'd rather die a maid . . . she said,
    And be buried all in my grave,
    Than I'd have such a nasty . . . coal-black smith,
    My maiden-name shall die.'

[348]

(9) Then she became a duck, a duck,
    To puddle in a peel,
And he became a rose-kaimd drake,
    To gie the duck a dreel.
      O bide, lady, bide, &c.

(10) She turnd hersell into a hare,
    To rin upon yon hill,
And he became a gude grey-hound,
    And boldly he did fill.
      O bide, lady, bide, &c.

(7) Then she became a turtle dow,
    To fly up in the air,
And he became another dow,
    And they flew pair and pair.
      O bide, lady, bide, &c.

(2) Then she became a duck,
    A duck all on the stream,
And he became a water-dog
    And fetch'd her back again.
      Hulloa, hulloa, &c.

(3) Then she became a hare,
    A hare upon the plain,
And he became a grey-hound dog,
    And fetch'd her back again.
      Hulloa, hulloa, &c.

(4) Then she became a fly,
    A fly all in the air,
And he became a spídér
    And fetch'd her to his lair.
      Hulloa, hulloa, &c.

The Sharp version will probably be felt to look like a somewhat enfeebled imitation of the other, with occasional substitutions in image and rhyme-word where the earlier text has been forgotten or has not been understood. Thus *harm* supplies the place of *wrong* to rhyme with *long*; and *die* fills the place of *have*, to rhyme with *grave*, because *have* has just occurred. *Stream* takes the place of the Scots form of "pool" (*peel*); and *dreel* not being understood, the rhyme is abandoned for an attempted assonance. The water-dog is borrowed with the line following from the next stanza, probably out of forgetfulness, or because *rose-combed* was too poetic to stick and the drake was anyhow acting obscurely in the next line. Similarly, *dow* not being understood and *fly* being supplied in the next line, a fly pursued by a spider is nearly inevitable, and the tetrameter shall halt for it. It is significant of a connection that identical rhymes, or traces thereof, appear at corresponding points in the two versions.

We must now try to account for the asymmetrical burden, and the parallel musical aberration, in Sharp. The burden as it now occurs in the tune is as follows:

Hulloa, hulloa, hulloa, hulloa, you coal-black smith,
    You have done me no harm;
You never shall have my maiden-name [*sic* in the MS.]
    That I have kept so long:
I'd rather die a maid, yes, but then she said,
    And be buried all in my grave
Than I'd have such a nasty, husky, dusky, musty,
              fusky, coal-black smith,
My maiden-name shall die.

The line-adjustment here is unauthorized: it has been adopted to enforce the fact revealed by the parallel above, that this matter is really stanzaic, all the alternate lines preserving their stanzaic length, but losing their rhymes as we have seen. The long lines, all but one, have become hypermetrical in varying degrees. The first appears to have been carried beyond itself by an excess of exuberance, and so also with the last. The first has been prolonged to the seven-stress length of two phrases, which will make an extra, short phrase in the tune at that point, and will need fitting into place as plausibly as may be. The last is prolonged just for hearty fun and will cause no embarrassment to the tune, for cumulative songs have familiarized folk-singers with the trick of adding as many repetitive bars of the same figure as serve the needs of the occasion. It is no more than holding the phonograph needle in the same groove for a couple of extra revolutions. The musical phrase can therefore be reduced to its true dimensions by simply dropping out the excess. The remaining hypermetrical line is just too short for a full half-quatrain, but quite too long to be crowded into four stresses or be ignored. We may therefore expect here a visible irregularity in the musical vehicle, which must be cut away if we wish to restore the tune to the regularity of its quatrain form.

The assumption here has been that these irregularities are in the main owing to rhetorical, verbal, causes—a matter of pulling a tune's just phrases this way and that to accommodate particular textual requirements. (On the other hand, the seven-stress—rather than five- or six-stress—length of the first line is in response also to the needs of the music.) Interacting forces of this kind are generally operative in folk-song as far back as we can bring actual evidence to bear. It might, on the contrary, be possible to argue that the lawless and free tune was the primitive condition out of which the regular stanzaic phrases were gradually refined as the musical stuff cooled and the slag was poured off. Such an argument would carry along with it the corollary that Sharp's text is really an earlier development than Buchan's more poetic, elaborate, and evolved piece, and Buchan could once again be stigmatized as a vile poetaster. Or the case could be used to demonstrate the so-called "epic process," hypothesized, but perhaps never observed as part of the action of tradition upon ballads. These opportunities are open to any one; but the task of persuading will be difficult, and I beg to be excused. I am the more confirmed in positing a precedent regularity by the fact that the stuff of Sharp's tune for this ballad seems to have been mined from the same vein as "An old woman poor and blind"—a tune enormously popular at the beginning of the eighteenth century, used with various broadside ballads, and in ballad-operas, and printed at least three times, to different texts, in D'Urfey's *Pills*. [Cf. Chappell, II, pp. 551ff. for references.] It was sung in both major and minor variants, and had generally two strains, thus accommodating two regular ballad quatrains.

As to the subject-matter of the present ballad, Child has called it "a base-born cousin of a pretty ballad known over all Southern Europe, and elsewhere (as among the Slavs), but in especially graceful forms in France." Without wishing to take issue with the master, one may observe that "base-born" is rather a moral or aesthetic, than a historical, judgment. At least one would assume that a form of the ballad in which magic was powerfully practiced was more primitive than one in which the magic was restricted to the limits of a play of fancy, or to poetic wishes, as it is in most of the Continental variants which Child cites. Child does not make the observation—though his placing the ballad next to two riddling ballads would suggest it—that in the latter guise the ballad allies itself with those contests in which opponents match wits in proposing equal impossibilities or solving each other's challenging questions in order to gain, or evade, a desired, or unwelcome, mate.

It is very probable that a song familiar in the West of England, and known in Ireland and New England, collected by Cecil Sharp under the name "Hares on the Mountains," is a derivative of this ballad. Magic has been rationalized out of existence, and along with it has gone the narrative element. Instead of these, we have a series of conditional statements expressing the idea that no matter what form the girls might take, the men would pursue and find them out. All the variants that I have seen are in triple time and seem at least distantly related. Sharp gathered five copies of this song and four copies of the closely related "Sally, my Dear." Of the latter, only the concluding stanzas pertain to the radical idea.

LIST OF VARIANTS

1. "The Two Magicians." Sharp MSS., 276/383, Clare College Library, Cambridge. Also, as "The Coal-Black Smith," in Cecil J. Sharp, *JFSS*, II (1905), p. 50; Cecil J. Sharp and Charles L. Marson, *Folk Songs from Somerset*, 1904, pp. 38-39; Cecil J. Sharp, *One Hundred English Folksongs* [1916], pp. 48-49; and in Sharp, *English Folksongs*, Selected Ed., Novello & Co., 1920. (Sparks)

APPENDIX—GROUP A

2. "Hares on the Mountains." Sharp MSS., 9/16. Also in Sharp and Marson, 1904, pp. 20-21; in Sharp [1916], pp. 142-43; and in Sharp, 1920. (Hooper, White)
3. "Hares on the Mountains." Sharp MSS., 925/. (Bailey)
4. "If fair maids was hares." Barry Collection, tr. MS. Bk. IV, No. 76, Harvard College Library.
5. "Hares on the Mountains." Sharp MSS., 274/. (Slade)

6. "Hares on the Mountains." Sharp MSS., 729/. (Small)
7. "Hares on the Mountains." Sharp MSS., 253/351. (Lock)
8. "If all the young maidens were blackbirds and thrushes." George Petrie, *The Complete Petrie Collection of Irish Music*, edited by Charles Villiers Stanford, 1902-5, No. 821.

GROUP B

9. "Sally my Dear." Sharp MSS., 933/. (Balsh)
10. "Sally my Dear." Sharp MSS., 1266/. (Harding)
11. "Sally, my Dear." Sharp MSS., 1129/1131. (Davis)
12. "O Sally, my Dear." Sharp MSS., 891/960. Also in Sharp and Marson, *Folk Songs from Somerset*, 3rd series, 1906, pp. 60-61; and Sharp, *One Hundred English Folk Songs* [1916], pp. 144-45. (Barnett)

TUNES WITH TEXTS

1. [The Two Magicians]

Sharp MSS., 276/383-84. Also, as "The Coal-Black Smith," in Sharp, *JFSS*, II (1905), p. 50; Sharp and Marson, 1904, pp. 38-39; and Sharp [1916], pp. 48-49. Sung by Mr. Sparks, a blacksmith, Minehead, August 8, 1904.

a I

O she looked out of the window
As white as any milk.
But he looked into the window
As black as any silk.
 Hulloa, hulloa, hulloa, hulloa,
 You coal-black smith!
 You have done me no harm.
 You never shall change my maiden name
 That I have kept so long.
 I'd rather die a maid,
 Yes, but then, she said,
 And be buried all in my grave
 Than I'd have such a nasty,
 Husky, dusky, musty, fusky
 Coal-black smith
 A maiden I will die.*

Then she became a duck
A duck all on the stream.
And he became a water-dog
And fetched her back again.
 Hulloa, &c.

Then she became a hare,
A hare upon the plain.
And he became a greyhound dog
And fetched her back again.
 Hulloa, &c.

O she look'd out of the win-dow as white as an-y milk,— But he look'd in-to the win-dow as black as an-y silk.— "Hul-loa, hul-loa, hul-loa, hul-loa, you coal-black smith! You have done me no harm;— You nev-er shall have my maid-en name that I have kept so long:— I'd rath-er die a maid, Yes!" but then she said, "And be bur-ied all in my grave— Than I'd have such a nas-ty, husk-y, dusk-y, must-y, fusk-y coal-black-smith,— My maid-en name shall die.

Then she be-came a duck,— A duck all on the stream,— And he be-came a wa-ter-dog And fetched her back a-gain.—

Then she became a fly,
A fly all in the air.
And he became a spider
And fetched her to his lair.
 Hulloa, &c.

* Sharp, *JFSS*: "My maiden name shall die."

2. [Hares on the Mountains]

Sharp MSS., 9/16. Also in Sharp and Marson, 1904, pp. 20-21; and Sharp [1916], pp. 142-43. Sung by Mrs. Louie Hooper and Mrs. Lucy White, Hambridge, September 1903.

m I

The original is in F.

Young women they'll run like hares on the mountains,
Young women they'll run like hares on the mountains.
If I were but a young man, I'd soon go a-hunting,
　　To my right fol diddle dero, To my right fol diddle dee.

Young women they sing like birds in the bushes,
Young women they sing like birds in the bushes.
If I was a young man, I'd go and bang the bushes,
　　To my right fol diddle dero, To my right fol diddle dee.

Young women they'll swim like ducks in the water,
Young women they'll swim like ducks in the water.
If I was a young man, I'd go and swim all after,
　　To my right fol diddle dero, To my right fol diddle dee.

3. "Hares on the Mountains"

Sharp MSS., 925/. Sung by William Bailey (60), Cannington, April 20, 1906.

p I

Young women they run like hares on the mountains
Young women they run like hares on the mountains
If I was a young man I'd soon go a hunting
Right fal the dal Right fal the dal Right fal the dal I dee.

4. [If fair maids was hares]

Barry Coll., tr. MS. Bk. IV, No. 76. Sung by Mrs. Sarah Carson, Boston, Mass., March 21, 1908; learned in County Tyrone.

a I/Ly (– VI)

If fair maids was hares, they'd run o'er the mountains,
If fair maids was hares, they'd run o'er the mountains,
Young men to be hounds, they would soon follow after
　　To me fol the deedle lol tol lol lol tol lol lee.

If fair maids was thrushes, they would sit on yon bushes,
If fair maids was thrushes, they would sit on yon bushes,
Young men to be blackbirds, they would break down their
　　　　　　　　　　　　　　　　　　　　branches,
　　To me fol the deedle lol tol lol lol tol lol lee.

5. "Hares on the Mountains"

Sharp MSS., 274/. Sung by Mrs. Slade, Minehead, August 8, 1904.

a I

Young women they sing like birds on the bushes
But if I was a young man I'd go and shake the bushes
Sing fal de dal ri fal de dal
Sing fal the dal the diddle dal de dee

6. "Hares on the Mountains"

Sharp MSS., 729/. Sung by Mrs. Eliza Small, Langport, December 30, 1905.

p I

If girls go swim like ducks on the water
All those young men will soon follow after
Sing Fal lal the diddle lal lal the diddle
    fal lal di dee

7. "Hares on the Mountains"

Sharp MSS., 253/351. Sung by Mrs. Lock, Muchelney Ham, August 2, 1904.

p I

If all those young men were as rushes a-growing,
Then all those pretty maidens will get scythes go mowing
[With Ri fol de dee Cal all the day Ri fol eye dee.]

If all those young men were as hares on the mountains
Then all those pretty maidens will get guns go a hunting

If all those young men were as ducks in the water
Then all those pretty maidens would soon follow after.

Note: The refrain is supplied from the tune-book MS.

GROUP B

9. [Sally my Dear]

Sharp MSS., 933/. Sung by Mrs. Balsh (66), Ubley, April 23, 1906.

a I

8. [If all the young maidens were blackbirds and thrushes]

Petrie, 1902-5, No. 821.

a D

'Pretty Polly my dear, shall I come up to see you?'
She laugh and reply, 'I'm afraid you'll undo me.'
Sing fal the diddle daddle i-day.

10. [Sally my Dear]

Sharp MSS., 1266/. Sung by James Harding, Stow-on-the-Wold, March 2, 1907.

a I/M

Sharp did not take down the words. There may be a dittograph in the bracketed notes.

11. "Sally my Dear"

Sharp MSS., 1129/1131. Sung by William Davis (76), Porlock Weir, September 7, 1906.

p I

With the music:

O Sally my dear will you come up to me
O Sally my dear will you come up to me
She laughed and replied I'm afraid you'll undo me
    Right fal the dal dal fal the dal dal
    Riddle diddle al the dee.

In the text-book as follows:

If young women could build like Blackbirds & Thrushes
There's many a young man would soon find out the nestes [*sic*]

[If young women could] swim like fishes in water
[There's many a young man would] strip & swim after

[If young women could] fly like birds in the air
[There's many a young man would] cock and let fire.

The variants are from the 1916 edition.

12. "O Sally, my Dear"

Sharp MSS., 891/960. Also in Sharp and Marson, 3rd series, 1906, pp. 60-61; and Sharp, [1916], pp. 144-45. Sung by John Barnett, Bridgwater, April 16, 1906.

a Æ/D

With the music:

O Sally my dear shall I come up to see you
O Sally my dear shall I come up to see you
She laugh & reply I'm afraid you'll undo me
 Sing fal the diddle i-do Sing whack fal the diddle day.

6. If blackbirds was blackbirds as thrushes was thrushes
 If blackbirds was blackbirds as thrushes was thrushes
 How soon the young men would go beating the bushes.
  Sing fal the diddle i do, Sing whack fal the diddle day.

7. Should young women be hares and race round the mountain
 Should young women be hares and race round the mountain
 Young men (would) take guns and they'd soon go a-hunting
  Sing fal the diddle i do, Sing whack fal the diddle day.

8. Should young women be ducks and should swim round the ocean
 Should young women be ducks and should swim round the ocean
 Young men would turn drakes and soon follow after.
  Sing fal the diddle i do, Sing whack fal the diddle day.

King John and the Bishop

CHILD NO. 45

THE stuff of this ballad, as Child's introduction makes very clear, is out of the storehouse of tradition. On the other hand, Child's parallels—an impressive array—are almost wholly drawn from *tales* both popular and literary. The earlier we get in the English records, the less does the ballad resemble traditional verse. Neither is there any later traditional form which I have seen that has shaken clear of its broadside associations. Here, then, we have a ballad that may have started its career, as a ballad, in close connection with writing, and that was refashioned and reprinted for broadside dissemination at frequent intervals, probably from the time of Elizabeth down to the nineteenth century. So far as we know, it never took hold in Scotland (although Child mentions a Faroe version of the nineteenth century), and its strongest lease on life has been where it could renew its forces by contact with the mother press.

There seems, then, no hope of working back toward an "uncontaminated" traditional ballad, and in this case external form is no determinant of purity. The various seventeenth-century broadsides, however, are directed to be sung to three different tunes, depending on the copy. The names of the tunes are "The Shaking of the Sheets," "Chievy-Chase," and "The King and the Lord Abbot." At best, then, we may infer that the makers of various versions of the ballad had one or another of these specific tunes in mind to guide them in shaping their stanzas. There is no cheat about this, because the tunes are of easily distinguishable patterns, and the texts in each case do go to the tunes designated—albeit stumblingly. Seventeenth-century variants of all three tunes are extant.

An attempt to determine the relative age of these tunes from external evidence will not lead to positive conclusions, nor enable us to fix the priority of the textual tradition. It is true that a song of "The Hunttis of Chevet" is mentioned in c. 1549, and we may assume that that ballad was a good deal older. But the earliest extant text of it has a disconcerting way of shifting from CM to LM; we have no equally early record of the proper tune; and, anyway, it need not be inferred that the earlier copies of "The King and the Bishop" (or "Abbot") were sung to the tune—any tune—of "Chevy Chase." (The tune best known as "Chevy Chase," employed in vulgar balladry *ad nauseam* in the seventeenth and eighteenth centuries, seems previously to have been called by the name of "Flying Fame," and was therefore probably borrowed for the use that gave it its common title: but it held its accustomed shape with a most wearisome persistence, and provides us with no clue to the present purpose.)

"The Shaking of the Sheets" is likewise old, and references to it are common in the second half of the sixteenth century. As a ballad-tune it would appear to have had an earlier vogue than the other. Moreover, "The Shaking of the Sheets," besides the fact that there are two distinct tunes of that name, became modified in the course of years almost out of recognition. The earliest extant copy (c. 1600) may be the one in William Ballet's lutebook (in tablature), in Trinity College, Dublin. This is a variant form of the tune printed in the Appendix to Hawkins' *History of Music* (reproduced below). The most striking thing about this tune, superficially considered, is that its two halves do not balance in length, being eight bars (i.e., four repeated) against six. The six bars break into three equal phrases, all with the same cadence. The tune thus has to modern ears a

curious, unfinished effect. Moreover, it must carry an odd number of lines of text. This textual problem is solved with a rhyming quatrain followed by three lines rhyming together. The inconvenience of the pattern seems to have been felt, because the tune was later modified to accommodate an ordinary double quatrain.

The other tune known as "The Shaking of the Sheets," or "The Night-Peece," makes its first known appearance in Playford's *Dancing Master*, 1650. As it is there printed, it will accommodate ten lines of CM text. But its second part is printed out in a triple repetition, and the last of the three may have been simply to fill out the stave. When danced, there was no necessary limit to the number of repetitions; but as a song the tune has properly four phrases, or eight if each half is sung twice. This tune, it will be apparent, does not go to the form of our ballad which is directed to be sung to "The Shaking of the Sheets." Neither, by the same token, does it go to the broadside texts of "The Dance of Death," although Chappell, by forcing dactyls into an iambic rhythm and repeating the last line without authority, has arbitrarily compelled it to serve in that capacity. Both in the venturesome and unusual stanza-form and in the archaic character of the tune, the song belongs to the sixteenth century, if not before. To find it printed late in the seventeenth century is to infer Elizabethan copies of the same pattern and to suggest a reason for remodeling in a newer mode. This form of the ballad, then, entitled "The Old Abbot and King Olfrey," although in the least popular vein of any, may be with some confidence assigned to a date as early as that of the more "popular" types.

The third tune remains to be considered. This is "The King and the Lord Abbot," a tune which is indicated for singing with the form of the ballad chosen by Child as his B-text. The broadsides of this type are entitled "A *new* Ballad of King John and the Abbot of Canterbury." From the adjective Child infers an older ballad, now lost. We need not grant too much weight to the adjective, either way, since the broadside press was utterly unscrupulous in its claims. If an Elizabethan ballad was printed as "a new ballad," a Restoration reprint was quite likely to repeat the phrase. Nevertheless, Child's assumption is in this case perhaps supported by the name of the tune, which is hardly suggested by the accompanying text. "To its own tune" would be the ordinary direction if text and tune had grown up together. The ballads of type B have a different stanza-form from the others, a four-line dactylic (= anapaestic) tetrameter pattern rhyming in couplets, followed by an end-refrain of "Derry down, down hey, derry down." This scheme entails a different musical vehicle. Since the latter cannot be a variant of either "Chevy Chase" or "The Shaking of the Sheets," it is reasonable to identify it with the tune which appears in various forms almost as early as the B texts, is printed with a B text by D'Urfey, and is for the next two hundred years generally used and known as "The Abbot of Canterbury." In spite of a great deal of superficial change, this tune has kept its basic outline with noteworthy fidelity, and there is no reason to suppose its earlier forms were very different. If, then, our B-text is really a rewriting, it is justifiable to infer a parent text used with previous variants of the same tune, and therefore having the same textual pattern. How far back this tune might go is hard to guess, but it cries sib to "Greensleeves" and "Packington's Pound," both characteristically Elizabethan.

Child's A-text is taken from the Percy Folio. There is nothing but the date of the MS. (c. 1640) to put it before the broadsides, except its length and perhaps greater elegance. The style of it is certainly not more "popular" than that of B, and it sounds copied from earlier print or manuscript. There is no indication of a tune to go with it, but the fact is worth mentioning that as it stands—without any refrain—it is the only version that will sing at all to the second tune of "The Shaking of the Sheets." The latter appears in Playford's *Dancing Master*, 1650, as "The Night Piece," and is reprinted by Chappell, I, p. 84. It might be corroborative of this possibility that eight of the ballad's thirty-eight stanzas (or nine of thirty-seven, if a two-line stanza be attached to its predecessor) have an additional couplet, and, as Playford's printing of this tune demonstrates, these would be absorbed with perfect ease by the tune's

expansibility—a fact not equally true of the other tunes for this ballad. If this tune is later than the other, as it sounds, and if this text was ever sung to it, we might take the folio copy as representing an intermediate stage in the ballad's development, between the types of "The old Abbot and King Olfrey" and "The King and the Bishop" in CM. On the other hand, in the absence of definite evidence on the point, it appears almost equally credible that the actual singers of the folio text have been few indeed.

It is at any rate only in the "Derry Down" pattern that the ballad has been perpetuated in traditional singing. In this form it has been found in our own century in the Midlands, and in New England, the Mid-West, and Far West within the last decade. It is perhaps significant of the prevailing Scotch-Irish roots of Appalachian tradition that it does not occur in so large a collection as Sharp's. Thanks to frequent transfusions of printer's ink, its condition is still vigorous wherever it appears; and for its sturdy merit a long succeeding life is still to be hoped.

LIST OF VARIANTS

1. "King John and the Abbot of Canterbury." Thomas D'Urfey, *Wit and Mirth; or, Pills to Purge Melancholy*, 1719-20, IV, pp. 28-31.
2. "King John and the Abbot of Canterbury." Edward F. Rimbault, *Musical Illustrations of Bishop Percy's Reliques of Ancient English Poetry*, 1850, p. 73. Also in William Chappell, *Popular Music of the Olden Time*, I [1855], p. 352.
3. "King John and the Abbot." William Chappell, *A Collection of National English Airs*, 1838-40, II, No. 9b, p. 5.
4. "The Bishop of Canterbury; or, King John." Sidney Robertson, UC/LC Folk-Record 4196 A. (Warde E. Ford)
5. "King John and the Bishop." Emelyn Elizabeth Gardner and Geraldine Jencks Chickering, *Ballads and Songs of Southern Michigan*, 1939, p. 379.
6. "The Abbot of Canterbury." Harvard College Library 25242.64F, fol. 234, (18th c.) broadside, "The Snipe."
7. "King John." Grainger MS., No. 138, New York Public Library, hectograph.
8. "King John and the Abbot; or, Derry Down." Chappell, *A Collection of National English Airs*, 1838-40, II, No. 9a, p. 5. Also in Chappell, *Popular Music of the Olden Time*, I [1855], pp. 350-52; John Watts, *The Musical Miscellany*,

1729-31, VI, p. 136; and Edward F. Rimbault, "Musical Illustrations of the Robin Hood Ballads," in John Mathew Gutch, *A Lytell Geste of Robin Hode, &c.*, 1847, II, p. 442.
9. "King John and the Bishop." Phillips Barry, *JAF*, XXI (1908), pp. 57-58. Also in Phillips Barry, *JAF*, XXII (1909), p. 73.
10. "Derry Down." Helen Hartness Flanders, and others, *The New Green Mountain Songster*, 1939, p. 176.
11. "The King's Three Questions." Helen Hartness Flanders and George Brown, *Vermont Folk-Songs & Ballads*, 1931, pp. 200-3.
12. "The Bishop of Canterbury." Lester A. Hubbard and LeRoy J. Robertson, *JAF*, LXIV (1951), pp. 43-44.

APPENDIX

13. "The shakinge of the sheetes." William Ballet's MS., p. 84. Trinity College, Dublin.
14. "The Shaking of the Shetes." Sir John Hawkins, *History of Music*, 1776, V, p. 469.
15. "The old Abbot and King Olfrey." John Playford, *The English Dancing Master*, 1650, reprinted 1933, p. (3). Also in Chappell, *Popular Music of the Olden Time*, I [1855], p. 85.

TUNES WITH TEXTS

1. [King John and the Abbot of Canterbury]

D'Urfey, 1719-20, IV, pp. 28-31.

m Minor, or D (inflected VII)

1. I'll tell you a Story, a Story anon,
   Of a Noble Prince, and his Name was King *John*;

For he was a Prince, a Prince of great might,
He held up great Wrongs, and he put down great Right,
Derry down, down, hey derry down.

2. I'll tell you a Story, a Story so merry,
Concerning the Abbot of *Canterbury*;
And of his House-keeping and high Renown,
Which made him repair to fair *London* Town.
Derry down, &c.

3. How now, Brother Abbot! 'tis told unto me,
That thou keep'st a far better House than I;
And for thy House-keeping and high Renown,
I fear thou hast Treason against my Crown.
Derry down, &c.

4. I hope my Liege, that you owe me no Grudge,
   For spending of my true gotten Goods;
   If thou dost not answer me Questions Three,
   Thy Head shall be taken from thy Body.
   Derry down, &c.

5. When I am set on my Steed so high,
   With my Crown of Gold upon my Head;
   Amongst all my Nobility, with Joy and much Mirth,
   Thou must tell me to One Penny what I am Worth.
   Derry down, &c.

6. And the next Question you must not flout,
   How long I shall be Riding the World about?
   And the Third Question thou must not shrink,
   But tell to me truly what I do think.
   Derry down, &c.

7. O These are hard Questions for my shallow Wit,
   For I cannot answer your Grace as yet;
   But if you will give me Three days space,
   I'll do my Endeavour to answer your Grace.
   Derry down, &c.

8. O Three Days space I will thee give,
   For that is the longest day thou hast to Live;
   And if thou dost not answer these Questions right,
   Thy Head shall be taken from thy Body quite.
   Derry down, &c.

9. And as the Shepherd was going to his Fold,
   He spy'd the old Abbot come riding along;
   How now Master Abbot, you're welcome home,
   What News have you brought from good King *John.*
   Derry down, &c.

10. Sad News, sad News, I have thee to give,
    For I have but Three Days space for to Live;
    If I do not answer Him Questions Three,
    My Head will be taken from my Body.
    Derry down, &c.

11. When He is set on His Steed so high,
    With His Crown of Gold upon His Head;
    Amongst all His Nobility, with Joy and much Mirth,
    I must tell Him to One Penny what He is worth.
    Derry down, &c.

12. And the next Question I must not flout,
    How long He shall be Riding the World about;
    And the Third Question I must not shrink,
    But tell to Him truly what he does Think.
    Derry down, &c.

13. O Master did you never hear it yet,
    That a Fool may learn a Wise Man Wit?
    Lend me but your Horse and your Apparel,
    I'll ride to fair *London* and answer the Quarrel.
    Derry down, &c.

14. Now I am set on my Steed so high,
    With my Crown of Gold upon my Head;
    Amongst all my Nobility, with Joy and much Mirth,
    Now tell me to One Penny what I am worth.
    Derry down, &c.

15. For Thirty Pence our Saviour was Sold,
    Amongst the false *Jews,* as you have been told;
    And Nine and Twenty's the Worth of Thee,
    For I think thou art One Penny worser than he.
    Derry down, &c.

16. And the next Question thou maist not flout,
    How long I shall be Riding the World about?
    You must Rise with the Sun, and Ride with the same,
    Until the next Morning he Rises again:
    And then I am sure, You will make no doubt,
    But in Twenty Four Hours you'll Ride it about.
    Derry down, &c.

17. And the Third Question thou must not shrink,
    But tell me truly what I do Think?
    All that I can do, and 'twill make your Heart Merry,
    For you think I'm the Abbot of *Canterbury,*
    But I'm his poor Shepherd as you may see,
    And am come to beg Pardon for he and for me.
    Derry down, &c.

18. The King he turn'd him about, and did Smile,
    Saying thou shalt be Abbot the other while;
    O no my Grace, there is no such need,
    For I can neither Write nor Read.
    Derry down, &c.

19. Then Four Pounds a Week will I give unto thee,
    For this merry true Jest thou hast told unto me;
    And tell the old Abbot when thou comest home,
    Thou hast brought him a Pardon from good King *John:*
    Derry down, down, hey derry down.

2. [King John and the Abbot of Canterbury]

Rimbault, 1850, p. 73. Also in Chappell, I [1855], p. 352.

a Æ/D (but inflected VII)

Rimbault says he extracted this tune from a "small oblong common-place book of music," dated on the flyleaf 1697. Presumably this was a MS. Rimbault thinks this an older form than that of the "common versions" of "Derry Down," such as those in the ballad operas (e.g., *The Beggar's Opera,* 1728; *The Village Opera,* 1729; *The Devil to Pay,* 1731; *The Boarding School,* 1733).

An ancient story Ile tell you anon
Of a notable prince, that was called King John;
And he ruled England with maine and with might,
For he did great wrong and maintain'd little right,
Derry down down down derry down.

The text is from Percy's broadside copy, which was amended by selected readings from his Folio MS.

3. [King John and the Abbot]

Chappell, 1838-40, II, No. 9b, p. 5.

a Æ/D

Chappell does not identify the source of this variant.

4. "The Bishop of Canterbury; or, King John"

Robertson, UC/LC Folk-Record 4196 A. Sung by Warde H. Ford, Central Valley, Calif., December 25, 1938; learned from his mother, Mrs. J. C. Ford, Crandon, Wisc.

p I/Ly

The first two phrases are repeated in stanzas 3 and 6 to accommodate the extra lines.

1. A story a story a story anon
   I'll tell unto thee concerning King John
   He had a great mind for to make himself merry
   So he called for the Bishop of Canterbury
   Lol li dol lay, lol li dol luddy, tri ol di dum day.

2. 'Good morning good morning' the old king did say
   'I've called you to ask you questions three
   And if you don't answer them all right
   Your head shall be taken from your body quite'
   Lol li dol lay, lol li dol luddy, tri ol di dum day.

3. 'My first question is and that without doubt
   How long I'll be trav'ling this whole world about
   And the next question is when I set in state
   With my gold crown upon my pate
   And all the nobility joined in great mirth
   You must tell to one penny just what I am worth'
   Lol li dol lay, lol li dol luddy, tri ol di dum day.

4. 'And the last question is and when I do wink
   You must tell to me presently what I do think
   (Next two lines forgotten)
   Lol li dol lay, lol li dol luddy, tri ol di dum day.

5. As the old Bishop was returning home
   He met his young shepherd and him all alone
   'Good morning good morning' the young man did say
   'What news do you bring from the old king today?'
   Lol li dol lay, lol li dol luddy, tri ol di dum day.

6. 'Oh very bad news' the old bishop did say
   'The king has asked me questions three
   And if I don't answer them all right
   My head shall be taken from my body quite'
   Lol li dol lay, lol li dol luddy, tri ol di dum day.

7. 'Well I'm sorry a man of such learning as thee
   Can't go back and answer the king's questions three
   But if you will lend me a suit of apparel
   I'll go to King John and settle the quarrel'
   Lol li dol lay, lol li dol luddy, tri ol di dum day.

8. 'A suit of apparel I freely will give
   And ten thousand pounds as sure as you live'
   And now the young shepherd has gone to King John
   To settle the quarrel that he had begun
   Lol li dol lay, lol li dol luddy, tri ol di dum day.

9. 'Good morning good morning' the young shepherd did say
   'I've called to answer your questions three
   Your first question is and that without doubt
   How long you'll be trav'ling this whole world about
   If you start with the sun and you travel the same
   In twenty-four hours you'll come back again'
   Lol li dol lay, lol li dol luddy, tri ol di dum day.

10. 'The next question is when you sit in state
    With your gold crown upon your pate
    And all the nobility joined in great worth (sic, for mirth)
    I'm to tell to one penny just what you are worth'
    Lol li dol lay, lol li dol luddy, tri ol di dum day.

11. 'For thirty gold pieces our dear Lord was sold
    By those old Jews so brazen and bold
    And for twenty-nine pieces I think you will do
    For I'm sure he was one piece better than you'
    Lol li dol lay, lol li dol luddy, tri ol di dum day.

12. 'The last question is and when you do wink
    I'm to tell to you presently what you do think
    And that I will do if 'twill make your heart merry
    You think I'm the Bishop of Canterbury'
    Lol li dol lay, lol li dol luddy, tri ol di dum day.

13. 'And that I am not as is very well known
    I am his young shepherd and him all alone'
    'Go tell the old Bishop, go tell him for me
    That his young shepherd has outwitted me'
    Lol li dol lay, lol li dol luddy, tri ol di dum day.

5. [King John and the Bishop]

Gardner and Chickering, 1939, p. 379. Sung by Henry R. Vaughan, Detroit, Mich., 1937; learned from his mother, in Vermont.

p I (– VI), ending on III

I'll tell you a story, a story anon,
Of a noble prince, and his name was King John;
For he was a prince and a prince of great might,
He held up great wrongs, and he put down great right,
To me down, down, diddy-i-down.

6. [The Abbot of Canterbury]

HCL 25242.64F, fol. 234 (18th c.) broadside, "The Snipe."

a Minor; or Æ (inflected VII)

7. "King John"

Grainger MS., No. 138. Sung by Joseph Skinner, Barrow-on-Humber, July 27, 1906.

a Æ

1. An ancient story I'll tell you anon,
   Of a notable King that was called King John,
   Who reüled over England with main & with might,
   Who did great wrong & maintained little right. Derry down.

2. An abbot who lived at Canterburý,
   Who for his housekeeping so rich & merrý;
   That for his housekeeping & wealth & renoun
   King John bade him hasten to fair London town. Derry down.

3. "Sir abbot," says John, "unto me it is told,
   More state than the King thou hast dared to uphold;
   For treason like this thou must forfeit thine head,
   Unless thou can answer 2 questions instead." Derry down.

4. "The first, I will ask thee most plainly to show
   How long round the world it'll take me to go,
   & at the next question thou mayest not shrink
   But tell me I pray thee, now what do I think." Derry down.

5. Then home rode the abbot his fate to bewail,
   & met his good shepherd & told him his tále.
   "Don't trouble thý brains, my goodmaster," said he,
   "For I'll go to King John & he'll think it is thee." Derry down.

6. In 3 weeks time his mule he bestrode,
   & üp to the King as the abbot he rode.
   "Sir abbot, yě're welcome, it's now quickly shown
   How long roun' the world it'll take to go." Derry down.

7. "You must start with the sun when at morn he doth rise,
   & travel with him all the day thro' the skies;
   & then thou need not make any doubt
   That in 24 hour thou'll ride it about." Derry down.

8. "Right well to my 1st question thou hast replied,
   Now tell me my 2nd & home thou shalt hie."
   "Yes, that I will do, it will make your grace merry;
   You think I'm the abbot of Canterbury." Derry down.

9. "But I'm his poor shepherd, as plain you can see,
   & I've come to beg pardon for him & for me."
   "O ho! here is gold, get thee gone.
   Tell the abbot he's pardoned by good King John."
   Derry down. Down, derry down, Derry down.

8. [King John and the Abbot; or, Derry Down]

Chappell, 1838-40, II, No. 9a, p. 5. Also in Chappell, I [1855], 350-52.

a Æ influence (but inflected VII)

Rimbault, 1847, II, p. 442, also prints this tune ("the *old* tune") in a different key, as from Watt's *Musical Miscellany*, 1729-31 ("Derry Down," VI, p. 136).

An ancient story I'll tell you anon,
Of a notable prince that was called King John;
And he rul'd over England with main and with might,
For he did great wrong, and maintain'd little right,
Derry down, down, hey, derry down. [Etc.]

Chappell follows Percy's text in the *Reliques*, II, Bk. III, No. 6, in the early editions.

9. [King John and the Bishop]

Barry, *JAF*, XXI (1908), pp. 57-58. Also in Barry, *JAF*, XXII (1909), p. 73.

m Æ

Barry's MSS. show that this variant came from Mrs. Mary E. Eddy, May 4, 1907, who sent the words her mother had sung. The transmitter was Mrs. S. A. Flint, of Providence.

1. . . . . . .
   . . . . . .

        For he did great wrong, and maintained little right.
        Chorus.—With my derry-i-down,
            Heigh-down,
            Derry-der-ray!

2. . . . . . "in his stead,
   With my crown of gold so fair on my head,"
   . . . .
   . . . .

3. . . . .
   . . . "in such (your) despite,
   Your head shall be taken from your body quite."

4. "My first question is, without any doubt,
   How long I'd be travelling this wide world about?"
   "You rise with the sun, go down with the same,
   In twenty-four hours you will it obtain.

5. . . . .
   . . . .
   . . . .
   . . . .

6. "Our Savior for thirty pieces was sold
   Unto the Jews, both wicked and bold,
   I think twenty-nine must be just your due,
   For I'm sure He was one piece better than you!"

7. "And from my third question you must not shrink,
   But tell me truly what I do think!"
   "My answer, here 't is, 't will make you quite merry,
   You think I'm the Bishop of old Canterbury!"

8. "But I'm his shepherd, as now you do see!"
   . . . .
   . . . .
   . . . .

9. . . . .
   . . . .
   "You bring him a pardon from good King John."

10. [Derry Down]

Flanders, and others, 1939, p. 176. Sung by Powell Smith, Glens Falls, N.Y. Here found with another song, "The Belle of Long Lake." From *The New Green Mountain Songster*, edited by Helen Hartness Flanders, Elizabeth Flanders Ballard, George Brown, and Phillips Barry; copyright 1939 by Helen Hartness Flanders.

a Æ

As Mrs. Flanders notes, the lumbermen sing other songs to "Derry Down," e.g., "The Little Brown Bulls." "Red Iron Ore" (Sandburg, 1927, p. 176) is also sung to another variant. The first half of the above is close to the common type of "Henry Martin" (250, q.v.).

11. "The King's Three Questions"

Flanders and Brown, 1931, pp. 200-3. Sung by George Farnham, Wardsboro, Vt., 1932; learned from his grandmother. Recorded by George Brown. From *Vermont Folk-Songs and Ballads*, edited by Helen Hartness Flanders and George Brown; copyright 1931 by Arthur Wallace Peach.

a π⁴

1. A story, a story, a story of one,
   'Twas of a great prince, his name was King John.
   He was a man and a man of great might,
   He tore down great barns and set up great right.
       To my derry I down, oh high down derry day.

2. Now it was to make the king merry,
   He sent for the Bishop of Can-te-ro-berry.
   He said, "Mr. Bishop, it is told to me,
   That you're a far greater scholar than me."
       To my derry I down, oh high down derry day.

3. "Now if you don't answer to my questions three,
   Your head will be taken from your body.
   And if you don't answer to all of them right,
   Your head will be taken from your body quite."
       To my derry I down, oh high down derry day.

4. "My first question is, When I'm in my state,
   With my crown of gold upon my pate.
   To all my nobility, joy and much mirth,
   You must tell to one penny what I am worth."
       To my derry I down, oh high down derry day.

5. "My second question is without any doubt,
How long I'll be traveling this whole world about.
My third question is that when I do wink,
You must tell me presently what I do think."
    To my derry I down, oh high down derry day.

6. Now as the Bishop was returning home
He met a poor shepherd and him all alone.
"Good morning, Mr. Bishop," the shepherd did say.
"What news do you bring from court today?"
    To my derry I down, oh high down derry day.

7. "Bad news, bad news," the Bishop did say,
"For if I don't answer King John's questions three,
My head shall be taken from my body.
And if I don't answer to all of them right,
My head shall be taken from my body quite."
    To my derry I down, oh high down derry day.

8. "His first question is, when he's in his state,
With his crown of gold upon his pate,
To all his nobility, joy and much mirth,
I must tell to one penny what he is worth."
    To my derry I down, oh high down derry day.

9. "His second question is, without any doubt,
How long he will be traveling this whole world about.
The third question is when he does wink,
I must tell him presently what he do think."
    To my derry I down, oh high down derry day.

10. "Now are you such a man of learning," says he,
"That you can't answer the king's questions three?
Now you give me a robe of your apparel,
I will go to King John and settle the quarrel."
    To my derry I down, oh high down derry day.

11. "A robe of apparel you shall have,
Ten thousand pounds as long as you live."
And now the shepherd, he is gone,
To answer the questions of King John.
    To my derry I down, oh high down derry day.

12. "Good morning, Mr. Bishop," the king did say,
"Have you come here to live or to die?"
"I hope your Grace will let me live,
If I do all your answers give."
    To my derry I down, oh high down derry day.

13. "Your first question is, when you're in your state,
With your crown of gold upon your pate.
To all your nobility joy and much mirth,
I must tell to one penny what you're worth."
    To my derry I down, oh high down derry day.

14. "For thirty pieces our Saviour was sold,
To the false Jews both brazen and bold.
Twenty-nine pieces must be your just due,
For I think him one piece better than you."
    To my derry I down, oh high down derry day.

15. "Your next question is, without any doubt,
How long you'll be traveling this whole world about.
Arise with the sun and go round with the same,
In twenty-four hours you will it obtain."
    To my derry I down, oh high down derry day.

16. "The third question is, that when you do wink,
I must tell you presently what you do think.
And now it is to make your Grace merry,
You think I'm the Bishop of Can-te-ro-berry.
But, you mistake, I am not he,
I am a poor shepherd of Salisburree."
    To my derry I down, oh high down derry day.

12. [The Bishop of Canterbury]

Hubbard and Robertson, *JAF*, LXIV (1951), pp. 43-44.
Sung by Mrs. Salley A. Hubbard, Salt Lake City, Utah,
February 10, 1946, and June 10, 1947; learned from her
brother, c. 1875.

a I/M, ending on IV

Lal the roo-loo, Lal the roo-loo, li-ful the day.

1. Old King John was a great noble Knight;
He built up all wrong and he tore down all right;
And when he got seated to make himself merry,
He sent for the Bishop of Canterbury.
Lal the roo-loo, Lal the roo-loo, li-ful the day.

2. "Good morning, Mr. Bishop, it's been told unto me
That you set a far better table than me,
And if you don't answer my questions three,
Your head shall be taken from your body.

3. "My first question is, while me and my estate,
With my golden crown all on my pate,
With all my nobility, joy and great mirth,
You must tell to one penny what I am worth.

4. "My second question is, without any doubt,
How long I'll be traveling this wide world about.
My third question is, when I do wink,
You must tell to me plainly what I do think."

5. The poor bishop on his return home,
He met a poor shepherd, and him all alone,
"Good morning, Mr. Bishop," the shepherd did say,
"What news have you brought from the king today?"

6. "Bad news, bad news," the bishop did say,
"For he has been asking me questions three,
And if I don't answer to them all right,
My head shall be taken from my body quite.

7. "His first question is, while he and his estate,
His golden crown all on his pate,
With all his nobility, joy and great mirth,
I must tell to one penny what he is worth.

8. "His second question is, without any doubt,
How long he'll be traveling this wide world about.
His third question is, when he does wink,
I must tell to him plainly what he does think."

9. "Give to me one suit of your apparel;
I'll go to King John and answer the farrell."
"One suit of my apparel I freely will give
And ten pounds a year as long as I live."

10. Now the poor shepherd and he is gone
To answer the questions of King John,
And if he don't answer to them all right,
His head will be taken from his body quite.

11. "Good morning, Mr. Bishop," the king did reply,
"Have you come here to live or to die?"
"If I don't answer to your questions three
I hope your grace will pardon me.

12. "Your first question is, while you and your estate,
With your golden crown all on your pate,
With all your nobility, joy and great mirth,
I must tell to one penny what you are worth.

13. "The Saviour for thirty bright pieces was sold
Among the false Jews so brazen and bold,
Twenty-nine pieces is your just due,
For I think he's one piece better than you.

14. "Your second question is, without any doubt,
How long you'll be traveling this wide world about.
You'll rise with the sun and keep in full pace,
And in twenty-four hours you'll end your race.

15. "Your third question is, when you do wink,
I must tell to you plainly just what you do think.
That if I do, it will make your heart merry;
You think I'm the Bishop of Canterbury."

16. The king looked the shepherd in the face with a smile,
Saying, "He shall reign bishop another while.
Go tell your bishop, go tell him for me
He keeps a good fellow while he keeps thee."

APPENDIX

13. "The shakinge of the sheetes"

William Ballet's lute MS., p. 84. Trinity College Library,
Dublin.

According to the tablature reading, the B in the first strain of
the tune must be B♮; but in the second strain B♭.

14. [The Shaking of the Shetes]

Hawkins, 1776, V, p. 469 (with a bass).

a M (but IV and VII inflected)

15. [The old Abbot and King Olfrey]

Playford, 1650, reprinted 1933, p. (3). Also in Chappell, I
[1855], p. 85. Playford's title is "The Night Peece." See
Chappell for other names.

p I

Chappell observes, loc. cit., that the tune of "The Shaking of the
Sheets" is mentioned as a country-dance in Misogonus, c. 1560. "The
Dance and Song of Death" was entered in the Stationer's Register,
1568-69. Chappell finds "The Night Piece" often between 1650 and
1783, in which latter year it is printed in The Vocal Enchantress.

Captain Wedderburn's Courtship

CHILD NO. 46

For the theme of this ballad Child has cited ancient parallels in European and Eastern folk-tales. It is not clear, however, that any other people has made a song of it; and there is nothing to prove that the British ballad is very old. If it is so, it must have been thoroughly overhauled in quite modern times. Even in the earliest texts (Scottish, of the later eighteenth century), the talk of livery-men and butlers' bells ringing supper has certainly a very incongruous sound mixed with the lady's primitive riddling conditions. In view of the proven antiquity of these riddles and their independent use in folk-song (cf. the Appendix to this ballad), it seems possible that the whole extant narrative frame is a recent (and highly inartistic) concoction, on the analogy of Child 1 and 2, but in more modern dress. The early texts are in much too sound a condition to have been long independent of writing, and we may suppose that broadside-makers are the persons who would concern themselves with this kind of manufacture.

The old wine, at any rate, has had savor enough to keep the ballad in vogue, particularly in Scotland and Ireland, down to our own day. American copies have doubtless come from one or the other of those countries, as there appears to be no English tradition for this ballad. The melodic tradition shows a fairly distinct cleavage between Scottish and Irish variants, with the Irish perhaps slightly in the lead. But one or two of those with an Irish character have been found on Scottish soil, and the racial distinction as between these two countries in folk-song is notoriously blurred at many points.

Both lines are mainly in the major tonality, with a strong Mixolydian leaning. The Irish tradition is likely to fall into the "Come-all-ye" pattern of tune. Most of the tunes in the first two groups are authentic or, occasionally, mixed. All are in duple time (including examples of 6/8 and 12/8). There are several variants which appear to me to end on other than tonic finals (on V and VI). One of these appears a mere fragment of a tune; the others are deliberate. A variant collected in California, but brought from Wisconsin, probably came out of the lumberman tradition, and goes to a tune associated with the Great Lakes song of "The Bigler's Crew," or "The Bigler," or "Bigerlow." This is also of the "Come-all-ye" type, but in the present instance Dorian.

LIST OF VARIANTS

GROUP A

1. "Captain Wedderburn." Greig MSS., I, p. 94, King's College Library, Aberdeen. (Pyper)
2. "Captain Wedderburn." W. Christie, *Traditional Ballad Airs*, II, 1881, p. 48.
3. "Captain Wedderburn's Courtship." Greig MSS., IV, p. 88. Also in Gavin Greig and Alexander Keith, *Last Leaves of Traditional Ballads and Ballad Airs*, 1925, p. 36(1c). (Robb)
4. "Captain Wedderburn." Greig MSS., III, p. 71. King's College Library, Aberdeen. (Murison)
5. "Captain Wedderburn's Courtship." Duncan MS., No. 285 (transcribed by W. Walker, Greig-Duncan MS.). Also in Greig and Keith, *Last Leaves*, 1925, p. 36(1a). (Alexander)
6. "The Laird o' Roslin's Daughter." John Ord, *The Bothy Songs & Ballads*, 1930, pp. 416-20.
7. "Captain Wedderburn's Courtship." Greig MSS., I, p. 165; text, Bk. 726, XVI, pp. 85ff. Also in Greig and Keith, *Last Leaves*, 1925, p. 36(1b). (Spence)
8. "The Earl o' Roslyn's Dochter." Harris MS., No. 15, Harvard College Library. Also in Francis James Child, *The English and Scottish Popular Ballads*, 1882-98, V, p. 414; text, I, pp. 421-22, 425.
9. "Captain Wedderburn's Courtship." Phillips Barry, *JAF*, XXIV (1911), pp. 335-36. Also in Phillips Barry, Fannie H. Eckstorm, and Mary W. Smyth, *British Ballads from Maine*, 1929, p. 97.

GROUP B

10. "Captain Wedderburn's Courtship; or, The Laird o' Roslin's Daughter." Greig MSS., II, p. 149; text, Bk. 729, XIX, p. 32. Also in Greig and Keith, *Last Leaves*, 1925, p. 36(2). (Mowat)

11. "The Duke of Rutland's Daughter." Hudson MS., No. 701, Boston Public Library. Also in Phillips Barry, *JAF*, XXIV (1911), p. 337.
12. "Captain Wedderburn's Courtship." Barry, Eckstorm, and Smyth, *British Ballads from Maine*, 1929, pp. 95(B)-96.
13. "Six Questions." W. Roy Mackenzie, *Ballads and Sea Songs from Nova Scotia*, 1928, pp. 391 and 14-15.
14. "Captain Wedderburn." Barry, Eckstorm, and Smyth, *British Ballads from Maine*, 1929, p. 96.
15. "Mr. Woodburn's Courtship." Emelyn Elizabeth Gardner and Geraldine Jencks Chickering, *Ballads and Songs of Southern Michigan*, 1939, pp. 141-42.
16. "Captain Wedderburn's Courtship." Phillips Barry Dictaphone Cylinders, No. 91, transcribed by S. P. Bayard, Harvard College Library MS., p. 24.
17. "Bold Robbington." Barry, Eckstorm, and Smyth, *British Ballads from Maine*, 1929, pp. 481 and 93-95.
18. "For my breakfast you must get a bird without a bone." George Petrie, *The Complete Petrie Collection of Irish Music*, edited by Charles Villiers Stanford, 1902-5, No. 777.
19. "Buff the Quilt." Helen Creighton and Doreen H. Senior, *Traditional Songs from Nova Scotia*, 1950, pp. 22-23. Also in Doreen H. Senior and Helen Creighton, *JEFDSS*, VI (December 1951), p. 85.
20. "Captain Wedderburn's Courtship." Creighton and Senior, 1950, pp. 23-24. Also in *JEFDSS*, VI (Dec. 1951), p. 84.
21. "Captain Wedderburn's Courtship." Creighton and Senior, 1950, pp. 24-25.
22. "Captain Woodstock." Helen Creighton, *Songs and Ballads from Nova Scotia*, 1933, pp. 6-7.
23. "For my breakfast you must get a bird without a bone." Petrie, *The Complete Petrie Collection of Irish Music*, 1902-5, No. 778.

24. "Mr. Woodburn's Courtship." Gardner and Chickering, *Ballads and Songs of Southern Michigan,* 1939, pp. 139-40.
25. "A Gentle Young Lady." George Korson, *Pennsylvania Songs and Legends,* 1949, pp. 35-36.

GROUP C

26. "Many Questions." Sidney Robertson, LC Archive of Folk-Song (4196 B1). (Warde H. Ford)

TUNES WITH TEXTS

GROUP A

1. [Captain Wedderburn]

Greig MSS., I, p. 94. Sung by Mrs. Pyper, Affath, December 1905.

a I/M, ending on VIII

The cadence of the first (double) phrase is that of the familiar bothy song, "Drumdelgie." The MS. reads as above; but the omission of an eighth beat in bars three and seven may be suspected to be inadvertent. The last two notes of bar 3 should probably be a dotted quarter and an eighth; and of bar 7, two dotted quarters.

> It's I must have to my supper
> A chicken without a bone
> It's I must have to my supper
> A cherry without a stone
> A cherry without a stone.

2. [Captain Wedderburn]

Christie, II, 1881, p. 48. Learned from his maternal grandfather.

a M, ending on V

Christie prints (II, p. 196) a variant of the same tune to "Sweet William and Fair Annie; or, The Nut-brown Bride" (73, q.v.).

> The Laird of Roslin's daughter
>   Walk'd through the wood her lane;
> And by cam' Captain Wedderburn,
>   A servant to the king.
> He says, "My pretty lady,
>   I pray, lend me your hand,
> And ye'll ha'e drums and trumpets
>   Always at your command." [Etc.]

Christie's text is borrowed and abridged.

3. [Captain Wedderburn's Courtship]

Greig MSS., IV, p. 88. Also in Greig and Keith, 1925, p. 36(1c). Sung by Miss Robb, Strichen.

a I/Ly, ending on VI

The first half of this tune belongs to the omnipresent type of "Lazarus" (cf. Broadwood and Maitland, 1893, p. 102, and *JFSS, passim,* under "Come all you worthy Christian Men").

4. [Captain Wedderburn]

Greig MSS., III, p. 71. Also in Greig-Duncan MS. 785, p. 35. Sung by James Murison, Doghillock, Whitehill, March 1908.

a I/M, ending on VIII

5. "Captain Wedderburn's Courtship"

Duncan MS., No. 285 (W. Walker). Also in Greig and Keith, 1925, p. 36(1a). Sung by R. Alexander, Udny, Aberdeenshire; "dates back 100 years."

a I/M, ending on VIII

A lady fair one May morning
   Went out to take a walk;
A noble lord he followed her,
   An' then began to talk.
He hysed her on his saddle bow,
   An' he's stown her awa,
An' ta'en her aff to his castle,
   To lay her next the wa'.

6. "The Laird o' Roslin's Daughter"

Ord, 1930, pp. 416-20.

a M, ending on VIII

The original employs notes of half the length of the above.

1. The Laird o' Roslin's daughter
      Walked through the woods her lane,
   And by cam' Captain Wedderburn,
      A servant to the King.
   He said unto his livery men,
      If it werna against the law,
   He'd tak' her to his ain bed
      And lay her neist the wa'.

2. "I'm walking here alane," she says,
      "Amang my father's trees,
   And you must let me walk alane,
      Kind sir, now, if you please;
   The supper bell it will be rung,
      And I'll be missed awa;
   Sae I winna lie in your bed
      At either stock or wa'."

3. He says, "My pretty lady,
      I pray give me your hand,
   And ye'll hae drums and trumpets
      Always at your command;
   And fifty men to guard you with
      That well their swords can draw;
   Sae we'll baith lie in ae bed
      And ye'll lie neist the wa'."

4. "Haud awa frae me," she says,
      "And pray lat gae my hand,
   The supper bell it will be rung,
      I can nae langer stand;
   My father he will angry be
      Gin I be missed awa,
   Sae I'll nae lie in your bed
      At either stock or wa'."

5. Then said the pretty lady,
      "I pray tell me your name?"
   "My name is Captain Wedderburn,
      A servant to the King.
   Though thy father and his men were here,
      O' them I'd have nae awe;
   But would tak' you to my ain bed
      And lay you neist the wa'."

6. He lichtit aff his milk-white steed,
      And set this lady on;
   And a' the way he walked on foot
      He held her by the hand;
   He held her by the middle jimp
      For fear that she should fa',
   To tak' her to his ain bed
      And lay her neist the wa'.

7. He took her to his lodging-house,
      His landlady looked ben:
   Says, "Mony a pretty lady
      In Edinbruch I've seen,
   But sic a lovely face as thine
      In it I never saw;
   Gae mak' her doun a down-bed
      And lay her at the wa'."

8. "O, haud awa frae me," she says,
      "I pray you lat me be,
   I winna gang to your bed
      Till ye dress me dishes three;
   Dishes three ye maun dress me,
      Gin I should eat them a',
   Afore I lie in your bed
      At either stock or wa'.

9. "It's ye maun get to my supper
      A cherry without a stane;
   And ye maun get to my supper
      A chicken without a bane;
   And ye maun get to my supper
      A bird without a ga';
   Or I winna lie in your bed,
      At either stock or wa'."

10. "It's when a cherry is in the blume,
      I'm sure it has nae stane;
   And when the chicken's in the shell,
      I wat it has nae bane.
   An' sin' the flood o' Noah,
      The doo she has nae ga';
   Sae we'll baith lie in ae bed,
      And ye'll lie neist the wa'."

11. "O haud your tongue, young man," she says,
      "Nor that gate me perplex;
   For ye maun tell me questions yet,
      And that is questions six.
   Questions six ye'll answer me,
      And that is three times twa;
   Afore I lie in your bed,
      At either stock or wa'.

12. "What's greener than the greenest grass?
      What's higher than the trees?

What's waur than an ill-woman's wish?
　　What's deeper than the seas?
What bird sings first? and whereupon
　　First doth the dew down fa'?
Ye'll tell afore that I lie down
　　At either stock or wa'."

13. "O, holly's greener than the grass;
　　Heaven's higher than the trees;
The deil's waur nor a woman's wish;
　　Hell's deeper than the seas;
The cock crows first; on cedar tap
　　The dew does first down fa';
So we'll baith lie in ae bed,
　　And ye'll lie neist the wa'."

14. "O, haud your tongue, young man," she says,
　　"And gie your fleechin' ower;
Unless ye find me ferlies,
　　And that is ferlies four.
Ferlies four ye maun find me,
　　And that is twa and twa;
Or I'll never lie in your bed
　　At either stock or wa'.

15. "It's ye maun get to me a plum
　　That in December grew;
And ye maun get a silk mantel
　　That waft was ne'er ca'd through;
A sparrow's horn; a priest unborn,
　　This nicht to join us twa;
Or I'll nae lie in your bed
　　At either stock or wa'."

16. "My father has some winter fruit
　　That in December grew;
My mother has an Indian gown
　　That waft was ne'er ca'd through;
A sparrow's horn is quickly found,
　　There's ane on ilka claw,
And twa upon the neb o' him;
　　And ye'll shall get them a'.

17. "There stands a priest outside the door
　　Just ready to come in;
Nae man can say that he was born,
　　Nae man, unless he sin;
A wild boar tore his mother's side,
　　He out o' it did fa';
Sae we'll baith lie in ae bed,
　　And ye'll lie neist the wa'."

18. Little kenned Grizzie Sinclair
　　That morning when she rose,
That this would be the hindmost
　　O' a' her maiden days.
But now there's no within the realm,
　　I think, a blyther twa;
And they baith lie in ae bed,
　　And she lies neist the wa'.

7. [Captain Wedderburn's Courtship]

Greig MSS., I, p. 165; text, Bk. 726, XVI, pp. 85ff. Also in Greig and Keith, 1925, p. 36(1b). Sung by J. W. Spence, April 1906.

a M, ending on VIII

1. The Laird o' Roslin's daughter
　Walked through the woods her lane
　Met in wi' Captain Wedderburn
　A servant to the king
　He said unto his serving man
　Were't not against the law
　I wad tak' her to my ain bed
　And lay her neist the wa'.

2. "I am walking here alane" she says,
　"Amang my father's trees
　And you must let me walk alane
　Kind sir now if you please
　The supper bell it will be rung
　And I'll be missed awa'
　Sae I winna lie in your bed
　Either at stock or wa'.

3. He says "My pretty lady
　I pray lend me your hand
　And ye'll hae drums & trumpets
　Always at your command
　And fifty men to guard you wi'
　That well their swords can draw
　Sae we'se baith lie in ae bed
　And ye'se lie neist the wa'."

4. "Haud awa frae me" she said
　And pray let gae my hand
　The supper bell it will be rung
　I can nae langer stand
　My father he will angry be
　Gin I be missed awa
　Sae I'll nae lie in your bed
　Either at stock or wa'.

5. Then said the pretty lady
　"I pray tell me your name"
　"My name is Captain Wedderburn
　A servant to the King
　Tho your father and his men were here
　O['] them I'd hae nae awe
　But wad tak ye to my ain bed
　And lay you neist the wa'."

6. "Oh haud awa frae me she says
　I pray you let me be
　I winna be in your bed
　Till ye dress dishes three
　Dishes three ye maun dress me
　Gin I should eat them a'
　Afore I lie in your bed
　Either at stock or wa'.

7. It's ye maun get to my supper
   A cherry without a stane
   And ye maun get to my supper
   A chicken without a bane
   And ye maun get to my supper
   A bird without a ga'
   Or I winna lie in your bed
   Either at stock or wa'."

8. It's when the cherry is in its bloom
   I'm sure it has nae stane
   And when the chicken is in its shell
   I'm sure it has nae bane
   The dove she is a gentle bird
   She flies withoot a ga'.
   Sae we'll baith lie in ae bed
   And ye'll lie neist the wa'.

9. Oh haud your tongue young man she says
   Nor that way me perplex
   For ye maun tell me questions
   And that is questions six
   Questions six ye maun tell me
   And that is three times twa
   Afore I lie in your bed
   Either at stock or wa'.

10. What's greener than the greenest grass?
    What's higher than the trees?
    What is worse than woman's wish?
    What's deeper than the seas?
    What bird sings first and
    Whereupon first doth the dew down fa'
    Tell me afore I lay me doon
    Between you & the wa'.

11. Holly's greener than the grass
    Heaven's higher than the trees
    The devil's worse than woman's wish
    Hell's deeper than the seas
    The cock craws first on cedar tap
    The dew doon first doth fa'.
    So we'll baith be in ae bed
    And ye'll lie neist the wa'.

12. Oh haud your tongue young man she says
    And gie your pleadin over
    And unless you find me ferlies
    And that is ferlies four
    Ferlies four ye maun find me
    And that is twa & twa
    Or I'll never lie in your bed
    Either at stock or wa'.

13. It's ye maun get to me a plum
    That in December grew
    And ye maun get a silk mantle
    That waft was ne'er ca'ed through
    A sparrow's horn, a priest unborn
    This night to join us twa
    Or I'll nae lie in your bed
    Either at stock or wa'.

14. My father he has winter fruit
    That in December grew

My mother has an Indian gown
That waft was ne'er ca'ed through
A sparrow's horn is quickly found
There's ane on ilka claw
And twa upon the nib o' him
And ye shall get them a'.

15. The priest he's standing at the door
    Just ready to come in
    Nae man can say that he was born
    Nae man unless he sin
    A wild boar tore his mother's side
    He oot o' it did fa'.
    Sae we'll baith lie in ae bed
    And ye'll lie neist the wa'.

16. Little thought this fair maid
    That morning when she raise
    That this wad be the hindmost
    O' a' her maiden days.
    But now there's no within the realm
    I think a blyther twa
    And they baith lie in ae bed
    And she lies neist the wa'.

8. [The Earl o' Roslyn's Dochter]

Harris MS., No. 15. Also in Child, 1882-98, V, p. 414; text, I, pp. 421-22, 425.

a M, ending on V (VII is inflected once, perhaps by mistake)

Cf. *CFQ*, I (1942), p. 194, on the reading of the MS.

1. The Earl o Roslin's dochter gaed out to tak the air;
   She met a gallant gentleman, as hame she did repair;

   I will take you wi me, I tell you, aye or no.

(?) 2. "I am Captain Wedderburn, a servant to the king.

   I will tak you wi me, I tell you, aye or no."

3. "I maun hae to my supper a bird without a bone;
   And I maun hae to my supper a cherry without a stone;
   An I maun hae a gentle bird that flies without a gaw,
   Before that I gae with you, I tell you, aye or na."

4. "When the bird is in the egg, I'm sure it has na bane;
   And whan the cherry's in the bud, I'm sure it has na
                                                  stane;

The dove it is a gentle bird, it flies without a gaw,
I will tak you wi me, I tell you, aye or na."

5. "'Tis I maun hae some winter fruit that in December
grew;
And I maun hae a gey mantle that waft neer ca'ed
through;
A sparrow's horn, a priest unborn, this nicht to join us
twa,
Before that I gae with you, I tell you, aye or na."

6. "My father has some winter fruit that in December
grew;
My mither has a gey mantle that waft neer ca'ed
through;
A sparrow's horn ye sune sall get, there's ane on evry
claw,
And twa upo the gab o it, and ye shall get them a'.

7. "The priest is standing at the yett, just ready to come in;
Nae man can say that he was born, nae man without a
sin;
He was haill cut frae his mither's side, and frae the
same let fa;
Sae I will tak you wi me, I tell you, aye or na."

9. [Captain Wedderburn's Courtship]

Barry, JAF, XXIV (1911), pp. 335-36. Also in Barry, Eckstorm, and Smyth, 1929, p. 97. From E. A. S., a native of County Down, in Boston, Mass.

p I/M

Barry's MSS. identify the donor as Elizabeth A. Smith, March 7, 1911. Barry believed all variants collected in Maine, Massachusetts, and Nova Scotia might come from a single Irish source.

1. A Gentleman's fair daughter walked down yon narrow lane,
She met with William Dixon, the keeper of the game,
"It's go away, young man," she said, "and do not me
perplex,
. . . . "

2. ". . . . .
Three questions you must answer me,
Before you lie in my bed, at either stock or wall!"

3. "What is rounder than the ring, what's higher than the tree,
What is worse than womankind, what's deeper than the
sea?"

"The globe is rounder than a ring, Heaven's higher than
the tree,
The devil's worse than womankind, Hell's deeper than
the sea!"

4. ". . . . .
. . . .
So you and I in one bed lie, and you'll lie next the wall!"

5. "What bird sings best, what flower blooms first, and where
the dew first falls?
Before I lie one night with you, at either stock or wall!"
"The thrush sings best, the heath blooms first, and there the
dew first falls,
So you and I in one bed lie, and you'll lie next the wall!"

6. "For my breakfast you must get me a bird without a bone,
The cherry without a stone, the bird without a gall,
. . . .
. . . ."

7. "The dove it is a gentle bird, it flies without a gall,
When the cherry is in the blossom, I'm sure it has no stone,
When the bird is in the egg, I'm sure it has no bone,
So you and I in one bed lie and you'll lie next the wall!"

8. "You must get to me some winter fruit that in December
grew,
You must get to me a silk mantle that weft did ne'er go
through,
A priest unborn, to make us both in one,
Before I lie one night with you, at either stock or wall!"

9. "My father has some winter fruit that in December grew,
My mother has a silk mantle that weft did ne'er go through,
Melchisedek's a priest unborn, and he'll make us both in one,
So you and I in one bed lie, and you'll lie next the wall!"

GROUP B

10. [Captain Wedderburn's Courtship; or, The Laird o' Roslin's Daughter]

Greig MSS., II, p. 149; text, Bk. 729, XIX, p. 32. Also in Greig and Keith, 1925, p. 36(2). Sung by J. Mowat, New Pitsligo, Aberdeenshire, September 1907.

p Æ/D

According to Keith, Last Leaves, p. 36, this tune occurs with other folksongs in the Greig country, e.g., "Dr. Stafford," "The Irish Girl," and "The Ploughman's Daughter" (Christie, II, p. 92).

1. The Laird o' Roslin's daughter walked through the wood
her lane
When by cam Captain Wedderburn a servant to the king
He said unto his servant man, were it not against the law
I wad tak her to my ain bed and lay her neist the wa'.

2. I'm walking here alone she said among my father's trees
And you must let me walk alone kind sir, now if you please
The supper bells they will be rung and I'll be missed awa
So I canna lie in your bed either at stock or wa'.

3. He says "My pretty lady I pray lend me your hand
And you'll get drums & trumpets always at your command
And fifty men to guard you an long's this sword can draw
And we'll baith lie in ae bed and you'll lie neist the wa.'

4. O says the pretty lady, I pray tell me your name
My name is Captain Wedderburn a servant to the king
Though your father were her[e] & all his men I would tak
you frae them a'
I wad tak you to my ain bed and lay you neist the wa'.

5. He jumped off his milk white steed & set this lady on
And all the way he walked on foot and held her by the hand
He held her by the middle jimp for fear that she should fa',
Til he took her to his ain bed (and) to lay her neist the wa'.

6. He took her to a lodging house, the landlady looked ben
Says Many's the pretty lady in Edinburgh I've seen
But such a pretty weel-faured face in it I never saw
You'll make her down a doon bed and lay her neist the wa'.

7. O says the pretty lady before you do gain me
It's you will dress me dishes yet & that is dishes three,
Dishes three you'll dress to me though I should eat them a'
Before I lie in your bed either at stock or wa'.

8. You will get to my supper a cherry without a stone
And you will get to my supper a chicken without a bone
And you will get to my supper a bird without a gall
Before I lie in your bed either at stock or wa'.

9. When the cherry is in its bloom, I'm sure it hath no stone
And when the chicken is in the egg, I'm sure it hath no
bone
The dove he is a gentle bird and flies without a gall
So we'll both lie in ae bed and you'll lie neist the wa'.

10. O say the pretty lady before you me perplex
You will tell me questions yet and that is questions six
Questions six you'll tell to me and that is three times two
Before I lie in your bed either at stock or wa'.

11. What's greener than the greenest grass, what's higher than
the trees
What is worse than woman's vice (hell's) what's deeper
than the sea
What was the first bird that crew and what did first doonfa
Before I lie in your bed either at stock or wa'.

12. Evergreen's greener than the grass, heaven's higher than
the trees
The devil is worse than woman's vice, hell's deeper than
the sea
The cock was the first bird that crew, the dew it did doonfa
So we'll baith lie in ae bed and you'll lie neist the wa'.

13. O says the pretty lady before I give you owre
You will tell me fairlies, and that is fairlies four
Fairlies four you'll tell to me and that is twa and twa
Before I lie in your bed either at stock or wa'.

14. You will give to me fruit that in December grew
You'll get to me a mantle that waft was ne'er ca'ed* through
A sparrow wi' a horn & a priest unborn this night to join
us twa
Before I lie in your bed either at stock or wa'.

15. My father had plums that in December grew
My mother had an Indian gown that waft was ne'er ca'ed*
through
A sparrow wi' a horn that's easily found, there's one on
every claw
And tow upon the gab o' it and you shall have them a'.

16. The priest is standing at the door, just ready to come in
No one can say that he was born no one unless he sin
A wound cut in his mother's side and he oot at it did fa'
So we'll baith be in ae bed and you'll lie neist the wa'.

17. Little did that fair maid think, that morning when she rose
That it would be the very last of all her maiden days
And in the parish where they lived there was not a blither
twa
And they both lay in one bed and she lay neist the wa'.

* MS.: ca'ad

11. [The Duke of Rutland's Daughter]

Hudson MS., No. 701. From E. Clements. Also in Barry
JAF, XXIV (1911), p. 337.

a I

The Duke of Rutland's daughter
Walked out the fields so green

12. [Captain Wedderburn's Courtship]

Barry, Eckstorm, and Smyth, 1929, pp. 95(B)-96. Sung by
T. Edward Nelson, Union Mills, New Brunswick, Canada,
1928. Melody recorded by George Herzog.

p I/M, ending on V

O, what is rounder than a ring?
What's higher than a tree?
What's worse than women all?
What's deeper than the sea?

This is a fragment of the familiar tune of "The Lowlands of Holland" (cf., e.g., LC/AAFS rec. 103, sung by Mrs. Carrie Grover, Gorham, Maine, 1941).

What tree buds first?
Where the dew first falls . . .

A globe is rounder than a ring,
A sky is higher than a tree,
The Devil is worse than women all,
Hell is deeper than the sea.

13. "Six Questions"

Mackenzie, 1928, p. 391; text, pp. 14-15. Sung by John Adamson, Westville, Pictou County, Nova Scotia. Text also in *JAF*, XXIII, 377, and Mackenzie, *The Quest of the Ballad*, 1919, pp. 108-110.

p I

1. The Duke of Merchant's daughter walked out one summer day;

   She met a bold sea captain by chance upon the way.
   He says, "My pretty fair maid, if it wasn't for the law
   I would have you in my bed this night, by either stock or wa'."

2. She sighed and said, "Young man, O do not me perplex,

   You must answer me in questions six before that I gang awa,
   Or before that I lie in your bed by either stock or wa'."

3. "O what is rounder than your ring? What's higher than the trees?

   Or what is worse than women's tongue? What's deeper than the seas?
   What bird sings first? What bird sings last? Or where does the dew first fall?
   Before that I lie in your bed by either stock or wall."

4. "The globe is rounder than your ring; sky's higher than the trees;

   The devil's worse than women's tongue; Hell's deeper than the seas;
   The roe sings first, the thirst sings last; on earth the dew first falls,
   Before that I lie in your bed by either stock or wall."

5. "You must get for me some winter fruit which in December grew;

   You must get for me a silken cloak that ne'er a waft went through;
   A sparrow's thorn, a priest new-born, before I gang awa,
   Before that I lie in your bed by either stock or wa'."

6. "My father's got some winter fruit which in December grew;

   My mother's got a silken cloak that ne'er a waft went through;
   A sparrow's thorns they're easy found—there's one on every claw;
   So you and I lie in one bed, and you lie next the wa'."

7. "You must get for my wedding supper a chicken without a bone;

   You must get for my wedding supper a cherry without a stone;
   You must get for me a gentle bird, a bird without a gall,
   Before that I lie in your bed by either stock or wall."

8. "O when the chicken's in the egg I'm sure it has no bone;

   And when the cherry's in full bloom I'm sure it has no stone;
   The dove it is a gentle bird—it flies without a gall,
   Before that I lie in your bed by either stock or wall."

9. He took her by the lily-white hand and led her through the hall;

   He held her by the slender waist for fear that she would fall;
   He led her on his bed of down without a doubt at all,
   So he and she lies in one bed, and he lies next the wall.

14. [Captain Wedderburn]

Barry, Eckstorm, and Smyth, 1929, p. 96. Sung by Mrs. James McGill, Chamcook, New Brunswick; learned in Scotland. Melody recorded by George Herzog.

a M

Herzog barred his copy in 12/8 time.

15. "Mr. Woodburn's Courtship"

Gardner and Chickering, 1939, pp. 141-42. Sung by Charles Muchler, Kalkaska, Mich., 1934; learned in a Pennsylvania lumber camp. (The title may properly belong only to number 24, below.)

m I

As I took a walk one May morning down by John Sander's
    lane,
Who should I spy but a pretty little maid, the keeper of the
    game?
I says to her, "My pretty fair maid, if it wasn't for the law,
I'd take you in my arms and roll you over next to the wall."

Says she, "Get away, you silly lad, and do not be perplexed,
Before you could lie in bed with me you must answer ques-
    tions six.
Six questions you must answer me and I will ask them all,
Then you and I in bed can lie and you lie next to the wall.

"Now what is rounder than a ring, what's higher than the
    trees?
What's worse than woman's tongue, what's deeper than the
    seas?
What bird sings first, and what one best, and where does
    the dew first fall?
And you and I in bed can lie and you lie next to the wall."

"This earth is rounder than a ring, heaven's higher than
    the trees.
The devil's worse than woman's tongue, hell's deeper than
    the seas.
The lark sings first, the hackey bird best, and the earth's
    where the dew first falls,"
And then I took this fair maid in my arms and rolled her
    over next to the wall.

16. [Captain Wedderburn's Courtship]

Barry Dict. Cyl., No. 91, transcribed by S. P. Bayard, Harvard College Library MS., p. 24. Sung by Mrs. S. M.
Harding.

m I/M

17. "Bold Robbington"

Barry, Eckstorm, and Smyth, 1929, p. 481; text, pp. 93-95.
Sung by Mrs. Annie V. Marston, West Gouldsboro, Maine,
June 28, 1929; learned in 1867.

m I

1. As I walked out one evening down by a strawberry lane,
It was there I saw Bold Robbington, the keeper of the game.
It is true I loved that handsome maid, and if it was not for
    the law,
I would take that fair maid round the waist and roll her
    away from the wall.

2. "Oh, hold your tongue, you silly man, and do not me per-
    plex,
Before that you can lie with me, you must answer questions
    six;
Six questions you must answer me, and I will put them all,
Then you and I in one bed shall lie, and you lie next to
    the wall.

3. "O what is rounder than a ring? What is higher than a
    tree?
What is worse than a woman's tongue? What is deeper
    than the sea?
What bird flies far the broad sea across? And where does
    the first dew fall?
Then you and I in one bed shall lie, and you lie next to
    the wall."

4. "This world is rounder than a ring; Heaven is higher than
    a tree;
The devil is worse than a woman's tongue; Hell is deeper
    than the sea;
The gull flies far the wide sea across, and there is where the
    first dew falls,
So you and I in the bed shall lie, and you lie next to the
    wall."

5. "O hold your tongue, you silly man, and do not bother me,
Before that you with me can lie, you must answer questions
    three;
Three questions you must answer me, and I will put them
    all,
Then you and I in the bed shall lie, and you lie next to
    the wall.

6. "You must get for me a winter fruit that in September
    grew,
You must get for me a silk mantle that never web went
    through,

A sparrow's thorn, a priest unborn, that shall make us one
and all,
Then you and I in the bed shall lie, and you lie next to
the wall."

7. "My father has a winter fruit that in September grew,
My mother has a silk mantle that never web went through;
A sparrow's thorn is easily found, for there is one on every
scroll,
Belshazzar was a priest unborn, so you lie next to the wall."

8. "For my breakfast you must get me a cherry without any
stone,
And for my dinner you must get me a chicken without any
bone,
And for my supper you must get me a bird without any
gall,
Then you and I in one bed shall lie, and you lie next to
the wall."

9. "Oh, when the cherry is in the bloom, I am sure it has no
stone,
And when the chicken is in the egg, I am sure it has no
bone;
The dove it is a gentle bird, and it flies without a gall,
So you and I in the bed shall lie, and you lie next to the
wall."

10. She found her Willie so manfully did Mary's heart enthrall,
He took this young girl by the waist; but—she didn't lie
next to the wall.

18. [For my breakfast you must get a bird without a bone]

Petrie, 1902-5, No. 777. Sung by R. A. Fitzgerald, County
Wexford.

a I

19. "Buff the Quilt"

Creighton and Senior, 1950, pp. 22-23. Also in Senior and
Creighton, *JEFDSS*, VI (December 1951), p. 85. Sung by
Dennis Smith, Chezzetcook, Nova Scotia, July 11, 1937.

a π^1, ending on II

1. As the duke's fair daughter of Scotaland was riding out one
day,
Two gentlemen from Ireland by chance did come that way.
Said one unto the other, "if it wasn't for the law,
I'd take this fair one in my arms, either by stock or wall."

2. "Hands off, hands off young man," said she, "hands off to
hide all shame,
But the supper bell will shortly ring and I'll be found awa'
And before I'll be found in your arms either by stock or wall,

3. "You must get for me some winter fruit that in the summer
grew,
You must get for me a silk made cloak that shuttle never
went through,
You must get for me that bonny bird that flies without a gall
And you and I will 'bove the quilt and you must pay for all."

4. "My father he has winter fruit that in the summer grew,
My mother has a silk made cloak that shuttle never went
through,
The dove she is a bonny bird that flies without a gall,
And you and I will 'bove the quilt and you must pay for all."

5. "Oh what is rounder than the ring, what higher than the
sky?
And what is worse than a woman, what is deeper than the
sea?
What bird sings best, what tree buds first, and where does
the dew first fall?
And you and I will 'bove the quilt and you must pay for all."

6. "The globe is rounder than the ring, heaven's higher than
the sky,
The devil is worse than a woman, hell's deeper than the sea,
The thrush sings best, the oak buds first on the earth when
the dew first falls,
And you and I will 'bove the quilt and you must pay for all."

7. "You must get for me a wedding supper, a chicken without
bones,
You must get for me a wedding supper, cherries without
stones,
A sparrow's horn and a priest unborn to marry us right awa'
Before I will lie in your arms either by stock or wall."

8. "Oh chickens when they're in the shell I'm sure they have
no bones,
And cherries when they're in the blossom I'm sure they have
no stones,
A sparrow's horns are easily found for there's one on every
claw,
Before I would lie in your arms by either stock or wall."

20. [Captain Wedderburn's Courtship]

Creighton and Senior, 1950, pp. 23-24. Sung by Tom
Young, Petpeswick, Nova Scotia, July 23, 1937. Also in
JEFDSS, VI (December 1951), p. 84.

a π^1, ending on II

1. As the duke's fair daughter of Scotaland was riding out one day
   Two gentlemen from Ireland by chance did come that way.
   Says one unto the other, "If it wasn't for the law,
   I'd take this fair one in my arms either by stock or wall."

2. "Oh what is rounder than a ring, what is higher than the sky,
   And what is worse than womankind, what's deeper than the sea,
   What tree buds first, what bird sings best and where does the dew first fall,
   Before I will lie in your arms, and you must pay for all."

3. "The globe is rounder than a ring, heaven's higher than the sky,
   The devil is worse than womankind, hell's deeper than the sea,
   The oak buds first and the thrush sings best on top where the dew first falls,
   Now you and I must 'bove the quilt and you must pay for all."

4. "You must get for me a wedding supper, chickens without bones,
   You must get for me a wedding supper, cherries without stones,
   You must get for me a bonny bird that flies without a gall
   Before I will lie in your arms, and you must pay for all."

5. "Chickens when they're in the shell I'm sure they have no bones,
   And cherries in their blossoms oh I'm sure they have no stones,
   The dove it is a gentle bird that flies without a gall,
   Now you and I must 'bove the quilt and you must pay for all."

6. "You must get for me some winter fruit that in December grows,
   You must get for me a silken webbed cloak that never a shadow went through,
   A sparrow's horns and a priest unborn to marry us right awa'
   Before I will lie in your arms and you must pay for all."

7. "My father has a winter fruit that in December grows,
   My mother has a silken webbed cloak that never a shadow went through,
   A sparrow's horns are easily found, there's one on every claw,
   Now you and I must 'bove the quilt and you must pay for all."

21. [Captain Wedderburn's Courtship]

Creighton and Senior, 1950, pp. 24-25. Sung by Ralph Huskins, Cape Sable Island, Nova Scotia.

m I (inflected VI)

Three questions I will give to you
If you can answer all
Then you and I in the bed shall lie
And you lie next to the wall.

For breakfast you must cook for me
Is a bird without a bone,
For dinner you must cook for me
Is a cherry without a stone,
For supper you must cook for me
Is a bird without a call
Then you and I in the bed shall lie
And you lie next to the wall.

Oh, when the bird is in its egg,
I'm sure it has no bone,
And when the cherry is in its bloom,
I'm sure it has no stone,
My father's got some gentle doves
Who will come without a call
Then you and I in the bed shall lie
And you lie next to the wall.

22. "Captain Woodstock"

Creighton, 1933, pp. 6-7. Sung by Richard Hartlan, South-East Passage, Nova Scotia.

a I

1. As I rode out one May morning
   Down by a shady lane,
   When I met with Captain Woodstock,
   The keeper of the game,
   He said unto his servant,
   "If it was not for the law
   I would have that maid in bed with me
   As she lay next to the wall."

2. "Oh, before you lay one night with me
   You must answer my questions six.
   What is rounder than a ring,
   What's higher than a tree?
   Oh, what is worse than woman's tongue,
   What deeper than the sea?
   What tree buds first and what bird sings best?
   Come answer my questions all
   Before you lay one night with me
   At either stock or wall."

3. "Oh, the world is rounder than a ring,
   Heaven's higher than a tree,
   The devil is worse than a woman's tongue,
   Hell's deeper than the sea.
   The oak buds first and the thrush sings best,
   I've answered your questions all,
   So shake you up that old straw bed,
   You must lay next to the wall."

4. "Oh, it's for my breakfast you must get
   Me chickens without bones,
   And for my dinner you must get
   Me cherries without stones,
   And for my supper you must get
   A bird without a gall
   Before I lay one night with you
   At either stock or wall."

5. "Oh, when a chicken is in the egg
   I'm sure it has no bones,
   And when a cherry's in blossom
   I'm sure it has no stones.
   The dove she is a gentle bird,
   She flies without a gall,
   So shake me up that old straw bed,
   We must lay close to the wall."

6. "Oh, bring to me a silken gown,
   A web that never went through,
   And you must get me a priest unborn
   To join us one and all,
   Before I lay one night with you
   At either stock or wall."

7. "Oh, my mother's got a silken gown,
   A web that never went through;
   Melchisedec is a priest unborn,
   He will join us one and all,
   So shake you up that old straw bed,
   You must lay next to the wall."

23. "For my breakfast you must get a bird without a bone"

Petrie, 1902-5, No. 778. Sung by Mr. Fitzgerald.

a I/M

24. "Mr. Woodburn's Courtship"

Gardner and Chickering, 1939, pp. 139-40. Sung by Mrs. Eliza Youngs, Greenville, Mich., 1934; learned from her mother.

a Æ/D

1. A nobleman's fair daughter walked down a narrow lane;
   She met with Mr. Woodburn, a keeper of the game.
   He said unto his servants, "If it wasn't for the law,
   This maid I'd have within my bed, and she would lie at the wall."

2. "Get you gone, young man," she said, "and do not trouble me;
   Before you lie one night with me, you must get me dishes three.
   Three dishes you must get for me; suppose I eat them all,
   Before you lie one night with me at either stock or wall."

3. "For my breakfast you must have a bird without a bone,
   And for my dinner you must have cherries without a stone,
   And for my supper you must have a bird without a gall,
   Before you lie one night with me at either stock or wall."

4. "When the bird is in the egg, it really has no bone;
   When cherries are in blossom, they really have no stone;
   The dove she is a gentle bird, she flies without a gall;
   So you and I in bed must lie, and you must lie at the wall."

5. "Get you gone, young man," she said, "and do not me perplex;
   Before you lie one night with me, you must answer questions six.
   Six questions you must answer me when I set forth them all
   Before you lie one night with me at either stock or wall.

6. "What is rounder than a ring, what's higher than a tree?
   What is worse than women, else what's deeper than the sea?

What bird sings best of three birds first, and where the
dew does fall?
Before you lie one night with me at either stock or wall."

7. "The globe is rounder than the ring, heaven's higher than
a tree.
The devil's worse than women, else hell's deeper than the
sea.
The thrush sings best of three birds first, and there the dew
does fall,
So you and I in bed must lie, and you must lie at the wall."

8. "Well, you must get me some winter fruit that in December
grew.
You must get me a mantle that weft it ne'er went through.
You must get me a sparrow's horn, a priest unborn to join
us one and all,
Before you lie one night with me at either stock or wall."

9. "My father has some winter fruit that in December grew,
And my mother has a mantle that weft it ne'er went
through.
A sparrow's horn is easy got, there's one on every claw;
Melchesik he was a priest unborn, so you must lie at the
wall."

10. . . . .
. . . .
Seeing she was so clever my heart she did enthrall,
I took her in my arms and rolled her from the wall."

25. "A Gentle Young Lady"

Korson, 1949, pp. 35-36. Sung by Albert E. Richter, South
Connellsville, Pa., 1946. Recorded by Samuel P. Bayard.

m Æ

1. Oh, a gentee young lady 'way down in yonders lane,
She met with Mister Woodbury, the keeper of the game.
Said Mister Woodbury to her, If it wasn't for the law
and all,
I would take this fair maid in my arms and roll her from
the wall.

2. Oh, go away, you foolish man, and don't you bother me;
Before you and I in one bed lie, you cook me dishes three.
Three dishes you will cook for me, and I will eat them all,
Before you and I in one bed lie, and I lie next the wall.

3. For my breakfast you cook for me a cherry without a stone,
For my dinner you will cook for me a bird that has no
bone;
For my supper you will fry for me a bird that has no gall,
Before you and I in one bed lie, and I lie next the wall.

4. Oh, a cherry when in its blossom, it hasn't any stone;
A chicken when in a egg, I know it has no bone.
The dove she is a gentle bird, she flies without a gall—
So jump into my arms, my love, and I roll you from the
wall!

5. Oh, go away, you foolish man, before you me perplex;
Before you and I in one bed lie, you answer questions six.
Six questions you will give to me, and I will name them all,
Before you and I in one bed lie, and I'll lie next to the wall.

6. What rounder is than my gold ring, what's deeper than the
sea,
What is worse than a woman's tongue, what's higher than
the tree?
What bird sings first, and which one best, and where does
the dew first fall?
Before you and I in one bed lie, and I lie next the wall.

7. Oh, this globe is rounder than your gold ring, hell's deeper
than the sea,
The devil is worse than a woman's tongue, heaven's higher
than the tree;
The lark sings first to which one best, and on the treetops
dew first falls,
So jump into my arms, my love, and I roll you from the
wall!

8. Oh, go away, you foolish man, and don't you bother me;
Before you and I in one bed lie, you get me articles three.
Three articles you will get for me, and I will use them all,
Before you and I in one bed lie, and I'll lie next to the wall.

9. First I want some farren fruit that in Car'lina grew;
Next I want a silk dallman* that never a warm male threw;
Next I want a sparrow's horn, it will do us one and all,
Before you and I in one bed lie, and I'll lie next the wall.

10. Oh, my father has some farren fruit that in Car'lina grew;
My mother has a silk dallman that never a warm male
threw;
The sparrow's horns are easy found, there's one for every
call (claw);
Saint Patrick is the preece and swarm†—so I'll roll you
from the wall.

11. Oh it's now to finish and conclude all these funny things,
This couple now is married, and happy as can be.
She's not so very handsome, nor not so very tall.
But still he takes her in his arms and rolls her from the
wall.

* This is possibly a perversion of *man-dall*, i.e., mantle. But perhaps for *dolman*.
† Originally, *priest unborn*.

GROUP C

26. "Many Questions"

Robertson, LC/AAFS No. 4196 B1. Sung by Warde H.
Ford, Central Valley, Calif., December 25, 1938.

a D

46. CAPTAIN WEDDERBURN'S COURTSHIP

Compare with this tune "The Bigler" (J. and A. Lomax, *Folk-Song: U.S.A.*, 1948, p. 149).

1. 'Go away from me you vulgar youth and let me quiet be;
Before one night I'd lie with you you must answer questions
three,
Answer questions three as I put them forth to you:
Then into bed with you I'll go and slumber next the wall.

2. 'For breakfast you must bring to me a bird without a bone;
For dinner you must bring to me cherries without any stone;
For supper you must bring to me a bird without a gall:
Then into bed with you I'll go and slumber next the wall.'

3. 'O when the chicken is in the eggshell, then I'm sure there's
not a bone;
When the cherry is in full blossom then I'm sure there's not
a stone;
The dove soars high, a timid bird, it soars without a gall:
Now into bed with me you'll go and you'll slumber next the
wall.'

4. 'Now go away from me, young man, and be off with your
tricks;
Before one night I'd lie with you you must answer ques-
tions six;
Answer questions six as I put them forth to you:
Then into bed with you I'll go and slumber next the wall.

5. 'What is rounder than any ring, what's deeper than the sea?
What is worse than woman's kind, what's higher than the
trees?
What bird sends forth its busy call and from whence do the
dewdrops fall?
Then into bed with you I'll go and I'll slumber next the
wall.'

6. 'Oh the earth is rounder than any ring, Hell's deeper than
the sea;
The devil is worse than woman's kind, skies are higher than
the tree;
The lark soars high, a timid bird, and from heaven the dewdrops fall.'
Then they two jumped in bed together and they bumped
against the wall.

Riddle Song

CHILD NO. 46, APPENDIX

ONE of the oldest songs in the language, this still keeps a strong hold on life. The earliest text of it that has come down is of about the same date as the earliest text of the first ballad in Child's canon—that is, of the mid-fifteenth century. In this earliest shape, the song lacks all extraneous circumstance, either of narrative frame (except the bare suggestion in "my sister sent me from oversea," &c.) or of refrain or burden. It is in long couplets, metrically so free and easy as to prove that their stress depended on the music which went with them. Doubtless, this was a dancing-song; it probably had a refrain or burden, not recorded, as do most of the later versions. Probably, again, the couplets were of seven stresses, i.e., ballad meter, as in the first version below. Unfortunately, the MS. (Sloane 2593) in which it occurs has no music. Whether it is anterior or posterior to the ballad (Child 46) of which it now forms a part is anyone's guess. My own guess is that it is of prior origin; but I do not know that I could produce very cogent arguments to support the conjecture. If it be, instead, a worn-down descendant of the ballad, it would be analogous to the "Scarborough Fair" variants of Child 2, which have little more of

a narrative framework for the "tasks" than is to be found here.

There is nothing in the musical tradition, so far as we know it, to connect the ballad and the song. The earliest tune that I have found is in a manuscript of about the mid-seventeenth century, or a little later (?): here it is clearly for dancing, and of a type not uncommon in that era. With one exception, later versions are all connected in one way or another; but fall into various subdivisions according to the refrain material with which at various points they have coalesced, or which they have discarded. At some period, the song picked up an acquaintance with another old ditty, "Go no more a-rushing," a version of which is printed, from an old MS. of Byrd's pieces formerly in Rimbault's possession, in Chappell, I, p. 158. Chappell notes that that tune also occurs in the Fitzwilliam Virginal Book as "Tell me, Daphne," (set by Giles Farnaby, ed. 1899, II, p. 446).

Most of the variants, in both main classes, are of major tonality, although it happens that the oldest of record is a melodic minor. Several are in gapped scales, π^1, π^2, and I/Ly. All but one, a somewhat anomalous Æolian tune from Dorset, are authentic.

LIST OF VARIANTS

GROUP A

1. "My Love gave me a cherry." Edinburgh University MS. DC.1.69, No. 2 (at back of MS.).
2a. "I'll Give My Love an Apple." Helen Creighton and Doreen H. Senior, *Traditional Songs from Nova Scotia*, 1950, p. 163(A).
2b. "I'll Give My Love an Apple." Creighton and Senior, 1950, p. 163(B).
3. "I will give my love an apple." H. E. D. Hammond, *JFSS*, III (1909), p. 114. Also on English Columbia, rec. WA 10686 (DB 335). (Clive Carey)
4. "A Paradox." M. H. Mason, *Nursery Rhymes and Country Songs*, 1878 [ed. of 1908], p. 24.
5. "The Riddle Song." Sharp MSS., 4155/2997, Clare College Library, Cambridge. Also in Cecil J. Sharp and Maud Karpeles, *English Folk Songs from the Southern Appalachians*, 1932, II, p. 191(C); and in *Novello's School Songs*, Set VII, No. 1318. (Dunagan)
6. "The Riddle Song." Sharp MSS., 4139/2987. Also in Sharp and Karpeles, 1932, II, p. 190(B). (Pace)
7. "The Riddle Song." Sharp MSS., 3621/2688. Also in Sharp and Karpeles, 1932, II, p. 190(A). (Wilson)
a. "I gave my love a cherry." Mellinger Edward Henry, *Folk-Songs from the Southern Highlands*, 1938, p. 141.
8. "I Gave My Love a Cherry." Elmer Griffith Sulzer, *Twenty-Five Kentucky Folk Ballads*, 1936, I, p. 5.

9. "Riddle Song." F. C. Brown MS., 16 a 4 J, Library of Congress, photostat. Text, *The Frank C. Brown Collection of North Carolina Folklore*, II, 1952, p. 49.

GROUP B

10. "Don't you go a-Rushing." Sabine Baring-Gould MSS., CXVI(1) and (A), Plymouth Public Library.
11. "Don't you go a-Rushing." Baring-Gould MSS., CXVI(2) and (B).
12. Don't You Go A-Rushing. Sharp MSS., 1224/1197. (Ware)

GROUP C

13. "Gifts from over the Sea." Emelyn Elizabeth Gardner and Geraldine Jencks Chickering, *Ballads and Songs of Southern Michigan*, 1939, p. 453.
14. "A Paradox." Mason, *Nursery Rhymes and Country Songs*, 1878 [ed. of 1908], p. 23.
15. "Perry Merry Dictum Dominee." Mary O. Eddy, *Ballads and Songs from Ohio*, 1939, p. 25.
b. "Piri-miri-dictum Domini." John Jacob Niles, *More Songs of the Hill-Folk*, Schirmer's American Folk-Song Series, Set 17, 1936, p. 12.
16. "Go No More a Rushing." William Alexander Barrett, *English Folk Songs* [1891], p. 62.

GROUP A

1. [My Love gave me a cherry]

Edinburgh Univ. MS. DC.1.69, No. 2 (at back of MS.).

a Æ (Melodic minor)

With this tune compare the following in Playford, *The English Dancing Master*, 1650 (reprinted 1933): "Confesse" (p. 19); "Hearts Ease" (p. 54); "Jack Pudding" (p. 56); "Dissembling Love" (p. 59). These are dance-tunes in the same style, though not variants.

My Love gave me a Cherry a Cherry without a stone
My Love gave me a Chicken a Chicken without a Bone
My Love gave me a Ringe a Ringe wthout a rim
My Love gave me a Child wench a Child wench a
[Child wench] a Child without mourninge.

2a. "I'll Give My Love an Apple"

Creighton and Senior, 1950, p. 163(A). Sung by Dennis Smith, Chezzatcook, Nova Scotia.

a Æ/D

1. I'll give my love an apple without e'er a core,
   I'll give my love a dwelling without e'er a door,
   I'll give my love a palace wherein she might be
   That she might unlock it without e'er a key.

2. How can there be an apple without e'er a core,
   How can there be a dwelling without e'er a door,
   How can there be a palace wherein she might be
   That she might unlock it without e'er a key?

3. My head is an apple without e'er a core,
   My mind is a dwelling without e'er a door,
   My heart is a palace wherein she might be
   That she might unlock it without e'er a key.

4. I'll give my love a cherry without e'er a stone,
   I'll give my love a chicken without e'er a bone,
   I'll give my love a baby and no crying.

5. How can there be a cherry without e'er a stone,
   How can there be a chicken without e'er a bone,
   How can there be a baby and no crying?

6. When the cherry's in blossom it has no stone,
   When the chicken's in the egg it has no bone,
   When the baby is a-getting there's no crying.

2b. "I'll Give My Love an Apple"

Creighton and Senior, 1950, p. 163(B). Noted by Nina Bartley Finn at a later singing.

a D

3. "I will give my love an apple"

Hammond, JFSS, III (1909), p. 114. Sung by Mr. J. Burrows, Sherborne, Dorset, July 1906. Also sung by Clive Carey on English Columbia, rec. WA 10686 (DB 335).

p Æ

Miss Gilchrist cites "Glenlogie" in Boulton, *Songs of the North*, n.d., I, pp. 2-4, as an analogous tune. Miss Broadwood presumes a Celtic origin and refers to a tune from County Antrim, published in *JIFSS*, I (1904), p. 58.

I will give my love an apple without e'er a core;
I will give my love a house without e'er a door;
I will give my love a palace wherein she may be,
And she may unlock it without e'er a key.

My head is the apple without e'er a core,
My mind is the house without e'er a door,
My heart is the palace wherein she may be,
And she may unlock it without e'er a key.

I will give my love a cherry without e'er a stone,
I will give my love a chick without e'er a bone,
I will give my love a ring, not a rent to be seen,
I will give my love children without any crying.

When the cherry's in blossom, there's never no stone,
When the chick's in the womb, there's never no bone,
And, when they're rinning running [the ring is running?],
                           not a rent's to be seen,
And, when they're [love-making],* they're seldom crying.

    * *Sic* Hammond, *pudoris causa* for *a-getting?*

4. [A Paradox]

Mason, 1878 [ed. of 1908], p. 24.

a I

This is an interesting variant of the "Villikens and Dinah" type.

My love sent me a chicken without a bone;
He sent me a cherry without a stone;
He sent me a Bible that no man could read;
He sent me a blanket without a thread.
So don't you go a-rushing, maids in May;
Don't you go a-rushing, maids, I pray;
For if you go a-rushing,
I'm sure to catch you blushing;
So gather up your rushes, and haste away.

How could there be a chicken without a bone?
How could there be a cherry without a stone?
How could there be a Bible that no man could read?
How could there be a blanket without a thread?
    So don't you go a-rushing, maids, in May,
    Don't you go a-rushing, maids, I pray;
        For if you go a-rushing,
        I'm sure to catch you blushing;
    So gather up your rushes, and haste away!

When the chicken's in the eggshell, there is no bone;
When the cherry's in the blossom, there is no stone;
When the Bible's in the press, no man can it read;
When the wool is on the sheep's back, there is no thread.
    So don't you go a-rushing, &c.

5. [The Riddle Song]

Sharp MSS., 4155/2997. Also in Sharp and Karpeles, 1932, II, p. 191(C). Sung by Mrs. Margaret Dunagan, St. Helen's, Lee County, Ky., October 12, 1917.

p π[1]

Sharp's MS. copy is in 2/2 time.

I gave my love a cherry without any stone,
I gave my love a chicken without any bone,
I gave my love a thimble without any ring,
I gave my love a baby and no crying.

How can (*or*, could) there be a cherry without any stone?
How can there be a chicken without any bone?
How can there be a thimble without any ring?
How can there be a baby and no crying?

The cherry's in the bloom without any stone,
The chicken's in the shell it's without any bone,
The thimble's a-rolling without any ring,
The baby's a-sleeping and no crying.*

    * Sharp's MS. note: "In Mr. Thomas's version, as given by Mrs. Thomas, this line was as follows:—'When the baby's in the belly, there's no cry within.'"

6. [The Riddle Song]

Sharp MSS., 4139/2987. Also in Sharp and Karpeles, 1932, II, p. 190(B). Sung by Mrs. Eliza Pace, Hyden, Ky., October 9, 1917.

p π[1]

I brought my love a cherry without any stone,
I brought my love a chicken without any bone,
I brought my love a thimble without any rim,
And I brought my love a baby and no cryin'.

How can there be a cherry without any stone?
How can there be a chicken without any bone?
How can there be a thimble without any rim?
How can there be a baby and no cryin'?

When the cherry's in the blossom it's without any stone,
When the chicken's in the egg it's without any bone,
When the thimble's a running it's without any rim,
When the baby's asleep there's no cryin'.

A cherry when it's blooming, it has no stone,
A chicken when it's pipping, it has no bone,
A ring when it's rolling, it has no end.

7. [The Riddle Song]

Sharp MSS., 3621/2688. Also in Sharp and Karpeles, 1932, II, p. 190(A). Sung by Mrs. Wilson, Pineville, Ky., May 2, 1917.

a π^2

Sharp's MS. copy is in A major.

A variant nearly allied to this is sung by Burl Ives on Keynote, rec. No. 6315, Album K-3. Also, the copy printed by M. E. Henry, 1938, p. 141, is very close. It may likewise be mentioned that a variant of "The Wagoner's Lad," sung by Buell Kazee on Brunswick, rec. No. 213B (069), is basically the present tune in triple time.

I gave my love a cherry that* has no stones,
I gave my love a chicken that has no bones,
I gave my love a ring that has no end,
I gave my love a baby that's no cry-en.

How can there be a cherry that has no stones?
How can there be a chicken that has no bones?
How can there be a ring that has no end?
How can there be a baby that's no cry-en?

A cherry when it's blooming it has no stones,
A chicken when it's pipping it has no bones,
A ring when it's rolling it has no end,
A baby when it's sleeping there's no cry-en.

* Sharp's MS. note: "It was difficult to hear whether Mrs. Wilson said 'it' or 'that.'"

8. "I Gave My Love a Cherry"

Sulzer, 1936, I, p. 5. Sung in Knott County, Ky.

a π^2

I gave my love a cherry, that had no stone,
I gave my love a chicken, that had no bone,
I gave my love a ring, without an end.

How can there be a cherry without a stone,
How can there be a chicken, without a bone,
How can there be a ring, without an end?

9. [Riddle Song]

Brown MS., 16 a 4 J. Collected by Mrs. Sutton, October 6, 1927. Text, *North Carolina Folklore*, II, 1952, p. 49. Sung by "a young girl who worked in a mica mill and had lived on the . . . ridge above the Toe River valley all her life."

p I/Ly, ending on V

I gave my love a cherry that had no stone,
I gave my love a chicken that had no bone,
I gave my love a ring that had no end,
Oh, I gave my love a baby with no crying.

Now where is there a cherry that has no stone?
And where is there a chicken that has no bone?
And where is there a ring that has no end?
Oh, who has seen a baby with no crying?

Oh, when a cherry's budding it has no stone,
And when a chicken's pipping it has no bone,
And when a ring's a-rolling it has no end,
Oh, when a baby's sleeping there's no crying.

GROUP B

10. [Don't you go a-Rushing]

Baring-Gould MSS., CXVI(1); text, (A). Sung by J. Helmore, South Brent, 1888; also from Samuel Fone, Mary Tavy, 1893. Noted by H. Fleetwood Sheppard.

a I/M

This copy suggests the outlines of "Son of a Gambolier."

Don't you go a rushing, Maids in May,
Don't you go a rushing, Maids I say.
Don't you go a rushing
Or you'll get a brushing,
Gather up your rushes, & go away.

I'll give you a chicken, that has no bone,
I'll give you a cherry, without a stone.
    I'll give you a ring
    That has not got a rim,
I'll give you an oak that has no limb.

How can you give a chicken that has no bone?
How can you give a cherry without a stone?
    How give a ring
    That has not got a rim?
How give an oak that has no limb?

When the chicken's in the egg it has no bone.
When the cherry is in bloom it has no stone.
    When a melting is the ring,
    It has not got a rim.
When the oak is in the acorn it has no limb.

Don't you go rushing maids, I say,
Don't you go rushing maids in May,
For if you go a rushing they're sure to get you blushing,
They'll steal all your rushes away.

I went a rushing 'twas in May,
I went a rushing maids you say,
I went a rushing, they caught me a blushing
And stole my rushes away.

When the chicken's in its yolk
There is no bone;
The cherry's in its blossom
There is no stone;
And when the baby's a-making
There's no squalling.

11. [Don't you go a-Rushing]

Baring-Gould MSS., CXVI(2); text (B). Sung by William Nichols, Whitchurch, May 27, 1890. Noted by H. Fleetwood Sheppard.

p I

Presumably the last three syllables but one (or two) in each stanza were repeated—unless there is scribal dittograph in the tune.

I'll get my love a home, wherein she may be,
Where she may be kept fast, without any key,
O my heart it is the house, wherein she may bide,
And not a key is wanted to keep her inside.

I'll get my love a cherry without any stone,
I'll get my love a chicken without any bone,
    [I'll give a ring
    That has not got a rim,
I'll get my love an oak that has no limb.]

[*The rest as in the previous copy,* A]

12. [Don't You Go A-Rushing]

Sharp MSS., 1224/1197. Sung by Mrs. Ware, Eley, Over Stowey, January 23, 1907.

p I

13. [Gifts from over the Sea]

Gardner and Chickering, 1939, p. 453. Sung by Charles Muchler, Michigan, 1934; learned c. 1879.

p π¹ (– VI)

I had four brothers over the sea,
Perry merry dinctum dominee;
And each sent a present unto me;
Partum, quartum, perry dee centum,
Perry merry dinctum dominee.

One sent a cherry that had no stone,
One sent a chicken without any bone.

The next sent a blanket without any thread,
And the next sent a book that couldn't be read.

When the cherry's in the blossom, it has no stone,
When the chicken's in the egg, it has no bone.

When the wool's on the sheep, it has no thread,
When the book's on the press, it can't be read.

14. [A Paradox]

Mason, 1878 [ed. of 1908], p. 23.

m I/Ly (– VI)

I have four brothers over the sea,
    Perry, merry, dictum, domine;
They each sent a present unto me,
    Perry, merry, dictum, domine.
        Partum quartum pare dissentum,
    Perry, merry, dictum, domine.

The first sent a chicken without any bone,
  Perry, &c.
The second a cherry without any stone,
  Perry, &c.
    Partum, &c.

The third sent a book that no man could read,
  Perry, &c.
The fourth sent a blanket without any thread,
  Perry, &c.
    Partum, &c.

How could there be a chicken without any bone?
  Perry, &c.
How could there be a cherry without any stone?
  Perry, &c.
    Partum, &c.

How could there be a book that no man could read?
  Perry, &c.
How could there be a blanket without any thread?
  Perry, &c.
    Partum, &c.

When the chicken is in the egg, it has no bone,
  Perry, &c.
When the cherry is in the blossom, it has no stone,
  Perry, &c.
    Partum, &c.

When the book is in the press, no man can it read,
  Perry, &c.
When the blanket is in the fleece, it has no thread,
  Perry, &c.
    Partum, &c.

15. "Perry Merry Dictum Dominee"

Eddy, 1939, p. 25. Sung by Lena Smith, Medina, Ohio.
Transmitted by Helen Hobart.

p π¹ (– VI)

I had four brothers over the sea;
  Perry merry dictum dominee;
And they each sent a present unto me.
  Partum quartum perry dicentum,
  Perry merry dictum dominee.

The first sent me cherries without any stones;
  Perry, *etc.*
The second sent a chicken without any bones.
  Partum, *etc.*

The third sent a blanket that had no thread;
The fourth sent a book that could not be read.

When the cherries are in bloom, they have no stones;
When the chicken's in the egg, it has no bones.

When the blanket's in the fleece, it has no thread;
When the book's in the press, it cannot be read.

16. [Go No More a-Rushing]

Barrett [1891], p. 62.

m Æ (inflected VII)

Go no more a rushing, maids, in May;
Go no more a rushing, maids, I pray;
Go no more a rushing, or you'll fall a blushing,
Bundle up your rushes and haste away.
You promised me a cherry without any stone,
You promised me a chicken without any bone,
You promised me a ring that has no rim at all,
And you promised me a bird without a gall.

How can there be a cherry without a stone?
How can there be a chicken without a bone?
How can there be a ring without a rim at all?
How can there be a bird that hasn't got a gall?
When the cherry's in the flower it has no stone;
When the chicken's in the egg it hasn't any bone;
When the ring it is a making it has no rim at all;
And the dove it is a bird without a gall.

Barrett's note: "This melody which is still to be heard in country places appears in Queen Elizabeth's Virginal Book with the same title, and probably was sung to the same words three hundred years ago."
The Elizabethan tune is properly "Tell me, Daphne." Cf. Chappell, *Popular Music*, I, 1855, p. 158.

Proud Lady Margaret

CHILD NO. 47

This ballad appears not to have wandered often beyond the Scottish boundaries. Reed Smith announced it, by title only, as found in America, but his copy is not discovered. No American tune is as yet on the record.

The three tunes below are of dates approximately fifty years apart, and seem to have no relation to one another. The first sounds as if drawn out of eighteenth-century hymnody, in keeping with the moralizing tone of the ballad as we have it. On the other hand, this may be no more than a pious influence acting on folk material. Such give-and-take between sacred and secular is, of course, not at all uncommon, especially in Scotland. The second tune is, according to Christie, a major variant of "The Laird abeen the Dee." The third sounds like a fragmentary recollection of the "Gilderoy" tune, worn down to a repeated double phrase.

It is again apparent that we have here no strong single tradition: nothing would indicate that these tunes had not been sharked up for a late text wherever they came conveniently to hand.

LIST OF VARIANTS

1. "The Knicht o' Archerdale." Harris Music MS., No. 1; text, Harris MS., fol. 7, No. 3, Harvard College Library. Also in Francis James Child, *The English and Scottish Popular Ballads*, 1882-98, V, pp. 414 and I, 430-31.
2. "Proud Lady Margaret." W. Christie, *Traditional Ballad Airs*, I, 1876, p. 28.
3. "Proud Lady Margaret." Greig MSS., IV, p. 39, King's College Library, Aberdeen. Also in Gavin Greig and Alexander Keith, *Last Leaves of Traditional Ballads and Ballad Airs*, 1925, p. 37.

TUNES WITH TEXTS

1. "The Knicht o' Archerdale"

Harris Music MS., No. 1; text, Harris MS., fol. 7, No. 3. Also in Child, 1882-98, V, p. 414; text, I, pp. 430-31.

a Æ

1. There cam a knicht to Archerdale,
   His steed was winder sma,
   An there he spied a lady bricht,
   Luikin owre her castle wa.

2. "Ye dinna seem a gentle knicht,
   Though on horseback ye do ride;
   Ye seem to be some sutor's son,
   Your butes they are sae side."

3. "Ye dinna seem a lady gay,
   Though ye be bound wi pride;
   Else I'd gane bye your father's gate
   But either taunt or gibe."

4. He turned aboot his hie horse head,
   An awa he was boun to ride,
   But neatly wi her mouth she spak:
   Oh bide, fine squire, oh bide.

5. "Bide, oh bide, ye hindy squire,
   Tell me mair o your tale;
   Tell me some o that wondrous lied
   Ye've learnt in Archerdale.

6. "What gaes in a speal?" she said,
   "What in a horn green?
   An what gaes on a lady's head,
   Whan it is washen clean?"

7. "Ale gaes in a speal," he said,
   "Wine in a horn green;
   An silk gaes on a lady's head,
   Whan it is washen clean."

8. Aboot he turned his hie horse head,
   An awa he was boun to ride,
   When neatly wi her mouth she spak:
   Oh bide, fine squire, oh bide.

9. "Bide, oh bide, ye hindy squire,
   Tell me mair o your tale;
   Tell me some o that unco lied
   You've learnt in Archerdale.

10. "Ye are as like my ae brither
    As ever I did see;
    But he's been buried in yon kirkyaird
    It's mair than years is three."

11. "I am as like your ae brither
    As ever ye did see;
    But I canna get peace into my grave,
    A' for the pride o thee.

12. "Leave pride, Janet, leave pride, Janet,
     Leave pride an vanitie;
If ye come the roads that I hae come,
     Sair warned will ye be.

13. "Ye come in by yonder kirk
     Wi the goud preens in your sleeve;
When you're bracht hame to yon kirkyaird,
     You'll gie them a' thier leave.

14. "Ye come in to yonder kirk
     Wi the goud plaits in your hair;
When you're bracht hame to yon kirkyaird,
     You will them a' forbear."

15. He got her in her mither's bour,
     Puttin goud plaits in her hair;
He left her in her father's gairden,
     Mournin her sins sae sair.

2. [Proud Lady Margaret]

Christie, I, 1876, p. 28.

a I/M

'Twas on a night, an ev'ning bright,
     When the dew began to fa',
Lady Marg'ret was walking up and down,
     Looking over her castle wa', &c.

The text is after Scott's *Minstrelsy*, III, pp. 32ff.; but Christie says the Aberdeenshire tradition followed Buchan, *Ancient Ballads and Songs*, 1828, I, pp. 91ff., "The Courteous Knight," or "Jolly Janet."

3. [Proud Lady Margaret]

Greig MSS., IV, p. 39. Also in Greig and Keith, 1925, p. 37.
Sung by Mrs. Gordon, New Deer, Aberdeenshire.

If on G, a Æ/D

When ye gang in at yon church door,
     With the yellow gold on your hair,
It's ye care more for your weel redd locks
     Than ye do for morning prayer.

The Two Brothers

CHILD NO. 49

THIS Scottish ballad was not known to the world until the beginning of the nineteenth century, and it appears latterly to have been lost to traditional memory in the land of its birth. No copy was found by Gavin Greig, nor has a copy been reported south of the Border. But the ballad was brought to America and for some reason has flourished in the new soil, both in New England and, especially, in the Southern mountains. It has been reported also from Missouri.

Since the early Scottish collectors failed to preserve a tune, the musical tradition is represented only in American variants. These are, however, fairly numerous. They show clear marks of family relationship wherever they have been collected, although they are by no means always melodically close. The ballad is thus a very favorable subject for study in the ways of variation. Rhythmically, a preference is shown for triple measure, in a proportion of about four variants to three. But the triple rhythm is generally complex, as 6/8, 6/4, 3/2, and rarely has been noted as 3/4. The rhythmical divergence does not often coincide with a melodic cleavage, and the following grouping takes no account of it. In this case, the tunes are grouped quite strictly according to the middle cadence, a method that seems here to provide a fairly satisfactory demarcation of the chief branches. The first group is composed of variants with a middle cadence on the tonic; the second, on the supertonic; the third, on the dominant; and the fourth, on the octave above. The fifth group contains anomalous cases. The second and third groups are most favored. Roughly speaking, all the tunes in Group A, and probably all but one in Group B, are in a major tonality; but Group C shows a drift toward minor tonality, and so does Group D. Mixolydian leanings appear in Groups C and D (and E). About a third of the total are genuinely hexatonic; five are pentatonic. Group B is consistently plagal; Group D, authentic; A and C are divided between plagal and authentic variants. No marked regional distinctions are discernible.

LIST OF VARIANTS

GROUP A

1. "The Two Brothers." Sharp MSS., 3770/2781, Clare College Library, Cambridge. Also in Cecil J. Sharp and Maud Karpeles, *English Folk Songs from the Southern Appalachians*, 1932, I, pp. 73(I)-74. (Huff)
2. "The Two Brothers." Vance Randolph, *Ozark Folksongs*, I, 1946, p. 80(D).
3. "The Two Little Boys." Randolph, I, 1946, p. 79(C).
4. "The Two Brothers." Winston Wilkinson MSS., 1935-36, p. 35(B), University of Virginia.
5. "The Two Brothers." Arthur Kyle Davis, Jr., *Traditional Ballads of Virginia*, 1929, pp. 563(E) and 151-52. (Maxie)
6. "Said Billy to Jimmy, 'Take my fine shirt.'" Asher E. Treat, *JAF*, LII (1939), p. 35.
7. "The Two Brothers." Phillips Barry, *BFSSNE*, No. 5 (1933), p. 6.
8. "The Two Brothers." John Harrington Cox, *Folk-Songs Mainly from West Virginia*, 1939, p. 15.

GROUP B

9. "The Two Brothers." Sharp MSS., 3634/2695. Also in Sharp and Karpeles, *Appalachians*, 1932, I, p. 72(H). (Sloane)
10. "The Two Brothers." Sharp MSS., 3533/2606. Also in Sharp and Karpeles, 1932, I, pp. 66(B)-67; and Davis, *Traditional Ballads of Virginia*, 1929, p. 564(H). (Smith)
11. "The Two Brothers." Sharp MSS., 3688/2747. Also in Sharp and Karpeles, 1932, I, pp. 71(G)-72. (Knuckles)
12. "The Two School Boys." Alton C. Morris, *Folksongs of Florida*, 1950, pp. 255-56.
13. "The Two Brothers." Randolph, *Ozark Folksongs*, I, 1946, pp. 76(A)-77.
14. "The Rolling away of the Stones." Eloise Hubbard Linscott, *Folk Songs of Old New England*, 1939, pp. 278-80.
15. "The Two Brothers." Sharp MSS., 4542/3182. Also in Sharp and Karpeles, *Appalachians*, 1932, I, pp. 74(J)-75. (Freeman)

16. "The Two Brothers." Sharp MSS., 3472/. (Johnson)
17. "The Two Brothers." Sharp MSS., 3458/2547. Also in Sharp and Karpeles, *Appalachians*, 1932, I, pp. 65(A)-66. (Roberts, Smith)
18. "The Two Brothers." Sharp MSS., 3490/. Also in Sharp and Karpeles, 1932, I, p. 69(E). (Ford)
19. "The Two Brothers." Sharp MSS., 3972/2856. Also in Sharp and Karpeles, 1932, I, pp. 69(F)-70; and Cecil J. Sharp, *American-English Folk-Ballads*, 1918, p. 7. (Dunagan)
20. "The Two Brothers." Alan Lomax, LC Archive of American Folk Song, Album 7, rec. 32A(541). (Mrs. Texas Gladden)

GROUP C

21. "Billy Murdered John." Phillips Barry, Fannie H. Eckstorm, and Mary W. Smyth, *British Ballads from Maine*, 1929, pp. 99-100.
22. "The Dying Soldier." E. C. and M. N. Kirkland, *Southern Folklore Quarterly*, II (1938), p. 66.
23. "The Two Brothers." Davis, *Traditional Ballads of Virginia*, 1929, pp. 563(A) and 147-48. (Shifflett)
24. "The Two Brothers." Sharp MSS., 3536/2612. Also in Sharp and Karpeles, *Appalachians*, 1932, I, p. 68(D); and Davis, 1929, p. 564(I). (Keeton)
25. "The Two Brothers." Sharp MSS., 3563/2633. Also in Sharp and Karpeles, 1932, I, p. 76(L). (Maples)
26. "John Gobillips." Herbert Halpert, LC/AAFS, rec. 2760 A3. (Polly Johnson)
27. "The Two Brothers." Sharp MSS., 4598/3216. Also in Sharp and Karpeles, *Appalachians*, 1932, I, pp. 75(K)-76. (Bennett)
28. "Two Born Brothers." Mary O. Eddy, *Ballads and Songs from Ohio*, 1939, pp. 26-27.
29. "John and William." Josephine McGill, *Folk-Songs of the Kentucky Mountains*, 1917, pp. 54-58.
30. "The Twa Brothers." Eddy, *Ballads and Songs from Ohio*, 1939, pp. 27-28.

TUNES WITH TEXTS

GROUP A

1. [The Two Brothers]

Sharp MSS., 3770/2781. Also in Sharp and Karpeles, 1932, I, pp. 73(I)-74. Sung by Mrs. Ollie Huff, Berea, Knox County, Ky., May 31, 1917.

p I

There's two little brothers going to school.
The oldest to the youngest called:
Come go with me to the green shady grove
And I'll wrestle you a fall.

They went to the green shady grove,
Where they wrestled up and down.
The oldest to the youngest said:
You've given me a deadly wound.

Rip my shirt from off my back,
Rip it from gore to gore,
And then tie up those bleeding wounds,
And they won't bleed no more.

He ripped his shirt off of his back,
Ripped it from gore to gore,
And then tied up those bleeding wounds,
And they did bleed no more.

When you go home tell mother dear,
If she isn't quarrelling about me,
Tell her I'm laid at the new church-yard,
Let be what church it may.

* * * * *

She mourned and she mourned,
She mourned for little Willie,
She nearly mourned him out of his grave
To come home and be with her.

2. [The Two Brothers]

Randolph, I, 1946, p. 80(D). Sung by Mrs. H. L. McDonald, Farmington, Ark., February 10, 1942; learned in 1910.

p I

The original is in 2/4 bars as far as the change of time; thereafter as here.

If you meet my father as you turn to go home,
He will ask you where is John,
You may tell him he's gone to the new bookstore,
To bring his new books home.

3. "The Two Little Boys"

Randolph, I, 1946, p. 79(C). Sung by Mrs. Mildred Tuttle, Farmington, Ark., December 31, 1941; learned from her father in Missouri.

p π¹

The original is written in notes of double the length of the present copy.

Oh two little boys were going to school,
Oh very fine boys were they,
On Friday evening they went home,
On Monday they went away.

Then Willie took out his pocket-knife,
It was very keen and sharp,
. . . .
He pierced his brother's heart.

Oh Willie, take off your hollow gown
And tear it from gore to gore,
And wrap it around the bleeding place
So it may bleed no more.

So Willie took off his hollow gown
And he tore it from gore to gore,
And he wrapped it around the bleeding wound,
But still it bled the more.

Oh Willie, when you go home tonight,
Mother'll ask you where I am,
Tell her I am gone to Heaven above,
Its pearls but to learn.

4. [The Two Brothers]

Wilkinson MSS., 1935-36, p. 35(B). Sung by Mrs. Kit
Williamson, Evington, Va., October 19, 1935.

p I (– VI)

Two brothers, dear brothers, walked out one day
To view the chestnut grove.
The youngest had a long, keen knife,
And he stoved it through the older one's heart.

5. [The Two Brothers]

Davis, 1929, p. 563(E); text, pp. 151-52. Sung by Dan
Maxie, Altavista, Va., May 9, 1914.

a I/M (– VI) (compass of fifth)

1. There were two brothers walked out one day,
   To view the chestnut grove.
   The oldest one drew a long pen-knife
   And stove it to the youngest one's heart.

2. "Dear brother, dear brother, pull off your coat,
   And bind my bleeding wound;
   Bind it up so neat and nice
   And it will not bleed any more.

3. "Dear brother, dear brother, when you go home
   My mama will ask for me;
   You may tell her I'm gone to London town
   To view the chestnut grove.

4. "Dear brother, dear brother, when you go home
   My papa will ask for me;
   You may tell him I'm with the little school-mates
   To bear the sad company home.

5. "Dear brother, dear brother, when you go home
   Little Sweetie will ask for me;
   You may tell her I'm dead, and in the clay cold ground,
   Whose face she will no more see.

6. "Dear brother, dear brother, go dig my grave,
   Go dig it both wide and deep;
   Lay my Bible under my head
   My Testament under my feet.
   My sword and my pistol lay by my side,
   As I was sound asleep.

7. "Little Sweetie, she will mourn,
   Little Sweetie, she will cry,
   Little Sweetie, she once loved me;
   But now I'm dead in the cold clay ground,
   Whose face she will no more see."

6. "Said Billy to Jimmy, 'Take my fine shirt' "

Treat, *JAF*, LII (1939), p. 35. Sung by Mrs. Maud G.
Jacobs and Pearl Jacobs Borusky, Bryant, Wisc., July 13,
1938; learned from William Hagerman in West Virginia.

a π¹

Said Billy to Jimmy, "Take my fine shirt,
Tear it from gore to gore,
And bind it upon my deadly wound."
But it still bled more and more.

"Bury my bow and my arrow at my side,
And my sounder* at my feet."

* This word was explained as meaning *hunting horn*.

7. [The Two Brothers]

Barry, *BFSSNE*, No. 5 (1933), p. 6. Sung by Josiah S. Kennison, Townshend, Vt., April 6, 1932 in Cambridge, Mass.

a I/M (–VI) (compass of fifth)

Barry notes that the same singer used this tune for "Little Sir Hugh" (155), and that it is a worn-down variant of the "Come-all-ye" air to which "Little Musgrave" (81) was sung by Mrs. Sarah Black, Southwest Harbor, Me.

Two brothers were going to school one day,
　Two brothers were going to school;
Instead of going to school that day,
　They thought the day too long,
　And they thought the day too long.

The elder one he drew a knife,
　A knife that was piercing sharp,
And he pierced it into his brother's side,
　And he pierced it into his heart.

"O dear, O dear, when you go home,
　If father should ask for me,
Just tell him I'm gone to yonder churchyard,
　To fight for Liberty.

"O dear, O dear, when you go home,
　If sister should ask for me,
Just tell her I've gone to yonder churchyard,
　To learn my lessons free.

"O dear, O dear, when you go home,
　If mamma should ask for me,
Just tell her I'm lying on yonder churchyard,
　And I'm mamma's boy no more."

8. [The Two Brothers]

Cox, 1939, p. 15. Sung by John A. Moore, Wheeling, W.Va., January 1927; learned from Mrs. Flora A. Williams.

a I

Oh Monday morning going to school, on Friday coming home,
I met those boys a-playing ball, those girls a-rolling stone;
They rassled up, they rassled down, and Johnnie fell to the
　　　　　　　　　　　　　　　　　　　　　　ground,
And out of his pocket a weapon flew, gave Johnnie a deadly
　　　　　　　　　　　　　　　　　　　　　　wound.

GROUP B

9. [The Two Brothers]

Sharp MSS., 3634/2695. Also in Sharp and Karpeles, 1932, I, p. 72(H). Sung by Mrs. Sudie Sloane, Barbourville, Ky., May 6, 1917.

p I/Ly

Sharp's MS. is noted in 3/4 time.
This may be one of the rare cases in which a foreign tune has influenced native tradition; the first two phrases more than suggest the German, "In einem kühlen Grunde" (Friedrich Glück, 1814).

Two little boys were going to school,
O very fine boys were they,
On Sunday evening they come home,
On Monday they go away,
On Sunday evening they come home,
On Monday they go away.*

O toss the ball, the pocket-knife,
Or can't you throw a stone?
I am too little, I am too young
Please, brother, leave me alone.

O Willie drew out his pocket-knife,
O it a-being keen and sharp,
Between the long ribs and the short
He pierced his brother's heart.

O Willie, pull off your morning gown,
And tear it from gore to gore,
Wrap up this bleeding wound of mine
And it will bleed no more.

O Willie pulled off his morning gown,
He tore it from gore to gore,
O Willie wrapped up the bleeding wound
And still it bled the more.

There's no little fishes in the brook
And no little girls to mourn,
But Willie will sigh and mourn for me
When I am dead and gone.

O tell our loving mother
What a change to see,

Just tell her I'm gone to the golden land
My prayer-books for to learn.

* Sharp and Karpeles, 1932, omit the last two lines of this stanza
and the next four stanzas.

10. [The Two Brothers]

Sharp MSS., 3533/2606. Also in Sharp and Karpeles, 1932,
I, pp. 66(B)-67; and Davis, 1929, p. 564(H). Sung by Mrs.
Rosie Smith, Charlottesville, Va., September 25, 1916.

p I

1. Two brothers they have just returned,
   Their pleasures are all sincere.
   I want to see my pretty Susie,
   The girl I loved so dear.

2. You're not the one that loved* Susie,
   And here I'll spill your blood.
   He drew a knife both keen and sharp
   And pierced it through his heart.

3. What will you tell my father dear
   When he calls for his son John?
   I'll tell him you're in the western woods
   A-learning your hounds to run.

4. What will you tell my mother dear
   When she calls for her son John?
   I'll tell her you're in the Tennessee
   A lesson there to learn.

5. What will you tell my pretty Susie
   When she calls for true love John?
   I'll tell her you're in your silent grave,
   Where never no more to return.

6. She took her bible in her hand,
   A-moaning† she went on.
   She moaned till she came to his silent grave.
   In search of her true love John.

7. What do you want, my pretty Susie?
   What do you want with me?
   I want a kiss from your clay cold lips,
   'Tis all I ask of thee.

8. If I were to kiss your rosy cheeks
   My breath it is so§ strong.
   If I were to kiss your ruby lips,
   You would not stay here long.

9. So now go home, my pretty Susie,
   And moan no more for me,
   For you may moan to Eternity,
   My face no more you'll see.

* 1932: "loves"
† Sharp MS. has, in parentheses, "(mourning?)."
§ 1932: "too"

11. [The Two Brothers]

Sharp MSS., 3688/2747. Also in Sharp and Karpeles, 1932,
I, pp. 71(G)-72. Sung by Mrs. Delia Knuckles, Barbourville, Knox County, Ky., May 16, 1917.

p I

1. O brother, O brother, play ball with me,
   Or will you either throw a stone,
   Or will you go to yon shady grove
   And there we'll wrestle and throw?

2. I'll not play ball* with you,
   Or either will I throw a stone;
   But if you'll go to yon shady grove
   There we will wrestle and throw.

3. O brother, O brother, you've wounded me,
   You've wounded me so bad.
   Go and tear my shirt from off my back
   And tear it from gore to gore,
   And wrap it around my bleeding wound
   That it won't bleed no more.

4. He tore his shirt from off his back,
   And tore it from gore to gore.
   And wrapped it around his bleeding wound
   That it might bleed no more.

5. If you meet my father, as you turn round home,
   Enquiring for his son John,
   Go tell him I've gone to Langford's Town
   To bring those new books home.

6. If you meet my mother, as you turn round home,
   Enquiring for her son John,
   Go tell her I'm gone to the cottage gate
   To learn to sing and pray.

7. If you meet my true love, as you turn round home,
   Enquiring for her true love John,
   Go tell her I'm buried in the old churchyard,
   And it's for her sake I'm gone.

8. He met his father, as he turned round home,
Enquiring for his son John.
O father, O father, he's gone to Langford's Town
To bring those new books home.

9. He met his mother, as he turned round home,
Enquiring for her son John.
O mother, O mother, he's gone to the cottage gate
To learn to sing and pray.

10. He met his true love, as he turned round home,
Enquiring for her true love John.
O true love, O true love, he's buried in the old
churchyard,
And it's for your sake he's gone.

11. They buried his bible at his head,
His testament at his feet,
And on his breast his little hymn-book,
That with them he might sleep.

* 1932: "play at ball"

12. "The Two School Boys"

Morris, 1950, pp. 255-56. Sung by Mrs. G. A. Griffin, Newberry, Fla.; learned from her father.

p π^1, ending on V (or a π^2)

1. There is two school boys in our town;
What fine school mates they'd be;
If I could be by the side of them
What fine school boys they'd be.

2. It's Monday morning go to school,
It's Saturday night go home;
It's combing back those curly locks;
It's bid them welcome home.

3. "Oh Brother, oh Brother, will you play ball,
Or will you scatter and stone?"
"I'm too little and I'm too young;
So, Brother, let me alone."

4. He drew his penknife in his hand,
Both keen and sharp;
Between his long ribs and his short
He rested his brother's heart.

5. "Oh Brother, oh Brother, when you go home
And my father asks for me,
Tell him I'm in some foreign land
A-wishing to come home."

6. "Oh Brother, oh Brother, when you go home
And my mother asks for me,
Tell her I'm in some foreign land
A-wishing to come home."

7. Little Old Tom went riding home,
Just as welcome as could be;
Who should he meet but his father dear;
"What news have you brought me?"

8. "Sad news, sad news, dear Father,
Sad news for thee;
My brother is in some foreign land
His lesson still to know."

9. Little Old Tom went riding home,
Just as welcome as could be;
Who should he meet but his mother dear,
"What news have you brought to me?"

10. "Sad news, sad news, dear Mother,
Sad news for thee;
My brother is in some foreign land
And wishing to come home."

11. Little Old Tom went riding home,
Just as welcome as could be;
Who should he meet but his fair Eleander dear;
"What news have you brought to me?"

12. "Sad news, sad news, fair Eleander dear,
Sad news for thee;
My brother is dead and is in cold clay,
And buried in Christian charm."

13. She harbored around her true love's grave,
Five weeks to a day;
He harbored the redbird out of the nest
And the red fish out of the sea.

14. "Go away, fair Eleander dear;
Go away from me,
For if you stay here to the day of your death,
You'll see no more of me."

13. [The Two Brothers]

Randolph, I, 1946, pp. 76(A)-77. Sung by Mrs. Emma L.
Dusenbury, Mena, Ark., November 24, 1939. Collected by
Professor F. M. Goodhue, Commonwealth College, Mena.

p I/Ly

1. I once did know two little boys,
An' pretty little boys was they,
I safely wished myself with them,
My playmates for to be.

2. A Monday mornin' they'd start to school,
A Saturday they'd return,
An' then they'd comb their yaller locks
To see their parents at home.

3. Oh Johnny, can you toss a ball,
Or can you throw a stone?
I am too little, I am too young,
Dear brother, let me alone.

4. Willie pulled out his big long knife,
An' it was keen an' sharp,
Between the long ribs an' the short
He pierced little Johnny's heart.

5. When Willie pulled off his loathy shirt
An' tore it from gore to gore,
An' wropped it round Johnny's bleedin' wound,
But still it bled the more.

6. Oh pick me up, dear brother, says he,
An' lay me out so straight,
Oh pick me up, dear brother, says he,
An' bury me at the gate.

7. If you meet mother, an' she's much concerned,
Just tell her I've went alone,
Just tell her I'm a-goin' to the old camp ground,
My prayer-book for to learn.

14. "The Rolling away of the Stones"

Linscott, 1939, pp. 278-80. Sung by Mrs. Mary E. Harmon,
Cambridge, Mass.; learned from her father.

p Æ/D (– VI; inflected VII)

This is like a New Brunswick copy of "Young Hunting" (68),
brought from Ireland. Cf. Barry, Eckstorm, and Smyth, 1929, p. 122.

1. Oh, will you go to the rolling of the stones
Or the tossing of the ball?
Or will you go and see pretty Susie
And dance among them all?

2. I will not go to the rolling of the stones
Or the tossing of the ball,
But I will go and see pretty Susie
And dance among them all.

3. They had not danced but one single dance
More than once or twice around
Before the sword that hung by Bell's side
Gave him his fatal wound.

4. They took him up and they carried him out,
For he was in distress,
They carried him and buried him all in the green woods,
Where he was content to rest.

5. Pretty Susie she came mourning by,
With a tablet on her arm.
   (*The next two lines are missing.*)

6. She charmed the fish all out of the sea,
And the birds all out of the nests,
Until she came where her true love lay,
Where he was content to rest.

15. [The Two Brothers]

Sharp MSS., 4542/3182. Also in Sharp and Karpeles, 1932,
I, pp. 74(J)-75. Sung by Mrs. Lucindie (G. K.) Freeman,
Marion, N.C., September 3, 1918.

p I/Ly

Cf. "Ain't goin' to rain no more."

1. Monday morning go to school,
Friday evening home.
Sister, comb my sweetheart's hair
And welcome her at home.

2. It's O brother, O brother, don't play no game of ball,
Brother don't cast no stone,
Don't play no other game
As we go marching home.

3. I won't play no game of ball,
Nor neither cast no stone,
I won't play no other game,
But sister won't let me alone.

4. Brother pulled out his little penknife,
It was both sharp and keen.
He pierced his own brother to the heart,
It made a dreadful wound.

5. O brother, O brother, pull off your little check shirt,
Stitched from gore to gore,
And bind it around this dreadful wound
And it will bleed no more.

6. Brother pulled off his little check shirt,
Stitched from gore to gore,
And bound it around his dreadful wound,
And it did bleed no more.

7. O brother, go dig my grave,
Dig it wide and deep,
Bury a bible at my head
And a prayer-book at my feet.

8. He buried his bible at his head,
His prayer-book at his feet.
A bow and arrow by his side,
And now he lies asleep.

16. [The Two Brothers]

Sharp MSS., 3472/. Sung by Mrs. Ellie Johnson (23), Hot Springs, N.C., September 16, 1916.

p I/Ly

Monday morning go to school
Friday evening home
Brother comb my sweetheart's hair
As we go walking home.

17. [The Two Brothers]

Sharp MSS., 3458/2547. Also in Sharp and Karpeles, 1932, I, pp. 65(A)-66. Sung by Mrs. Lizzie Roberts and Mrs. Smith, Hot Springs, N.C., September 15, 1916.

p I/Ly

Variant (a) is Mrs. Smith's.

1. Monday morning go to school,
   Friday evening home.
   Brother, comb my sweetheart's hair
   As we go welcome* home.

2. Brother, won't you play a game of ball?
   Brother, won't you toss a stone?
   Brother, won't you play no other game
   As we go marching home?

3. I can't play no game of ball,
   I can't toss no stone,
   I can't play no other game.
   Brother, leave me alone.

4. Brother took out his little penknife,
   It was sharp and keen.
   He stuck it in his own brother's heart,
   It caused a deadly wound.

5. Brother, take off your little check shirt,
   Stitched from gore to gore;
   Bind it around the deadly wound.
   It won't bleed no more.

6. Brother took off his little check shirt,
   Stitched from gore to gore;
   Bound it around the deadly wound.
   It didn't bleed no more.

7. Brother, O brother, go dig my grave,
   Dig it wide and deep.
   Bury my bible at my head,
   My hymn book at my feet.

8. He buried his bible at his head,
   His hymn book at his feet,
   His bow and arrow by his side,
   And now he's fast asleep.

* 1932: "walking"

18. [The Two Brothers]

Sharp MSS., 3490/. Also in Sharp and Karpeles, 1932, I, p. 69(E). Sung by Mrs. Carrie Ford, Black Mountain, N.C., September 18, 1916.

p I/Ly

Its Monday morning go to school
Friday evening home
Brother comb my sweetheart's hair
And welcome her in home.

19. [The Two Brothers]

Sharp MSS., 3972/2856. Also in Sharp and Karpeles, 1932, I, pp. 69(F)-70; and, with piano accompaniment, in Sharp, 1918, p. 7. Sung by Mrs. Margaret Dunagan, St. Helen's, Lee County, Ky., September 5, 1917.

p I

1. O brother, can you toss the stone,
   Or can you play the ball?
   I am too little, I am too young,
   Go, brother, let me alone.

2. His brother took his little penknife,
   He hung it up* by his side,
   He put it deeply deathly wound
   As it hung by his side.

3. O brother, take my holland shirt,
   And rip it from gore to gore;
   You tie it around my bleeding wound
   And still it'll bleed no more.

4. His brother took his holland shirt
   And ripped it from gore to gore;
   He tied it around his bleeding wound,
   But still it bled the more.

5. O brother, take me on your back,
   Carry me to Chesley Town;
   You dig me a deep and large, wide grave
   And lay me there so sound.

6. You put my bible at my head,
   My solberd (psalter?) at my feet,
   My little bow and arrow at my side,
   And sounder I will sleep.

7. His brother took him on his back,
   He carried him to Chesley Town;
   He dug him a deep and large, wide grave
   And laid him there so sound.

8. He put his bible at his head,
   His solberd at his feet,
   His little bow and arrow at his side,
   So sounder he will sleep.

9. O brother, as you go home at night
   And my mother asks for me,
   You tell her I'm along with some schoolboys,
   So merry I'll come home.

10. And if my true love asks for me,
    The truth to her you'll tell;
    You'll tell her I'm dead and in grave laid
    And buried in Chesley Town.

11. With my bible at my head,
    My solberd at my feet,
    My little bow and arrow at my side,
    And sounder I will sleep.

12. And as his brother went home at night,
    His mother asked for him.
    He told he's along with some schoolboys,
    So merry he'll come home.

13. And then his true love asked for him;
    The truth to her he told.
    He told he was dead and in grave laid
    And buried in Chesley Town.

14. With his bible at his head,
    His solberd at his feet,
    His little bow and arrow at his side,
    So sounder he will sleep.

15. And then his true love put on small hoppers
    And tied them with silver strings.
    She went hopping all over her true love's grave
    A twelve-months and a day.

16. She hopped the red fish out of the sea,
    The small birds out of their nests;
    She hopped her true love out of his grave,
    So he can't see no rest.

17. Go home, go home, you rambling reed;
    Don't weep nor mourn for me;
    If you do for twelve long years,
    No more you'll see of me.

* 1932: *del.* up

20. [The Two Brothers]

Lomax, LC/AAFS, Album 7, rec. 32A(541). Sung by Mrs.
Texas Gladden, Salem, Va., 1941.

m π¹

1. "Oh, brother, oh brother, can you play ball
      Or roll a marble stone?"
   "No, brother, no, brother, I can't play ball
      Nor roll a marble stone."*

2. He took his tomahawk from him
      And hacked him across the breast.
   "Say, now, brother, I reckon you can't play ball
      Nor roll a marble stone."

3. "Oh, take my hunting shirt from me
      And tear it from gore to gore,
   And wrap it around my bleeding breast
      That it might bleed no more."

4. He took his hunting shirt from him
      And tore it from gore to gore,
   And wrapped it around his bleeding breast,
      But it still bled the more.

5. "Oh, brother, when you go home to-night,
      My mother will ask for me.
   You must tell her I'm gone with some little schoolboys.
      To-morrow night I'll be at home.

6. "My dear little sister will ask for me.
      The truth to her you must tell.
   You must tell her I'm dead and in grave laid
      And buried at Jesseltown.

7. "Oh, take me up, oh, on your back
  And carry me to Jesseltown,
  And dig a hole and lay me in
    That I might sleep so sound."

8. He took him up, oh, on his back
    And carried him to Jesseltown,
  And dug a hole and laid him in
    That he might sleep so sound.

9. He laid his bible under his head,
    His tomahawk at his feet,
  His bow and arrow across his breast
    That he might sleep so sweet.

* The last two lines of each stanza are repeated.

GROUP C

21. "Billy Murdered John"

Barry, Eckstorm, and Smyth, 1929, pp. 99-100. Sung by
Mrs. Susie Carr Young, Brewer, Maine, 1926; learned from
her grandmother. Melody recorded by George Herzog.

p I (– VI)

"O Billy, O Billy, [you have]* come home!
And where is my true-love John?"
"The last time I saw him he was in the greenwood
A-learning the hounds to run."

*   *   *   *   *

"If you should kiss my cherry cheeks,
Your breath would smell so strong;
If you should kiss my ruby, ruby lips,
Your life would not last long."

*   *   *   *   *

And Susan came with sobs of pain,
With tears all in her eyes.
She mourns by the flocks of the merry, merry brooks,
For she's been where her own true-love lies.

* Words in brackets inserted by Mrs. Young to fill out the tune.

22. "The Dying Soldier"

E. C. and M. N. Kirkland, *SFQ*, II (1938), p. 66. Sung by
Miss Nanie McNew, Carlisle, Ky., July 25, 1937. Recorded
by Dr. Claudius Capps.

m I/Ly

This has typical affiliations with "Barbara Allen" (84; cf., e.g.,
Sharp and Karpeles, 1932, I, p. 191[I]). Cf. also "Lizie Wan" (51)
and "Edward" (13).

Oh, Willie, take my highland shirt,
Tear it from gore to gore,
And wrop it around my bleeding wounds,
And I will bleed no more.

Willie took his highland shirt,
Tore it from gore to gore,
And wropt it around his bleeding wounds;
He still bled more and more.

Oh, Willie, take me on your back
And carry me to the church door,
And lay me down on the cold ground
And I will bleed no more.

Willie took him on his back
And carried him to the church door,
And laid him down on the cold ground
And he bled more and more.

Oh, Willie, go dig my grave,
Dig it both wide and deep,
And place my prayer book by my side,
A marble stone at my head and feet.

23. [The Two Brothers]

Davis, 1929, p. 563(A); text, pp. 147-48. Sung by Etta
Shifflett, Blackwell's Hollow, Va., November 10, 1919. Collected by John Stone.

a π¹

1. There were two brothers in one school.
    One evening coming home
  The oldest said to the youngest one,
    "Let's have a wrestle and fall."

2. The oldest threw the youngest one,
    He threw him to the ground,
  And out of his pocket he drew a pen knife
    And gave him a deadly wound.

3. "Pull off, pull off your woolen shirt
        And tear it from gore to gore
    And wrap it around your bleeding wound,
        And it will bleed no more."

4. So he pulled off his woolen shirt
        And tore it from gore to gore,
    He wrapped it around his bleeding wound
        And it did bleed no more.

5. "Pick me all up upon your back
        And carry me to yonder churchyard,
    And dig my grave both wide and deep
        And gently lay me down."

6. "What must I tell your loving father
        When he calls for his son John?"
    "Tell him I'm in some lonely green wood
        Teaching young hounds to run."

7. "What must I tell your loving mother
        When she calls for her son John?"
    "Tell her I'm in some graded school,
        A good scholar to never return."

8. "What must I tell your loving Susie
        When she calls for her dear John?"
    "Tell her I'm in my lonely grave,
        My books to carry back home."

9. When loving Susie heard of this,
        She took her horn and blew;
    She charmed the birdies from the nest
        And the fishes out of the sea.

10. She charmed young Johnny from his grave
        He said, "Susie, what do you want?"
    "One sweet kiss from your sweet lips
        Is all my heart doth crave."

11. "Go home, go home, my loving Susie,
        And weep no more for me,
    For one sweet kiss from my sweet lips
        Will cause your days short on."

24. [The Two Brothers]

Sharp MSS., 3536/2612. Also in Sharp and Karpeles, 1932,
I, p. 68(D); and Davis, 1929, p. 564(I). Sung by Mr. Ozro
Keeton (25), Mount Fair, Brown's Cove, Va., September
26, 1916.

a M

Sharp wrote this in 6/8 time originally.

But when young Suse came to know this
She charmed the birds all out of their nests,
And charmed young John all out of his grave,
Where he was resting in peace.

O what do you want with me, young Suse,
O what do you want with me?
I want one kiss from your sweet lips
And then I can rest in peace.

Sharp MS. and Davis, 1929: "Mr. Keeton could not remember any
more of the song. The following lines were given by his mother."

Two little boys was going to school
And they fell all into a play.

. . . .
And split from gore to gore

. . . .
That it may bleed no more.

"Tell them I have done learned my lessons
And gone in the mountains to train my hounds to run."

25. [The Two Brothers]

Sharp MSS., 3563/2633. Also in Sharp and Karpeles, 1932,
I, p. 76(L). Sung by Mrs. James A. Maples, Bird's Creek,
Sevierville, Tenn., April 16, 1917.

a M (– VI)

Little Willie, can't* you throw a ball,
Nor even cast a stone?
No, I'm too small to throw a ball,
Or even cast a stone.

Little Willie had a new penknife
Which was both keen and sharp
He pierced little Johnnie to the side
And quickly touched his heart.

Go bury my Bible at my head,
My Testament at my feet,
And if any of them ask for me,
Pray tell them I'm asleep.

* 1932: "can"

26. "John Gobillips"

Halpert, LC/AAFS rec. 2760 A3. Sung by Mrs. Polly Johnson, Wise, Va., 1939.

a I/M (compass of sixth)

Variant reading (a) accommodates the extra line in stanza 3.

'John Gobillips, go take my fine shirt
    And tear it from gore to gore
And wrap my bleeding wounds in hit
    That they may bleed no more.'

John Gobillips he tuck his fine shirt
    And he tore it from gore to gore
And he wrapped his bleeding wounds in hit
    But they still bled more and more.

'John Gobillips, go dig my grave
    And dig it both wide and deep
And bury my Bible under my head
    And my bow or knife at my side
    That I may sleep the more.'

27. [The Two Brothers]

Sharp MSS., 4598/3216. Also in Sharp and Karpeles, 1932, I, pp. 75(K)-76. Sung by Mrs. Virginia Bennett, Burnsville, N.C., September 13, 1918.

a D/M

This suggests the "House Carpenter" family: the American tradition of "The Daemon Lover" (243).

1. On Monday morning going to school
    And Friday evening coming home:
    The ladies all a-rolling a ball,
    And the gents a-throwing a stone.

      * * * * *

2. He wrestled him up and he wrestled him down,
    Till he wrestled him to the ground.

      * * * * *

3. What will you tell to my father dear
    When he calls for his son John?
    I'll tell that I left you in the Mackintaw woods
    A-learning your hounds to run.

4. What will you tell to your mother dear
    When she calls for her son John?
    I'll tell that I left you in the old school-house
    With a long, long lesson to learn.

5. What will you tell to your sister Susan dear
    When she calls for her brother John?
    I'll tell that I left you in the cold grave-yard,
    No more for her to see.

6. She took her banjo in her arms,
    Her harp strung to her back.
    She harped till she harped the fowls from the air
    And the fishes from the sea.

7. She harped till she harped brother John from his grave.
    Sister, what do you want with me?
    One sweet kiss from your sweet ruby lips,
    This world's not long for me.

28. "Two Born Brothers"

Eddy, 1939, pp. 26-27. Sung by Mrs. Anna E. Housley, Canton, Ohio; learned from her mother.

m D

Cf. with this especially "The House Carpenter" (243); also Appalachian variants "Young Hunting" (68) and "Lady Isabel and the Elf Knight" (4, e.g., Sharp and Karpeles, I, p. 10[F]). One of Miss Eddy's singers used the tune for "Lord Thomas and Fair Elinor" (73). Cf. Eddy, 1939, p. 29, a copy learned in Tennessee.

1. Once there were two brothers
    Who loved each other well,
    On Monday morning going to school,
    On Saturday coming home.

2. "Oh, brother will you wrestle,
    Will you wrestle up and down,
    Or will you go to the green shade,
    Or to the milk-white stone?"

3. "I will neither go to the green shade tree,
    Nor to the milk-white stone,
    But here upon this pretty green grass
    I will wrestle you up and down."

4. They wrestled up and they wrestled down,
    They wrestled up and down,
    Till out of William's pocket a pen-knife flew
    Which gave John a deathly wound.

5. "Take off, take off my Holland shirt,
    And tear it from gore to gore,
    And wrap it around my bleeding wound;
    Perhaps it will bleed no more."

6. He took off, took off his Holland shirt,
   And tore it from gore to gore,
   And wrapped it around his bleeding wound,
   But still it bled more and more.

7. "Oh, what shall I tell to your mother
   When she asks for her son John?"
   "Tell her I've gone to a distant land
   Where many a poor man's gone."

8. "And what shall I tell to your father
   When he asks for his son John?"
   "Tell him I've gone to a distant school
   My books are there to bring home."

9. "And what shall I tell to your true love
   When she asks for her true lover John?"
   "Tell her I'm dead and buried under sod;
   In West Chester lies my bones."

10. She wept, she wept from door to door,
    She wept from door to door,
    Until she had wept this young man out of his grave;
    No rest could she find no more.

11. "Go home, go home, you lovely maid,
    And weep and weep no more,
    For as surely as you do, you surely will rue
    Until the day you die."

29. "John and William"

McGill, 1917, pp. 54-58.

a D (– II; inflected VII)

This beautiful variant has relations with "Young Hunting" (68)
and "Lady Gay" (79).

1. O John and William walkèd out one day
   To view the iron band.
   Says John to William, "At any price
   We'd better turn home again."

2. "O no," says William, "That can never be
   That we'll return again,
   For I'm the one loves pretty Susanne
   And I will murder thee."

3. "What will you tell to my mother dear,
   When she askès for her son John?"
   "I left him at the cottage school
   His lessons for to learn."

4. "What will you tell to my father dear,
   When he askès for his son John?"
   "I left him in the high wild woods
   A-learnin' his hounds to run."

5. "What will you tell to my pretty Susanne
   When she askès for her true love John?"
   "I left him in the grave-lie deep,
   Never more to return."

6. She mourned the fish all out of the sea,
   The birds all out of the nest;
   She mourned her true love out of his grave
   Because that she could not rest.

7. "What do you want, my pretty Susanne,
   What do you want with me?"
   "A kiss or two from your pretty bright lips
   Is all that I ask of thee."

8. "Go home, go home, my pretty Susanne,
   Go home, go home," said he;
   "If you weep and mourn all the balance of your days
   You'll never more see me."

30. [The Twa Brothers]

Eddy, 1939, pp. 27-28. Sung by Mrs. James Robertson,
Perrysville, Ohio; learned in Missouri.

a Æ

"Can you throw a stone,
    Or can you toss a ball?"
"I am too little, I am too young,
    Pray, brother, let me be."

He pulled his little penknife,
    It being keen and sharp,
And pierced it through and through
    Poor Johnny's heart.

"When you chance to see my old mother,
    And she inquires for me,
Tell her I've gone to join my little school mates,
    No more of me she'll see.

"Go, dig my grave both wide and deep,
    And bury my Bible at my head,
My hymn book at my feet,
    My bow and arrow by my right side,
The sweeter that I might sleep."

GROUP D

31. [The Two Brothers]

Sharp MSS., 3534/2609. Also in Sharp and Karpeles, 1932,
I, pp. 67(C)-68; and Davis, 1929, p. 563. Sung by Mr.

Nuel Walton, Mount Fair, Brown's Cove, Va., September 26, 1916.

a M (inflected VII)

Sharp noted this originally in 6/8 time.

1. One evening, one evening,
   Two brothers gone from school.
   The oldest said to the youngest one:
   Let's take a wrastle fall.

2. The oldest threw the youngest down,
   He threw him to the ground,
   And from his pocket came a penknife
   And give him a deathless wound.

3. Pull off, pull off, your woolen shirt,
   And tear it from gore to gore,
   And wrap it around this deathless wound,
   And that will bleed no more.

4. He pulled off his woolen shirt,
   And tore it from gore to gore,
   And wrapped it around this deathless wound,
   And it did bleed no more.

5. It's take me up all on your back
   And carry me to yonder churchyard,
   And dig my grave both wide and deep
   And gentle lie me down.

6. What will you tell your father
   When he calls for his son John?
   You can tell him I'm in some low green woods
   A-learning young hounds to run.

7. What will you tell your mother
   When she calls for her son John?
   You can tell her I'm in some graded school,
   Good scholar to never return.

8. What will you tell your true love
   When she calls for her dear John?
   You can tell her I'm in some lonesome grave,
   My books to carry home.

*   *   *   *   *

9. One sweet kiss from your clay, clay lips
   Will bring my day short on.

32. [The Two Brothers]

Sharp MSS., 4168/3006. Also in Sharp and Karpeles, 1932, I, p. 76(M). Sung by Mrs. Florence Fitzgerald, Afton, Va., April 23, 1918.

a M (– VI)

There was* two brothers a-going to school,
A-going to the very same school;
The oldest says to the youngest one:
Let's take a wrestle and fall.

The very first fall the old one gave,
He threw him to the ground,
He drew a knife from his pocket
And gave him a deathly wound.

Pick me up, pick me up all in your arms,
And carry me to yonders church ground,
And dig my grave both wide and deep
And gently lie me down.

He picked him up all in his arms
And carried him to yonders church ground
And dug his grave both wide and deep
And gently lay him down.

What must I tell my mother dear
This evening as I go home?
Just tell her I'm gone to the Olgen woods
My books all for to bring home.

What must I tell little Susie dear
This evening as I go home?
Just tell her I am in the Olgen woods
A-learning young hounds to run.

*   *   *   *   *

One sweet kiss from your cold clay lips
Is all I want of thee.

* 1932: "were"

33. [The Two Brothers]

Davis, 1929, p. 564(F); text, pp. 152-53. Sung by Mrs. Rosie Morris, Elkton, Va., August 30, 1922. Collected by Martha M. Davis.

a Æ (inflected II)

1. There were two brothers all in one school.
   One evening coming home
   The oldest said to the youngest one,
   "Let's go out in the green grass and wrestle and fall."

2. First he threw, he threw on the lea (or, he threw a Lee)
   He threw him on the ground,
   Out of his pocket a pen-knife he drew
   And gave him a deathly wound.

The E♭ in bar 8 belies the mode.

3. "Pull off, pull off my holland shirt
    And tear it from gore to gore
And wrap it round my bleeding wounds,
    So I won't bleed no more."

4. He pull-ed off his holland shirt
    And tore it from gore to gore
And wrapped it round his bleeding wounds,
    But still he bled the more.

5. "O pick me up upon your back,
    And carry me to yonder graveyard,
And dig my grave both wide and deep
    And lay me gently down."

6. "What must I tell your loving mother
    When she asks for her son John?"
"Tell her I've gone to Jersey School,
    My books are all to send home."

7. "What must I tell your loving father
    When he asks for his son John?"
"Tell him I've gone to low green woods,
    A-learning young hounds to run."

8. "What must I tell your loving Susie
    When she asks for her dear John?"
"Tell her I'm dead and in my grave,
    A good scholar never to return."

9. She took her flute all in her hand,
    She blew it more and more,
She charmed the birds out of their nests
    And the fish out of the sea.

10. . . . .
    She charmed young Johnny out of his grave
    Where he was lying asleep.

11. "What do you want, my loving Susie,
    What do you want with me?"
"It's one sweet kiss from your clay lips,
    That's all I want with thee."

34. [The Two Brothers]

Wilkinson MSS., 1935-36, p. 34(A). Sung by Alice Bruce, Harriston, Va., October 9, 1935.

a Æ/D (inflected III, VII)

What must I tell your father
Tonight when I go home?
Tell him I'm in some lonesome woods
A-learning the hounds to run.

What must I tell to Sadie
Tonight when I go home?
Tell her I'm in the cold, cold coffin
With my pale face turned to the wall.

35. [The Two Brothers]

Wilkinson MSS., 1935-36, p. 38(D). Sung by Z. B. Lam, Standardsville, Va., November 3, 1935.

a D

36. [The Two Brothers]

Wilkinson MSS., 1935-36, pp. 39-40(E). Sung by T. Henry Lam, Elkton, Va., November 6, 1935.

a D

1. Pull off, pull off, the haulin' shirt,
    And tear it from gore to gore.
    And wrap it around this bleeding wound
    So it may bleed no more.

2. He pulled off the haulin' shirt,
    And tore it from gore to gore
    And wrapped it around the bleeding wound,
    And still it bled the more.

3. O what must I tell your loving mother,
   This night when I go home?
   You can tell her I'm in young Chester's Gap,
   With lets no more to roam.

4. O what must I tell your loving father,
   This night when I go home?
   You can tell him I'm down in the low green woods,
   A-learning young hounds to run.

5. O what must I tell your loving Susie,
   This night when I go home?
   You can tell her I'm dead and in my grave,
   To never more return.

6. She taken her flute all in hand,
   She played it more and more.
   She charmed the little fish out of the sea, and the birds
      all out of their nest.
   She charmed Sweet William all out of his grave where he
      was lying at rest.

7. O what do you want, my loving Susie?
   O what do you want? says he.
   Just one sweet kiss from your clay lips
   Is all I crave from thee.

8. Go home, go home, my loving Susie,
   Go home, go home, says he.
   If one sweet kiss from my clay lips
   Is all you crave from me.

4. Take off, take off, your woolen shirt,
   And tear it from gore to gore.
   And wrap it around my bloody wound,
   So it won't bleed anymore.

5. He took off his woolen shirt.
   He tore it from gore to gore.
   He wrapt it around his bloody wound,
   But still it bled the more.

6. What must I tell your loving old father,
   This night when I go home?
   Tell him I'm in some lonely greenwoods
   A-learning young hounds to run.

7. What must I tell your loving old mother,
   This night when I go home?
   Tell her I'm at some college school
   My books to carry home.

8. What must I tell your loving little Susie,
   This night when I go home?
   Tell her I'm in some lonely church yard
   To never turn back (home) no more.

9. He picked him up all on his back,
   And carried him to yonder's church yard.
   He dug his grave both wide and deep
   And gently laid him down.

10. She took her banjo all in her arms,
    . . . .
    She charmed the fishes out of the sea,
    Young Johnny out of his grave.

37. [The Two Brothers]

Wilkinson MSS., 1935-36, pp. 36-37(C). Sung by Mrs. Mary McAllister, Grottoes, Va., October 30, 1935.

a D

1. One evening two brothers was going from school;
   They fell into a play.
   The oldest said to the youngest one:
   Let's take a wrestle and fall.

2. The oldest threw the youngest down;
   He threwed him on the ground.
   And out of his pocket a pen-knife drew,
   And give him a deathly wound.

3. Pick me up, pick me up, all on your back,
   And carry me to yonder's church yard.
   And dig my grave both wide and deep
   And gently lie me down.

38. "Martyr John"

Flanders and Olney, 1953, pp. 230-32. Sung by Mrs. Lily Delorme, Cadyville, N.Y., August 16, 1943. From *Ballads Migrant in New England*, edited by Helen Hartness Flanders and Marguerite Olney; copyright 1953 by Helen Hartness Flanders.

p Æ/D (inflected VII); or Harmonic Minor

1. It was Martyr John who died of late
   By his older brother's hand
   As he walked o'er to take the air
   And to view the pleasant land.

2. "O brother dear, when shall we return
   From a-viewing the pleasant land?"
   He answered him, "You never can return
   For I have mercy none."

3. "Then what will you tell to my old father
   When he'll call for his son John?"
   "O I'll tell him that you've gone to the merry Greenwood
   A-learning your hounds to run."

4. "Then what will you tell to my old mother
When she calls for her son John?"
"O I'll tell her that you've gone to fair Starksborotown
Your lessons for to learn."

5. "Then what will you tell to my pretty Susan
When she calls for her true-love John?"
"O I'll tell her that you are dead and in your grave laid
Never, never more to return."

6. Then he drew his dagger from his side
And he pierced his brother through
And he laid him down by the clear running brook
Saying: "Now, there's an end of you!"

7. Then he went home to his old father
Who said, "Where is my son John?"
"O he is in the merry Greenwood
A-learning his hounds to run."

8. And then upspoke his old mother
Saying: "Where is my son John?"
"O he has gone to fair Starksborotown
His lessons for to learn."

9. And then upspoke his pretty Susan
Saying, "Where is my true love John?"
"O he is dead and in his grave laid
Never, never more to return."

10. O she took her dagger in her hand
And she run along the clear running brook
And she run to the place where in the field
And the birds were in their nests.

11. And she mourned her true love out of his grave
O I'm sure that he could not rest.

12. "O what do you want, my pretty Susan,
O why do you mourn for me?"
"One kiss from your clay-cold lips
It's all that I want of thee."

13. "Go home! Go home! my pretty Susan
And worry no more for me
For you must have known from the day of your doom
I never can return to you."

39. [The Twa Brothers]

Creighton and Senior, 1950, pp. 25-26. Sung by Mrs. R. W.
Duncan and Richard Hartlan, Nova Scotia.

m π¹

Will you go to the footing of the hills
Or to the marvelous hall,
Or will you go to the merry green fields
To dance amongst them all.

"No I won't go to the footing of the hills
Nor to the marvelous hall,
But I will go to the merry green fields
For to dance amongst them all."

Now Willie had a little pen knife
It being both keen and sharp,
And betwixt the short ribs and the long
He pierced his brother to the heart.

"Oh it's when you get home to my own mother dear
She'll enquire for her son John,
You can tell her that he's there in old Engaland
A-learning the hounds for to run.

"And when you get there in old Engaland
She'll enquire for her love John,
You can tell her that he's dead and into his grave
And perhaps he never will return."

She flung her apron all over her head
And she mourned the streets all round,
Until she mourned her true love out of his grave,
For rest he never had none.

40. [The Two Brothers]

Randolph, I, 1946, pp. 77(B)-78. Sung by J. Will Short,
Galena, Mo., August 15, 1941; learned from his mother,
near Marionville, Mo., c. 1890.

a M

The rhythm here is puzzling and has been left as received. But it
may probably have been triple (i.e., 3/2) rather than duple.

1. One Monday morning a-going to school,
And in the evening a-coming home,
A-coming home to my parents dear,
My yellow hair for to comb.

2. Now brother dear, can you roll a stone
Or throw a ball?
No brother, I'm too little and young,
Pray brother, let me alone.

3. Now he drew a sword from his side
Which was all covered with gold,
And pierced it into his own brother's side,
From that the blood did flow.

4. Now brother dear, take your shirt off o' your back,
And rip it from gore to gore,
And tie up these bleeding wounds
So they will bleed no more.

5. Now he took his shirt all off o' his back,
And he ripped it from gore to gore,
And tied up those bleeding wounds
But still they bled the more.

6. Now brother dear, when you go home,
My mother will ask for me,
You may tell her I'm along with my little school mates,
So early I'll be home.

7. Now brother dear,
My father will ask for me,
You may tell him I'm a-lyin' in my grave cold,
My face he never shall see.

8. Now brother dear, take me all in your arms,
And carry me over to your church yard,
And lay me in my grave so low.

9. And bury my Bible all under my head,
My bow-and-arrow by my side,
My spelling-book all under my feet,
So soundly I may sleep.

APPENDIX

41. "Edward Ballad"

Flanders and Olney, 1953, pp. 96-99. Sung by George J.
Edwards, Burlington, Vt., January 22, 1934; from family
tradition. From *Ballads Migrant in New England*, edited
by Helen Hartness Flanders and Marguerite Olney; copyright 1953 by Helen Hartness Flanders.

a I, ending on III (inflected IV)

The original time-signature is 12/8.
Melodically, this version is as disturbingly independent as it is
textually. The tune resembles material used for Child 283 ("Saddle
to Rags," "The Silly Old Man"). The words are a too literary
rifacimento of "The Two Brothers" and "Edward" (13) combined.

1. It was in the Mid-Lothian Country,
Up near the Pentland hills,
Two brothers met one summer's day
To test their strength and skill.

2. Edward was the eldest one,
And John was the younger man;
They were equally matched in every way
To try what valor can.

3. "Shall we go to the school grounds?
Or will we remain at the Hall?
But, better we go to the greenwood,
To see which of us must fall."

4. "No, we'll not go to the school grounds,
Nor will we remain at the Hall,
But we will go to Roslyn woods
To see which of us will fall."

5. They struggled long for the mastery,
Till shadows told the end of the day,
When Edward waxed wroth at his failure,
And with his sword did his brother slay.

6. "Brother, raise me up and help me to walk;
Take me to yon stream so fair;
Wash the blood from out my wounds
So they will bleed no more."

7. He raised his brother upon his feet,
And helped him to the stream so fair.
Frantically he bathed his bloody wounds,
But they bled more and more.

8. "Now, brother, I know that I must die,
And I conjure you ere I go,
That you will not tell the folks at home
How this happened, nor let them know.

9. "Now lift me up, upon your back,
And take me to the churchyard fair;
Dig my grave both broad and deep
And lay my body there.

10. "You will place my arrows at my head;
My bow put at my feet;
My sword and buckler at my side
As though I were asleep.

11. "When you go home to my true love,
She'll ask for her lover John;
Say you left me in the churchyard fair
But you fear I'll never come home.

12. "When you go home to our sister,
She'll ask for her brother John;
Tell her I've gone to Stirling Carse
To see the king upon his throne.

13. "When you go home to our parents,
They'll ask you, 'Where is John?'
Tell them I'm at the Abbot's house
Studying there alone."

14. When he came home to John's true love,
She asked for her lover John.
He said, "I left him in the fair churchyard
And I fear he will never come home."

15. When he came home to his sister,
She asked for her brother John;
He told her he had gone to the Carse of Stirling
To the king upon his throne.

16. When he came home to his parents,
They asked for their son John;
"I left him at the Abbot's school
To study there alone."

17. "What blood is that on thy coat front, Edward?
It's as red as it can be."
"It's the blood of my great hawk
That uncle gave to me."

18. "Hawk's blood was never so red, son;
Come, and tell the truth to me."
"It is the blood of my greyhound, mother,
He would not run for me."

19. "That's not the blood of a hound, son;
That is very plain to see,
Is it not the blood of thy brother John?
Come, and tell the truth to me."

20. "It is the blood of brother John
O mother! Woe is me;
I slew him in a fit of rage,
Now the truth I have told to thee.

21. "You have always told me, mother,
Eldest sons must ne'er give in,

The family name and title
Must always be sure to win."

22. "What penance will you do, son,
To wipe away the stain?"
"I'll sail away across the seas,
And never come back again."

23. "What will you leave your wife and son,
If you sail beyond the sea?"
"I'll leave them my towers and hall, mother,
Which mean nothing now to me."

24. "What will you leave your mother, Edward,
Who has been so fond of thee?"
"I'll leave with her the memory of
Wrong counsel given me."

25. "When will you return, my son?
I shall long thy face to see."
"When the sunlight and moonbeams meet on the
green,
And that will never be."

Lizie Wan

CHILD NO. 51

THIS ballad, which might have been supposed to have died a hundred and fifty years ago, has surprisingly been recovered in late copies on both sides of the Atlantic. The theme is one not much affected in the last century. But the music gives evidence of a continuous and unbroken tradition, which would seem to indicate that where this ballad has been learned it has neither made a vague impression nor become confused. On the contrary, it may be much more generally known than appears from the record, and kept close from casual collectors—strangers at best.

There appears to be a definite, if unconscious, association in folk tradition between this ballad and "Edward." Such a con-nection is suggested both melodically and textually. The fact might lend some countenance to Barry's interpretation of "Ed-ward" as a ballad on the incest-theme, although there is no hint of this on the surface of any text except, possibly, the (famous) Dalrymple-Percy version.

Perhaps all copies of the present ballad's tune should be classed as plagal majors, although the Vermont copies have the dropped ending (Mixolydian), and the Kentucky copy lacks the seventh (I/M). One copy only is of English record.

Melodic relations may be noted with "The Unquiet Grave" (78) and "Little Musgrave" (81).

LIST OF VARIANTS

1a. "Fair Lucy." Phillips Barry Dictaphone Cylinders, No. 90, transcribed by S. P. Bayard, Harvard College Library MS., p. 23.

1b. "Fair Lucy." Barry MSS., Bk. I, No. 51 A, Harvard College Library.

2. "Lizzie Wan." Sharp MSS., 3838/2810, Clare College Library, Cambridge. Also in Cecil J. Sharp and Maud Karpeles, *English Folk Songs from the Southern Appalachians*, 1932, I, p. 89.

3. "Lucy." W. P. Merrick and Ella Bull, *JEFDSS*, I (1932), p. 53.

4. "Fair Lucy." Helen Hartness Flanders, *BFSSNE*, No. 7 (1934), p. 7(1).

5a. "Fair Lucy." Flanders, *BFSSNE*, No. 7 (1934), p. 7(2).

5b. "Fair Lucy." Helen Hartness Flanders and Marguerite Olney, *Ballads Migrant in New England*, 1953, pp. 143-45.

6. "Fair Lucy." Alton C. Morris, *Folksongs of Florida*, 1950, pp. 257-59.

TUNES WITH TEXTS

1a. "Fair Lucy"

Barry Dict. Cyl., No. 90, transcribed by S. P. Bayard, Harvard College Library MS., p. 23. Sung by Mrs. Myra Daniels.

p I

1b. "Fair Lucy"

Barry MSS., Bk. I, No. 51 A. Tr. by Barry from dictaphone. Sung by Mrs. Myra Daniels, Calais, Vt., at Allston, Mass., October 26, 1934; learned from her grandfather, Chester Chase, of Plymouth, Mass., who moved to Woodbury, Vt.

p I

2. [Lizzie Wan]

Sharp MSS., 3838/2810. Also in Sharp and Karpeles, 1932, I, p. 89. Sung by Benjamin J. Finlay, Manchester, Clay County, Ky., August 10, 1917.

p I/M

Compare "Edward" (13) in Sharp and Karpeles, 1932, I, p. 50(F), and "The Cruel Mother" (20), a Kentucky variant in *JFSS*, II, p. 109, from Esther White.

1. Fair Lucy sitting in her father's room,
   Lamenting and a-making her mourn;
   And in steps her brother James:
   O what's fair Lucy done?

2. It is time for you to weep,
   Lamenting and a-making your mourn.
   Here's a babe at my right side,
   And it is both mine and yourn.

3. O what will you do when your father comes home?
   Dear son, come tell to me.
   I'll set my foot into some little ship
   And I'll sail plumb over the sea.

4. O what will you do with your house and land?
   Dear son, come tell to me.
   I'll leave it here, my old, dear mother;
   Be kind to my children three.

5. O what will you do with your pretty, little wife?
   Dear son, come tell to me.
   She can set her foot in another little ship
   And follow after me.

6. Back home, back home will you return?
   Dear son, come tell to me.
   When the sun and moon sets in yon hill,
   And I hope that'll never be.

3. "Lucy"

Merrick and Bull, *JEFDSS*, I (1932), p. 53. Sung by Mrs.
Dann, Cottenham, Cambridgeshire.

p I

Compare especially with Somerset copies of "The Unquiet Grave"
(78), e.g., Sharp MSS., 917/, 2124/.

"O what shall you do with your houses and your lands,
My son, pray tell unto me."
O I shall leave them all to my childeren so small,
By one, by two, by three.

"O, when shall you turn to your own wife again?
My son, pray tell unto me."
"When the sun and the moon rises over yonder hill,
I hope that may never, never be."
When the sun, etc.

"O what shall you do when your father comes to know?
My son, pray tell unto me."
I shall dress myself in a new suit of blue,
And gang (or sail) to some far country.
I shall dress," etc.

"O, is this the blood of our greyhound
Or the blood of our Lucee?"
"O, this is not the blood of our greyhound,
But the blood of our Lucee."
O, this is not," etc.

. . . .

O, what did he do there? you very soon shall hear.
He shed poor Lucy's blood.

4. "Fair Lucy"

Flanders, *BFSSNE*, No. 7 (1934), p. 7(1). Sung by Mrs.
Alice Slayton Sicily, North Calais, Vt., July 28, 1933. From
Bulletin of the Folk-Song Society of the Northeast, No. 7
(1934), edited by Phillips Barry; copyright 1934 by the
Folk-Song Society of the Northeast.

p I, ending on *V*; or a M

1. Fair Lucy was sitting in her own cabin door,
   Making her laments alone;
   Who should come by but her own mother dear,
   Saying, "What makes Fair Lucy mourn?"

2. "I have a cause for to grieve," she said,
   "And a reason for to mourn;
   For the babe that lies in the cradle asleep,
   Dear mother, it is his own."

3. Fair Lucy was sitting in her own cabin door,
   Making her laments alone;
   Who should come by but her own brother dear,
   Saying, "What makes Fair Lucy mourn?"

4. "I have a cause for to grieve," she said,
   "And a reason for to mourn;
   For the babe that lies in the cradle asleep,
   Dear brother, it is your own."

5. He took her by the lily-white hand
   And he led her into the woods;
   What he did there, I never can declare,
   But he spilt Fair Lucy's blood.

6. "O, what is that upon your frock,
   My son, come tell to me."
   "It is one drop of Fair Lucy's blood,
   And that you plainly can see."

7. "What will your father say to you,
   When he returns to me?"
   "I shall step my foot on board a ship,
   And my face he never shall see."

8. "What will you do with your three little babes,
   My son, come tell to me?"
   "I shall leave them here at my father's command,
   For to keep him companee."

9. "What will you do with your pretty little wife,
   My son, come tell to me?"
   "She shall step her foot on board a ship,
   And sail the ocean with me."

10. "What will you do with your houses and lands,
    My son, come tell to me?"
    "I shall leave them here at my father's command,
    For to set my children free."

11. "When will you return again,
My son, come tell to me?"
"When the sun and the moon set on yonders green hill,
And I'm sure that never can be."

5a. [Fair Lucy]

Flanders, *BFSSNE*, No. 7 (1934), p. 7(2). Sung by Elmer
George, East Calais, Vt.; learned from Mr. Slayton fifty
years earlier. From *Bulletin of the Folk-Song Society of the
Northeast*, No. 7 (1934), edited by Phillips Barry; copyright 1934 by the Folk-Song Society of the Northeast.

p I, ending on *V*; or a M

5b. "Fair Lucy"

Flanders and Olney, 1953, pp. 143-45. Sung by Elmer
George, East Calais, Vt., July 30, 1933; learned fifty years
earlier. From *Ballads Migrant in New England*, edited by
Helen Hartness Flanders and Marguerite Olney; copyright
1953 by Helen Hartness Flanders.

p I, ending on *V*; or a M

(Repeat last two lines in each verse.)

1. Fair Lucy was sitting in her own father's hall,
Making her lamency mourn,
When who should come there but her own brother dear,
Saying; "What makes fair Lucy mourn?"

2. "O I have a cause for to grieve," she said,
"And a reason for to mourn;
For the babe that lies in yon cradle asleep,
Dear Brother, it is your own."

3. He took her by the lily-white hand
And led her into the woods
And what he done there I never shall disclose
But he spilt fair Lucy's blood.

4. "O what is that upon your frock,
My son, come tell to me?"
"It is just one drop of fair Lucy's blood
And that you plain can see."

5. "O what will your father say to you,
My son, come tell to me?"
"I shall step my foot on board of a ship
And my face he never shall see."

6. "What will you do with your pretty little babe,
My son, come tell to me?"
"I shall leave them here at my father's command
For to keep him company."

7. "O what will you do with your houses and your lands
My son, come tell to me?"
"I shall leave them here at my father's command
For to set my children free."

8. "O what will you do with your pretty little wife
My son, come tell to me?"
"She shall step her foot on board of the ship
And sail away with me."

9. "O when will you return again?
My son, come tell to me?"
"When the sun and the moon meet on yonders green hills
And I'm sure that never will be."

6. "Fair Lucy"

Morris, 1950, pp. 257-59. Sung by Mrs. G. A. Griffin, Newberry, Fla., 1937.

a π²

1. Fair Lucy a-setting in her father's hall,
A-weeping all of her moans,
And who did appear but her own fair mother,
A-saying, "What's fair Lucy done, done, done?"
A-saying, "What's fair Lucy done?"

2. "O Mother, O Mother, it's enough to make a wife weep;
It's enough to make a wife moan,
To think of the babe's in my body now,
And brother's the owner of thine, thine, thine,
And brother's the owner of thine."

3. Fair Lucy a-setting in her father's hall,
A-weeping all of her moans,
And who did appear but her own fair sister,
A-saying, "What's fair Lucy done, done, done?"
A-saying, "What's fair Lucy done?"

4. "O, Sister, O Sister, it's enough to make a wife weep;
It's enough to make a wife moan,
To think of the babe's in my body now,
And brother's the owner of thine, thine, thine,
And brother's the owner of thine."

5. Fair Lucy a-setting in her father's hall,
A-weeping all of her moans,
And who did appear but her own fair brother,
A-saying, "What's fair Lucy done, done, done?"
A-saying, "What's fair Lucy done?"

6. "O Brother, O Brother, it's enough to make a wife weep;
It's enough to make a wife moan,
To think of the babe's in my body now,
And you are the owner of thine, thine, thine,
And you are the owner of thine."

7. He takened her by her lily-white hand,
And he led her off in the woods;
And there he 'bused fair Lucy's body all around,
And he shed fair Lucy's blood, blood, blood,
And he shed fair Lucy's blood.

8. "O what's that blood on your coat?
My son come tell it to me."
"It is the blood of the little grey horse
That walked all under me, me, me,
That walked all under me."

9. "O what's that blood that's on your vest?
My son come tell it to me."
"It is the blood of my old grey goose,
That made a bed for me, me, me,
That made a bed for me."

10. "O what's the blood that's on your shirt?
My son come tell it to me."
"O it's the blood of my sister, fair Lucy,
And Mother, a gaily deed, deed, deed,
And Mother, a gaily deed."

11. "O what's you going to do when your father comes home?
My son come tell it to me."
"I'll set my foot on the gallant ship
And I'll sail all over the sea, sea, sea,
And I'll sail all over the sea."

12. "O when are you coming back home any more?
My son come tell it to me."
"When the sun and moon set on yonder hill,
Which I hope will never be, be, be,
Which I hope will never be."

The King's Dochter Lady Jean

CHILD NO. 52

THIS is another ballad of which only a Scottish tradition is known. It is a little hard to see why Child did not rank it as a version of his No. 50 ("The Bonny Hind"), for it shows no more divergence from that ballad than do the versions of a number of others which he has united, e.g., "Lady Isabel" (4), "Leesome Brand" (15).

Three of the five recorded tunes were collected by Greig at the beginning of the present century. They are all variants of a single type, related, as Keith notes, to one of the tunes for "The Douglas Tragedy" (7). The other two are of older record, and marks of relationship are not easy to make out. Because of rhythmical effect, however, and of general melodic contour, the earliest one, recorded by Motherwell in 1827, may perhaps be a distant variant. The other, taken down by Christie in Banffshire about the middle of the last century, seems apart from the rest. There are, I believe, no American variants.

LIST OF VARIANTS

GROUP A

1. "Lady Jean." William Motherwell, *Minstrelsy: Ancient and Modern*, 1827, App'x No. 23 and p. xxi.
2. "Castle Ha's Daughter." W. Christie, *Traditional Ballad Airs*, I, 1876, p. 228.

GROUP B

3. "Fair Rosie Ann." Greig MSS., III, p. 166; text, Bk. 742, XXXII, pp. 86ff., King's College Library, Aberdeen. Also in Gavin Greig and Alexander Keith, *Last Leaves of Traditional Ballads and Ballad Airs*, 1925, p. 39(a).
4. "Fair Rosie Ann." Greig MSS., IV, p. 72. Also in Greig and Keith, 1925, p. 40(b).
5. "Fair Rosie Ann." Greig MSS., IV, p. 27. Also in Greig and Keith, 1925, p. 40(c).

TUNES WITH TEXTS

GROUP A

1. [Lady Jean]

Motherwell, 1827, App'x No. 23; text, p. xxi. Noted by Andrew Blaikie, Paisley.

p Æ

This may be compared especially with C. K. Sharpe's copy of "The Cruel Mother" (20). Cf. also "The Sprig of Thyme" (Sharp, *One Hundred English Folksongs*, 1916, No. 34, p. 79).

The king's young daughter was sitting in her window
    Sewing at her fine silken seam,
She luikit out at her braw bower window
    And she saw the leaves growin' green, my love,
    And she saw the leaves growing green.

2. [Castle Ha's Daughter]

Christie, I, 1876, p. 228. Sung by an old woman in Banffshire. Christie's text is revamped out of Buchan, *Ancient Ballads and Songs*, 1828, I, pp. 241-245.

a Æ

The second half of the tune (doubtless Christie's manufacture) has been lowered an octave in transposition.

GROUP B

3. [Fair Rosie Ann]

Greig MSS., III, p. 166; text, Bk. 742, XXXII, pp. 86ff. Also in Greig and Keith, 1925, p. 39(a). Sung by Alexander Robb, New Deer, Aberdeenshire, March 1909.

a I

1. Fair Rosie Ann sat on her castle wa',
    Sewing at her satin seam,
    And she's awa to good greenwoods
    Some nuts for to pull & bring hame.

Keith notes the relation with "The Douglas Tragedy" (7). Cf. also the English variants of "Lady Isabel and the Elf Knight" (4).

2. She hadna pulled a nut, a nut,
    A nut but barely three,
When a young man entered into the wood,
    To ruin her fair bodie[.]

3. Oh cam' ye here to pull my nuts?
    Or cam' ye here to be my slave?
Or cam' ye here, kind sir, she said,
    For to put me in my grave?

4. I came nae here to pull your nuts,
    Nor I came nae to be your slave,
But your mantle or your maidenhead
    Some o' them I maun have[.]

5. It's if ye tak' my mantle, she said,
    My mother can caird & spin,
But if ye tak' my maidenhead
    There's nae pardon for the sin.

* * * * *

6. Since ye've gotten your wills (sic) o' me,
    Your wills o' me ye've ta'en,
Would you be so good, kind sir, she said,
    As to tell me your name?

7. My name, my name, fair maid, he said,
    My name I'll never deny,
For I'm Lord Barnet's ae only son,
    And he never had another but I.

8. If ye be Lord Barnet's ae only son,
    There's little between thee & me,
For I'm Lord Barnet's ae daughter,
    And he never had another but me.

9. Heel weel, heel weel, my sister dear,
    Heel weel, heel weel, on me;
For I wish my ship she had been wrecked,
    And sunk to the bottom of the sea.

10. Fair Rosie Ann sat in good greenwoods,
    Lamentin' for what she had done,
When her mother entered into the wood,
    Says, What ails thee, fair Rosie Ann?

11. As I cam' in by yon high high hill,
    And in by yon high castle wa',
Oh heavy, heavy was the stone
    That on my foot did fa'.

12. O fair Rosie Ann, dry up your tears,
    And come awa hame wi' me,
For your brother John is new come home,
    Is new come home from sea.

13. Haud your tongue, dear mother, she said,
    Oh haud your tongue frae me;
For he may be made welcome by a' the hoose,
    But he'll never be made welcome by me.

4. [Fair Rosie Ann]

Greig MSS., IV, p. 72. Also in Greig and Keith, 1925, p. 40(b). Sung by Mrs. Sangster, Cortiecram, Mintlaw.

a I

He may be made welcome by your mother dear,
He may be made welcome by thee.
He may be made welcome by all in the house
But he'll never be made welcome by me.

5. [Fair Rosie Ann]

Greig MSS., IV, p. 27. Also in Greig and Keith, 1925, p. 40(c). Sung by Mrs. Dunbar, Longhill of Crimond.

a I

Young Beichan

CHILD NO. 53

This ballad, whatever its earlier history may have been, has enjoyed in the last century, and apparently still enjoys, a popularity as great as almost any ballad in the record. It is a popularity which has been frequently fortified in its verbal text by the broadside press; but the remarkably wide spread of a vigorous and consistent musical tradition proves with equal clarity that there has been no interruption in oral transmission. For access to a printed tune can only have been possible in very recent years, and then hardly among the class of singers from whom ninety-nine per cent of our variants have been gathered. What has occurred, we may suppose, is that singers have continuously learned the song from other singers; but that, knowing it so, they have refreshed or revised their notions of the words from time to time by the sight of the printed ballad-sheets. Moreover, the occasional discovery, by collectors, of a good many manuscript collections of "song-ballets" among undeniably "folk" singers, provides further evidence of a practice which, while it can have done little to increase the poetic merit of these old things, must yet have done much to prevent the extremes of mutilation by dullness or forgetfulness, and must often have enabled them to survive at all. Thus, far from agreeing with Scott's Jenny Laidlaw that printing (or writing) would stop the singing of her ballads, we should rather conclude that it was one of the most potent aids in keeping them alive. Jenny was only expressing the usual distrust of the uninstructed for "book-learning." And what has been true for the nineteenth century must have been true for the eighteenth, seventeenth, and even sixteenth, though in ever lessening degree as literacy became more and more restricted. It is natural to suppose that anyone who loved to sing narrative songs, and who had experienced the annoyances of forgetfulness, would be glad to put himself beyond the reach of such annoyance by securing a record if he could. That he did not more often succeed is our misfortune as well as his. Of course, the breath of life itself lay in the music, which made him wish to keep the songs in mind and perpetuated oral transmission. He would not sing from book, but would merely resort to his copy upon need. Nevertheless, tradition, for at least the last three hundred years, is inextricably bound up with writing, whether printed or manuscript, and we must reckon this element a potent and positive force in our study, rather than the purely negative and deleterious influence it has been too generally accounted. All this is not to deny the vulgarity and relative inferiority of many of the texts so perpetuated: it is merely to insist that an inferior text is better than no text at all. No text at all, for one thing, must have meant, sooner or later, no tune at all; and the value of the music gathered from singing tradition with the merest orts of texts is beyond argument.

There is no extant tune for the present ballad earlier than the earliest verbal records—that is to say, than the second half of the eighteenth century.* It is an interesting, and may be a significant, fact in the development of the musical tradition that the earliest tunes we have are in common time, and the vast majority of later ones in triple time. It is also a fact that most of the nineteenth-century records are in 3/4, and of the twentieth-century in 3/2, time; but this, probably, indicates no real difference in the singing—only a change in the conventions of notation. The change (if there was one) from duple to triple rhythm, however, would be significant because it might confirm our hypothesis, already suggested, that five-time and three-time, when they take the pattern, as they generally do in the variants here to be seen, of [musical notation] and [musical notation], are traditional developments or extensions of common or duple time. The probable sequence is as follows, although some of the steps might be skipped:

[musical notation] to [musical notation]

to [musical notation] to [musical notation]

(= [musical notation]) or to [musical notation]

(= [musical notation]) Cf. *Western Folklore*, XI (October 1952), p. 245.

There is in the following list a considerable number of variants which, to judge by the preponderant evidence, have been wrongly barred in duple time instead of triple. Most, but not all, such cases are from inexpert hands, and can be readily corrected. There is but one true 6/8 variant in the lot. A lone variant in 2/4, published by Joyce, seems actually 3/2; and a solitary variant in 2/2, printed by Karpeles in 1932, might as well be given as 4/4, and was so set down by Sharp in his manuscripts. The question of barring 3/2 time is vexing, but does not really affect the tune as it is heard. Miss Karpeles, I believe, has regularly altered Sharp's manuscript barring of the 3/2 tunes, feeling, with justice perhaps, that the bar should come before the emphatic held note. Yet, inasmuch as this course obscures the possible historical development suggested above, the manuscript barring has an argument in its favor, and I have followed the manuscript in most cases. It is noteworthy that all the 5/4 variants were collected, by Sharp, in Somerset. The same collector found none in that rhythm in the Appalachians (but many in 3/2).

The identity of the tune has persisted with quite remarkable clarity through most of the variants noted. Apart from half a dozen cases that seem to have stronger affiliations elsewhere, there is hardly any question of membership in the large class, and the following groups comprise not distinct traditions but subdivisions according to where the mid-cadences lie. Of these, the group with mid-cadence on the fifth is nearly twice as large as its nearest competitor in popularity, with mid-cadence on the supertonic. The rest are thrown together for convenience, in this order: seven on the mediant, three on the tonic, five on the octave, and one each on the fourth and sixth. As to cadences of other phrases, the variants with mid-cadence on the fifth show a marked preference for ending the first phrase on the

*It should be noted that there was another ballad, current on seventeenth-century broadsides, which went by the name of "Bateman," or "Young Bateman," with alternative title, "A Warning for Maidens." (Cf. Roxburghe, I, 501.) This has nothing to do with the present ballad. It was popular enough to give its name to the tune, for use with other ballads like "James Harris" (Roxburghe, I, 502; cf. Child 243). The tune specified for Roxburghe, I, 501, however, is "The Ladies Fall"; and that ballad is elsewhere (e.g., Pepys, I, 510) directed to be sung to "In Pescod Time," which was also sometimes used for "Chevy Chase." (Cf. Child 162 and Chappell, I, pp. 195-97.)

tonic, a preference which appears in about half the examples; while perhaps a quarter of them cadence first on the lower fifth. Those with mid-cadence on the second even more strongly prefer (if weak endings are counted) to cadence the first phrase on the lower fifth. All the variants with mid-cadence at the octave end the first phrase on the tonic; and those again with mid-cadence on the third prefer the lower fifth for the cadence of the first phrase.

In the groupings which follow, no distinction is kept between 3/4 and 3/2 variants. Within each group, the arrangement is generally by range, authentic or plagal, and thereafter roughly by mode, from I/Ly to Æolian. In classifying, the first-phrase cadence in this family has appeared more indicative than the opening stresses since it is steadier. The groups as a whole are determined according to the cadence of phrase 2, in the following order: the group with mid-cadence on the fifth comes first; then that with mid-cadence on the second; then the variants with mid-cadence on the third, the tonic, octave, fourth, and sixth, in turn.

A ballad called "The Turkish Lady" (found, e.g., in Christie, 1876, I, p. 246; Barry, *JAF*, XXIII, p. 450; Merrick, *JEFSS*, I, p. 113), of a Turkish beauty who fell in love with an English slave, appears to have no genuine connection with the present ballad.

LIST OF VARIANTS

GROUP Aa

1. "Lord Bakeman." Helen Hartness Flanders and Marguerite Olney, *Ballads Migrant in New England*, 1953, pp. 54-57.
2. "Lord Bateman." Barry MSS., Bk. I, No. 53C, Harvard College Library.
3. "Lord Bateman." Vance Randolph, *Ozark Folksongs*, I, 1946, pp. 81(A)-83. Also in Vance Randolph, *Ozark Mountain Folk*, 1932, p. 197.
4. "Lord Bacon." Barry MSS., Bk. I, No. 53D.
5. "Lord Bateman." Sharp MSS., 355/, Clare College Library, Cambridge. (Chapman)
6. "Lord Bateman." Helen Creighton and Doreen H. Senior, *Traditional Songs from Nova Scotia*, 1950, pp. 28-29.
7. "Lord Batesman." Randolph, *Ozark Folksongs*, I, 1946, pp. 86(E)-88.
8. "Lord Bateman." Phillips Barry, Fannie H. Eckstorm, and Mary W. Smyth, *British Ballads from Maine*, 1929, pp. 106(A)-108.
9. "Lord Baykim." Patrick Weston Joyce, *Old Irish Folk Music and Songs*, 1909, No. 617, p. 317.
10. "Lord Batesman." Sharp MSS., 3259/. Also in Cecil J. Sharp and Maud Karpeles, *English Folk Songs from the Southern Appalachians*, 1932, I, p. 80(C). (Z. Rice)
11. "Lord Bakeman." Helen Hartness Flanders and George Brown, *Vermont Folk-Songs & Ballads*, 1931, pp. 204-8.
12. "Lord Bateman." Frank Kidson, *JFSS*, I (1904), p. 240(1).
13. "Lord Bateman." Creighton and Senior, *Traditional Songs from Nova Scotia*, 1950, p. 31.
14. "Lord Bateman." Sharp MSS., 3859/2820. Also in Sharp and Karpeles, *Appalachians*, 1932, I, pp. 83(G)-86. (Smith, Patrick)
15. "Lord Bateman." Sharp MSS., 4884/. (Hughes)
16. "Lord Bateman." Sharp MSS., 807/. (Shuttler)
17. "Lord Bateman." Charlotte Sophia Burne, *Shropshire Folk-Lore*, 1884-86, pp. 651 and 547-48.
18. "Lord Bateman." Sharp MSS., 4849/. (Carpenter)
19. "Lord Bateman." Sharp MSS., 992/. (Burland)
20. "Lord Bateman." Lucy E. Broadwood and J. A. Fuller Maitland, *English County Songs* (1893), pp. 62-63.
21. "Lord Bateman." Lucy E. Broadwood, *Sussex Songs*, n.d., No. 22, p. 43.
22. "Lord Bakeman." W. Roy Mackenzie, *Ballads and Sea Songs from Nova Scotia*, 1928, pp. 393 and 16-19.
23. "Lord Bateman." Sharp MSS., 663/. (Jeffreys)
24. "Lord Bateman." Sharp MSS., 735/. (Southwood)
25. "Lord Bateman." Sharp MSS., 4919/. (Alcock)
26. "Lord Bateman." Sharp MSS., 878/. (Coombes)
27. "Lord Bateman." Sharp MSS., 2358/. (Benfield)
28. "Lord Bateman." Percy Grainger MS., No. 171, New York Public Library. (Thompson)
29. "Lord Bateman." Sharp MSS., 1071/. (Stokes)
30. "Lord Bateman." Sharp MSS., 1085/. (Carter)
31. "Lord Bateman." Sharp MSS., 1561/. (Jarrett)
32. "Lord Bateman." Sharp MSS., 2278/. (Corbett)
33. "Lord Bateman." Grainger MS., No. 174. Also in Percy Grainger, *JFSS*, III (1909), pp. 195-99. (Wray)
34. "Lord Bateman." Grainger MS., No. 170. Also in Percy Grainger, *JFSS*, III (1909), p. 192. (Taylor)
35. "Lord Bateman." Louis W. Chappell, *Folk-Songs of Roanoke and the Albemarle*, 1939, pp. 18-20.
36. "Young Beichan; or, Lord Bacon." Sharp MSS., 3168/2305. Also in Sharp and Karpeles, *Appalachians*, 1932, I, pp. 77(A)-79. (Banks)
37. "The Loving Ballad of Lord Bateman." George Cruikshank, *The Loving Ballad of Lord Bateman*, 1839. Also in Francis James Child, *The English and Scottish Popular Ballads*, 1882-98, I, pp. 476-77.
38. "Young Beichan." Phillips Barry, *JAF*, XXII (1909), p. 78.
39. "The Jailer's Daughter." Dorothy Scarborough, *A Song Catcher in Southern Mountains*, 1937, pp. 410 and 212-13.
40. "Lord Bakeman." Sidney Robertson, LC Archive of American Folk Song, rec. 3811 A1 and 2, B1. (George Vinton Graham)
41. "Young Beichan." Sharp MSS., 3999/2882-83. Also in Sharp and Karpeles, *Appalachians*, 1932, I, p. 87(J). (Carter)
42. "Young Beichan." Sharp MSS., 3860/2823-24. Also in Sharp and Karpeles, 1932, I, p. 87(I). (Jones)
43. "Lord Bateman." Sharp MSS., 3971/. (Bagley)
44. "Lord Bateman." Randolph, *Ozark Folksongs*, I, 1946, p. 85(C).
45. "Lord Beichan and Susie Pye." George R. Kinloch, *Ancient Scottish Ballads*, 1827, App'x to p. 260 and pp. 260-70.
46. "Lord Bateman." Sharp MSS., 4156/. (Clapp)
47. "The Turkish Lady." Arthur Kyle Davis, Jr., *Traditional Ballads of Virginia*, 1929, pp. 565(I) and 171.
48. "Lord Bateman." Sharp MSS., 4119/. (Price)
49. "Lord Bateman." Sharp MSS., 4037/. (Stamper)
50. "Lord Bateman." Sharp MSS., 4065/. (Unnamed)
51. "The Turkish Lady." Jean Thomas, *Devil's Ditties*, 1931, pp. 86-87.
52. "Lord Bateman." Sharp MSS., 3757/. (Vaughan)
53. "Turkish Lady." John Harrington Cox, *Traditional Ballads Mainly from West Virginia*, 1939, pp. 19-20.
54. "A Turkish Lady." Cox, 1939, pp. 16-18.
55. "Lord Bateman and the Turkish Lady." Davis, *Traditional Ballads of Virginia*, 1929, pp. 565(D) and 165-66.

56. "Lord Beichan." J. Collingwood Bruce and John Stokoe, *Northumbrian Minstrelsy*, 1882, pp. 64-69.
57. "Young Beichan." Sharp MSS., 3568/2634-35. Also in Sharp and Karpeles, *Appalachians*, 1932, I, p. 86(H). (Williams)
58. "Lord Beichan." W. Christie, *Traditional Ballad Airs*, I, 1876, p. 30.

GROUP A b

59. "Lord Bateman." Sharp MSS., 2371/. (Hayden)
60. "Lord Bateman." Sharp MSS., 545/. (Fido)
61. "Lord Bateman." Sharp MSS., 595/. Also in Cecil J. Sharp, *English Folksong. Some Conclusions*, 1907, p. 80(1); and Sabine Baring-Gould and Cecil J. Sharp, *English Folk-Songs for Schools* [1906], No. 11, p. 24. (Williams)
62. "Lord Bateman." Sharp MSS., 712/. (Young)
63. "Lord Bateman." Sharp MSS., 355/479. (Wyatt)
64. "Lord Bateman." Creighton and Senior, *Traditional Songs from Nova Scotia*, 1950, pp. 26-28.
65. "Lord Bateman." Grainger MS., No. 173. (Leaning)
66. "Lord Bateman." Dr. Clague, *JFSS*, VII (1926), p. 315.
67. "Lord Bateman." Sharp MSS., 3936/. (Short)
68. "Lord Brechin, or Bechin." Greig MSS., II, p. 149; text, Bk. 729, XIX, pp. 15-19, King's College Library, Aberdeen. (Mowat)
69. "Young Beichan." Sharp MSS., 3957/. Also in Sharp and Karpeles, *English Folk Songs from the Southern Appalachians*, 1932, I, p. 88(L). (Creech)
70. "Lord Brechin." Greig MSS., IV, p. 14; text, Bk. 764, LIV, pp. 50ff. Also in Gavin Greig and Alexander Keith, *Last Leaves of Traditional Ballads and Ballad Airs*, 1925, p. 43(b). (Cruickshank)
71. "Lord Beichan." A. Reid, *Rymour Club Miscellanea*, I (1910), p. 114.
72. "Lord Brechin." Greig MSS., IV, p. 26. Also in Greig and Keith, *Last Leaves*, 1925, p. 43(a). (Dunbar)
73. "Lord Beichan." Greig MSS., IV, p. 174. (Angus)
74. "Young Beichan." Greig MSS., I, p. 28. Also in Greig and Keith, *Last Leaves*, 1925, p. 43(c). (Knowles)
75. "Young Beichan." Greig MSS., IV, p. 130. Also in Greig and Keith, 1925, p. 43(d). (Dickie)
76. "Lord Brechin." Greig MSS., I, p. 28; text, Bk. 712, II, p. 37, King's College Library, Aberdeen. (Clark)
77. "Lord Beaconet." Greig MSS., I, p. 28. (Pyper)
78. "Young Beichan." Duncan MS., No. 266, transcribed by W. Walker, in Greig-Duncan MS. 785. Also in Greig and Keith, *Last Leaves*, 1925, p. 43(e). (Harper)
79. "Lorde Bateman." Joseph Crawhall, *Olde Tayles Newlye Relayted*, 1883, No. 8, pp. 1-23.
80. "Lord Bateman's Castle." Emelyn Elizabeth Gardner and Geraldine Chickering, *Ballads and Songs of Southern Michigan*, 1939, pp. 143-45.
81. "Lord Bateman (?)." Greig MSS., II, p. 134. (Milne)
82. "Lord Beichan." Greig MSS., III, p. 162. (Harrison)
83. "Lord Brechin." Greig MSS., IV, p. 88. (Robb)
84. "Lord Brechin." Greig MSS., IV, p. 138. (Corbett)
85. "Lord Bateman." Frank Kidson, *JFSS*, I (1904), p. 240(2).
86a. "Lord Bateman." Sharp MSS., 450/566-67. (Glover)
86b. "Lord Bateman." Sharp MSS., 750/. Also in Sharp, *English Folksong. Some Conclusions*, 1907, p. 80(2). (Glover)
87. "Lord Bateman." Barry, Eckstorm, and Smyth, *British Ballads from Maine*, 1929, pp. 119(E)-21.
88. "Young Beichan." Winston Wilkinson MSS., 1935-36, pp. 41-43(A2), University of Virginia.
89. "Young Beichan." Wilkinson MSS., 1935-36, pp. 41-43(A1).
90. "Young Beichan." Wilkinson MSS., 1935-36, pp. 44-45(B).
91. "Lord Bakeman." Phillips Barry Dictaphone Cylinders, No. 86, transcribed by S. P. Bayard, Harvard College Library MS., p. 17.
92. "Lord Bateman." Sharp MSS., 695/722-76. Also in Sharp, *Folk Songs from Somerset*, 3rd series, 1906, pp. 28-31; and Sharp, *English Folksong. Some Conclusions*, 1907, pp. 22-23. Also in Sharp, *English Folksongs*, Selected Ed., Novello and Co., 1920. (Larcombe)
93. "Lord Wetram." Cox, *Traditional Ballads Mainly from West Virginia*, 1939, pp. 21-23.
94. "Young Becon." Harris MS., No. "27" (=26), Harvard College Library. Also in Child, *The English and Scottish Popular Ballads*, 1882-98, V, p. 415.

GROUP AC

95. "Lord Bateman." Sharp MSS., 3698/. (Berea students) Also, as "Turkish Lady," in James Watt Raine, *The Land of Saddle-bags*, 1924, pp. 109-11.
96. "Lord Batesman; or, The Turkish Lady." Mary Wheeler and Clara Gregory Bridge, *Kentucky Mountain Folk-Songs*, 1937, pp. 89-100.
97. "Lord Bateman." Pleaz Mobley, Argonaut pressing, private dubbing, 1937. Text, Artus M. Moser, LC Archive of American Folk Song, Album 12, rec. 56A and B. (Pleaz Mobley)
98. "Lord Batesman; or, The Turkish Lady." Loraine Wyman and Howard Brockway, *Lonesome Tunes* [1916], pp. 58-61.
99. "Lord Batesman." Sharp MSS., 3131/? Also in Sharp and Karpeles, *Appalachians*, 1932, I, pp. 79(B)-80. (Hindman students)
100. "Lord Bateman." Frank Kidson, *Traditional Tunes*, 1891, pp. 33-36.
101. "Lord Akeman." Maud Karpeles, *Folk Songs from Newfoundland*, 1934, pp. 88-92.
102. "Lord Bateman." Sharp MSS., 4526/. Also in Sharp and Karpeles, *Appalachians*, 1932, I, p. 87(K). (Blackett)
103. "Lord Bateman." Sharp MSS., 3309/. (Gentry)
104. "Young Behan." Mellinger Edward Henry, *Folk-Songs from the Southern Highlands*, 1938, pp. 55(A)-58.
105. "A Gentleman of the Courts of England." Theodore Garrison, *Forty-five Folk Songs Collected from Searcy County, Arkansas* (University of Arkansas, M.A. thesis), 1944, pp. 16-18.
106. "Lord Batesman." Sharp MSS., 3180/. Also in Sharp and Karpeles, *Appalachians*, 1932, I, p. 81(E). (Sands)
107. "Lord Bateman." Sharp MSS., 3277/. Also in Sharp and Karpeles, 1932, I, p. 81(D). (Rice)
108. "Lord Bateman." Sharp MSS., 3772/. (Kilburn)
109. "Lord Bateman." Sharp MSS., 3020/. (Aimers)
110. "Lord Beechman." Sharp MSS., 3597/2657. Also in Sharp and Karpeles, *Appalachians*, 1932, I, pp. 81(F)-83. (Ray)
111. "Lord Bateman." Reed Smith, *South Carolina Ballads*, 1928, pp. 104-6.

GROUP B

112. "Young Bekie." Ritson-Tytler-Brown MS., pp. 38-47, Harvard College Library.

GROUP A a

1. "Lord Bakeman"

Flanders and Olney, 1953, pp. 54-57. Sung by Asa Davis, Milton, Vt., June 23, 1939; learned from his grandfather, Charles Atkins, of Duxbury, Vt. From *Ballads Migrant in New England*, edited by Helen Hartness Flanders and Marguerite Olney; copyright 1953 by Helen Hartness Flanders.

a I

The variants are from the later recording, in the H. H. Flanders Collection of New England Folk Songs, Middlebury College, Vermont, Vol. I. (LP phonographic disc)

1. In India lived a noble lord,
   Whose riches were beyond compare;
   He was the darling of his parents,
   And of his estate the only heir.

2. Oh, he had gold and he had silver,
   And he had houses of high degree,
   But he could never be contented,
   Until a voyage he had been to sea.

3. He sail-ed east, he sail-ed west,
   Until he came to the Turkish shore.
   There he was taken and put in prison,
   Where he could neither see nor hear.

4. For seven long months he lay lamenting,
   He lay lamenting in iron chains.
   There happened to be a brisk young lady,
   Who released him out of his iron bands.

5. The jailer had an only daughter,
   And a brisk young lady gay was she.
   As she was a-walking across the floor,
   She chanced Lord Bakeman to see.

6. She stole the keys of her father's prison,
   And vowed Lord Bakeman she would set free.
   She went into the prison door,
   And opened it without delay.

7. "Have you got gold, have you got silver?
   And have you houses of high degree?
   What will you give to the lady fair,
   If she from bondage will set you free?"

8. "Yes, I've got gold and I've got silver,
   And I have houses of high degree
   And I'll give them all to the lady fair,
   If she from bondage will set me free."

9. "I do not want your gold nor silver,
   Nor your houses of high degree.
   All I want for is to make me happy,
   And all I crave is your fair bodee."

10. "Let us make a bargain and make it strong,
    For seven long years it shall stand:
    You shall not marry no other woman,
    Nor I'll not marry no other man."

11. The seven long years had gone and passed.
    The seven long years were at an end.
    She pack-ed up all her rich gay clothing,
    Saying: "Now I'll go and seek a friend."

12. She sail-ed east, she sail-ed west,
    Until she came to the Indian shore.
    There she could never be contented
    Till for Lord Bakeman she did inquire.

13. She inquired for Lord Bakeman's palace
    At every corner of the street.
    She did inquire for Lord Bakeman's palace,
    Of every person she chanced to meet.

14. And when she came to Lord Bakeman's palace,
    She knocked so loud upon the ring,
    There was no one so ready as the brisk young porter
    To arise and let this fair lady in.

15. "Oh, is this Lord Bakeman's palace?
    And is the Lord himself within?"
    "Oh, yes, oh, yes," cries the brisk young porter.
    "He and his new bride have just entered in."

16. She wept, she wept, she wrung her hands,
    Crying, "Alas, I am undone.
    I wish I was in my native country,
    Across the seas there to remain.

17. "Tell him to send me an ounce of bread,
    And a bottle of his wine so strong,
    And ask him if he has forgot the lady
    Who released him out of his iron bands."

18. The porter went unto his master,
    He knelt so low upon one knee.
    "Arise, arise, my brisk young porter,
    And tell to me what the matter is."

19. "There is a lady stands at your gate
    And she doth weep most bitterly.
    I think she is the finest creature
    That ever I chanced my eyes to see.

20. "She's got more rings on her four fingers,
    And around her waist a diamond band;
    She's got more gold about her clothing
    Than your bride and all her kin.

21. "She wants you to send her an ounce of bread,
    And a bottle of your wine so strong,
    And ask you if you have forgot the lady
    Who released you out of your iron bands?"

22. He jumped into the middle of the floor,
    He smashed the table in pieces three.
    "You came here on a horse and saddle,
    You may ride home in a coach and three."

23. Then up spoke his new bride's mother,
    And she was a lady of high degree,
    " 'Tis you have married my only daughter,
    Why, she is none the worse for thee."

24. "But since my fair one has arrived,
    A second wedding there shall be.
    Your daughter came on a horse and saddle,
    She may ride home in a coach and three."

25. He took his fair lady by the hand;
    He led her over the marble stone.
    He changed her name from Susannah Fayer*
    To be the wife of Lord Bakeman.

26. He took her by the lily-white hand,
    He led her through from room to room,
    He changed her name from Susannah Freeman
    To be the wife of Lord Bakeman.

27. He took her by the lily-white hand,
    He led her across the marble stone,
    He changed her name from Susannah Freeman
    To be the wife of Lord Bakeman.

* For fair?

2. [Lord Bateman]

Barry MSS., Bk. I, No. 53C. Sung by Gertrude Leach,
Boston, Mass., July 2, 1907.

a I/Ly

Lord Bateman was a noble Lord,
A n[oble Lord of high degree . . .

3. "Lord Bateman"

Randolph, I, 1946, pp. 81(A)-83. Sung by Mrs. Lenore
Evans, Jane, Mo., September 5, 1927.

a I/Ly

The same tune appears in Randolph, 1932, p. 197, as from Zeke
Langley, this time written in 6/8 time. The latter would better have
been written as 3/4, and one may surmise that so the original might
have been sung.

1. Lord Bateman was a noble lord,
   A noble lord of high degree,
   He shipped himself on board a ship,
   Some foreign country for to see.

2. He sail-ed East, he sail-ed West
   Till he come into Turkey,
   An' there he was taken an' put into prison,
   Until his life was quite weary.

3. In this here prison there grew a tree,
   It grew so very stout an' strong,
   An' he was chain-ed by the middle
   Until his life was almost gone.

4. The Turk he only had one daughter,
   The fairest creature eye ever did see,
   She stole the key of her father's prison,
   She says I'll set Lord Bateman free.

5. Have you got houses, have you got lands?
   An' does Northumberland belong to thee?
   An' what would you give to the fair young lady
   Who out of prison would set you free?

6. Oh I've got houses an' I've got lands,
   An' half of Northumberland belongs to me,
   An' I'd give it all to the fair young lady,
   That out of prison would set me free.

7. Then she took him to her father's palace,
   An' give to him the best of wine,
   An' every health she drunk to him was:
   Lord Bateman, I wish that you was mine.

8. For seven long years I'll make a vow,
   An' seven long years I'll keep it strong,
   If you will not wed no other woman,
   I will not wed no other man.

9. Then she took him down to her father's harbor,
   An' give to him a ship of fame,
   Farewell, farewell to you, Lord Bateman,
   I fear I never shall see you again.

10. When seven long years was gone an' past,
    An' fourteen days, well known to me,
    She packed up her gay gold an' clothings,
    An' says Lord Bateman she would see.

11. When she come to Lord Bateman's castle,
    So boldly there she rang the bell,
    Who's there? Who's there? cried the young proud porter,
    Who's there, who's there, unto me tell!

12. O is this here Lord Bateman's castle?
    An' is his lordship here within?
    Oh yes, oh yes, cried the young proud porter,
    He's just now taken his young bride in.

13. Tell him to send me a slice of cake,
    An' a bottle of the best of wine,
    An' not to forget the fair young lady
    That did release him when close confined.

14. Away, away went the young proud porter,
    Away, away went he
    Until he come unto Lord Bateman
    When on his bended knees fell he.

15. What news, what news, my young proud porter,
    What news, what news have you brought unto me?
    Oh, there is the fairest of fair young ladies
    That ever my two eyes did see!

16. She has got rings on every finger,
    An' on one of 'em she has got three;
    She's got as much gold round her middle
    As would buy Northumberland of thee!

17. She tells you to send her a slice of cake,
    An' a bottle of the best of wine,
    An' not to forget the fair young lady
    That did release you when close confined.

18. Lord Bateman in a passion flew,
    He broke his sword in splinters three,
    I'll give all my father's wealth and riches
    Now, if Sophia has crossed the sea!

19. Then up spoke his young bride's mother,
    Who never was heard to speak so free,
    Don't you forget my only daughter,
    Even if Sophia has crossed the sea.

20. I own I've made a bride of your daughter,
    But she's none the better nor worse for me,
    She come to me on a horse an' saddle,
    An' she can go back in a carriage an' three.

21. Then another marriage was prepared,
    With both their hearts so full of glee,
    I'll range no more to foreign countries
    Since my Sophia has crossed the sea.

4. [Lord Bacon]

Barry MSS., Bk. I, No. 53D. Miss Bessie Osgood's transcript of Perkins MS. 1790, owned by Mrs. Holden, Boston, Mass.

a I

There is a bass in the MS. copy, but no words are given. The Perkins MS. has 2/4, which Barry reduces to 3/4 and also to 4/4.

5. [Lord Bateman]

Sharp MSS., 355/. Sung by Mrs. Jane Chapman, West Harptree, Somerset, August 25, 1904.

a π[1]

This is allied to a branch of the "Barbara Allen" tunes.

Lord Bateman was a noble Lord
A noble Lord of high degree
He shipped himself in a border vessel
Some foreign country to go and see.

6. [Lord Bateman]

Creighton and Senior, 1950, pp. 28-29. Sung by Dennis Smith, Chezzetcook, Nova Scotia.

a M

The original timing is 6/4.

1. In India lived a noble lord,
   His riches they were beyond compare,
   But still he would not be contented
   Until a voyage he had been to sea.

2. He sailèd east he sailèd west
   Until he came to the Turkish shore,
   There he was taken and put in prison
   Where he could neither see nor hear.

3. The jailor had one only daughter
   A nice young lady fair was she,
   She stole the keys of her father's prison
   And swore Lord Bateman she would set free.

4. "Let us make a bargain and make it strong,
   For seven long years oh it shall stand,
   You'll never wed with no other woman
   Or me with any other man."

5. When seven long years was gone and past,
   When seven long years was to an end,
   She packed up all her rich clothing
   Saying, "Now I'll go and seek my friend."

6. Then she sailèd East and she sailèd West
   Enquired for Lord Bateman's palace.
   Every person she chanced to meet
   . . . .

7. . . . .
   She knocked upon the door,
   There was none so ready as the brisk young porter
   To rise and let this fair lady in.

8. "Oh is this Lord Bateman's palace,
   And is the lord himself within?
   And ask him if he knows the lady
   That set him free from yon iron claws?"

9. "There is a lady at your door
   And she does weep most bitterlee,
   I think she is the finest lady
   That ever my two eyes did see.

10. "She's got more gold on her four fingers
    And around her waist a diamond chain,
    She's got more gold about her clothing
    Than your new bride and all her kin.

11. "She wants you to send her an ounce of bread
    And a bottle of your wine so strong,
    And ask her if she knows the lady
    That let you free from yon iron strong."

12. He stamped his feet upon the floor
    And broke the table in pieces three,
    "Here's adieu to you my wedded bride
    For this fair lady I must go see."

13. He took her by the lily white hand
    And led her through from room to room,
    And he changed her name for Susannah fair
    And she's now called the wife of Lord Bateman.

7. "Lord Batesman"

Randolph, I, 1946, pp. 86(E)-88. Sung by Wiley Hembree, Farmington, Ark., December 12, 1941; learned from his parents, near Farmington, c. 1899.

a π[1]

1. Lord Batesman was a brave young man,
   As brave a young man as you ever did see,
   He bundled up his rings and jewels
   And vowed strange countries he'd go see.

2. He flew east and he flew west
   He flew among some . . . . . Turks,
   Those Turks they did so badly abuse him
   That he became wearied of his life.

3. Those Turks they took and put him in prison,
   They bound him down in every way,
   They fed him on just bread and water,
   Just bread and water once a day.

4. Those Turks they had a lovely daughter,
   As fair a young miss as you ever did see,
   She stole the keys of her father's prison
   And vowed Lord Batesman she would set free.

5. She taken him down in her father's cellar,
   The best of drinks that they had was wine,
   She drank her health in every . . . . . to him,
   And said Lord Batesman, I wish you was mine.

6. They made a bargain and they made it strong,
   For seven long years to stand,
   And if you will wed no other lady
   I'm sure I'll wed no other man.

7. She taken him down unto the sea shore,
   To watch him sail far over the main,
   Saying farewell, farewell my own dear creature,
   When shall I see your fair face again?

8. She dwell-ed there for seven long years,
   For seven long years and three,
   She bundled up her rings and jewels
   And vowed Lord Batesman she'd go see.

9. She rode, she rode till she come to a castle,
   And there so loudly she did ring,
   Who's there, who's there? cried the proud young porter,
   That rings so shrill and won't come in.

10. Is this then Lord Batesman's castle,
    Or is it a place that he dwells in?
    Oh yes, oh yes, it's Lord Batesman's castle,
    But just today he brought his new bride in.

11. Is this, is this the truth you're telling,
    Which I suppose it for to be,
    I wisht I had my . . . . .
    And back in my own country free.

12. You go before your worthy master
    Down on your bended knees,
    And ask him if he don't remember
    A Turkish lady that set him free.

13. He went before his worthy master
    Down on his bended knees,
    Says at your gate there stands a-waiting
    As fair a young miss as you ever did see.

14. She has a ring on every finger
    And on the middle one she had three,
    She told me to ask if you didn't remember
    A Turkish lady that set you free.

15. Lord Batesman bowed, not a word was spoken,
Not a word but three,
I'll forfeit all my land and livin'
If Susy Fair has crossed the sea.

16. Up stepped, up stepped his new bride's mother,
A very well-spoken old lady was she,
Says will you forsake my own fair daughter
And marry you a Turkish lady?

17. Your daughter is fair, I must acknowledge,
But what is she to the worth of me?
She came to me on a horse and saddle
And I'll send her away on coaches three.

18. He taken Susy by her lily-white hand,
He led her into . . . . . room,
He changed her name from Susy Fair
And now she's called Lady Batesman.

8. "Lord Bateman"

Barry, Eckstorm, and Smyth, 1929, pp. 106(A)-108. Sung
by Mrs. Susie Carr Young, Brewer, Maine; learned from
her family, c. 1925. Melody recorded by George Herzog.

a I/M

1. In England lived a noble lord,
His riches were beyond compare;
He was the darling of his parents
And of their estates the only heir.

2. He had gold and he had silver,
He had houses of high degree;
But yet he never could be contented
Until a voyage he had been to sea.

3. He sailèd east and he sailèd west
Until he came to the Turkish shore,
Where he was taken and put in prison,
Where he could neither see nor hear.

4. The jailer had an only daughter
And she was a lady of high degree;
She stole the keys of her father's prison,
Saying: "Lord Bateman I will set free!"

5. And they made a solemn promise
For seven long yeärs it should stand,
That he would wed with no other woman
And she would wed with no other man.

6. When seven long years had come and gone,
When seven long years had passed away,
She packed up all of her richest clothing,
Saying: "Lord Bateman, I'll go and see."

7. She sailèd east and she sailèd west
[Until she came to a foreign land,
And to a city full of strange people
Whose words she hardly could understand.]*

8. She inquired for Lord Bateman's palace
At ev'ry corner of the street,
She inquired for Lord Bateman's palace
Of ev'ry person she chanced to meet.

9. And when she came to Lord Bateman's palace
And knockèd loudly at the ring.
There was none so ready as a young porter
To rise and let the fair lady in.

10. "Oh! isn't this Lord Bateman's palace?
And is the noble Lord within?"
"Oh! yes," replied this brisk young porter,
"He and his new bride have just walked in."

11. "Tell him to send me an ounce of bread
And a bottle of his wine so strong;
And ask him if he has forgot that lady
Who set him free from his iron chains."

12. "There is a lady at your door;
She asks you for to let her in;
She wears more gold about her clothing
Than your new bride and all her kin.

13. "She asks you to send her an ounce of bread
And a bottle of your wine so strong,
And asks if you have forgot that lady
That set you free from your iron chains."

14. He stamped his foot upon the floor,
He broke the table in pieces three,
Saying: "Since my fair one has arrivèd
A second wedding there shall be."

15. Then upspake his new bride's mother,
And she was a lady of high degree,
Saying: "Will you forsake my only daughter
And so disgrace my family?"

16. "Your daughter came with a horse and saddle;
She may go home with a coach and three;
And here's Adieu to my new bride,
For a second wedding there shall be."

17. He took the lady by the hand
And led her into his palace home;
He changed her name to Susannah Fair
And she's the wife of Lord Bateman.

* Editor's note: "Mrs. Young feels uncertain as to the authenticity
of the words in brackets."

9. [Lord Baykim]

Joyce, 1909, No. 617, p. 317. From the Forde Collection.

a M

It seems fairly certain that the timing of this copy should be triple, and not duple; and I have ventured to make the change.

10. [Lord Batesman]

Sharp MSS., 3259/. Also in Sharp and Karpeles, 1932, I, p. 80(C). Sung by Mrs. Zippo Rice, Rice Cove, Big Laurel, N.C., August 15, 1916.

a M

Sharp's barring starts after the initial upbeat.

Lord Batesman was a nobleman
A valiant soldier he set sail
He put his foot into some little boat
And declared some strange land he'd go and see

11. "Lord Bakeman"

Flanders and Brown, 1931, pp. 204-8. Sung by Josiah Samuel Kennison, Townshend, Vt., August 23, 1930; learned from his mother, whose father came from England. From *Vermont Folk-Songs and Ballads*, edited by Helen Hartness Flanders and George Brown; copyright 1931 by Arthur Wallace Peach.

a M

The timing has been left here as in the former printed copy, so that the reader may test his own feeling; but normally it would be made to conform with the variants preceding and following.

1. Lord Bakeman, he was a noble lord
And he had riches of high degree,
But never could he be contented
Until a voyage he had been to sea,
But never could he be contented
Until a voyage he had been to sea.

2. He sail-ed East and he sail-ed West
Until he came to the Turkey shore,
And there he was taken and put in prison
Where he could neither see nor hear,
And there he was taken and put in prison
Where he could neither see nor hear.

3. Seven long months he lie lamented,
He lie lamented in iron bonds,
Until he spied a calm-eyed damsel
Who set him free from his iron bonds,
Until he spied a calm-eyed damsel
Who set him free from his iron bonds.

4. She was walking across the floor;
She chanced Lord Bakeman for to see;
She stole the keys of her father's prison
Saying, "Now Lord Bakeman, I'll set free."
She stole the keys of her father's prison
Saying, "Now Lord Bakeman, I'll set free."

5. "Have you got gold, have you got silver,
Or have you houses of high degree?
And what will you give to this fair lady
If she from bondage will set you free?
And what will you give to this fair lady
If she from bondage will set you free?"

6. "Yes. I've got gold and I've got silver
And I've got houses of high degree;
All these I'll give to this fair lady
If she from bondage will set me free,
All these I'll give to this fair lady
If she from bondage will set me free."

7. "I want none of your gold nor silver
Nor none of your houses of high degree,
But all I ask to make me happy
For all I crave is your fair body,
But all I ask to make me happy
For all I crave is your fair body."

8. "Let us make a bargain and make it strong,
And seven long years that it shall stand,
That you shan't wed no other woman
Nor I shan't wed no other man,
That you shan't wed no other woman
Nor I shan't wed no other man."

9. When seven long years were gone and passed
And seven long months were at an end,
She then picked up her richest clothing,
Saying, "Now I'll go to seek my friend,"
She then picked up her richest clothing,
Saying, "Now I'll go to seek my friend."

10. She sail-ed East and she sail-ed West
Until she came to the Indee shore,
And there she inquired for Lord Bakeman's palace
In every corner of the street,
And there she inquired for Lord Bakeman's palace
To every one she chanced to meet.

11. "Is this Lord Bakeman's palace
Or is the Lord himself within?"
"Yes, yes, oh yes," cries the brisk young porter,
"He and his new bride has just entered in,

Yes, yes, oh yes," cries the brisk young porter,
"He and his new bride has just entered in."

12. Then she did wring her lily white hands.
Then she did weep most bitterly,
Saying, "I wish I was back across the ocean
In my own country for to stay,"
Saying, "I wish I was back across the ocean
In my own country for to stay."

13. "Go ask Lord Bakeman to send me one ounce of bread
And a bottle of his wine so strong,
And ask if he has forgotten the lady
Who set him free from his iron bonds,
And ask if he has forgotten the lady
Who set him free from his iron bonds."

14. Away, away run the brisk young porter
And down upon his bended knees,
"Arise, arise, my brisk young porter
And tell me what the matter is,
Arise, arise, my brisk young porter
And tell me what the matter is."

15. "There stands a lady at your gate
And she doth weep most bitterly,
I think she is the fairest lady
That ever my eyes could wish to see,
I think she is the fairest lady
That ever my eyes could wish to see.

16. "She has a ring on every finger
And on her forefinger she has three.
She's got more gold about her clothing
Than your new bride and all her kin,
She's got more gold about her clothing
Than your new bride and all her kin.

17. "She sent me for an ounce of bread
And a bottle of your wine so strong,
And to ask if you'd forgotten the lady
Who set you free from your iron bonds,
And to ask if you'd forgotten the lady
Who set you free from your iron bonds."

18. He stamped his foot on the marble floor.
He split the table in pieces three,
Saying, "Adieu, adieu, to the wedded bride,
And this fair lady I'll go to see,"
Saying, "Adieu, adieu, to the wedded bride,
And this fair lady I'll go to see."

19. Then up steps the new bride's mother,
She being a lady of high degree,
Saying, "You've married my only daughter
And she's a lady of high degree.
I wish to God that Silky Friar
Had died before she'd crossed the sea."

20. "Yes, I married your only daughter
But she is none the worse for me,
She came to me on a horse and saddle
She shall go back in a coach so free,
She came to me on a horse and saddle
She shall go back in a coach so free."

21. He took her by her lily white hand
And led her across the marble floor,
He changed her name from Silky Friar
She's now the wife of Lord Bakeman,
He changed her name from Silky Friar
She's now the wife of Lord Bakeman.

12. "Lord Bateman"

Kidson, *JFSS*, I (1904), p. 240(1). Sung in Shropshire.

a M

Lord Bateman was a noble Lord,
A noble Lord of high degree.
He put his foot upon shipboard,
Some foreign country he would go see.

13. "Lord Bateman"

Creighton and Senior, 1950, p. 31. Sung by Lawson Sanford, East Walton, Nova Scotia.

a M

The original timing is 6/4. In the last bar of line 2, the half-note may have been dotted, or the last two notes twice as long.

She wants you to send her a piece of bread,
And a glass of your wine so strong,
She asked if you remember the maiden
That set you free from your prison chain.

14. [Lord Bateman]

Sharp MSS., 3859/2820. Also in Sharp and Karpeles, 1932, I, pp. 83(G)-86. Sung by Mrs. Nanny Smith and Mrs. Polly Patrick, Goose Creek, Manchester, Clay County, Ky., August 16, 1917.

a π^2

1. There was a noble lord,
A noble lord was he.
He shipped himself on board a ship,
Some foreign country he would see.

2. He sailed East and he sailed West
Until he come to Turkey,
And there was he put into prison
Until his life grew weary.

3. All in this prison there grew a tree
So very stout and strong,
And he was fastened to this tree
Until his life was almost gone.

4. The Turks they had one only daughter,
The fairest creature eyes ever did see.
She stole the keys of her father's prison,
And said: Lord Bateman I will free.

5. Have you houses, have you got land?
Does Northumberland belong to thee?
And what will you give to the fair young lady
That out of prison will set you free?

6. I have houses and I have land,
Half of Northumberland belongs to me,
And I'll give it all to the fair young lady
That out of prison will set me free.

7. Then she took him to her father's table
And gave to him the best of wine;
And every health she drunk unto him:
O Lord Bateman, I wish that you were mine.

8. Then she led him to her father's harbour
And gave to him a ship of mine.
Farewell, farewell to you, Lord Bateman,
I fear I'll never see you again.

9. With these I'll make a vow,
And seven long years I'll hold it strong.
If you will wed no other woman,
I will wed no other man.

10. Seven long years had come and gone,
Fourteen days well known to thee.
She dressed herself in her fine, gay, gold clothing,
And says: Lord Bateman I'll go see.

11. And when she come to Lord Bateman's castle
And there she tingled at the bell.
Who's there, who's there? cried the proud young porter.
Who's there,* Unto me tell.

12. Is this Lord Bateman's castle,
And is his lordship here within?
This is Lord Bateman's castle;
He's just now taken a young bride in.

13. Go tell him to send me a slice of cake,
A bottle of the best wine,
And not to forget the fair young lady
That did release him from close confine.

14. Away, away went the proud young porter,
Until Lord Bateman he did see.
What news, what news, my proud young porter?
What news,† have you brought unto me?

15. There is the fairest young lady
That ever my eyes did see;
She has a ring on every finger,
On one she wears three.

16. She says for you to bring her a slice of cake,
A bottle of the best wine,
And not to forget the fair young lady
That did release you from close confine.

17. Lord Bateman in a passion flew,
His sword he broke in pieces three.
I'll forsake my house and all my living
If Sophie hasn't crossed the sea.

18. Then up spoke the young bride's mother
Who was never heard to speak so free:
O don't you forsake my only daughter,
Although Sophie have crossed the sea.

19. I own I've made a bride of your only daughter;
She's none the worse by me.
She come here on her own horse and saddle,
I'll send her home in a coacheree.

20. O then the wedding was prepared;
It's both their hearts is full of glee.
I'll range no more in a foreign country
So Sophie has crossed the sea.

* Sharp and Karpeles, 1932, add a second "who's there?"
† Sharp and Karpeles, 1932, add a second "what news?"

15. "Lord Bateman"

Sharp MSS., 4884/. Sung by Robert Hughes (63), Buckingham Union, September 8, 1922.

a M (inflected VII)

However it be with the tune, this text seems unlikely to survive till morning.

Lord Bateman was he was, he was, he was,
A nobleman of high degree
Lord Bateman was, he was, he was
A nobleman of high degree.

16. [Lord Bateman]

Sharp MSS., 807/. Sung by Oliver Shuttler (68), a stone-breaker, Dundon, January 20, 1906.

a M (inflected VII)

17. [Lord Bateman]

Burne, 1884-86, p. 651; text, pp. 547-48. Sung by Sally Withington, Edgmond, 1879; noted by J. Smart.

a M

1. Lord Bateman was a noble lord,
   A noble lord of high degree,
   He shipped himself upon a ship
   Some foreign country for to see.

2. He sealéd* east, he sealéd west,
   Until he came to [proud] Turkey,
   Where he was taken and pŭt i'prison,
   Until his life it was weary.

3. This Turk he had one only daughter,
   The fairest creature I ever did see,
   She stole the keys of her father's prison,
   Saying, 'Lord Bateman I will set free.'

4. She took him to her father's arbour,
   And gave to him the best of wine,
   And every health she drank unto him,
   'I wish, Lord Bateman, you were mine.'

5. 'Now seven years I'll make a vow,
   And seven years I'll keep it strong,
   If you will wed with no other woman,
   I will wed with no other man.'

6. The seven years were over and past,
   And forty days were over and gone,
   When she packed up her gay gold clothing,
   And said, 'Lord Bateman I will go see.'

7. When she got to Lord Bateman's castle
   So boldly she rung the bell,
   O who was so ready as the young proud porter
   For to let this fair creature in?

8. 'Is this Lord Bateman's castle?' she says,
   'Or is his lordship now within?'
   'O yes, O yes,' cried the young proud porter,
   'He's just now taken his young bride in.'

9. 'Tell him to send me a slice of bread,
   And a bottle of the best of wine,
   And not to forget the fair young lady
   That did release him when close confined.'

10. Away, away, went the young proud porter,
    Away, away, away went he,
    Until he came to Lord Bateman's chamber,
    He fell down on his bended knee.

11. 'O there is one of the fairest creatures,
    That ever my two eyes did see,
    She has got rings on every finger,
    On one of them she has got three,
    And as much gay gold about her middle
    As would buy all Northumberland.

12. 'She bids you give her a slice of bread,
    And a bottle of the best of wine,
    And not to forget the fair young lady
    That did release you when close confined.'

13. Then Lord Bateman flew in a passion,
    And broke his sword in splinters three,
    Saying 'I'll give all my father's riches
    If Sophia has crossed the sea!'

14. Then up and spake the young bride's mother,
    (She never was heard to speak so free),
    'You'll not forget my only daughter
    If Sophia has crossed the sea!'

15. 'Take back, take back your daughter, Madam,
    She's neither better nor worse for me,
    She came to me with a horse and saddle,
    She shall go back with a coach and three!'

* That is, "sailed."

18. [Lord Bateman]

Sharp MSS., 4849/. Sung by William Carpenter (82), Ross Workhouse, September 2, 1921.

a M (inflected VII)

Lord Bateman was a noble Lord
A noble lord of high degree
He shipped himself on board a ship
Some foreign country to go & see

19. [Lord Bateman]

Sharp MSS., 992/. Sung by William Burland, Stogursey, August 11, 1906.

a M

20. [Lord Bateman]

Broadwood and Maitland (1893), pp. 62-63. "Tune from Mrs. Wilson"; sung in Northamptonshire.

a M

1. Lord Bateman was a noble lord,
    A noble lord of high degree;
   He shipped himself on board a ship,
    Some foreign country he would go see.

2. He sailèd east, he sailèd west,
    Until he came to proud Turkey,
   Where he was taken into prison,
    Until of his life he was quite weary.

3. In this prison there grew a tree,
    It grew so stout, it grew so strong;
   And he was chained all by the middle
    Until his life was almost gone.

4. The turnkey (or "The Turk, he") had one only daughter,
    The fairest that all eyes did see;
   She stole the keys of her father's prison,
    And said Lord Bateman she would set free.

5. "Have you got houses, have you got land,
    Does half Northumberland belong to you?
   What would you give to that fair young lady
    That out of prison would set you free?"

6. "I have got houses, I have got land,
    And half Northumberland belongs to me;
   All this I would give to the fair young lady
    That out of prison would set me free."

7. She took him to her father's hall,
    And gave to him the best of wine;
   And all the healths she drank with him,
    "I wish, Lord Bateman, that you was mine.

8. "Seven years I will make a vow,
    Seven years I will keep it strong;
   If you will wed with no other woman,
    I will wed with no other man."

9. Seven years been gone and past,
    And fourteen days to keep it strong,
   She packed up all her gay clothing,
    And said, Lord Bateman she would go see.

10. And when she came to Lord Bateman's castle,
    There she boldly rang the bell;
   "Who's there, who's there?" cried the proud young porter,
    "Who's there I pray now unto me tell."

11. "Is this, is this Lord Bateman's castle?
    And is his lordship here within?"
   "O yes, it is Lord Bateman's castle,
    And he's just now returned with a new bride in."

12. "Tell him to send me a slice of bread
    And a bottle of the best wine;
   And not to forget the fair young lady
    That did release him when close confined."

13. Away, away went this proud young porter,
    Away, away, away went he;
   Until he came to Lord Bateman's chamber,
    Then on his bended knees fell he.

14. "What news, what news have you, my porter,
    What news have you brought unto me?"
   "There is one of the fairest creatures
    That ever my two eyes did see.

15. "She has got rings on every finger,
    And on one she has got three;
   She's as much gay gold all about her middle
    As would buy half Northumberlee.

16. She bids you send her a slice of bread,
    And a bottle of the best wine;
   And not to forget that fair young lady
    Who did release you when close confined."

17. Then up and spoke the young bride's mother,
    That was never heard to speak so free;
   "You'll not forget my only daughter,
    If so Sophia has crossed the sea."

18. Lord Bateman then flew in a passion,
    And broke his sword in splinters three
   "She came to me with horse and saddle,
    And she may go back with coach and three."

19. Then he prepared another wedding,
    With both their hearts so full of glee;
   "I'll give up all my father's riches,
    If so Sophia has crossed the sea."

By permission of Messrs. J. B. Cramer & Co., Ltd., London

21. [Lord Bateman]

Broadwood, n.d., No. 22, p. 43.

a M

Lord Bateman he had a mind to travel
Into some foreign country;
Where he was taken and put in prison,
Till of his life he was quite weary.

22. "Lord Bakeman"

Mackenzie, 1928, p. 392; text, pp. 16-19. Sung by Alexander Harrison, Maccan, Cumberland County, Nova Scotia.

a M

1. In India there lived a noble lord,
 His riches was beyond compare.
He was the darling of his parents,
 And of their estate an only heir.

2. He had gold and he had silver,
 And he had houses of high degree,
But still he never could be contented
 Until a voyage he had been to sea.

3. He sailéd east and he sailéd west
 Until he came to the Turkish shore,
Where he was taken and put in prison,
 Where he could neither see nor hear.

4. For seven long months he lay lamenting,
 He lay lamenting in iron bands,
There happening to see a brisk young lady,
 Who set him free from his iron chains.

5. The gaoler had one only daughter,
 A brisk young lady gay was she;
As she was walking across the floor,
 She chanced Lord Bakeman for to see.

6. She stole the keys of her father's prison,
 And said Lord Bakeman she would set free.
She went unto the prison door
 And opened it without delay.

7. "Have you got gold, or have you got silver?
 Have you got houses of high degree?
What will you give the fair lady,
 If she from bondage will set you free?"

8. "Yes, I've got gold and I've got silver,
 And I've got houses of high degree.
I'll give them all to the fair lady,
 If she from bondage set me free."

9. "It's not your silver nor your gold,
 Nor yet your houses of high degree;
All that I want to make me happy
 And all that I crave is your fair body.

10. "Let us make a bargain and make it strong,
 For seven long years it shall stand:
You shall not wed no other woman,
 Nor I'll not wed no other man!"

11. When seven long years were gone and past,
 When seven long years were at an end,
She packed up all her richest clothing,
 Saying, "Now I'll go and seek my friend."

12. She sailéd east, she sailéd west,
 Until she came to the Indian shore,
And there she never could be contented
 Till for her true love she did inquire.

13. She did inquire for Lord Bakeman's palace
 At every corner of the street.
She inquired after Lord Bakeman's palace
 Of every person she chanced to meet.

14. And when she came to Lord Bakeman's palace
 She knocked so loud upon the ring,
There's none so ready as the brisk young porter
 To rise and let this fair lady in.

15. She asked if this was Lord Bakeman's palace,
 "Or is the lord himself within?"
"Yes, yes," replied the brisk young porter,
 "He and his bride have just entered in."

16. "Ask him to send me one ounce of bread,
 And a bottle of his wine so strong,
And ask him if he's forgot the lady
 That set him free from his iron chains."

17. The porter went unto his master
 And bowed low upon his knees.
"Arise, arise, my brisk young porter,
 And tell me what the matter is."

18. "There is a lady stands at your gate,
 And she doth weep most bitterly.
I think she is as fine a creature
 As ever I wish my eyes to see.

19. "She's got more rings on her four fingers,
 And round her waist has diamond strings.
She's got more gold about her clothing
 Than your new bride and all her kin.

20. "She wants you to send one ounce of bread,
 And a bottle of your wine so strong,
And asks if you have forgot the lady
 That set you free from your prison chains."

21. He stamped his feet upon the floor,
    He broke the table in pieces three.
  "Here's adieu to you, my wedded bride,
    For this fair lady I will go and see!"

22. Then up spoke his new bride's mother,
    And she was a lady of high degree:
  " 'Tis you have married my only daughter."
    "Well, she's none the worse for me!"

23. "But since my fair one has arrived,
    A second wedding there shall be.
  Your daughter came on a horse and saddle,
    She may return in a coach and three."

24. He took this fair lady by the hand,
    And led her over the marble stones.
  He changed her name from Susannah fair,
    And now she is the wife of Lord Bakeman.

25. He took her by the lily-white hand,
    And led her through from room to room.
  He changed her name from Susannah fair,
    And she is called the wife of Lord Bakeman.

23. [Lord Bateman]

Sharp MSS., 663/. Sung by Mr. Jeffreys (86), Cheddar, September 16, 1905.

a M

    Lord Bateman was a noble Lord
    A noble Lord of high degree
    He shipped himself on board a ship
    Some foreign country he would go and see

24. [Lord Bateman]

Sharp MSS., 735/. Sung by Mrs. James Southwood, Bridgwater, January 1, 1906.

a M

25. [Lord Bateman]

Sharp MSS., 4919/. Sung by Joseph Alcock (78), Sibford Gower, September 17, 1922.

a M

    Lord Bateman was a noble lord
    A noble lord of high degree
    He shipped himself on board a ship
    Some foreign country for to see

26. [Lord Bateman]

Sharp MSS., 878/. Sung by Mrs. Coombes, Bridgwater, April 14, 1906.

a M

27. [Lord Bateman]

Sharp MSS., 2358/. Sung by Charles Benfield (68), Bould, September 4, 1909.

a M (inflected III)

28. [Lord Bateman]

Grainger MS., No. 171. Sung by Mr. Thompson, of Barrow, at Brigg, May 7, 1906.

a M (inflected III)

29. [Lord Bateman]

Sharp MSS., 1071/. Sung by William Stokes, Chew Stoke, August 27, 1906.

a D (inflected III)

Lord Bateman in a passion flew
And broke his sword in splinters three
He swore he'd have another wedding O
Since Sophia had crossed the Sea

30. [Lord Bateman]

Sharp MSS., 1085/. Sung by Mrs. Ellen Carter (71), Cheddar Cliffs, August 28, 1906.

a D (inflected III)

33. "Lord Bateman"

Grainger MS., No. 174. Also in Grainger, *JFSS*, III (1909), pp. 195-99. Sung by George Wray, Barton-on-Humber, Lincolnshire, at Briggs, Lincs., August 4, 1904.

a D—M (inflected III)

31. [Lord Bateman]

Sharp MSS., 1561/. Sung by Mrs. Jarrett, Bridgwater, January 7, 1908.

a D (inflected III)

32. [Lord Bateman]

Sharp MSS., 2278/. Sung by Henry Corbett, Snowshill, August 13, 1909.

a D (inflected III)

9. When seven long years aden (and) fōérteen days,
When for seven long years è well known to me,
She fetched úp all her gay clothing
And crossed the seas to Lord Bateman;
She fetched úp all her gay clothing
And crossed the seas to Lord Batemun.

Mr. Grainger's rather special phonetic symbols have been slightly reduced.

34. [Lord Bateman]

Grainger MS., No. 170. Also in Grainger, *JFSS*, III (1909), p. 192. Sung by Joseph Taylor, Brigg, Lincolnshire, July 28, 1906.

a D

Lord Bateman was aden (an) noble Lord,
A noble Lord of sòme high dègéree; (degree)
He shipped himsedelf (self) on board of a ship,
Sóm (some) foreign còuntéry he would go see.

He sailed east and he sailed west,
Until he came to péroud Turkey,
Where he was taken and put in prisun
Until his élife it è grēö (grew) quite weary.

And in this prisun there grēö (grew) a tree,
It grēö so large and it grēö so strong;
Where he was chēned (chained) around the middle
Until his è life it è was almost gone.

1. Lord Bateman was āden (a) noble lord,
Ā noble lord of high degree;
He shipped himself on board of ship,
Some foreign counteries he would go see.

2. He sailed east and he sailed west,
Ontil he came to the proud Turkey;
Where he was taken, put into prison,
Ontil his life it grew quite weary;
Where he was taken, put into prison,
Ontil his life it grew quite weary.

3. And in this prison there grēö (grew) a tree,
It grew so stout and it grew so strong;
Where he was chēned (chained) by the middle
Until his life it was almost gone;
Where he was chēned by the middle
Until his life it was almost gone.

4. Thē Turkē he 'ád but one onlī daughter,
The fairest creature my eyes dār (did e'er?) see;
She stole the keys from her father's pidilow (pillow),
And sād (said) Lord Bateman should be set free;
She stole the keys from her father's pidilow,
And sād Lord Bateman should be set free.

5. 'Have you got houses, have you got land,
Or does Northumberland belong to you?'
"I would give it all to that fair young lady
That out of prisun would set me free;
I would give it all to that fair young lady
That out of prisun would set me free."

6. Then she took him to hérér (her) father's pâlace,
And gave to him thē best of wine,
And ev'ry health that she drunk unto him;
'I wish, Lord Batemun, thē (thy) heart was mine.'
And ev'ry health that she drunk unto him;
'I wish, Lord Batemun, thē heart was mine.'

7. Then she took him to hérér father's 'arbour,
And gave to him a ship of fame;
Saying; 'adieu, adieu, my dear Lord Bateman,
I'm afraid I shall never see thy face again.'

8. 'For seven long years I will make a vow;
For seven long years, and I'll keep it strong;
If you do get wed to no óther woman
I will get wed to no óther man.'

His jailor 'àd bùt one honly (only) daughter,
The fairest creature my two eyes did see;
She stole the keys of her father's prisun,
And said Lord Batemun she would set free.

35. "Lord Bateman"

Chappell, 1939, pp. 18-20. Sung by Charles Tillett,
Wanchese, N.C., text, 1924; tune, 1935.

a I/Ly

1. In India lived a noble lord,
   And he had riches beyond compare.
   He was the darling of his parents,
   Of the estate an only heir.

2. He sailed east and he sailed west,
   He sailed till he came to the Turkish shore,
   And there he was taken and put in prison
   Where he could neither see nor hear.

3. The jailer had one only daughter,
   A lady young and gay was she;
   She stole the keys of her father's prison
   And said, Lord Bateman I will set free.

4. She went unto the prison door,
   She opened it without delay.

5. Have you gold or have you silver?
   Or have you houses of high degree?
   Or what will you give to this fair lady
   If she'll from bondage set you free?

6. I have gold and I have silver,
   I have houses of high degree,
   I'll give it all to the fair lady
   If she'll from bondage set me free.

7. I don't want your gold and silver,
   Neither your houses of high degree;
   All I want to make me happy,
   All I want is your pure body.

8. Let's make a bargain and make it strong,
   And seven long years it shall stand;
   For you to wed no other woman
   And I will wed no other man.

9. They made a bargain and made it strong,
   Though seven long years it did not stand;
   For he did wed another woman,
   But she didn't wed another man.

10. Six long years was done and over,
    And seven long years was now to an end;
    She packed all up her richest clothing,
    Says, I'll go and seek a friend.

11. She sailed east and she sailed west,
    She sailed till she came to India's shore;
    Yet she never could be contented,
    For her true-love she did inquire.

12. She inquired for Lord Bateman's palace,
    At every corner of the street;
    And she inquired for Lord Bateman's palace
    Of every one she chanced to meet.

13. When she came to Lord Bateman's palace
    She tingled loud at the ring;
    None so ready as a brisk young porter
    To rise and let her in.

14. Saying, Is this Lord Bateman's palace,
    Or is the lord himself within?
    O yes, replied the brisk young porter,
    For he and his new bride have just walked in.

15. I wish I was back to my native country,
    Across the seas there to remain.

16. Tell him to send me an ounce of bread
    And a bottle of his wine so strong;
    And ask if he had forgot the lady
    That set him free from his prison bonds.

17. He stamped his foot upon the floor
    And broke the table in pieces three;
    Adieu, adieu to my wedded wife,
    For this fair lady I'll go and see.

18. Then up steps the new bride's mother,
    She being a lady of high degree;
    Says, You've gone and married my daughter
    And this the second wedding will be.

19. Your daughter came on a horse and saddle,
    And she'll go back on a coach so free;
    Your daughter came on a horse and saddle,
    And she'll go back on a coach so free.

20. He took Susannah by the hand
    And led her in from room to room;
    He changed her name from Susannah Fair,
    And now she is the wife of Lord Bateman.

36. [Young Beichan; or, Lord Bacon]

Sharp MSS., 3168/2305. Also in Sharp and Karpeles, 1932,
I, pp. 77(A)-79. Sung by "Granny" Banks, White Rock,
N.C., July 28, 1916.

a I/M (– VI)

1. Lord Bacon was a nobleman,
   As fine as any you should see;
   He'd gathered all his silks and rubies,
   The Turkish land he'd go and see.

Originally noted in 4/4.

2. He first blowed East and then blowed West,
   And he blowed down to the Turkish land.
   The Turks they got him and so sadly used him,
   To love* his life he was quite wearied.

3. They bored a hole in his left shoulder
   And nailed him down unto a tree.
   They gave him nothing but bread and water,
   And bread and water but once a day.

4. The Turks they had but one fair daughter,
   As fair a one as you should see.
   She stole the keys of the prison strong
       (or, She stole the jail keep from her father)
   And vowed Lord Bacon she would set free.

5. She said: Have you got any land or living,
   Or have you any dwelling free?
   Would you give it all to a prince's daughter
   If she would set you free?

6. Then he says: I've got a land and living
   And I have got a dwelling free,
   And I'll give it all to you, (my) pretty creature,
   If you will do that thing for me.

7. She went on to her master's cellar
   And from her father stole a jail key.
   She opened the dungeon both deep and wide,
   And vowed Lord Bacon she would set free.

8. Then she took him to her master's (or father's) cellar
   And drawed some of the best port wine,
   And drink a health, you pretty creature,
   I wish, Lord Bacon, you were mine.

9. And then they drawed each other's notes of love
   And seven years they were to stand.
   He vowed he'd marry no other woman
   Unless (or, Until) she† married some other man.

10. Then she took him on to the sea-side
    And left him sailing over the main:
    Fare-ye-well, fare-ye-well, you pretty creature.
    O when shall I see you again?

11. When seven years was passed and gone,
    And seven months and almost three,
    She gathered all her silks and rubies
    And vowed Lord Bacon she'd go and see.

12. When she got to Lord Bacon's hall
    She knocked so far below the ring.
    Who's there, who's there (or, O yes, O yes), said the bold
       proud porter,
    Who knock so hard fain would come in?

13. Is this Lord Bacon's hall, she said,
    Or is there any man within?
    O yes, O yes, said the bold, proud porter,
    This day has fetched him a young bride in.

    * * * * *

14. She says: Now you've married some other woman
    And I have married no other man,
    I wish I had my notes of love,
    Straight back I'd go to the Turkish land.

15. She's got a ring on every finger
    And on her middle one she's got three,
    And gold around her neck a-plenty
    To buy all Cumberland of thee.

16. Then up spoke the young bride's mother,
    An angry spoken old thing was she,
    Saying: Would you quit my own fair daughter
    And take up with a Turkish lady?

17. He said: You may take your daughter home with you,
    For I'm sure she's none the worse of me.
    For the prettiest thing stands there a-waiting
    That ever my two eyes did see.

18. He took her by the lily-white hand
    And took her to her father's cellar,
    And drawed some of the best port wine,
    Saying: Drink a health, you pretty creature,
    Who freed me from such a prison strong.

19. He took her by the lily-white hand
    And gently led her to his hall,
    And changed her name from Pretty Nancy,
    And called her name, it was Noble Jane.

    * 1932: "leave"
    † 1932: "or, Until she had"

37. [The Loving Ballad of Lord Bateman]

Cruikshank, 1839. Also in Child, 1882-98, I, pp. 476-77.
According to Kidson (*JFSS*, I, p. 241), Cruikshank learned
his tune from a street singer nicknamed "Tripe Skewer,"
who used to sing it outside a public house at Battle Bridge
(King's Cross).

a I

1. Lord Bateman was a noble lord,
       A noble lord of high degree;
   He shipped himself all aboard of a ship,
       Some foreign country for to see.

2. He sailed east, he sailed west,
    Until he came to famed Turkey,
Where he was taken and put to prison,
    Until his life was quite weary.

3. All in this prison there grew a tree,
    O there it grew so stout and strong!
Where he was chained all by the middle,
    Until his life was almost gone.

4. This Turk he had one only daughter,
    The fairest my two eyes eer see;
She steel the keys of her father's prison,
    And swore Lord Bateman she would let go free.

5. O she took him to her father's cellar,
    And gave to him the best of wine;
And every health she drank unto him
    Was, 'I wish, Lord Bateman, as you was mine.'

6. 'O have you got houses, have you got land,
    And does Northumberland belong to thee?
And what would you give to the fair young lady
    As out of prison would let you go free?'

7. 'O I've got houses and I've got land,
    And half Northumberland belongs to me;
And I will give it all to the fair young lady
    As out of prison would let me go free.'

8. 'O in seven long years, I'll make a vow
    For seven long years, and keep it strong,
That if you'll wed no other woman,
    O I will wed no other man.'

9. O she took him to her father's harbor,
    And gave to him a ship of fame,
Saying, Farewell, farewell to you, Lord Bateman,
    I fear I never shall see you again.

10. Now seven long years is gone and past,
    And fourteen days, well known to me;
She packed up all her gay clothing,
    And swore Lord Bateman she would go see.

11. O when she arrived at Lord Bateman's castle,
    How boldly then she rang the bell!
'Who's there? who's there?' cries the proud young porter,
    'O come unto me pray quickly tell.'

12. 'O is this here Lord Bateman's castle,
    And is his lordship here within?'
'O yes, O yes,' cries the proud young porter,
    'He's just now taking his young bride in.'

13. 'O bid him to send me a slice of bread,
    And a bottle of the very best wine,
And not forgetting the fair young lady
    As did release him when close confine.'

14. O away and away went this proud young porter,
    O away and away and away went he,
Until he come to Lord Bateman's chamber,
    When he went down on his bended knee.

15. 'What news, what news, my proud young porter?
    What news, what news? Come tell to me:'
'O there is the fairest young lady
    As ever my two eyes did see.

16. 'She has got rings on every finger,
    And on one finger she has got three;
With as much gay gold about her middle
    As would buy half Northumberlee.

17. 'O she bids you to send her a slice of bread,
    And a bottle of the very best wine,
And not forgetting the fair young lady
    As did release you when close confine.'

18. Lord Bateman then in passion flew,
    And broke his sword in splinters three,
Saying, 'I will give half of my father's land,
    If so be as Sophia has crossed the sea.'

19. Then up and spoke this young bride's mother,
    Who never was heard to speak so free;
Saying, 'You'll not forget my only daughter,
    If so be as Sophia has crossed the sea.'

20. 'O it's true I made a bride of your daughter,
    But she's neither the better nor the worse for me;
She came to me with a horse and saddle,
    But she may go home in a coach and three.'

21. Lord Bateman then prepared another marriage,
    With both their hearts so full of glee,
Saying, 'I will roam no more to foreign countries,
    Now that Sophia has crossed the sea.'

The text has been decanted out of Cockney by the hand of Child.

38. [Young Beichan]

Barry, *JAF*, XXII (1909), p. 78. Sung by N. A. C., Rome, Pa., August 7, 1907.

a I/M (–II)

This is Barry's reading of a sol-fa script devoid of time-values. The singer may have conformed to triple time. The identification in Barry's MS. is Mrs. N. A. Chaffee.

39. "The Jailer's Daughter"

Scarborough, 1937, p. 410; text, pp. 212-13. Sung by Polly Morris, Yellow Branch, Pirkey, Va., c. 1932; learned from her father. The text is from her written copy.

If D tonic, a M, ending on IV; if G tonic, p I

This copy terminates unexpectedly, and is perhaps a Mixolydian ending on IV. If so, it reverses the usual tendency to drop from Major to a Mixolydian ending.

1. I sailed east, I sailed west,
    I sailed on to Kentucky shore,
There I was taken and put in Prison,
    and never expected freedom no more.

2. The jailer had as fairer daughter
    as ever my too eyes did see.
She stold the keys of her father's treasure
    and said lord Bateman she would set free.

3. She taken him to her father's seller,
    and there they drinked of the wine so strong,
And every health she drinked unto him
    and wished lord Bateman he was her own.

4. She taken him to her father's closet
    And bargains made was one, two, three,
That he was to marry no other lady
    nor she was to marry no other man.

5. For seven long years he stayed away,
    For seven long years was one, two, three.
She picked up her gold and diamonds,
    and said lord Bateman she would go see.

6. She rode till she came to lord Bateman's casle,
    And there so loud she rapted the ring,
There was none so ready as lord Bateman waiten
    to arise and let her in.

7. Is this here where lord Batemen lives,
    or is he now at home?
He is just now setting at his table,
    He is just now brought his new bride home.

8. O tell him to send me a slice of his bread,
    and tell him a glass of his wine so strong;
And tell him never to forget the lady
    that freed him of his Prison strong.

9. O yonder stands as fair a lily
    as ever my too eyes did see;
She has more gold about her neck
    that would buy the bride of your company.

10. Said tell you to send her a slice of your bread,
    and tell you a glass of your wine so strong,
And tell you never to forget the lady
    that freed you of your Prison so strong.

11. He sent her a glass of his wine so strong,
    and sliced his bread in peaces three.
Said, Come on, Porter and take your daughter,
    for she is none of the worse by me.

12. She came here on a horse and saddle,
    She will go away in a coach with me
So fair you well to the land of the living,
    since my Susie now have crossed the sea.

40. "Lord Bakeman"

Robertson, LC/ACFS, rec. 3811 A1 and 2, B1. Sung by George Vinton Graham, San Jose, Calif., October 12, 1937.

a D/M

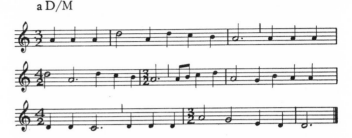

1. In India there lived a noble lord
    And he had houses of high degree;
But there he never could be contented
    Until he had been a voyage at sea.

2. Then he sailed east and he sailed west
    Until he came to the Turkish shore
And there he was taken and put in prison
    Where he could neither see nor hear.

3. The jailor had an only daughter
    And she was a lady fair to see.
She had stole the keys to her father's prison
    And she said Lord Bakeman she would set free.

Spoken: Then she enters the prison yard and unlocks the gate and is speaking to Lord Bakeman, and she said to him:

4. 'What will you give to the fair lady
    If she'll from bondage set you free?'

5. 'Oh, I have houses and I have money
    And I have houses of high degree,
All these I'll give to the fair lady,
    If she'll from bondage set me free.'

6. 'Then we'll make a bargain and we'll make it strong
    For seven long years that it shall end,
That you won't wed no other woman
    And I won't wed no other man.'

7. When seven long years were at an end,
    When seven long years had passed and gone,
She packed up all her richest clothing,
    Saying, 'Now I'll go and seek my friend.'

8. Then she sailed east and she sailed west
    Until she came to the India shore;
And there she never could be contented
    Until for Lord Bakeman she did inquire.

9. At every corner of the street
    She did inquire for Lord Bakeman's palace.
'Yes, yes' replied a (?)base young porter,
    'He and his bride have just stepped in.'

10. She wrung her hands and she tore her hair
    Just like a lady in despair.
    'Now and I wish I was in my native country,
    Across the sea there to remain.

11. (Will you tell your noble lord To send)
    'Take a message to your noble lord:
    Tell him to send one ounce of bread
    And a bottle of his wine so strong,
    And ask if he's forgot the lady
    Who set him free from his prison chains.'

12. 'There is a lady stands at your gates
    And she does weep most bitterly.
    I think she is the finest creature
    That ever I wish my eyes to see.

13. 'She wants you to send one ounce of bread
    And a bottle of your wine so strong,
    And ask if he's forgot the lady
    Who set him free from his prison chains.'

14. He stomped so loud upon the floor,
    He broke the table in pieces three:
    'Here's adieu, adieu, my wedded bride,
    For this fair one I'll go and see.'

15. Then up spoke his new bride's mother
    And she was a lady of high degree:
    'And it's if you have married my only daughter
    But she is none the worse for thee.'

16. 'Your daughter came with a horse and saddle,
    She shall return with a coach and three.'

· · · · · · · · · · ·
  · · · · · · · · · ·

17. He took her by the lily-white hand,
    He changed her—

Spoken: He changed her name from Susanna fair,
         She is now called the wife of Lord Bakeman.

41. [Young Beichan]

Sharp MSS., 3999/2882-83. Also in Sharp and Karpeles,
1932, I, p. 87(J). Sung by Mrs. Frances Carter, Beattyville,
Lee County, Ky., September 8, 1917.

a M/D

To this style of the tune-family belong many variants of a song
on a related theme, variously known as "The Broken Token," "The
Single Sailor," "A Fair Maid in her Garden Walking," etc.
Sharp and Karpeles, 1932, give only one stanza.

1. A gentleman from the courts of England,
   A gentleman of a high degree;
   He lived uneasy and discontented
   Until he took a voyage on sea.

2. He sailed East, he sailed West,
   He sailed till he come to a Turkish shore,
   And there he was caught and put in prison,
   No hopes of freedom for ever more.

3. The gaoler had one only daughter,
   She was just as pretty as pretty could be;
   She stole the keys of her father's prison
   And she vowed Lord Bateman she would set **free**.

4. She led him down in her father's cellar,
   She gave him of the wine so strong;
   She told him never to forget that lady
   Who freed him from the prison strong.

5. She led him to the harbour
   And there she bargained a ship for him,
   Saying: A bargain, a bargain, I will make with you,
   A bargain, a bargain of seven long years;
   That you won't marry no other woman,
   Nor I won't marry no other man.

6. Then seven long years being passed and over
   And seven long years and two or three,
   She bundled up her gold and diamonds
   And she vowed Lord Bateman she would go see.

7. She sailed East, she sailed West,
   She sailed from some Turkish shore.
   And there she spied the finest castle
   That she ever her two eyes did see.

8. She said: Is this Lord Bateman's castle,
   Or is he himself within?
   O yes, this is Lord Bateman's castle,
   He just has brought his new bride in.

9. Tell him I want a piece of Lord Bateman's bread
   And a bottle of his wine so strong.
   And tell him never to forget that lady
   Who freed him from his prison strong.

10. It's seven long years I've been your porter,
    It's seven long years and two or three,
    But at your gates stands the fairest damsel
    That ever my two eyes did see.

11. She says she wants a piece of Lord Bateman's bread
    And a bottle of your wine so strong;
    Says tell you never to forget that lady
    Who freed you from the prison strong.

12. So he rose up all in a passion,
    He split the table in pieces three,
    Saying: Fare you well to my new companion,
    If my Susanne has crossed the sea.

13. Said: To-day I married your daughter,
    But she ain't none the worse of me,
    And she rode here on a horse and saddle,
    And she may ride back in a coach and three.

14. He took her by the lily-white hand,
    He led her over the marble stone;
    He changed her name from Susannay fair,
    She's the wife of Lord Bateman now.

42. [Young Beichan]

Sharp MSS., 3860/2823-24. Also in Sharp and Karpeles, 1932, I, p. 87(I). Sung by Mrs. Cis Jones, Goose Creek, Manchester, Ky., August 16, 1917.

a π²

Sharp and Karpeles, 1932, omit all but the first stanza of the text.

1. There was a young man in old England dwelling,
He was tossed East, he was tossed West,
He was tossed on some Turkey shore.
He was imprisoned by the Turks
Where he could neither stand nor walk.

2. The Turks they had a lovely daughter,
A very handsome girl indeed.
She says; Young man, have you gold and silver,
Or riches to a high degree.

3. He says: Kind Madam, I've gold and silver
And riches to a high degree.
I'll give them all to the lady fairest
Who out of prison will set me free.

4. She stole the keys of her father's dwelling
And freed him from his iron bands.
She took him by the lily-white hand,
Two or three rooms into she led him.
And of the wine so strong she gave him.
Every health she drunk unto him
And wished Lord Baker might be her own.

* * * *

5. There was seventeen long years had come and gone,
And eighteen had entered in.
She dressed herself in men's clothing,
And said young Baker she would go see.

6. She rode and she rode till she came to Baker's castle,
And there she tingled at the ring.
She says: Is this Lord Baker's castle,
Or is it the lord himself within?

7. He jumped up and from his table,
He bursted it into splinters three.
I'll forsake my land and living
If Miss Susannah ain't crossed the sea.

8. He took her by the lily-white hand,
Two or three rooms into he led her,
And of the wine so strong he gave her
And says: Susannah shall be mine.

9. She says: Is this Lord Baker's bride
That he's just this day brought in?
He says: O lady, you can take your daughter;
She ain't none the worse by me.
She come here on her own horse and saddle,
I'll send her home in coaches three.

10. How he soon thought on his Susannah fair
Who freed him from his iron bands.
He took her by the lily-white hand
And he soon altered her name from Susannah fair
And called her young Baker's landlady.

43. [Lord Bateman]

Sharp MSS., 3971/. Sung by Mrs. Bagley, Beattyville, Ky., September 5, 1917.

a π²

A gentleman of the courts of England
A gentleman of high degree
He lived uneasy and discontented
Until he took a voyage to sea.

44. "Lord Bateman"

Randolph, I, 1946, p. 85(C). Sung by Miss Jewell Perriman, Jenkins, Mo., February 28, 1941.

a π³

They bored a hole through his left shoulder
And in that hole a rope did tie,
They made him draw the carts of iron
Till he was sick and like to die.

A Turkish slave loved a maiden fair,
And she was of a high degree . . . .

45. [Lord Beichan and Susie Pye]

Kinloch, 1827, App'x to p. 260; text, pp. 260-70.

a M

1. Young Beichan was in London born,
   He was a man of hie degree;
   He past thro' monie kingdoms great,
   Until he cam unto Grand Turkie.

2. He view'd the fashions of that land,
   Their way of worship viewed he;
   But unto onie of their stocks
   He wadna sae much as bow a knee:

3. Which made him to be taken straight,
   And brought afore their hie jurie;
   The savage Moor did speak upricht,
   And made him meikle ill to dree.

4. In ilka shoulder they've bor'd a hole,
   And in ilka hole they've put a tree;
   They've made him to draw carts and wains,
   Till he was sick and like to dee.

5. But young Beichan was a Christian born,
   And still a Christian was he;
   Which made them put him in prison strang,
   And cauld and hunger sair to dree;
   And fed on nocht but bread and water,
   Until the day that he mot dee.

6. In this prison there grew a tree,
   And it was unco stout and strang;
   Where he was chained by the middle,
   Until his life was almaist gane.

7. The savage Moor had but ae dochter,
   And her name it was Susie Pye;
   And ilka day as she took the air,
   The prison door she passed bye.

8. But it fell ance upon a day,
   As she was walking, she hear him sing;
   She listen'd to his tale of woe,
   A happy day for young Beichan!

9. "My hounds they all go masterless,
   My hawks they flee frae tree to tree,
   My youngest brother will heir my lands,
   My native land I'll never see."

10. "O were I but the prison-keeper,
    As I'm a ladie o' hie degree,
    I soon wad set this youth at large,
    And send him to his ain countrie."

11. She went away into her chamber,
    All nicht she never clos'd her ee;
    And when the morning begoud to dawn,
    At the prison door alane was she.

12. She gied the keeper a piece of gowd,
    And monie pieces o' white monie,
    To tak her thro' the bolts and bars,
    The lord frae Scotland she lang'd to see:—
    She saw young Beichan at the stake,
    Which made her weep maist bitterlie.

13. "O hae ye got onie lands," she says,
    "Or castles in your ain countrie?
    It's what wad ye gie to the ladie fair
    Wha out o' prison wad set you free?"

14. "It's I hae houses, and I hae lands,
    Wi' monie castles fair to see,
    And I wad gie a' to that ladie gay,
    Wha out o' prison wad set me free."

15. The keeper syne brak aff his chains,
    And set Lord Beichan at libertie:—
    She fill'd his pockets baith wi' gowd,
    To tak him till his ain countrie.

16. She took him frae her father's prison,
    And gied to him the best o' wine;
    And a brave health she drank to him,—
    "I wish, Lord Beichan, ye were mine!

17. It's seven lang years I'll mak a vow,
    And seven lang years I'll keep it true;
    If ye'll wed wi' na ither woman,
    It's I will wed na man but you."

18. She's tane him to her father's port,
    And gien to him a ship o' fame,—
    "Farewell, farewell, my Scottish lord,
    I fear I'll ne'er see you again."

19. Lord Beichan turn'd him round about,
    And lowly, lowly, loutit he:—
    "Ere seven lang years come to an end,
    I'll tak you to mine ain countrie."

* * * * *

20. Then whan he cam to Glasgow town,
    A happy, happy man was he;
    The ladies a' around him thrang'd
    To see him come frae slaverie.

21. His mother she had died o' sorrow,
    And a' his brothers were dead but he;
    His lands they a' were lying waste,
    In ruins were his castles free.

22. Na porter there stood at his yett;
    Na human creature he could see;
    Except the screeching owls and bats,
    Had he to bear him companie.

23. But gowd will gar the castles grow,
    And he had gowd and jewels free;
    And soon the pages around him thrang'd,
    To serve him on their bended knee.

24. His hall was hung wi' silk and satin,
  His table rung wi' mirth and glee;
He soon forgot the lady fair,
  That lows'd him out o' slaverie.

25. Lord Beichan courted a lady gay,
  To heir wi' him his lands sae free,
Ne'er thinking that a lady fair
  Was on her way frae Grand Turkie.

26. For Susie Pye could get na rest,
  Nor day nor nicht could happy be,
Still thinking on the Scottish Lord,
  Till she was sick and like to dee.

27. But she has builded a bonnie ship,
  Weel mann'd wi' seamen o' hie degree;
And secretly she stept on board,
  And bid adieu to her ain countrie.

28. But whan she cam to the Scottish shore,
  The bells were ringing sae merrilie;
It was Lord Beichan's wedding day,
  Wi' a lady fair o' hie degree.

29. But sic a vessel was never seen,
  The very masts were tapp'd wi' gold!
Her sails were made o' the satin fine,
  Maist beautiful for to behold.

30. But whan the lady cam on shore,
  Attended wi' her pages three,
Her shoon were of the beaten gowd,
  And she a lady of great beautie.

31. Then to the skipper she did say,
  "Can ye this answer gie to me—
Where are Lord Beichan's lands sae braid?
  He surely lives in this countrie."

32. Then up bespak the skipper bold,
  (For he could speak the Turkish tongue,)—
"Lord Beichan lives not far away,
  This is the day of his wedding."

33. "If ye will guide me to Beichan's yetts,
  I will ye well reward," said she,—
Then she and all her pages went,
  A very gallant companie.

34. When she cam to Lord Beichan's yetts,
  She tirl'd gently at the pin,
Sae ready was the proud porter
  To let the wedding guests come in.

35. "Is this Lord Beicham's house," she says,
  "Or is that noble Lord within?"
"Yes, he is gane into the hall,
  With his brave bride, and monie ane."

36. "Ye'll bid him send me a piece of bread,
  Bot and a cup of his best wine;
And bid him mind the lady's love
  That ance did lowse him out o' pyne."

37. Then in and cam the porter bold,
  I wat he gae three shouts and three,—
"The fairest lady stands at your yetts,
  That ever my twa een did see."

38. Then up bespak the bride's mither,
  I wat an angry woman was she,—
"You micht hae excepted our bonnie bride,
  Tho' she'd been three times as fair as she."

39. "My dame, your daughter's fair enough,
  And aye the fairer mot she be!
But the fairest time that e'er she was,
  She'll na compare wi' this ladie.

40. She has a gowd ring on ilka finger,
  And on her mid-finger she has three;
She has as meikle gowd upon her head,
  As wad buy an Earldom o' land to thee.

41. My lord, she begs some o' your bread,
  Bot and a cup o' your best wine,
And bids you mind the lady's love
  That ance did lowse ye out o' pyne."

42. Then up and started Lord Beichan,
  I wat he made the table flee,—
"I wad gie a' my yearlie rent
  'Twere Susie Pye come owre the sea."

43. Syne up bespak the bride's mother,—
  She was never heard to speak sae free,—
"Ye'll no forsake my ae dochter,
  Tho' Susie Pye has cross'd the sea?"

44. "Tak hame, tak hame, your dochter, madam,
  For she is ne'er the waur o' me;
She cam to me on horseback riding,
  And she sall gang hame in chariot free."

45. He's tane Susie Pye by the milk-white hand,
  And led her thro' his halls sae hie,—
"Ye're now Lord Beichan's lawful wife,
  And thrice ye're welcome unto me."

46. Lord Beichan prepar'd for another wedding,
  Wi' baith their hearts sae fu' o' glee;
Says, "I'll range na mair in foreign lands,
  Sin Susie Pye has cross'd the sea.

47. Fy! gar a' our cooks mak ready;
  And fy! gar a' our pipers play;
And fy! gar trumpets gae thro' the toun,
  That Lord Beichan's wedded twice in a day!"

46. [Lord Bateman]

Sharp MSS., 4156/. Sung by Mrs. Margaret Clapp, New York, N.Y., November 16, 1917; learned from her mother, who learned it from her mother in Dundee, Scotland.

a D—M—Æ (inflected III and VI)

This copy is surprisingly chromatic and hard to classify modally.

He gied the table such a kick
That it gar'd the cups and the cannels flee
I wad my life cried young Bateman
It is Susie Pye come o'er the sea.

There was a man who lived in England, and he
  was of some high degree;
And he became uneasy and discontented
Some foreign land some land to see.

47. "The Turkish Lady"

Davis, 1929, p. 565(I); text, p. 171. Sung by Mrs. M. Leake, Harrisonburg, Va., November 21, 1918. Collected by Martha M. Davis.

a D (–II)

This copy seems rhythmically ambiguous: it might have been basically 3/2.

"I sailed east, I sailed west,
  I sailed to the Turkey shore,
And there I was taken and put in prison
  With hopes of freedom nevermore."

48. [Lord Bateman]

Sharp MSS., 4119/. Sung by Mrs. Eliza Price, Hyden, Ky., October 3, 1917.

p π[1]

With this copy we leave the authentic range for the plagal.

He sailed East and he sailed West
He sailed till he came to the Turkish shore
And there they took him and put him in prison
He lived in hopes no freedom more.

49. [Lord Bateman]

Sharp MSS., 4037/. Sung by Mrs. Marthy Stamper, Hindman, Ky., September 18, 1917.

p π[1]

50. [Lord Bateman]

Sharp MSS., 4065/. Sung by girls at Hindman School, Hindman, Ky., September 20, 1917.

p π[1]

There was a man who lived in London,
He was of some high degree,
He became uneasy and discontented,
Some fair land, some land to see.

51. "The Turkish Lady"

Thomas, 1931, pp. 86-87. Sung in Kentucky.

p π[1]

1. Lord Bakeman was a noble lord.
   He was a lord of high degree.
   He could not rest or be contented
   Until he had voyaged across the sea.

2. He sailed east and he sailed westward
   Until he reached the Turkish shore;
   And there he was taken and put in prison;
   He lived in hopes of freedom no more.

3. Lord Bakeman rose up from the table
   He bursted it to splinters three,
   Saying, "I'll bet my houses and my lands
   That the Turkish lady has crossed the sea."

* * * * * *

4. "Have you houses or have you lands
    Or are you of some high degree?
    Would you give it all to the Turkish lady
    If out of prison would set you free?"

5. "I have houses and I have lands
    And I am of some high degree;
    I would give it all to the Turkish lady
    If out of prison she'd set me free."

6. They made a vow and they made it strong
    Seven long years and two and three,
    "If you won't marry no other woman
    It's I won't marry no other man."

7. Seven long years I will make a vow, sir,
    Seven long years and two and three,
    She gathered up her rich gay clothing
    And she said "Lord Bakeman, I will go see."

52. [Lord Bateman]

Sharp MSS., 3757/. Sung by Mrs. M. E. Vaughan, Berea, Ky., May 29, 1917.

p π¹

The second half-note was dotted in the MS., probably inadvertently.

53. "Turkish Lady"

Cox, 1939, pp. 19-20. Sung by Catharine E. Sutherland, Hindman, Ky., December 20, 1925.

p π¹

1. There was a man in England born,
    And he was of some high degree;
    He became uneasy, discontented,
    Some far land, some land to see.

2. He sailed east and he sailed west,
    He sailed all over the Turkish shore,
    Till he was caught and put in prison,
    Never to be released any more.

3. The Turk he had one only daughter,
    And she was of some high degree;
    She stole the key to her father's castle,
    Declared Lord Batesman she'd set free.

4. She took him down to the lower cellar,
    She drew him a drink of the strongest wine;
    And every moment seemed an hour,—
    "O Lord Batesman, if you were mine!"

5. "Let's make a vow, let's make a promise,
    Let's make a vow, let's make it stand;
    You vow you'll marry no other woman,
    I'll vow I'll marry no other man."

6. They made a vow, they made a promise,
    They made a vow, they made it stand;
    He vowed he'd marry no other woman,
    She vow'd she'd marry no other man.

7. Seven long years had rolled around,
    It seemed as though it were twenty-three;
    She packed up her gay golden clothing,
    And declared Lord Batesman she'd go see.

8. Seven long years had rolled around,
    It seemed as though it were twenty-nine;
    She packed up her gay golden clothing,
    Declared Lord Batesman she'd go find.

9. She went till she came to the gate, she tingled,
    It was so loud that she wouldn't come in;
    "Who's there? Who's there?" cried a proud young porter,
    "Who's there! Who's there? unto me tell."

10. "Oh, is this Lord Batesman's . . .

54. "A Turkish Lady"

Cox, 1939, pp. 16-18. Sung by Camilla Dennis; learned from schoolchildren, Hindman, Ky., 1922-23.

p I/Ly

1. There was a man he lived in London,
    And he was of some high degree,
    He became uneasy, discontented,
    Some fair land, some land to see.

2. O he sailed East, O he sailed West,
    He sailed all over the Turkish shore,
    Till he was caught and put in prison,
    Never to be released any more.

3. The Turk he had but one lone daughter,
    And she was of some high degree,
    She stole the keys to her father's dwelling,
    Declared Lord Batesman she'd set free.

4. She took him down to the lowest cellar,
    She drew him a drink of the strongest wine,
    Every moment seemed an hour;
    "O Lord Batesman, if you were mine!"

5. "Let's make a vow, let's make a promise,
    Let's make a vow, let's make it stand;
   You vow you'll marry no other woman,
    I'll vow I'll marry no other man."

6. They made a vow, they made a promise,
    They made a vow, they made it stand;
   He vowed he'd marry no other woman,
    She vowed she'd marry no other man.

7. Seven long years have rolled around,
    It seemed as though it were twenty-three;
   She packed up her gay gold and clothing,
    Declared Lord Batesman she'd go see.

8. Seven long years have rolled around,
    It seemed as though it were twenty-nine;
   She packed up her gay gold and clothing,
    Declared Lord Batesman she'd go find.

9. She went till she came to the gate, she tingled,
    It was so loud but she wouldn't come in;
   "Who's there, who's there?" cried a young porter,
    "Who's there, who's there, unto me tell?"

10. "O is this Lord Batesman's castle,
     And is his Lordship here within?"
    "O yes, this is Lord Batesman's castle,
     He's just now taken his young bride in."

11. Away, away went this young porter,
     Away, away and away went he,
    Until he came unto Lord Batesman,
     And down he fell upon his knee.

12. "What news, what news, my proud young porter,
     What news, what news have you brought me?"
    "O there is the fairest of all young ladies
     That ever my two eyes did see."

13. "O she's got rings on every finger,
     And on one of them she's got three,
    And more gay gold about her middle,
     Than would buy Northumberland for thee."

14. "She bids you remember a piece of bread,
     She bids you remember a glass of wine,
    She bids you remember a Turkish lady,
     Who freed you from cold iron bands."

15. Then Lord Batesman into a passion flew,
     He broke his sword into splinters three;
    "I'll give all my father's wealth and riches,
     If Sophia has crossed the sea."

16. Then up spoke his young bride's mother,
     She never'd been known to speak so free;
    "Don't you forget my only daughter,
     Although Sophia has crossed the sea."

17. "I own I've made a bride of your daughter,
     She's none the better or worse for me;
    She came to me on a horse and saddle,
     She shall go back in a carriage and three."

18. Then another marriage was prepared,
     With all their hearts so full of glee;
    "No more I'll range in foreign waters,
     Since Sophia has crossed the sea."

55. "Lord Bateman and the Turkish Lady"

Davis, 1929, p. 565(D); text, pp. 165-66. Sung by Sam Pritt, Barber, Va., November 28, 1924. Collected by B. C. Moomaw, Jr.

p I/M

We may suspect a triple-time behind this unskillfully noted copy.

1. There was a man in bondage brought,
    And he was of some high degree,
   Was captured by the Turkish nation,
    They worked that man both night and day.

2. There was a lady in that place,
    And she was of the Turkish too,
   She stole the keys to her father's dwelling,
    And so Lord Bateman's freedom bought.

3. She took him to her father's hall,
    She treated him on the wine so strong,
   And every health that she drank unto him
    She cried, "Lord Bateman, an thou wert mine.

4. "Let's make a promise, let's make it strong,
    Let's make it lasting seven years long.
   If you no other woman's be,
    No man on earth shall marry me."

5. Seven years had passed and almost three,
    Lord Bateman never a word had heard,
   He fell in love with a fair young damsel,
    This very day made her his bride.

6. Seven years had passed and almost three,
    This lady ne'er one word had heard.
   She gathered up her gay rich clothing
    And for Lord Bateman's hall she sailed.

7. "Is this Lord Bateman's hall?" she cried,
    "Is Lord Bateman on the inner side?"
   "No interruptions are here permitted.
    This very day brought home his bride."

8. "O who is this that's at my door,
    That knocks so loud and won't come in?
   O open wide to this loud knocking,
    And bid the opposite on the inner side."

9. "There is a lady at your door,
      And she is of some high degree.
    She wears a gold ring on each forefinger
      And on the others she wears three.

10. "She bids you mind of the wine so strong,
      She bids you mind of the roaring sea,
    She bids you mind of the Turkish Lady
      That out of bondage set you free."

11. Lord Bateman rose on hearing this,
      His table he did smash in three.
    "I owe my life to this Turkish Lady
      Who out of bondage set me free.

12. "Go take my bride to her father's hall,
      Oh, she is none the worse by me;
    Oh, she came here on horse and saddle,
      But take her back in coaches fine."

56. [Lord Beichan]

Bruce and Stokoe, 1882, pp. 64-69. Sung in Northumberland.

p I (lacks VI; inflected IV)

1. Lord Beichan was a noble lord,
      A noble lord of high degree;
    He shipped himself on board a ship,
      He longed strange countries for to see.

2. He sailed east, he sailed west,
      Until he came to proud Turkey,
    Where he was ta'en by a savage Moor,
      Who handled him right cruellie.

3. For he viewed the fashions of that land,
      Their way of worship viewed he;
    But to Mahound or Termagant
      Would Beichan never bend a knee.

4. So on each shoulder they've putten a bore,
      In each bore they've putten a tye,
    And they have made him trail the wine,
      And spices on his fair bodie.

5. They've casten him in a donjon deep
      Where he could neither hear nor see;
    For seven long years they've kept him there,
      Till he for hunger's like to dee.

6. And in his prison a tree there grew,
      So stout and strong there grew a tree,
    And unto it was Beichan chained,
      Until his life was most weary.

7. This Turk he had one only daughter,
      Fairer creature did eyes ne'er see;
    And every day as she took the air,
      Near Beichan's prison passed she.

8. And bonny, meek, and mild was she,
      Tho' she was come of an ill kin;
    And oft she sighed, she knew not why,
      For him that lay the donjon in.

9. O! so it fell upon a day,
      She heard young Beichan sadly sing;
    And aye and ever in her ears,
      The tones of hapless sorrow ring—

10. "My hounds they all go masterless,
      My hawks they flee from tree to tree,
    My younger brother will heir my land,
      Fair England again I'll never see."

11. And all night long no rest she got,
      Young Beichan's song for thinking on;
    She's stown the keys from her father's head,
      And to the prison strong is gone.

12. And she has ope'd the prison doors,
      I wot she opened two or three,
    Ere she could come young Beichan at—
      He was locked up so curiouslie.

13. But when she came young Beichan before,
      Sore wondered he that maid to see!
    He took her for some fair captive—
      "Fair ladye, I pray of what countrie?"

14. "Have you got houses? have you got land?
      Or does Northumberland 'long to thee?
    What would ye give to the fair young ladye
      That out of prison would set you free?"

15. "I have got houses, I have got lands,
      And half Northumberland 'longs to me—
    I'll give them all to the ladye fair
      That out of prison will set me free.

16. "Near London town I have a hall,
      With other castles two or three;
    I'll give them all to the ladye fair
      That out of prison will set me free."

17. "Give me the troth of your right hand,
      The troth of it give unto me,
    That for seven years ye'll no lady wed,
      Unless it be along with me."

18. "I'll give thee troth of my right hand,
      The troth of it I'll freely gie,
    That for seven years I'll stay unwed,
      For kindness thou dost show to me."

19. And she has bribed the proud warder,
      With golden store and white money,
    She's gotten the keys of the prison strong,
      And she has set young Beichan free.

20. She's gi'en him to eat the good spice cake,
      She's gi'en him to drink the blood-red wine;
    And every health she drank unto him—
      "I wish, Lord Beichan, that you were mine;"
    And she's bidden him sometimes think on her
      That so kindly freed him out of pine.

21. She's broken a ring from off her finger,
    And to Beichan half of it gave she:
"Keep it to mind you of that love
    The lady bore that set you free."

22. O she took him to her father's harbour,
    And a ship of fame to him gave she;
"Farewell, farewell to you, Lord Beichan,
    Shall I e'er again you see?

23. "Set your foot on the good ship board,
    And haste ye back to your own countrie,
And before seven years have an end
    Come back again, love, and marry me."

24. Now seven long years are gone and past,
    And sore she longed her love to see,
For ever a voice within her breast
    Said "Beichan has broken his vow to thee."
So she's set her foot on the good ship board,
    And turned her back on her own countrie.

25. She sailed east, she sailed west,
    Till to fair England's shore came she,
Where a bonnie shepherd she espied,
    Feeding his sheep upon the lea.

26. "What news, what news, thou bonnie shepherd?
    What news hast thou to tell to me?"
"Such news I hear, ladye," he said,
    "The like was never in this countrie.

27. "There is a wedding in yonder hall,
    (I hear the sound of the minstrelsie),
But young Lord Beichan slights his bride
    For love of one that's ayond the sea."

28. She's putten her hand in her pocket,
    Gi'en him the gold and white monie—
"Here, take ye that, my bonnie boy,
    For the good news thou tell'st to me."

29. When she came to Lord Beichan's gate
    She tirled softly at the pin,
And ready was the proud warder
    To open and let this ladye in.

30. When she came to Lord Beichan's castle,
    So boldly she rang the bell—
"Who's there, who's there?" cried the proud porter
    "Who's there? unto me come tell?"

31. "O! is this Lord Beichan's castle?
    Or is that noble lord within?"
"Yea, he's in the hall among them all,
    And this is the day of his weddin'."

32. "And has he wed another love,
    And has he clean forgotten me?"
And sighing, said that ladye gay:
    "I wish I was in my own countrie."

33. And she has ta'en her gay gold ring,
    That with her love she brake so free—
"Gie him that, ye proud porter,
    And bid the bridegroom speak to me.

34. "Tell him to send me a slice of bread,
    And a cup of blood-red wine,
And not to forget the fair young ladye
    That did release him out of pine."

35. Away and away went the proud porter,
    Away and away and away went he,
Until he came to Lord Beichan's presence,
    Down he fell on his bended knee.
"What aileth thee, my proud porter,
    Thou art so full of courtesie?"

36. "I have been porter at your gates,
    Its thirty long years now, and three,
But there stands a ladye at them now
    The like of her I ne'er did see.

37. "For on every finger she has a ring,
    And on her mid-finger she has three,
And as much gay gold above her brow
    As would an earldom buy to me;
And as much gay clothing round about her
    As would buy all Northumberlea."

38. Its out then spak' the bride's mother—
    Aye, and an angry woman was she—
"Ye might have excepted the bonnie bride,
    And two or three of our companie."

39. "O hold your tongue, ye silly frow,
    Of all your folly let me be,
She's ten times fairer than the bride
    And all that's in your companie.

40. "She asks one sheave of my lord's white bread,
    And a cup of his red, red wine;
And to remember the ladye's love
    That kindly freed him out of pine."

41. Lord Beichan then in a passion flew,
    And broke his sword in splinters three—
"O, well a day," did Beichan say,
    "That I so soon should married be;
For it can be none but dear Saphia
    That's crossed the deep for love of me."

42. And quickly hied he down the stair,
    Of fifteen steps he made but three,
He's ta'en his bonnie love in his arms,
    And kist and kist her tenderlie.

43. "O, have you taken another bride,
    And have ye quite forgotten me,
And have ye quite forgotten one
    That gave you life and libertie?"

44. She looked over her left shouther,
    To hide the tears stood in her e'e—
"Now fare thee well, young Beichan," she says,
    "I'll try to think no more on thee."

45. "O! never, never, my Saphia,
    For surely this can never be,
Nor ever shall I wed but her
    That's done and dreed so much for me."

46. Then out and spak' the forenoon bride—
      "My lord, your love is changed soon;
   At morning I am made your bride,
      And another's choose ere it be noon!"

47. "O sorrow not, thou forenoon bride,
      Our hearts could ne'er united be,
   You must return to your own countrie,
      A double dower I'll send with thee."

48. And up and spak' the young bride's mother,
      Who never was heard to speak so free—
   "And so you treat my only daughter,
      Because Saphia has cross'd the sea."

49. "I own I made a bride of your daughter,
      She ne'er a whit the worse can be,
   She came to me with her horse and saddle,
      She may go back in her coach and three."

50. He's ta'en Saphia by the white hand,
      And gently led her up and down,
   And aye as he kist her rosy lips,
      "Ye're welcome, dear one, to your own."

51. He's ta'en her by the milk-white hand,
      And led her to yon fountain stane,
   Her name he's changed from Saphia,
      And he's called his bonny love Lady Jane.

52. Lord Beichan prepared another marriage,
      And sang with heart so full of glee—
   "I'll range no more in foreign countries,
      Now since my love has crossed the sea."

57. [Young Beichan]

Sharp MSS., 3568/2634-35. Also in Sharp and Karpeles,
1932, I, p. 86(H). Sung by Solomon Williams, Emert's
Cove, Sevierville, Tenn., April 18, 1917.

p I

Through more than half its length, this tune is nearly identical
with Mrs. Harris' "Sir Colin" (No. 61, Child V, p. 415).

1. In London lived a worthy man,
      As worthy a man as ever was known.
   O he got uneasy and discontented,
      Taken abroad the Turkish shore.

2. And there they cast him into prison
      Where he could neither see nor hear.
   O the king had a daughter and only daughter,
      As kind a little damsel as ever was seen.
   O she stole the keys of her father's prison,
      And, Lord Bateman, I'll set you free.

3. Have you land or have you money?
      Have you living of a high degree?
   O would you give it to a kind young lady
      Who out of trouble would set you free?

4. I've got land and I've got money,
      I have living of a high degree;
   So freely I'd give it to a kind young lady
      Who out of trouble would set me free.

5. She took him by the lily-white hand
      And led him to her own room door,
   And every drink that she drank unto him:
      O Lord Bateman, I wish you was mine.

6. Then I'll make a vow and a solemn promise,
      I'll make promise and it shall stand.
   O if you never marry no other lady,
      I'll never marry no other man.

7. Then I'll wait seven long years,
      Then I'll wait one year more,
   And if you don't sail back in that time,
      Some other man might gain your time.

8. Then she waited seven long years,
      Then she waited one year more.
   She picked up her aged parents,
      For old England she did go.

9. She sailed East, she sailed West,
      She sailed to Lord Bateman's hall,
   Saying: Is this now not Bateman's castle,
      Or is it now not known as he?

10. O so quick spoke up a brisk young porter:
      He and his new bride's just come in.
   I'll bid you to ask him if he don't remember
      The lady that freed him from Turkish shore.

11. O will you ask him to remember
      Of the wines he drank so free.
   Then he turned unto his master,
      Gave raps one, two or three,
   Saying: The prettiest little damsel that I ever saw
      Is standing here at your hall door.

12. She wears gold rings on every finger,
      On her middle one she wears three;
   All the gold that's round about her
      Would buy your bride and company.

13. Then he fell across the table
      And broke it into pieces of three,
   Saying: I'll sacrifice of all I'm worth
      If Susie Fye has crossed the sea.

14. Then in came the new bride's mother,
      A-saying that Susie Fye would die.
   I'm afraid that you'll forsake my daughter
      On account of Susie Fye.

15. Madam, if I forsake your daughter,
      She'll be none the worse by me;
   She came to me without a horse or saddle,
      I'll take her back in a coach.

16. Lord Bateman has married early in the morning,
    Wed again before noon.
    O in London lived as worthy a man,
    As worthy a man as ever was known.

58. [Lord Beichan]

Christie, I, 1876, p. 30. Sung by old people in Aberdeen-shire and Moray.

m M

This copy is so far from the norm as to suggest a different tra-dition entirely. Christie relates it to "The Lass of Bennochie," which he prints next (I, p. 32), and to "The Gallant Grahams."

Young Beichan was in London born,
    He was a man of hie degree;
He past through monie kingdoms great,
    Until he cam' unto Grand Turkie. [Etc.]

Christie's text is adapted from Kinloch's, q.v., *ante*, No. 45.

GROUP Ab

59. [Lord Bateman]

Sharp MSS., 2371/. Sung by Shepherd Hayden (83), Bampton, September 7, 1909.

p I (inflected VII)

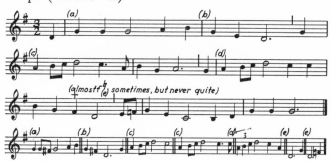

Of the copies with mid-cadence on II, all but the last pair are plagal in range.

60. [Lord Bateman]

Sharp MSS., 545/. Sung by Mrs. Fido (70), Langport, August 11, 1905.

p I

Lord Bateman was a noble Lord
A noble Lord of high degree

61. [Lord Bateman]

Sharp MSS., 595/. Also in Sharp, 1907, p. 80(1); and Baring-Gould and Sharp [1906], No. 11, p. 24. Sung by Mrs. Susan Williams, Haselbury Plucknett, August 23, 1905.

p I (inflected VII)

The MS. shortens the cadence-notes, as here.

Lord Bateman was a noble Lord
A noble Lord of high degree
He shipped himself on board a ship
Some foreign country to go and see

62. [Lord Bateman]

Sharp MSS., 712/. Sung by Mrs. Harriet Young, West Chinnock, December 28, 1905.

p I (inflected VII)

Lord Bateman was a noble Lord
A noble Lord of high degree
He bought a ship and went on board him
Swearing strange countries to go and see

63. [Lord Bateman]

Sharp MSS., 355/479. Sung by Mrs. Wyatt, East Harptree, August 24, 1904.

p I (− VI)

Compare this with the Mixolydian copy, in duple time, of "William Taylor" (Sharp, 1916, No. 71, p. 160). Cf. also "Yonder Stands a Lovely Creature."

Lord Bateman was a noble lord,
A noble lord of high degree,
He shipped himself in a border vessel
Some foreign country to go and see.

He travelled east, he travelled west
Till he came to Northumberlee
When he was taken and put in prison
Till his life was almost gone.

64. "Lord Bateman"

Creighton and Senior, 1950, pp. 26-28. Sung by Enos Hart-lan, South-East Passage, Nova Scotia.

p I

1. Lord Bateman was a noble lord
A noble lord of high degree,
He shipped himself aboard a ship
Some foreign country would go see.

2. He sailèd east, he sailèd west
Until he came to proud Turkey
Where he was taken and put in prison
Until his life grew quite weary.

3. And in that prison there grew a tree,
It grew so stout and it grew so strong
Where he was chained round his middle
Until his life was almost gone.

4. The Turk he had one only daughter
The fairest creature that ever eye did see,
She stole the keys of her father's prison
And swore Lord Bateman she would set free,

5. "Have you got houses, have you got land,
Or does Northumberland belong to thee?
What would you give to the first young lady
That out of prison would set you free?"

6. "I have got houses, I have got land,
And half of Northumberland belongs to me,
I'd give it all to the first young lady
That out of prison would set me free."

7. Then she takes him to her father's harbour
And gave to him a ship of fame
Saying, "Fare you well my own Lord Bateman,
I fear I ne'er shall see you again."

8. It's seven long years they made a vow
And seven long years they kept it strong
Saying if you will wed with no other woman
Then I'll wed with no other man.

9. The seven long years are gone and past
And fourteen days well known to me,
She packèd up all of her gay clothes
And swore Lord Bateman she would go see.

10. Away, away and away went she
Until she came to Lord Bateman's door,
Now boldly then she rang the bell,
"Who's there? Who's there? come tell to me."

11. "Is this Lord Bateman's castle within,
Or is his lordship within?"
"Oh no, oh no," cried the young proud porter,
"He's just now taking his young bride in."

12. "Tell him to send me a slice of bread
And a bottle of the best of wine,
And every health I drink unto him
I wish Lord Bateman that you were mine."

13. "I did not make a bride of your daughter,
She's neither the worse nor the better for me,
She came to me in her horse and saddle,
She may go home in her coach and three."

14. It's now Lord Bateman prepared another marriage
With both their hearts so full of glee,
And not forgetting the fair young lady
That St. Sofia is cross to see.

65. [Lord Bateman]

Grainger MS., No. 173. Sung by George Leaning, Brigg, Lincolnshire, August 4, 1906.

p M

Lord Bateman was aden (a) noble Lord,
    And a Lord of high degree.
He sailèd east and he sailèd ė west
    Ŭdentil he came to peroud Turkey,
Where he was taken and put in prison
    Ŭntil his days they grew quite weàry.

Then this jailor hàd bùt one daughter;
    She swore Lord Bateman she would go see;
She stole the keys of her father's pèrison;
    She went and said: "Let (?Set) Lord Batemuden free.

"Have you got houses, have you got land,
    And livin' in yōėr own countèry?
What would you give to a fair young lady
    Who out of prison would set you free?"

"Yes, I've got houses, and I've got land,
    And livin' in my own countéry;
I'll give it all to a fair young lady
    Who out of prison would set me free."

"Will you to me then ā promise make,
    And seven years to keep it strong:
You'll never marry no óther woman
    Except I mårry with sóme óther mån?"

"Yes, I will then thåt promise make,
    And seven years I'll keep it strong:
I'll never marry no other woman
    Except you mårry with sóme óther mån."

Six years was over and seven gōne;
    She thought she would go see Lord Batemuden's
                                                        home,

66. [Lord Bateman]

Clague, *JFSS*, VII (1926), p. 315. Sung on the Isle of Man.

p π[1]

67. [Lord Bateman]

Sharp MSS., 3936/. Sung by Mrs. Mary Ann Short, Pine Mountain, Ky., August 29, 1917.

p π[1]

She stamped her foot on the gate
The screams she gave were one, two, three
I wish I was at home with mother, she said
Back home across the sea.

68. [Lord Brechin, or Bechin]

Greig MSS., II, p. 149; text, Bk. 729, XIX, pp. 15-19. Sung by J. Mowat, New Pitsligo, September 1907.

p I/M

1. Lord Brechin was as great a lord
   As ever lived in the north countrie
   And he has set his ship in order
   The Turkish countrie for to see.

2. He sailed east so did he west
   Until he came to the Turkish quay
   And he was taken and put in prison
   Until his life was in misery.

3. The Turk he had an only daughter
   A fairer creature I never saw
   She stole the keys of her father's prison
   Swore Lord Brechin she would set free.

4. Have you lands & have you houses
   Does all Northumberland belong to thee
   Would you give it all to a fair lady
   Out of prison to set you free.

5. I have lands & I have houses
   And all Northumberland belongs to me
   I'll give it all to a fair young lady
   Out of prison to set me free.

6. She has taen him to her father's cellar
She gave him there a glass o' wine
And every health that she drank unto him
I wish Lord Brechin that ye were mine.

7. She's ta'en him to her father's harbour
She's given him there a ship o' fame
Farewell, farewell to you Lord Brechin
I hope I'll never see you here again.

8. But I'll make a vow & I'll keep it true
In seven long years & I'll keep it strong
That you will wed no .other woman
And I will wed no other man.

9. Seven long years they were gone & past
And fourteen days were well known to be
She bundled up her gay gold clothing
Swore Lord Bechin she would go see.

10. When she came to Lord Bechin's castle
So nimbly at the bell she rang
Who's there, who's there cried the bold young porter
Who's there, who's there, come tell to me.

11. Is this Lord Bechin's castle
And is his Lordship just now in
O yes, o yes cries the bold young porter
He is just a taking his young bride in.

12. You will bid him bring a slice of bread
A slice of bread & a glass of wine
He has forgot yon Turkish lady
That did relieve him in close confine.

13. Away away ran the bold young porter
Away, away, away, ran he
Until he came to Lord Bechin's chamber
So bendly on his knees fell he.

14. Get up, get up my bold young porter
Get up, get up, get up cried he
Get up, get up my bold young porter
And tell the news that ye have for me.

15. There is a lady stands at your gate sir,
A fairer creature did I never see.
She has as much gold hanging round her middle
As would buy a lease o' land to thee.

16. On every finger she's got a ring
On the mid finger she has got three
She has as much gold above her brow
As would buy a lease o' land to thee.

17. You're bidden bring a (gla) slice of bread
A slice of bread & a glass o' wine
You have forgot yon Turkish lady
That did relieve you in close confine.

18. Lord Bechin he flew in a passion
He brake his sword in splinters three
And swore by all his lands & houses
Sweet Susanna had crossed the seas.

19. She says "Have you wed a bonnie bride
And have you quite forsake me
I wish that I were home again
And in my own countrie."

20. I have not wed a bonnie bride
Nor have I quite forsaken thee
She has come here on a horse & saddle
She may go back wi' a coach & three.

69. [Young Beichan]

Sharp MSS., 3957/. Also in Sharp and Karpeles, 1932, I, p. 88(L). Sung by Mrs. Berry Creech, Greasy Creek, Pine Mountain, Ky., August 31, 1917.

p π[1]

In England lived a noble Lord,
His riches was beyond compare.
He had gold and he had silver;
He had houses and high degree.

70. "Lord Brechin"

Greig MSS., IV, p. 14; text, Bk. 764, LIV, pp. 5off. Also in Greig and Keith, 1925, p. 43(B). Sung by Mrs. Cruickshank, New Deer, Aberdeenshire.

p M

1. Lord Brechin was a noble man
    A gentle Lord of high degree
He put himself on board a ship
    Some foreign countries for to see.

2. He sailed east & he sailed west
    He sailed into fair Turkey
Until he was taken & put in prison
    And there his life it was misery.

3. The Turk he had one only daughter
    The fairest creature you ever did see
She stole the keys of her father's prison
    And swore Lord Brechin she would set free.

4. Have you got houses, have you got land, love,
    Or does Northumberland belong to thee?
What would you give to a fair young lady
    If out of prison would set you free?

5. Yes, I've got houses & I've got land love
   And Northumberland does belong to me
   I will give them all to a fair young lady
   If out of prison she would set me free.

6. Seven long years I'll make a vow
   And seven long years I'll keep it true
   And if you marry no other woman
   I will not marry no other man.

7. Now seven long years it was past & over
   And seven long years it was thought to her
   She has packed up her gay good clothing
   And swore Lord Brechin she would go & see.

8. When she came to Lord Brechin's castle
   So loud, so loud, she did ring the bell,
   Who is there, who is there, cried the young bold porter
   Who is there, who is there, come pray me tell?

9. Oh is this called Lord Brechin's castle,
   Or is his lordship now within?
   Yes this is called Lord Brechin's castle
   He's just now taken a young bride in.

10. Oh bid him bring a slice of bread
    And a bottle of his best red wine
    And not forget on his Turkish Lady
    Who did relieve him from close confine

11. Away, away ran the young bold porter
    As fast as ever he could flee
    And when he came to Lord Brechin's chamber
    On his bended knees fell he.

12. What news, what news, my bold young porter,
    What news, what news, have you brought to me?
    To understand she is the fairest lady
    Ever my two eyes did see.

13. She has a gold ring on every finger
    And one of them she has got three
    She has as much gold hanging round her waist
    It would buy all Earl & set him free.

14. Lord Brechin he flew in a passion
    And broke his sword in splinters three
    I'll wager a' my lands & rents
    It's fair Susanna crossed the sea.

15. Out it spake the young bride's mother
    She was never heard to speak so free
    You'll not forget my only daughter,
    Though fair Susanna has crossed the sea.

16. I own I made a bride of your daughter
    She was never the better nor the worse of me
    She came to me with a horse & saddle
    I'll send her back with a coach & three.

17. Now they have prepared for another marriage
    And both their hearts they were full o' glee
    I'll rove no more in a foreign country
    Since fair Susanna has crossed the sea.

71. "Lord Beichan"

Reid, *RCM*, I, (1910), p. 114. Sung by Bruce J. Home, Edinburgh, November 1906; traditional in Edinburgh, c. 1850.

p I—M (inflected VII)

Three-time is the right signature for this variant.

Lord Beichan was a noble Lord,
A noble Lord and of high degree;
He sail'd to many foreign countries,
Until he came to fair Turkee.

This Turcoman he had a daughter,
Her name was callèd Susan Pye;
And ev'ry day within her garden,
Lord Beichan's prison she passèd by.

Reid's note: "Mr. Home heard the melody of 'Lord Beichan' sung on the streets of Edinburgh sixty years ago, and believes it to be a genuine and very fine old setting of the ancient ballad, which appears in several collections."

72. "Lord Brechin"

Greig MSS., IV, p. 26. Also in Greig and Keith, 1925, p. 43(a). Sung by Mrs. Dunbar, Longhill of Crimond, Aberdeenshire.

p M

Lord Beichan was a noble lord,
A nobleman of high degree,
And he has put his ship in order,
A foreign country to go and see.

73. [Lord Beichan]

Greig MSS., IV, p. 174. Sung by J. Angus.

p M

1. Lord Brechin was as high a lord
   As ever was in this north country
   And he has put his good ship in order
   The Turkish countries to go & see.
   He sailed east so and he sailed west
   Until he came to thy Turkish shore
   And he was taken and put in prison
   Until his life it was nearly gone

2. There was a tree grew up the prison
   It grew so stout and so very strong
   And he was chained down by the middle
   Until his life it was nearly gone
   This jailer had an only daughter
   A fairer creature you never did see
   She stole the keys of her father's prison
   And swore Lord Brechin she would set free.

74. [Young Beichan]

Greig MSS., I, p. 28. Also in Greig and Keith, 1925, p. 43(c). Sung by J. D. Knowles, Buckie, 1904.

p M

Lord Bateman was a noble lord,
    Likewise a lord of high degree.
He shipped himself in a ship of fame,
    Some foreign country to go & see.

3. O hae ye houses or hae ye lands
   Or dis a' Northumber land belang to thee
   Or what would you give unto a young lady
   If out o' prison she could set you free
   It's I hae horses an' I hae land
   And a' Northumberland belangs to me
   I would give them all to you young lady
   If oot o' prison ye could set me free.

4. She has ta'en him to her father's cellar
   She has given to him a glass o' wine
   And every health, that she drank to him
   Says, I wish Lord Brechin that ye were mine
   Seven long years I will make a vow,
   And seven long years I'll keep it true
   If ye will wed wi' no other woman,
   It's I will wed wi' no other man.

75. [Young Beichan]

Greig MSS., IV, p. 130. Also in Greig and Keith, 1925, p. 43(d). Sung by J. Dickie, Belfast.

p I—M (inflected VII)

5. She has ta'en him to her father's shore
   She has given to him a ship of fame,
   Says farewell, farewell unto you Lord Brechin
   I'm afraid I'll never see you again
   But when seven long years were past & gone
   And other three days will seem to be
   She packed up her gay good blocking
   And swore Lord Brechin, she would go see.

6. And when she came to Lord Brechin's castle
   So nimbly at the bell she rang
   Whose there, whose there, cries the bold young porter
   Whose there, whose there, come tell to me.
   O, is this Lord Brechin's castle
   Or is his Lordship just now in.
   O yes, o yes, it is Lord Brechin's castle
   He is just a-taking his young bride in.

76. "Lord Brechin"

Greig MSS., I, p. 28; text, Bk. 712, II, p. 37. Sung by Mrs. Clark, Bruckley, November 1905.

p M (inflected VII)

7. You will bid him send a slice o' bread
   A slice o' bread and a glass o' wine
   And not forget on the Turkish lady
   That did relieve him when close confined.
   Away, away, ran the bold young porter
   Away, away and away ran he
   Away, away ran the bold young porter
   And on his bended knees fell he.

8. What news, what news, my bold young porter,
   What news, what news, hae ye brought to me

What news, what news my bold young porter
That ye do bow so low to me
There is a lady stands at your gate
A fairer creature you never did see
She has as much gold hanging round her brow
As would buy the lands o' Northumberland.

9. She has a ring on every finger
And on her mid finger she's got three
She has as much gold hanging round her body
As would buy the land o' Northumberland.
You are bidden send her a slice o' bread
A slice o' bread and a glass o' wine
And not forget on the Turkish lady
That did relieve you when close confined.

10. Lord Brechin he flew in a passion
He broke his sword in splinters three
I'll wager a' my father's lands
That young Susanna has crossed the sea
Then out did speak his young bride's mother
She never was heard to speak so free
I'll surely not forsake my daughter
Though the Turkish lady has crossed the sea.

11. It is true I made a bride of your daughter
She's none the better nor the waur o' me
She came to me with a horse & saddle
But I'll send her back with a coach & three
So he has ta'en his Turkish lady
And he did lead her through the room
And he has changed her name from young Susanna
Till Lady Brechin of high renown.

77. "Lord Beaconet"

Greig MSS., I, p. 28. Sung by Mrs. Pyper, Affath, White-hill, 1904.

p M

Lord Beaconet was a noble lawyer,
A gentle lord of high degree;
He's put himself on board a ship,
Some foreign countries for to see.

78. [Young Beichan]

Duncan MS., No. 266 (W. Walker). Also in Greig and Keith, 1925, p. 43(e). Sung by Mrs. Harper, Cluny; learned from her mother.

p I/M

Keith, *loc.cit.* above, observes that this tune was also used for "The Beggar Laddie" (280), although Greig's copies of the latter have characteristic differences.

79. [Lorde Bateman]

Crawhall, 1883, No. 8, pp. 1-23. (Done in the manner of an ancient wood-block, and very incorrect).

Probably intended p M (inflected VII)

The old cut is so casually drawn as to be nearly useless on the side of meter, and the above reading is largely conjectural in timing. But perhaps no irregularities were intended by the transcriber.

1. Lorde Bateman was a noble Lorde,
A noble Lorde, and of high degree—
He ship't himself all on board of ship,
It's some foreign countrie he would go see.

2. He sailed East and he sailed West,
Untill he came unto faire Turkie,
Where he was taken and put in prison,
Until of life he grew quite wearie.

3. Now, in this prison there grew a tree,
It grew sae stout and it grew sae strong,
Where he was chained all by his middle,
Until his life it was almost gone.

4. This Turke he had an onlie daughter,
The most beauteous damsel my eyes did ever see,
She stole the keys of her Father's prison,
And swore Lorde Bateman she would set free.

5. Have you got houses, have you got lands,
Does half Northumberland belong to thee,
What will you give to that faire young maiden,
That out of Turkie prison sets you free.

6. Oh, I've got houses, and I've got lands,
Half of Northumberland belongs to me,
All these I'll give to the fayre young damsel
That out of Turkie prison sets me free.

7. For seven long yeares I will make a vow
For seven long yeares I will keep it strang,
If you will wed with no other woman,
Its, I will wed with no other man.

8. And then she brought him a loaf of bread,
    And a bottel of the best of wine,
And every health that she drank unto him
    Was—I wish, Lorde Bateman, that you was mine.

9. Then she broke a ring from off her finger,
    And to Lorde Bateman one half gave she,
Saying, keepe it to mind you of the love,
    The Ladye bore to you that set you free.

10. Then she took him to her Father's harbour,
    And gave to him a ship of fame—
Farewell, farewell—my deare Lorde Bateman,
    I fear I ne'er shall see thy face again.

11. Oh, set your foot on good ship board,
    And haste ye back to your ain countrie,
Before seven long yeares shall have an end,
    Mind, come back again my love, and marry me.

12. Lorde Bateman turn'd him round about
    An' loving look't at that lovely she,
Ere seven long yeares shall come to an end,
    I'll tak' you hame to my ain countrie.

13. And when he'd come to London Town,
    A happie, happie man was he,
And ladies faire around him thranged,
    To welcome him frae slaverie.

14. His mother'd lang been i' the mools,
    His brothers a' were deid but he—
His landes were lying a' awaste—
    In ruins were his castles tae.

15. Nae porter stood there at his yett
    Nae creature therein could he see
Forbye the bats an' screechin' owls,
    There's nane to bear him companie.

16. But mailins sune mak' castles rise—
    He had baith gowd an' jewels free—
Faire ladies still around him thranged
    To cheer him wi' their companie.

17. Now, seven long yeares they are past and gane,
    And sore she long'd her true love to see,
She packed up all her gaie clothing,
    And swore Lorde Bateman she would go see.

18. She sailed East and she sailed West
    Till to faire Englands shore came she,
Where she espied a bonnie shepherd,
    A feeding of his sheep upon the lea.

19. What news, what news, my bonnie shepherd,
    What news hast thou for to tell to me,
Such news I hear, faire maiden dear,
    The like was ne'er in this countrie.

20. There is a wedding in yonder hall,
    Hark to the sound of the minstrelsie,
But young Lorde Bateman he slights his bride,
    For love of one beyond the sea.

21. She put her hand intil her pouch,
    An' gied him red an' white monie—
Here, tak' ye that my bonnie boy,
    For the guid news ye tell to me.

22. And then she went to Lord Batemans castle,
    And so boldly did she ring the bell—
Who's there, who's there, cried the proud young porter,
    Who's there, who's there, come unto me tell.

23. O is this young Lorde Batemans castle,
    And is his Lordship here within,
Give this to him, you proud young porter,
    The damsel waits who with him broke a ring.

24. Tell him to send me a shive of bread,
    And a bottel of the best of wine,
And to remember the faire young damsel,
    That did release him out of close confine.

25. Away, away went the proud young porter—
    Away, away, and away went he,
Until he came to Lorde Batemans presence,
    Where, down he fell upon his bended knee.

26. Oh, I've been porter at your gates,
    Its thirty long yeares now and three,
And there stands a ladye at them now,
    The like of her my eyes did never see.

27. She has a ring upon every finger,
    And upon one of them she has got three,
And as much gold above her brow,
    As would buy all Northumberlea.

28. Its, out then spake the young brides mother,
    Aye, and an angry wife was she,
'Ye might have excepted the bonnie bride
    And two or three of our companie.

29. Lorde Bateman in a passion flew,
    And broke his sword into splinters three,
'She's ten times fairer than the bride
    And all thats in this companie.

30. Then quickly hied he down the staires,
    Of fifteen steps he made but three,
He took his bonnie love in his arms,
    And kist, and kist her tenderlie.

31. Then up and spake the young brides mother,
    Who ne'er was heard for to speak so free,
Its thus you treat my onlie daughter,
    Because Sophia she has crost the sea.

32. 'I own I made a bride of your daughter,
    She's ne'er the better nor the worse for me,
She came to me on her horse and saddle,
    She may go home in a coach and three.'

33. Then he took Sophia by the hand,
    And gently led her up and down,
And aye he kist her rosy lips,
    Saying ye're welcome dearest to your owne.

34. An' hae ye ta'en anither bride,
       An' had ye quite forgotten me,
    An' was the maiden quite out o' mind
       That ga'e ye life an' libertie.

35. She lookit owre her left shoulder,
       To hide the tear drop in her ee—
    Now, fare ye weel my dear Lord Bateman,
       I'll try to think nae mair on thee.

36. Oh, no, no, never, Sophia dear—
       Oh surely this can never be—
    None other will I wed but her,
       That's dune an' dreed sae much for me.

37. Then he prepared another wedding,
       And sang, with heart so full of glee,
    'I'll range no more in foreign countries,
       Since my own true love has crost the sea.

38. He's ta'en her by the milk-white hand,
       An' led her to the Fountain Stane—
    He's changed her name frae Sophia,
       An' ca'd her his sweet Lady Jane.

39. Its fye, then, gar our Cooks make readie—
       An' fye, gar a' our Pipers play—
    An' fye, gar a' our trumpets sound—
       Lord Bateman's twice wed in ae daie.

80. "Lord Bateman's Castle"

Gardner and Chickering, 1939, pp. 143-45. Sung by Mrs.
Ethel White Roth, Detroit, Mich., 1935; learned from her
mother, who came from Scotland.

p I (inflected VII) and p. M

A quarter rest has been omitted after each phrasal cadence.

1. Lord Bateman was a noble lord,
       And of his lordship a high degree.
    He set his foot on the ship of fame
       Some foreign countries to go and see.

2. He sailèd east, he sailèd west,
       He sailèd unto fair Turkey;
    And there he was taken and put in prison,
       Till of his life he was quite weary.

3. The jailer had an only daughter,
       And she was fair as she could be.
    She took the keys of her father's prison
       And said, "Lord Bateman I'll go and see."

4. She said, "Have you got gold and silver,
       Have you got riches of high degree?
    What would you give to some fair young lady
       If she from prison would set you free?"

5. He said, "I have both gold and silver,
       And I have riches of high degree,
    And I would give all of my father's riches
       If she from prison would set me free."

6. "For seven long years I will make a promise,
       For seven long years I will make it stand,
    If you will wed with no other lady,
       I will wed with no other man."

7. When seven long years were past and ended,
       And fourteen days were no more to be,
    She packed up all her costly jewels
       And said, "Lord Bateman I'll go and see."

8. And when she came to Lord Bateman's castle,
       She loud, loud rapped at the bell.
    "Who's there, who's there?" cries the bold young porter,
       "Who's there, who's there? I pray you tell."

9. She said, "Is this Lord Bateman's castle,
       Or is his lordship himself within?"
    He said, "This is Lord Bateman's castle,
       He's just now taken his young bride in."

10. "Go bid him send me a slice of bread,
        Likewise a bottle of his best wine,
     And to remember the Turkish lady
        Who did release him when close confined."

11. Away, away ran the bold young porter,
        As fast as ever he could flee;
     And when he came to Lord Bateman's chamber,
        He fell down on his bended knee.

12. "What news, what news, my bold young porter?
        What news, what news have you brought to me?"
     He said, "There is the fairest lady
        That ever my two eyes did see.

13. "She has a ring on every finger,
        On some of them she has got three;
     And she has more gold around her middle
        Than would buy all of this country.

14. "She bade you to send her a slice of bread,
        Likewise a bottle of your best wine,
     And to remember the Turkish lady
        Who did release you when close confined."

15. Lord Bateman flew in an angry passion
        And brake his sword in pieces three.
     He said, "I'll give all my father's riches
        Since fair Susanna's come to me."

16. Then up spoke the bride's old mother,
    She was never known to speak so free,
    "And would you slight my only daughter
    Since fair Susanna has come to thee?"

17. "I've only made a bride of your daughter,
    She's none the better nor worse for me.
    She came to me on her horse and saddle;
    She may go home in her coach and three."

18. This couple's preparing for another wedding
    With both their hearts so full of glee.
    "No more I'll roam to foreign countries
    Since fair Susanna has come to me."

81. [Lord Bateman (?)]

Greig MSS., II, p. 134. Sung by M. Milne, August 1907.

p M (inflected VII)

82. [Lord Beichan]

Greig MSS., III, p. 162. Sung by John Harrison; sent by
George Shearer, New Byth, March 1909.

p M (inflected VII)

Lord Beichan was a noble lord,
    A nobleman of high degree,
And he has put his ship in order
    A foreign country to go see.

83. "Lord Brechin"

Greig MSS., IV, p. 88. Sung by Miss Robb, Strichen.

p M (inflected VII)

84. "Lord Brechin"

Greig MSS., IV, p. 138. Sung by G. Corbett; learned from
his mother.

p M

85. "Lord Bateman"

Kidson, *JFSS*, I (1904), p. 240(2). Sung near Nottingham.

p M (inflected VII)

Lord Bateman was a noble Lord,
A noble Lord of high degree;
He set his foot all on shipboard,
Some foreign countries he would go see.

He sailed east: he sailed west:
Until he came to proud Turkey,
Where he was ta'en and put in prison
Until his life was most weary.

And in the prison there grew a tree,
It grew so stout and grew so strong
Where he was chained by the middle,
Until his life was almost gone, &c., &c.

86a. [Lord Bateman]

Sharp MSS., 450/566-67. Sung by Mrs. Glover, Huish
Episcopi, December 24, 1904.

p I

1. Lord Bateman was a noble man,
   A noble man of courage,
   He slipped his foot on some board of rigging
   Some foreign country he would go and see.

2. He sailed East, he sailed low,
   Until he came to Torquay,
   There he got took and put in prison
   And sweared his life it was a misery.

3. This turnkey had but one only daughter
   The finest woman my eyes did see
   She stole the keys of her father's prison
   And said Lord Bateman she would set free.

4. 'Twas seven years and almost three
   She packed up her gay young clothing
   And sweared Lord Bateman she would go and see.

5. So when she came to Lord Bateman's castle
   Slowly she ringed but not walked in.
   Who's there, who's there, cried that young porter,
   Who's there, who's there, pray tell to me.

6. For I have houses and I have lands
   And I am humble and at your command
   So I'll give it all to that proud young lady
   What did relieve me of my misery.

7. So up spoke her old gay mother
   What never spoke so free before.
   She's got more gold hang round her middle
   That'll buy Lord Bateman and all his crew.

8. I only want to make a bride of your daughter,
   She's none the better or worse for me,
   She may come here on her horse and saddle
   I'll send her back in her coach and three.

9. So seven years I will make a woe
   And seven years I will keep at hold.
   If you'd out wed with another woman
   I will not wed with another man.

86b. [Lord Bateman]

Sharp MSS., 750/. Also in Sharp, 1907, p. 80(2). Sung by
Mrs. Glover, Huish Episcopi, December 5, 1906.

p I (inflected VII)

(a) only first stanza   (b) extra ♩ sometimes in this and other bars

The F naturals were sometimes nearly sharps.

87. "Lord Bateman"

Barry, Eckstorm, and Smyth, 1929, pp. 119(E)-21. Sung by
Dr. R. L. Grindle, Mount Desert, Maine, 1928; learned
from his mother. Melody recorded by George Herzog.

m π¹

1. I'll sing to you about Lord Bateman,
   Of all his journeyings o'er land and sea,
   How he got in and out of prison
   All through the help of a fair lady.

2. He sailèd south, he sailèd east,
   Until he came to a foreign shore,
   Here he was taken and put in prison
   Where he could see the light no more.

3. Long days and nights he lay in prison,
   With never a hope of liberty,
   And not a ray of light from heaven
   To cheer him in his misery.

4. At length there came into the prison
   A lady fair to hear and see,
   Whose jeweled hand and costly raiment
   Proclaimed her a lady of high degree.

5. Said he, "I have lands and costly treasures,
   Also a house of high degree,
   And all of these shall be thine forever
   If from this prison you'll set me free."

6. "I want none of your costly treasures,
   Nor none of your house of high degree,
   But what I want to make me happy
   Is just your own fair body."

7. When from the prison walls delivered,
   Straightway he sailed to his native shore;
   There seven long years he watched and waited,
   But his old deliverer came no more.

8. And so he wed a comely lady,
   And to his palace did repair;
   At another gate his old deliverer
   Was waiting and inquiring there.

9. Said she, "Is this Lord Bateman's palace,
   And is Lord Bateman now within?"
   "O yes, Lord Bateman and his lady
   With wedding guests have just passed in."

10. She wrung her hands with bitter weeping,
    And cried aloud, "Lord, pity me!
    And ask Lord Bateman has he forgotten
    The lady who did set him free."

11. He wrung his hands and tore his raiment,
And kicked the table in pieces three,
Saying, "There's lately been one wedding,
And another wedding there now shall be."

88. [Young Beichan]

Wilkinson MSS., 1935-36, pp. 41-43(A2). Sung by H. B.
Shiflett, Dyke, Va., April 16, 1936.

p I (– VI)

89. [Young Beichan]

Wilkinson MSS., 1935-36, pp. 41-43(A1). Sung by H. B.
Shiflett, Dyke, Va., April 16, 1936.

p I

1. I traveled East and I traveled West,
I traveled over Kentucky shore;
And there I was taken and put in prison,
And freedom I never expect no more.

2. The jailer had a beautiful daughter,
As ever any one did see.
She stole the key to her father's treasure,
And said, Lord Bateman she would set free.

3. They went into her father's closet,
And there they made bargains one, two, three.
That he was to marry no other lady,
Nor she was to marry no other man.

4. They went into her father's cellar,
And there they drank a very strong wine.
And every health that she drank with him,
She wished Lord Bateman, he was mine.

5. Oh seven long years he been gone on sea,
Oh seven long years he's been gone from me.
She picked up her gold and diamonds,
And said: Lord Bateman, I'll go see.

6. She rode till she came to Lord Bateman's castle,
And there she jingled on the ring.
And there was none so ready as Lord Bateman's waiter,
To rise and welcome her in.

7. Is Lord Bateman at his castle,
Or is he at his home?
He is setting at his wedding table,
He has just brought his new bride home.

8. Oh tell him to bring me a slice of bread,
And also a glass of his wine so strong.
Oh ask him if he has forgot the lady
That freed him from his prison bond.

9. He brought a slice of his bread,
And also a glass of his wine so strong.
I have not forgot the lady
That freed me from my prison bond.

10. Oh land lord take back your daughter,
For she is none the worse by me.
Farewell, farewell, to the land of living,
Since my Susanna have crossed the sea.

90. [Young Beichan]

Wilkinson MSS., 1935-36, pp. 44-45(B). Sung by Polly
Morris, Pirkey, Va., April 23, 1936.

p I

1. I sailed East, I sailed West,
I sailed on to Kentucky shore.
There I was taken and put in prison,
And never expected freedom more.

2. She taken him to her father's cellar,
And there they drank of very strong wine.
And every health she drank unto him,
I wish Lord Bateman, he was mine.

3. She taken him to her father's closet,
And bargains they made, one, two, three.
That he was to marry no other lady,
And she was to marry no other man.

4. The jailor had as fair daughter
As ever my two eyes did see.
She stole the keys of her father's treasures,
And said, Lord Bateman she would go see.

5. For seven long years he stayed away,
For seven long years was one, two, three.
She pick up her gold and diamonds,
And said, Lord Bateman she would go see.

6. She rode until she came to Lord Bateman's castle,
   And there so loud she rapped at the ring.
   There was none so ready as Lord Bateman's waiter,
   To rise and let her in.

7. Is this here where Lord Bateman lives?
   Or is he now at home?
   He's just now sitting at his table,
   He's just now brought his new bride home.

8. Go tell him to send me a slice of his bread,
   And tell him a glass of his wine so strong.
   And tell him never to forget his lady,
   That freed him of his prison strong.

9. Yonder stands as fair a lady
   As ever my two eyes did see.
   She has more gold about her middle,
   Than will buy your bride and your company.

10. Say, tell you to send her a slice of your bread,
    And tell you a glass of your wine so strong.
    And tell you never to forget the lady,
    That freed you of your prison so strong.

11. He sent her a glass of his wine so strong,
    And sliced his bread in pieces three.
    Say, come on porter and take your daughter,
    For she is none the less by me.

12. She came here on a horse and saddle,
    She'll go away in a coach with me.
    So fare you well to the land of living,
    Since my Susanna has crossed the sea.

91. [Lord Bakeman]

Barry Dict. Cyl., No. 86, transcribed by S. P. Bayard,
Harvard College Library MS., p. 17. Sung by Mrs. Eva
Cooley. The transcription here has been simplified and
abridged.

p I/Ly

92. [Lord Bateman]

Sharp MSS., 695/772-76. Also in Sharp, 3rd series, 1906,
pp. 28-31, with accompaniment; and Sharp, 1907, pp. 22-23.
Sung by Henry Larcom(be), Haselbury Plucknett, December 26, 1905.

p Æ/D

1. Lord Bateman was a noble Lord,
   A noble lord of high degree,
   He shipped himself on a board a ship
   Some foreign country to go and see.

This extraordinarily fine copy, it will be observed, is the only
variant with minor tonality in this group.

2. He sailèd East, he sailèd West,
   He sailèd into proud Turkey,
   Where he was taken and put in prison
   Until his life was quite weary.

3. And in this prison there growed a tree,
   It growed so stout, it growed so strong,
   He was chained up all by the middle,
   Until his life was almost gone.

4. This Turk he had one only daughter,
   The fairest creature that ever you see,
   She stole the keys of her father's prison
   And swore Lord Bateman she would set free.

5. Have you got lands, have you got livings,
   Or dost Northumberland belongs to thee?
   What will you give to a fair young lady
   If out of prison she'll set you free?

6. Yes, I've got lands and I've got livings
   And half Northumberland belong to me
   And I'll give it all to a fair young lady
   If out of prison she will set me free.

7. She took him to her father's cellar
   And give to him the best of wine,
   And every health that she drinked unto him.
   I wish, Lord Bateman, that you were mine.

8. Seven long years we will make a vow,
   And seven long years we will keep it strong.
   If you will wed with no other woman,
   I will never wed with no other man.

9. She took him to her father's harbour
   And give to him a ship of fame.
   Farewell, farewell, to you Lord Bateman,
   I'm afraid I never shall see you again.

10. Now seven long years is agone and past
And fourteen days well known to me.
She packèd up all her gay clothing
And swore Lord Bateman she'd go and see.

11. And when she came to Lord Bateman's castle
So boldly how she did ring the bell.
Who's there, who's there? cried the young proud porter,
Who's there, who's there? come quickly tell.

12. O is this called Lord Bateman's castle,
O is his lordship here within?
O yes, O yes, cries the young proud porter,
He has just now taken his young bride in.

13. You tell him to send me a slice of bread
And a bottle of the best of wine
And not forgetting that fair young lady
That did release him when he was close confined.

14. Away, away, went this proud young porter,
Away, away, away went he,
Until he came to Lord Bateman's chamber
Down on his bended knees fell he.

15. What news, what news, my young proud porter,
What news, what news hast thou brought to me?
There is the fairest of all young ladies
That ever my two eyes did see.

16. She have got rings on every finger,
Round one of them she have got three.
She have gold enough around her middle
To buy Northumberland that belongs to thee.

17. She tells you to send her a slice of bread
And a bottle of the best of wine
And not forgetting that fair young lady
That did release you when you were close confined.

18. Lord Bateman then in a passion flew,
He broke his sword in splinters three,
Saying: I will give you all my father's riches
And if Sophia have acrossed the sea.

19. O then up spoke this young bride's mother
Who was never heard to speak so free,
Saying: You'll not forget my only daughter
For if Sophia have acrossed the sea.

20. I only made a bride of your daughter,
She's neither the better nor worse for me.
She came to me over horse and saddle,
She may go back in a coach and three.

21. Lord Bateman prepared for another marriage,
So both their hearts so full of glee.
I will range no more to foreign countries
Now since Sophia have acrossed the sea.

93. [Lord Wetram]

Cox, 1939, pp. 21-23. Sung by Frances Sanders, Morgantown, W.Va., June 1924; learned from Emma Hewitt.

a I/M

1. Lord Wetram was a gentleman,
A gentleman of high degree;
This young man never could be contented
Till he had taken a voyage to sea.

2. He sailed east and he sailed west,
He sailed till he came to the Turkish shore,
And there he was taken and put in prison,
Where he could see nor hear no more.

3. The jailor had a lovely daughter,
A lovely daughter of high degree;
She stole the keys from her father's prison,
And said she'd set Lord Wetram free.

4. She led him through her father's garden,
She led him down to the sea-beaten shore,
Saying, "Fare thee well, young Susan Pious,
I fear I ne'er shall see you more."

5. "Three long years I will wait for you,
Another one I'll wait also,
And then, my dear, if you don't cross over,
Another fair one I must adore."

6. Three long years had come and ended,
Another one had come also;
She dressed herself in rich attainments,
And to hunt Lord Wetram she did go.

7. She sailed east until she came to his mansion,
She knocked so loudly at the inn;
It's then spoke up the bold, proud porter,
"Who knocks so loud, would fain come in?"

8. "Oh, Sir is this Lord Wetram's dwelling,
And is that noble young man within?"
"Yes, Miss, this is Lord Wetram's dwelling;
He's just brought home his darling queen."

9. She wrung her hands and she bitterly cried,
"Oh, I wish I were back home again;
I wish I had never come here,
Or ventured over the raging main."

10. "Go ask him for three cuts of bread
And a little bottle of his strongest wine,
And ask him if he don't remember
Who freed him from his iron chain."

11. It's up then went the bold, proud porter
And on his bended knees he fell,
Saying, "At your door stands the fairest lady
That my two eyes beheld."

12. Up rose Lord Wetram from the table
    And to his wedding did say,
    "I've forfeited all my lands and living,
    Young Susan Pious has come for me."

13. It's up then spoke the young bride's father,
    And to Lord Wetram he began:
    "Would you for the sake of young Susan Pious
    Go and forsake your darling queen?"

14. "Tis true," said he, "I married your daughter
    And to maintain her I did agree;
    She came to me on her horse and saddle,
    She may go back with her coach and three."

15. He took her by the lily white hand
    And he led her over the marble stone,
    Saying, "Your name shall be changed from young Susan
                                                      Pious
    And be called the bride of Lord Wetram."

94. "Young Becon"

Harris MS., No. "27" (=26). Also in Child, 1882-98, V, p. 415.

a I

The sixteenths in the penultimate bar are given in the MS. as eighths.

The Harris copy is one of the oldest in the record and quite unlike most of the rest. Mrs. Harris' daughter noted that her mother sang No. 106 to the tune of "Young Becon," but as given in the MS. her tune to No. 106 ("My husband built for me a Bowr") differs markedly.

GROUP AC

95. [Lord Bateman]

Sharp MSS., 3698/. Sung by four Berea students, Berea, Ky., May 20, 1917. Also, as "Turkish Lady," in Raine, 1924, pp. 109-11.

p π¹

The tune as given by Raine, 1924, pp. 109-11, is identical with the primary form above. I have therefore omitted the second copy, but appended Raine's text to the fragment collected by Sharp.

Lord Bateman was a noble Lord,
A noble Lord of high degree,
He shipped himself on board a ship
Some foreign country to go and see.

———

1. Lord Bateman was a noble lord,
   He thought himself of high degree;
   He could not rest nor be contented
   Until he had voyaged across the sea.

2. He sailed east and he sailed westward
   Until he reached the Turkish shore;
   And there he was taken and put in prison;
   He lived in hopes of freedom no more.

3. The Turkish had one only daughter,
   The fairest creature eye ever did see.
   She stole the keys to her father's prison,
   Saying, "Lord Bateman I'll set free."

4. "Have you got houses? have you got lands, sir?
   Or do you live at a high degree?
   What will you give to the fair young lady
   That out of prison will set you free?"

5. "I've got houses, and I've got lands, love—
   Half of Northumberland belongs to me,
   And I'll give it all to the Turkish Lady
   If she from prison will set me free."

6. "Seven long years I'll make a vow, sir,
   Seven more by thirty-three,
   And if you'll marry no other lady,
   No other man shall marry me."

7. Then she took him to her father's harbor,
   And gave to him a ship of fame;
   "Farewell, farewell, to you, Lord Bateman,
   I fear I never shall see you again."

8. For seven long years she kept her vow, sir,
   And seven more by thirty-three.
   She gathered all her gay, fine clothing,
   Saying, "Lord Bateman I'll go see."

9. She sailed east and she sailed westward,
   Until she reached the English shore;
   And when she came to Lord Bateman's castle,
   She lighted down before the door.

10. "Are these Lord Bateman's gay, fine houses?
    And is his lordship here within?"
    "Oh yes, oh yes," cried the proud young porter,
    "He has just taken his young bride in."

11. "Go tell him to send me a slice of cake,
    And draw me a glass of the strongest wine,
    And not to forget the fair young lady,
    That did release him when close confined."

12. "What news, what news, my proud young porter,
    What news, what news have you brought to me?"
    "Oh, there is the fairest of all young ladies
    That ever my two eyes did see."

13. "She has got rings on every finger,
And on one of them she has got three;
And she's as much gold around her middle
As would buy Northumberland of thee."

14. "She tells you to send her a slice of cake,
And draw her a glass of the strongest wine,
And not forget the fair young lady
That did release you when close confined."

15. Lord Bateman rose from where he was sitting,
His face did look as white as snow,
Saying, "If she is the Turkish Lady,
With her, love, I'm bound to go."

16. Oh, then, he spoke to the young bride's mother,
"She's none the better nor worse for me;
She came to me on a horse and saddle,
And she may go back in a carriage and three.

17. "Your daughter came here on a horse and saddle
And she may return in a chariot free,
And I'll go marry the Turkish Lady
That crossed the roaring sea for me."

96. [Lord Batesman or, The Turkish Lady]

Wheeler and Bridge, 1937, pp. 89-100.

p π¹

1. There was a man who lived in England
He was of some high degree;
He became uneasily discontented,
Some foreign lands, some lands for to see.

2. He sailed east, he sailed west,
He sailed all over the Turkish shore,
Till he was caught and put in prison,
Never to be released anymore.

3. The Turk he had one lovely daughter,
The loveliest mine eyes did ever see;
She stole the keys to her father's palace,
And swore Lord Batesman she'd set free.

4. She took him down to the lowest cellar,
She poured him a glass of the strongest wine,
Saying, "Every moment seems an hour!
O, Lord Batesman, if you were mine!"

5. They made a vow, they made a promise,
They made a vow, they let it stand;
He vowed he'd marry no other woman,
She vowed she'd marry no other man.

6. Seven long years had rolled around;
It seemed as though it were twenty three.
"But if he's gone for seven years longer,
No other man can marry me."

7. Seven long years had rolled around;
It seemed as though it were twenty nine;
She bundled up her fairest clothing,
And swore Lord Batesman she'd go and find.

8. She went till she came to the gate; she tingled;
How boldly then she rang the bell.
"Who's there? Who's there?" cried the proud young porter,
"O come unto me, and quickly tell!"

9. "O is this here Lord Batesman's dwelling,
And is his Lordship within?"
"O yes! O yes!" cried the proud young porter,
He's just now bringing his young bride in."

10. "Go remember him of a piece of bread,
Go remember him of a glass of wine,
Go remember him of the Turkish Lady
Who set him free from close confine."

11. Away and away went this proud young porter,
Away and away, and away went he,
Until he came to Lord Batesman's chamber,
When he fell down on bended knee.

12. "What news? What news? my proud young porter?
What news, what news do you bring to me?"
"There is a lady at your gate, sir,
Fairer than your bride will ever be.

13. "She has got gold rings on ev'ry finger,
And on one she has got three,
With as much gold around her middle,
As would buy the half of Northumberlee.

14. "She bids you remember a piece of bread,
She bids you remember a glass of wine,
She bids you remember the fair young lady,
Who set you free from the cold iron bond."

15. He stamped his foot upon the floor,
The table he broke in pieces three,
Saying "I'll forsake both lands and dwelling
For the Fair Ladye who set me free."

16. Then Lord Batesman into a passion flew,
He broke his sword in splinters three,
Saying "I'll forsake both land and honor,
If Sophia has crossed the sea."

17. Then up spoke the young bride's mother,
An angry, outspoken old thing was she:
"Don't you forget mine only daughter,
In Sophia has crossed the sea."

18. "I own I made a bride of your daughter,
She's none the better or worse for me;
She came to me in a horse and saddle,
She shall go back in a carriage and three."

19. Another wedding was prepared,
With both their hearts so full of glee;
No more he roams in foreign waters,
Since Sophia has crossed the sea.

97. "Lord Bateman"

Mobley, Argonaut pressing, private dubbing (1937); text, Moser, LC/AAFS, Album 12, rec. 56A and B. Sung by Pleaz Mobley, Manchester, Ky., at Harrogate, Tenn., 1943.

p π[1]

1. Lord Bateman was a noble lord,
   He held himself of high degree,
   He would not rest nor be contented
   Until he'd voyaged across the sea.

2. He sailed east and he sailed westward,
   Until he reached the Turkish shore,
   And there they took him and put him in prison,
   He never expected his freedom any more.

3. Now the Turk he had one only daughter,
   As fair a maiden as eyes did see,
   She stole the keys to her father's prison,
   Saying, "Lord Bateman I'll set free."

4. "Have you got house, have you got land, sir,
   Do you hold yourself of high degree,
   What would you give the Turkish lady
   If out of prison I'll set you free?"

5. "Well, I've got house and I've got land, love,
   Half of Northumberland belongs to me,
   I'll give it all to the Turkish lady
   If out of prison you'll set me free."

6. She took him to her father's harbor
   And gave to him a ship of fame,
   "Farewell, farewell to thee, Lord Bateman,
   I fear I'll never see you again."

[6a. "For six long years I'll make a vow, sir,
   Then seven more, 'bout thirty-three,
   If you will marry no other maiden,
   No other man will marry me."]

7. For seven long years she kept that vow true,*
   Then seven more, 'bout thirty-three,
   Then she gathered all her gay, fine clothing,
   Saying, "Lord Bateman I'll go see."

8. She sailed east and she sailed westward
   Until she reached the English shore,
   And when she came to Lord Bateman's castle,
   She alighted down before the door.

9. "Is this Lord Bateman's fine castle,
   And is his lordship here within?"
   "Oh, yes, oh yes," cried the proud young porter,
   "He's just taken his young bride in."

10. "What news, what news, my proud young porter,
    What news, what news do you bring to me?"
    "Oh, there's the fairest of all young ladies
    That ever my two eyes ever did see.

11. She says for you to send a slice of cake, sir,
    And draw a glass of the strongest wine,
    And not forget the proud young lady
    That did release you when confined."

12. Lord Bateman rose from where he was sitting,
    His face did look as white as snow,
    Saying, "If this is the Turkish lady,
    I'm bound with her love to go."

13. And then he spoke to the young bride's mother,
    "She's none the better nor worse for me,
    She came to me on a horse and saddle,
    I'll send her back in chariots three.

14. She came to me on a horse and saddle,
    I'll send her back in a chariot free,
    And I'll go marry the Turkish lady
    That crossed the roaring sea for me."

The additional stanza, 6a, was sung in the Argonaut rendition, but omitted when Moser recorded the song.

98. "Lord Batesman; or, The Turkish Lady"

Wyman and Brockway [1916], pp. 58-61. Sung in Letcher County, Ky.

p π[1]

1. There was a man who lived in England,
   He was of some high degree;
   He became uneasily discontented,
   Some foreign land, some lands to see.

2. He sailed east and he sailed west,
   He sailed all over the Turkish shore,
   Till he was caught and put in prison
   Never to be released any more.

3. The Turk he had but the one lone daughter,
   The fairest my eyes did ever see,
   She stole the keys from her father's dwelling
   And declared Lord Batesman she'd set free.

4. She led him down to the lower cellar
   And drew him a drink of the strongest wine,
   Saying "Every moment seems an hour
   O Lord Batesman if you were mine."

5. "Let's make a vow, let's make a promise,
   Let's make a vow, let's make it stand:
   You vow you'll marry no other woman
   I'll vow I'll marry no other man."

In the MS., Sharp at first barred this variant after the first note and so forward; but indicated the above as an alternative way.

6. They made a vow, they made a promise,
   They made a vow, they made it stand:
   He vowed he'd marry no other woman
   She vowed she'd marry no other man.

7. Seven long years had rolled around
   It seemed as though it were twenty-three,
   And if he's gone some seven years longer
   There is no other man can marry me.

8. Seven long years had rolled around
   It seemed as though it were twenty-nine,
   She bundled up her finest clothing
   And declared Lord Batesman she'd go find.

9. She went 'til she came to the gate, she tingled,
   How boldly then she rang the bell:
   "Who's there? Who's there?" cried the proud young
                                                porter,
   "O come unto me and quickly tell."

10. "O is this here Lord Batesman's castle
    And is his lordship here within?"
    "O yes, O yes," cried the proud young porter,
    "He's just now taking his young bride in."

11. "Go remember him of a piece of bread,
    Go remember him of a glass of wine,
    Go remember him of the Turkish lady
    Who freed him from the cold iron bond."

12. O away and away went this proud porter,
    O away and away and away went he
    Until he came to Lord Batesman's chamber
    When he went down on his bended knee.

13. "What news? What news? my proud young porter,
    What news? What news? Come tell to me."
    "There is a lady at your gate, sir,
    Fairer than your new bride ever can be."

14. "She has got rings on every finger
    And on one finger she has three,
    With as much gay gold about her middle
    As would buy half Northumberlee.

15. "O she bids you remember a piece of bread,
    O she bids you remember a glass of wine,
    O she bids you remember the fair young maid
    Who set you free from close confine."

16. He stamped his foot upon the floor
    And burst the table in pieces three:
    Says "I forsake both lands and dwellings
    For the fair ladye who set me free."

99. "Lord Batesman"

Sharp MSS., 3131/? Also in Sharp and Karpeles, 1932, I, pp. 79(B)-80. Sung by girls at Hindman School, Knott County, Ky., September 20, 1907.

p π¹

1. There was a man who lived in England
   And he was of some high degree;
   He became uneasy, discontented,
   Some fair land, some land to see.

2. He sailed East, he sailed West,
   He sailed all over the Turkish shore,
   Till he was caught and put in prison,
   Never to be released any more.

3. The Turk he had but one lone daughter,
   She was of some high degree;
   She stole the keys from her father's dwelling,
   And declared Lord Batesman she'd set free.

4. She led him down to the lower cellar
   And drew him a drink of the strongest wine,
   Every moment seemed an hour.
   O Lord Batesman, if you were mine!

5. Let's make a vow, let's make a promise,
   Let's make a vow, let's make it stand;
   You vow you'll marry no other woman,
   I'll vow I'll marry no other man.

6. They made a vow, they made a promise,
   They made a vow, they made it stand;
   He vowed he'd marry no other woman,
   She vowed she'd marry no other man.

7. Seven long years had rolled around,
   It seemed as if it were twenty-nine,
   She bundled up her finest clothing,
   And declared Lord Batesman she'd go find.

8. She went till she came to the gate, she tingled
   It was so loud, but she wouldn't come in,
   Is this your place, she cried, Lord Batesman,
   Or is it that you've let yours, brought your
                                      new bride in?

9. Go remember him of a piece of bread,
   Go remember him of a glass of wine,
   Go remember him of the Turkish lady
   Who freed him from the iron, cold bonds.

10. He stamped his foot upon the floor,
    He burst the table in pieces three,
    Saying: I'll forsake both land and dwelling
    For the Turkish lady that set me free.

11. She went till she came to the gate, she tingled,
    It was so loud, but she wouldn't come in,
    She's got more gold on her little finger
    Than your new bride and all your kin.

The text is from the printed copy; it has not been located in the MS.

100. "Lord Bateman"

Kidson, 1891, pp. 33-36. Sung by Mrs. Holt, Alderhill, Meanwood.

p I

1. Lord Bateman was a noble Lord,
       A noble Lord of high degree;
   He put himself all on a ship,
       Some foreign countries he would go see.

2. He sailèd east and sailèd west,
       Until he came to fair Turkey,
   Where he was taken and put in prison,
       Until his life was quite weary.

3. And in this prison there grew a tree,
       It grew so stout and it grew so strong,
   Where he was chained by the middle,
       Until his life was almost gone.

4. The Turk he had an only daughter,
       The fairest creature ever my eyes did see;
   She stole the keys of her father's prison,
       And swore Lord Bateman she would set free!

5. "Have you got houses, have you got lands?
       Or does Northumberland belong to thee?
   What would you give to the fair young lady,
       That out of prison would set you free?"

6. "I have got houses, I have got lands,
       And half Northumberland belongs to me;
   I'll give it all to the fair young lady,
       That out of prison would set me free."

7. Oh, then she took him to her father's palace,
       And gave to him the best of wine,
   And every health she drank unto him—
       "I wish, Lord Bateman, that you were mine."

8. "Now, for seven long years, I'll make a vow,
       For seven long years, and keep it strong,
   If you will wed no other woman,
       That I will wed no other man."

9. Oh, then she took him to her father's harbour,
       And gave to him a ship of fame;
   "Farewell, farewell, my dear Lord Bateman,
       I'm afraid I shall never see you again."

10. Now, seven long years were gone and past,
        And fourteen long days well known to me
    She packed up her gay clothing,
        And Lord Bateman she would go see.

11. And then she came to Lord Bateman's castle,
        So boldly now she rang the bell;
    "Who's there?" cried the young porter,
        "Who's there—now come unto me tell?"

12. "Oh, is this Lord Bateman's castle,
        And is his Lordship here within;"
    "O yes, O yes," cried the proud young porter,
        "He's just taking his young bride in."

13. "Oh, then tell him to send me a slice of bread,
        And a bottle of the best wine;
    And not forgetting the fair young lady,
        That did release him when close confined."

14. Away, away, went that proud young porter,
        Away, away, and away went he,
    Until he came to Lord Bateman's door,
        Down on his bended knees fell he.

15. "What news, what news, my young porter,
        What news have you brought unto me?"
    "There is the fairest of all young ladies,
        That ever my two eyes did see.

16. "She has got rings on every finger,
        And round one of them she has got three;
    And such gay gold hanging round her middle,
        That would buy Northumberland for thee.

17. "She tells you to send her a slice of bread,
        And a bottle of the best wine;
    And not forgetting the fair young lady,
        That did release you when close confined."

18. Lord Bateman then in a passion flew,
        And broke his sword in splinters three,
    Saying, "I will give all my father's riches,
        If that Sophia has crossed the sea."

19. Then up spoke this bride's young mother,
        Who never was heard to speak so free—
    "You'll not forget my only daughter,
        If Sophia has crossed the sea."

20. "I own I made a bride of your daughter,
        She's neither the better nor worse for me;
    She came to me with a horse and saddle,
        She may go home in a coach and three."

21. Lord Bateman prepared another marriage,
        With both their hearts so full of glee;
    "I'll range no more in foreign countries,
        Now since Sophia has cross'd the sea."

101. "Lord Akeman"

Karpeles, 1934, II, pp. 88-92. Sung by William Holloway, King's Cove, Bonavista Bay, Newfoundland, September 25, 1929. The text given according to the collector's MS.

m I; G tonic, ending on III

1. Lord Akeman was a noble lord,
   A noble lord of a high degree;
   He shipped himself on board of a vessel
   Foreign countries for to go see.

2. He sailed East and he sailed West
   Until he came to proud Turkey.
   'Twas there he was taken and put in prison
   Until his life was most weary.

3. By the side of the prison there grew a tree;
   It grew so mighty stout and long.
   He was tied to that right round his middle
   Until his life was almost gone.

4. The gaoler had one only daughter,
   One of the fairest creatures I have ever seen.
   She stole the keys of her father's prison,
   And said Lord Akeman she would set free.

5. Have you got houses, or have you got land?
   Or is any of Northumberland belongs to thee?
   What would you give to any fair maiden
   Who from this prison would set you free?

6. Yes, I've got houses and I got land,
   And half Northumberland belongs to me.
   I would give it all to any lady
   Who from this prison would set me free.

7. Seven long years you made a promise,
   Fourteen days he kept it strong;
   If you don't wed with no other woman,
   Sure I won't wed with no other man.

8. Seven long years have passed and over,
   And fourteen days being well known to her,
   She pack-ed up her 'mosquey' clothing,
   And she said Lord Akeman she'd go to see.

9. When she sees Lord Akeman's castle
   So merrily she rang the bell.
   Who's there, who's there? asked the proud young porter,

   I pray unto me tell.

10. Is Lord Akeman within? she says,
    Or is her ladyship within that hall?
    O yes, O yes, says the proud young porter,
    It's just after bringing a young bride in.

11. Go tell him to send me a slice of his best bread,
    And a bottle of his best wine,
    And not to forget the fair young maiden
    Who released him from his close combine.

12. Away ran the proud young porter,
    Down on his knees he fell to pray,
    Saying: I have seen one of the fairest creatures
    That ever my eyes would wish to see.

13. On every finger she has rings,
    And on one of them she has got three,
    And the golden robes around her middle
    I know Northumberland belongs to she.

14. Lord Akeman rose then in a passion
    And threw his sword in pieces three,
    Saying: I'll go no more to foreign countries
    Since young Sophia have a-crossed the sea.

15. Then up speaks the young bride's mother,
    Who was never known to speak so free,
    Saying: Are you going to leave my daughter
    Since young Sophia have a-crossed the sea?

16. I owe my bride I made out of your daughter,
    It's neither the better nor the worse for thee;
    She came to me in a horse and saddle,
    And I'll send her home in a coach and three.

102. [Lord Bateman]

Sharp MSS., 4526/. Also in Sharp and Karpeles, 1932, I, p. 87(K). Sung by Joe Blackett, Meadows of Dan, Va., August 28, 1918.

a M

She wears a gold ring on all of her fingers
And on the middle finger three;
And the chain that she wears around her middle
Would buy your bride and company[.]
He sailed, he sailed the ocean around*
Until he came to the Turkish shore,
And there he was taken and put in prison,
Where he c[oul]d neither see nor hear.

* 1932: "ocean round"

103. [Lord Bateman]

Sharp MSS., 3309/. Sung by Mrs. Gentry (54), Hot Springs, N.C., August 24, 1916.

a π² (compass of sixth)

Lord Beehan's to Glasgow's gone
The Turks took him a prisoner

104. "Young Behan"

Henry, 1938, pp. 55(A)-58. Sung by Laura Harmon, Cade's Cove, Blount County, Tenn., August 1928; learned from her father.

a π² (compass of sixth)

1. Young Behan from Glasgow gone,
   All these fine Turkish for to view.
   They bored a hole through his right shoulder
   And through and through they drew a key,
   And plunged him into the dungeon dark
   Where the light of day he no more could see.

2. The gaoler had a beautiful daughter;
   Oh, a beautiful daughter was she.
   She now to the gaol window is gone
   To call young Behan, to hear his voice.

3. "Have you any houses and lands?
   Have you any buildings free?
   Or what would you give to a pretty girl,
   To set you at your liberty?"

4. "The Glasgow town, it is all mine,
   Besides the castles two or three;
   And them I'll give to a pretty girl,
   That will set me at my liberty."

5. "Give to me your faith and troth
   And your right hand you will marry me,
   And pay down ninety thousand pounds
   And I'll set you at your liberty."

6. She took him by his pale white hand
   And led him up the marble walk
   Where the sugar, bread, and wine so red
   Was all to comfort his fair body.

7. They made a league between them both
   For seven long years and one day.
   "And if you don't come within that time,
   The blame all on you I will lay."

8. The seven long years has just been gone
   This lady a-thinking the time great long.
   "I'll go search for my young Behan;
   I know no where or within what land."

9. Her father built her a little ship
   And set it on the raging sea;
   And in that ship put gold enough
   To bear her own sweet company.

10. She floated low, she floated high;
    Some turf of (= and) stone she chanced did spy,
    As she went cracking her pretty white fingers
    As the lords and knights went talking by.

11. She went to young Behan's gate
    And dingled at the ring.
    "Wait a while," the porter said,
    "I'll quickly rise and let you in."

12. "Is this young Behan's hall,
    Or is it his knight within?"
    .   .   .   .
    .   .   .   .

13. On her fingers she wore rings,
    And on her middle finger three.
    She twisted a ring from a middle finger
    And gave the porter for his fee.

14. "Here is a lady at your gate,
    As fair as your two eyes ever did see."
    "I'll lay my like," Lord Behan says,
    "Miss Susie Price's come over the seas."

15. He kicked a table with his foot,
    And drew it down on his knee,
    And made cup, pans, and silver cans—
    All into flinders they did fly.

16. "Have you wedded any other woman?
    I am sure I've wedded no other man.
    Come, pay me down ninety thousand pounds
    And I'll go home to my native land."

17. "No, love, don't talk so;
    It's whether you marry, or let it be,
    I'll wed you to my older brother
    If with him content you'd be."

18. "I wish you luck with your older brother,
    But I don't want no such a man.
    Come, pay me down my portion small
    And I'll return to the Turkish land."

19. "No, love, don't talk so;
    Whether you marry him, or let that be,
    I'll marry you to my younger brother
    If with him content you'd be."

20. "I wish you luck with your younger brother,
    But I don't want no such a man.
    Come, pay me down ninety thousand pounds
    And I'll go home to my native land."

21. "No, love, don't talk so;
    It's whether you marry him, or let that be,
    I'll wed you to my own self,
    If with me content you'd be."

22. Up spoke his new bride;
    Oh, but she spoke desperately:
    "You've married as fair a lady
    As ever your two eyes did see."

23. "Yes, you are fair and very fair,
    And fair as ever need to be.
    If you were nine times fairer than ever you was,
    You wouldn't be as fair by one-tenth degree."

24. Up spoke his new bride's mother;
    Oh, but she spoke angrily:
    "Did you ever hear or know the like before,
    To wed a damsel in the morning soon
    And to wed to another just after noon?"

25. "You may have your brown girl.
    I am sure she is none the worse by me.
    Before I'd hear of my darling complain
    I'd like all this town in exchange."

26. He took her by her lily white hand
    And led her up a marble stair.
    He changed her name from Miss Susie Price
    And called her the Queen of Glasgow Geen
                                    (=Green).

105. "A Gentleman of the Courts of England"

Garrison, 1944, pp. 16-18. Sung by Mrs. Daisy Turner,
Marshall, Ark., April 1941.

a π²

This tune was originally noted in 4/4 time, but the note-values
are unchanged.

1. A gentleman of the courts of England,
       A gentleman of the high degree,
   He seemed to grow more discontented
       Till he taken a tantrum out on the sea.

2. He sailed east and he sailed west
       Until he came to the Turkish shore,
   And there he was caught and put in prison,
       No hope of freedom anymore.

3. The old jailer had a very nice daughter,
       A daughter of a high degree;
   She stole the keys of her father's prison
       And said Lord Bateman she'd set free.

4. Have you gold or have you silver?
       Have you money at a high degree?
   Could you afford to give it to a lady,
       One that would now set you free?

5. I have gold and I have silver,
       I have money at a high degree,
   And I can afford to give it to a lady,
       One that will now set me free.

6. She takened him down to her father's cellar,
       Drawed glasses of old port wine,
   And every health that she drank to him
       She'd cry, "Lord Bateman, I wish you were mine."

7. Seven long years had passed and over,
       Seven long years and two or three.
   She gathered up her gold and diamonds
       And said Lord Bateman she'd go see.

8. She rode and she rode till she came to his castle;
       She knocked so loud she made it ring,
   And none was so ready as his bold, bright porter
       To rise and see who wanted in.

9. Sir, is this Lord Bateman's castle,
       Or is he within?
   Oh yes, oh yes, he has just this day
       Gone and brought a new bride in.

10. Go tell him I want a slice of his bread,
        A bottle of his wine so strong;
    And tell him he must never forget the lady
        That freed him from his prison bond.

11. Sir, stands at your gate a fair damsel
        As ever my two eyes did see;
    She wears a gold ring on her little finger,
        And on her others two or three.

12. She said she wanted a slice of your bread
        And a bottle of your wine so strong,
    And to tell you you must never forget the lady
        Who freed you from your prison bond.

13. Up rose Lord Bateman from the table,
        And sliced his bread in pieces three,
    Saying, "Fare you well to the land of the living,
        Since my Susannah's crossed the sea."

14. "Sir, today I've married your daughter,
        And she is none the worse by me.
    She rode here a horse and saddle,
        And she may return in a coach with thee."

106. "Lord Batesman"

Sharp MSS., 3180/. Also in Sharp and Karpeles, 1932, I,
p. 81(E). Sung by Mrs. Mary Sands (45), Allanstand,
July 31, 1916.

a D/M

The barring of the MS. starts after the first note and so proceeds.

Lord Batesman was a noble young man
And as fair a one as you'd wish to see
And he put his foot on a little boaten
And he vowed some strange land he would go and see

107. [Lord Bateman]

Sharp MSS., 3277/. Also in Sharp and Karpeles, 1932, I,
p. 81(D). Sung by Mrs. Rosie Rice, Big Laurel, N.C.,
August 17, 1916.

a D/M

The barring of the MS. begins after the first note. The signature
is that of D major.

They bored a hole in his left shoulder
And nailed him down to the wood
They give him nothing but bread and water
But bread and water once a day.

108. [Lord Bateman]

Sharp MSS., 3772/. Sung by Mrs. Maud Kilburn, Berea,
Ky., May 31, 1917.

a π²

He sailèd East and he sailèd Westward
Until he came to the Turkey shore;
And the Turks they put him in prison.
He lives in hopes of freedom no more.

109. [Lord Bateman]

Sharp MSS., 3020/. Sung by Miss Aimers, Rothgar, Ireland,
at Stratford-on-Avon, August 15, 1914; learned from her
mother, who learned it in turn from her mother.

a D

Lord Beichan was in London born
But foreign countries he longed to see
He sailed East and he sailed West
Until he came unto Turkey

He viewed the customs of that land
Their ways & customs viewèd he
But unto any of their gods
He would not so much as bow the knee.

Sharp's MS. note: "The rest of the words as in the Scottish ballad
books. Beichan pronounced Beckan."

110. "Lord Beechman"

Sharp MSS., 3597/2657. Also in Sharp and Karpeles, 1932,
I, pp. 81(F)-83. Sung by May Ray, Lincoln Memorial University, Harrogate, Tenn., April 25, 1917.

p Æ/D(?) (Perhaps a D/M ending on V)

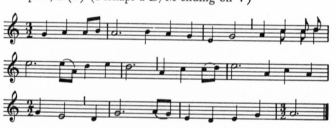

1. A gentleman from the courts of England,
   A gentleman of a high degree,
   But yet he could not rest contented
   Until he ploughed the raging sea.

2. O he rode East and he rode West,
   And he rode till he came to the Turkey shore;
   There he was caught and put in prison,
   No hopes for freedom any more.

3. The Turks they had a beautiful lady,
   And she's as kind as kind could be.
   She stole the keys of her father's castle,
   Saying: My Lord Beechman I'll go and see.

4. O have you house and have you land?
   And are you a man of a high degree?
   And will you will it to any young lady
   Who from this prison will set you free?

5. O I have house and I have land
And I am a man of high degree,
And I will will it to any young lady
Who from this prison will set me free.

6. She took him up to her father's castle
And there she ordered wine so strong,
And every glass that she drank with him:
I wish, Lord Beechman, you was my own.

7. She took him down to her father's hall,
And there she ordered a ship for him,
Saying: Fare you well, my own true love.
Saying: Fare you well till we meet again.

8. It's seven long years I'll make this bargain,
It's seven long years give you my hand,
That you will wed no other woman
And I will marry no other man.

9. O seven long years had done passed over,
Seven long years, one, two, or three.
She gathered up her golden jewelry,
Saying: My Lord Beechman I'll go see.

10. She rode till she came to Lord Beechman's castle,
And at the door she made a ring.
Lord Beechman sent his footman runner
To see who might wish to come in.

11. Pray tell me is this Lord Beechman's castle?
And is the lord himself at home?
O yes, this is Lord Beechman's castle.
He has this day brought a new bride home.

12. Go tell him I want a piece of his bread
And also a glass of his wine so strong;
And ask him if he has forgotten the lady
Who freed him from the prison so strong.*

13. There stands at your gate the prettiest lady
That ever my two eyes did see,
And on her right hand she wears a ring,
And on her left one, two or three,
And around her waist the gold and jewelry
To buy your bride and company.

14. She said she wanted a piece of your bread
And also a glass of your wine so strong,
And asked you if you had forgotten the lady
That freed you from your† prison so strong.

15. Lord Beechman rose up from his table,
And bursted it in splinters three,
Saying: Here, woman, take back your daughter,
My dear Susanne has come to me.

16. Saying: Here, woman, take back your daughter,
I'm sure she's none the worst by me,
For she came here in a horse and saddle,
She can go back in two coachmen free.

17. He took Susanne by her lily-white hand
And led her through rooms two or three.
Her name was put on the house enrolment,
Lord Beechman's landlady.

* 1932: "long"
† 1932: "the"

111. [Lord Bateman]

Smith, 1928, pp. 104-6. Sung by Ada Taylor Graham, Columbia, S.C., 1924; learned from her mother and grandmother.

a I

1. Lord Bateman lived in London Town,
And was of high degree!
He swore he could not rest a minute
Till he had sailed o'er the sea.

2. He sailed east, he sailed west;
He sailed to a far countree,
Where he was taken and put in prison
Where he could neither hear nor see.

3. His keeper had an only daughter,
And she was of a high degree.
She stole the keys of her father's prison
And swore she'd set Lord Bateman free.

4. . . . .

5. And there they made a solemn vow,
For seven long years they let it stand;
That he should marry no other woman,
And she should marry no other man.

6. . . . .

7. When seven long years had rolled away,
And another year had fully come,
She packed up all her gay rich clothing
And went to seek for Lord Bateman.

8. . . . .

9. She knocked so loud, she knocked so clearly
She made the castle gates to ring.
"Oh, who is there?" cried the brisk young porter,
"Who's there a-waiting to come in?"

10. She asked, "Is this Lord Bateman's castle?
And is Lord Bateman now within?"
"Ah yes! ah yes!" cried the brisk young porter,
"He and his bride have just come in."

11. "Go ask him for a piece of bread,
And ask him for some wine so strong,
And ask him if he still remembers
Who freed him from his iron bonds."

12. . . . .

"At your gate stands the fairest lady
That my two eyes have ever seen.

13. "She has a ring on every finger,
    And on the middle one she has three,
And round her neck is a golden necklace
    Fit for the bride and company.

14. "She asks you for a piece of bread,
    She asks you for some wine so strong,
She asks you if you still remember
    Who freed you from your iron bonds."

15. . . . .

16. He smote his fist upon the table,
    And broke it into pieces three,
Crying, "Ah I know, I know that lady,
    Her name it must be Susy Free."

17. . . . .

18. . . . .

    "I brought her here on a horse and saddle,
        I'll send her away in a coach and three."

19. Then he took Susie Free by the lily-white hand,
        And he led her o'er the threshold stone,
    Saying, "Now your name it shall be changed
        Your name shall now be Lady Bateman."

GROUP B

112. [Young Bekie]

Ritson-Tytler-Brown MS., pp. 38-47. Sung by Mrs. Brown,
Aberdeen.

Probably a I, ending on V

Note that this is the only CM variant in the "Beichan" album. But
Child's A copy, also from Mrs. Brown—the present is Child C with
slight verbal differences—is in LM, like all the rest.
I cannot persuade myself that the final here is the true tonic. The
tune has none of the Mixolydian feeling.

Young Bekie was as brave a knight
    As ever sail'd the sea,
An' he's ta'en him to the court of France
    To serve for meat and fee.
He had nae been in the French court
    A twelvemonth nor sae long
Till he fell in love wi' the kings daughter,
    An' was thrown in prison strong.
The king he had but ae daughter,
    Burd Isbel was her name,
An' she has to the prison-house gane
    To hear the prisoners moan.
"O gin a lady would borrow me,
    At her stirrup-foot i would run;

Or gin a widow would borrow me,
    I'd swear to be her son;
Or gin a virgin would borrow me,
    I'd wed her wi' a ring,
I'd gi' her ha's, i'd gi' her bow'rs,
    The bonny tow'r o' Lin."
O barefoot, barefoot gi'd she but,
    An' barefoot came she ben,
It was nae for want o' hose and sheen,
    Nor time to put them on,
But a' for fear her father dear
    Had heard her making din;
She's stown the keys o' the prison-house door
    An' latten the prisoner gang[.]
O whan she saw him young Bekie,
    Her heart was wond'rous sair,
For the mice but and the bold rottens
    Had cutted his yallow hair.
She's gi'n him a shaver for his beard,
    A comber for his hair,
Five hundred pound in his pocket,
    To spend and nae to spare.
She's gi'n him a steed was good in need,
    An' a sadle o' royal bone,
A leash o' hounds of ae litter,
    An' Hector called one.
Atween this twa a vow was made,
    'Twas made full solemnly,
That ere three years was come and gone
    Well marry'd they should be.
He had nae been in's ain country
    A twelvemonth till an end
Till he's forc'd to marry a dukes daughter,
    Or than lose a' his land.
Ohon! alas! says young Bekie,
    I know no' what to dee,
For i can no' win to burd Isbel,
    An' she kens nae to come to me.
It fell once upon a day,
    Burd Isbel fell asleep,
An' up it starts the Belly-blind,
    An' stood at her bed-feet.
"O waken, waken, burd Isbel,
    How can you sleep sae soun',
Whan this is Bekies marriage-day,
    An' the marriage going on?
Ye do ye to your mithers bow'r,
    Think neither sin nor shame,
An' tak' ye twa o' your mithers Marys
    To keep you frae thinking lang.
Ye dress yoursel' i' the scarlet red,
    Your Marys in dainty green,
An' ye put girdles about your middles
    Would buy an earldome.
Ye put nae money in your pocket,
    But barely guineas three,
And that to gie to the proud porter,
    To bid him speak you wi'.
O ye gang down to yon sea-side,
    An' down by yon sea-strand,
Sae bonny will the Holland boats
    Come rowing till your hand.
Ye set your milk-white foot on board,
    Cry Hail ye, dominee!

And i shall be the steerer o't,
    To row you o'er the sea."
She's ta'en her to her mithers bow'r,
    Thought neither sin nor shame,
An' she took twa o' her mithers Marys
    To keep her frae thinking lang.
She dress'd hersel i' the red scarlet,
    Her Marys in dainty green,
An' they pat girdles about their middles
    Would buy an earldome.
An' they gi'd down to yon sea-side,
    An' down by yon sea-strand,
Sae bonny did the Holland boats
    Come rowing to their hand.
She set her milk-white foot on board,
    Cry'd Hail ye, dominee!
And the Belly-blind was the steerer o't
    To row her o'er the sea.
Whan she came to young Bekies yate,
    She heard the music play,
Sae well she kent frae a' she heard
    It was his wedding-day.
She's pitten her hand in her pocket,
    Gi'n the porter guineas three:
"Tak' ye that, ye proud porter,
    Bid the bride-groom speak to me."
O whan that he came up the stair,
    He fell low down on's knee,
He hail'd the king, and he hail'd the queen,
    An' he hail'd him young Bekie:
"O i've been porter at your yates
    This thirty years and three,
But there's three ladys at them now,
    Their like i ne'er did see.
There's ane of them dress'd in red scarlet,
    An' twa in dainty green,

An' they ha' girdles about their middles
    Would buy an earldome."
Then out it spake the bierly bride,
    Was a' gowd to the chin,
"Gin they be braw without, she says,
    Wese be as braw within.["]
It's nae to anger the king, he says,
    Nor yet to vex your grace,
But the blackest bit o' the sole o' her fit
    Is whiter nor your face.
Then up it starts him young Bekie,
    An' the tears was in his ee,
"I'll lay my life it's bird Isbel,
    Come o'er the sea to me."
O quickly ran he down the stair,
    An' whan he saw 'twas she,
He kindly took her in his arms,
    An' kiss'd her tenderly.
"O ha' you forgotten, young Bekie,
    The vow you made to me,
Whan i took you out o' prison strong,
    Whan you was condemn'd to dee?
I ga' you a steed was good in need,
    An' a sadle o' royal bone,
A leash o' hounds of ae litter,
    And Hector called one."
It was well kent what the lady said,
    That it was no a lee,
For at ilka word 'at the lady spake
    The hound fell at her knee.
"Take hame, take hame your daughter,
    A blessing gae her wi',
For i man marry my burd Isbel,
    That's come o'er the sea to me."
"Is this the custom o' your house,
    Or the fashion o' your lan',
To marry a maid in a May morning,
    An' send her hame at even?"